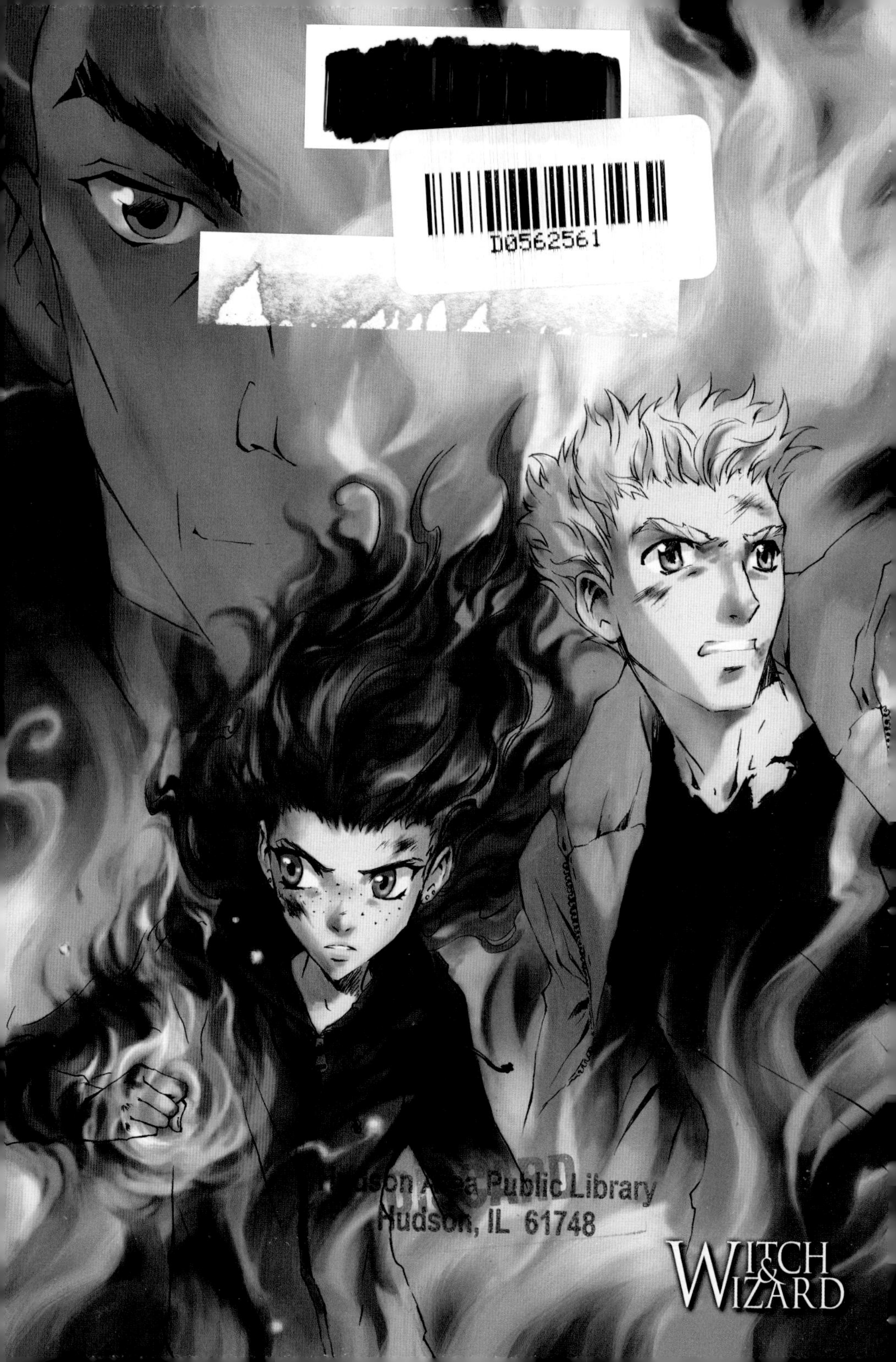
WITCH
&
WIZARD

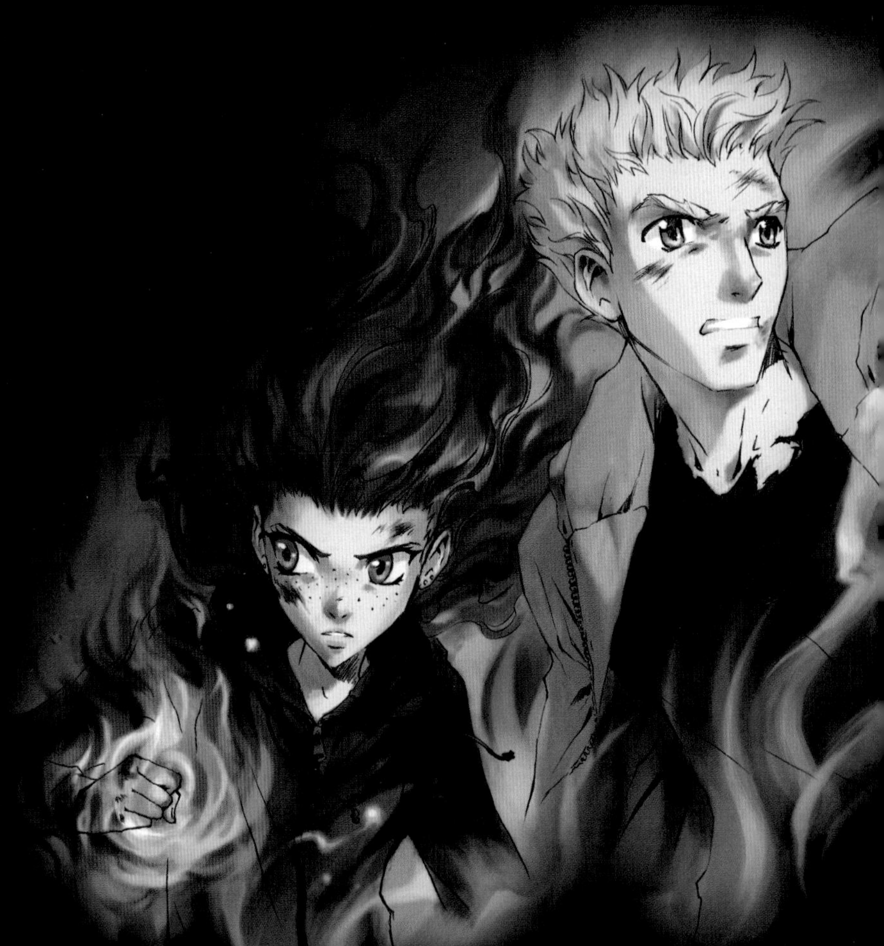

WITCH & WIZARD

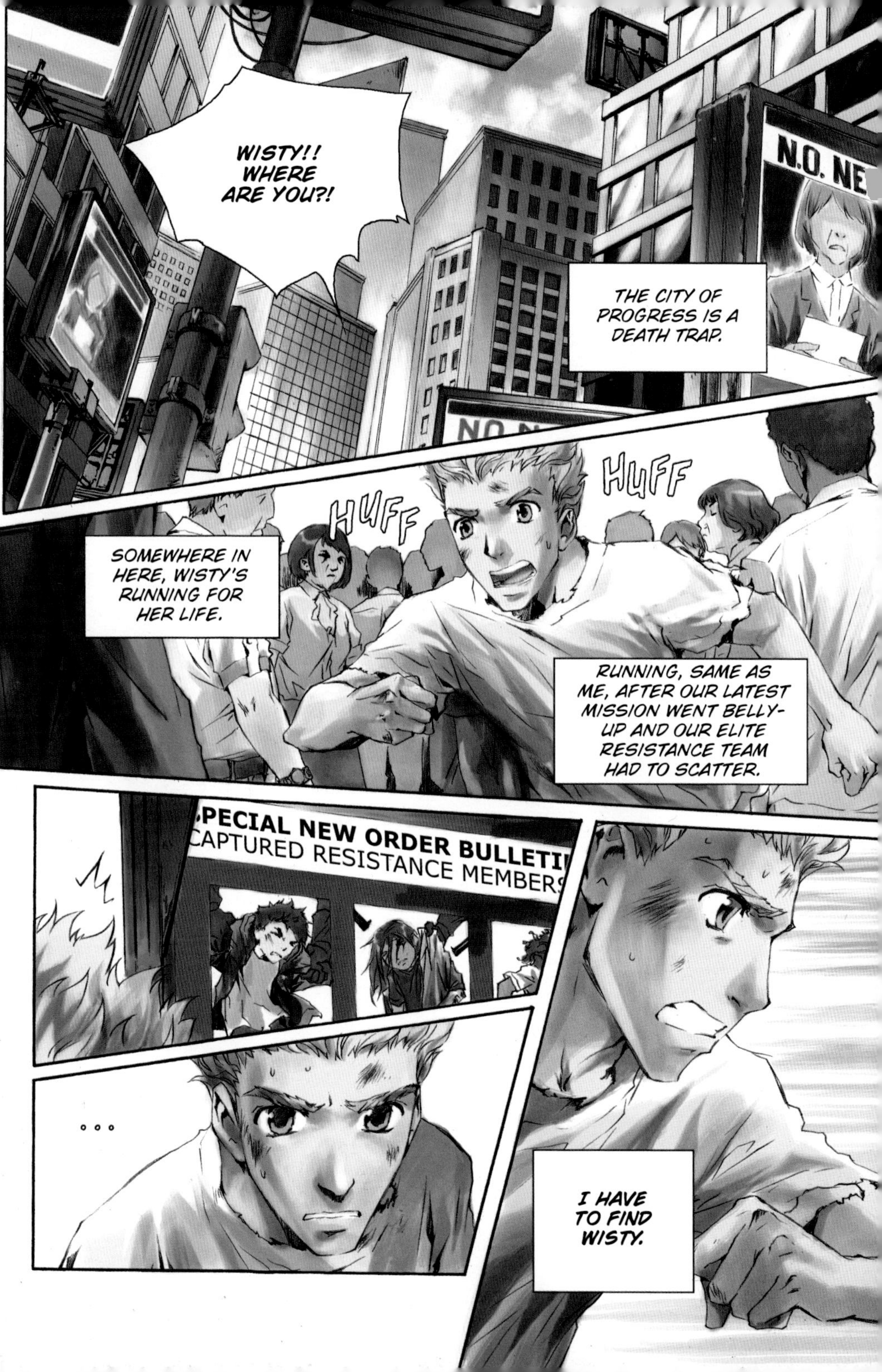
WISTY!! WHERE ARE YOU?!
N.O. NE
THE CITY OF PROGRESS IS A DEATH TRAP.
NO N
HUFF
HUFF
SOMEWHERE IN HERE, WISTY'S RUNNING FOR HER LIFE.
RUNNING, SAME AS ME, AFTER OUR LATEST MISSION WENT BELLY-UP AND OUR ELITE RESISTANCE TEAM HAD TO SCATTER.
SPECIAL NEW ORDER BULLETI
CAPTURED RESISTANCE MEMBERS
...
I HAVE TO FIND WISTY.

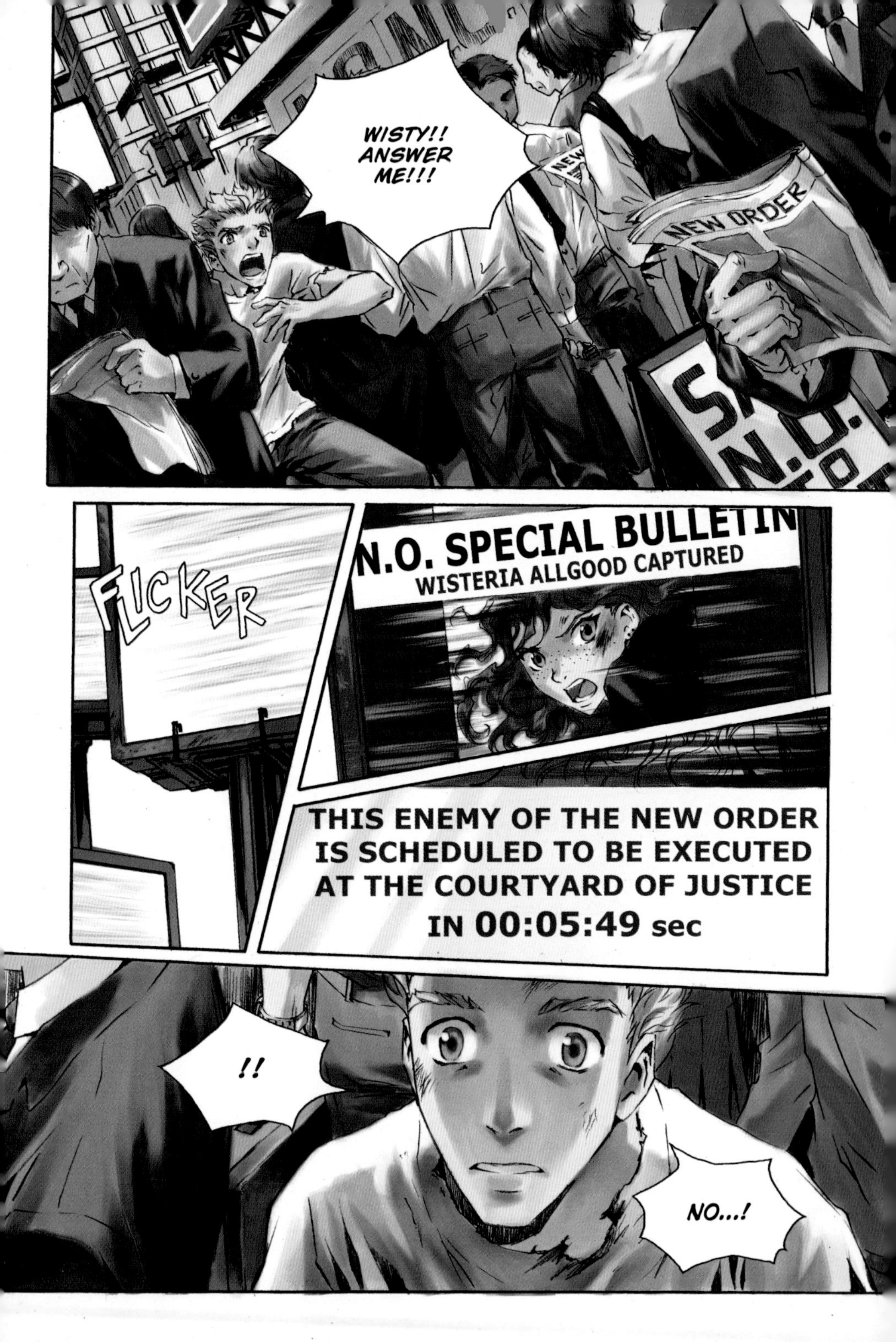
WISTY!! ANSWER ME!!!
NEW ORDER
FLICKER
N.O. SPECIAL BULLETIN
WISTERIA ALLGOOD CAPTURED
THIS ENEMY OF THE NEW ORDER IS SCHEDULED TO BE EXECUTED AT THE COURTYARD OF JUSTICE IN 00:05:49 sec
!!
NO...!

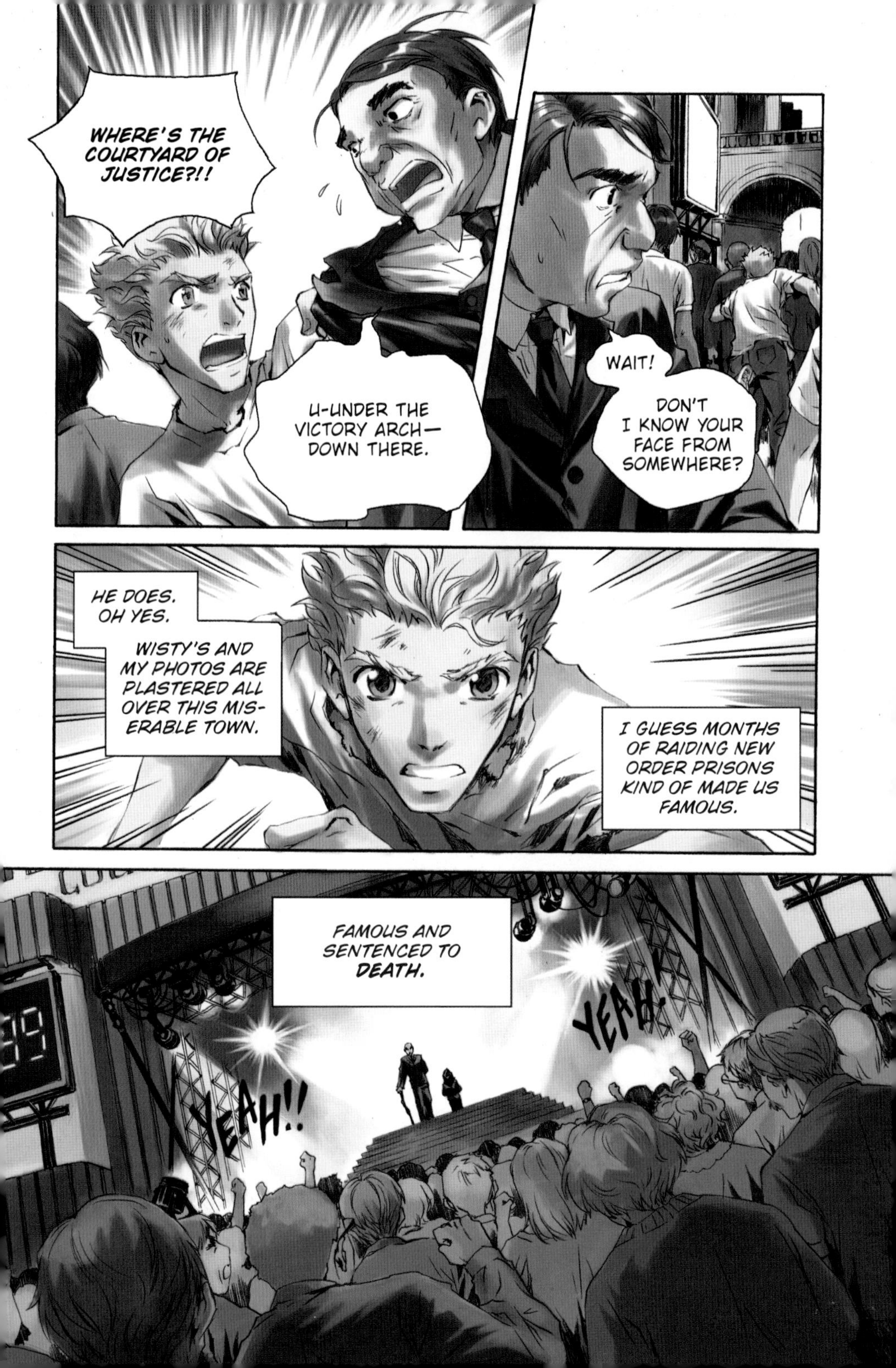
WHERE'S THE COURTYARD OF JUSTICE?!!
U-UNDER THE VICTORY ARCH— DOWN THERE.
WAIT!
DON'T I KNOW YOUR FACE FROM SOMEWHERE?
HE DOES. OH YES.
WISTY'S AND MY PHOTOS ARE PLASTERED ALL OVER THIS MIS-ERABLE TOWN.
I GUESS MONTHS OF RAIDING NEW ORDER PRISONS KIND OF MADE US FAMOUS.
FAMOUS AND SENTENCED TO **DEATH.**
YEAH!
YEAH!!

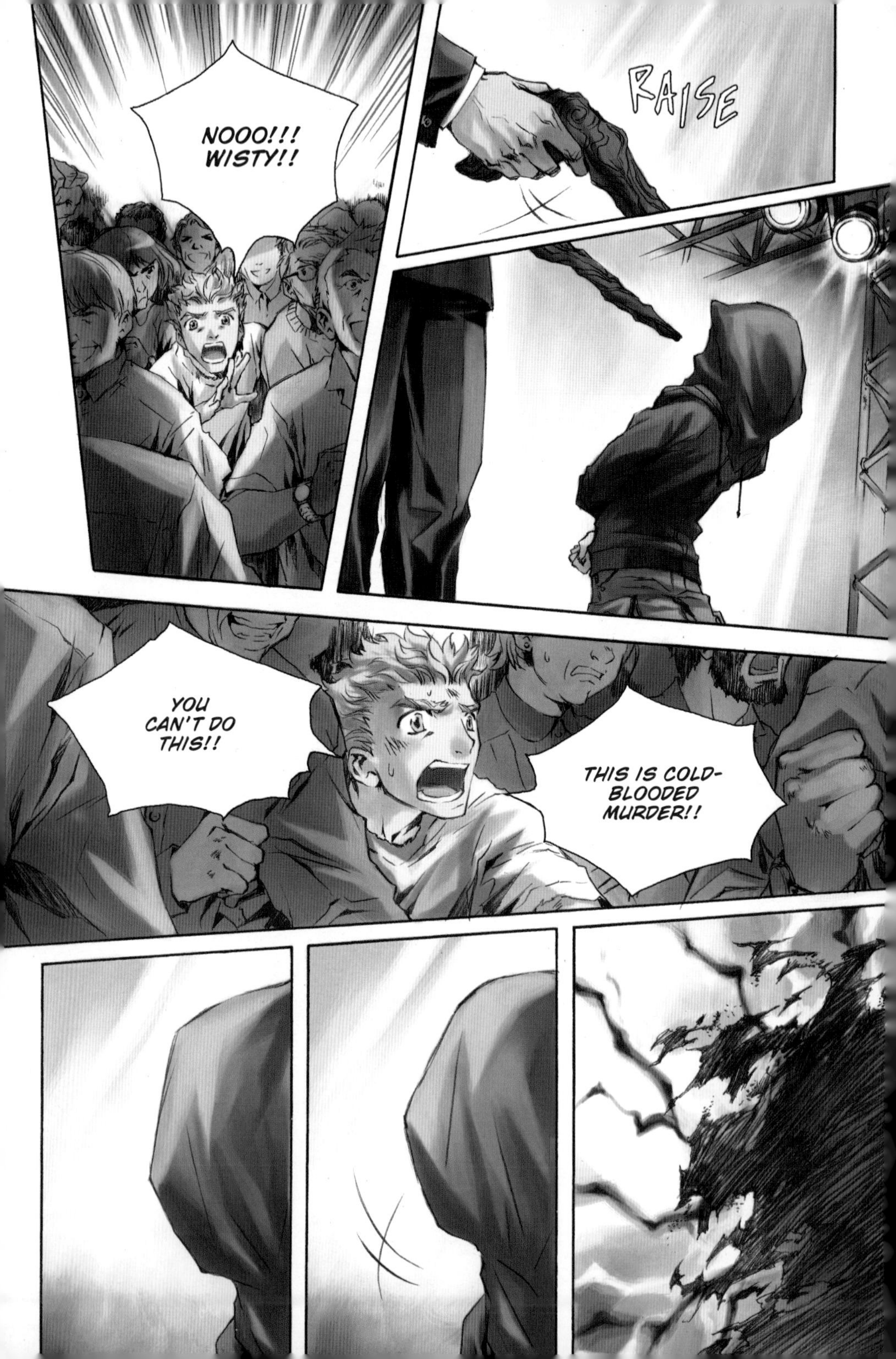
NOOO!!! WISTY!!
RAISE
YOU CAN'T DO THIS!!
THIS IS COLD-BLOODED MURDER!!

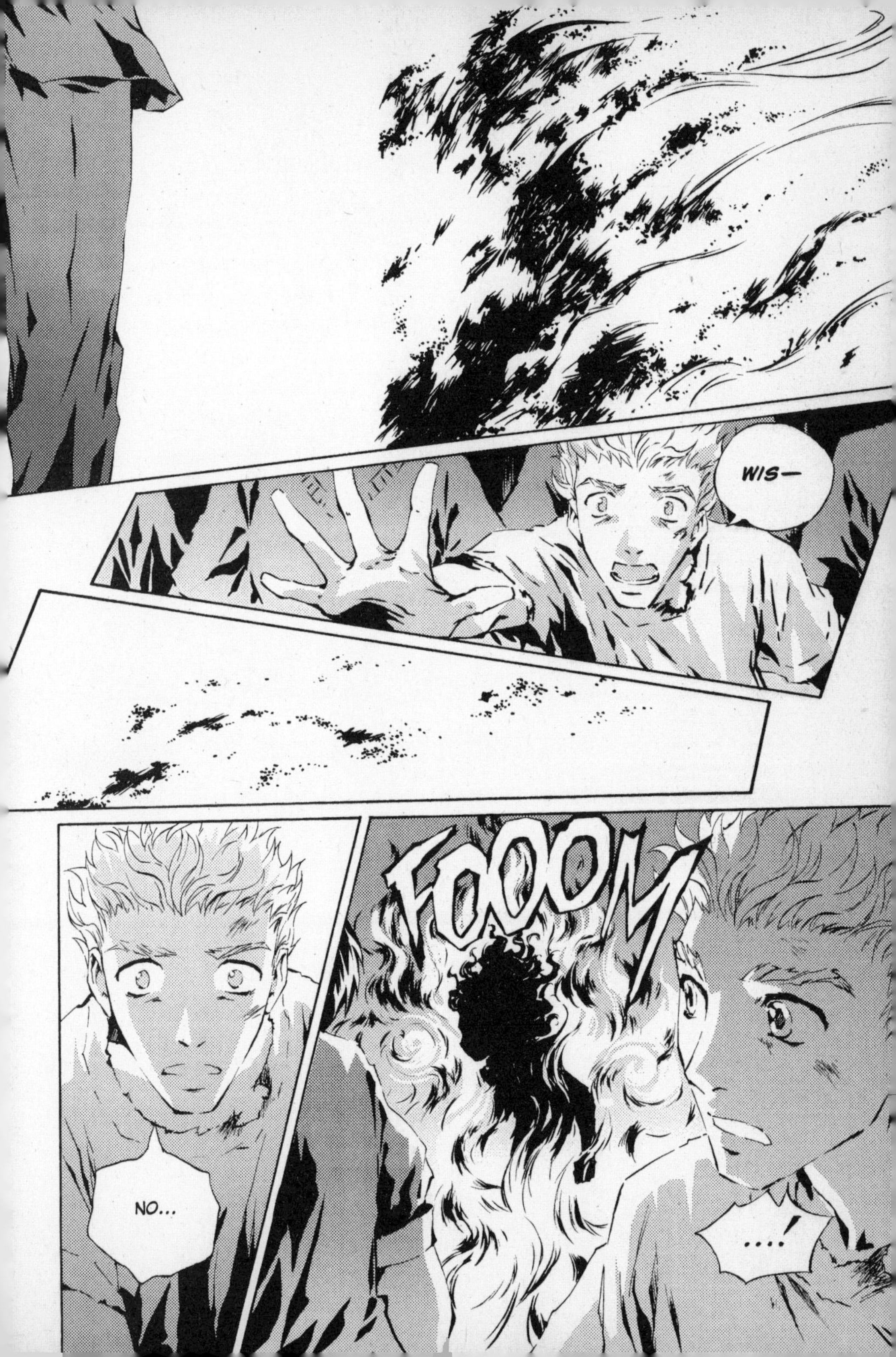
WIS—
NO...
FOOOM
....!

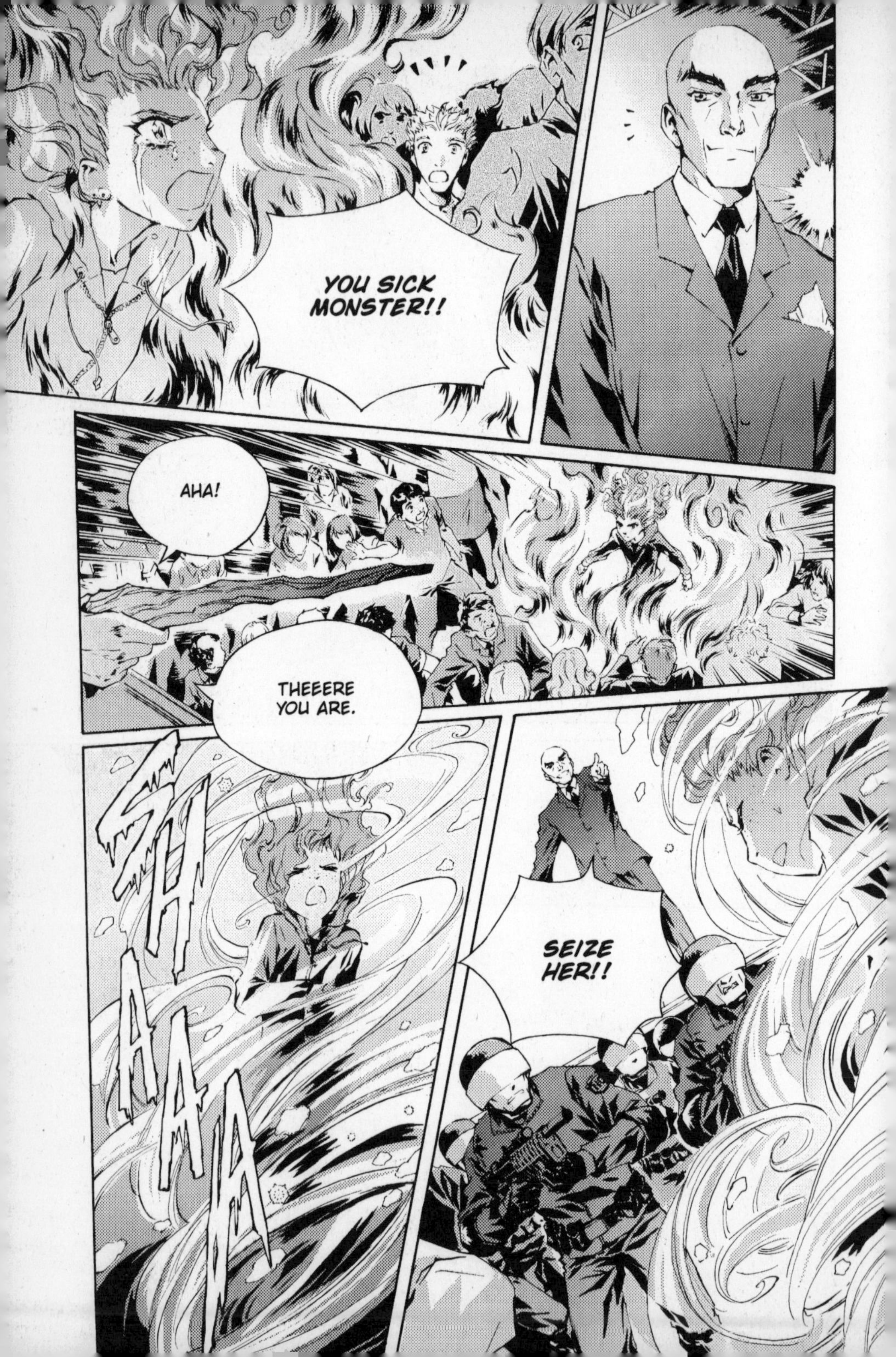
YOU SICK MONSTER!!
AHA!
THEEERE YOU ARE.
SHAAAA
SEIZE HER!!

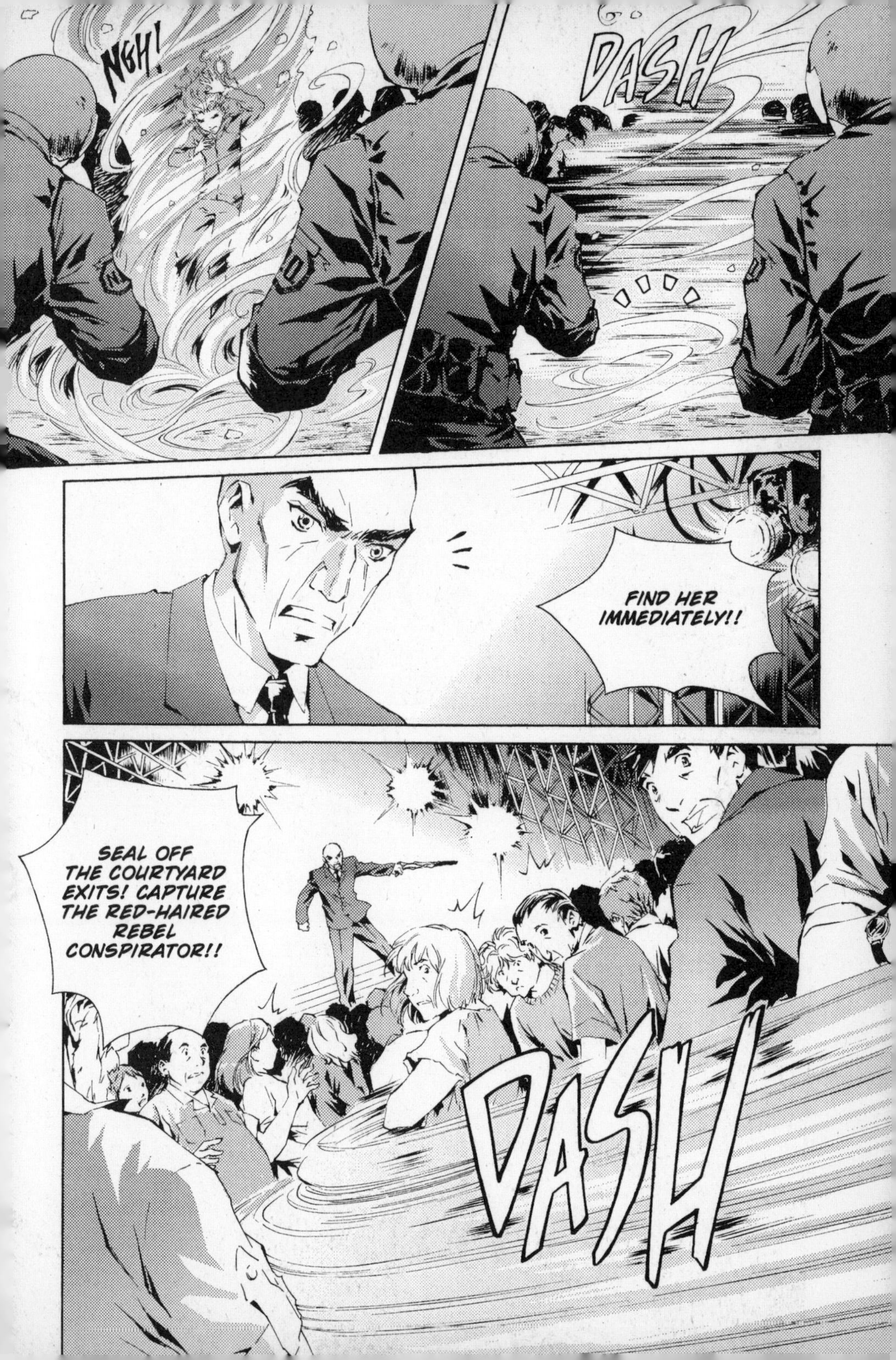
NGH!
DASH
FIND HER IMMEDIATELY!!
SEAL OFF THE COURTYARD EXITS! CAPTURE THE RED-HAIRED REBEL CONSPIRATOR!!
DASH

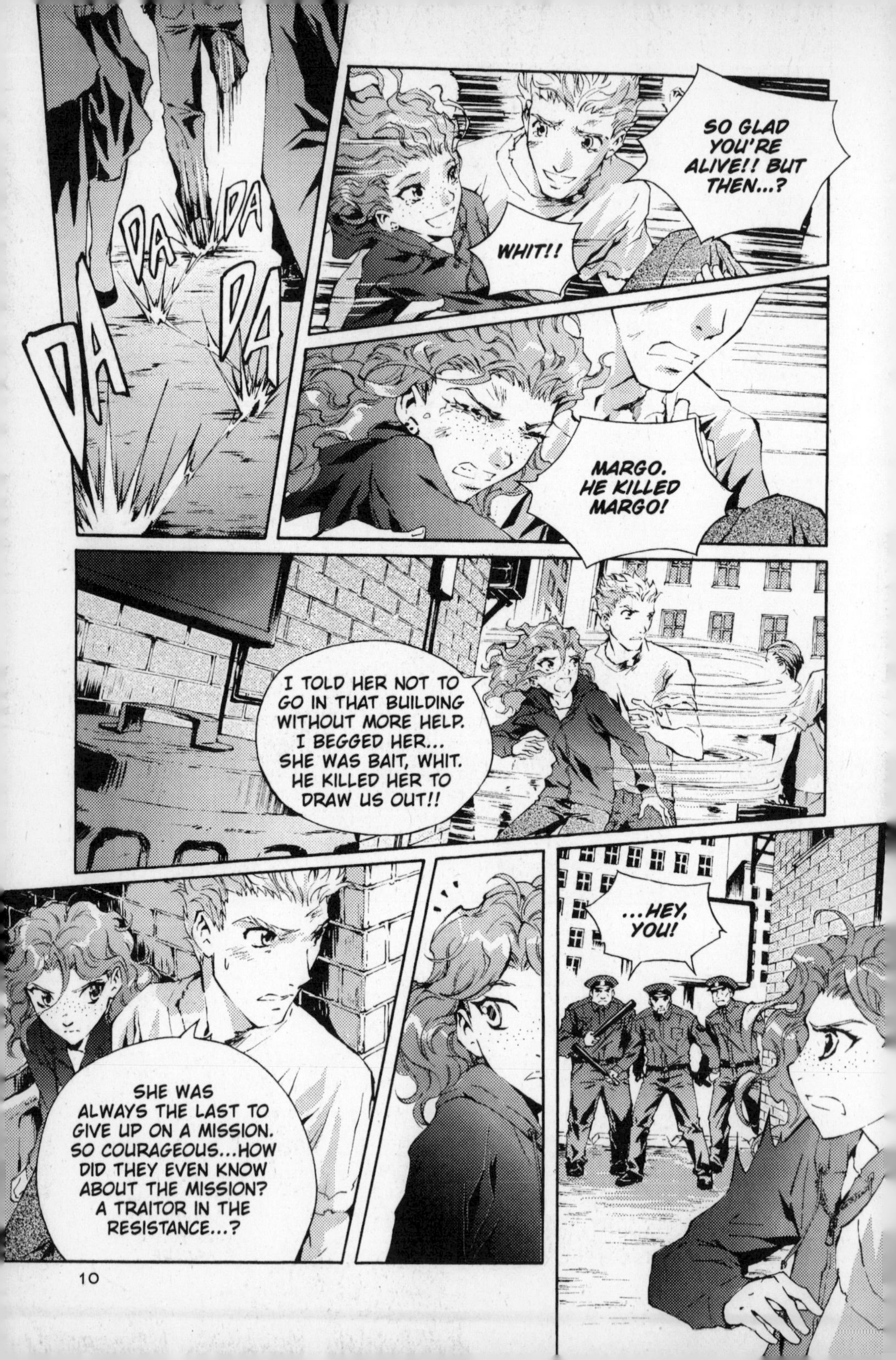
DA
DA
DA
DA
DA
WHIT!!
SO GLAD YOU'RE ALIVE!! BUT THEN...?
MARGO. HE KILLED MARGO!
I TOLD HER NOT TO GO IN THAT BUILDING WITHOUT MORE HELP. I BEGGED HER... SHE WAS BAIT, WHIT. HE KILLED HER TO DRAW US OUT!!
SHE WAS ALWAYS THE LAST TO GIVE UP ON A MISSION. SO COURAGEOUS...HOW DID THEY EVEN KNOW ABOUT THE MISSION? A TRAITOR IN THE RESISTANCE...?
...HEY, YOU!

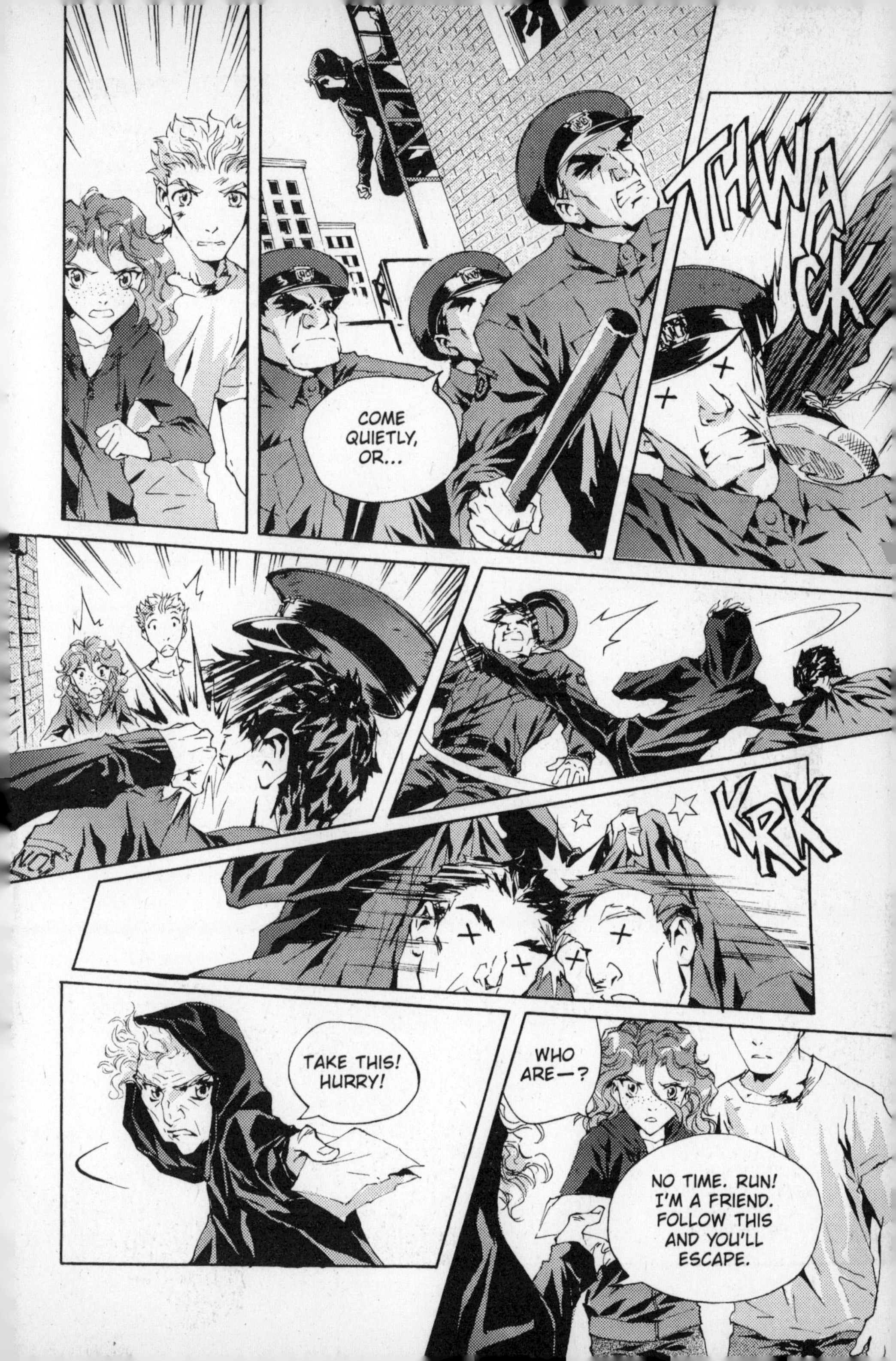
COME QUIETLY, OR...
THWACK
KRK
TAKE THIS! HURRY!
WHO ARE—?
NO TIME. RUN! I'M A FRIEND. FOLLOW THIS AND YOU'LL ESCAPE.

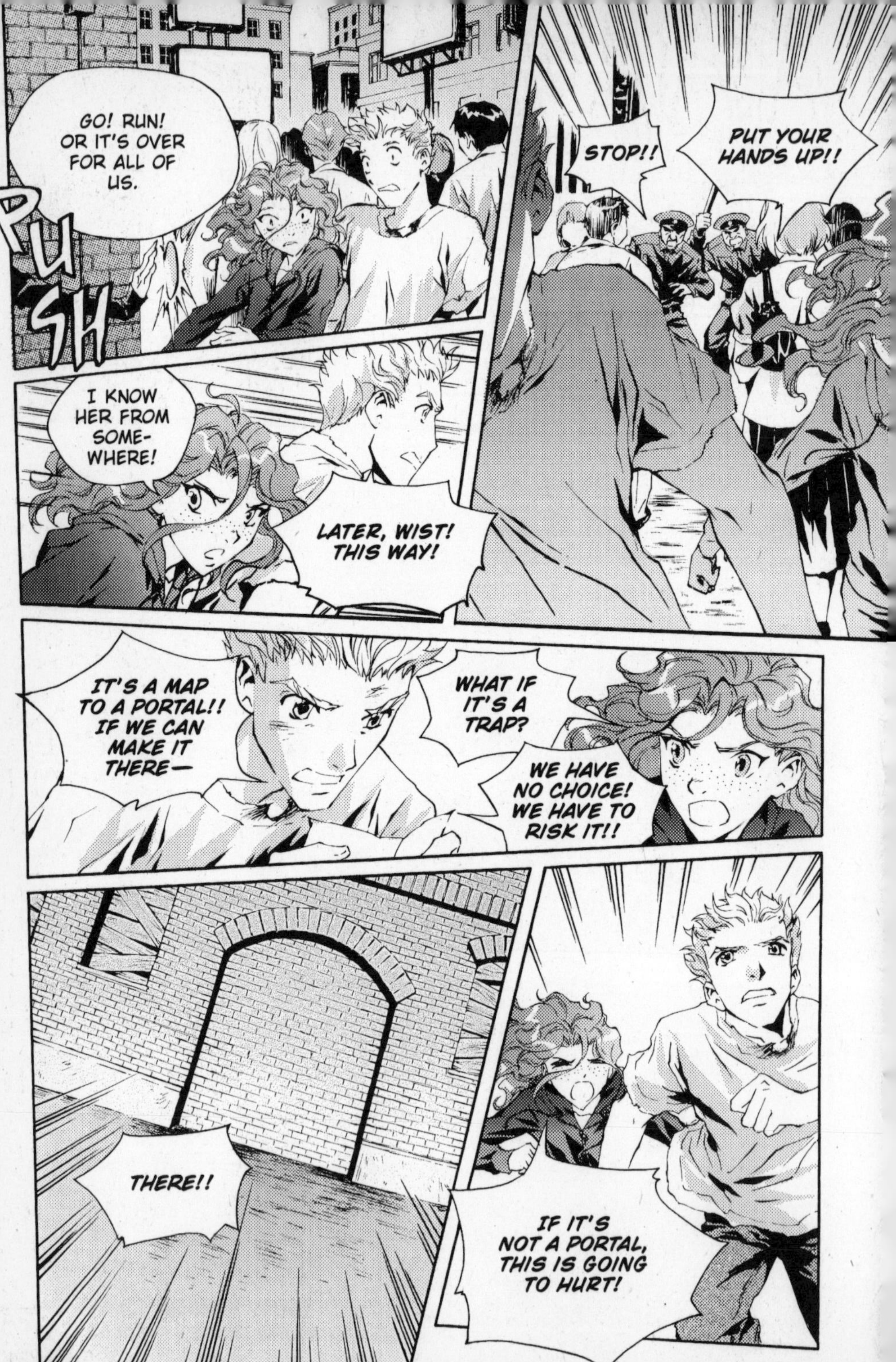
GO! RUN! OR IT'S OVER FOR ALL OF US.
PUSH
STOP!!
PUT YOUR HANDS UP!!
I KNOW HER FROM SOME-WHERE!
LATER, WIST! THIS WAY!
IT'S A MAP TO A PORTAL!! IF WE CAN MAKE IT THERE—
WHAT IF IT'S A TRAP?
WE HAVE NO CHOICE! WE HAVE TO RISK IT!!
THERE!!
IF IT'S NOT A PORTAL, THIS IS GOING TO HURT!

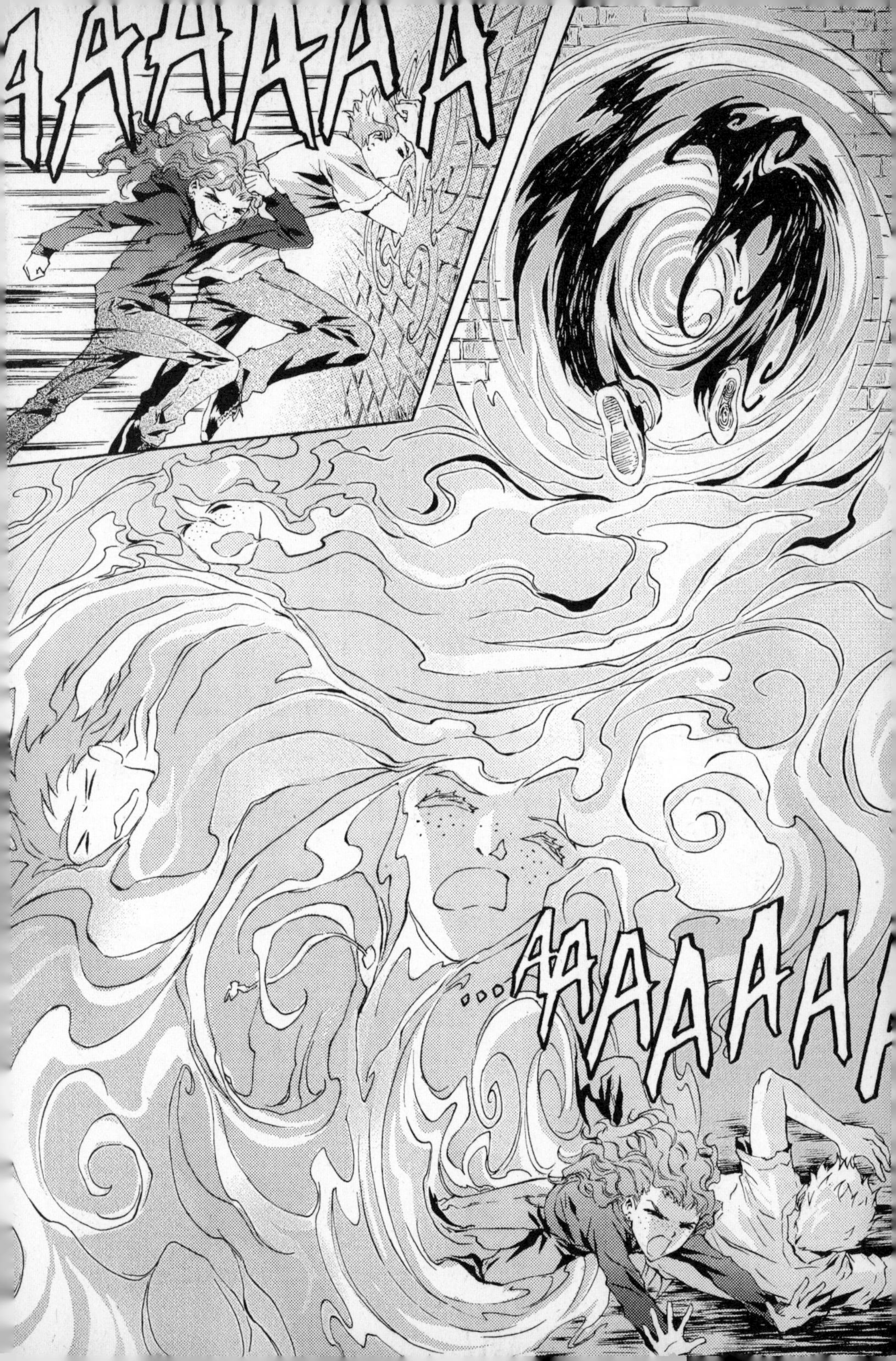
AAHAAA
...AAAAAA

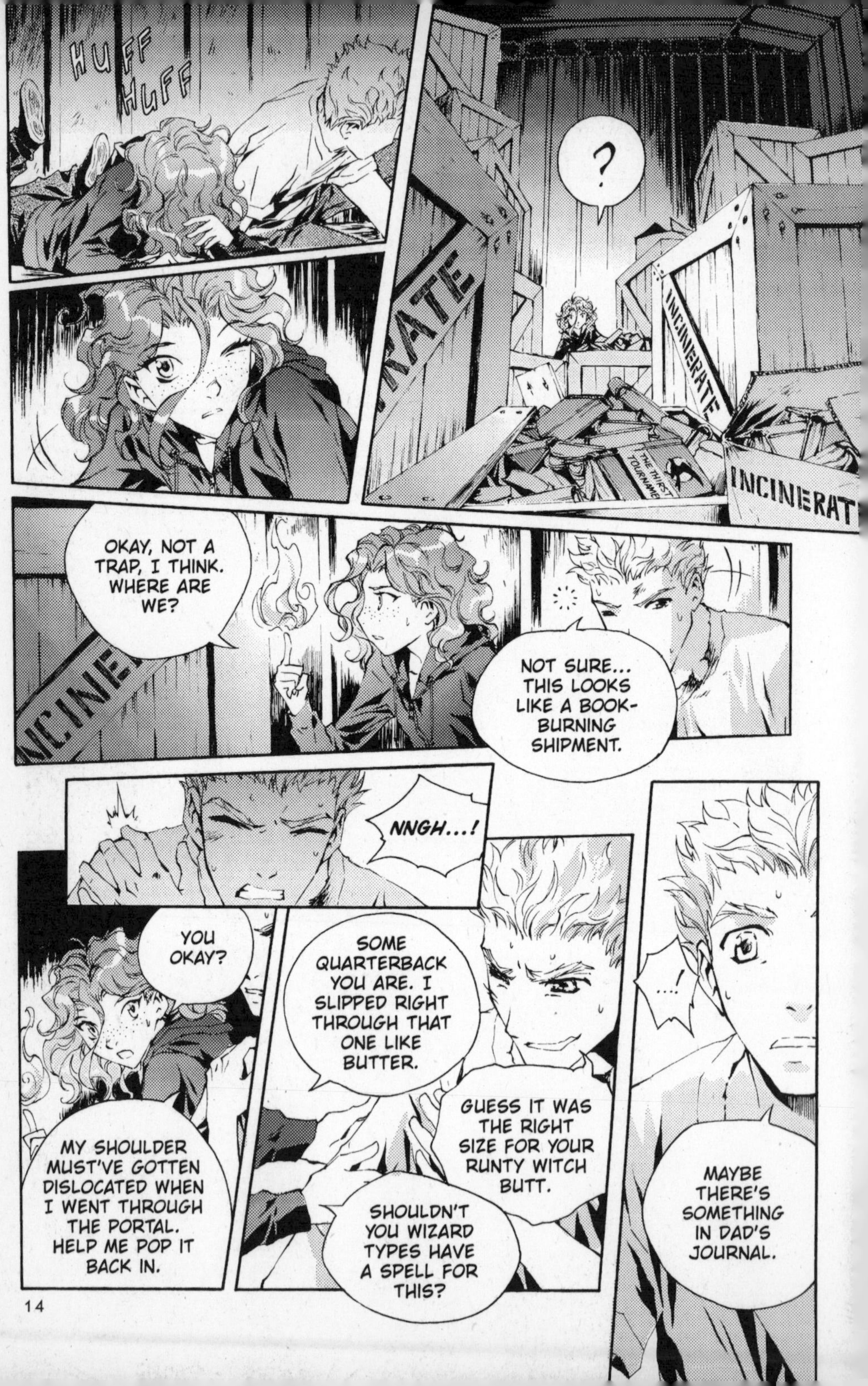

HUFF HUFF
?
INCINERATE
INCINERAT
OKAY, NOT A TRAP, I THINK. WHERE ARE WE?
NOT SURE... THIS LOOKS LIKE A BOOK-BURNING SHIPMENT.
NNGH...!
YOU OKAY?
MY SHOULDER MUST'VE GOTTEN DISLOCATED WHEN I WENT THROUGH THE PORTAL. HELP ME POP IT BACK IN.
SOME QUARTERBACK YOU ARE. I SLIPPED RIGHT THROUGH THAT ONE LIKE BUTTER.
GUESS IT WAS THE RIGHT SIZE FOR YOUR RUNTY WITCH BUTT.
SHOULDN'T YOU WIZARD TYPES HAVE A SPELL FOR THIS?
...!
MAYBE THERE'S SOMETHING IN DAD'S JOURNAL.

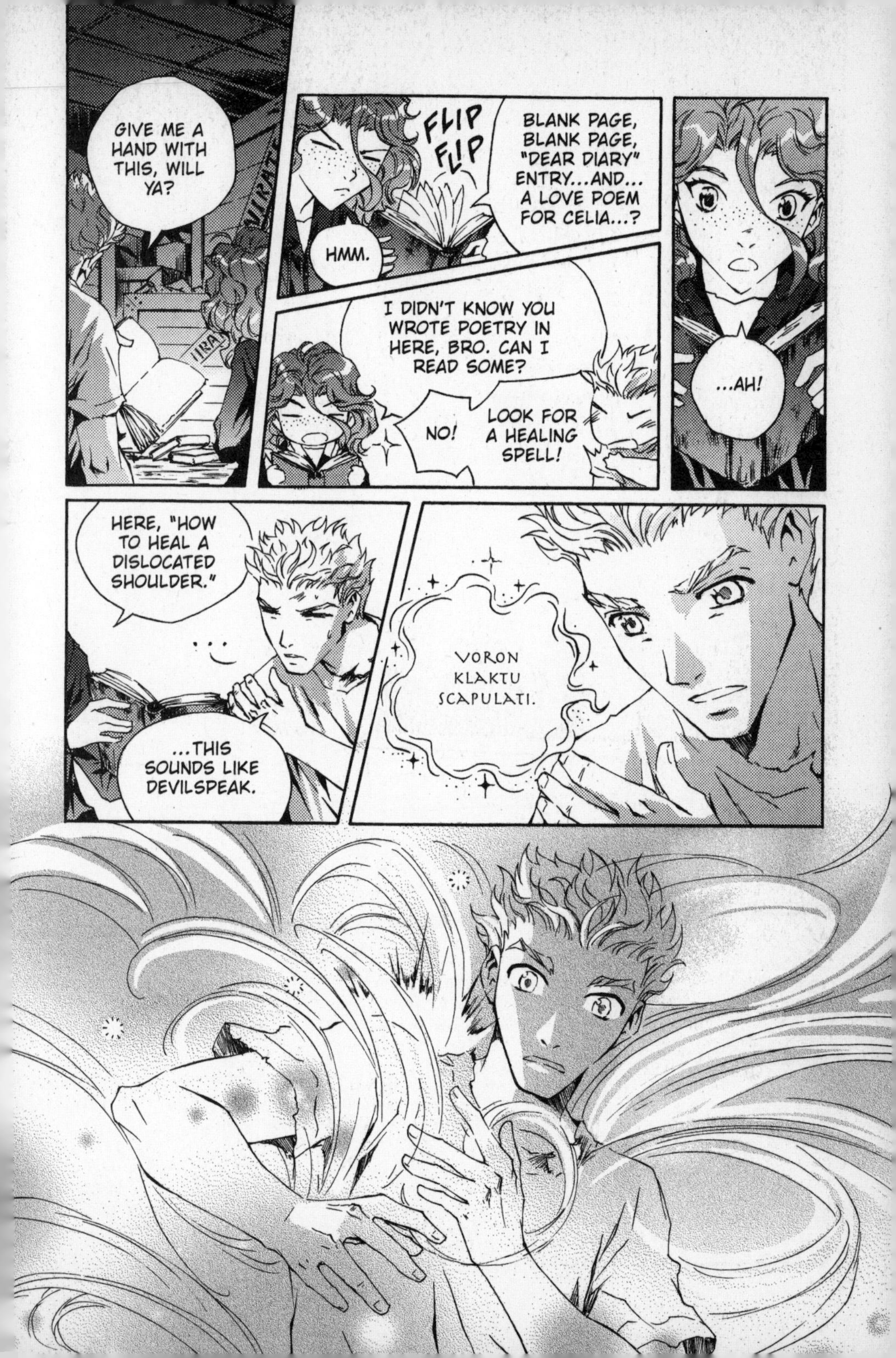
GIVE ME A HAND WITH THIS, WILL YA?
IRA
FLIP FLIP
HMM.
BLANK PAGE, BLANK PAGE, "DEAR DIARY" ENTRY...AND... A LOVE POEM FOR CELIA...?
I DIDN'T KNOW YOU WROTE POETRY IN HERE, BRO. CAN I READ SOME?
NO!
LOOK FOR A HEALING SPELL!
...AH!
HERE, "HOW TO HEAL A DISLOCATED SHOULDER."
...
...THIS SOUNDS LIKE DEVILSPEAK.
VORON KLAKTU SCAPULATI.

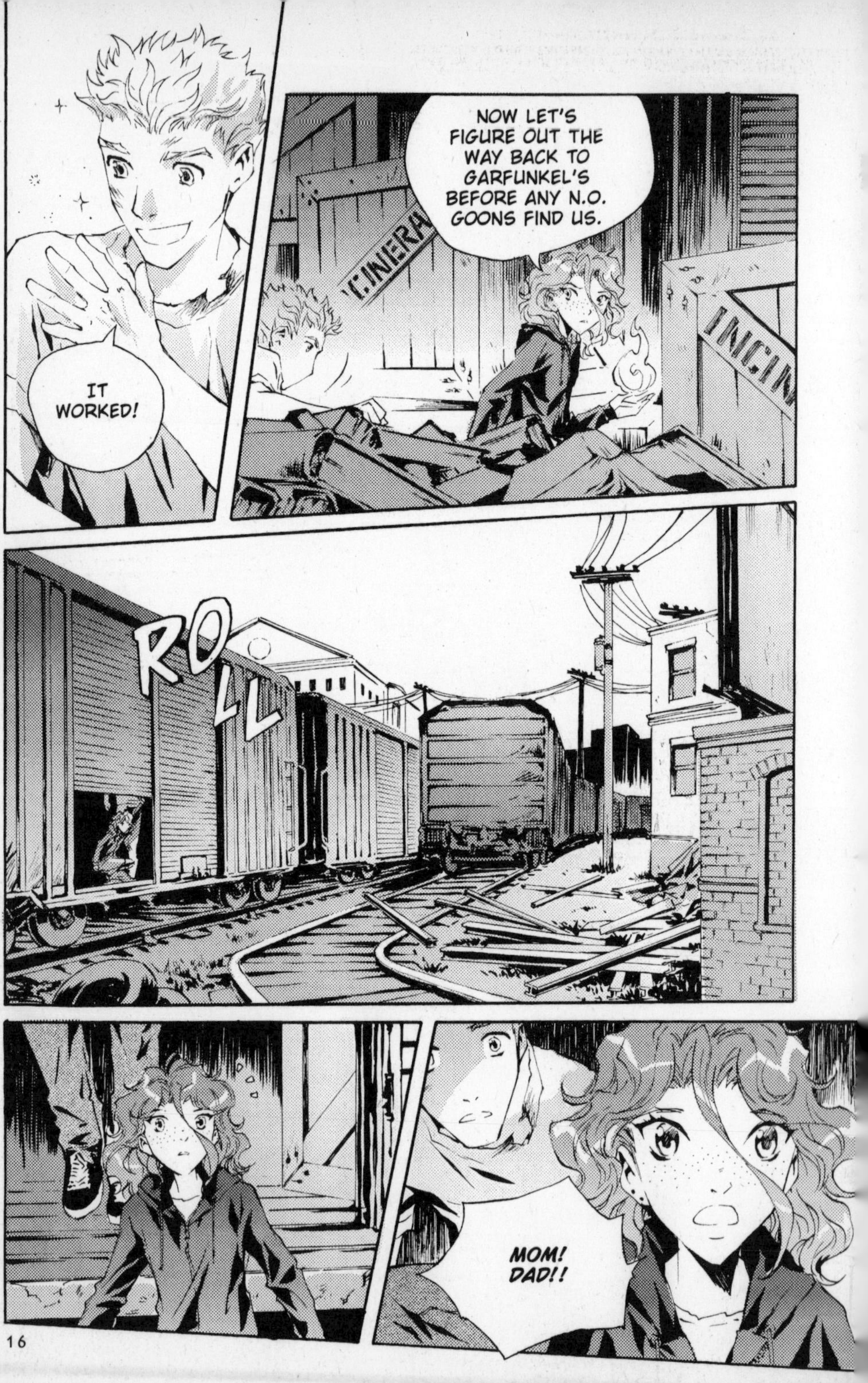
IT WORKED!
NOW LET'S FIGURE OUT THE WAY BACK TO GARFUNKEL'S BEFORE ANY N.O. GOONS FIND US.
CINERA
INCIN
ROLL
MOM! DAD!!

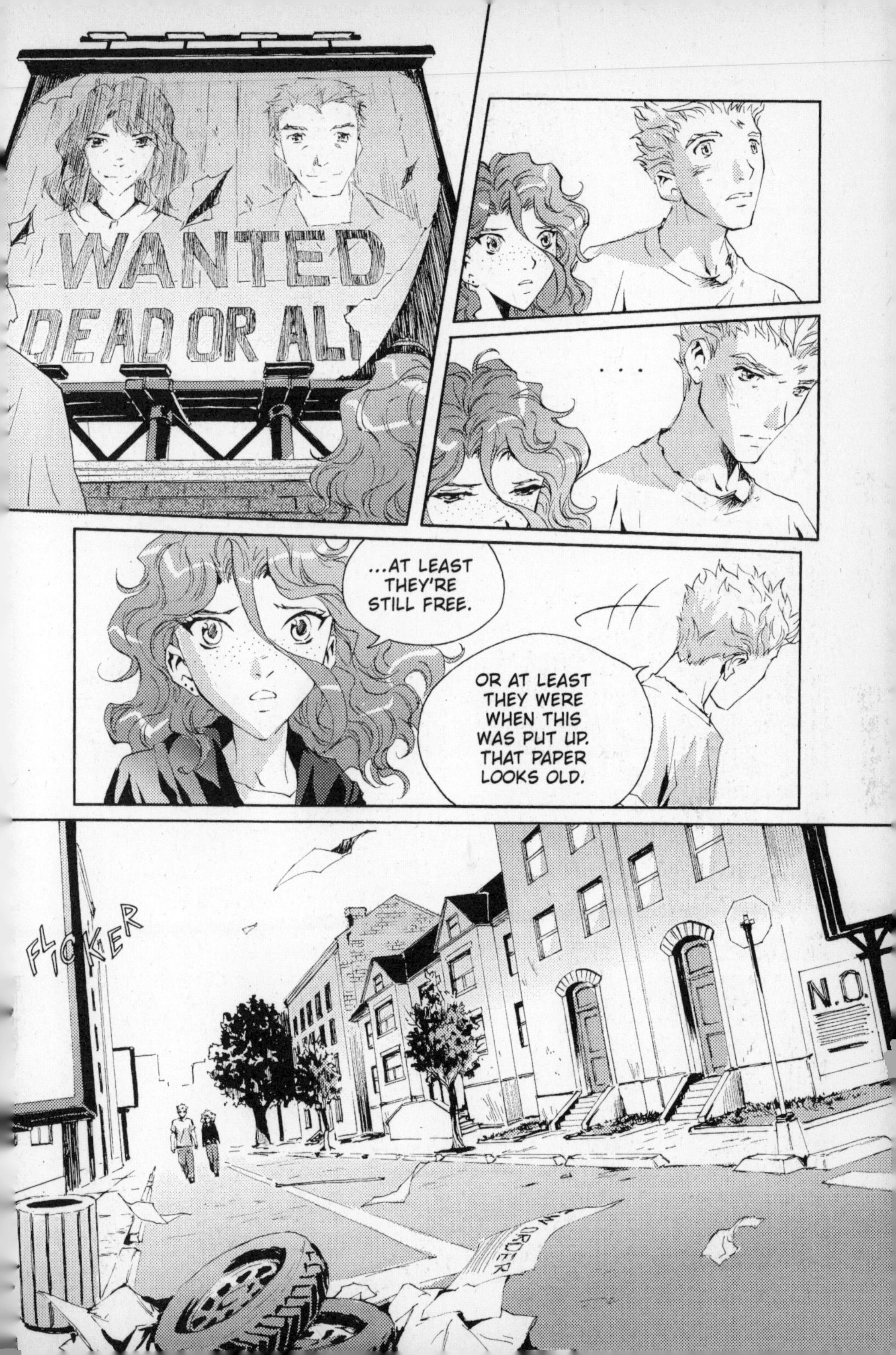
WANTED
DEAD OR AL
...
...AT LEAST THEY'RE STILL FREE.
OR AT LEAST THEY WERE WHEN THIS WAS PUT UP. THAT PAPER LOOKS OLD.
FLICKER
N.O.

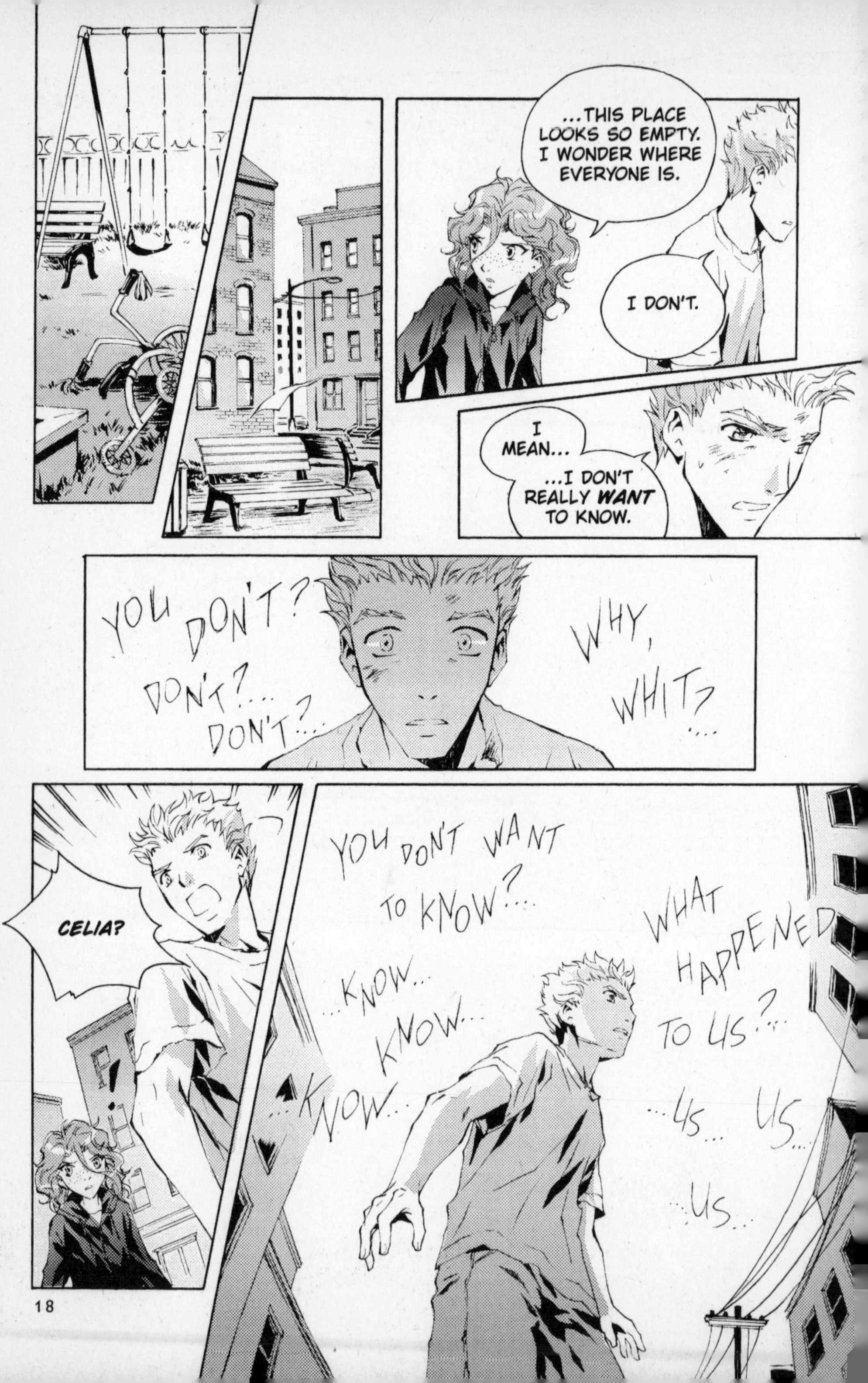
...THIS PLACE LOOKS SO EMPTY. I WONDER WHERE EVERYONE IS.
I DON'T.
I MEAN...
...I DON'T REALLY *WANT* TO KNOW.
YOU DON'T? DON'T?... DON'T?...
WHY, WHIT?...
CELIA?
YOU DON'T WANT TO KNOW?...
...KNOW... KNOW... ...KNOW...
WHAT HAPPENED TO US?...
...US... US... ...US...

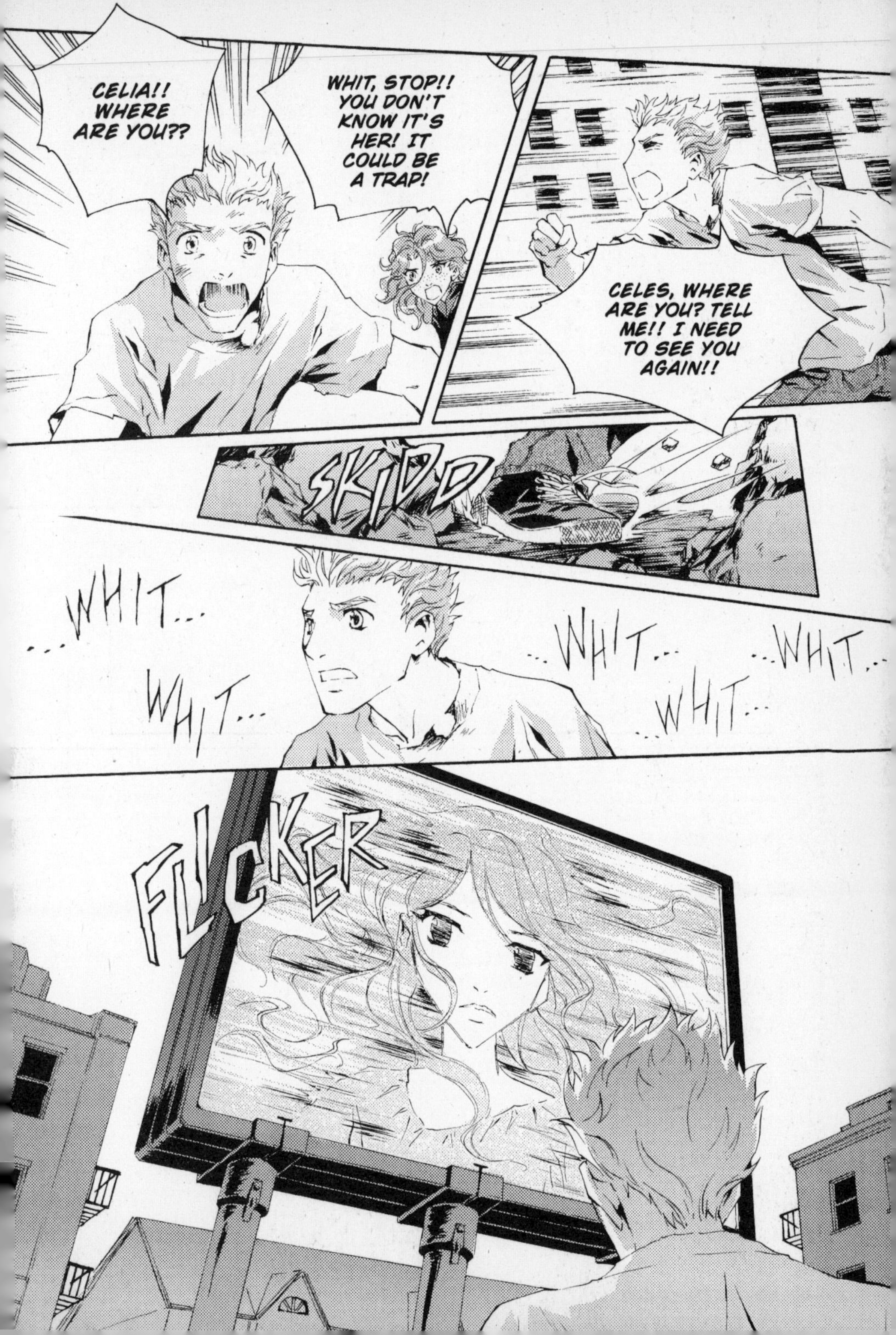
CELIA!! WHERE ARE YOU??
WHIT, STOP!! YOU DON'T KNOW IT'S HER! IT COULD BE A TRAP!
CELES, WHERE ARE YOU? TELL ME!! I NEED TO SEE YOU AGAIN!!
SKIDD
...WHIT...
WHIT...
...WHIT...
...WHIT...
...WHIT...
FLICKER

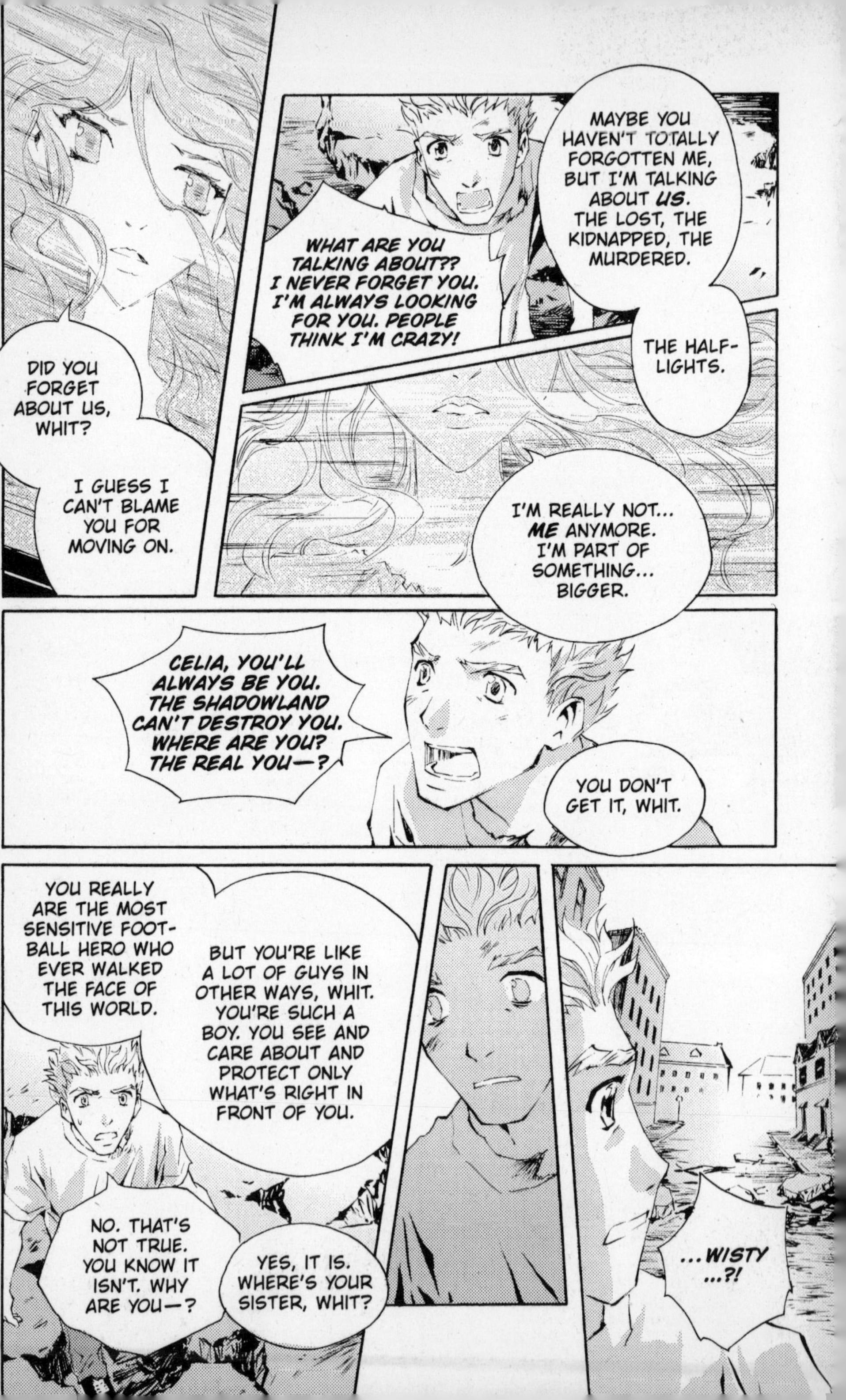
DID YOU FORGET ABOUT US, WHIT?
I GUESS I CAN'T BLAME YOU FOR MOVING ON.
WHAT ARE YOU TALKING ABOUT?? I NEVER FORGET YOU. I'M ALWAYS LOOKING FOR YOU. PEOPLE THINK I'M CRAZY!
MAYBE YOU HAVEN'T TOTALLY FORGOTTEN ME, BUT I'M TALKING ABOUT US. THE LOST, THE KIDNAPPED, THE MURDERED.
THE HALF-LIGHTS.
I'M REALLY NOT... ME ANYMORE. I'M PART OF SOMETHING... BIGGER.
CELIA, YOU'LL ALWAYS BE YOU. THE SHADOWLAND CAN'T DESTROY YOU. WHERE ARE YOU? THE REAL YOU—?
YOU DON'T GET IT, WHIT.
YOU REALLY ARE THE MOST SENSITIVE FOOT-BALL HERO WHO EVER WALKED THE FACE OF THIS WORLD.
BUT YOU'RE LIKE A LOT OF GUYS IN OTHER WAYS, WHIT. YOU'RE SUCH A BOY. YOU SEE AND CARE ABOUT AND PROTECT ONLY WHAT'S RIGHT IN FRONT OF YOU.
NO. THAT'S NOT TRUE. YOU KNOW IT ISN'T. WHY ARE YOU—?
YES, IT IS. WHERE'S YOUR SISTER, WHIT?
...WISTY ...?!

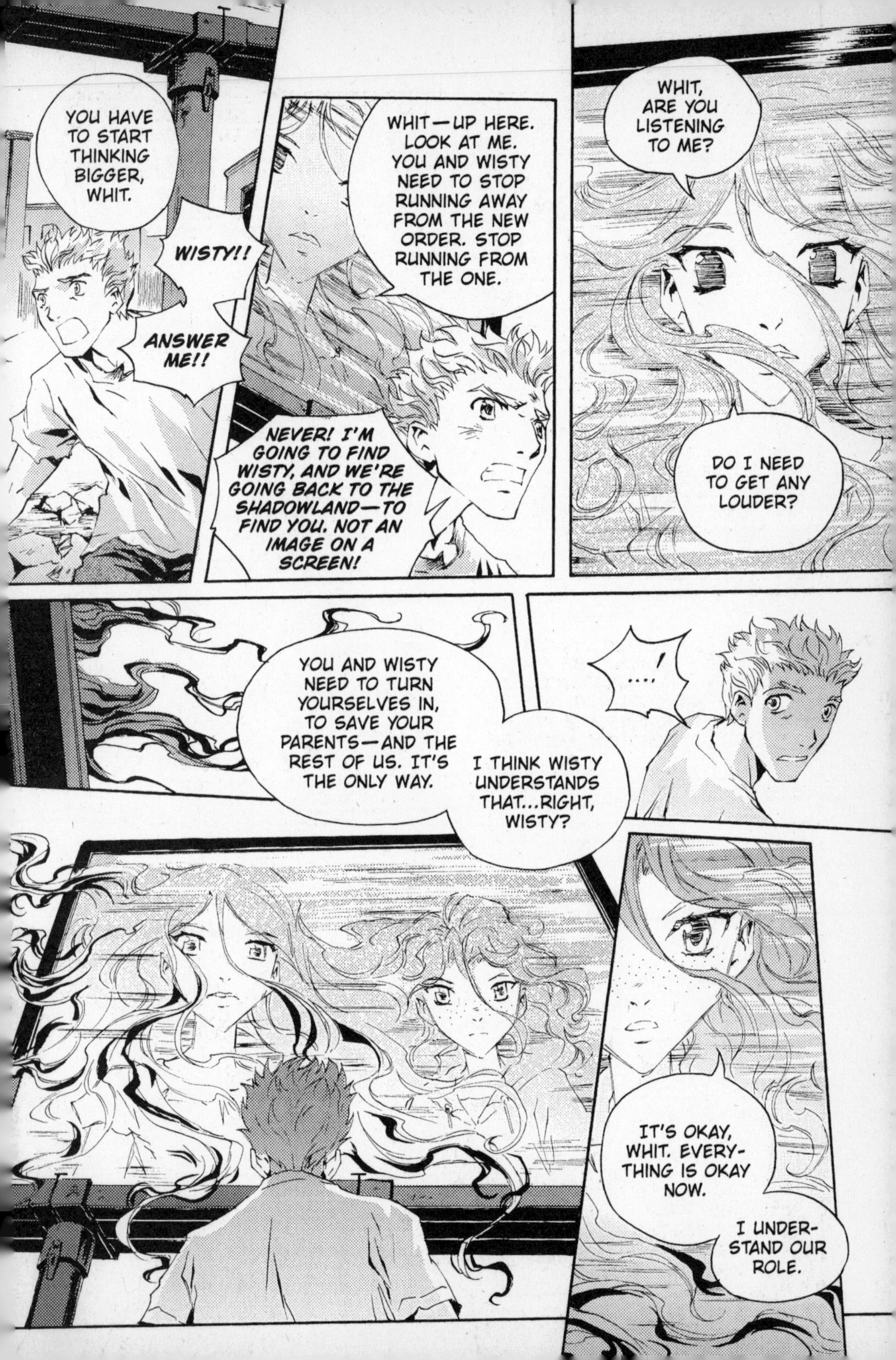

YOU HAVE TO START THINKING BIGGER, WHIT.
WISTY!!
ANSWER ME!!
WHIT—UP HERE. LOOK AT ME. YOU AND WISTY NEED TO STOP RUNNING AWAY FROM THE NEW ORDER. STOP RUNNING FROM THE ONE.
NEVER! I'M GOING TO FIND WISTY, AND WE'RE GOING BACK TO THE SHADOWLAND—TO FIND YOU. NOT AN IMAGE ON A SCREEN!
WHIT, ARE YOU LISTENING TO ME?
DO I NEED TO GET ANY LOUDER?
YOU AND WISTY NEED TO TURN YOURSELVES IN, TO SAVE YOUR PARENTS—AND THE REST OF US. IT'S THE ONLY WAY.
I THINK WISTY UNDERSTANDS THAT...RIGHT, WISTY?
...!
IT'S OKAY, WHIT. EVERY-THING IS OKAY NOW.
I UNDER-STAND OUR ROLE.

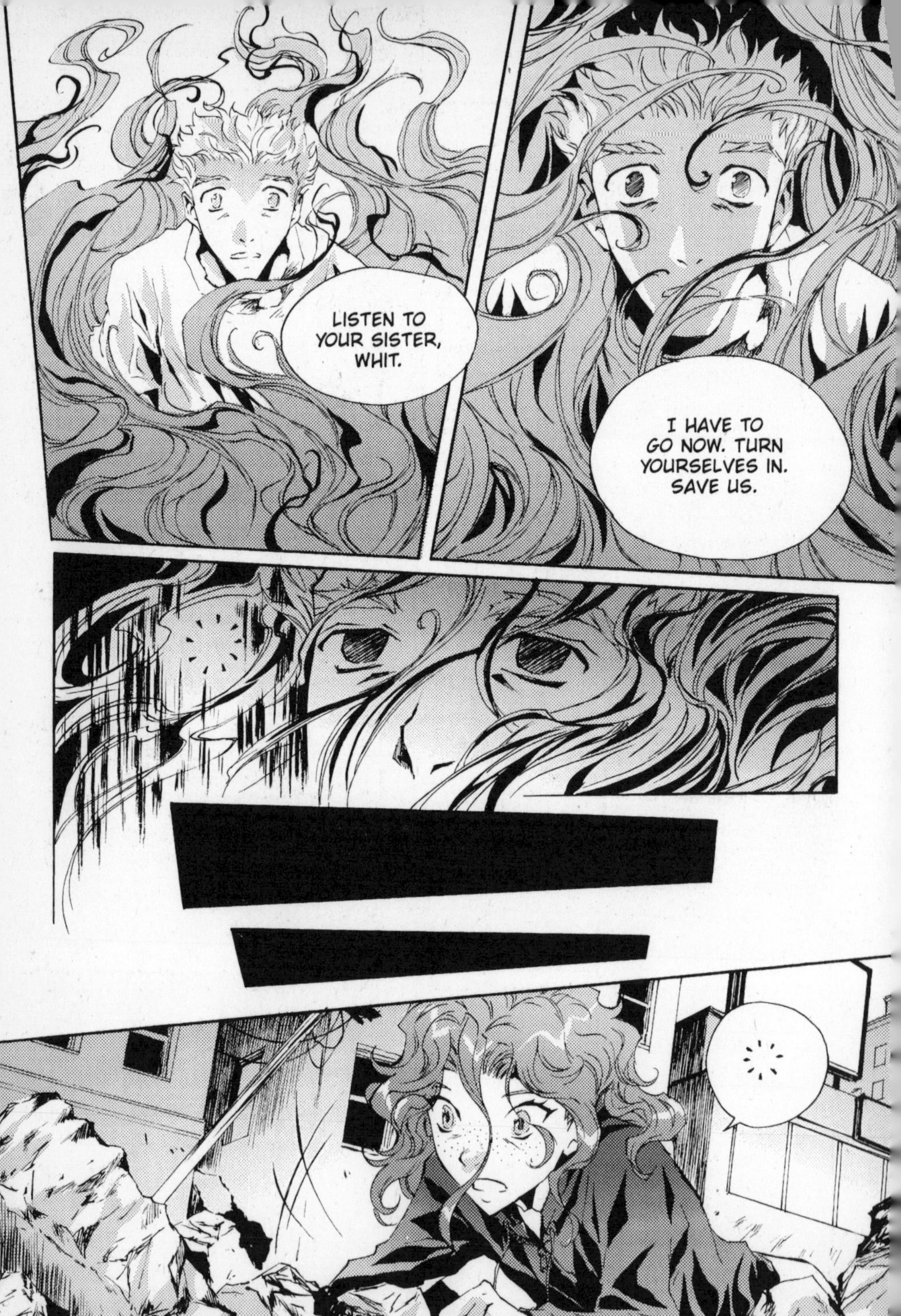
LISTEN TO YOUR SISTER, WHIT.
I HAVE TO GO NOW. TURN YOURSELVES IN. SAVE US.

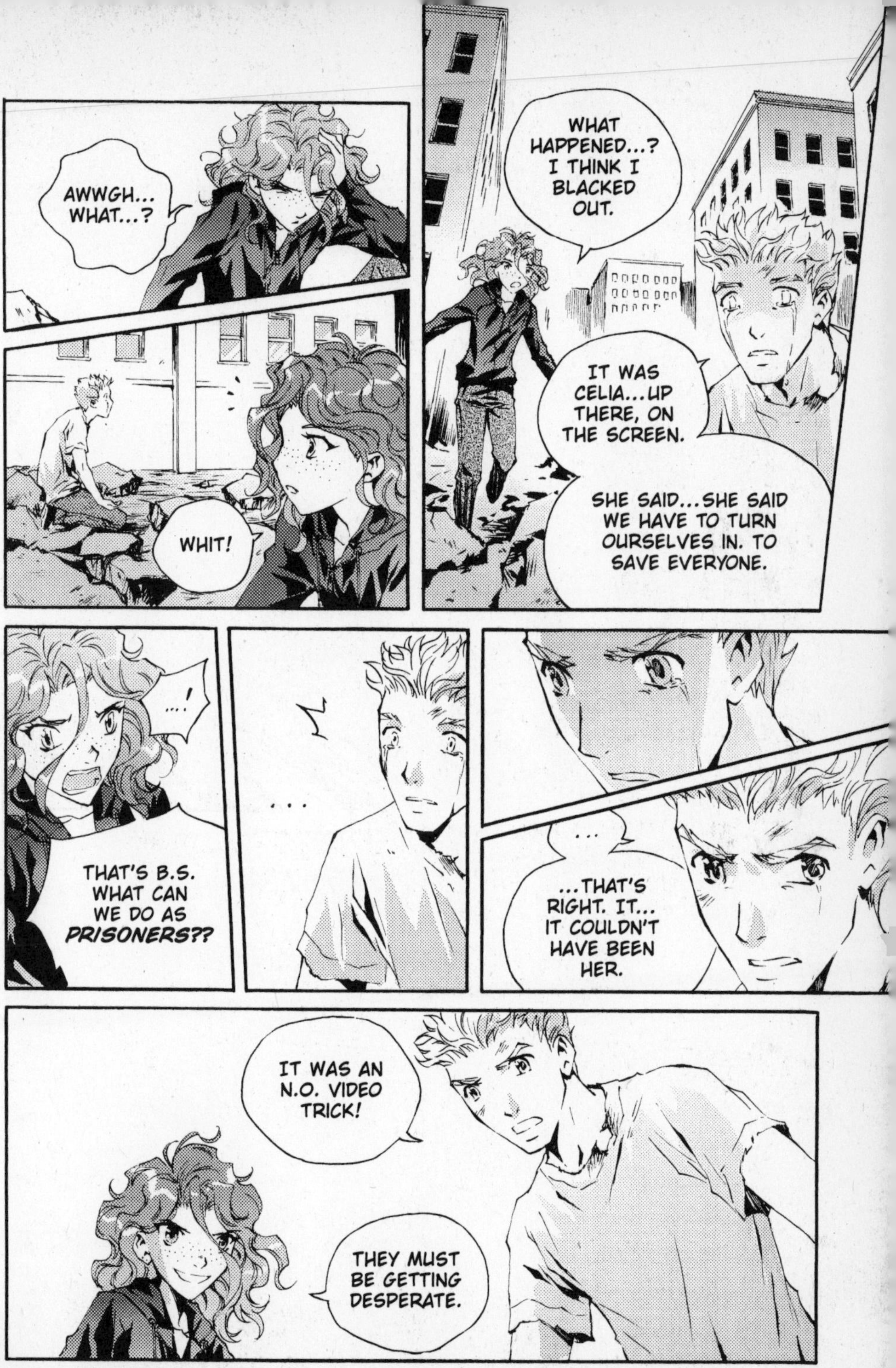
AWWGH... WHAT...?
WHIT!
WHAT HAPPENED...? I THINK I BLACKED OUT.
IT WAS CELIA...UP THERE, ON THE SCREEN.
SHE SAID...SHE SAID WE HAVE TO TURN OURSELVES IN. TO SAVE EVERYONE.
...!
THAT'S B.S. WHAT CAN WE DO AS *PRISONERS??*
...
...
...THAT'S RIGHT. IT... IT COULDN'T HAVE BEEN HER.
IT WAS AN N.O. VIDEO TRICK!
THEY MUST BE GETTING DESPERATE.

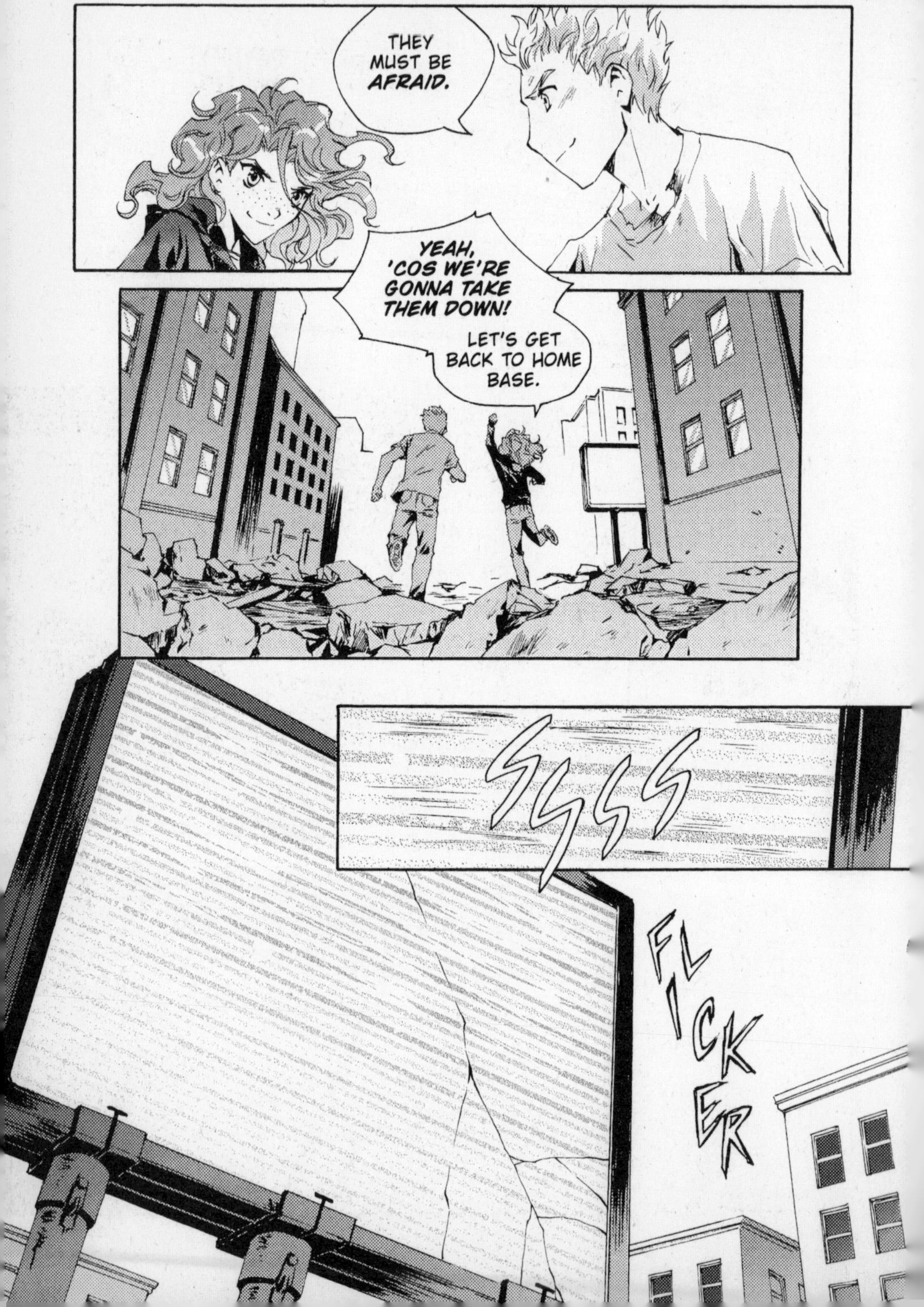
THEY MUST BE AFRAID.
YEAH, 'COS WE'RE GONNA TAKE THEM DOWN!
LET'S GET BACK TO HOME BASE.
SSSS
FLICKER

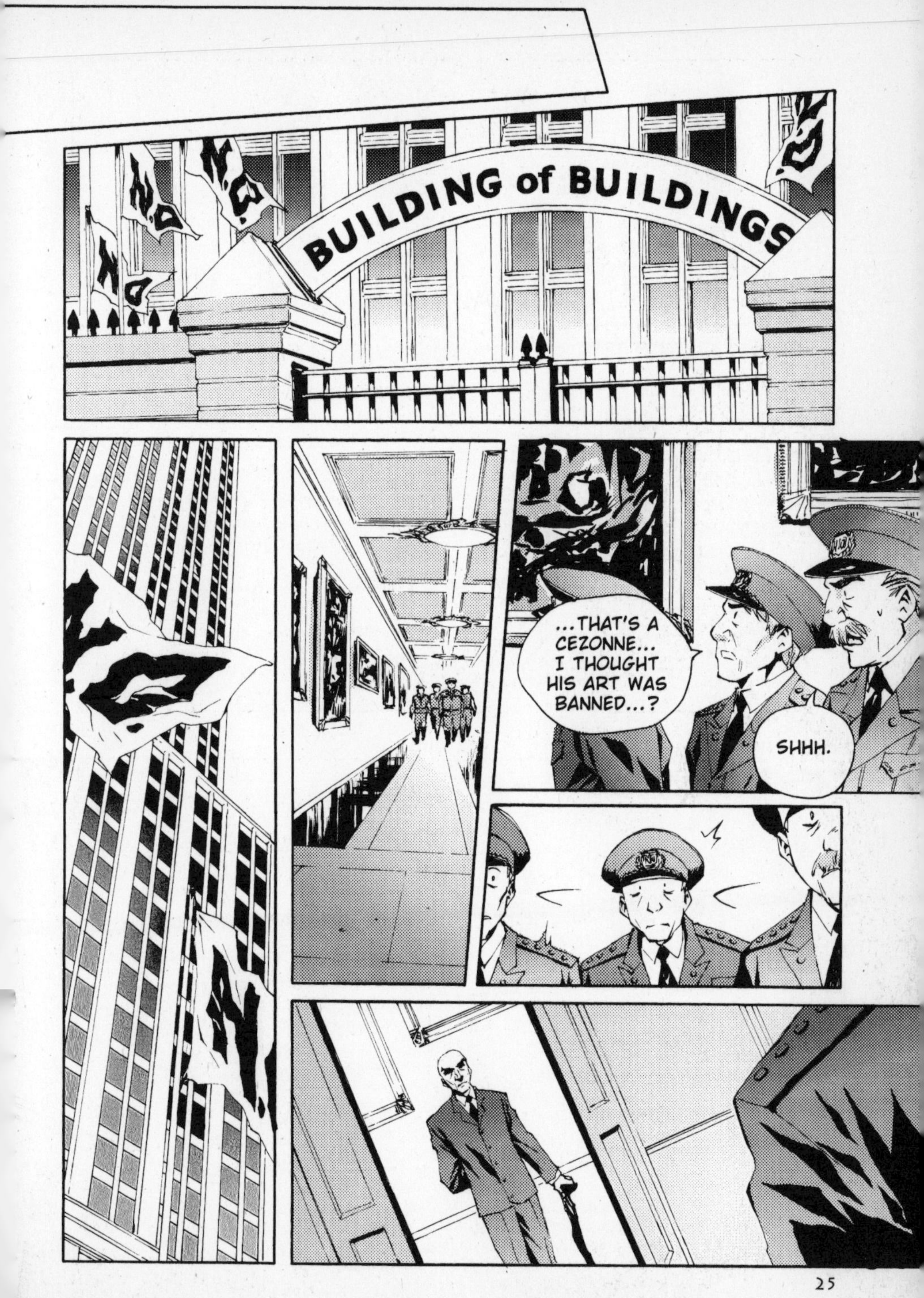
BUILDING of BUILDINGS
...THAT'S A CEZONNE... I THOUGHT HIS ART WAS BANNED...?
SHHH.

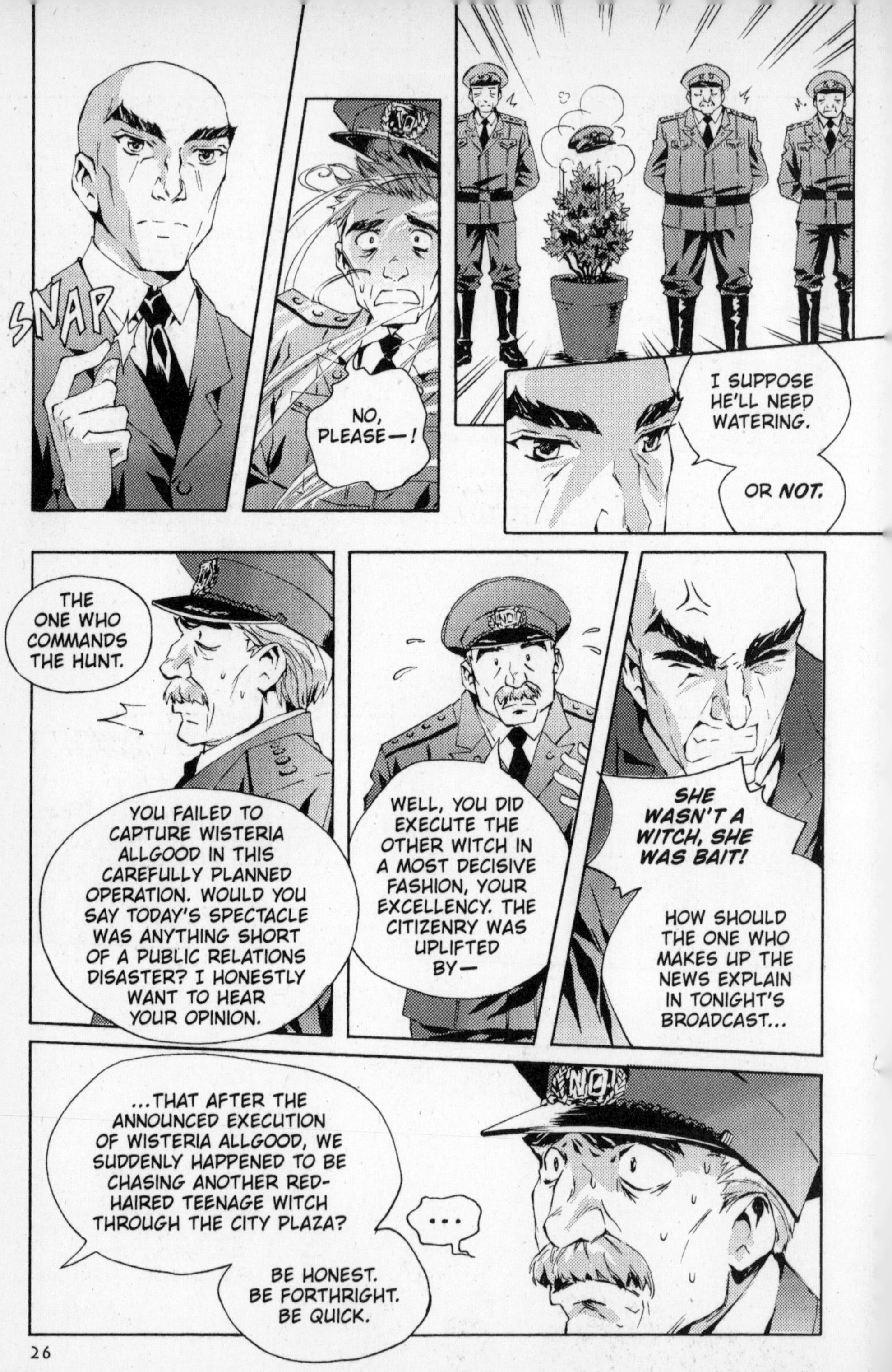
SNAP
NO, PLEASE—!
I SUPPOSE HE'LL NEED WATERING.
OR *NOT.*
THE ONE WHO COMMANDS THE HUNT.
YOU FAILED TO CAPTURE WISTERIA ALLGOOD IN THIS CAREFULLY PLANNED OPERATION. WOULD YOU SAY TODAY'S SPECTACLE WAS ANYTHING SHORT OF A PUBLIC RELATIONS DISASTER? I HONESTLY WANT TO HEAR YOUR OPINION.
WELL, YOU DID EXECUTE THE OTHER WITCH IN A MOST DECISIVE FASHION, YOUR EXCELLENCY. THE CITIZENRY WAS UPLIFTED BY—
SHE WASN'T A WITCH, SHE WAS BAIT!
HOW SHOULD THE ONE WHO MAKES UP THE NEWS EXPLAIN IN TONIGHT'S BROADCAST...
...THAT AFTER THE ANNOUNCED EXECUTION OF WISTERIA ALLGOOD, WE SUDDENLY HAPPENED TO BE CHASING ANOTHER RED-HAIRED TEENAGE WITCH THROUGH THE CITY PLAZA?
...
BE HONEST. BE FORTHRIGHT. BE QUICK.

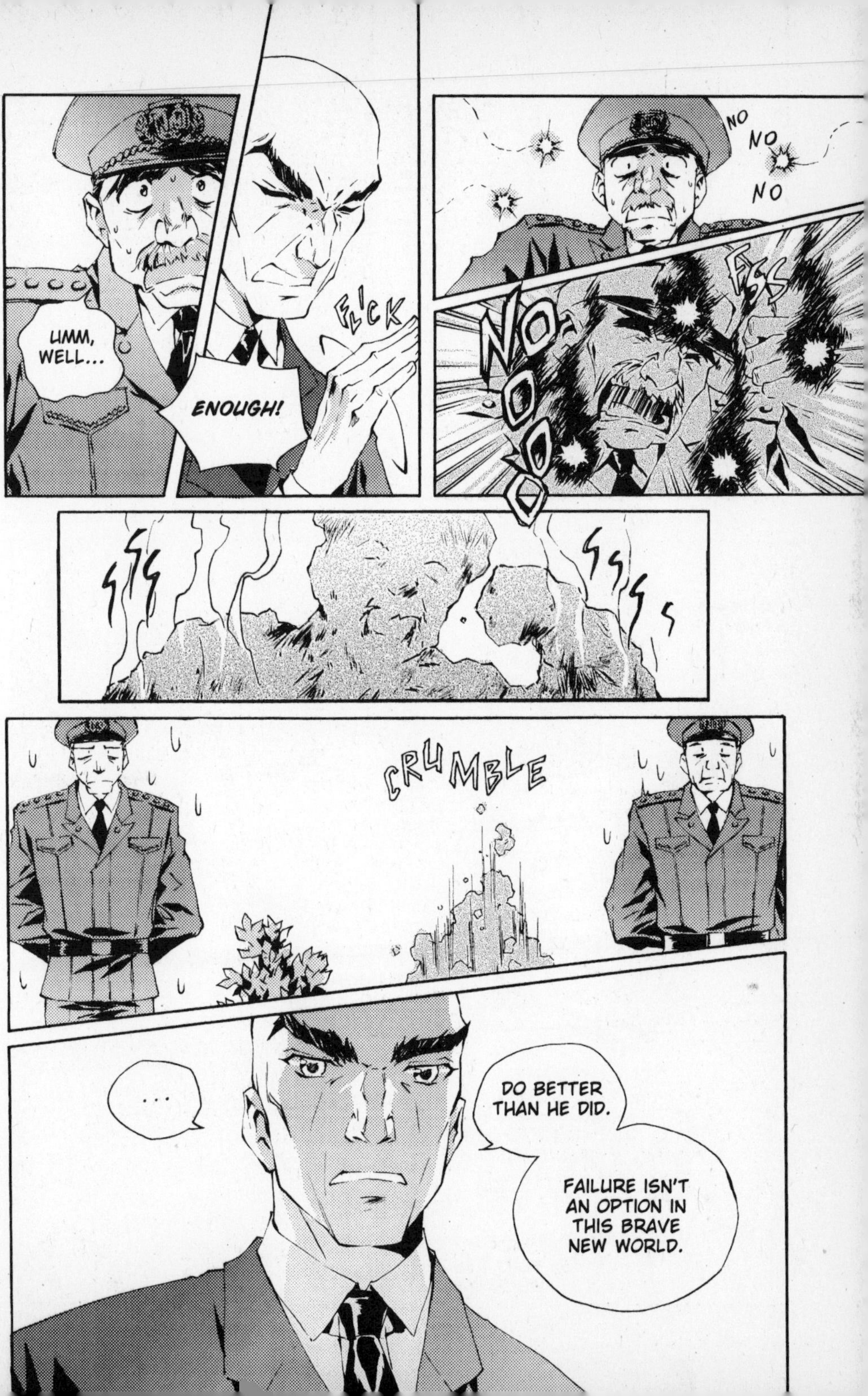
UMM, WELL...
ENOUGH!
FLICK
NO
NO
NO
FSS
NOOOOOO
CRUMBLE
...
DO BETTER THAN HE DID.
FAILURE ISN'T AN OPTION IN THIS BRAVE NEW WORLD.

WITCH
&
WIZARD

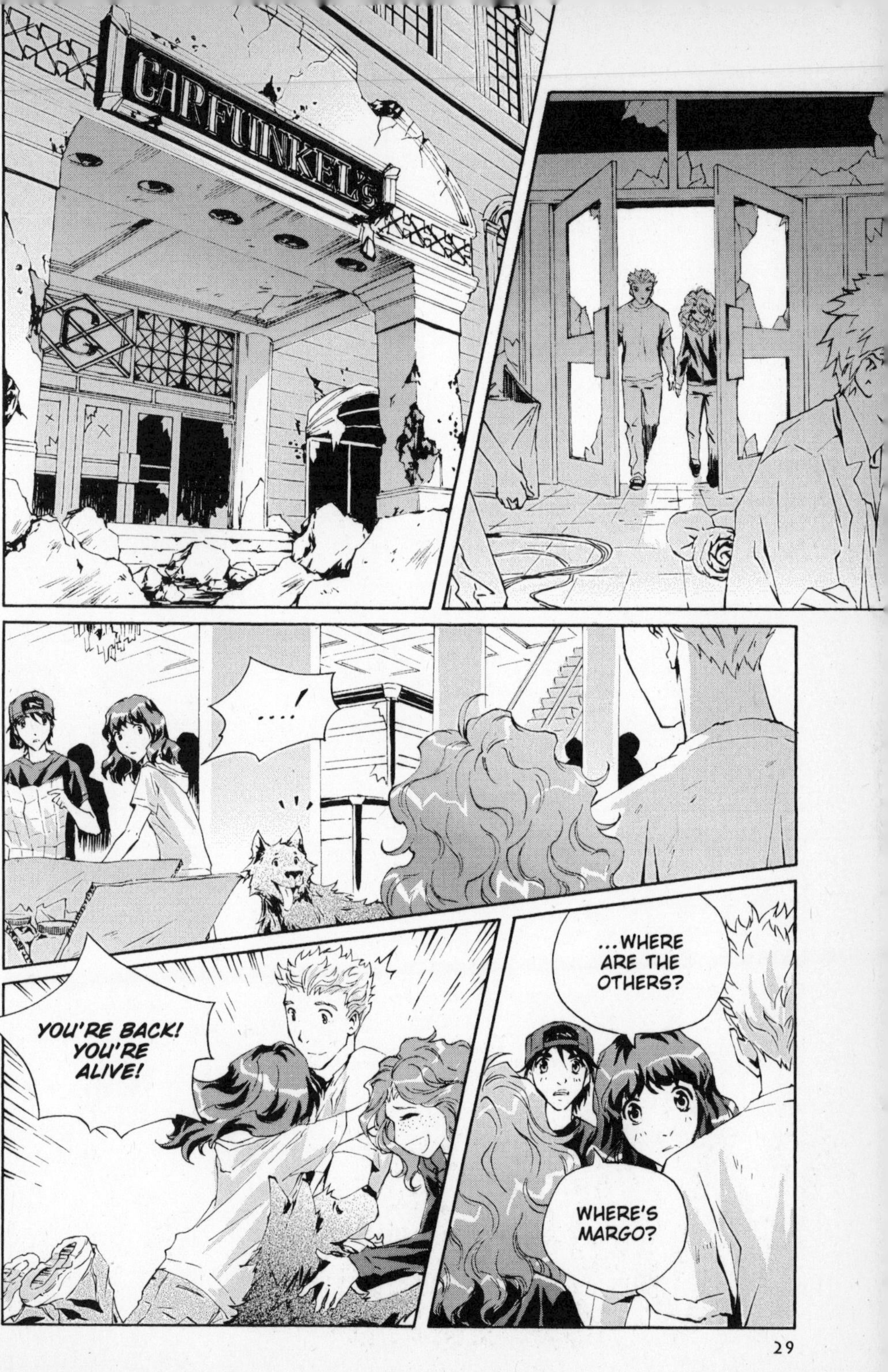
GARFUNKEL'S
...!
YOU'RE BACK! YOU'RE ALIVE!
...WHERE ARE THE OTHERS?
WHERE'S MARGO?

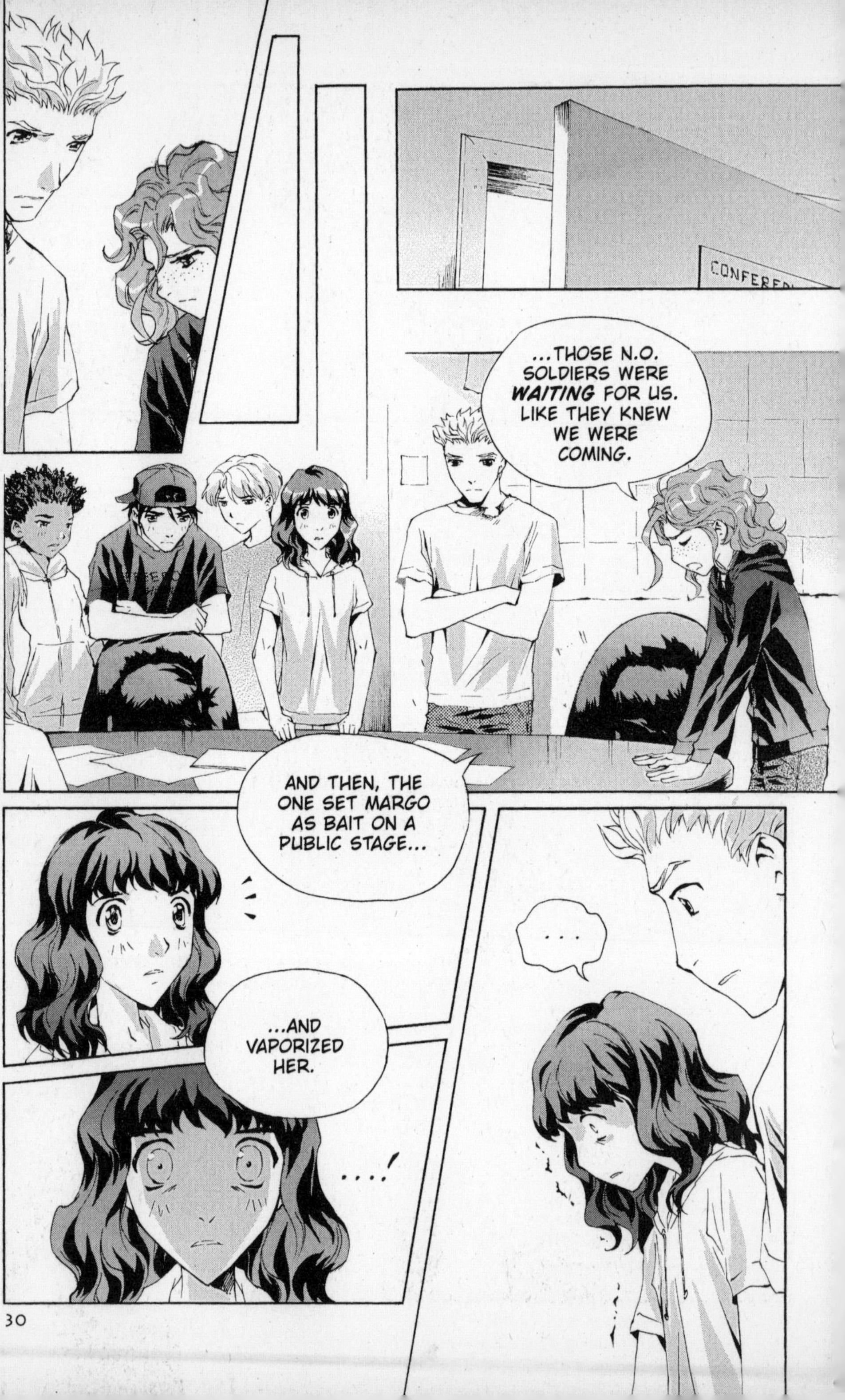
...THOSE N.O. SOLDIERS WERE *WAITING* FOR US. LIKE THEY KNEW WE WERE COMING.
AND THEN, THE ONE SET MARGO AS BAIT ON A PUBLIC STAGE...
...AND VAPORIZED HER.
....!
...

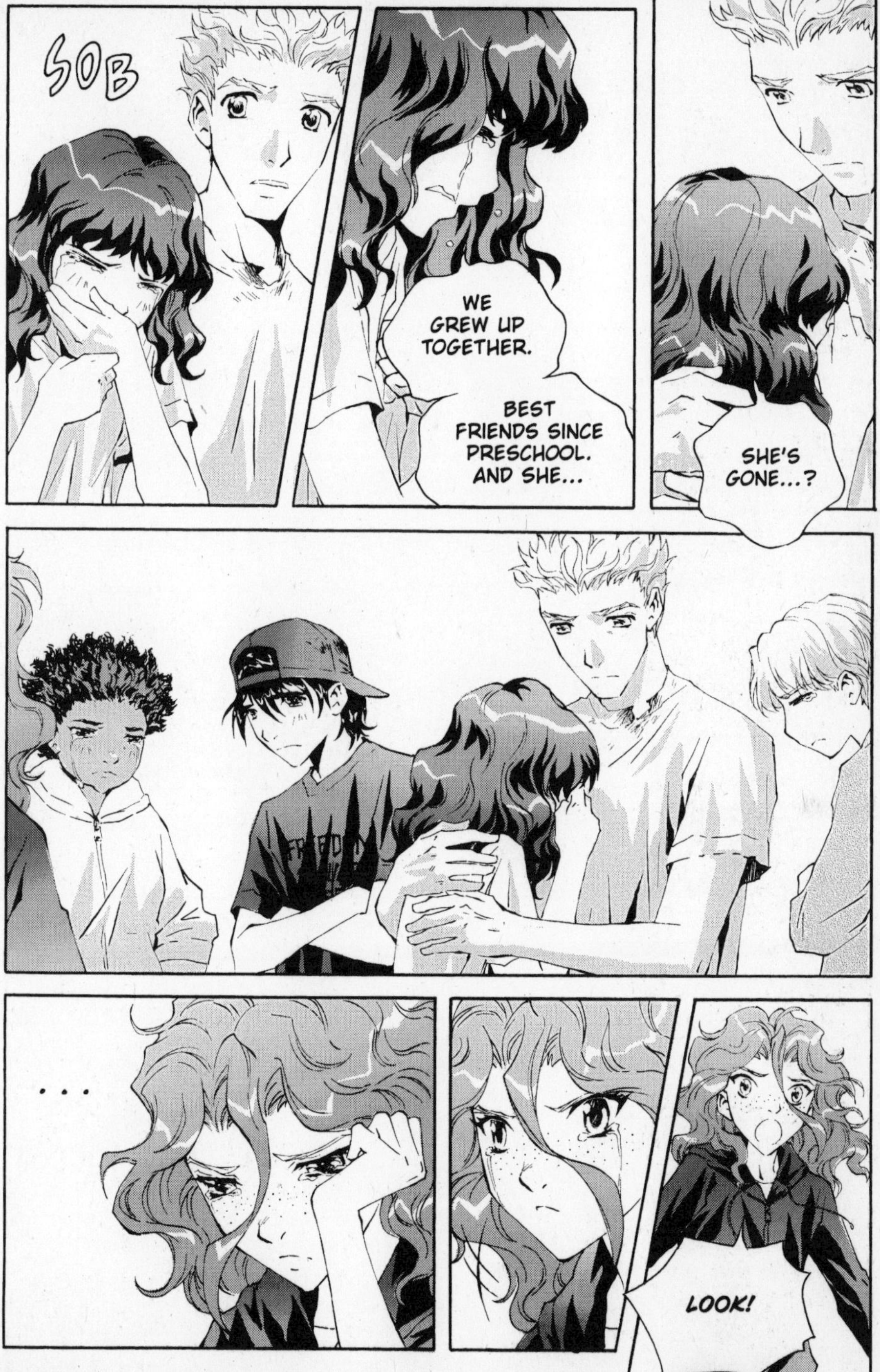
SOB
WE GROW UP TOGETHER.
BEST FRIENDS SINCE PRESCHOOL. AND SHE...
SHE'S GONE...?
...
LOOK!

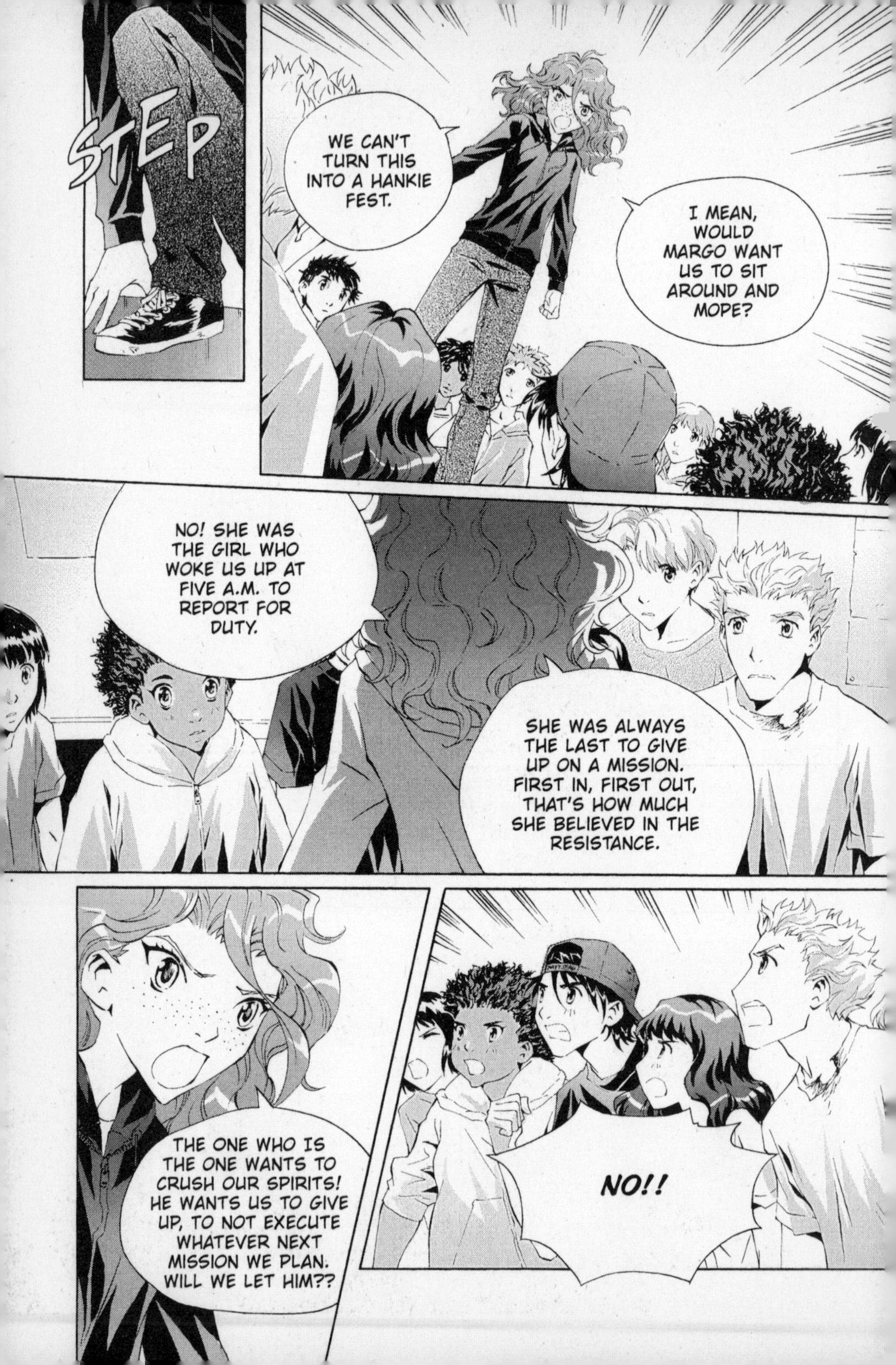
STEP
WE CAN'T TURN THIS INTO A HANKIE FEST.
I MEAN, WOULD MARGO WANT US TO SIT AROUND AND MOPE?
NO! SHE WAS THE GIRL WHO WOKE US UP AT FIVE A.M. TO REPORT FOR DUTY.
SHE WAS ALWAYS THE LAST TO GIVE UP ON A MISSION. FIRST IN, FIRST OUT, THAT'S HOW MUCH SHE BELIEVED IN THE RESISTANCE.
THE ONE WHO IS THE ONE WANTS TO CRUSH OUR SPIRITS! HE WANTS US TO GIVE UP, TO NOT EXECUTE WHATEVER NEXT MISSION WE PLAN. WILL WE LET HIM??
NO!!

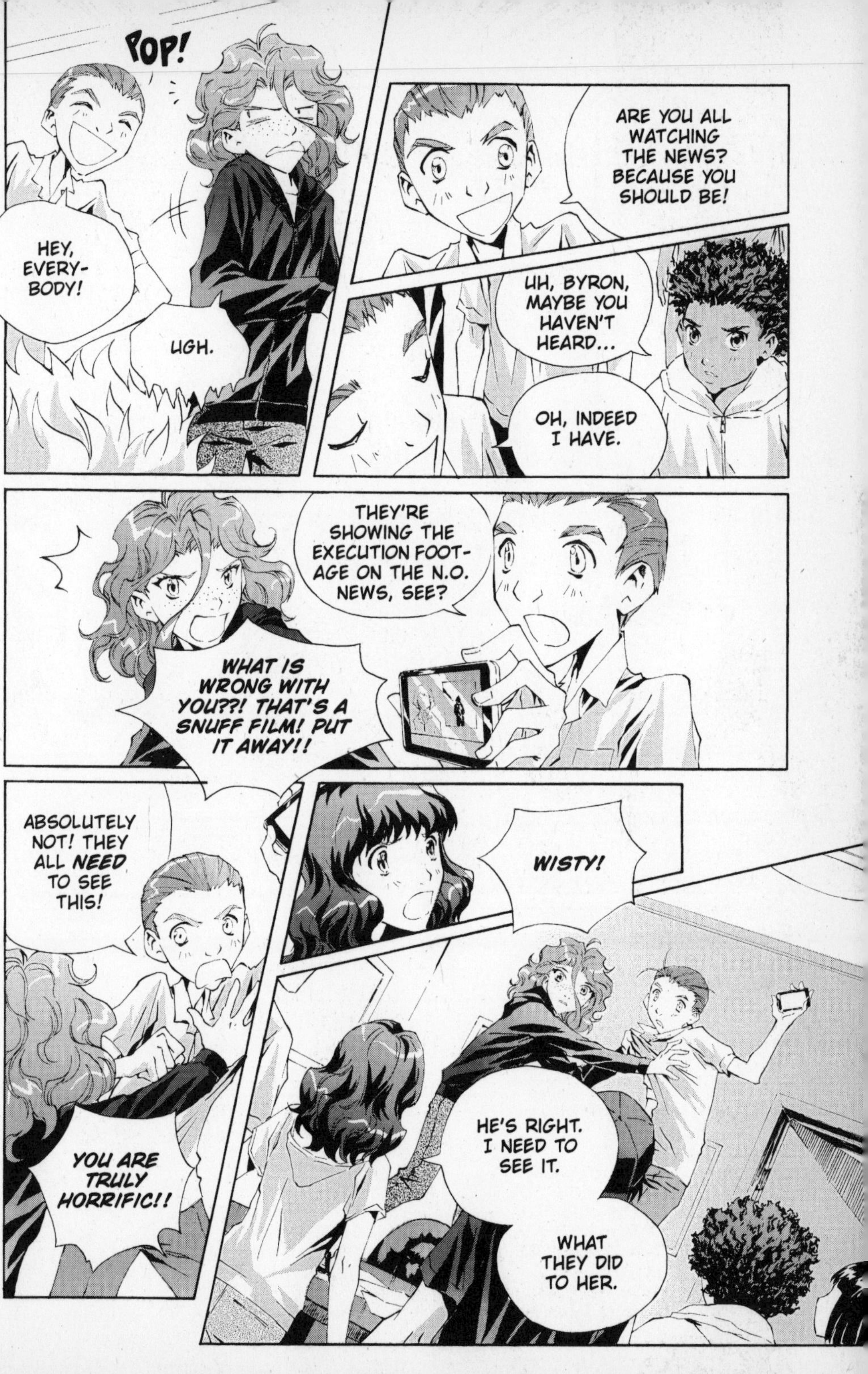
POP!
HEY, EVERY-BODY!
UGH.
ARE YOU ALL WATCHING THE NEWS? BECAUSE YOU SHOULD BE!
UH, BYRON, MAYBE YOU HAVEN'T HEARD...
OH, INDEED I HAVE.
THEY'RE SHOWING THE EXECUTION FOOT-AGE ON THE N.O. NEWS, SEE?
WHAT IS WRONG WITH YOU??! THAT'S A SNUFF FILM! PUT IT AWAY!!
ABSOLUTELY NOT! THEY ALL NEED TO SEE THIS!
YOU ARE TRULY HORRIFIC!!
WISTY!
HE'S RIGHT. I NEED TO SEE IT.
WHAT THEY DID TO HER.

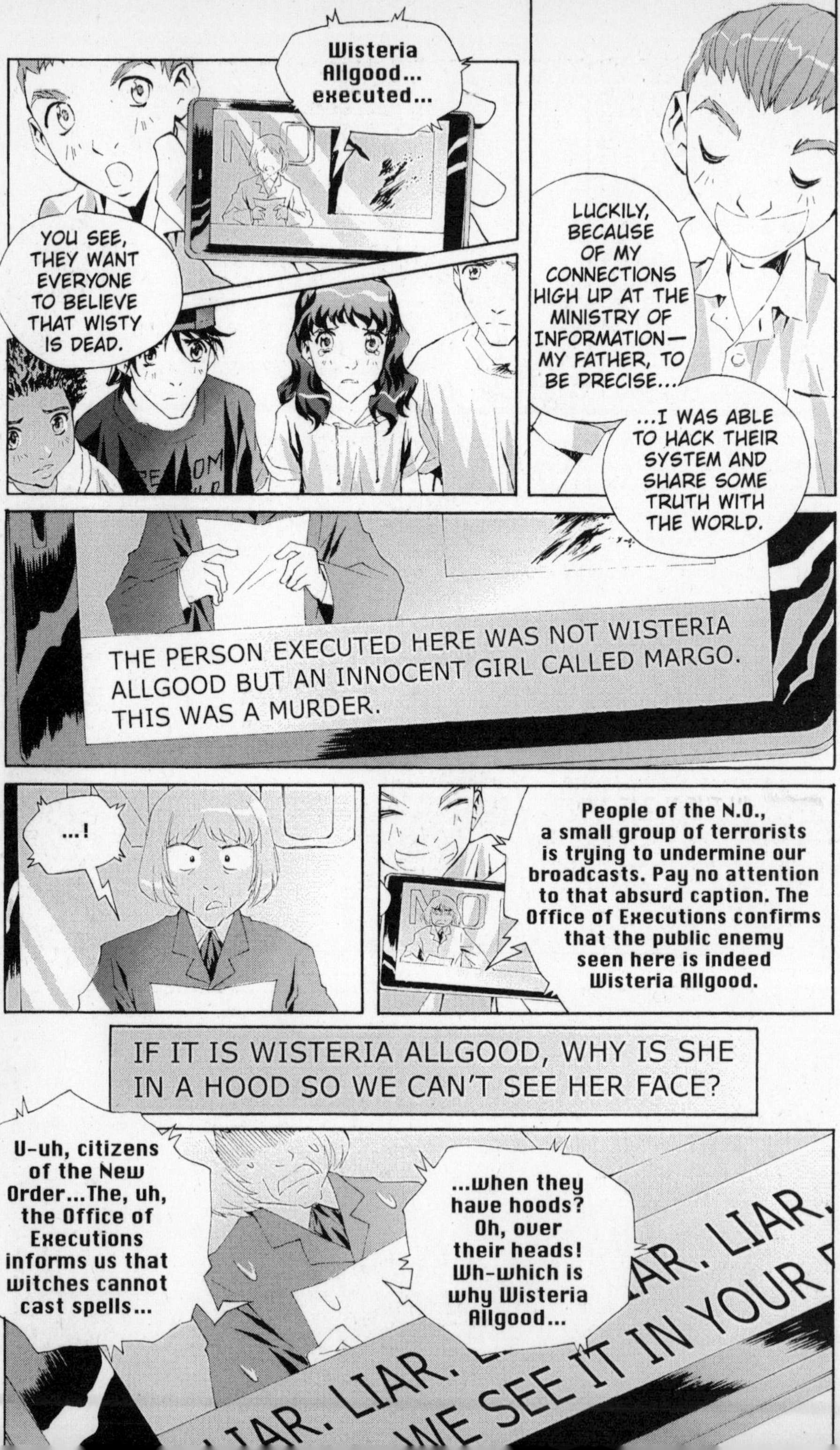
Wisteria Allgood... executed...
YOU SEE, THEY WANT EVERYONE TO BELIEVE THAT WISTY IS DEAD.
LUCKILY, BECAUSE OF MY CONNECTIONS HIGH UP AT THE MINISTRY OF INFORMATION—MY FATHER, TO BE PRECISE...
...I WAS ABLE TO HACK THEIR SYSTEM AND SHARE SOME TRUTH WITH THE WORLD.
THE PERSON EXECUTED HERE WAS NOT WISTERIA ALLGOOD BUT AN INNOCENT GIRL CALLED MARGO. THIS WAS A MURDER.
...!
People of the N.O., a small group of terrorists is trying to undermine our broadcasts. Pay no attention to that absurd caption. The Office of Executions confirms that the public enemy seen here is indeed Wisteria Allgood.
IF IT IS WISTERIA ALLGOOD, WHY IS SHE IN A HOOD SO WE CAN'T SEE HER FACE?
U-uh, citizens of the New Order...The, uh, the Office of Executions informs us that witches cannot cast spells...
...when they have hoods? Oh, over their heads! Wh-which is why Wisteria Allgood...
LIAR. LIAR.
LIAR. LIAR.
WE SEE IT IN YOUR

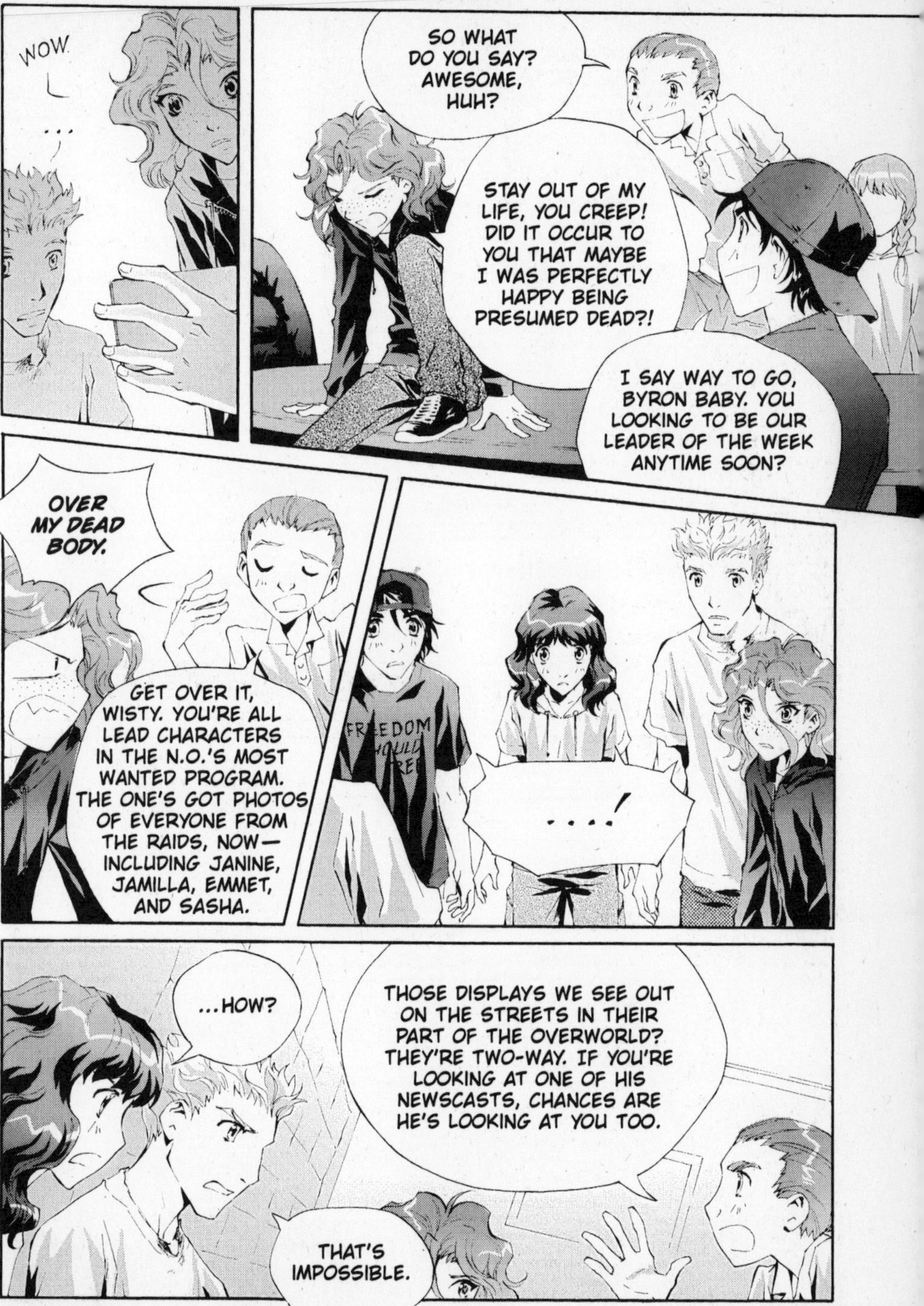
WOW.
...
SO WHAT DO YOU SAY? AWESOME, HUH?
STAY OUT OF MY LIFE, YOU CREEP! DID IT OCCUR TO YOU THAT MAYBE I WAS PERFECTLY HAPPY BEING PRESUMED DEAD?!
I SAY WAY TO GO, BYRON BABY. YOU LOOKING TO BE OUR LEADER OF THE WEEK ANYTIME SOON?
OVER MY DEAD BODY.
GET OVER IT, WISTY. YOU'RE ALL LEAD CHARACTERS IN THE N.O.'S MOST WANTED PROGRAM. THE ONE'S GOT PHOTOS OF EVERYONE FROM THE RAIDS, NOW— INCLUDING JANINE, JAMILLA, EMMET, AND SASHA.
FREEDOM
...!
...HOW?
THOSE DISPLAYS WE SEE OUT ON THE STREETS IN THEIR PART OF THE OVERWORLD? THEY'RE TWO-WAY. IF YOU'RE LOOKING AT ONE OF HIS NEWSCASTS, CHANCES ARE HE'S LOOKING AT YOU TOO.
THAT'S IMPOSSIBLE.

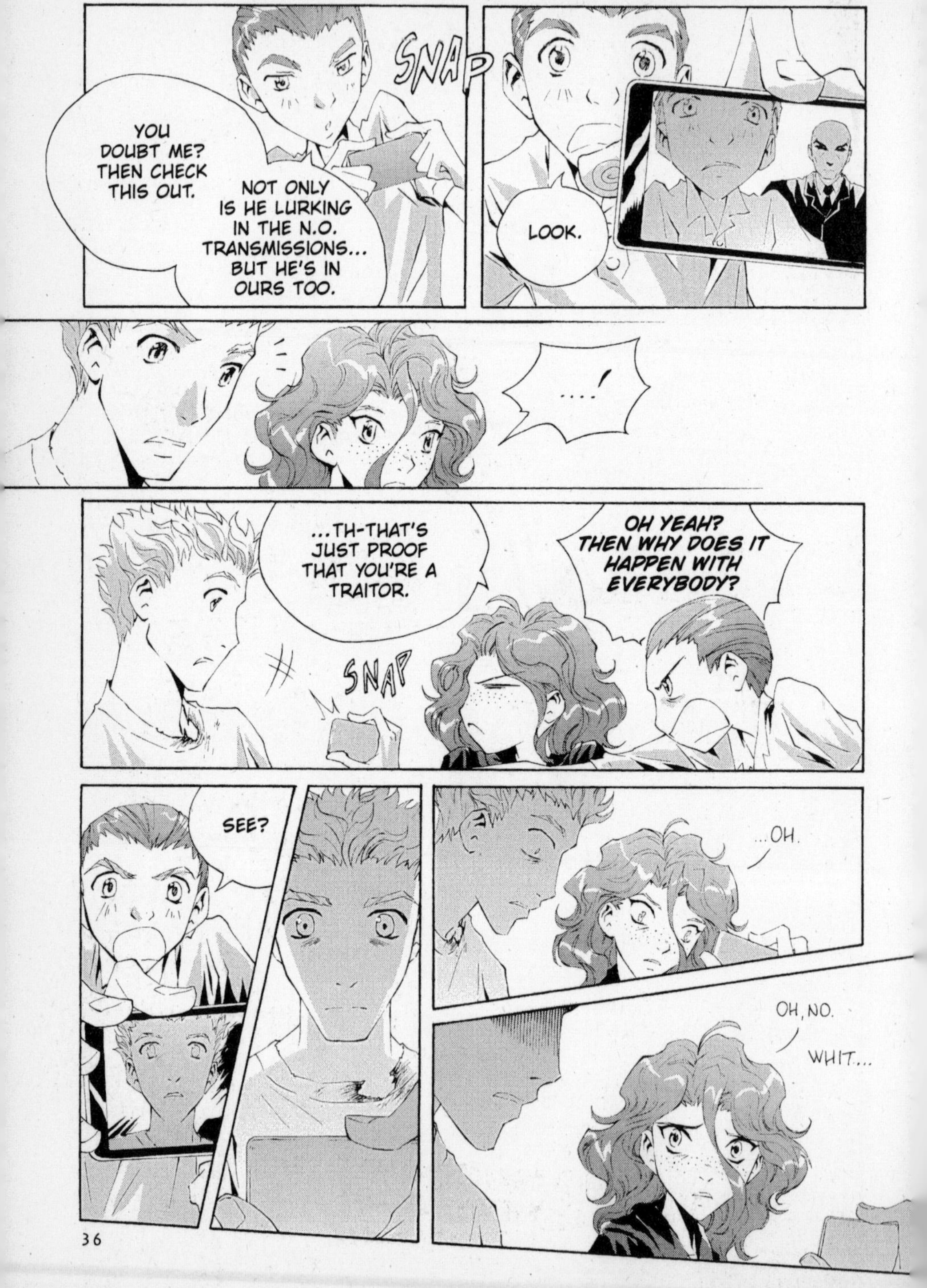
YOU DOUBT ME? THEN CHECK THIS OUT.
NOT ONLY IS HE LURKING IN THE N.O. TRANSMISSIONS... BUT HE'S IN OURS TOO.
SNAP
LOOK.
....!
...TH-THAT'S JUST PROOF THAT YOU'RE A TRAITOR.
SNAP
OH YEAH? THEN WHY DOES IT HAPPEN WITH EVERYBODY?
SEE?
...OH.
OH, NO.
WHIT...

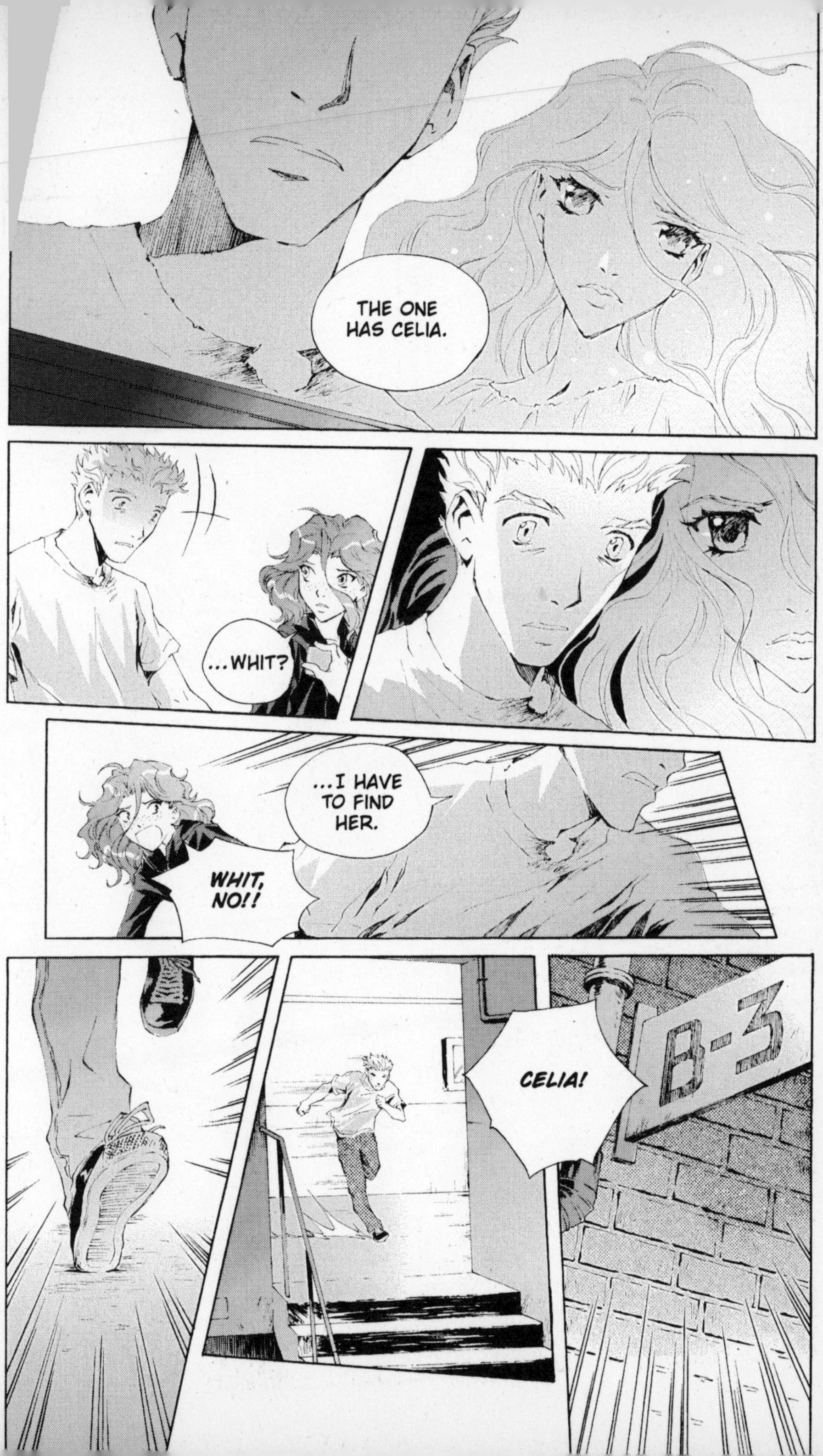
THE ONE HAS CELIA.
...WHIT?
...I HAVE TO FIND HER.
WHIT, NO!!
CELIA!
B-3

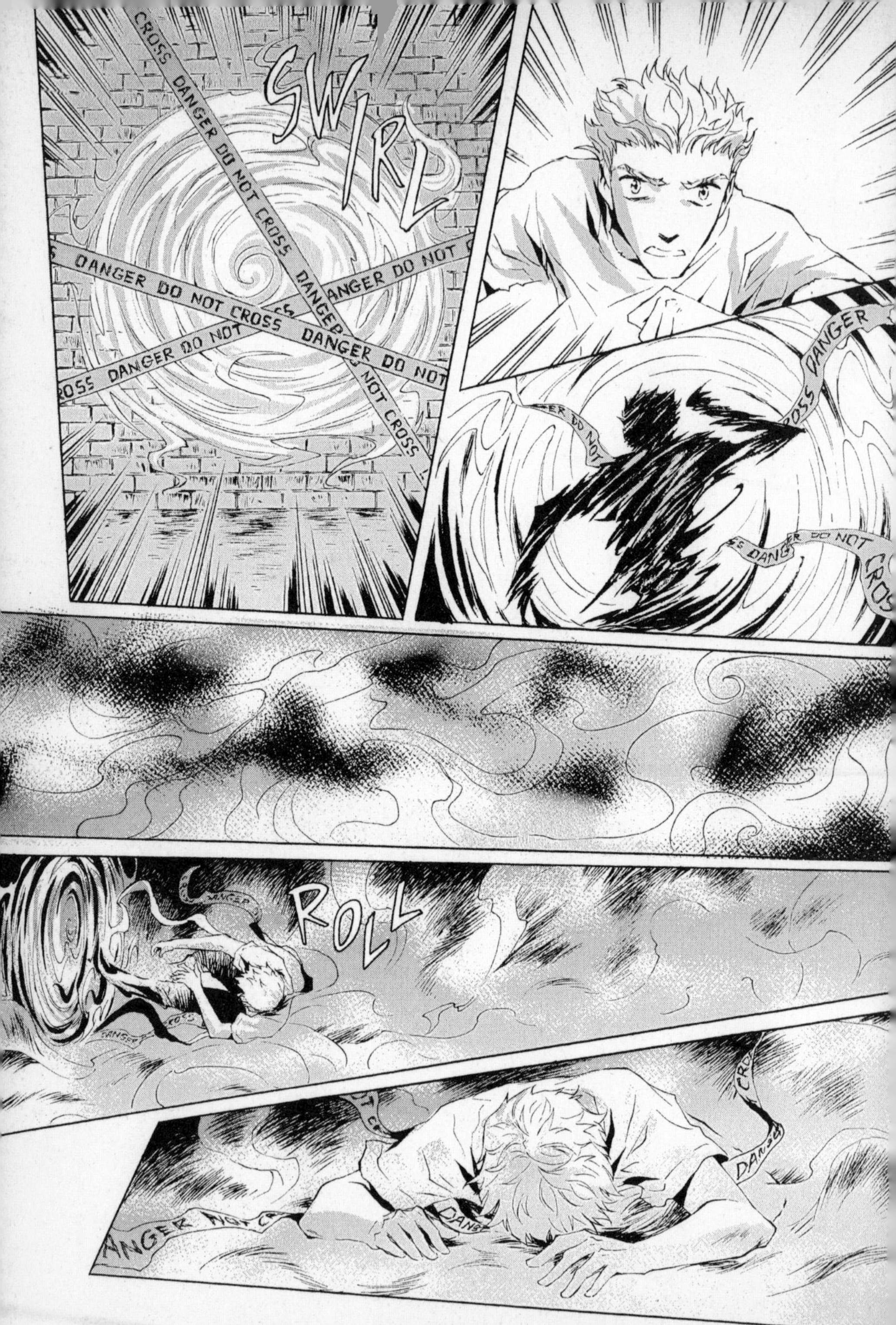

SWIRL
CROSS DANGER DO NOT CROSS
DANGER DO NOT CROSS
DANGER DO NOT
CROSS DANGER DO NOT
DANGER DO NOT
DANGER DO NOT CROSS
DANGER
CROSS
DANGER DO NOT
DANGER DO NOT
CROSS
ROLL

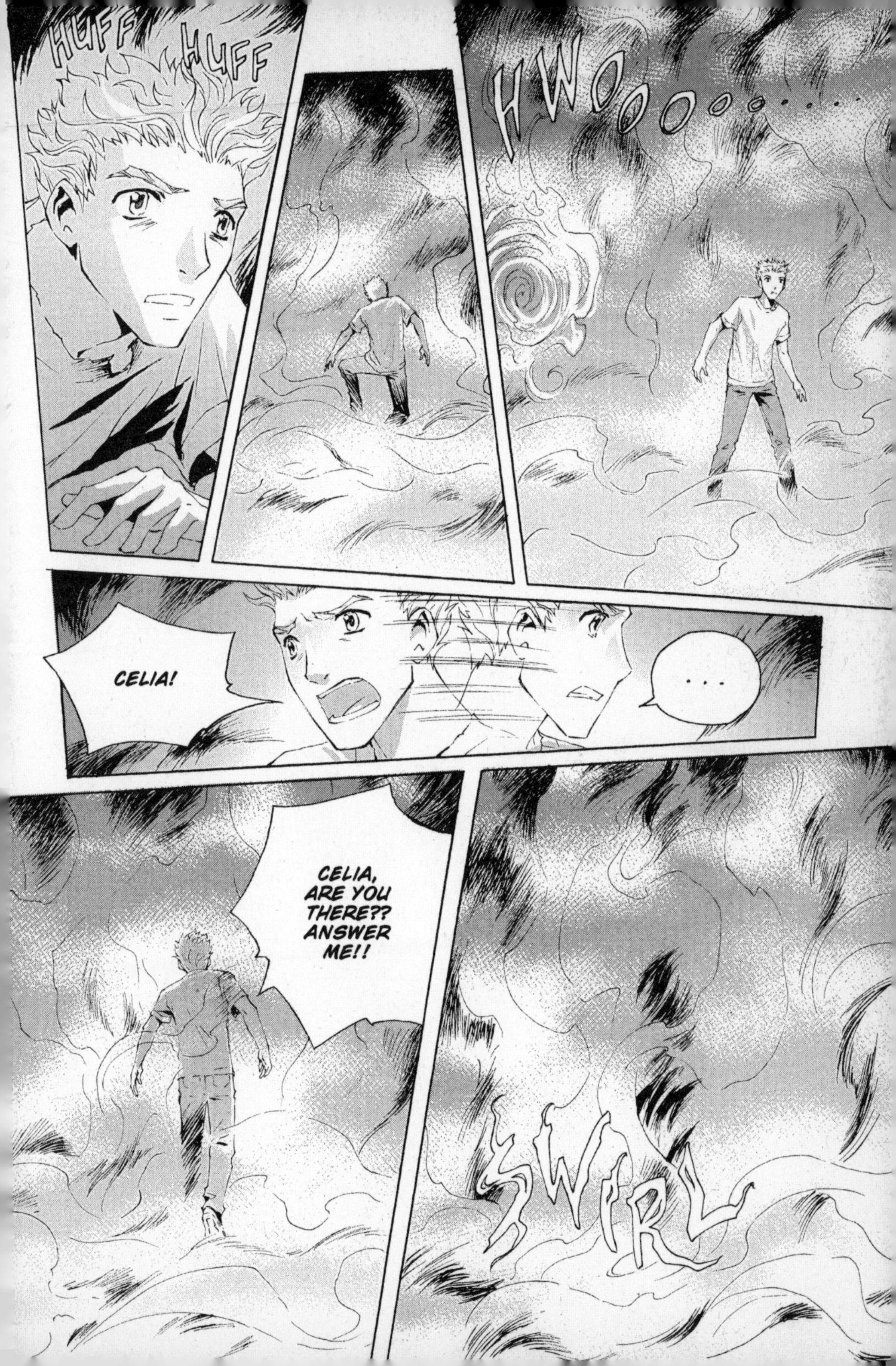
HUFF HUFF
HWOOOOO....
CELIA!
...
CELIA, ARE YOU THERE?? ANSWER ME!!
SWIRL

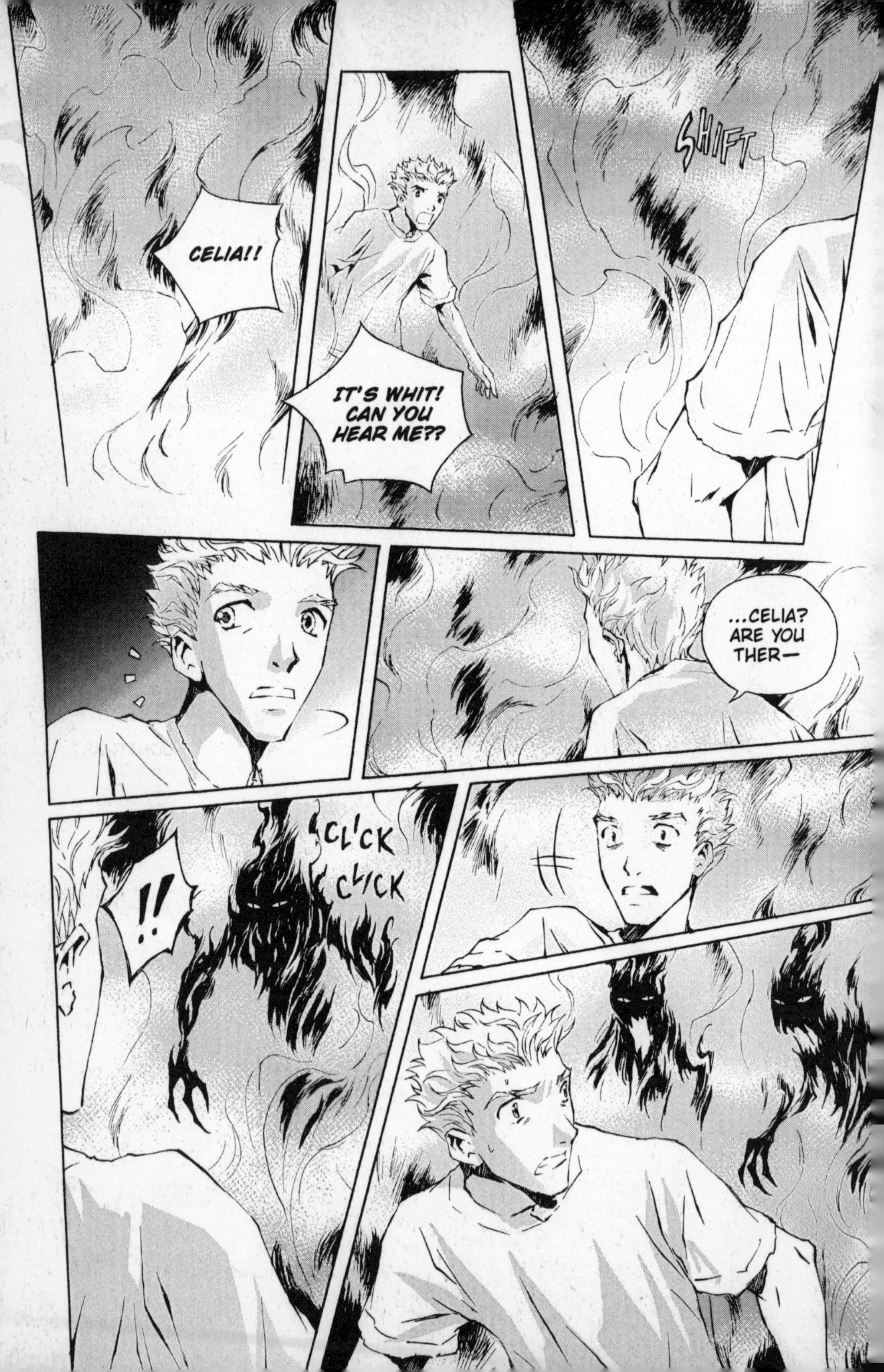

CELIA!!
IT'S WHIT! CAN YOU HEAR ME??
SHIFT
...CELIA? ARE YOU THER—
!!
CLICK
CLICK

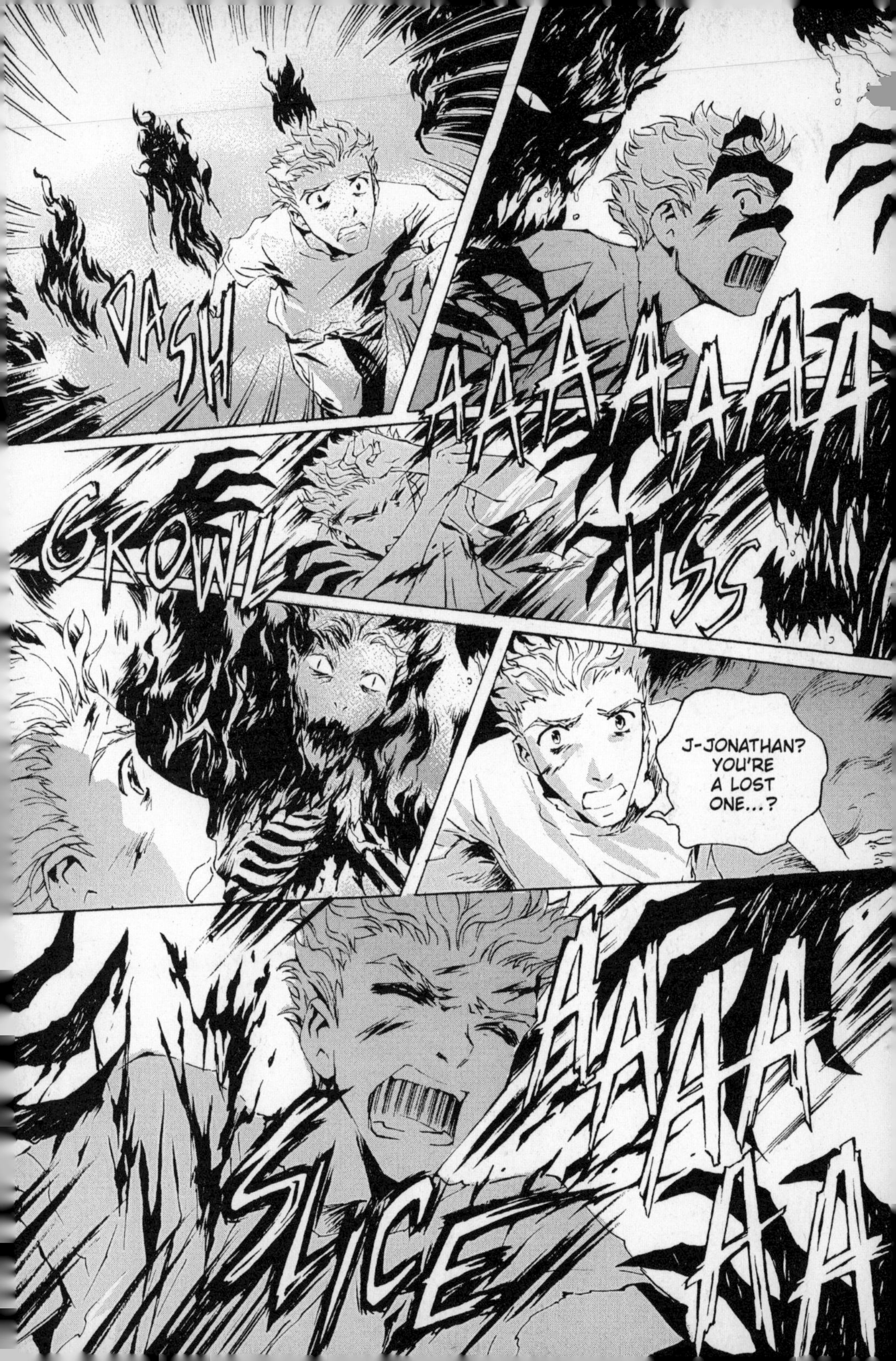
DASH
AAAAAA
GROWL
HISS
J-JONATHAN? YOU'RE A LOST ONE...?
SLICE
AAAAAA

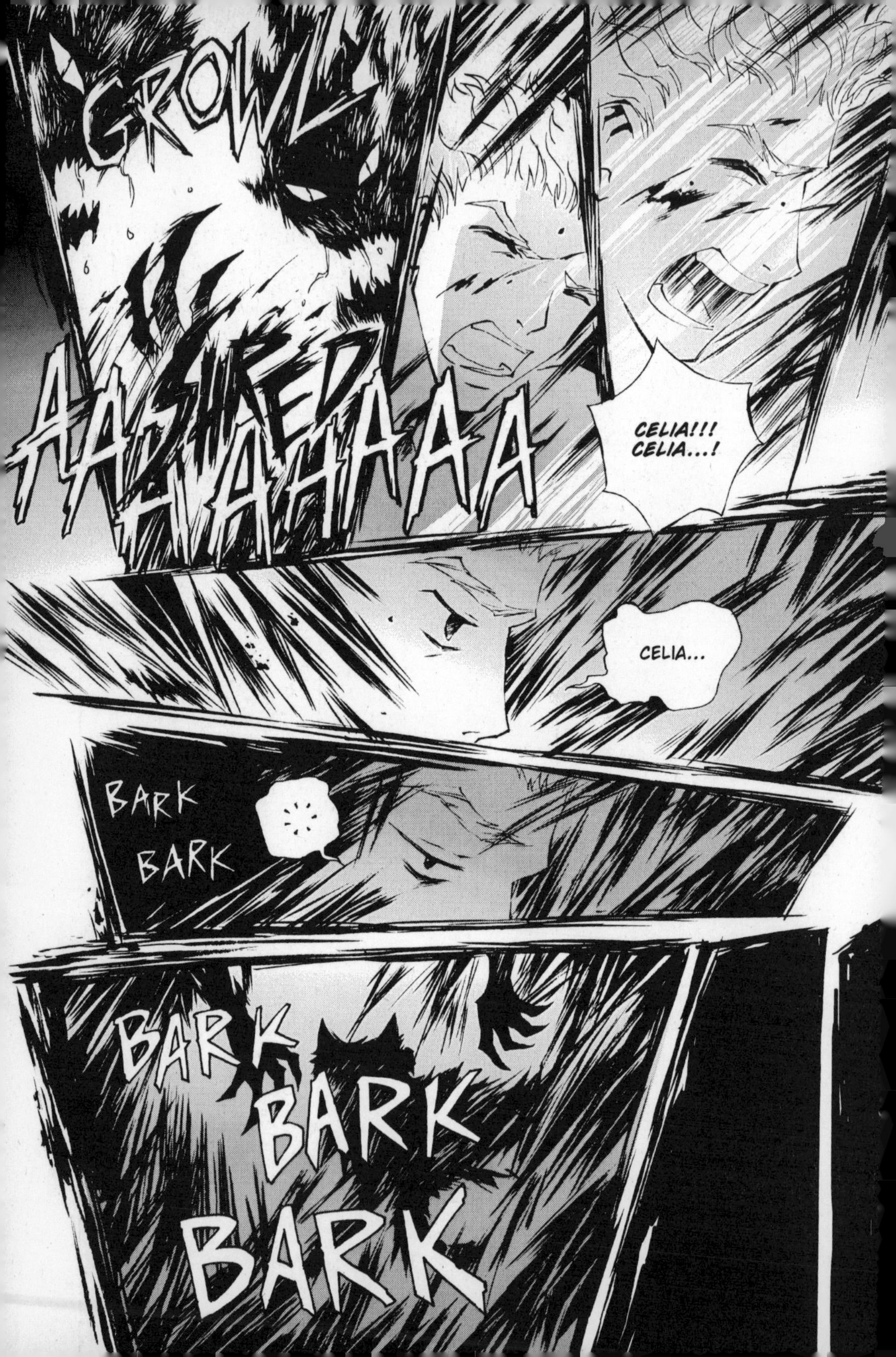
GROWL
CELIA!!!
CELIA...!
CELIA...
BARK
BARK
BARK
BARK
BARK

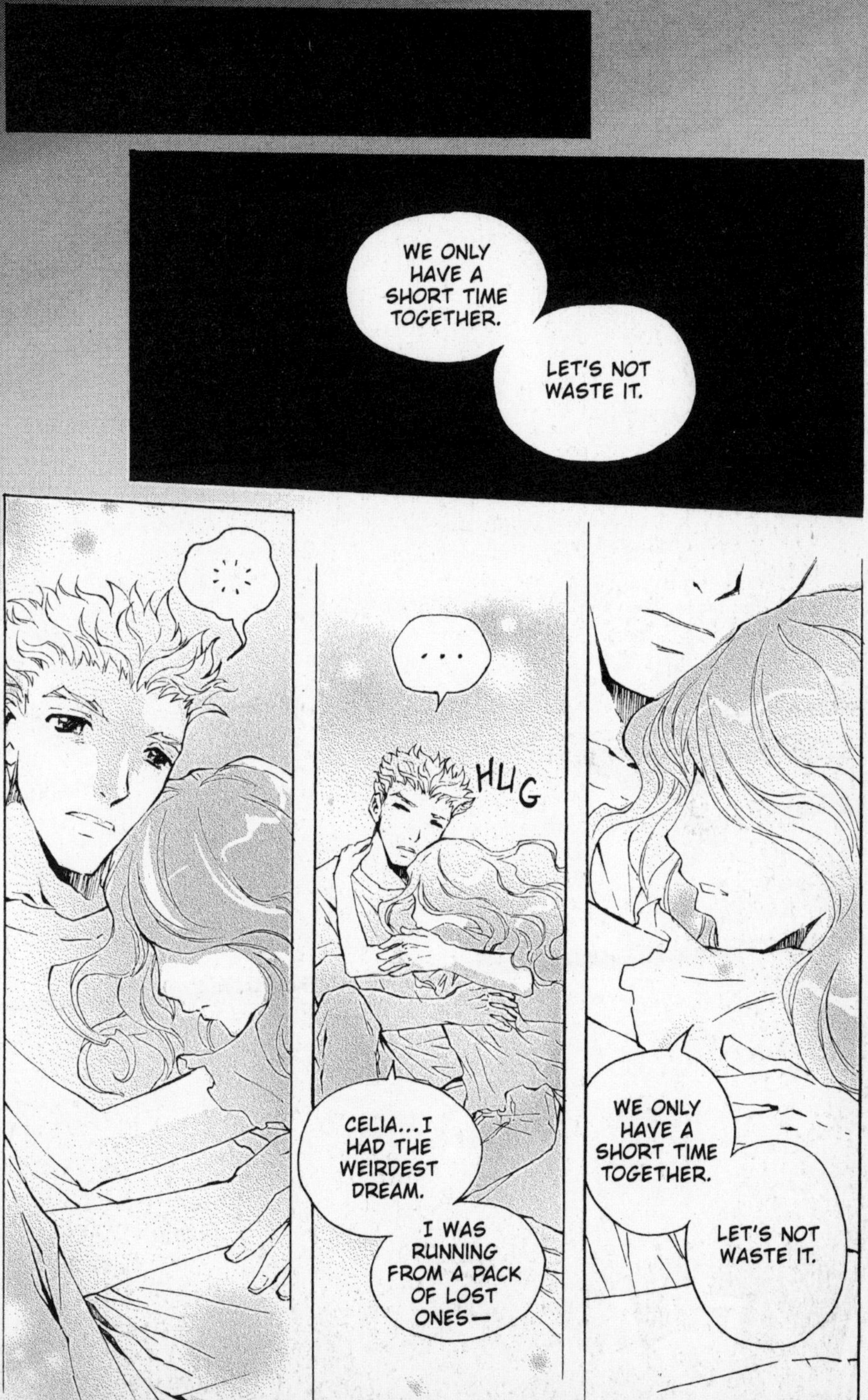
WE ONLY HAVE A SHORT TIME TOGETHER.
LET'S NOT WASTE IT.
...
HUG
CELIA...I HAD THE WEIRDEST DREAM.
I WAS RUNNING FROM A PACK OF LOST ONES—
WE ONLY HAVE A SHORT TIME TOGETHER.
LET'S NOT WASTE IT.

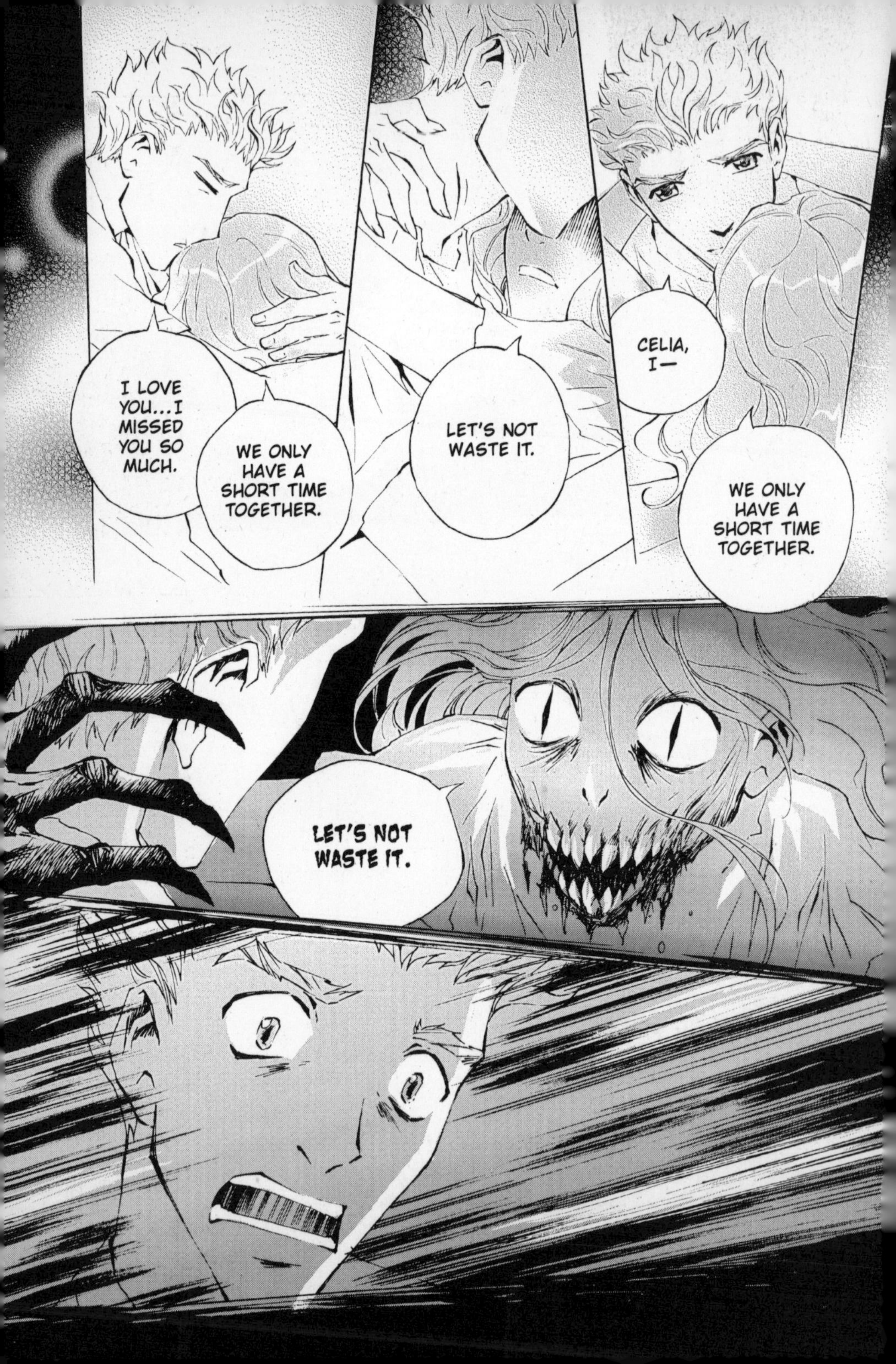
I LOVE YOU...I MISSED YOU SO MUCH.
WE ONLY HAVE A SHORT TIME TOGETHER.
LET'S NOT WASTE IT.
CELIA, I—
WE ONLY HAVE A SHORT TIME TOGETHER.
LET'S NOT WASTE IT.

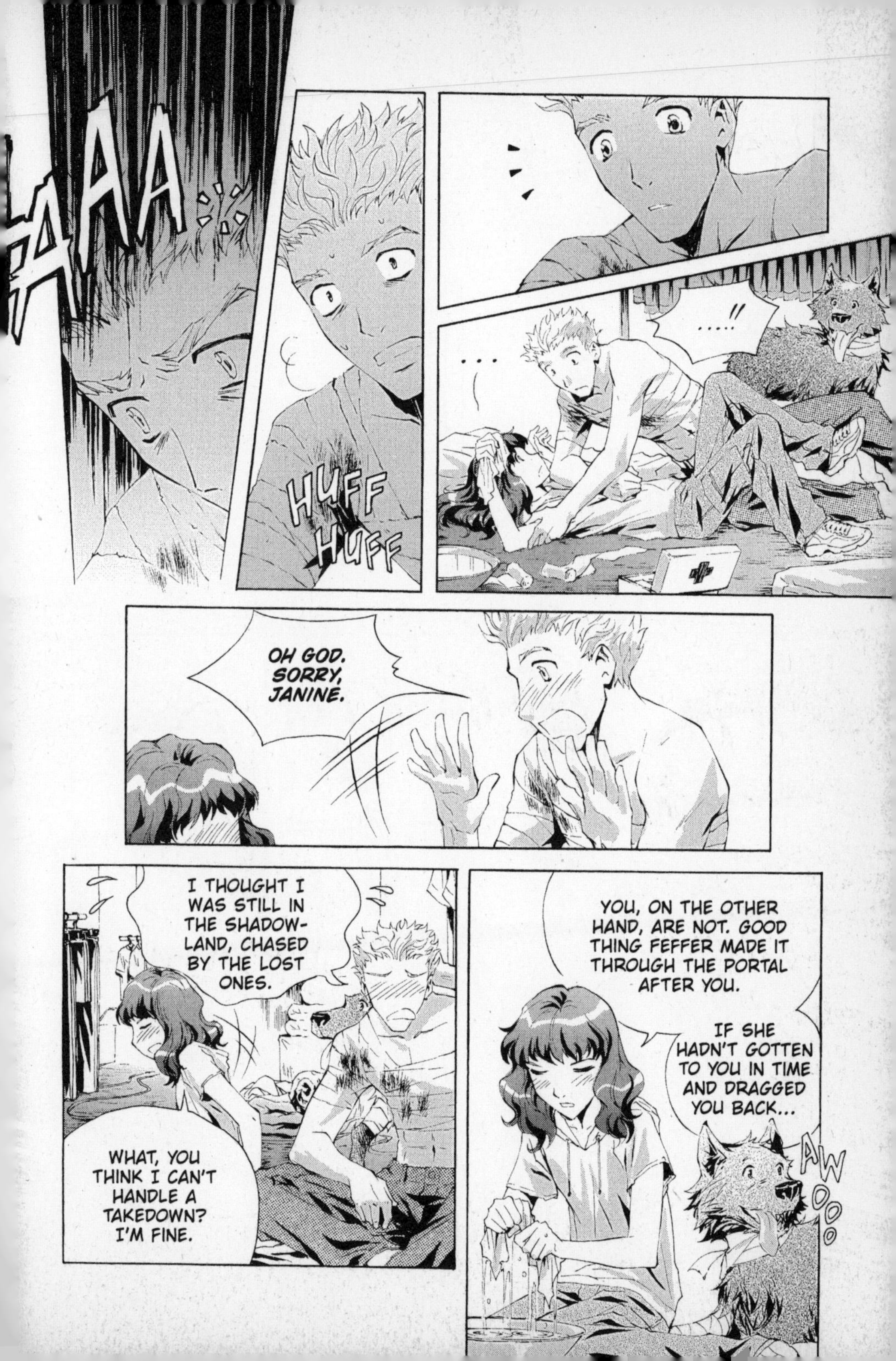

HAAA
HUFF
HUFF
...
.....!!
OH GOD. SORRY, JANINE.
I THOUGHT I WAS STILL IN THE SHADOW-LAND, CHASED BY THE LOST ONES.
WHAT, YOU THINK I CAN'T HANDLE A TAKEDOWN? I'M FINE.
YOU, ON THE OTHER HAND, ARE NOT. GOOD THING FEFFER MADE IT THROUGH THE PORTAL AFTER YOU.
IF SHE HADN'T GOTTEN TO YOU IN TIME AND DRAGGED YOU BACK...
AWOOO

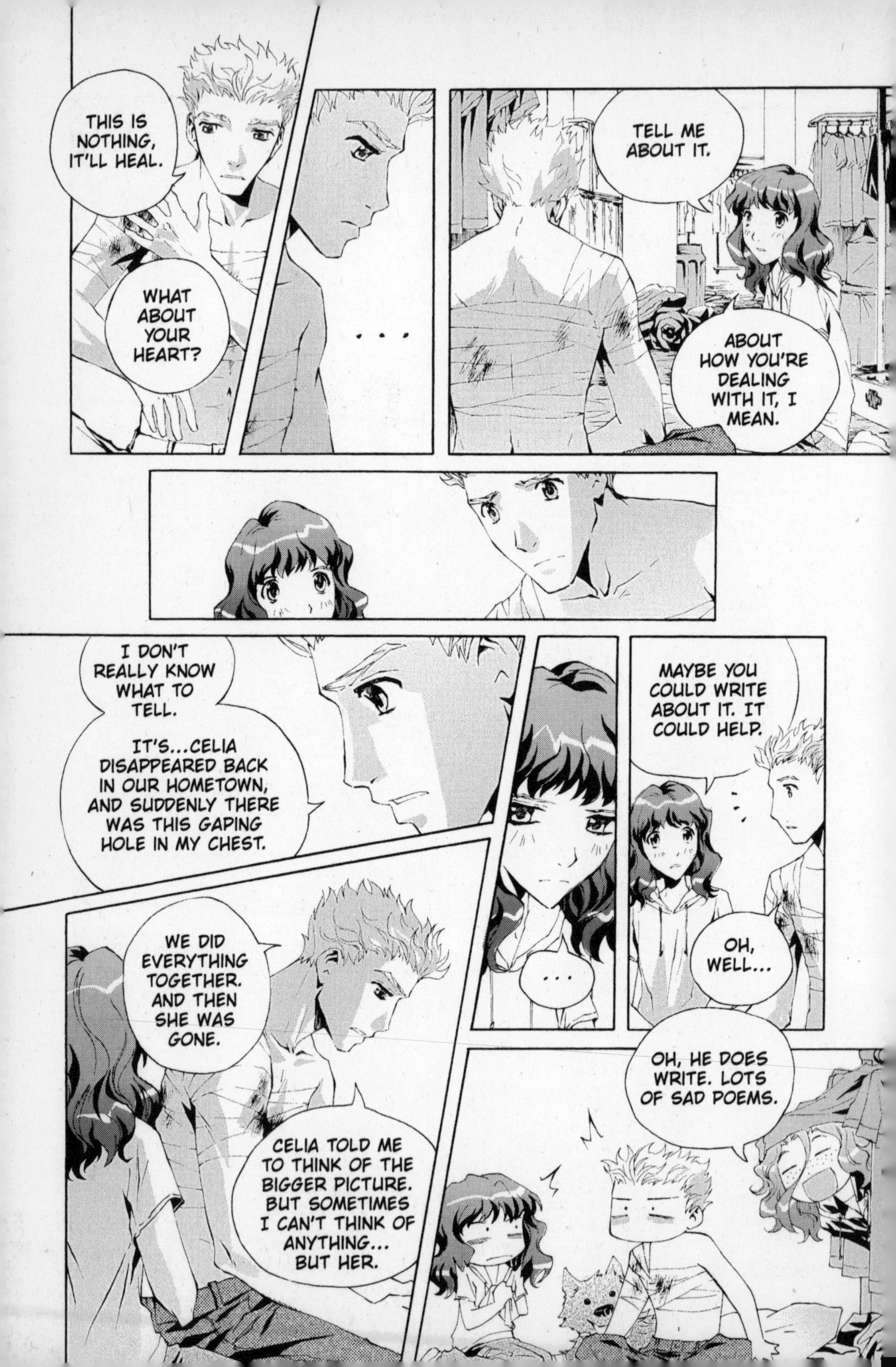
THIS IS NOTHING, IT'LL HEAL.
WHAT ABOUT YOUR HEART?
...
TELL ME ABOUT IT.
ABOUT HOW YOU'RE DEALING WITH IT, I MEAN.
I DON'T REALLY KNOW WHAT TO TELL.
IT'S...CELIA DISAPPEARED BACK IN OUR HOMETOWN, AND SUDDENLY THERE WAS THIS GAPING HOLE IN MY CHEST.
...
MAYBE YOU COULD WRITE ABOUT IT. IT COULD HELP.
OH, WELL...
WE DID EVERYTHING TOGETHER. AND THEN SHE WAS GONE.
CELIA TOLD ME TO THINK OF THE BIGGER PICTURE. BUT SOMETIMES I CAN'T THINK OF ANYTHING... BUT HER.
OH, HE DOES WRITE. LOTS OF SAD POEMS.

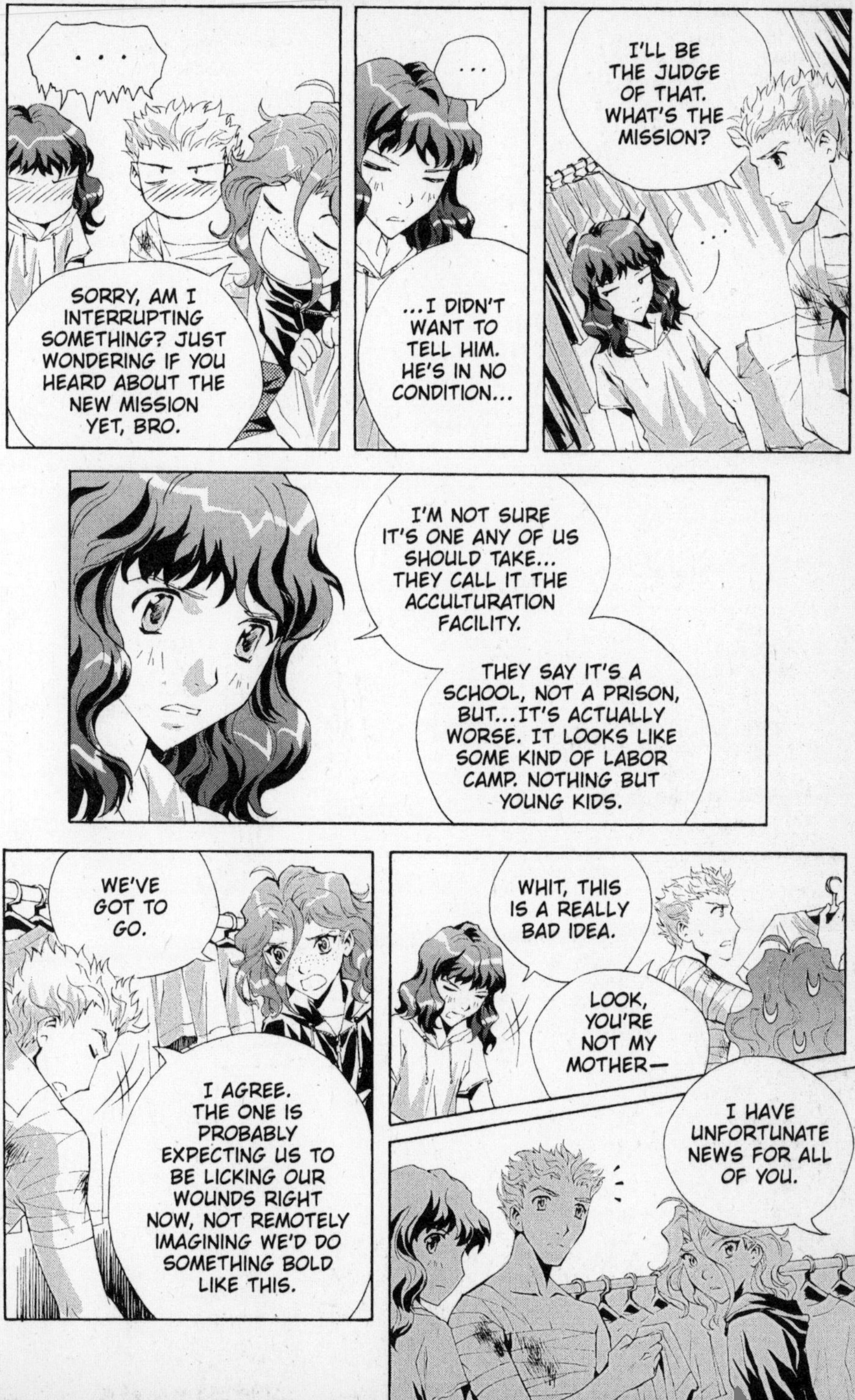
...
SORRY, AM I INTERRUPTING SOMETHING? JUST WONDERING IF YOU HEARD ABOUT THE NEW MISSION YET, BRO.
...
...I DIDN'T WANT TO TELL HIM. HE'S IN NO CONDITION...
I'LL BE THE JUDGE OF THAT. WHAT'S THE MISSION?
...
I'M NOT SURE IT'S ONE ANY OF US SHOULD TAKE... THEY CALL IT THE ACCULTURATION FACILITY.
THEY SAY IT'S A SCHOOL, NOT A PRISON, BUT...IT'S ACTUALLY WORSE. IT LOOKS LIKE SOME KIND OF LABOR CAMP. NOTHING BUT YOUNG KIDS.
WE'VE GOT TO GO.
I AGREE. THE ONE IS PROBABLY EXPECTING US TO BE LICKING OUR WOUNDS RIGHT NOW, NOT REMOTELY IMAGINING WE'D DO SOMETHING BOLD LIKE THIS.
WHIT, THIS IS A REALLY BAD IDEA.
LOOK, YOU'RE NOT MY MOTHER—
I HAVE UNFORTUNATE NEWS FOR ALL OF YOU.

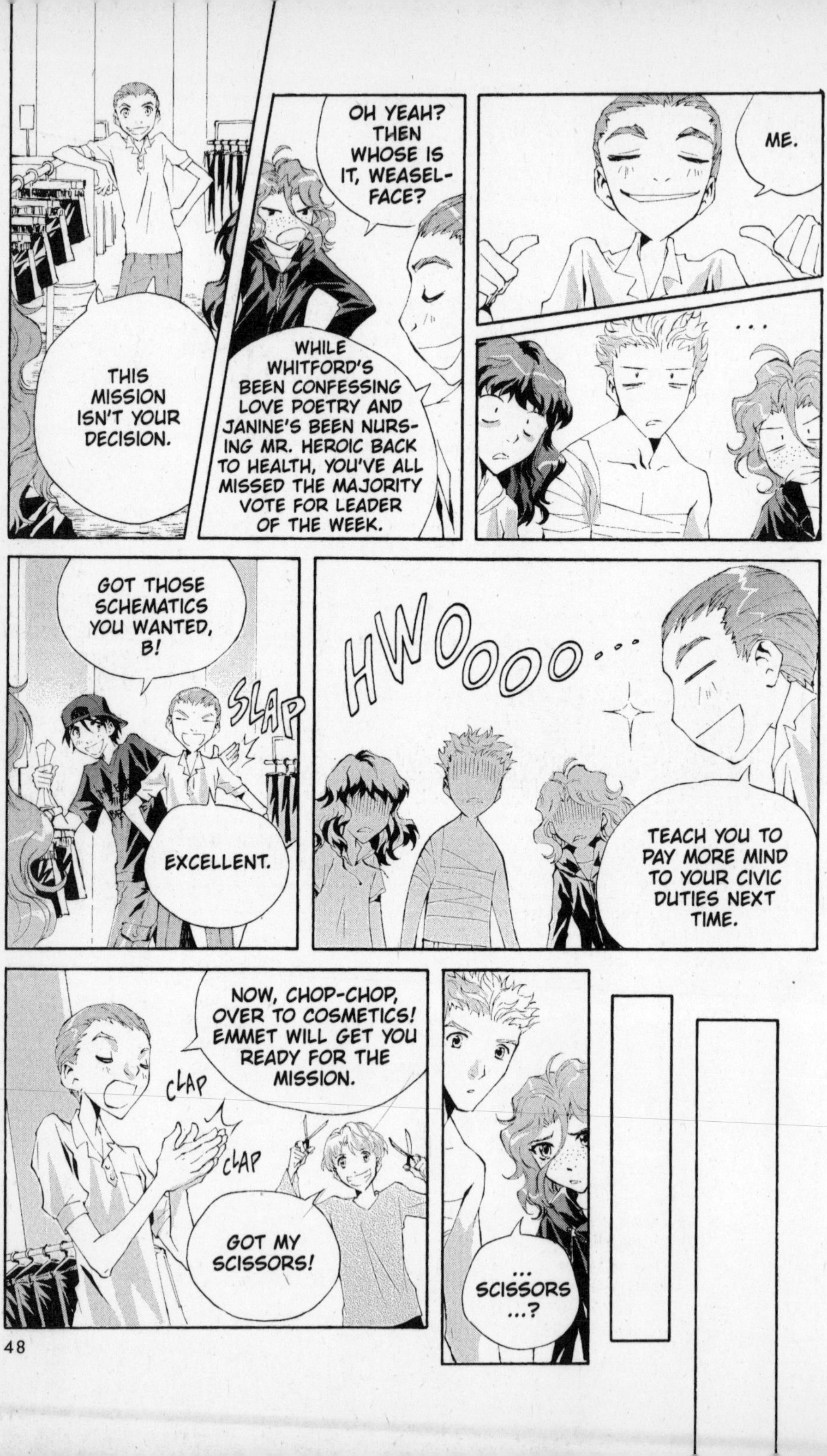
THIS MISSION ISN'T YOUR DECISION.
OH YEAH? THEN WHOSE IS IT, WEASEL-FACE?
WHILE WHITFORD'S BEEN CONFESSING LOVE POETRY AND JANINE'S BEEN NURSING MR. HEROIC BACK TO HEALTH, YOU'VE ALL MISSED THE MAJORITY VOTE FOR LEADER OF THE WEEK.
ME.
...
GOT THOSE SCHEMATICS YOU WANTED, B!
SLAP
EXCELLENT.
HWOOOO...
TEACH YOU TO PAY MORE MIND TO YOUR CIVIC DUTIES NEXT TIME.
NOW, CHOP-CHOP, OVER TO COSMETICS! EMMET WILL GET YOU READY FOR THE MISSION.
CLAP
CLAP
GOT MY SCISSORS!
...SCISSORS...?

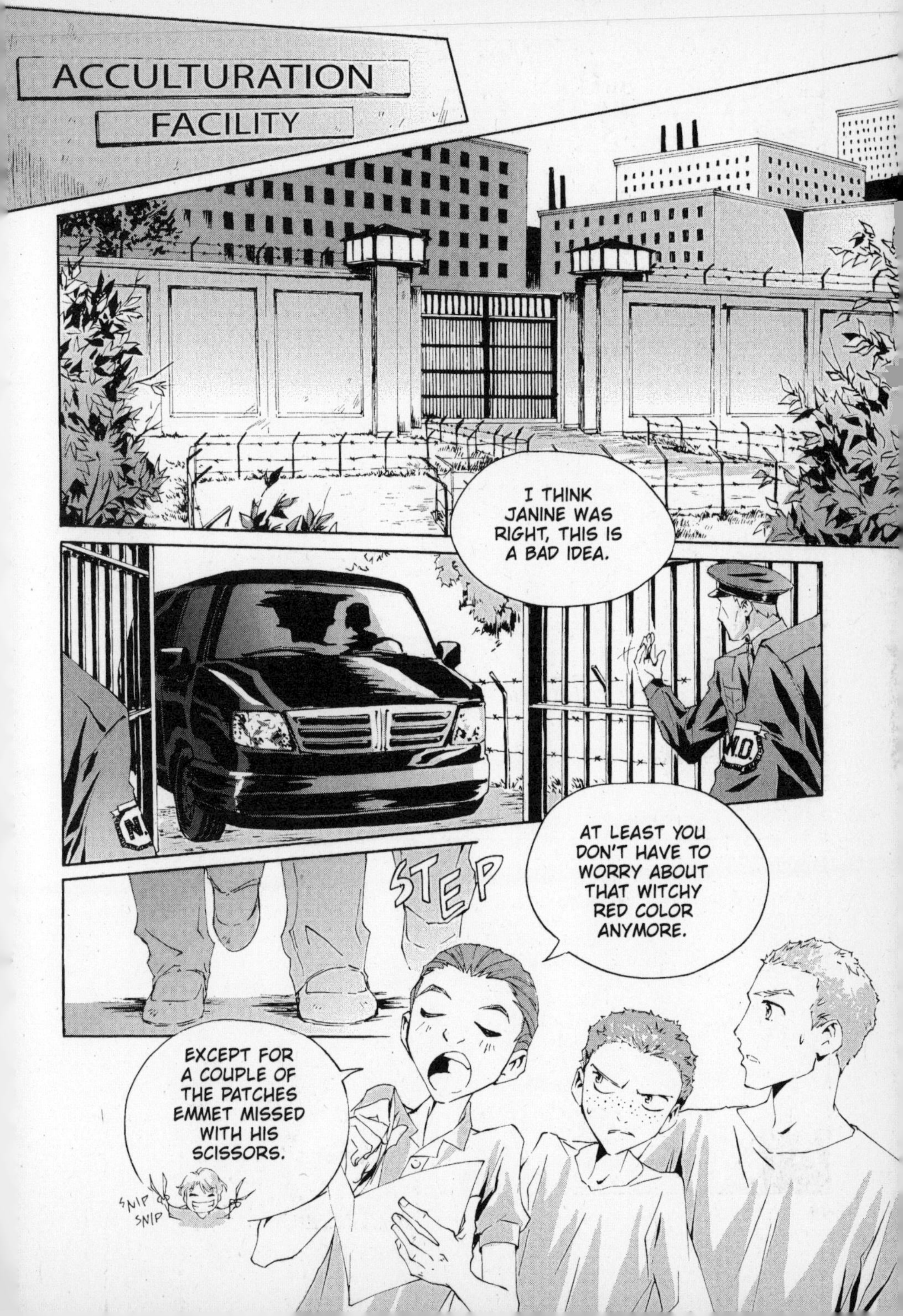
ACCULTURATION
FACILITY
I THINK JANINE WAS RIGHT, THIS IS A BAD IDEA.
W.D.
N.
STEP
AT LEAST YOU DON'T HAVE TO WORRY ABOUT THAT WITCHY RED COLOR ANYMORE.
EXCEPT FOR A COUPLE OF THE PATCHES EMMET MISSED WITH HIS SCISSORS.
SNIP SNIP

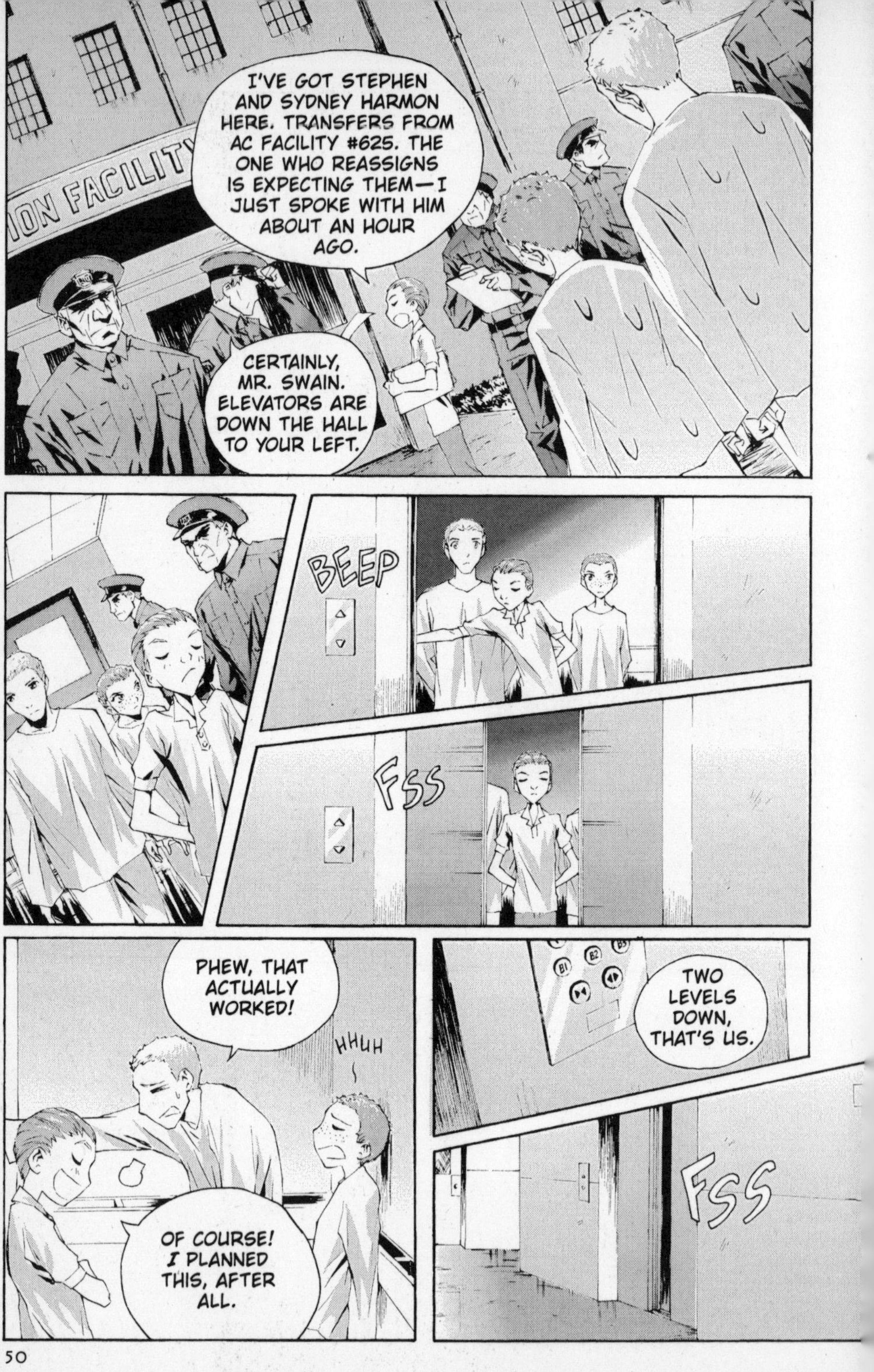
ION FACILITY
I'VE GOT STEPHEN AND SYDNEY HARMON HERE. TRANSFERS FROM AC FACILITY #625. THE ONE WHO REASSIGNS IS EXPECTING THEM—I JUST SPOKE WITH HIM ABOUT AN HOUR AGO.
CERTAINLY, MR. SWAIN. ELEVATORS ARE DOWN THE HALL TO YOUR LEFT.
BEEP
FSS
PHEW, THAT ACTUALLY WORKED!
HHUH
OF COURSE! I PLANNED THIS, AFTER ALL.
TWO LEVELS DOWN, THAT'S US.
FSS

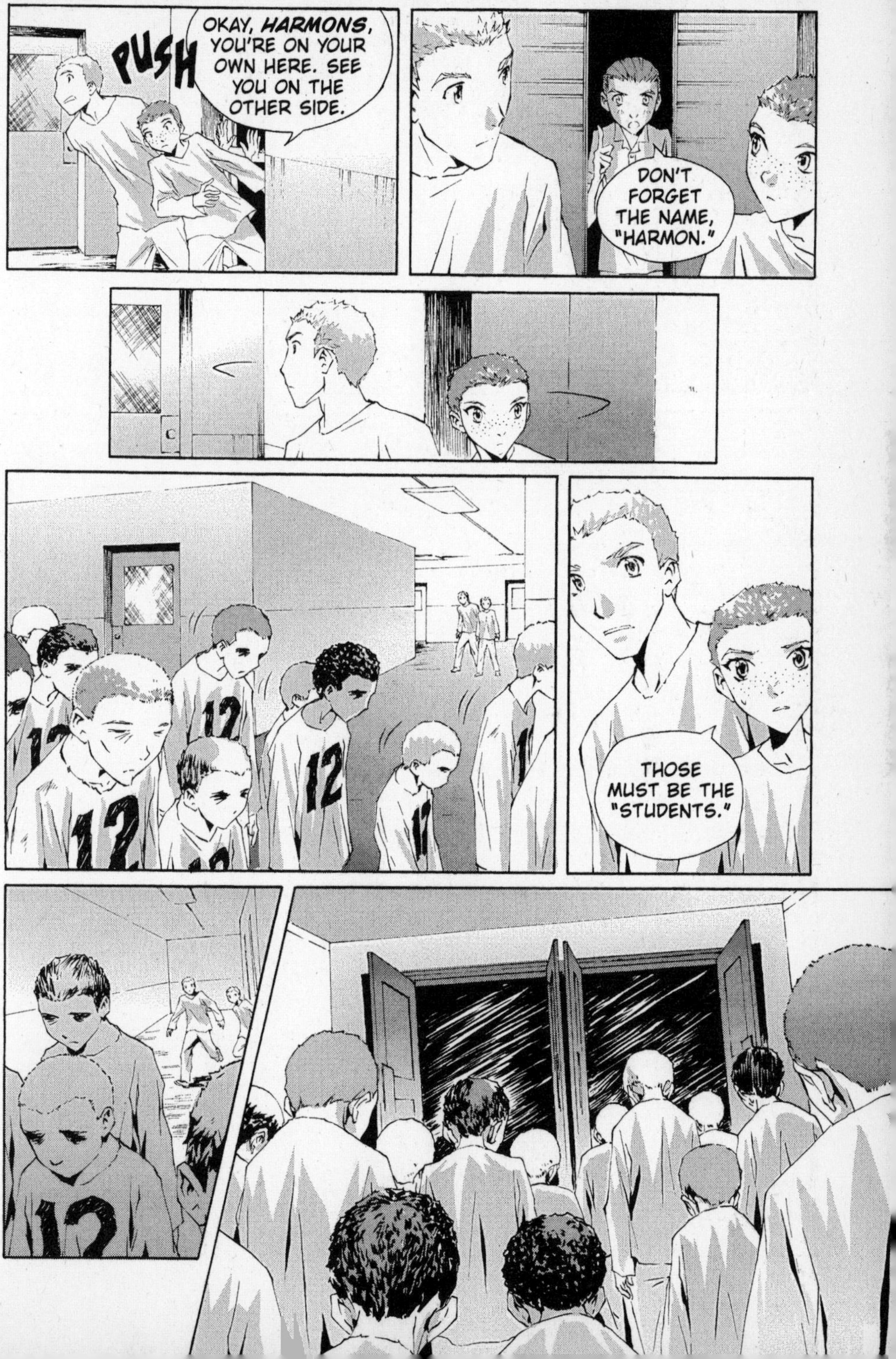
PUSH
OKAY, HARMONS, YOU'RE ON YOUR OWN HERE. SEE YOU ON THE OTHER SIDE.
DON'T FORGET THE NAME, "HARMON."
THOSE MUST BE THE "STUDENTS."

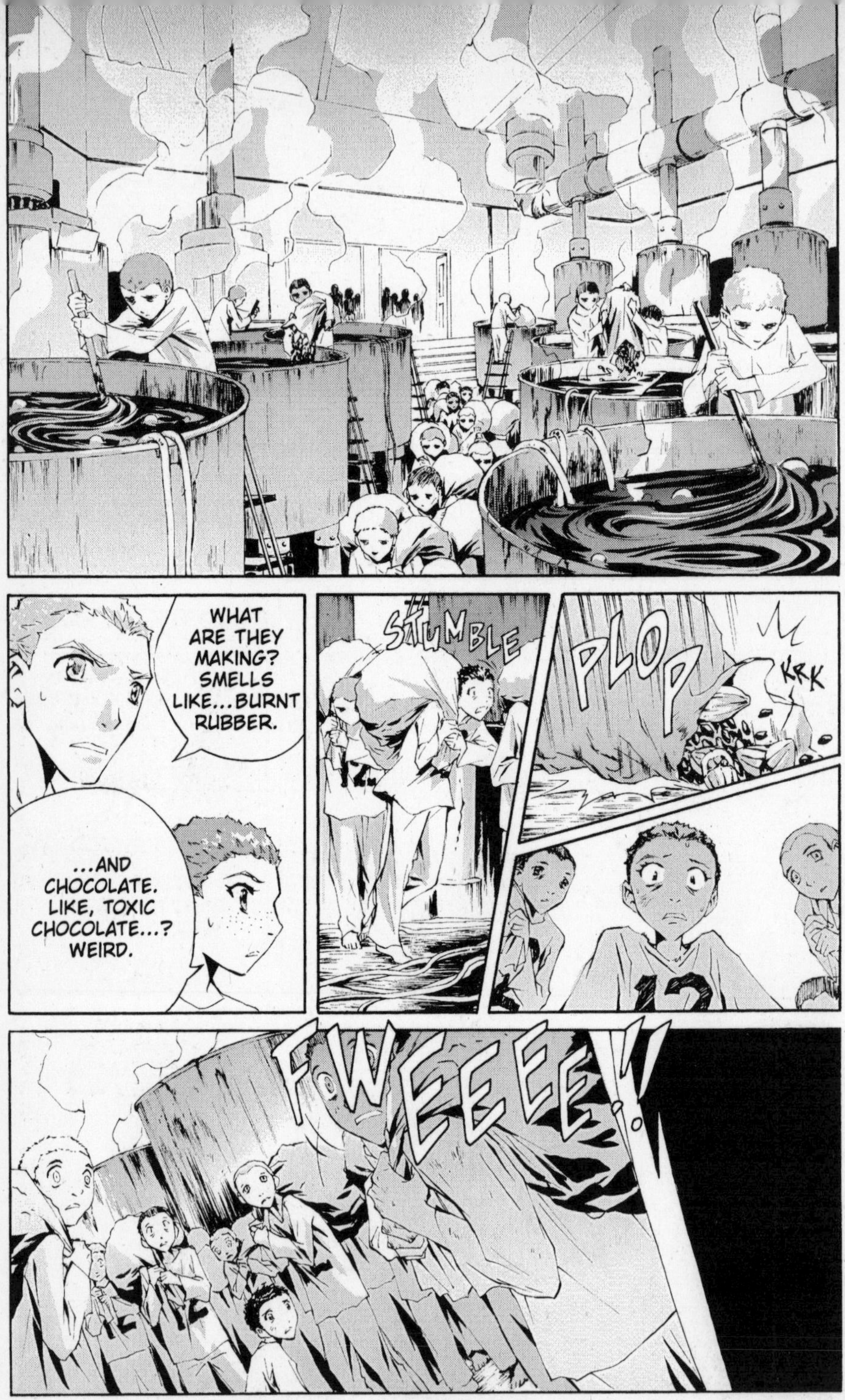
WHAT ARE THEY MAKING? SMELLS LIKE...BURNT RUBBER.
...AND CHOCOLATE. LIKE, TOXIC CHOCOLATE...? WEIRD.
STUMBLE
PLOP
KRK
FWEEEE!!

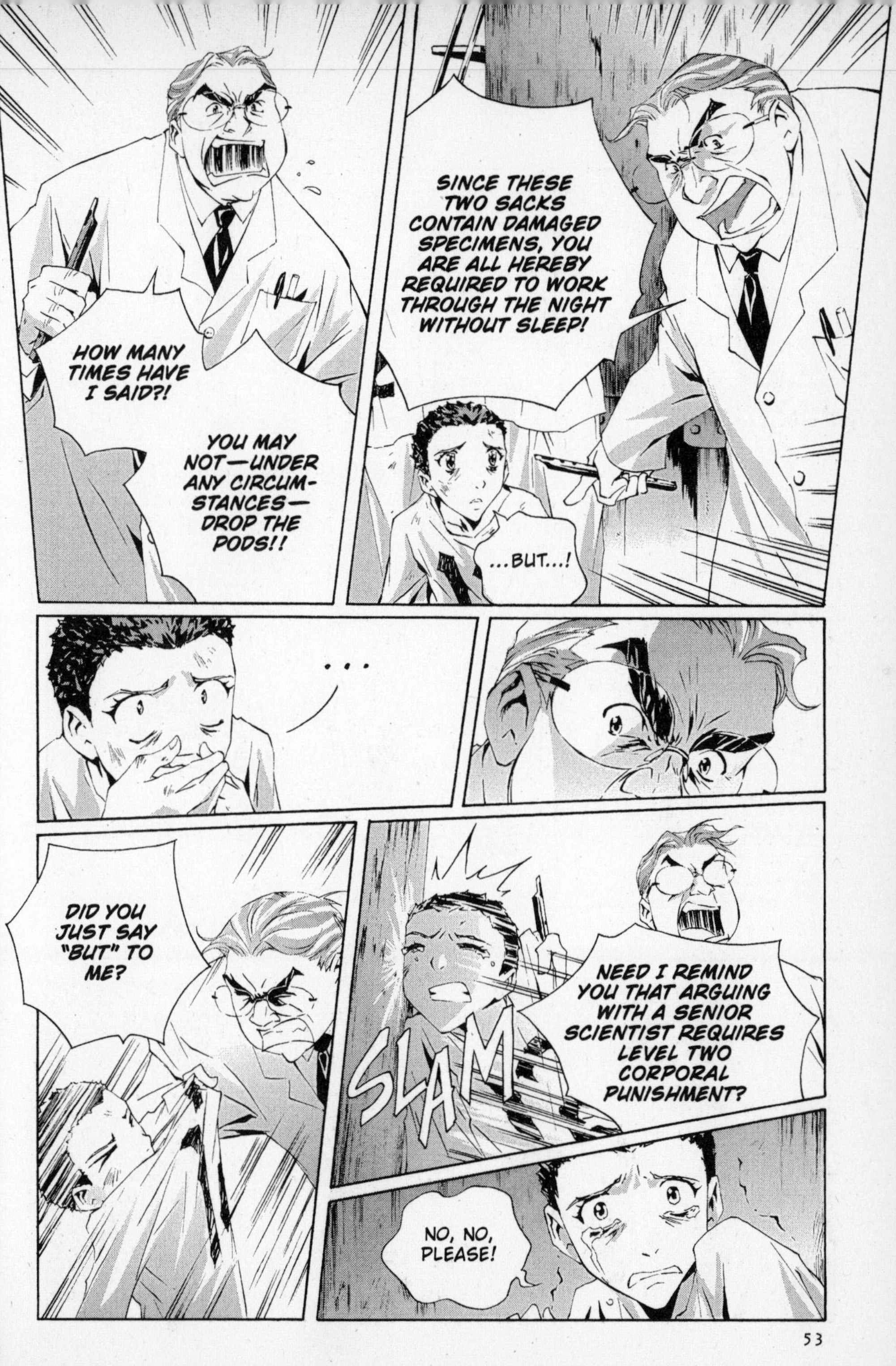
HOW MANY TIMES HAVE I SAID?!
YOU MAY NOT—UNDER ANY CIRCUM-STANCES—DROP THE PODS!!
SINCE THESE TWO SACKS CONTAIN DAMAGED SPECIMENS, YOU ARE ALL HEREBY REQUIRED TO WORK THROUGH THE NIGHT WITHOUT SLEEP!
...BUT...!
...
DID YOU JUST SAY "BUT" TO ME?
NEED I REMIND YOU THAT ARGUING WITH A SENIOR SCIENTIST REQUIRES LEVEL TWO CORPORAL PUNISHMENT?
SLAM
NO, NO, PLEASE!

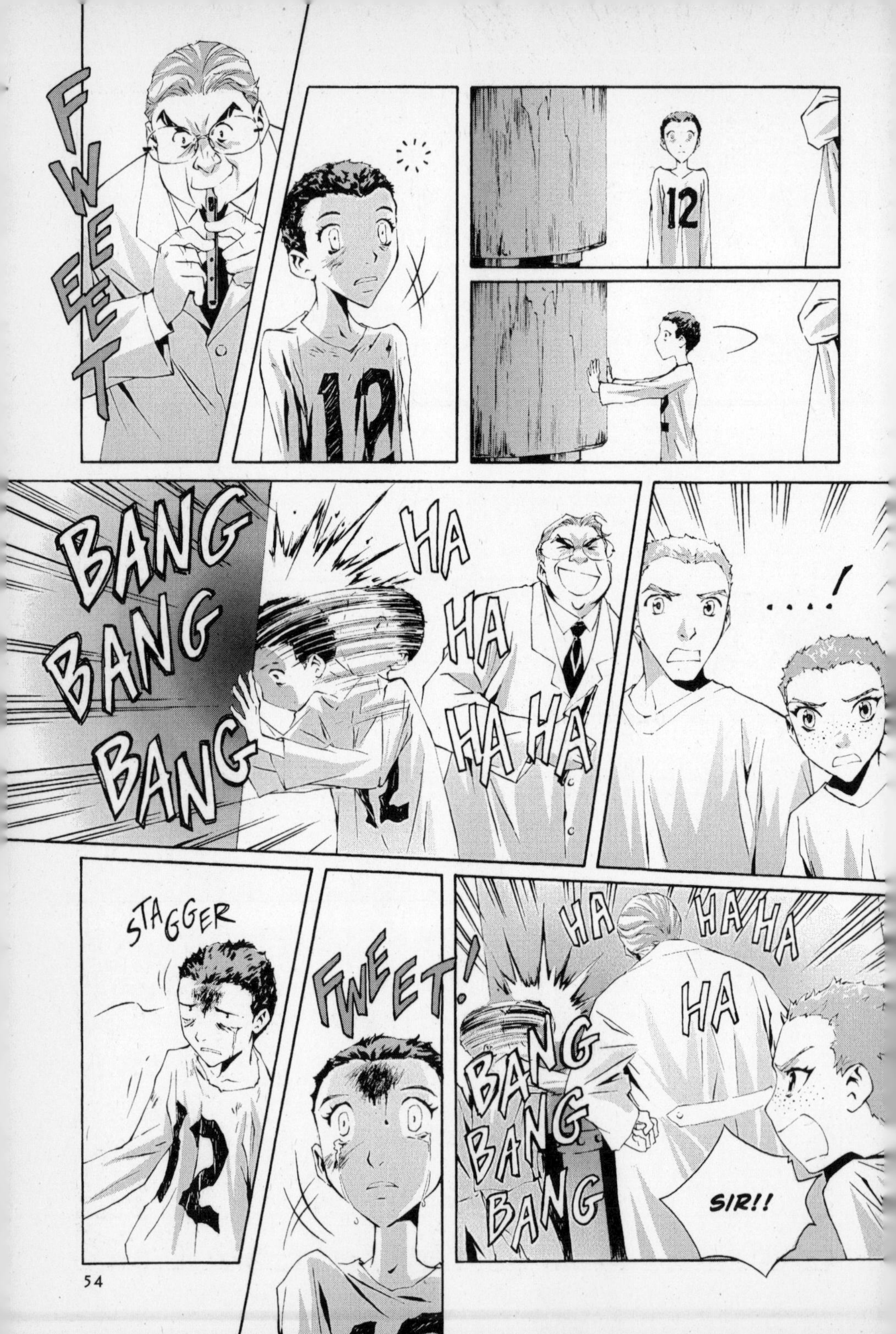
FWEEEET
BANG
BANG
BANG
HA
HA
HA HA
...!
STAGGER
FWEET!
HA
HA HA HA
HA
BANG
BANG
BANG
SIR!!

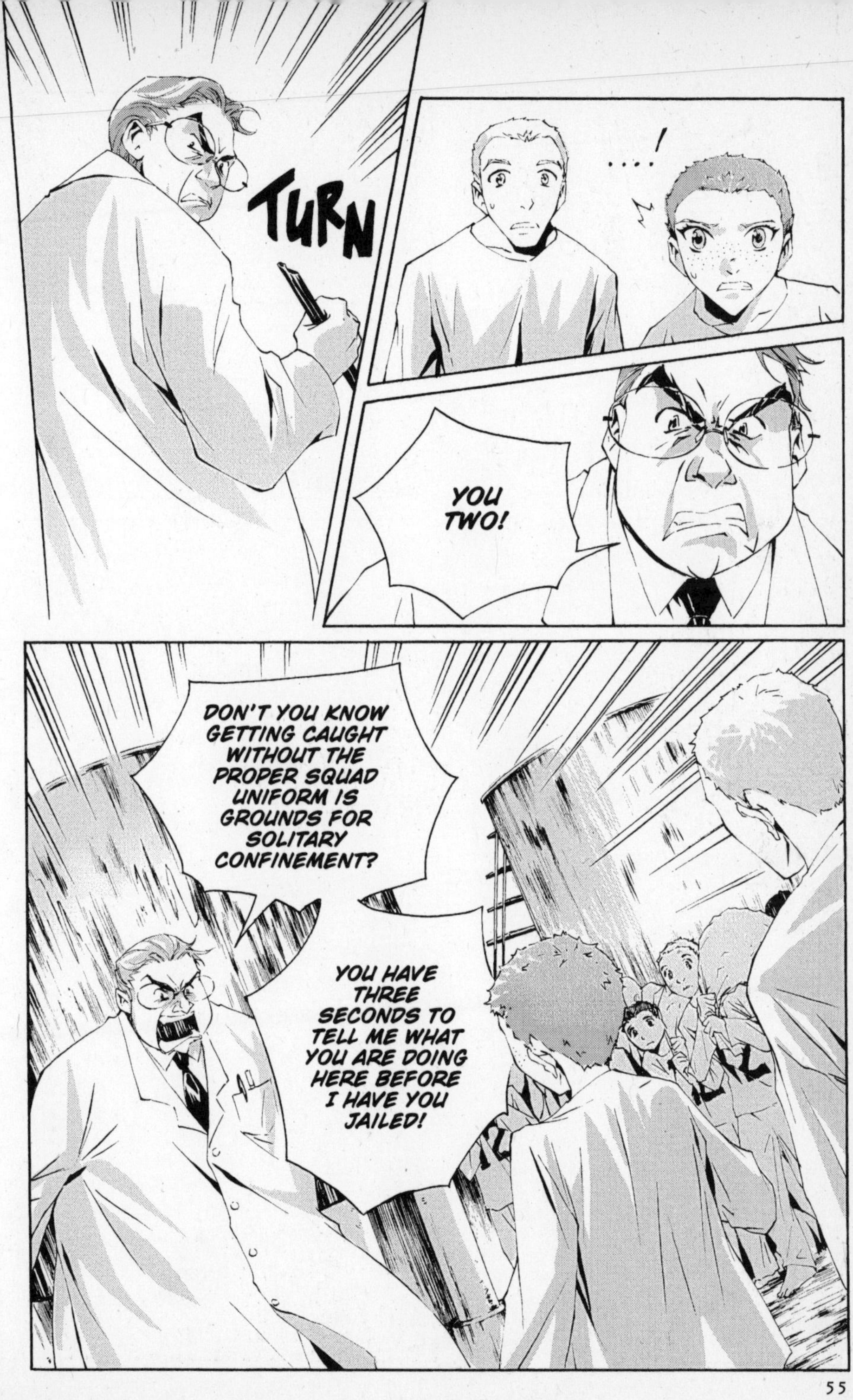
TURN
...!
YOU TWO!
DON'T YOU KNOW GETTING CAUGHT WITHOUT THE PROPER SQUAD UNIFORM IS GROUNDS FOR SOLITARY CONFINEMENT?
YOU HAVE THREE SECONDS TO TELL ME WHAT YOU ARE DOING HERE BEFORE I HAVE YOU JAILED!

WITCH & WIZARD

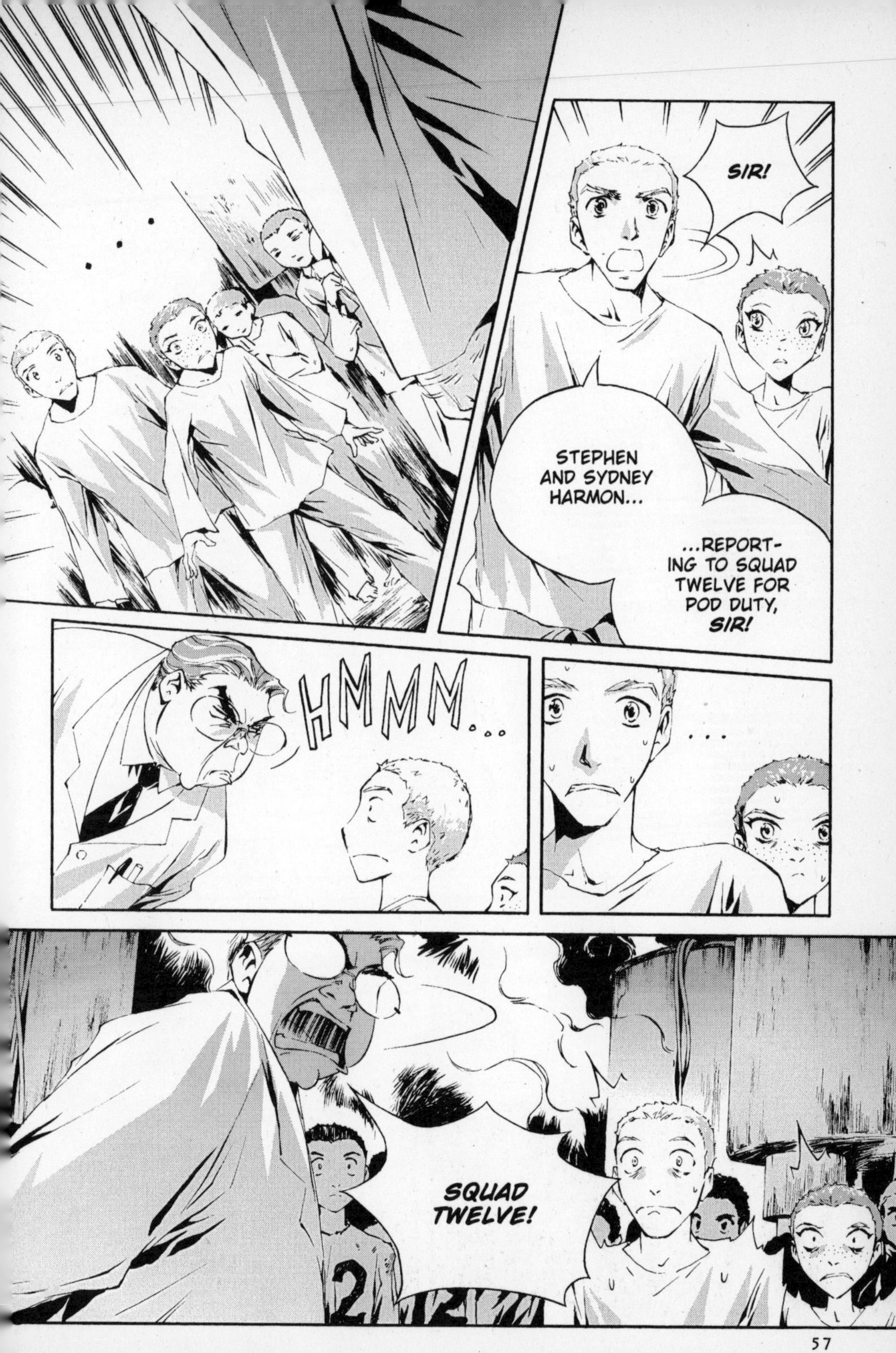

...
SIR!
STEPHEN AND SYDNEY HARMON...
...REPORTING TO SQUAD TWELVE FOR POD DUTY, SIR!
HMMM...
...
SQUAD TWELVE!

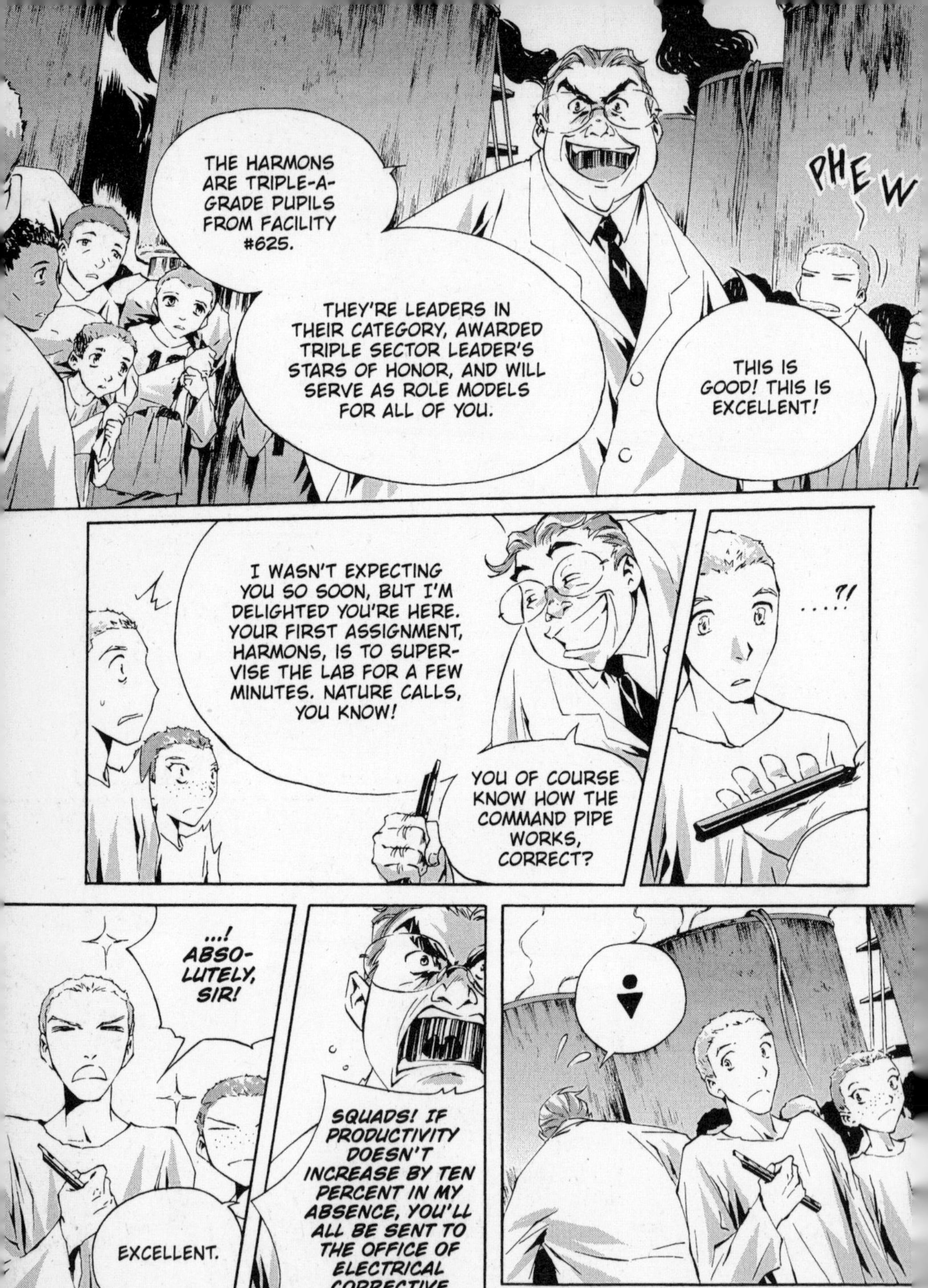
THE HARMONS ARE TRIPLE-A-GRADE PUPILS FROM FACILITY #625.
THEY'RE LEADERS IN THEIR CATEGORY, AWARDED TRIPLE SECTOR LEADER'S STARS OF HONOR, AND WILL SERVE AS ROLE MODELS FOR ALL OF YOU.
PHEW
THIS IS GOOD! THIS IS EXCELLENT!
I WASN'T EXPECTING YOU SO SOON, BUT I'M DELIGHTED YOU'RE HERE. YOUR FIRST ASSIGNMENT, HARMONS, IS TO SUPER-VISE THE LAB FOR A FEW MINUTES. NATURE CALLS, YOU KNOW!
YOU OF COURSE KNOW HOW THE COMMAND PIPE WORKS, CORRECT?
....?!
...! ABSO-LUTELY, SIR!
EXCELLENT.
SQUADS! IF PRODUCTIVITY DOESN'T INCREASE BY TEN PERCENT IN MY ABSENCE, YOU'LL ALL BE SENT TO THE OFFICE OF ELECTRICAL CORRECTIVE PUNISHMENTS!

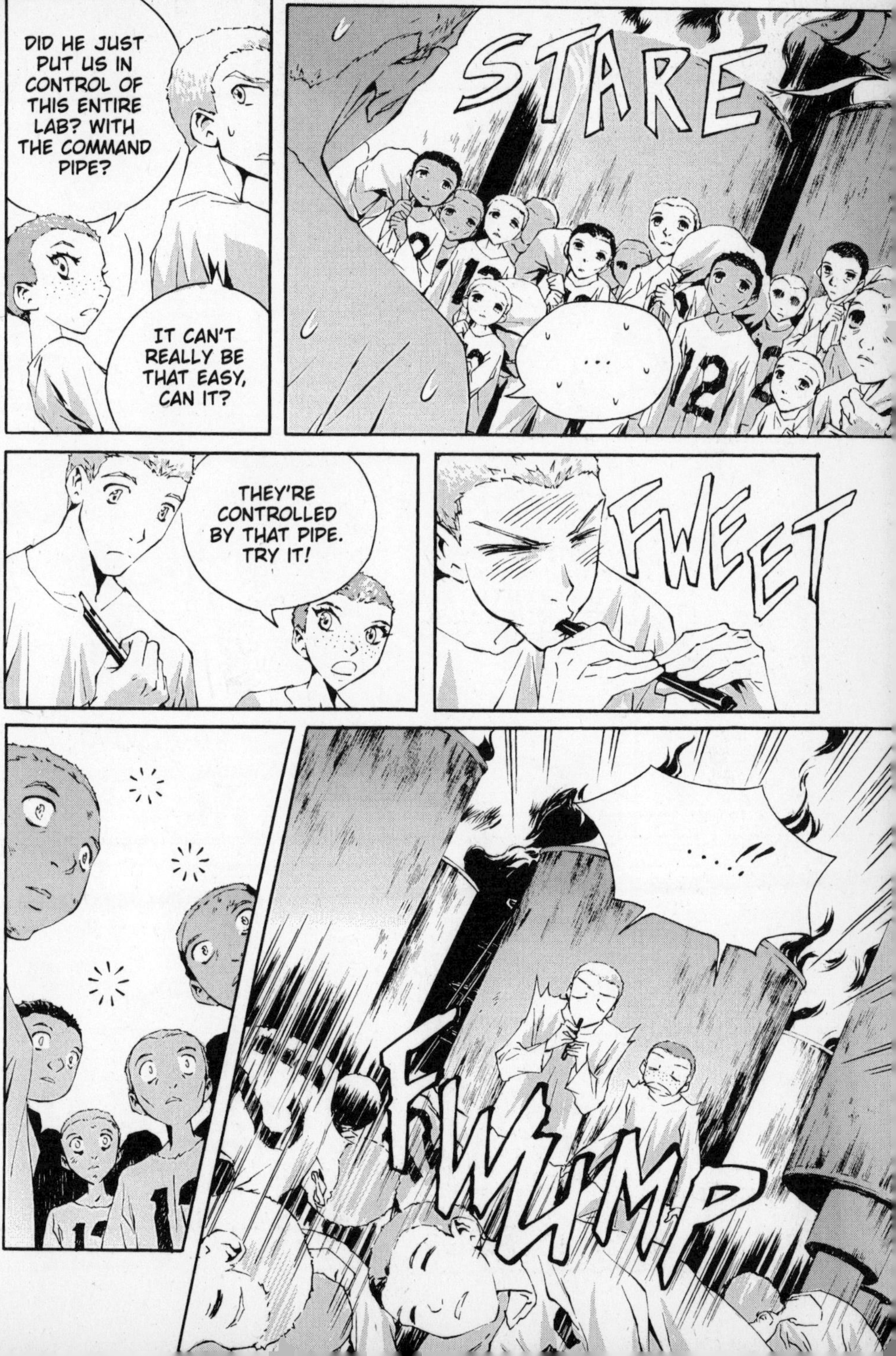
DID HE JUST PUT US IN CONTROL OF THIS ENTIRE LAB? WITH THE COMMAND PIPE?
IT CAN'T REALLY BE THAT EASY, CAN IT?
STARE
...
THEY'RE CONTROLLED BY THAT PIPE. TRY IT!
FWEET
...!!
FWUMP

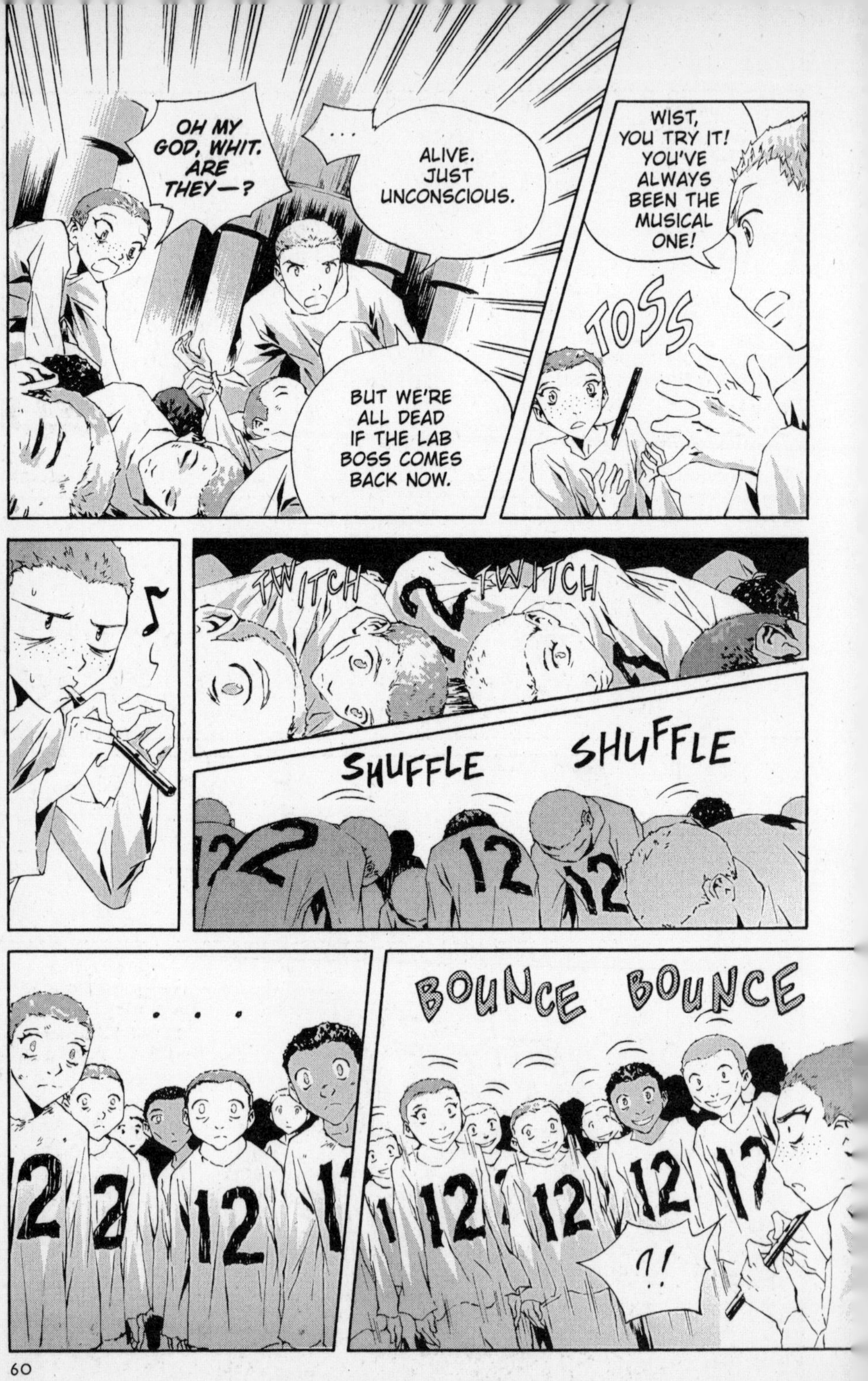
OH MY GOD, WHIT. ARE THEY—?
. . .
ALIVE. JUST UNCONSCIOUS.
BUT WE'RE ALL DEAD IF THE LAB BOSS COMES BACK NOW.
WIST, YOU TRY IT! YOU'VE ALWAYS BEEN THE MUSICAL ONE!
TOSS
TWITCH
TWITCH
SHUFFLE
SHUFFLE
. . .
BOUNCE
BOUNCE
?!

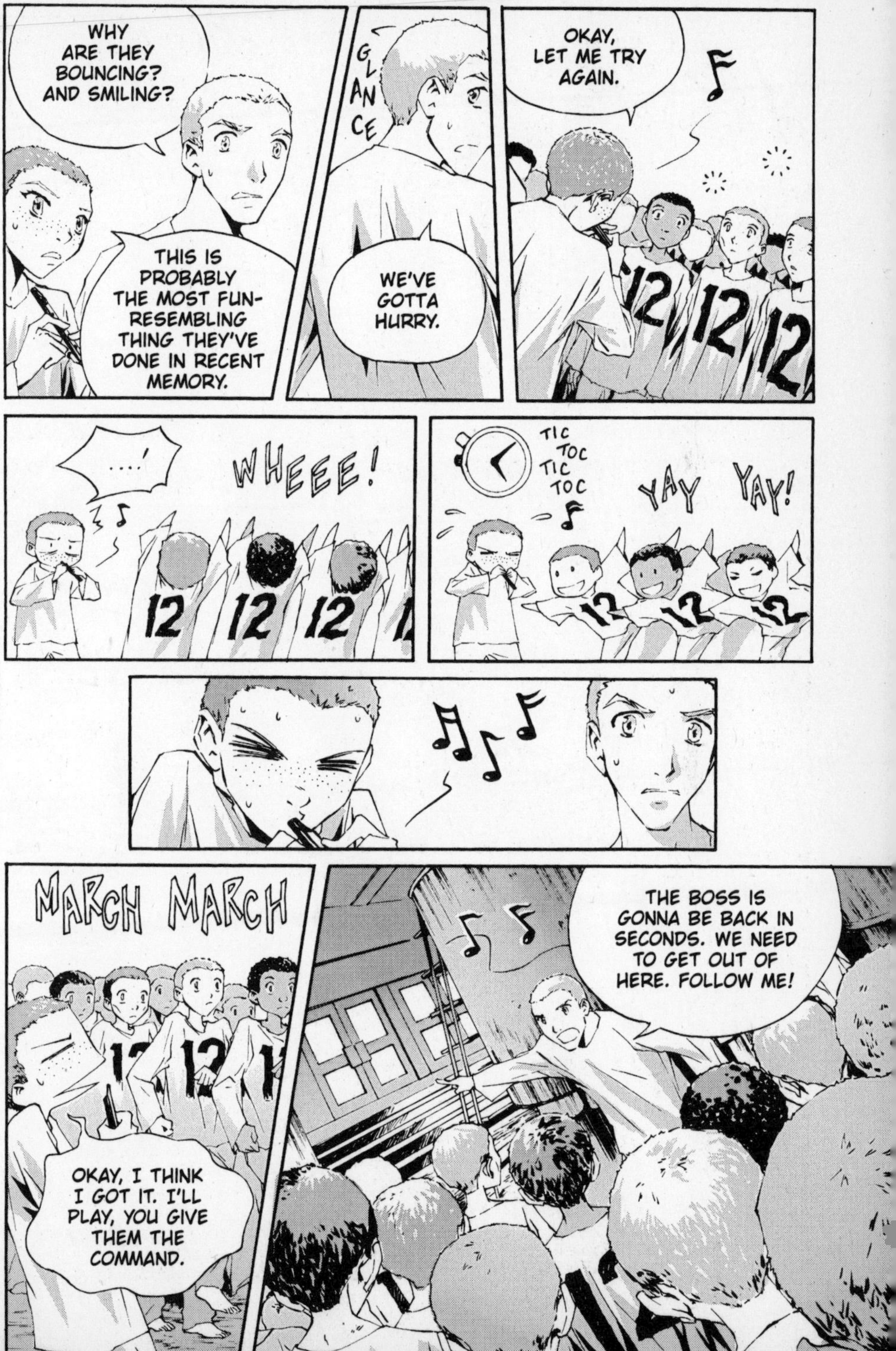
WHY ARE THEY BOUNCING? AND SMILING?
THIS IS PROBABLY THE MOST FUN-RESEMBLING THING THEY'VE DONE IN RECENT MEMORY.
GLANCE
WE'VE GOTTA HURRY.
OKAY, LET ME TRY AGAIN.
12
12
12
....!
WHEEE!
12
12
12
TIC TOC TIC TOC
YAY YAY!
12
12
12
MARCH MARCH
12
12
OKAY, I THINK I GOT IT. I'LL PLAY, YOU GIVE THEM THE COMMAND.
THE BOSS IS GONNA BE BACK IN SECONDS. WE NEED TO GET OUT OF HERE. FOLLOW ME!

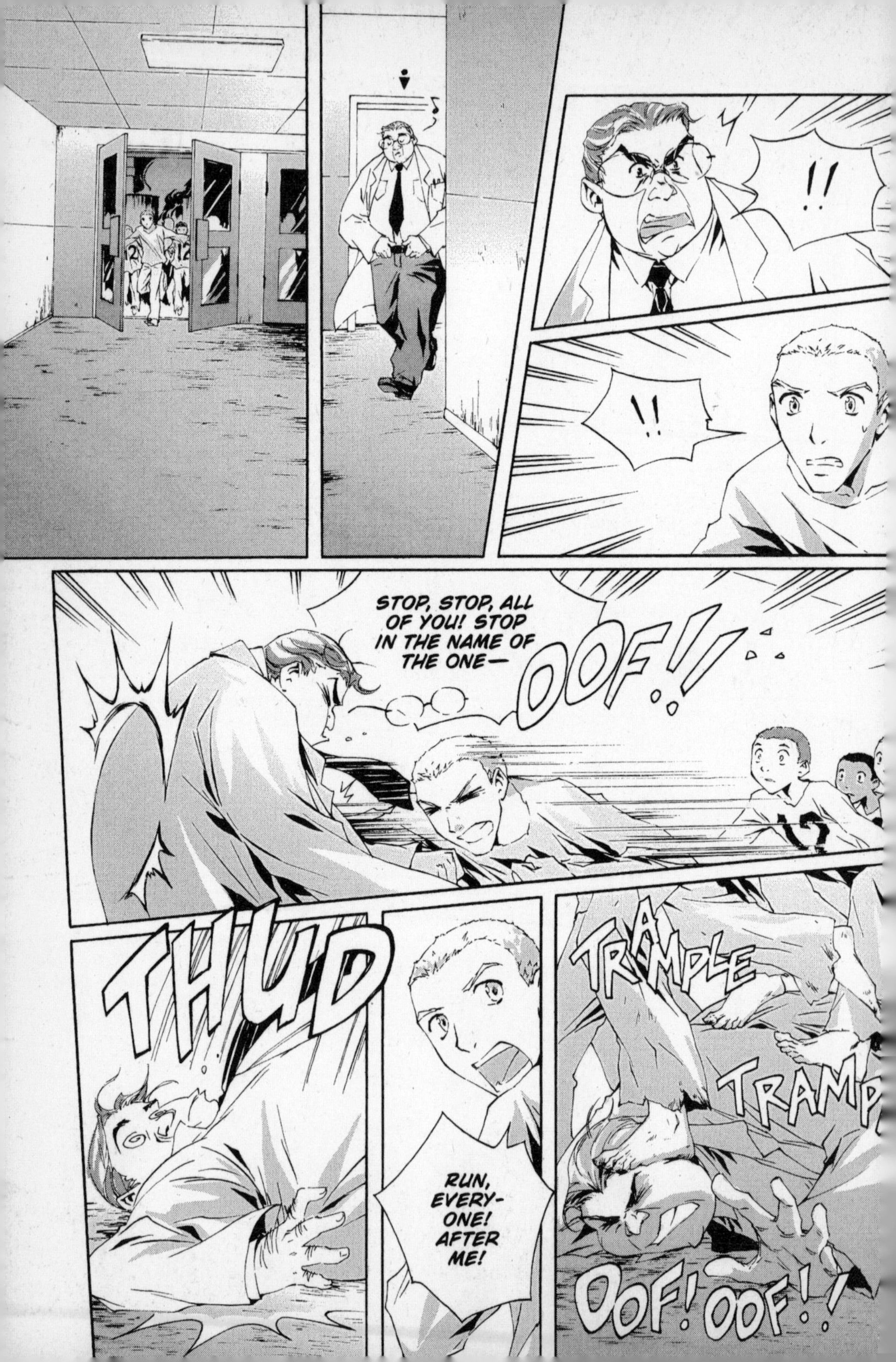
!!
!!
STOP, STOP, ALL OF YOU! STOP IN THE NAME OF THE ONE—
OOF!!
THUD
RUN, EVERY-ONE! AFTER ME!
TRAMPLE
TRAMP
OOF! OOF!!

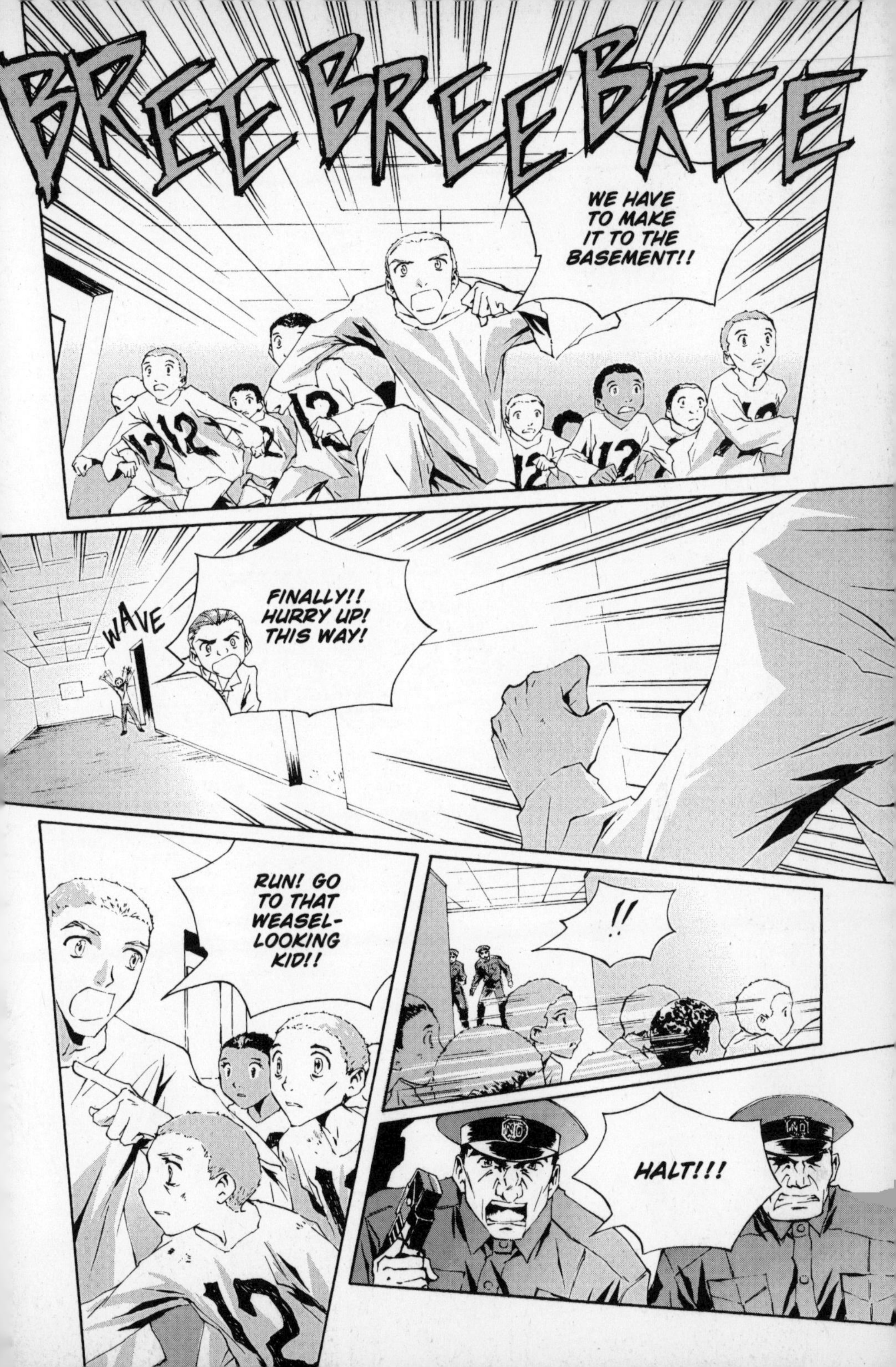
BREE BREE BREE
WE HAVE TO MAKE IT TO THE BASEMENT!!
WAVE
FINALLY!! HURRY UP! THIS WAY!
RUN! GO TO THAT WEASEL-LOOKING KID!!
!!
HALT!!!

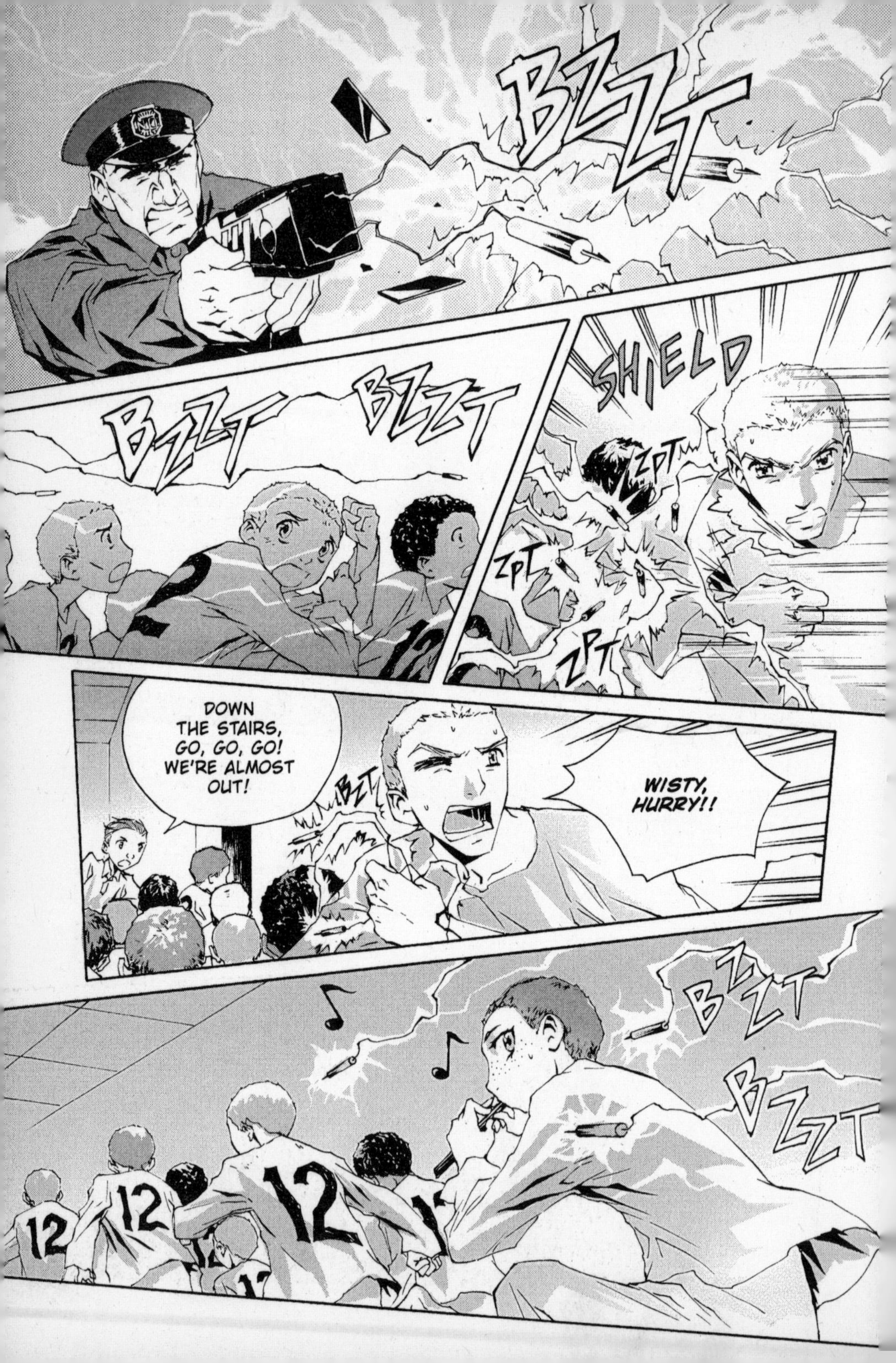
BZZZT
BZZT
BZZZT
SHIELD
ZPT
ZPT
ZPT
DOWN THE STAIRS, GO, GO, GO! WE'RE ALMOST OUT!
BZT
WISTY, HURRY!!
BZZZT
BZZT

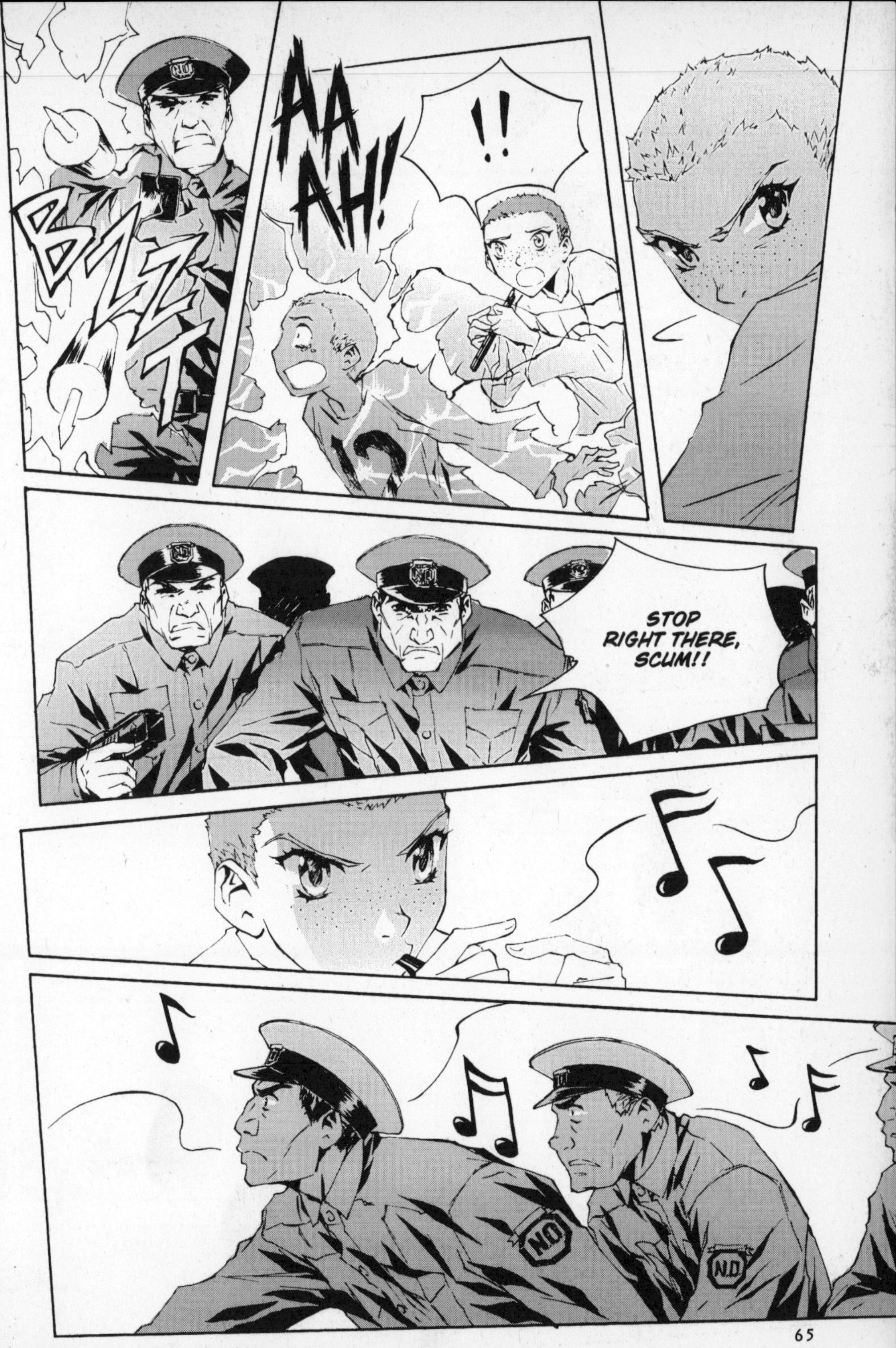
BZZZT
AAAH!
!!
STOP RIGHT THERE, SCUM!!

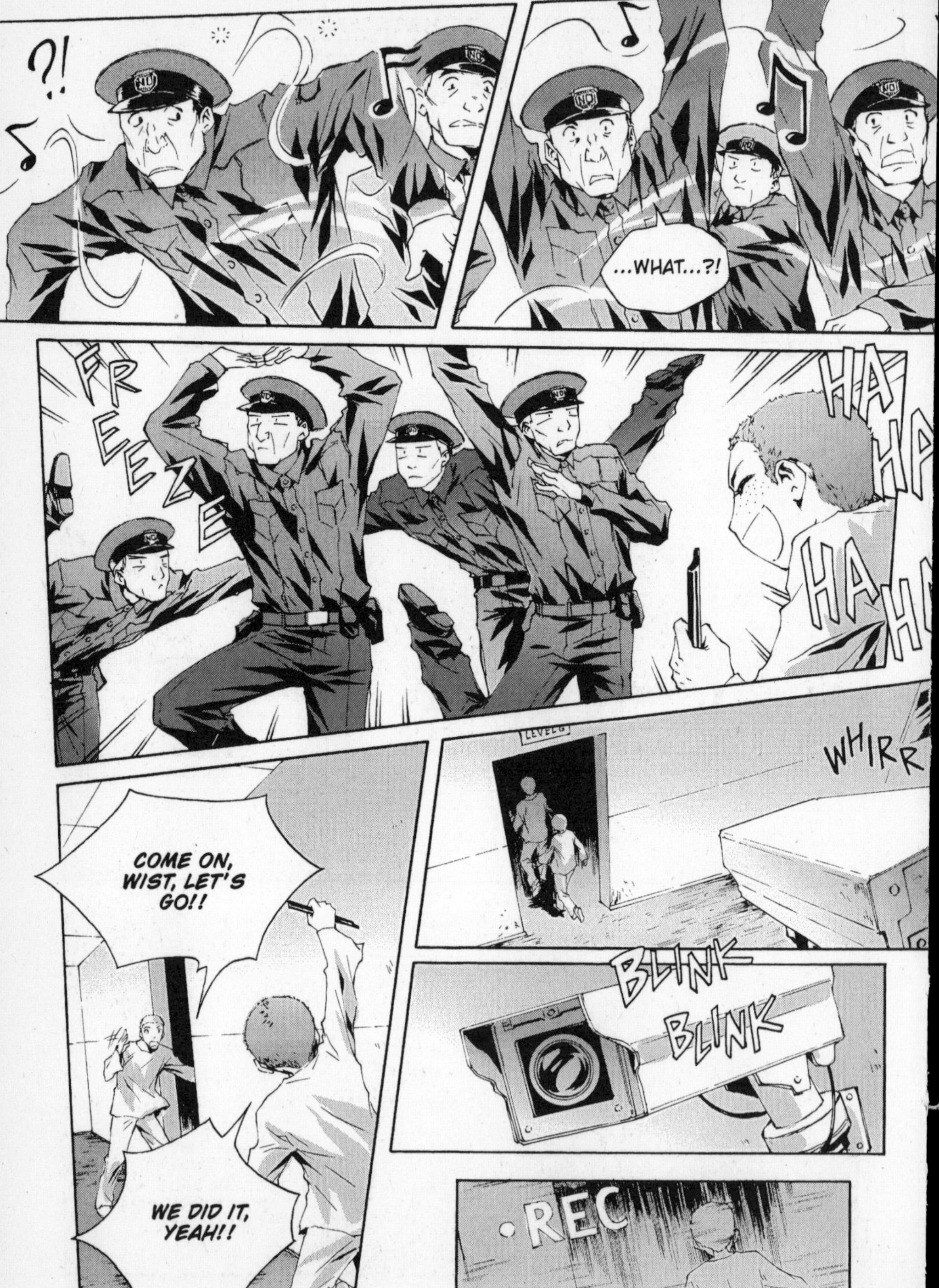
?!
...WHAT...?!
FREEZE
HA HA
HA
COME ON, WIST, LET'S GO!!
WE DID IT, YEAH!!
WHIRR
BLINK BLINK
REC

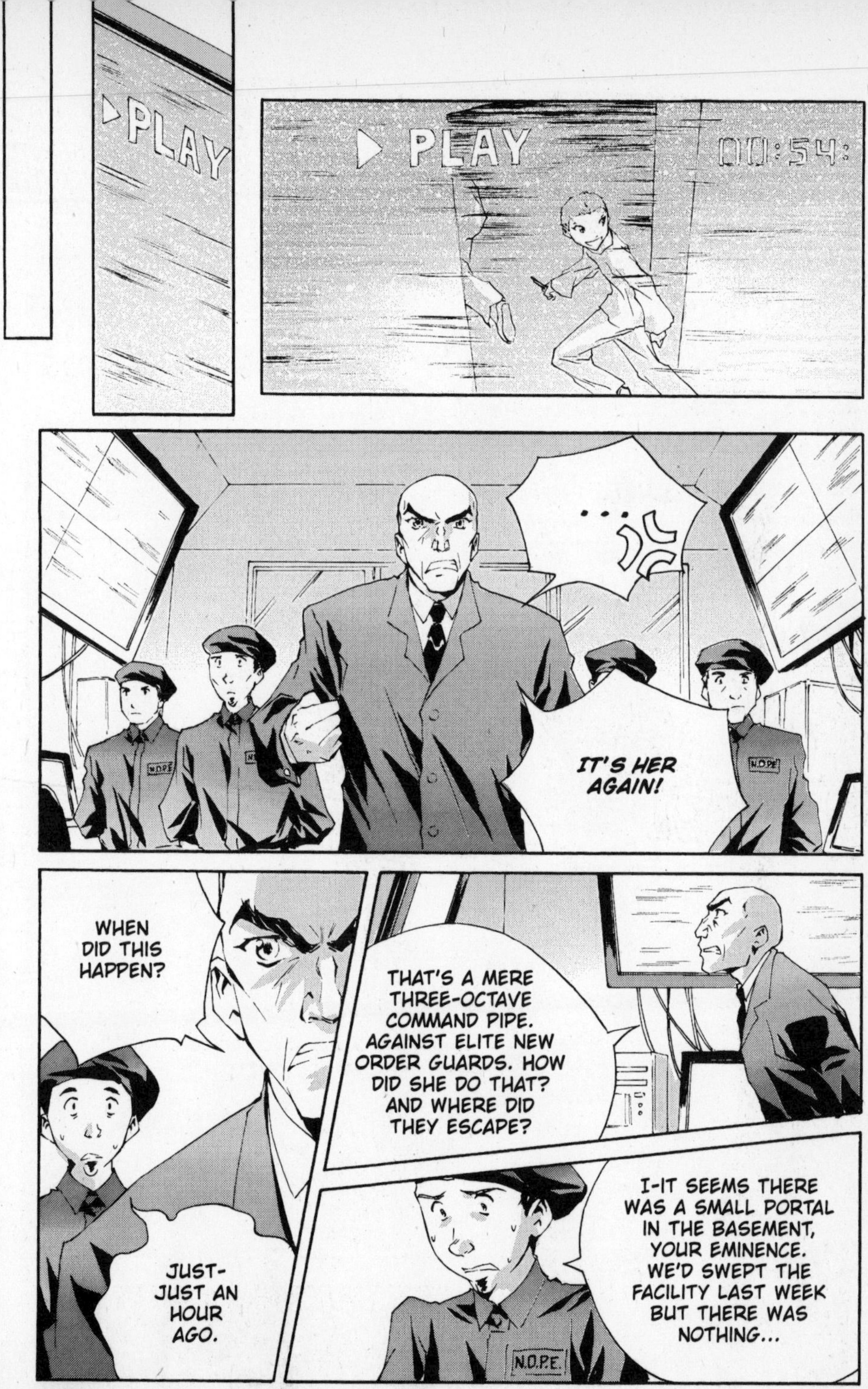
PLAY
PLAY
00:54:
...
IT'S HER AGAIN!
WHEN DID THIS HAPPEN?
JUST- JUST AN HOUR AGO.
THAT'S A MERE THREE-OCTAVE COMMAND PIPE. AGAINST ELITE NEW ORDER GUARDS. HOW DID SHE DO THAT? AND WHERE DID THEY ESCAPE?
I-IT SEEMS THERE WAS A SMALL PORTAL IN THE BASEMENT, YOUR EMINENCE. WE'D SWEPT THE FACILITY LAST WEEK BUT THERE WAS NOTHING...

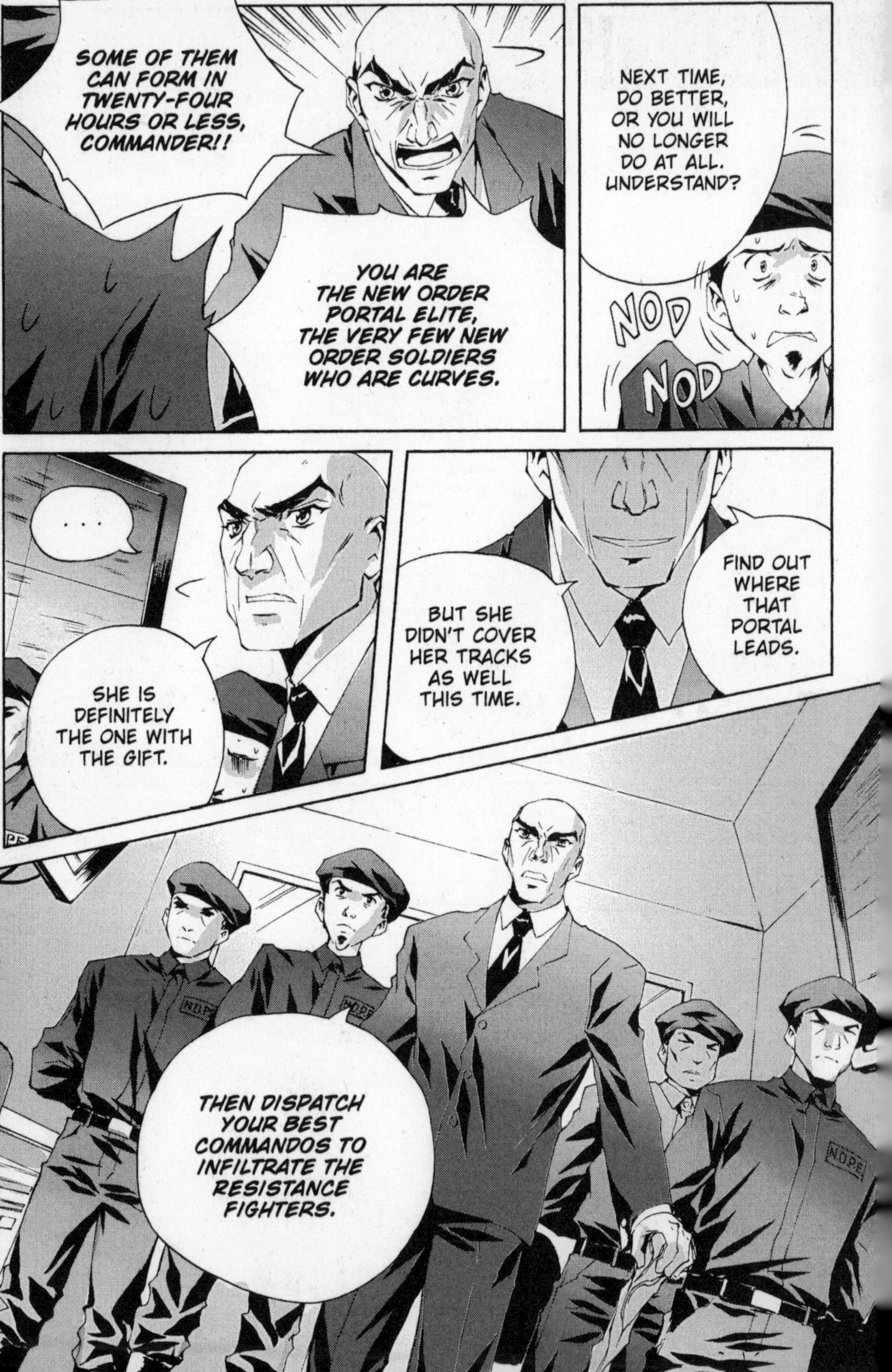
SOME OF THEM CAN FORM IN TWENTY-FOUR HOURS OR LESS, COMMANDER!!
YOU ARE THE NEW ORDER PORTAL ELITE, THE VERY FEW NEW ORDER SOLDIERS WHO ARE CURVES.
NEXT TIME, DO BETTER, OR YOU WILL NO LONGER DO AT ALL. UNDERSTAND?
NOD
NOD
. . .
SHE IS DEFINITELY THE ONE WITH THE GIFT.
BUT SHE DIDN'T COVER HER TRACKS AS WELL THIS TIME.
FIND OUT WHERE THAT PORTAL LEADS.
THEN DISPATCH YOUR BEST COMMANDOS TO INFILTRATE THE RESISTANCE FIGHTERS.

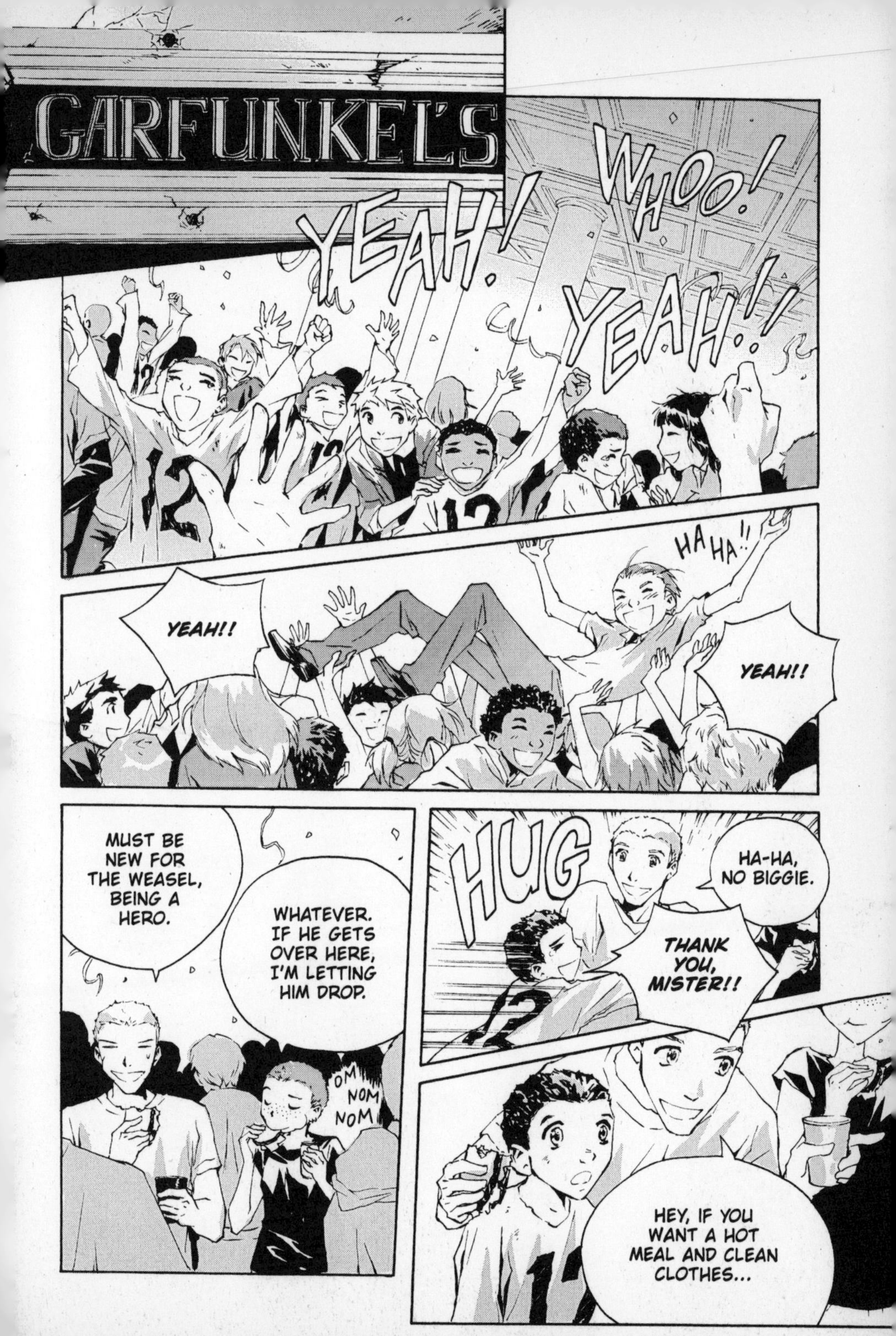
GARFUNKEL'S
YEAH!
WHOO!
YEAH!!
HA HA!!
YEAH!!
YEAH!!
MUST BE NEW FOR THE WEASEL, BEING A HERO.
WHATEVER. IF HE GETS OVER HERE, I'M LETTING HIM DROP.
OM NOM NOM
HUG
HA-HA, NO BIGGIE.
THANK YOU, MISTER!!
HEY, IF YOU WANT A HOT MEAL AND CLEAN CLOTHES...

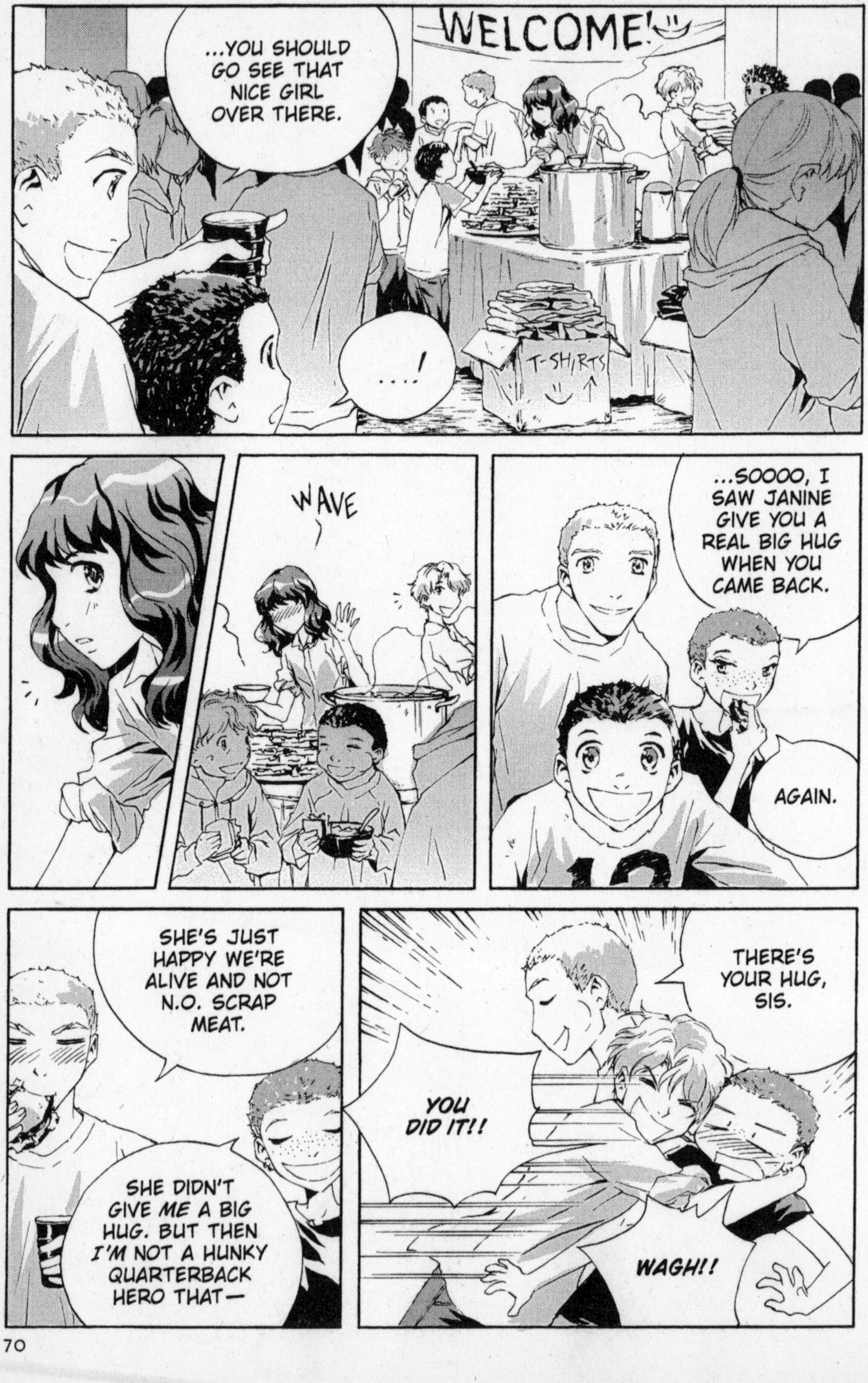
WELCOME!
...YOU SHOULD GO SEE THAT NICE GIRL OVER THERE.
T-SHIRTS
...!
WAVE
...SOOOO, I SAW JANINE GIVE YOU A REAL BIG HUG WHEN YOU CAME BACK.
AGAIN.
SHE'S JUST HAPPY WE'RE ALIVE AND NOT N.O. SCRAP MEAT.
SHE DIDN'T GIVE *ME* A BIG HUG. BUT THEN *I'M* NOT A HUNKY QUARTERBACK HERO THAT—
THERE'S YOUR HUG, SIS.
YOU DID IT!!
WAGH!!

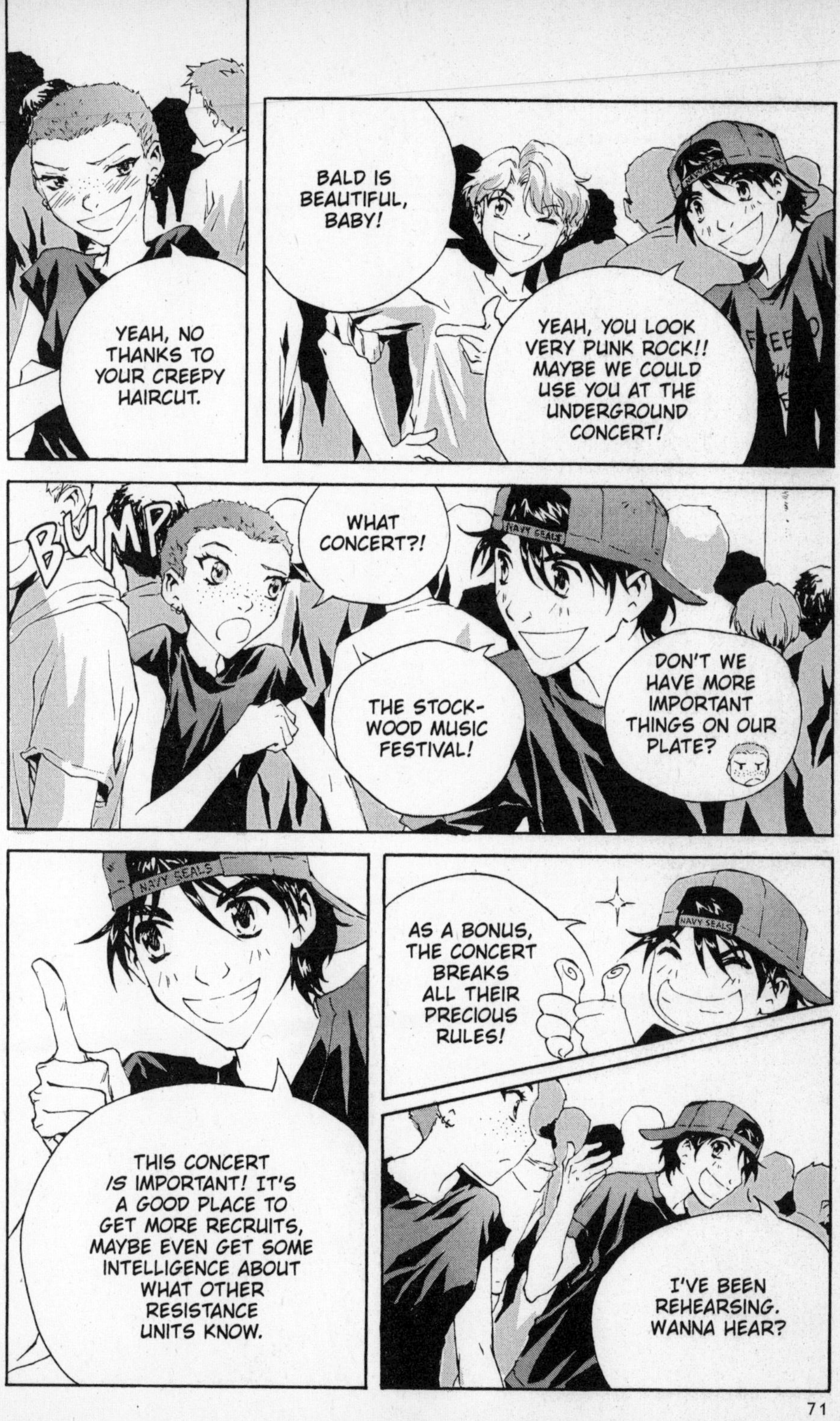
YEAH, NO THANKS TO YOUR CREEPY HAIRCUT.
BALD IS BEAUTIFUL, BABY!
YEAH, YOU LOOK VERY PUNK ROCK!! MAYBE WE COULD USE YOU AT THE UNDERGROUND CONCERT!
BUMP
WHAT CONCERT?!
THE STOCK-WOOD MUSIC FESTIVAL!
DON'T WE HAVE MORE IMPORTANT THINGS ON OUR PLATE?
THIS CONCERT *IS* IMPORTANT! IT'S A GOOD PLACE TO GET MORE RECRUITS, MAYBE EVEN GET SOME INTELLIGENCE ABOUT WHAT OTHER RESISTANCE UNITS KNOW.
AS A BONUS, THE CONCERT BREAKS ALL THEIR PRECIOUS RULES!
I'VE BEEN REHEARSING. WANNA HEAR?

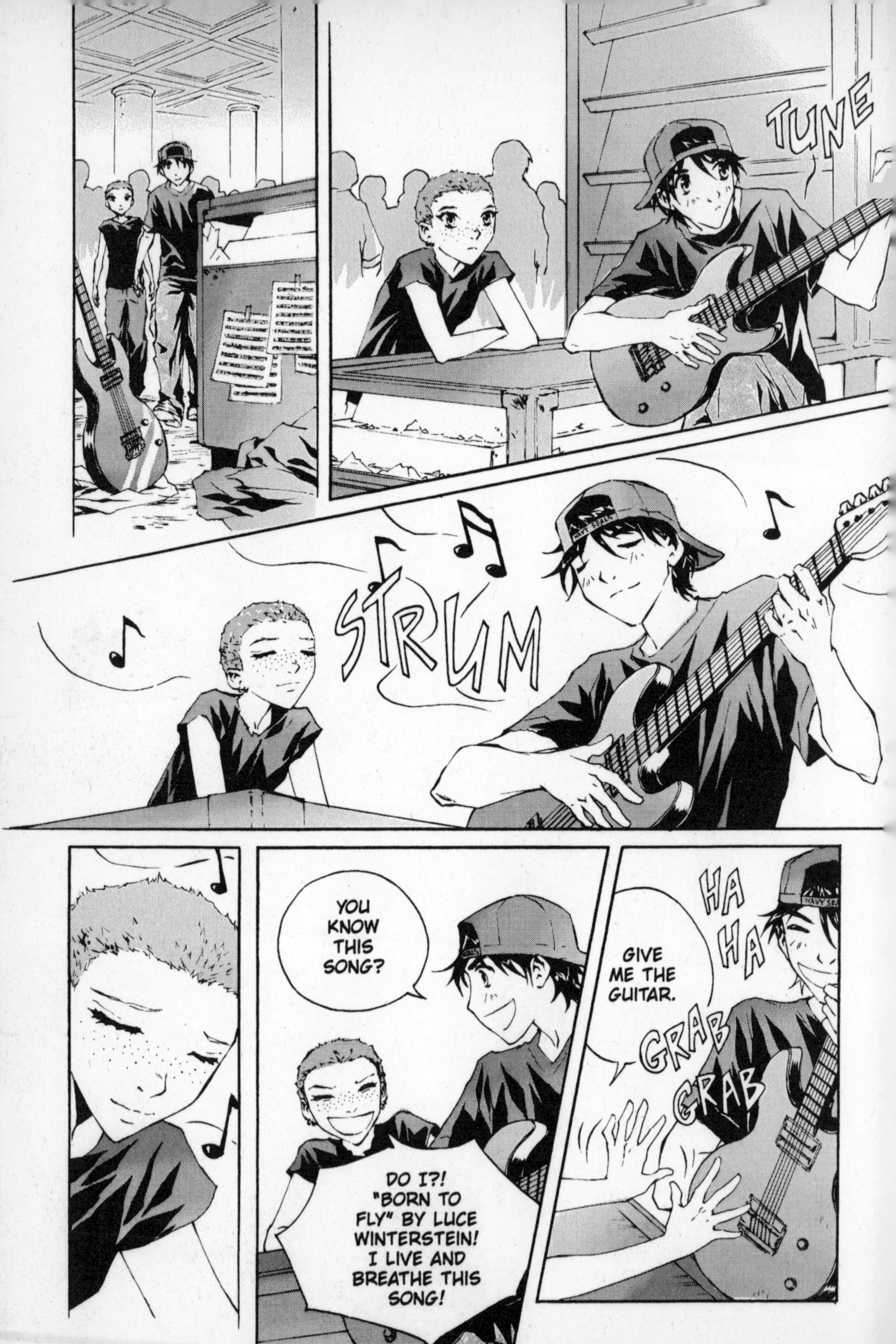
TUNE
STRUM
YOU KNOW THIS SONG?
DO I?! "BORN TO FLY" BY LUCE WINTERSTEIN! I LIVE AND BREATHE THIS SONG!
HA HA
GIVE ME THE GUITAR.
GRAB
GRAB

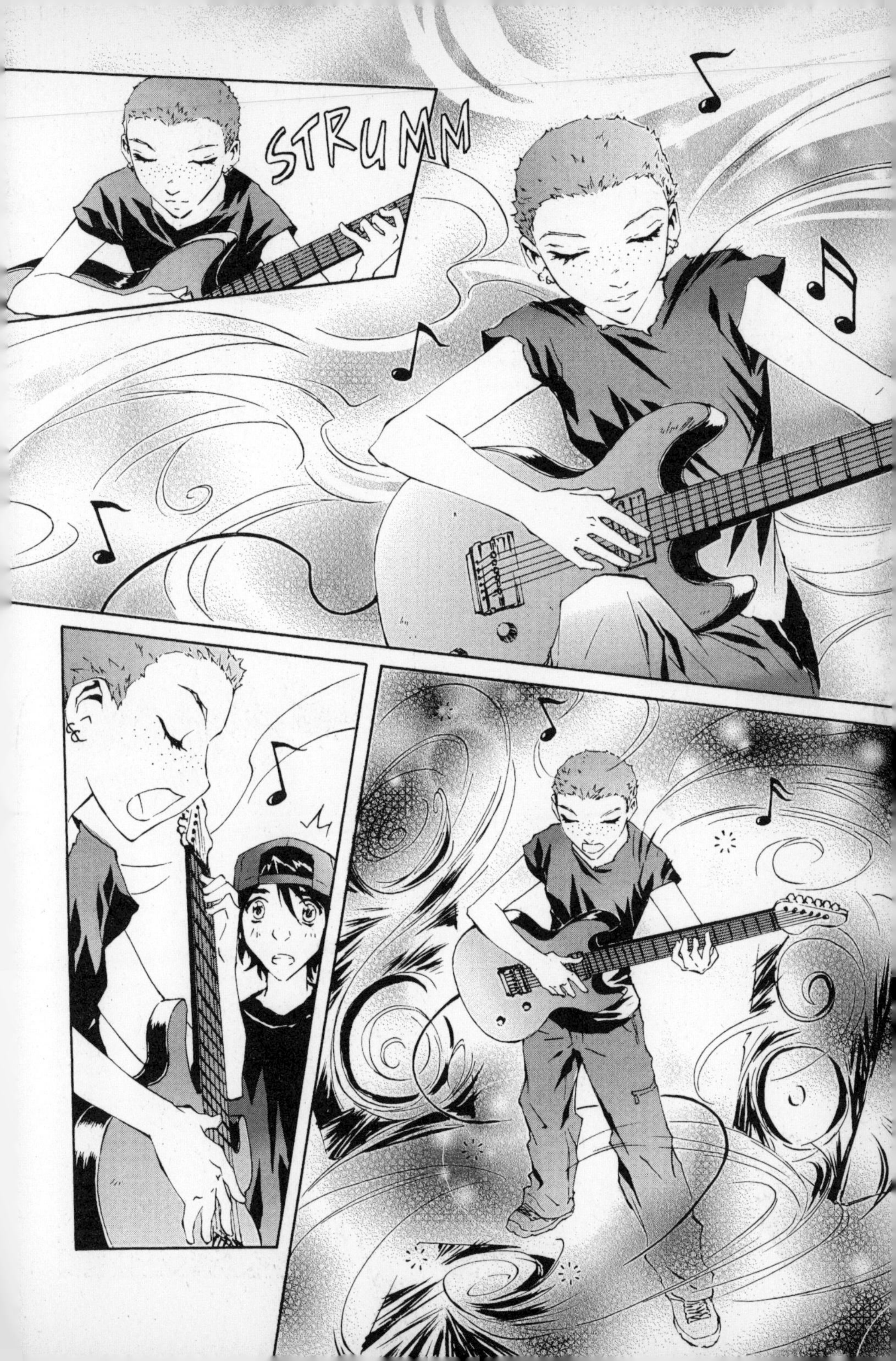
STRUMM

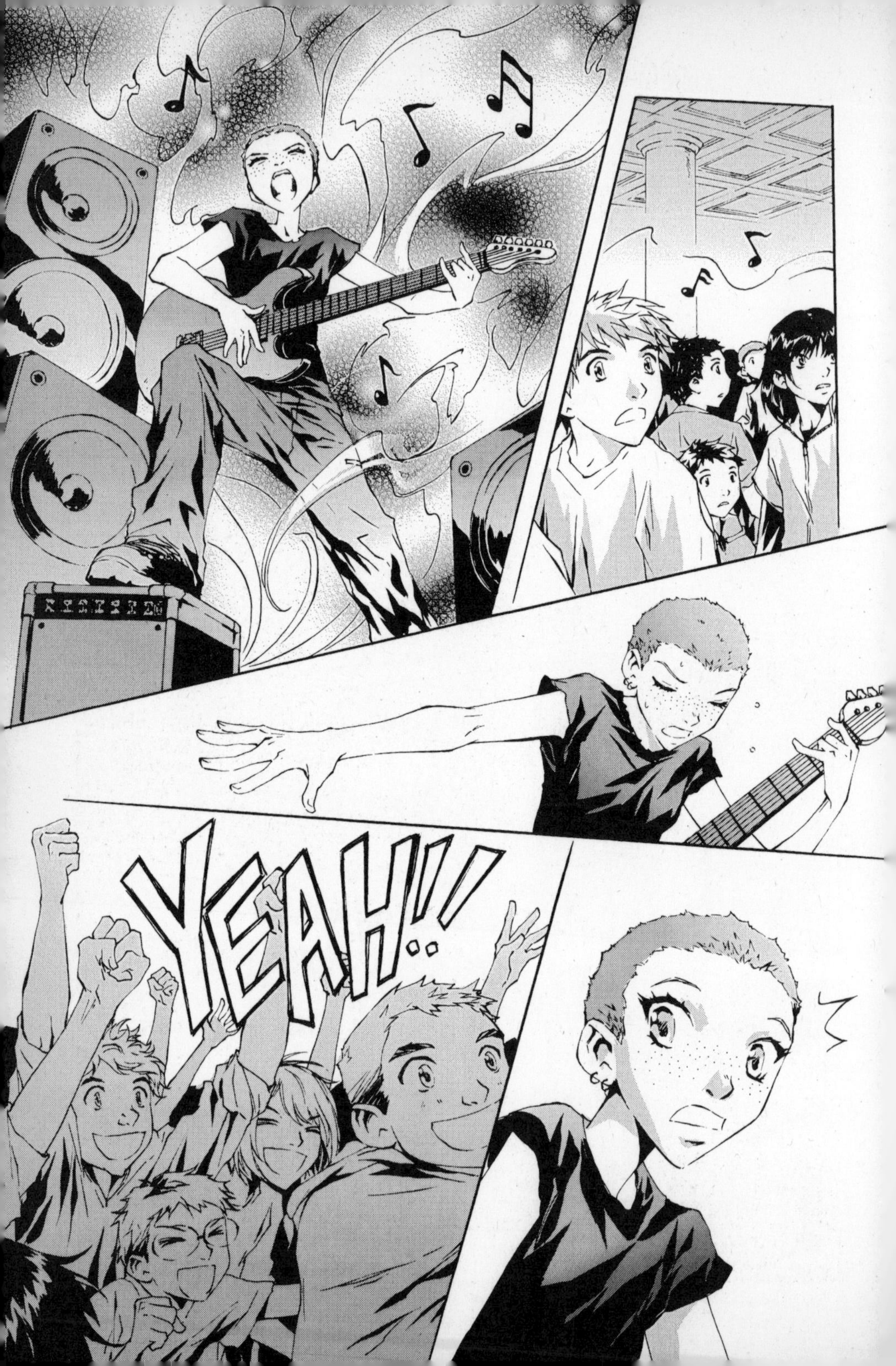
YEAH!!

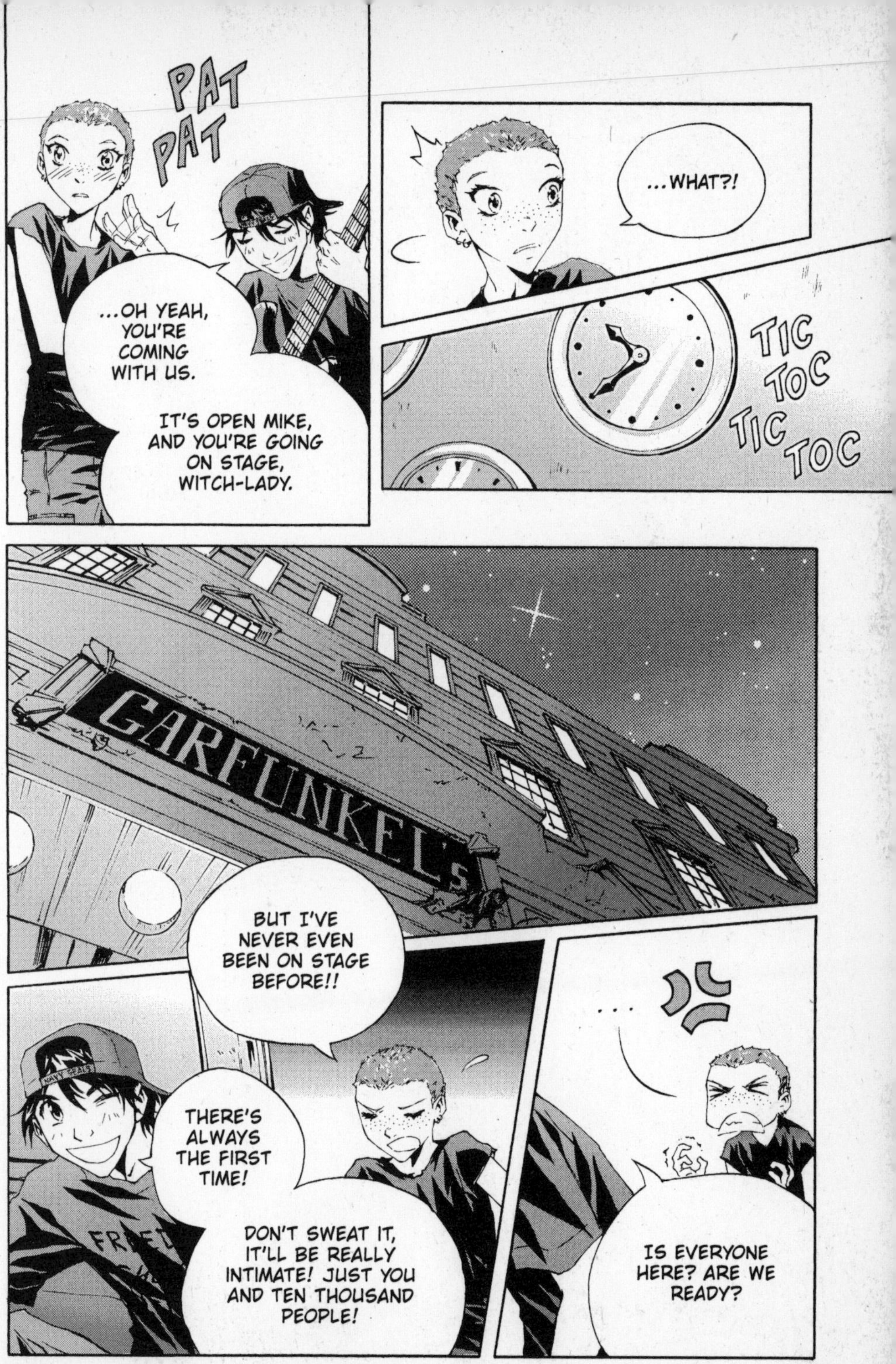
PAT PAT
...OH YEAH, YOU'RE COMING WITH US.
IT'S OPEN MIKE, AND YOU'RE GOING ON STAGE, WITCH-LADY.
...WHAT?!
TIC TOC TIC TOC
GARFUNKEL's
BUT I'VE NEVER EVEN BEEN ON STAGE BEFORE!!
THERE'S ALWAYS THE FIRST TIME!
DON'T SWEAT IT, IT'LL BE REALLY INTIMATE! JUST YOU AND TEN THOUSAND PEOPLE!
...
IS EVERYONE HERE? ARE WE READY?

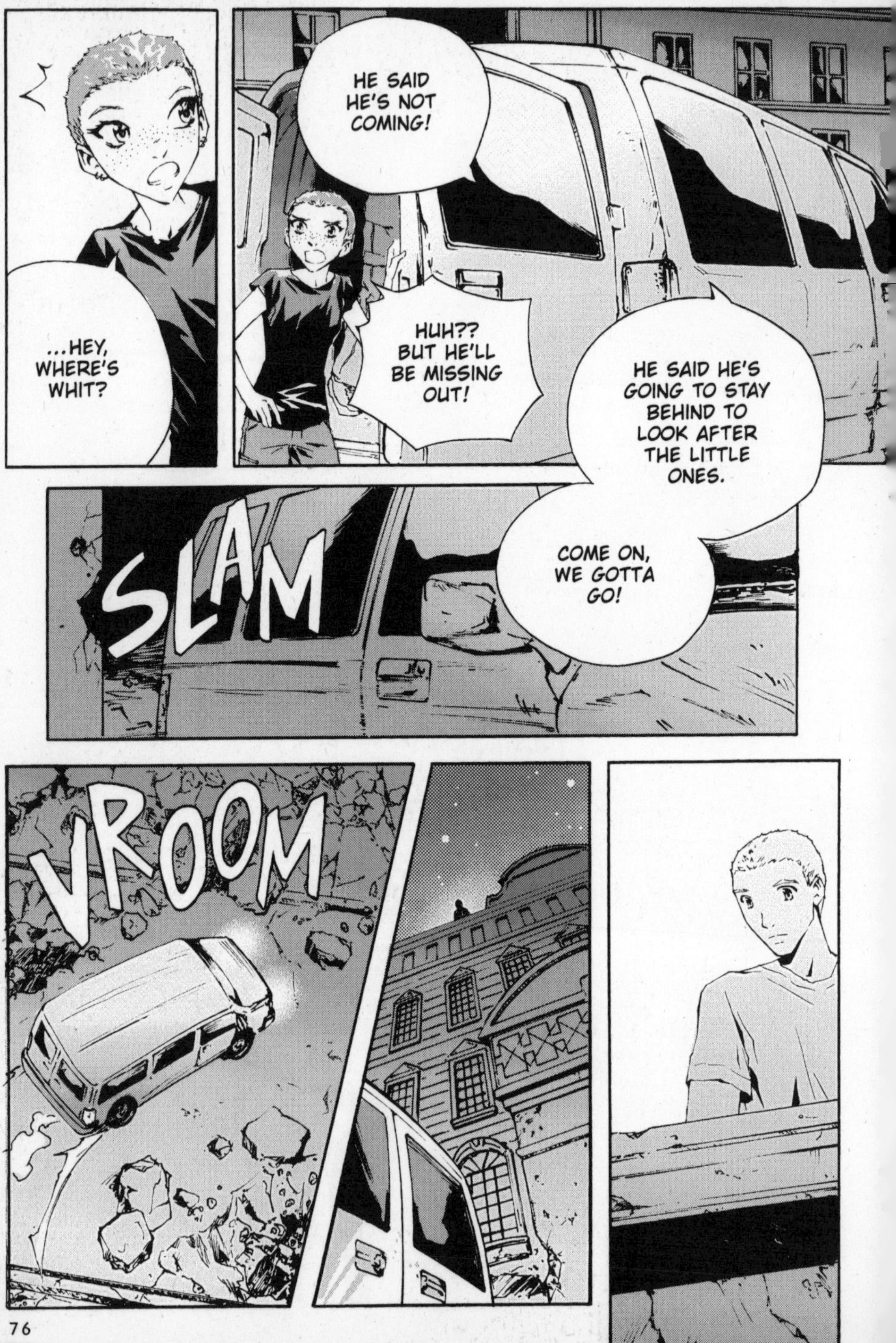
...HEY, WHERE'S WHIT?
HE SAID HE'S NOT COMING!
HUH?? BUT HE'LL BE MISSING OUT!
HE SAID HE'S GOING TO STAY BEHIND TO LOOK AFTER THE LITTLE ONES.
SLAM
COME ON, WE GOTTA GO!
VROOM

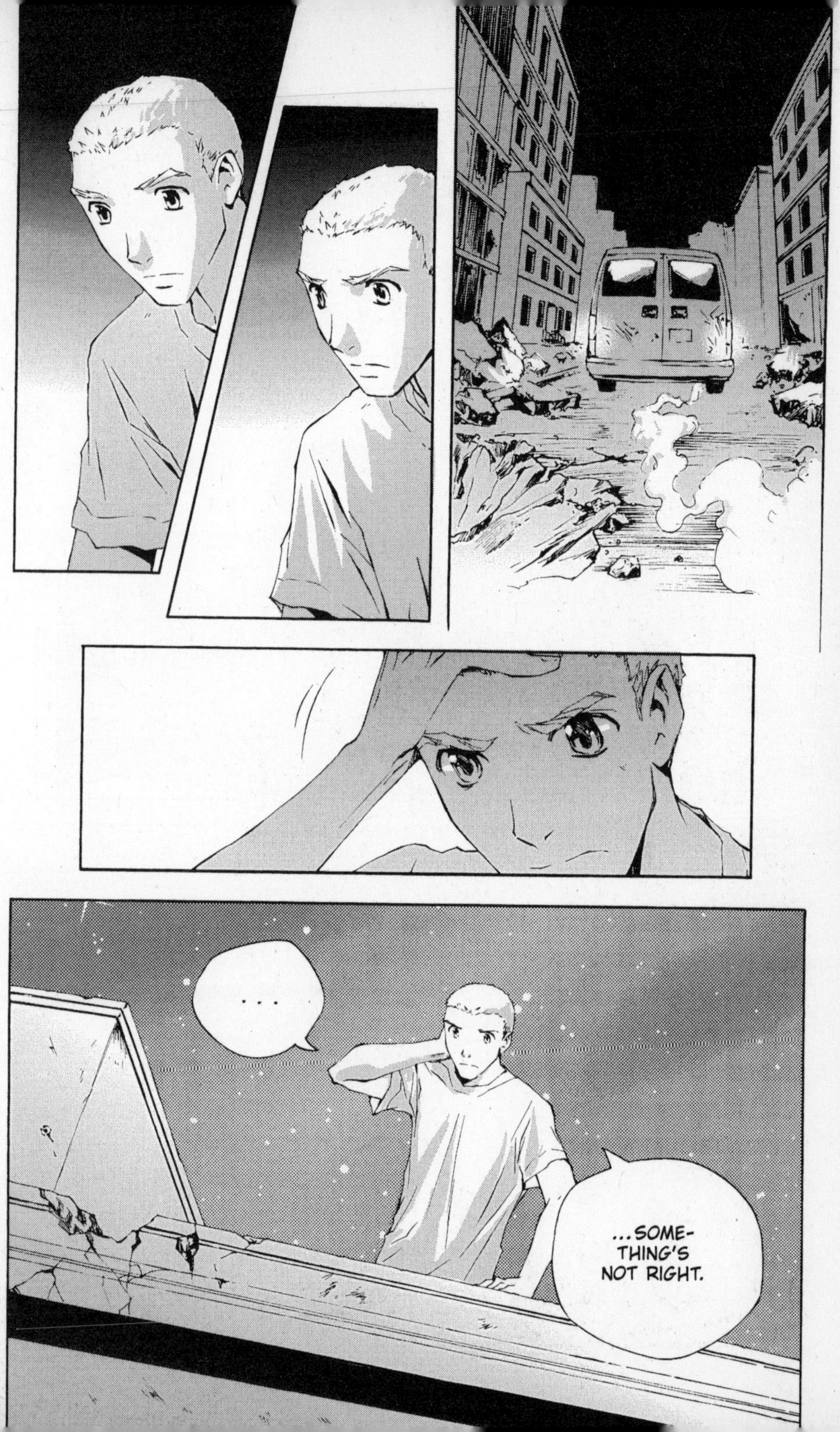
...
...SOME-THING'S NOT RIGHT.

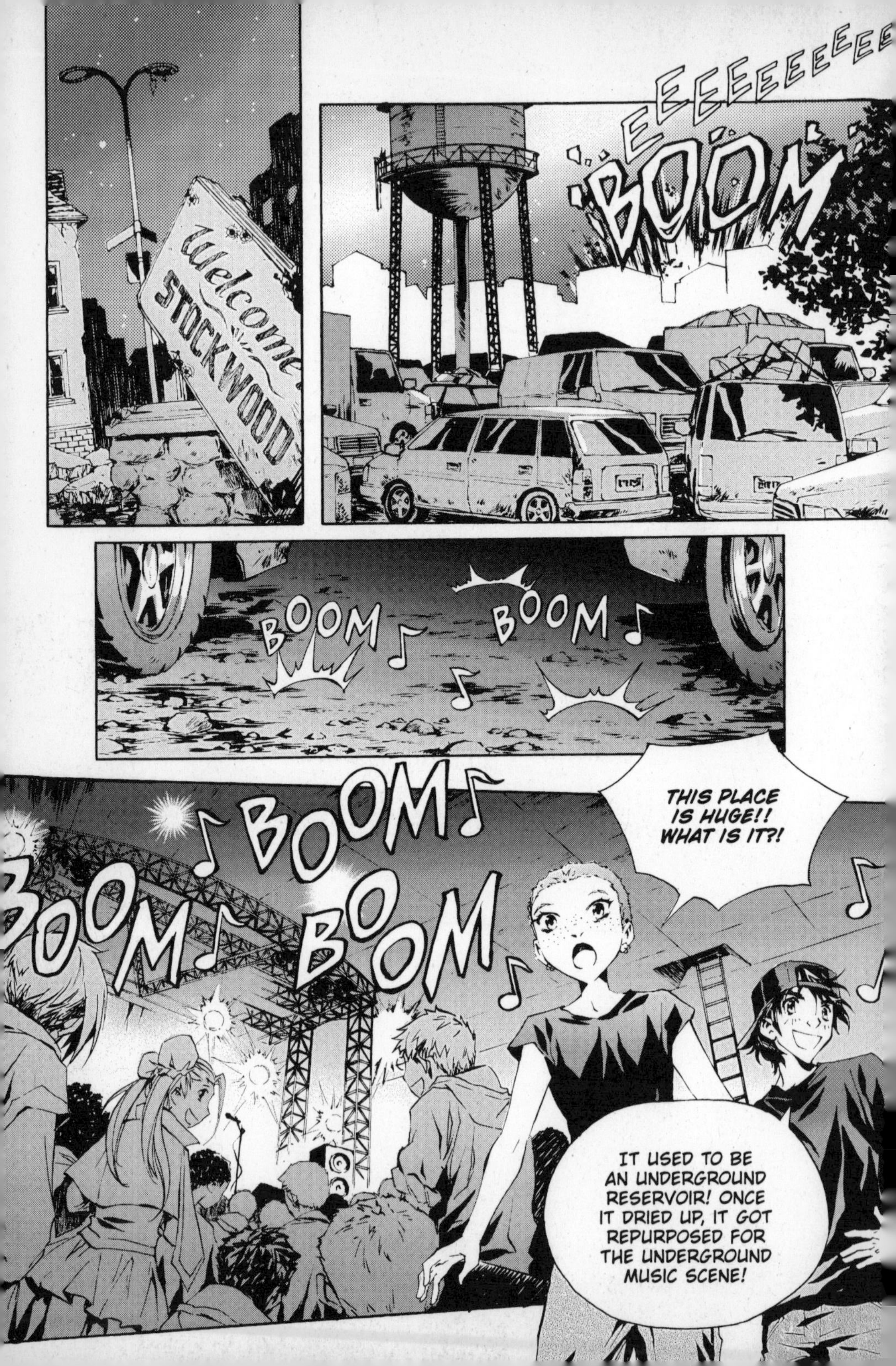

Welcome
STOCKWOOD
EEEEEEEEEEE
BOOM
BOOM BOOM
BOOM BOOM BOOM BOOM
THIS PLACE IS HUGE!! WHAT IS IT?!
IT USED TO BE AN UNDERGROUND RESERVOIR! ONCE IT DRIED UP, IT GOT REPURPOSED FOR THE UNDERGROUND MUSIC SCENE!

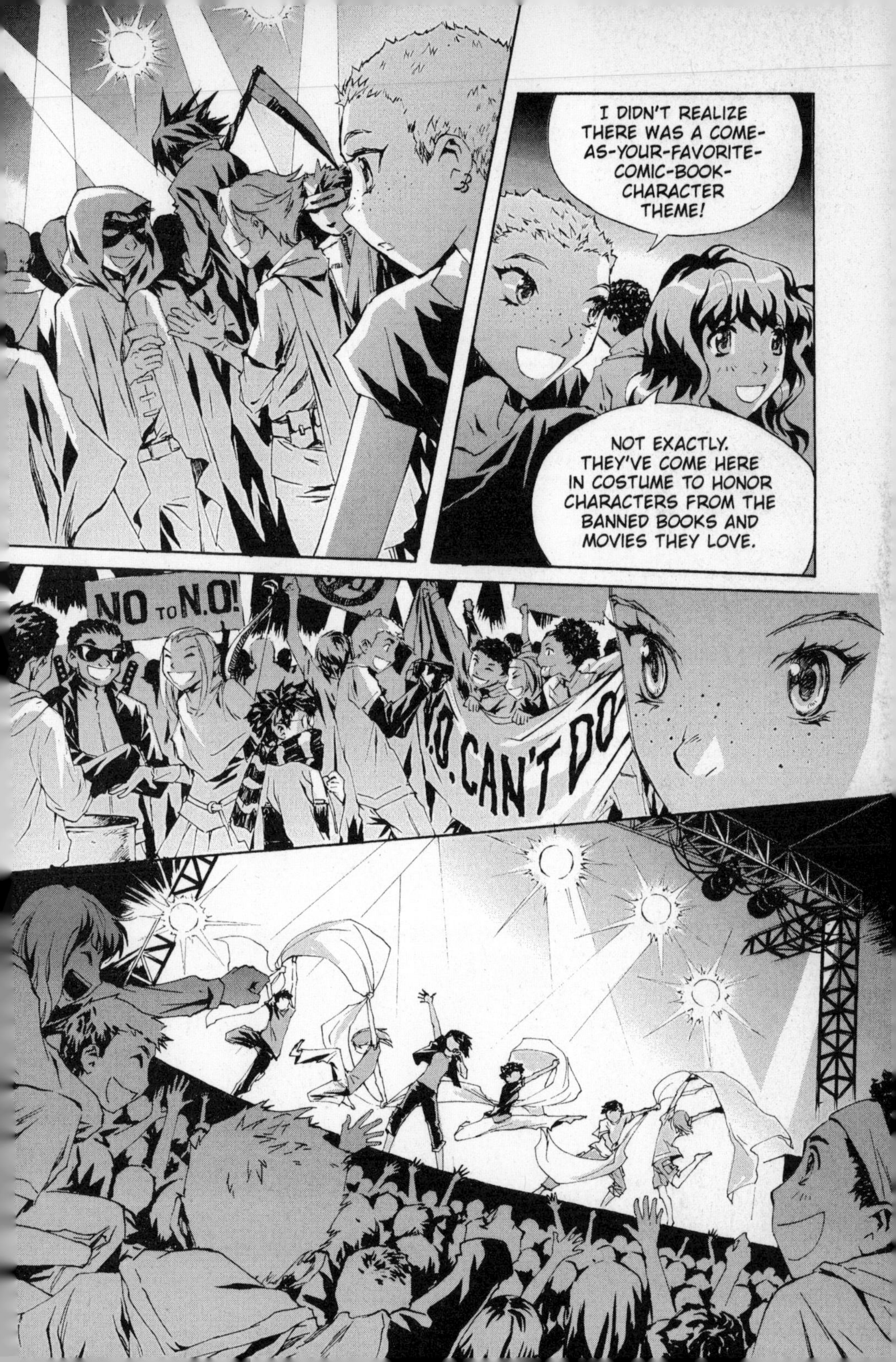
I DIDN'T REALIZE THERE WAS A COME-AS-YOUR-FAVORITE-COMIC-BOOK-CHARACTER THEME!
NOT EXACTLY. THEY'VE COME HERE IN COSTUME TO HONOR CHARACTERS FROM THE BANNED BOOKS AND MOVIES THEY LOVE.
NO TO N.O!
.O. CAN'T DO

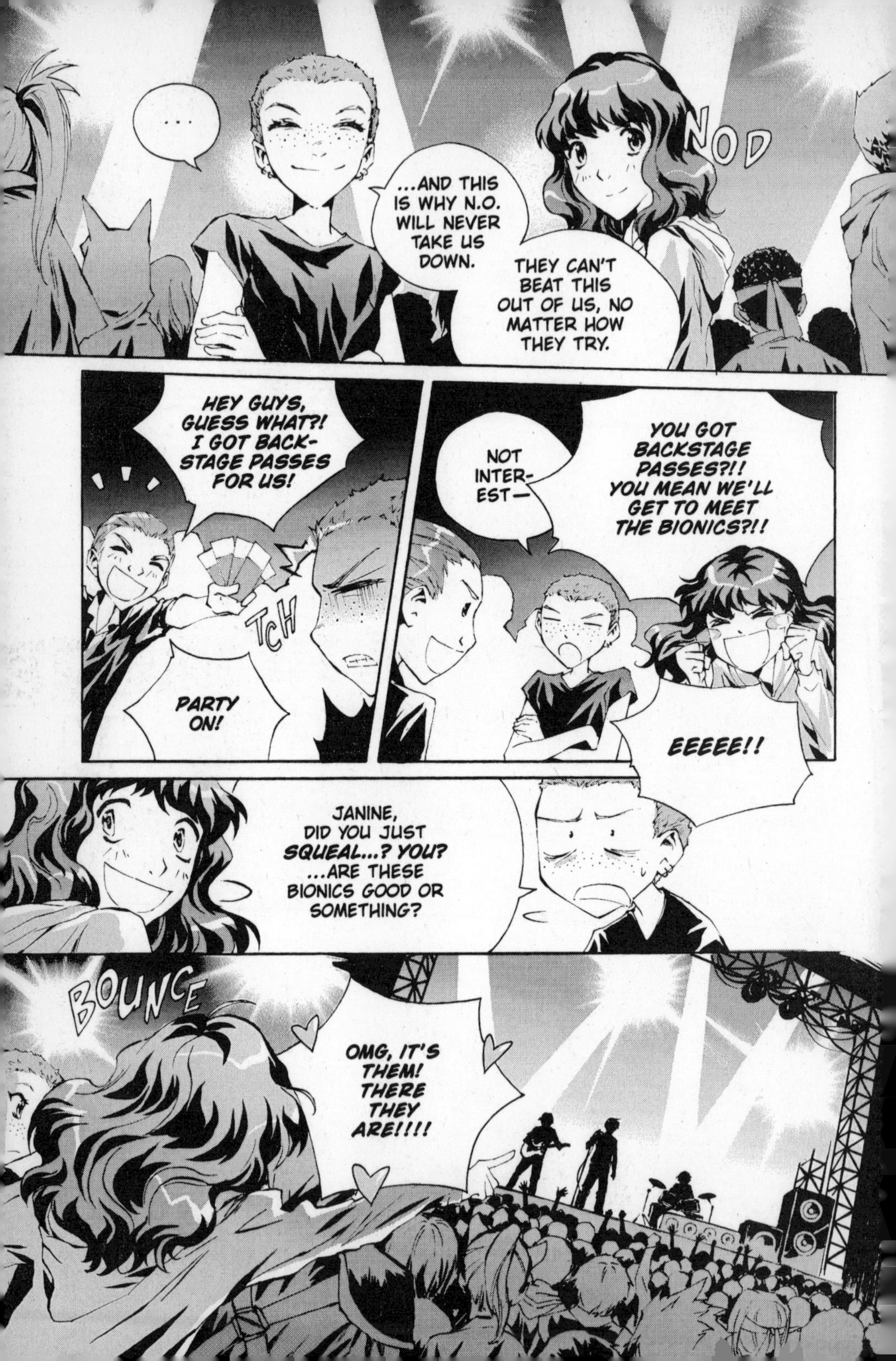

...
...AND THIS IS WHY N.O. WILL NEVER TAKE US DOWN.
NOD
THEY CAN'T BEAT THIS OUT OF US, NO MATTER HOW THEY TRY.
HEY GUYS, GUESS WHAT?! I GOT BACK-STAGE PASSES FOR US!
TCH
PARTY ON!
NOT INTER-EST—
YOU GOT BACKSTAGE PASSES?!! YOU MEAN WE'LL GET TO MEET THE BIONICS?!!
EEEEE!!
JANINE, DID YOU JUST SQUEAL...? YOU? ...ARE THESE BIONICS GOOD OR SOMETHING?
BOUNCE
OMG, IT'S THEM! THERE THEY ARE!!!!

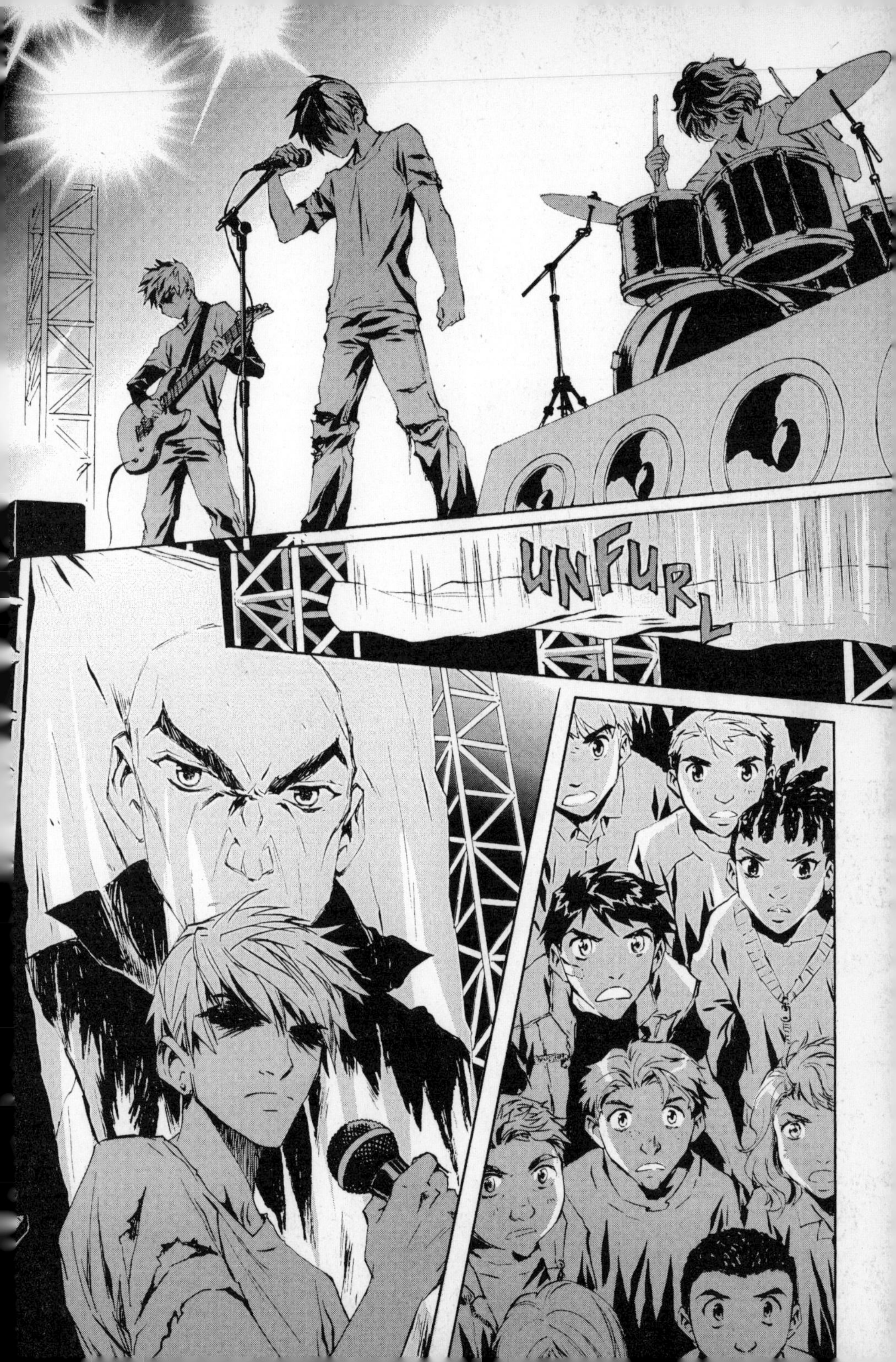
UNFURL

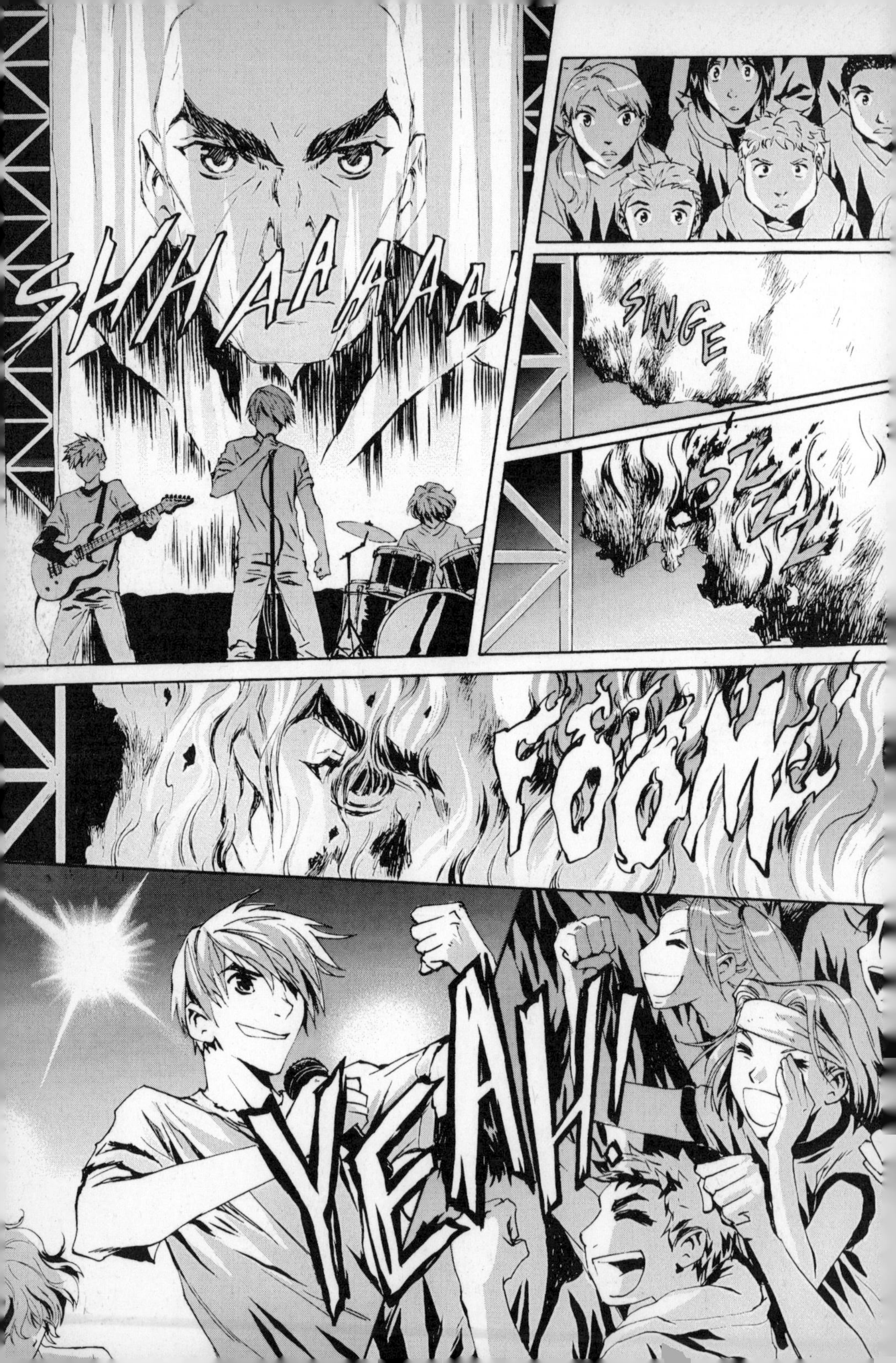
SHHAAAAA!
SINGE
SIZZ
FOOM!
YEAH!

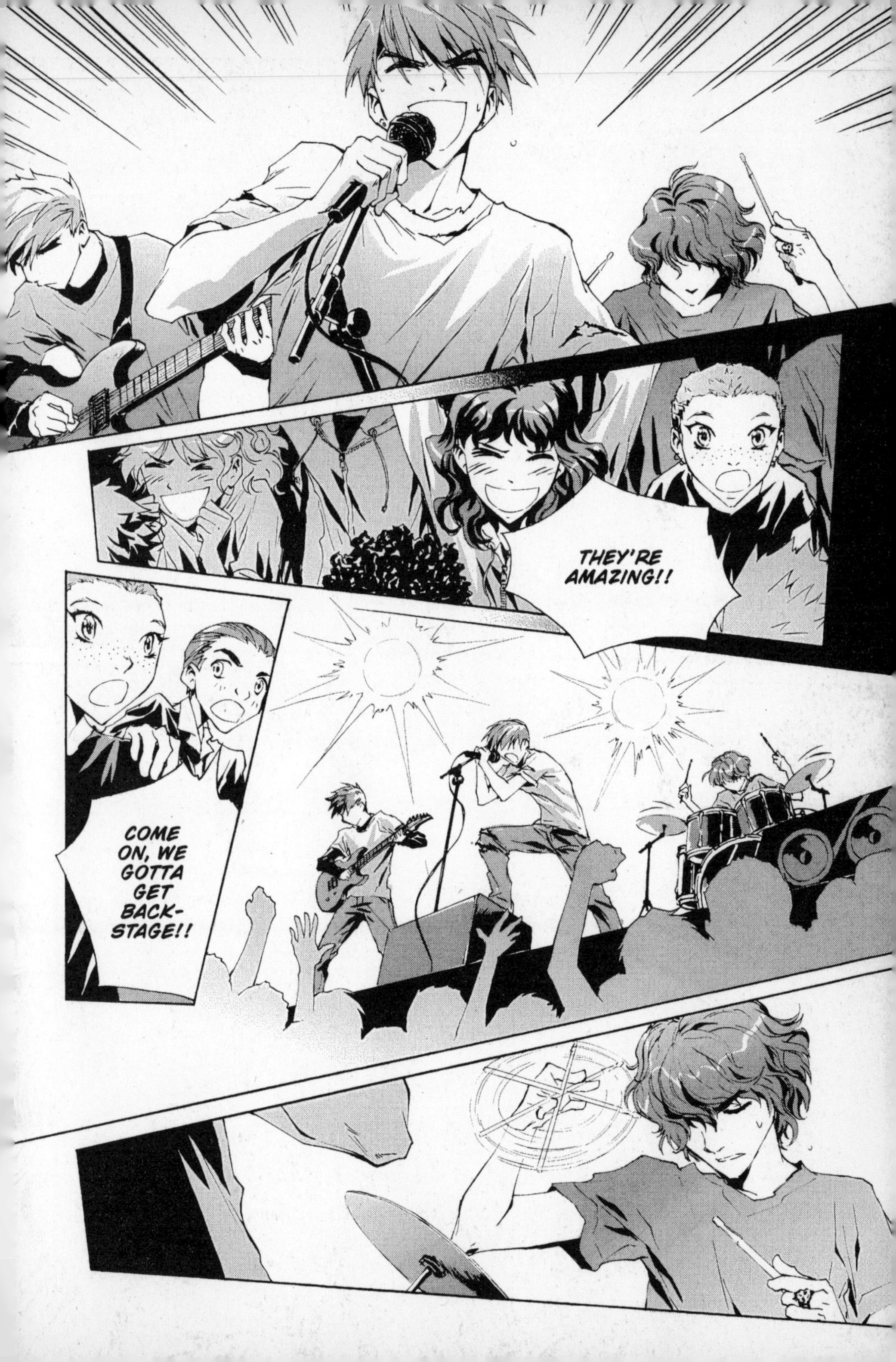
THEY'RE AMAZING!!
COME ON, WE GOTTA GET BACK-STAGE!!

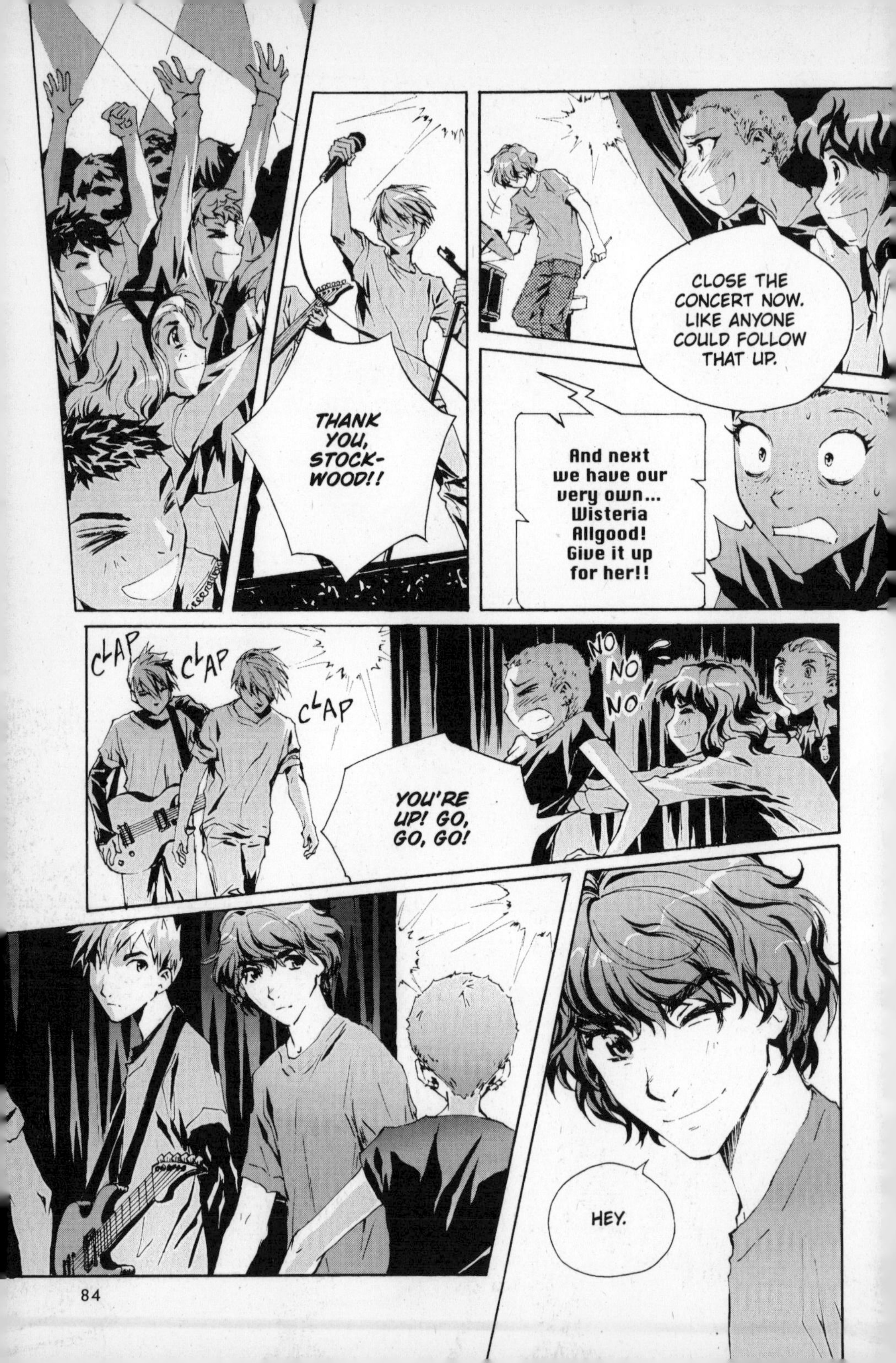
THANK YOU, STOCK-WOOD!!
CLOSE THE CONCERT NOW. LIKE ANYONE COULD FOLLOW THAT UP.
And next we have our very own... Wisteria Allgood! Give it up for her!!
CLAP
CLAP
CLAP
NO
NO
NO
YOU'RE UP! GO, GO, GO!
HEY.

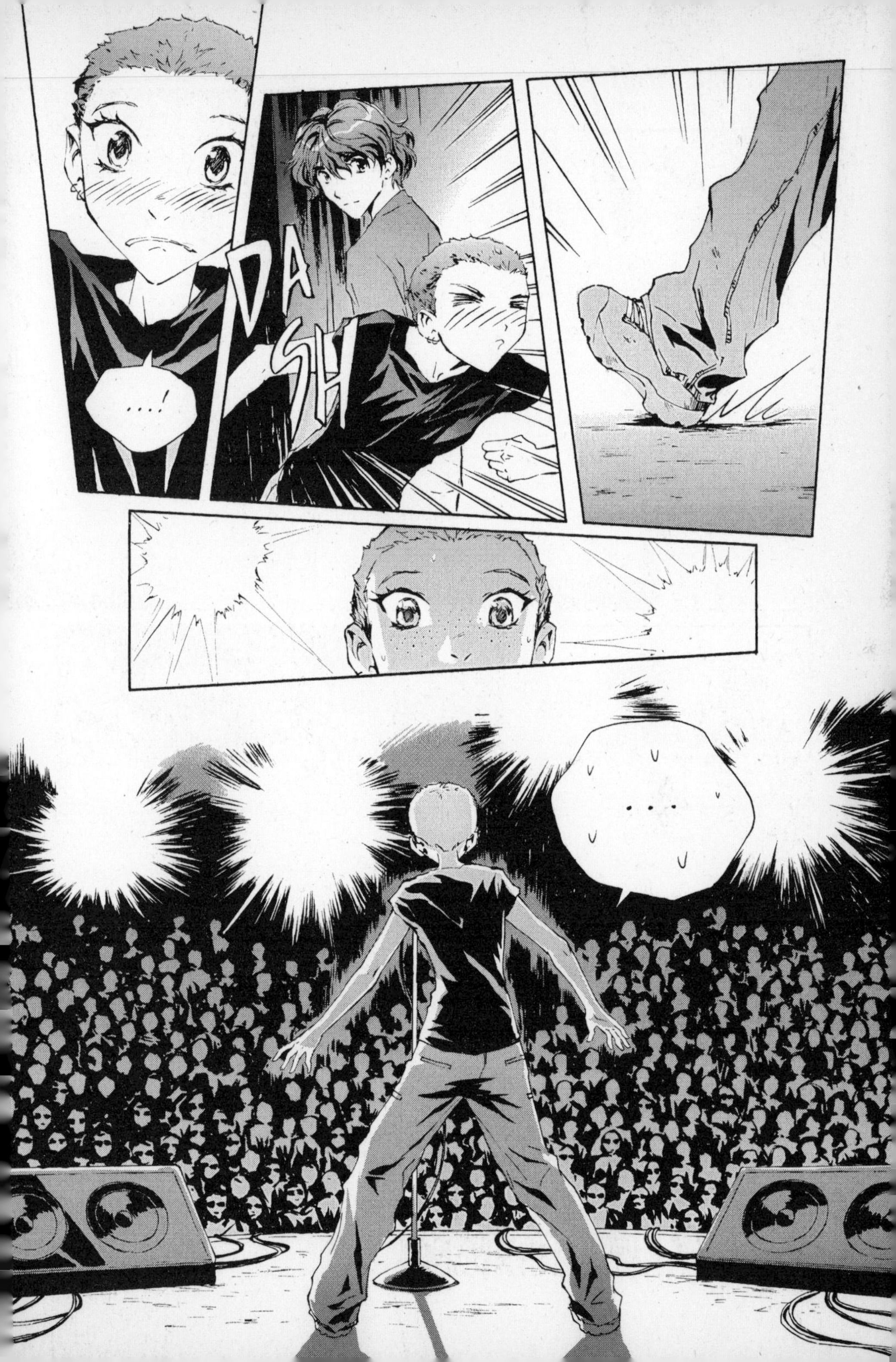
....!
DASH
...

WITCH & WIZARD

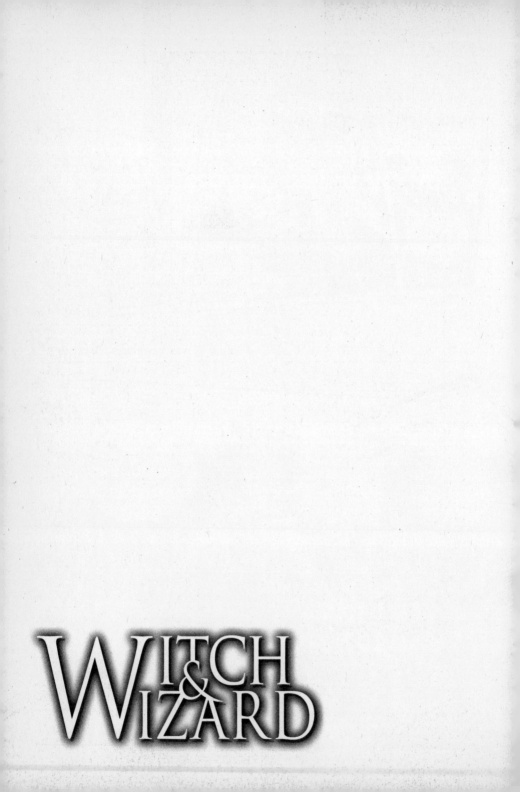

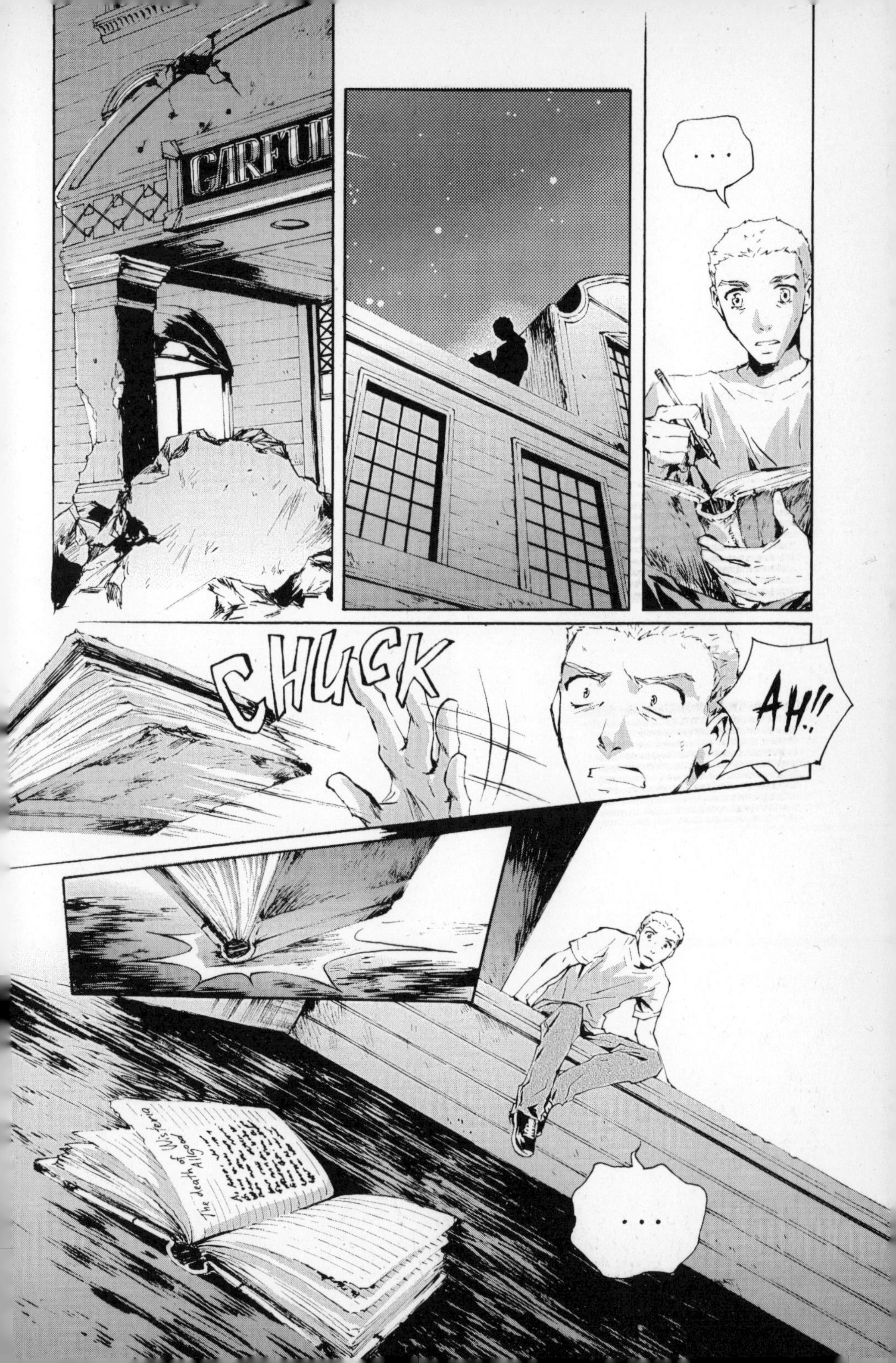
. . .
CHUCK
AH!!
The death of Wisteria Allgood
. . .

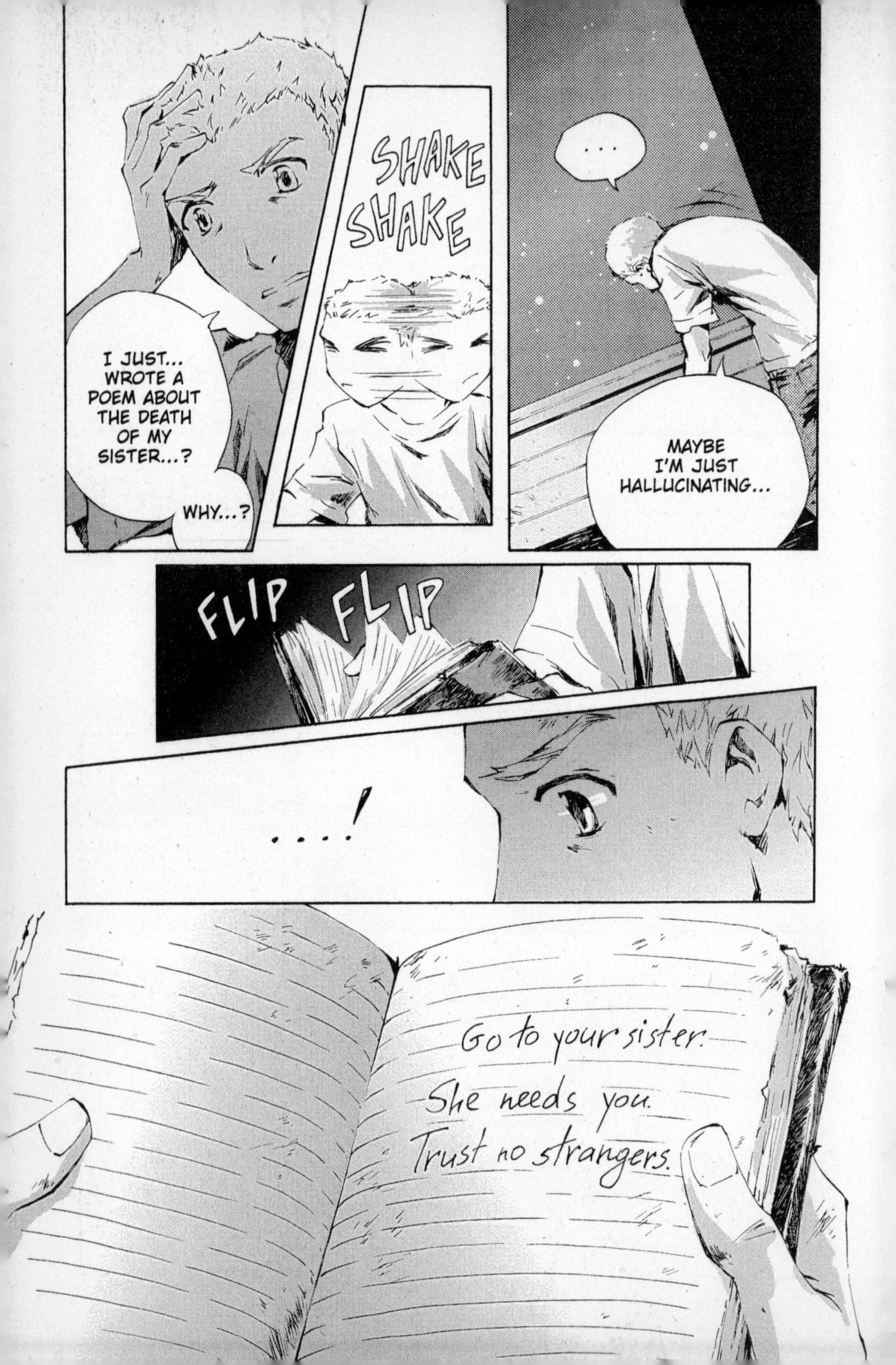
I JUST... WROTE A POEM ABOUT THE DEATH OF MY SISTER...?
WHY...?
SHAKE SHAKE
...
MAYBE I'M JUST HALLUCINATING...
FLIP FLIP
...!
Go to your sister.
She needs you.
Trust no strangers.

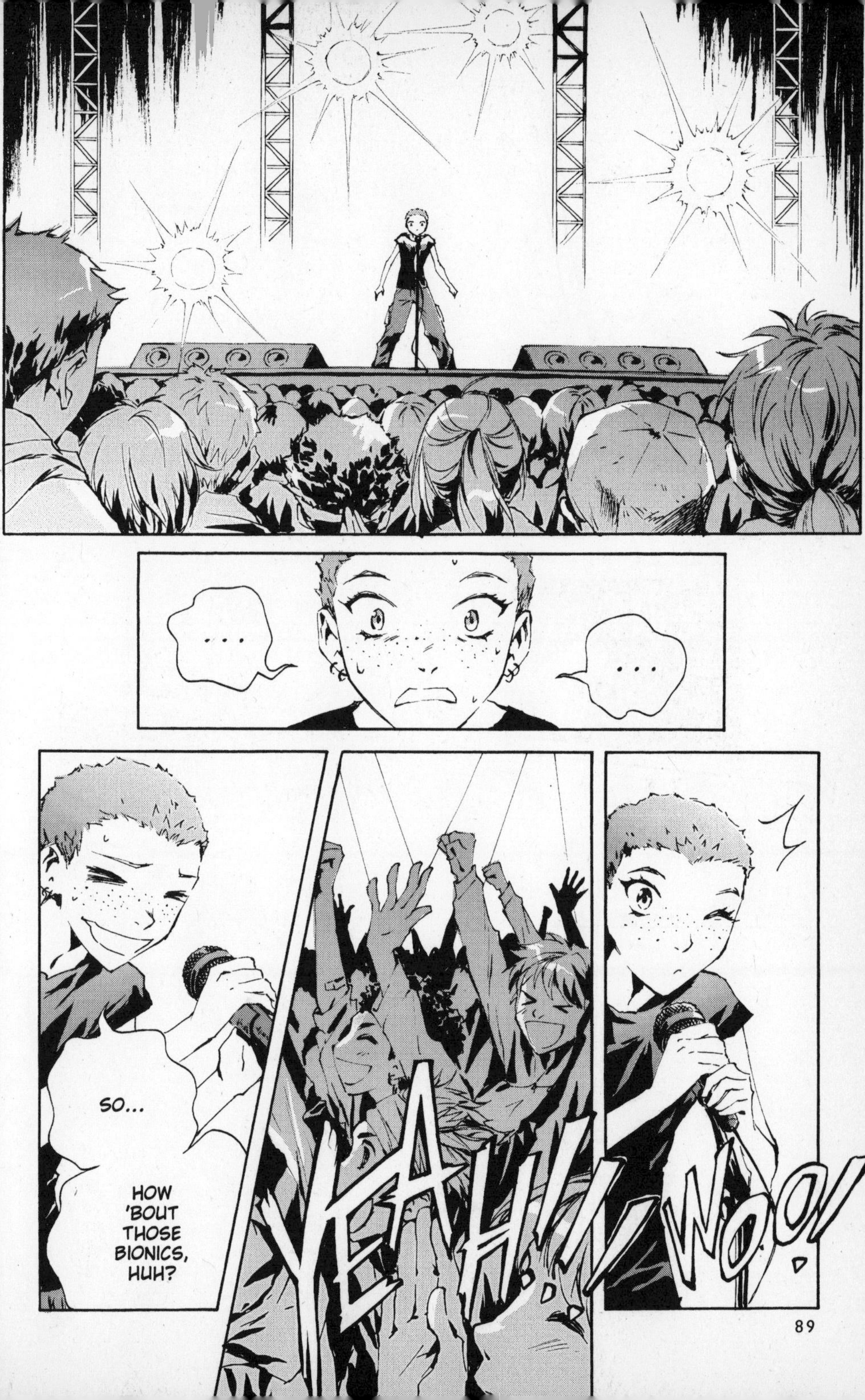
...
...
SO...
HOW 'BOUT THOSE BIONICS, HUH?
YEAH!!
WOO!

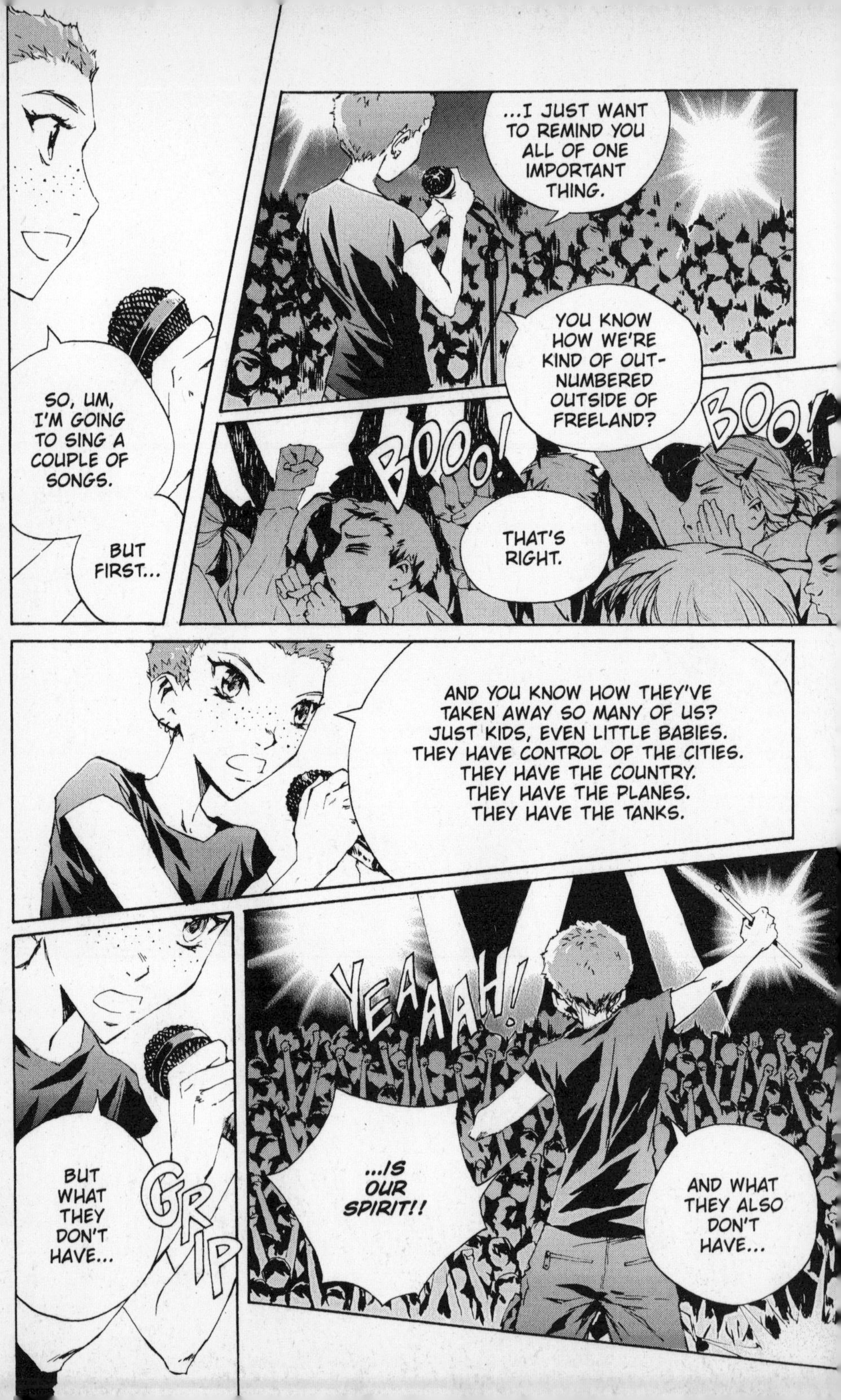
SO, UM, I'M GOING TO SING A COUPLE OF SONGS.
BUT FIRST...
...I JUST WANT TO REMIND YOU ALL OF ONE IMPORTANT THING.
YOU KNOW HOW WE'RE KIND OF OUT-NUMBERED OUTSIDE OF FREELAND?
BOOO!
BOOO!
THAT'S RIGHT.
AND YOU KNOW HOW THEY'VE TAKEN AWAY SO MANY OF US? JUST KIDS, EVEN LITTLE BABIES. THEY HAVE CONTROL OF THE CITIES. THEY HAVE THE COUNTRY. THEY HAVE THE PLANES. THEY HAVE THE TANKS.
BUT WHAT THEY DON'T HAVE...
GRIP
YEAAAH!
...IS OUR SPIRIT!!
AND WHAT THEY ALSO DON'T HAVE...

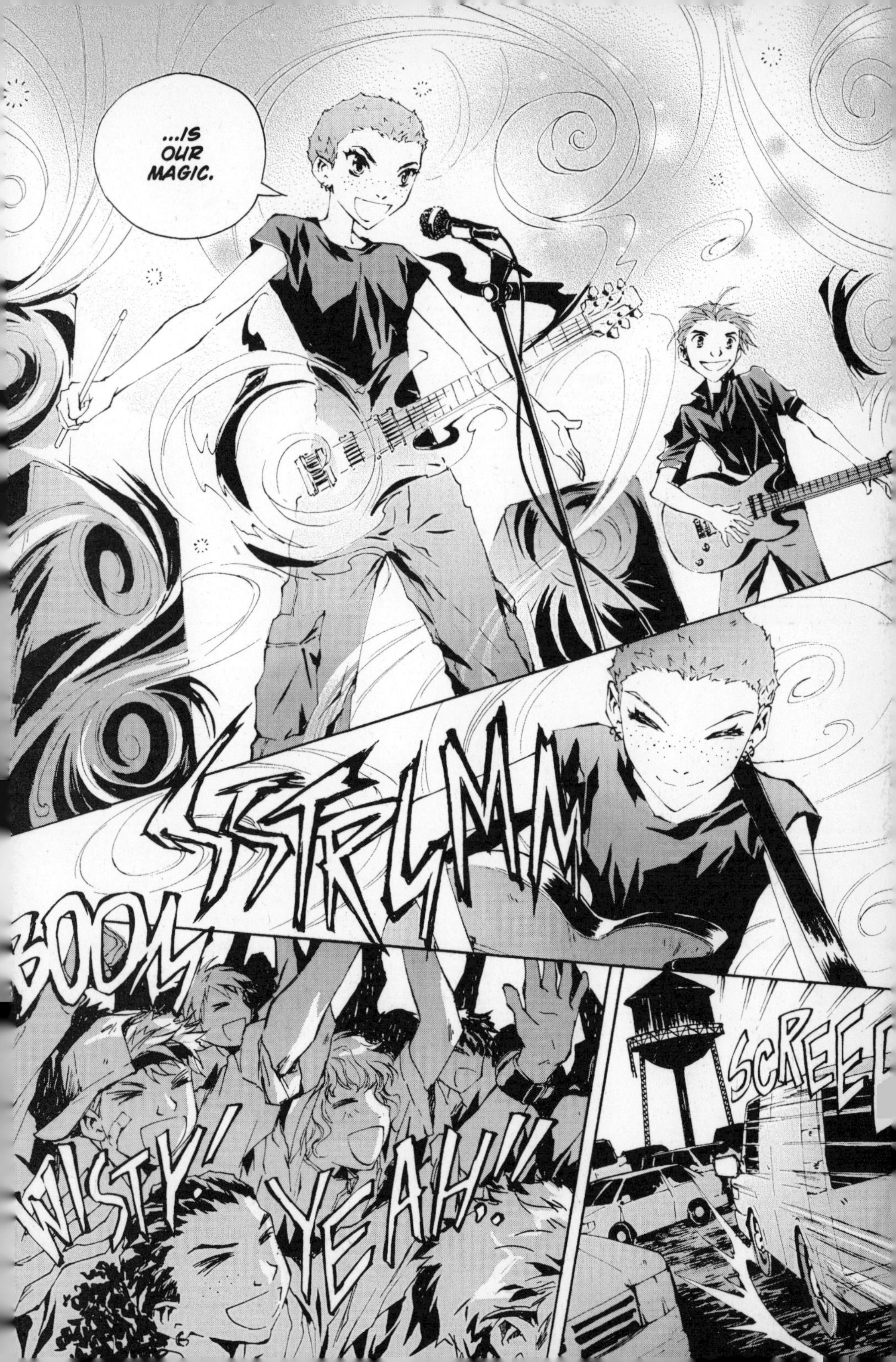
...IS OUR MAGIC.
SSTRLMM
BOOM
WISTY!
YEAH!!
SCREEE

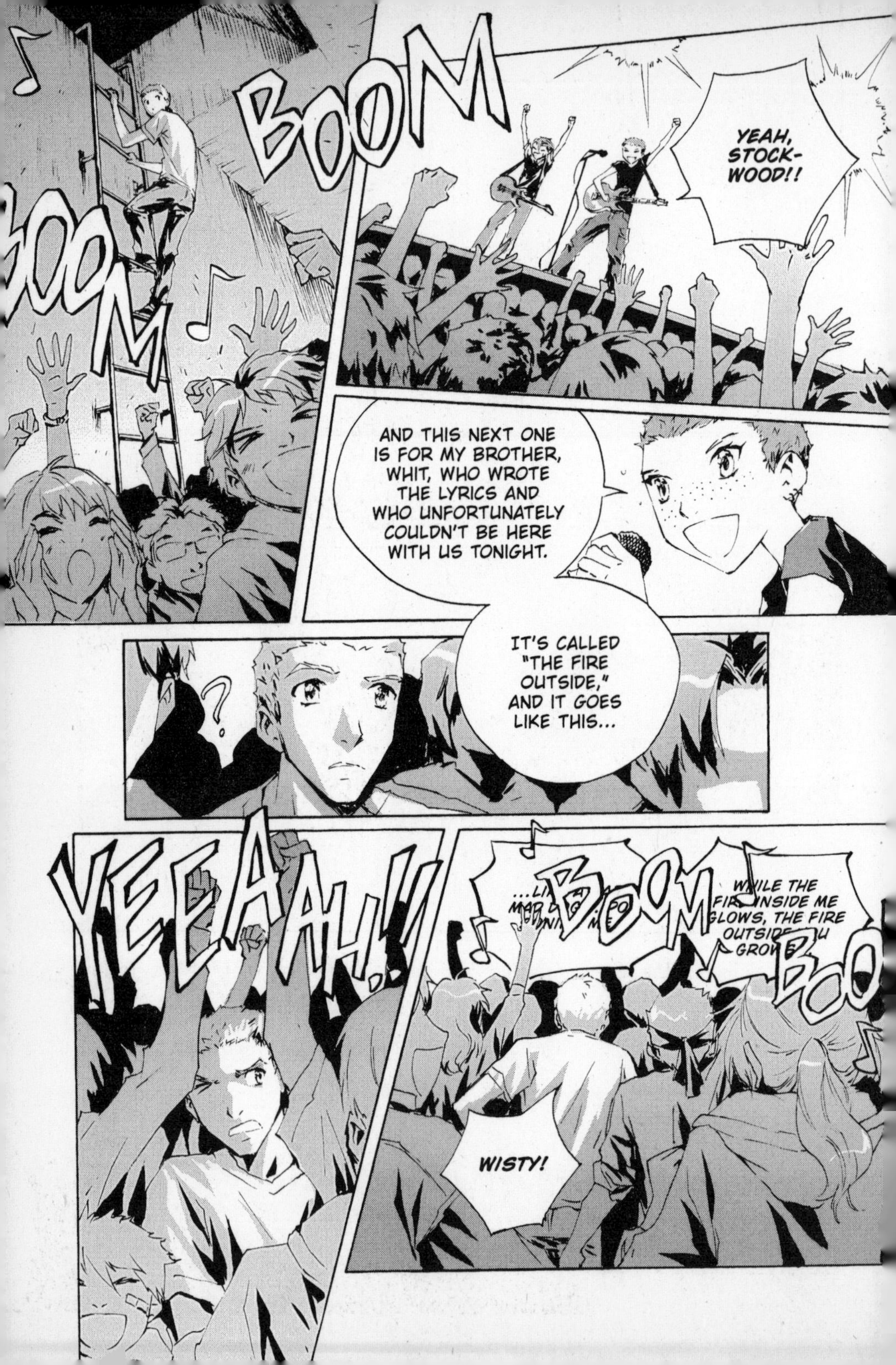
BOOM
BOOM
BOOM
YEAH, STOCK-WOOD!!
AND THIS NEXT ONE IS FOR MY BROTHER, WHIT, WHO WROTE THE LYRICS AND WHO UNFORTUNATELY COULDN'T BE HERE WITH US TONIGHT.
IT'S CALLED "THE FIRE OUTSIDE," AND IT GOES LIKE THIS...
YEEAAH!!
BOOM
WHILE THE FIR INSIDE ME GLOWS, THE FIRE OUTSID U GROW
BOOM
WISTY!

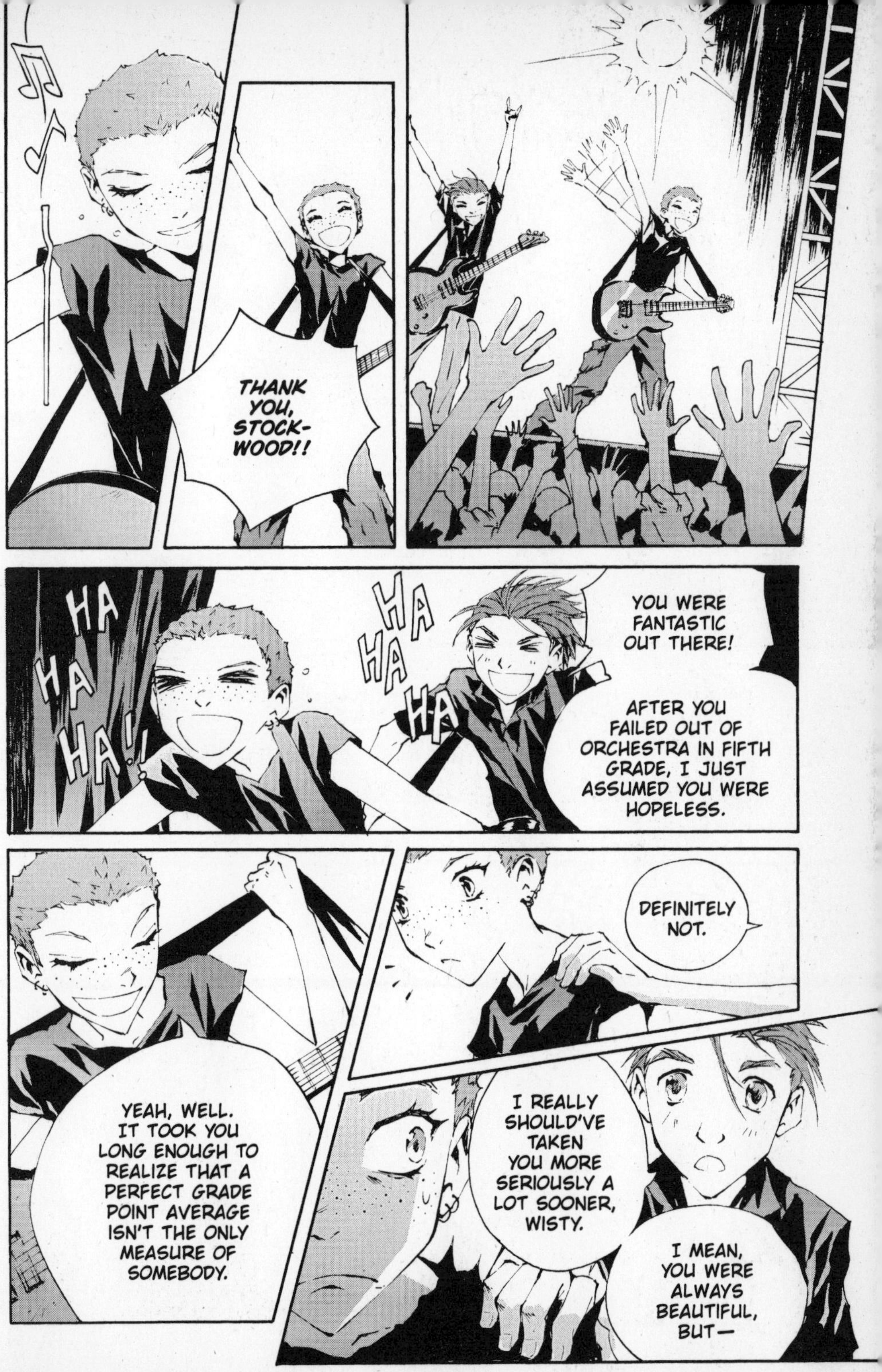
THANK YOU, STOCK-WOOD!!
HA HA HA!!
HA HA HA HA
YOU WERE FANTASTIC OUT THERE!
AFTER YOU FAILED OUT OF ORCHESTRA IN FIFTH GRADE, I JUST ASSUMED YOU WERE HOPELESS.
YEAH, WELL. IT TOOK YOU LONG ENOUGH TO REALIZE THAT A PERFECT GRADE POINT AVERAGE ISN'T THE ONLY MEASURE OF SOMEBODY.
DEFINITELY NOT.
I REALLY SHOULD'VE TAKEN YOU MORE SERIOUSLY A LOT SOONER, WISTY.
I MEAN, YOU WERE ALWAYS BEAUTIFUL, BUT—

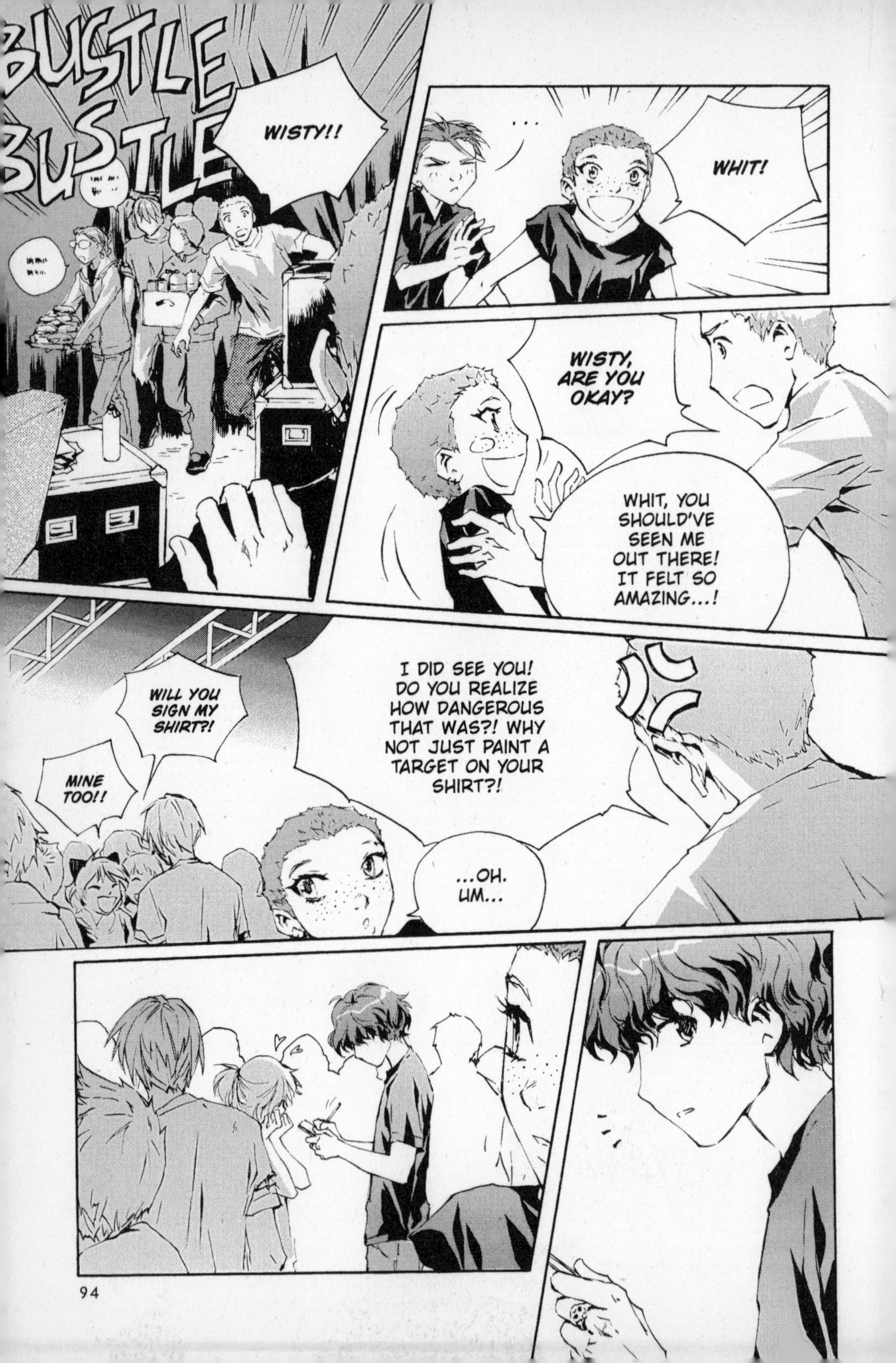
BUSTLE BUSTLE
WISTY!!
...
WHIT!
WISTY, ARE YOU OKAY?
WHIT, YOU SHOULD'VE SEEN ME OUT THERE! IT FELT SO AMAZING...!
WILL YOU SIGN MY SHIRT?!
MINE TOO!!
I DID SEE YOU! DO YOU REALIZE HOW DANGEROUS THAT WAS?! WHY NOT JUST PAINT A TARGET ON YOUR SHIRT?!
...OH. UM...

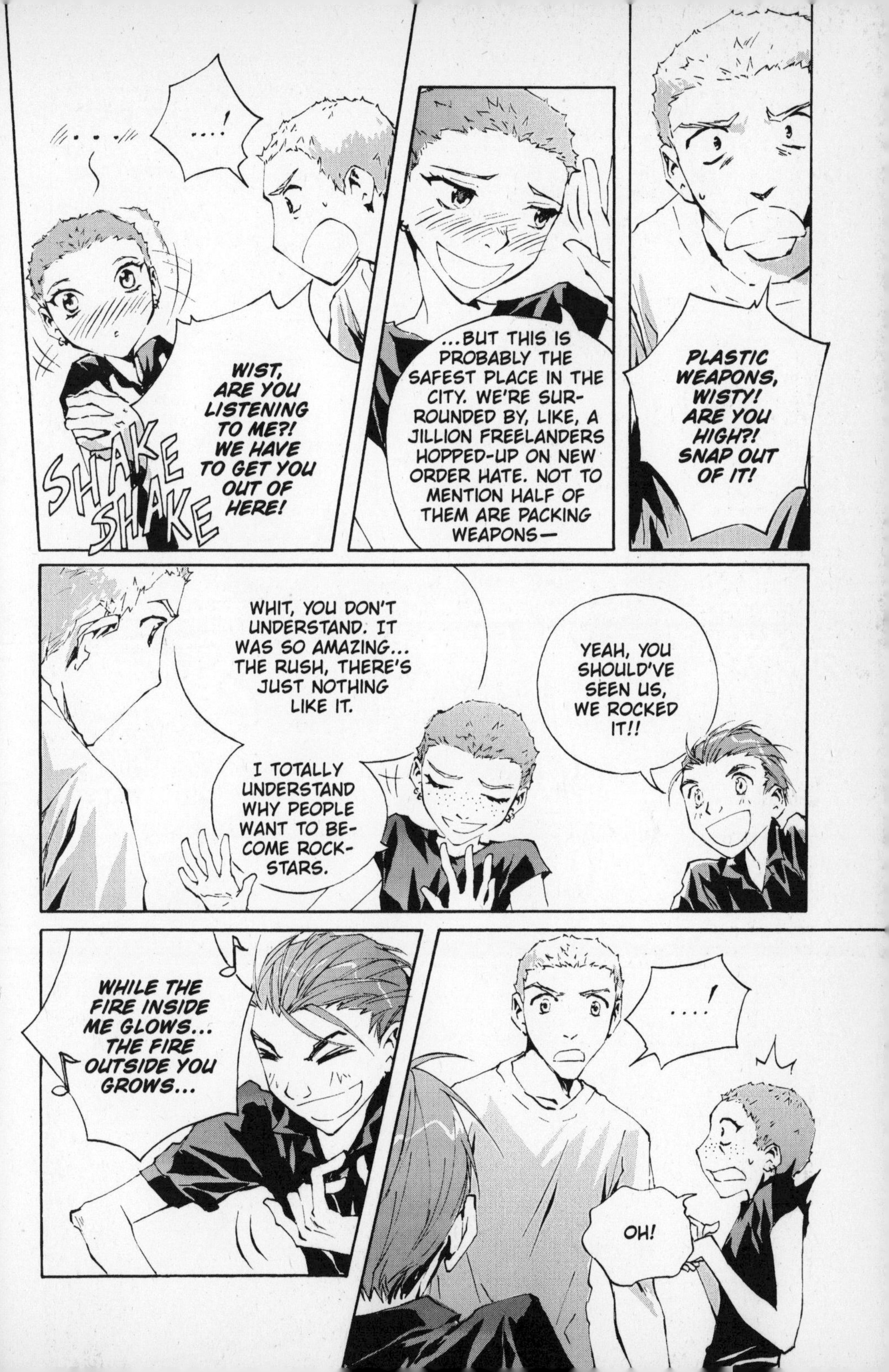
. . . . . .
. . . .!
WIST, ARE YOU LISTENING TO ME?! WE HAVE TO GET YOU OUT OF HERE!
SHAKE SHAKE
...BUT THIS IS PROBABLY THE SAFEST PLACE IN THE CITY. WE'RE SURROUNDED BY, LIKE, A JILLION FREELANDERS HOPPED-UP ON NEW ORDER HATE. NOT TO MENTION HALF OF THEM ARE PACKING WEAPONS—
PLASTIC WEAPONS, WISTY! ARE YOU HIGH?! SNAP OUT OF IT!
WHIT, YOU DON'T UNDERSTAND. IT WAS SO AMAZING... THE RUSH, THERE'S JUST NOTHING LIKE IT.
I TOTALLY UNDERSTAND WHY PEOPLE WANT TO BECOME ROCKSTARS.
YEAH, YOU SHOULD'VE SEEN US, WE ROCKED IT!!
WHILE THE FIRE INSIDE ME GLOWS... THE FIRE OUTSIDE YOU GROWS...
. . . .!
OH!

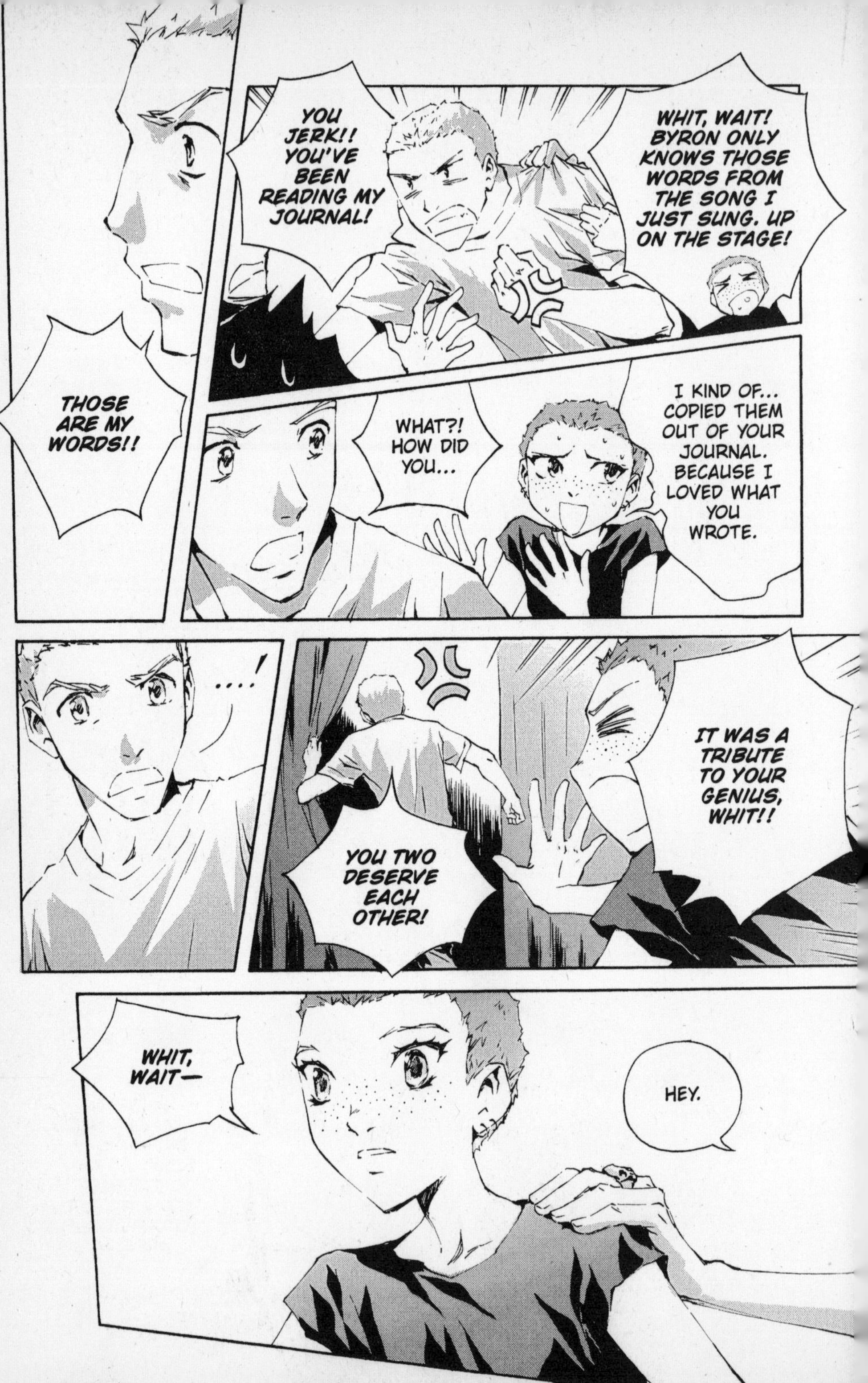
THOSE ARE MY WORDS!!
YOU JERK!! YOU'VE BEEN READING MY JOURNAL!
WHIT, WAIT! BYRON ONLY KNOWS THOSE WORDS FROM THE SONG I JUST SUNG. UP ON THE STAGE!
WHAT?! HOW DID YOU...
I KIND OF... COPIED THEM OUT OF YOUR JOURNAL. BECAUSE I LOVED WHAT YOU WROTE.
....!
IT WAS A TRIBUTE TO YOUR GENIUS, WHIT!!
YOU TWO DESERVE EACH OTHER!
WHIT, WAIT—
HEY.

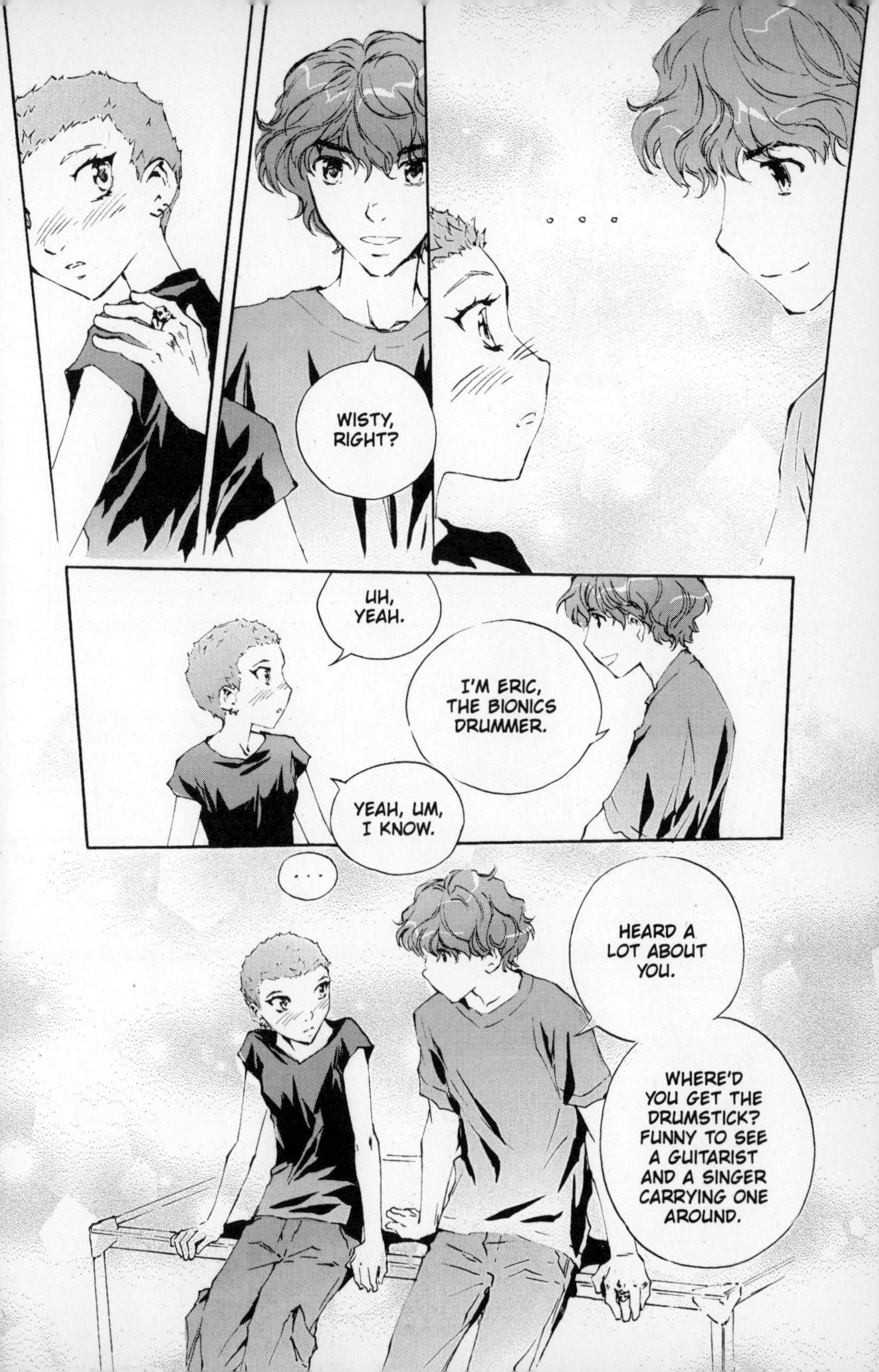
WISTY, RIGHT?
...
UH, YEAH.
I'M ERIC, THE BIONICS DRUMMER.
YEAH, UM, I KNOW.
...
HEARD A LOT ABOUT YOU.
WHERE'D YOU GET THE DRUMSTICK? FUNNY TO SEE A GUITARIST AND A SINGER CARRYING ONE AROUND.

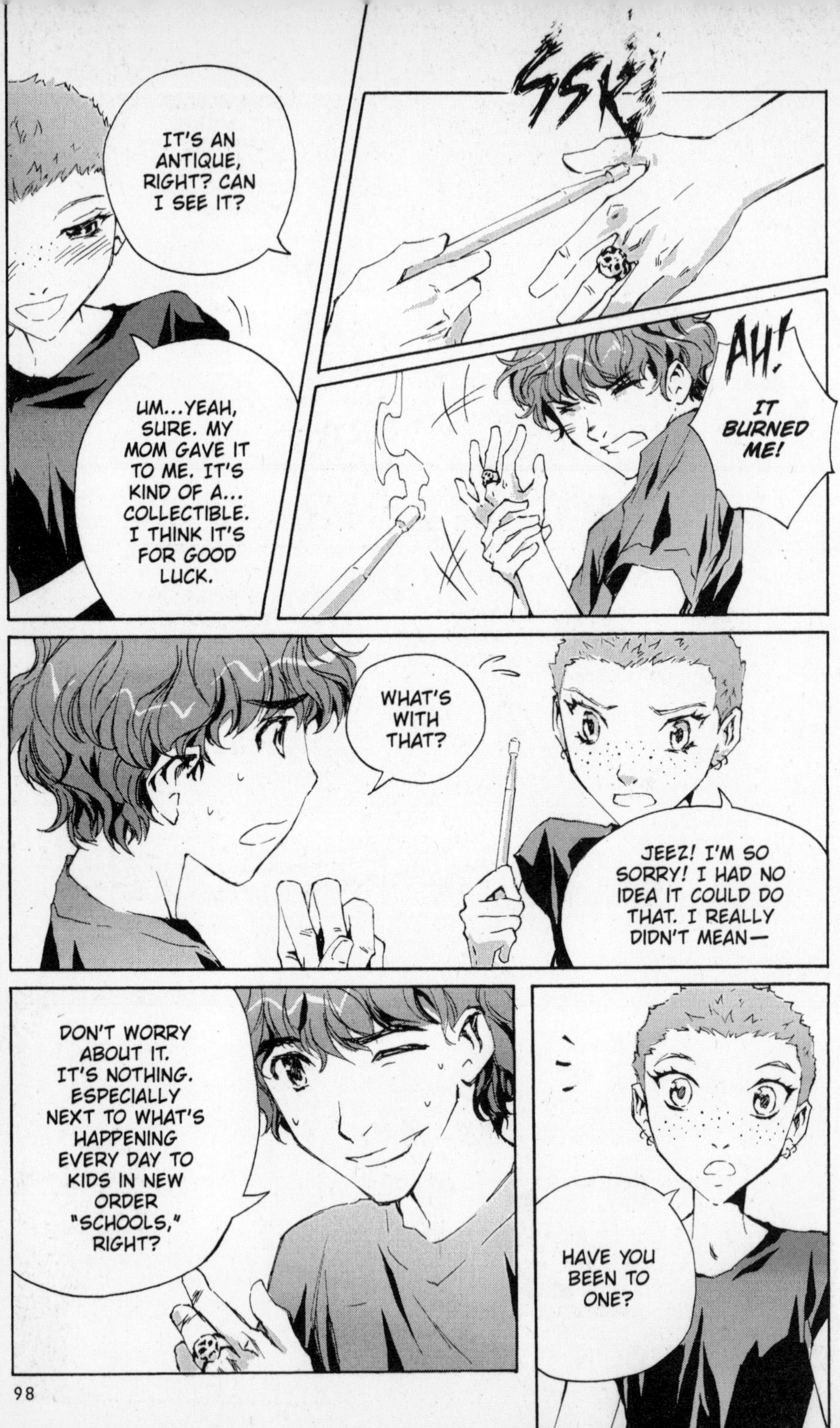
IT'S AN ANTIQUE, RIGHT? CAN I SEE IT?
UM...YEAH, SURE. MY MOM GAVE IT TO ME. IT'S KIND OF A... COLLECTIBLE. I THINK IT'S FOR GOOD LUCK.
SSK
AH!
IT BURNED ME!
WHAT'S WITH THAT?
JEEZ! I'M SO SORRY! I HAD NO IDEA IT COULD DO THAT. I REALLY DIDN'T MEAN—
DON'T WORRY ABOUT IT. IT'S NOTHING. ESPECIALLY NEXT TO WHAT'S HAPPENING EVERY DAY TO KIDS IN NEW ORDER "SCHOOLS," RIGHT?
HAVE YOU BEEN TO ONE?

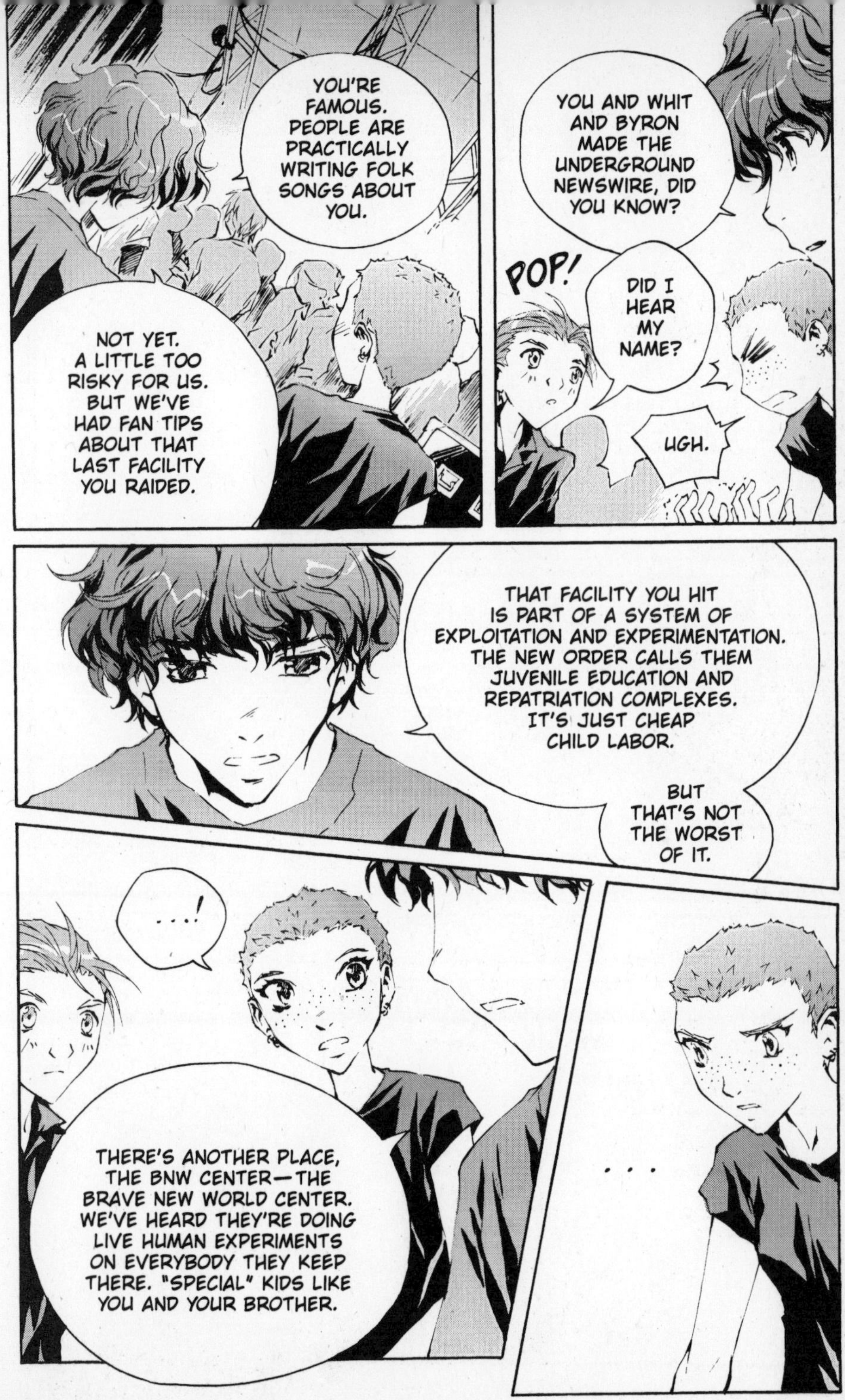
YOU'RE FAMOUS. PEOPLE ARE PRACTICALLY WRITING FOLK SONGS ABOUT YOU.
NOT YET. A LITTLE TOO RISKY FOR US. BUT WE'VE HAD FAN TIPS ABOUT THAT LAST FACILITY YOU RAIDED.
YOU AND WHIT AND BYRON MADE THE UNDERGROUND NEWSWIRE, DID YOU KNOW?
POP!
DID I HEAR MY NAME?
UGH.
THAT FACILITY YOU HIT IS PART OF A SYSTEM OF EXPLOITATION AND EXPERIMENTATION. THE NEW ORDER CALLS THEM JUVENILE EDUCATION AND REPATRIATION COMPLEXES. IT'S JUST CHEAP CHILD LABOR.
BUT THAT'S NOT THE WORST OF IT.
...!
THERE'S ANOTHER PLACE, THE BNW CENTER—THE BRAVE NEW WORLD CENTER. WE'VE HEARD THEY'RE DOING LIVE HUMAN EXPERIMENTS ON EVERYBODY THEY KEEP THERE. "SPECIAL" KIDS LIKE YOU AND YOUR BROTHER.
...

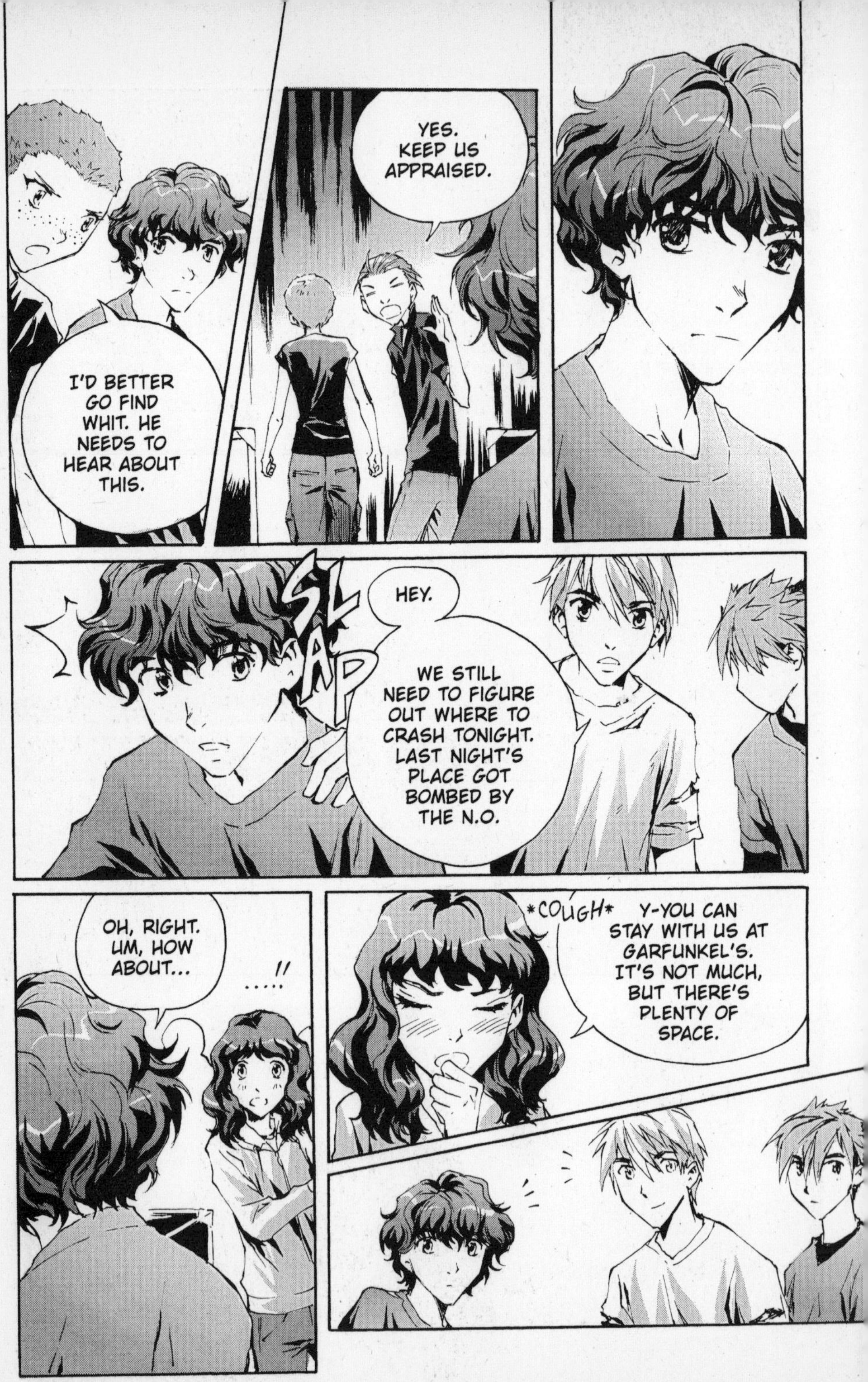
I'D BETTER GO FIND WHIT. HE NEEDS TO HEAR ABOUT THIS.
YES. KEEP US APPRAISED.
SLAP
HEY.
WE STILL NEED TO FIGURE OUT WHERE TO CRASH TONIGHT. LAST NIGHT'S PLACE GOT BOMBED BY THE N.O.
OH, RIGHT. UM, HOW ABOUT...
....!!
COUGH
Y-YOU CAN STAY WITH US AT GARFUNKEL'S. IT'S NOT MUCH, BUT THERE'S PLENTY OF SPACE.

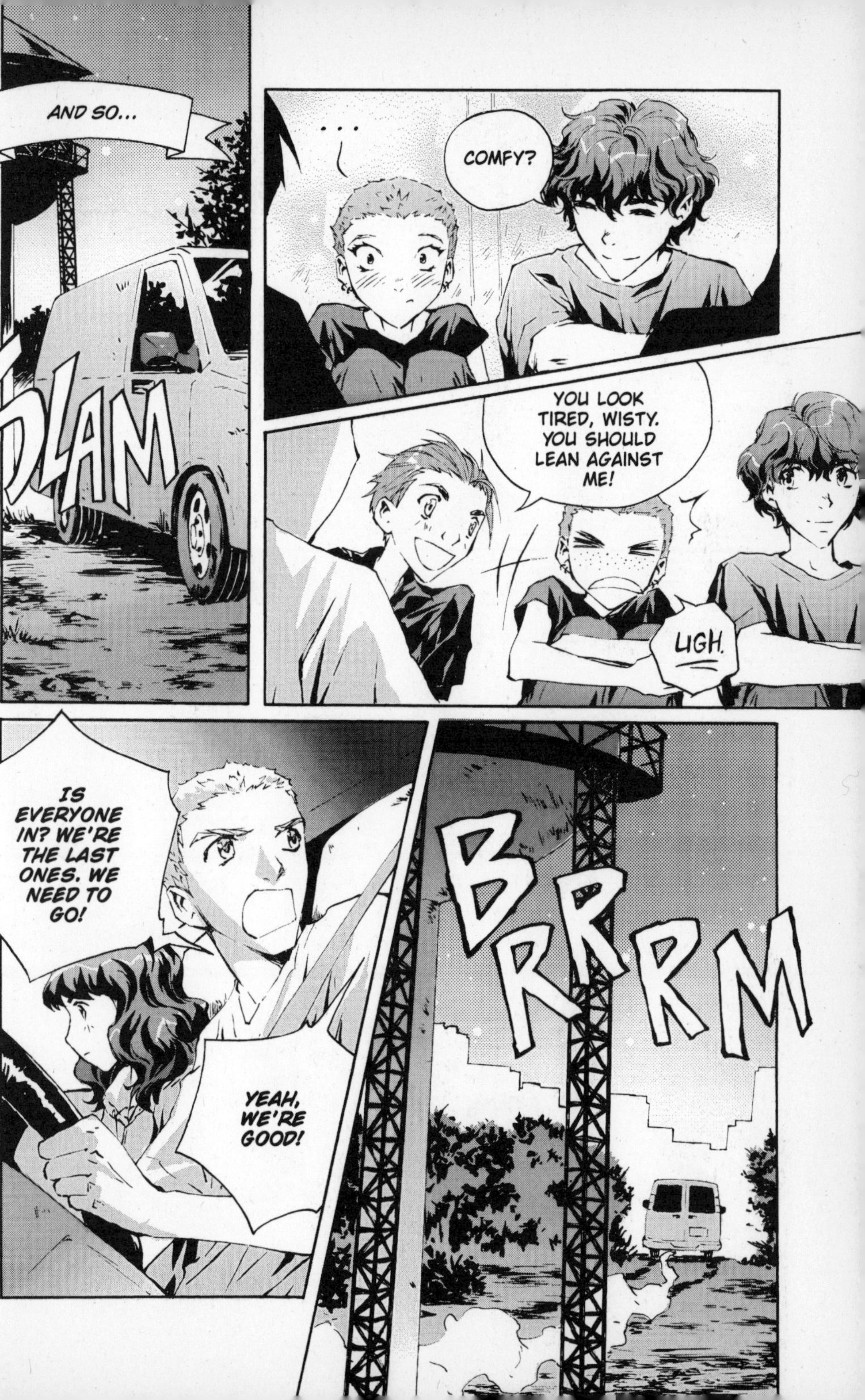
AND SO...
SLAM
...
COMFY?
YOU LOOK TIRED, WISTY. YOU SHOULD LEAN AGAINST ME!
UGH.
IS EVERYONE IN? WE'RE THE LAST ONES. WE NEED TO GO!
YEAH, WE'RE GOOD!
BRRRM

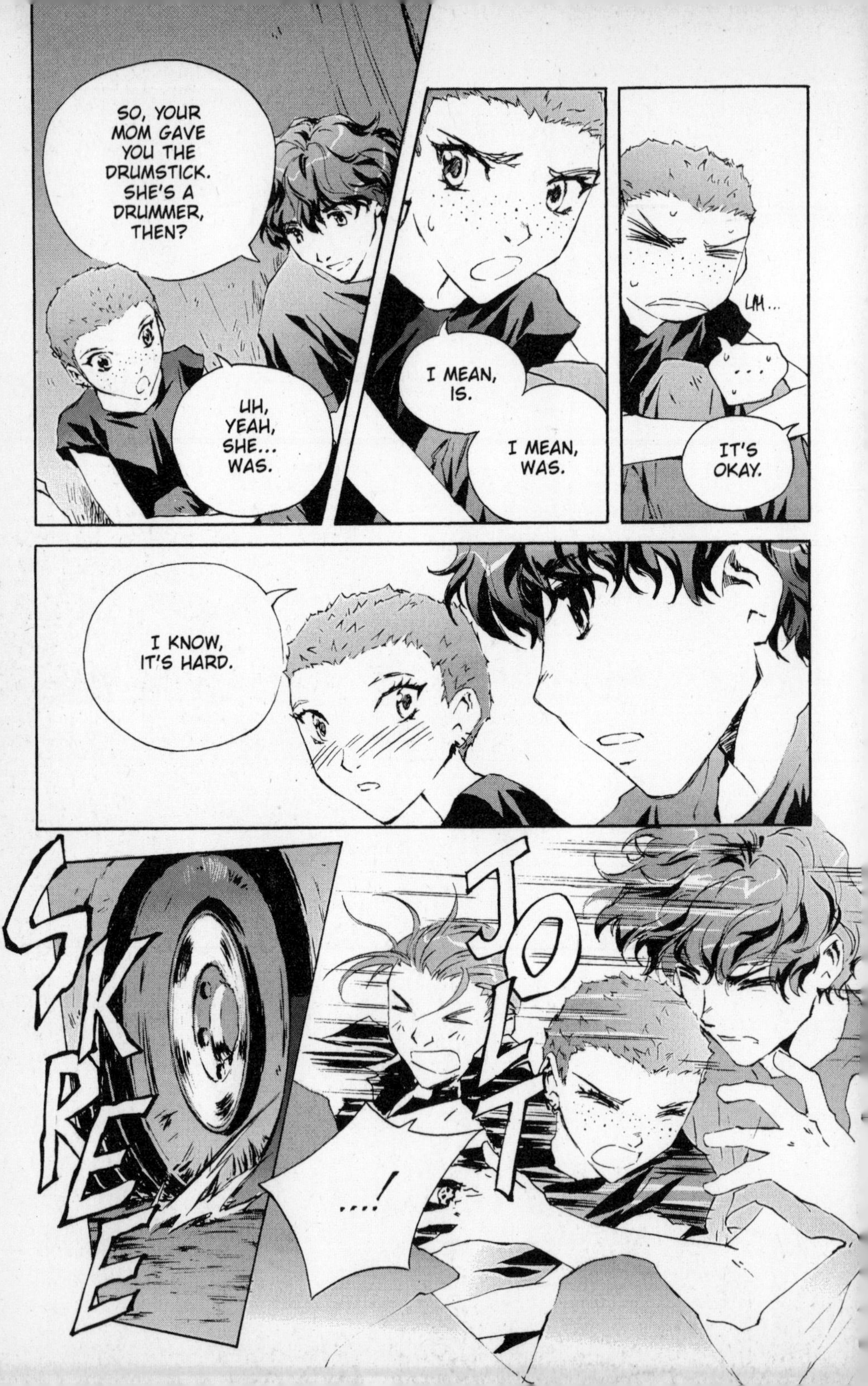
SO, YOUR MOM GAVE YOU THE DRUMSTICK. SHE'S A DRUMMER, THEN?
UH, YEAH, SHE... WAS.
I MEAN, IS.
I MEAN, WAS.
UH...
...
IT'S OKAY.
I KNOW, IT'S HARD.
SKREEE
JOLT
...!

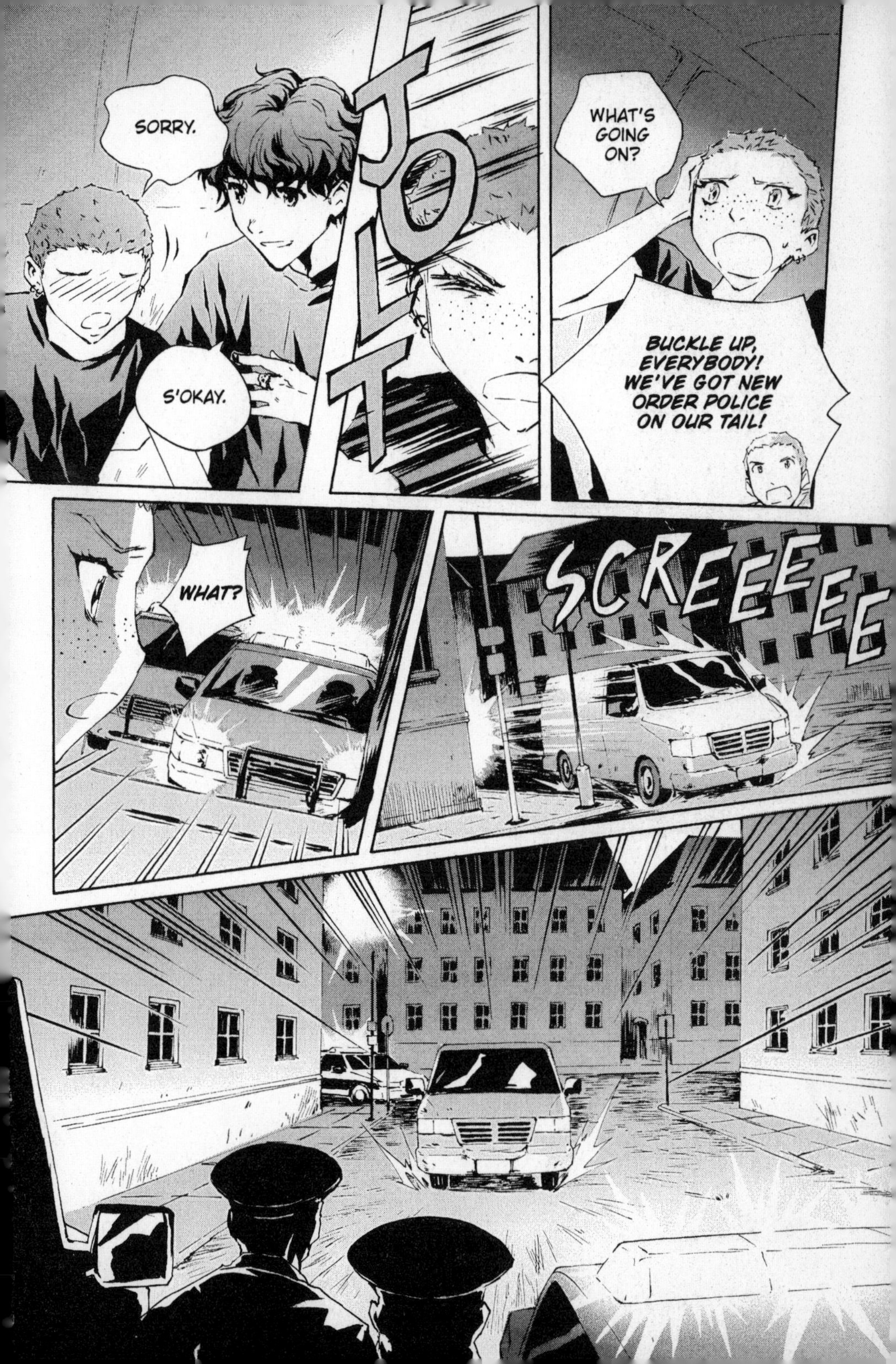
SORRY.
S'OKAY.
JOLT
WHAT'S GOING ON?
BUCKLE UP, EVERYBODY! WE'VE GOT NEW ORDER POLICE ON OUR TAIL!
WHAT?
SCREEEEEE

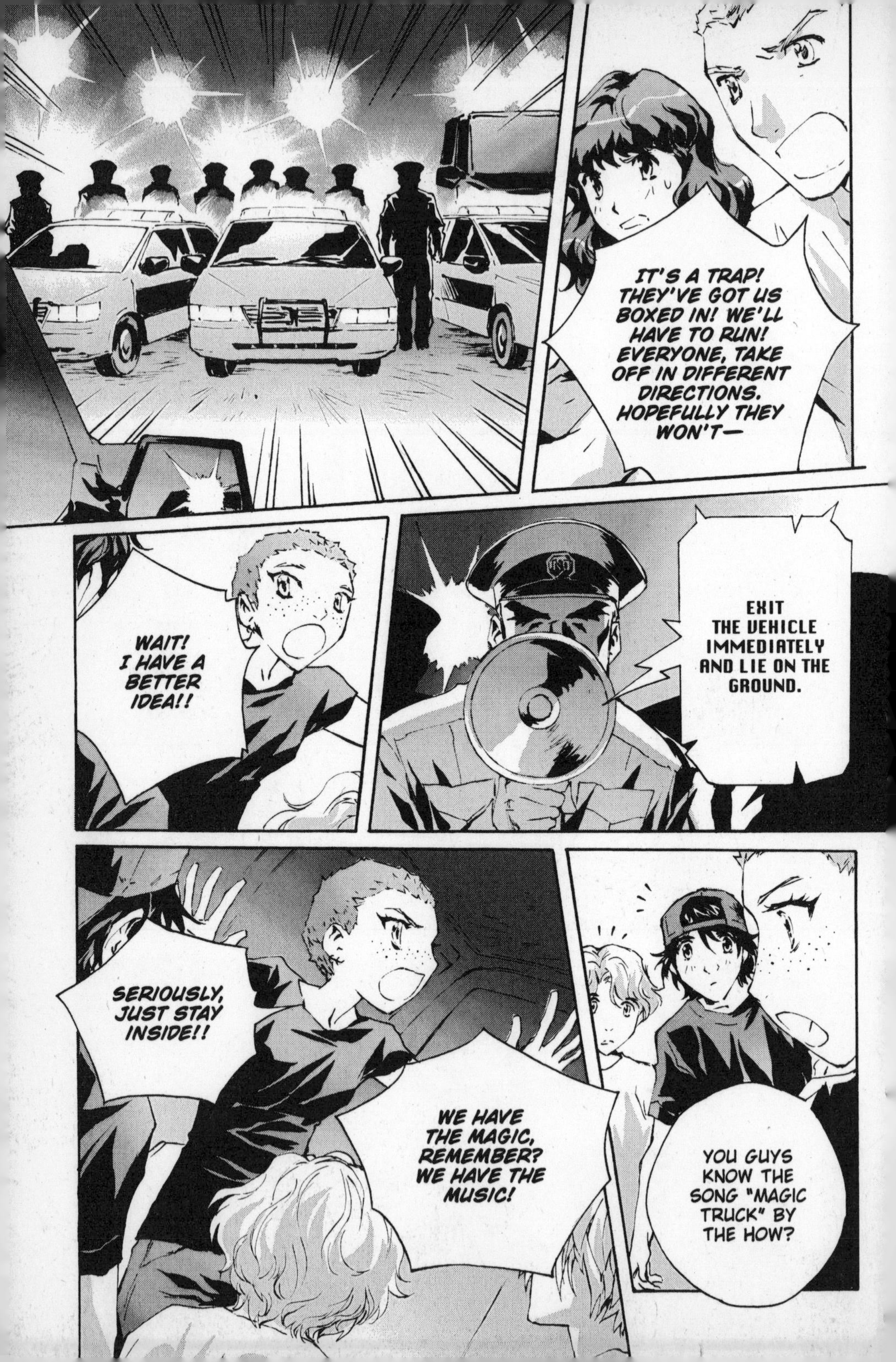
IT'S A TRAP! THEY'VE GOT US BOXED IN! WE'LL HAVE TO RUN! EVERYONE, TAKE OFF IN DIFFERENT DIRECTIONS. HOPEFULLY THEY WON'T—
WAIT! I HAVE A BETTER IDEA!!
EXIT THE VEHICLE IMMEDIATELY AND LIE ON THE GROUND.
SERIOUSLY, JUST STAY INSIDE!!
WE HAVE THE MAGIC, REMEMBER? WE HAVE THE MUSIC!
YOU GUYS KNOW THE SONG "MAGIC TRUCK" BY THE HOW?

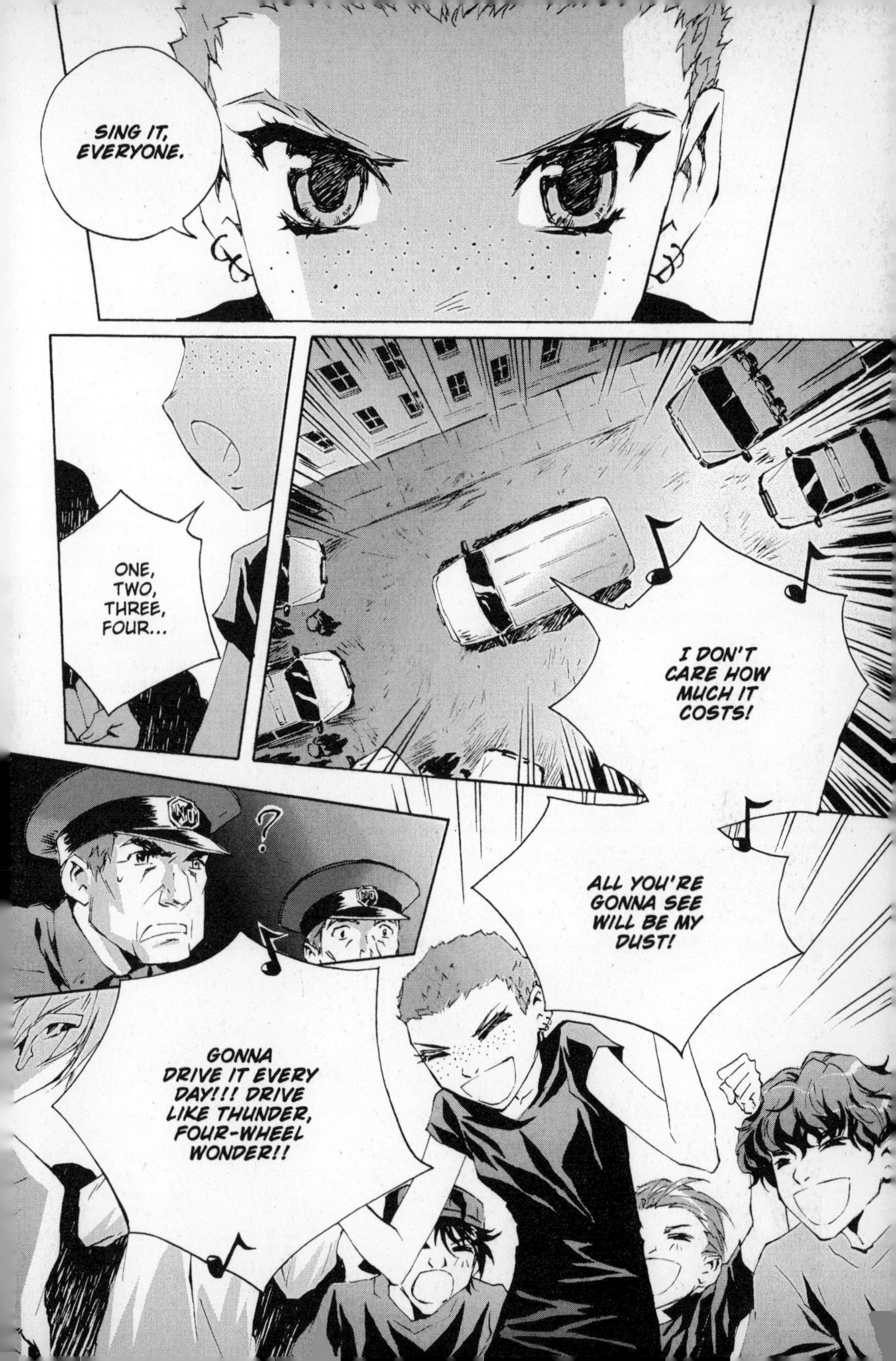
SING IT, EVERYONE.
ONE, TWO, THREE, FOUR...
I DON'T CARE HOW MUCH IT COSTS!
?
ALL YOU'RE GONNA SEE WILL BE MY DUST!
GONNA DRIVE IT EVERY DAY!!! DRIVE LIKE THUNDER, FOUR-WHEEL WONDER!!

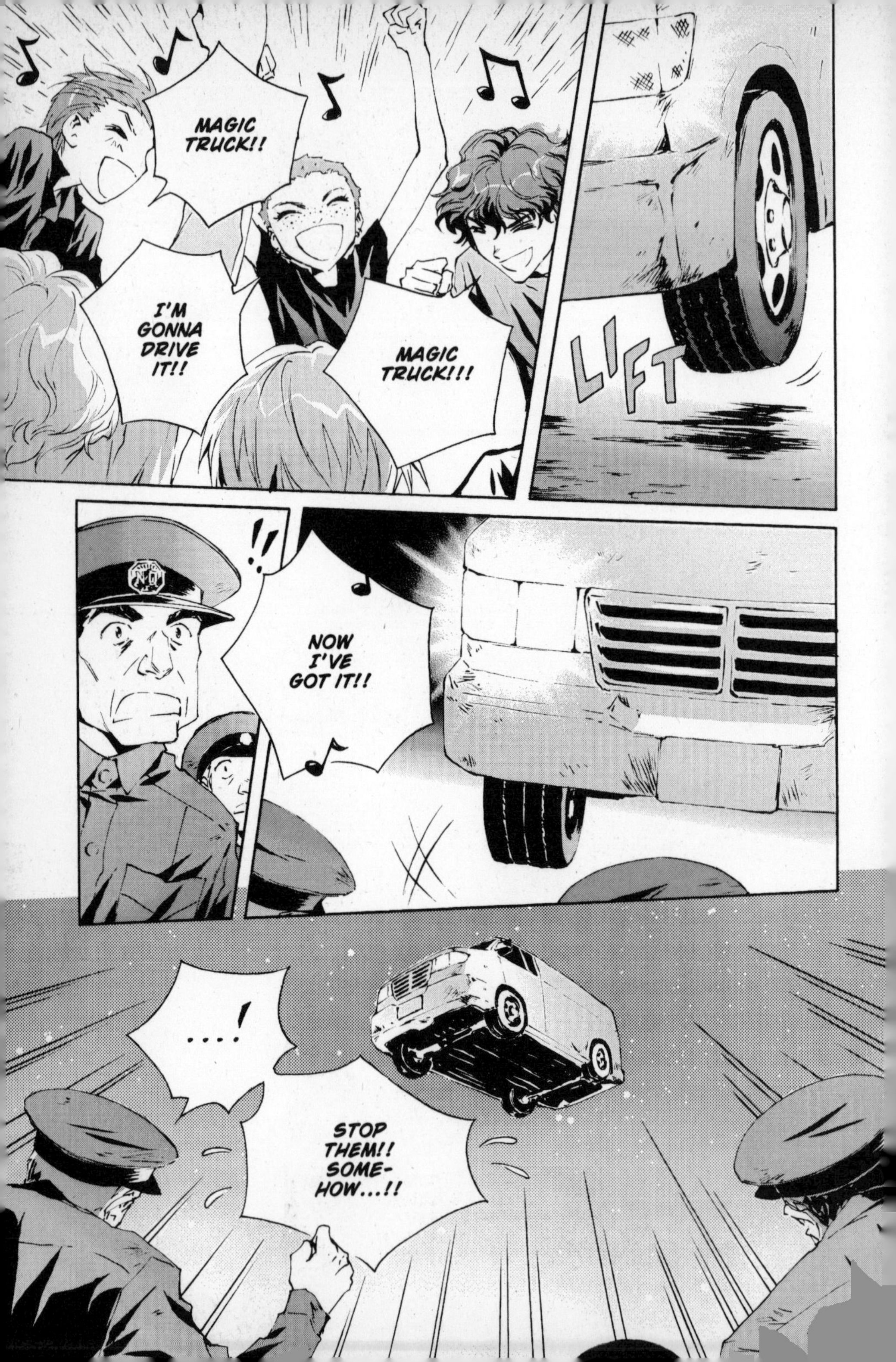
MAGIC TRUCK!!
I'M GONNA DRIVE IT!!
MAGIC TRUCK!!!
LIFT
!!
NOW I'VE GOT IT!!
...!
STOP THEM!! SOME-HOW...!!

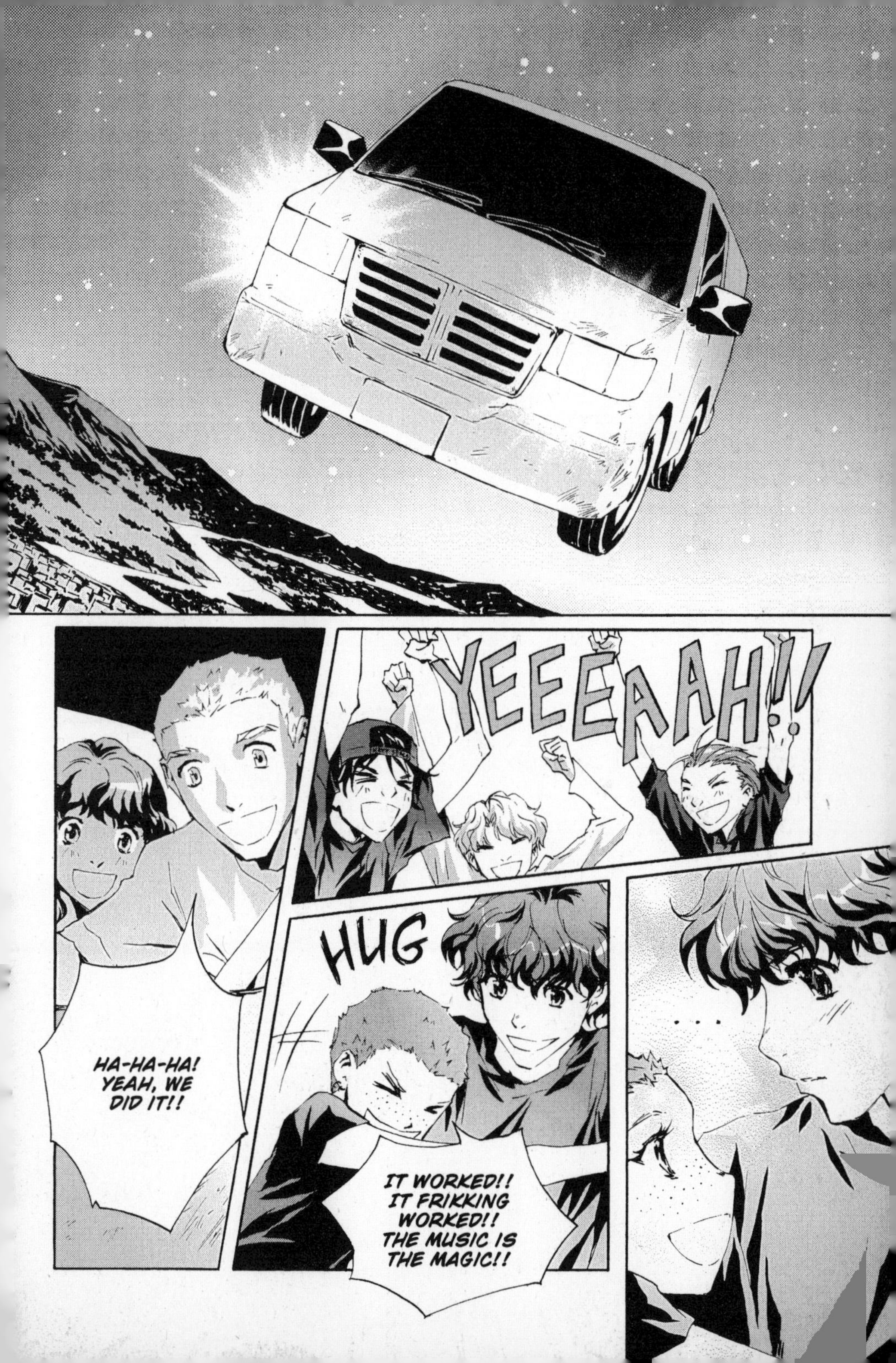
YEEEAAH!!
HA-HA-HA! YEAH, WE DID IT!!
HUG
IT WORKED!! IT FRIKKING WORKED!! THE MUSIC IS THE MAGIC!!
...

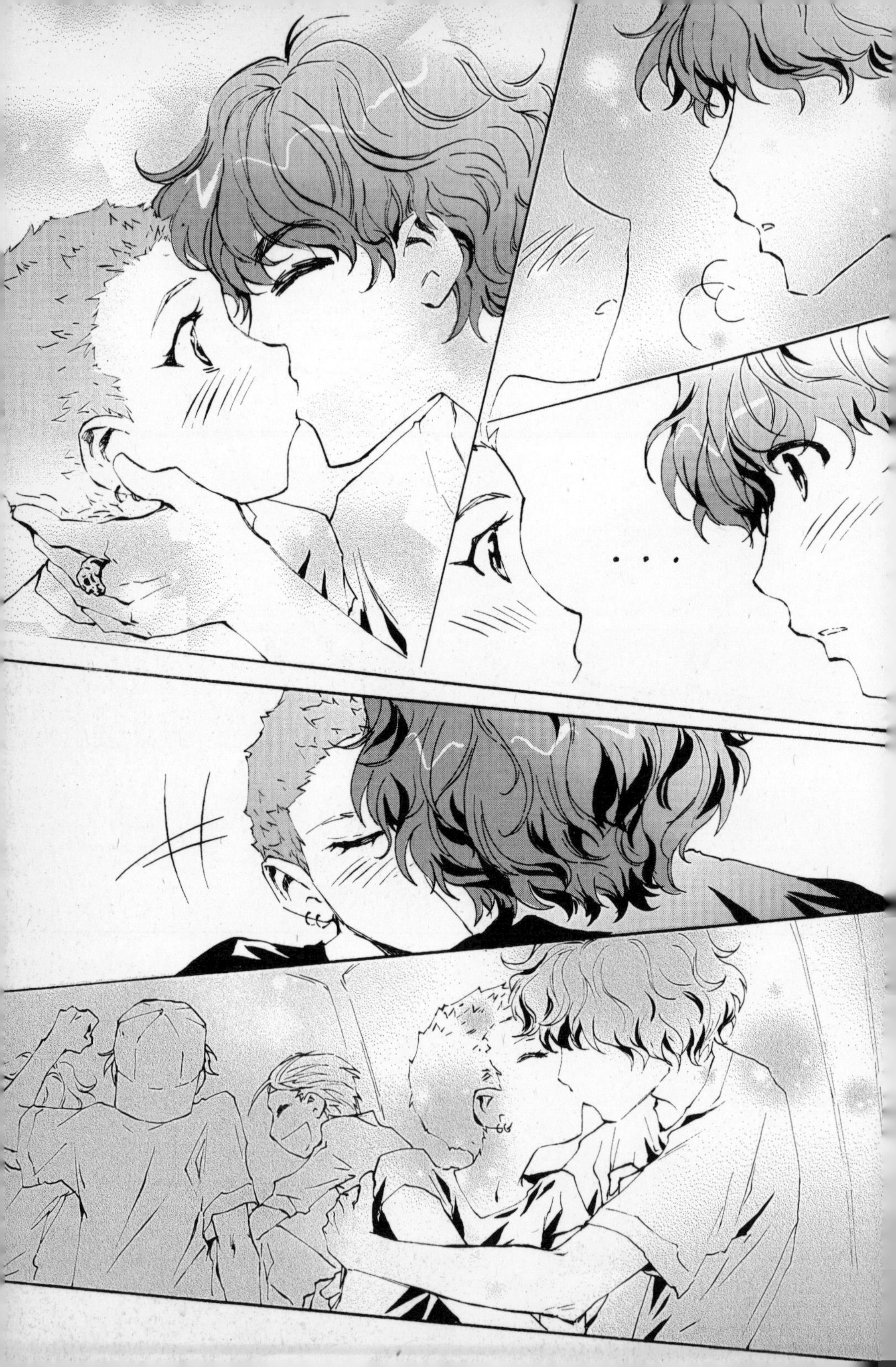
• • •

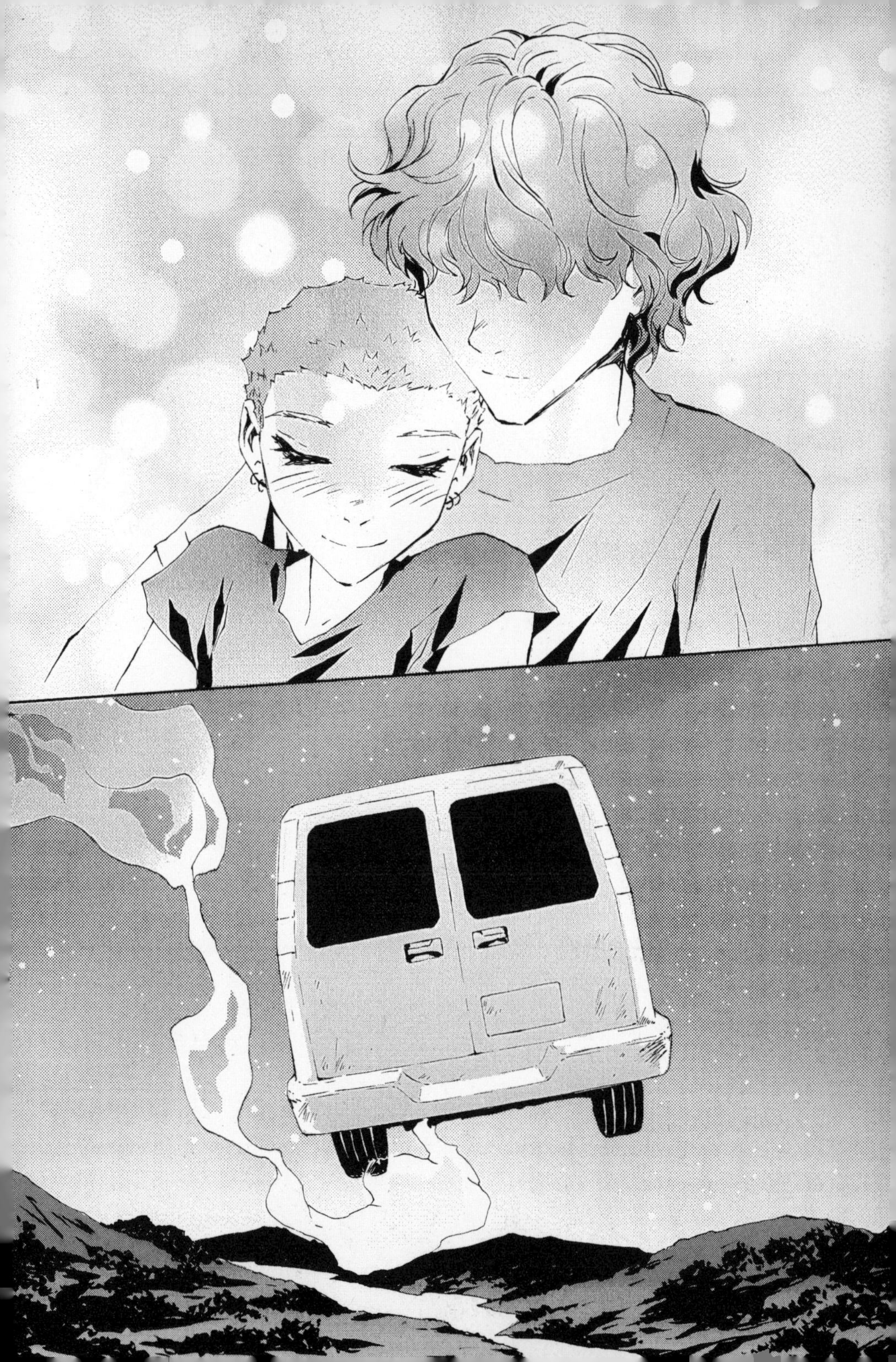

WITCH & WIZARD

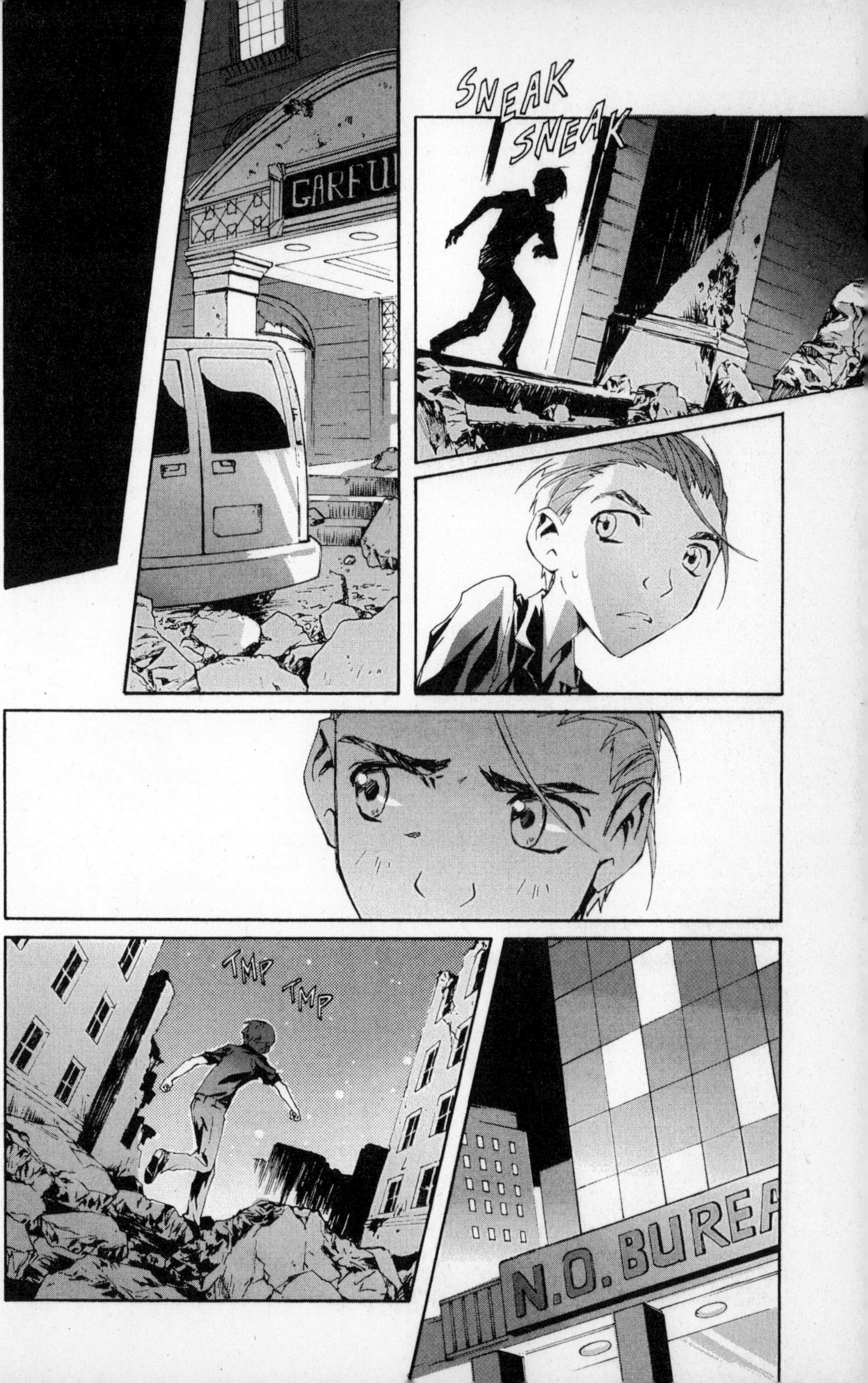
GARFU
SNEAK
SNEAK
TMP
TMP
N.O. BUREA

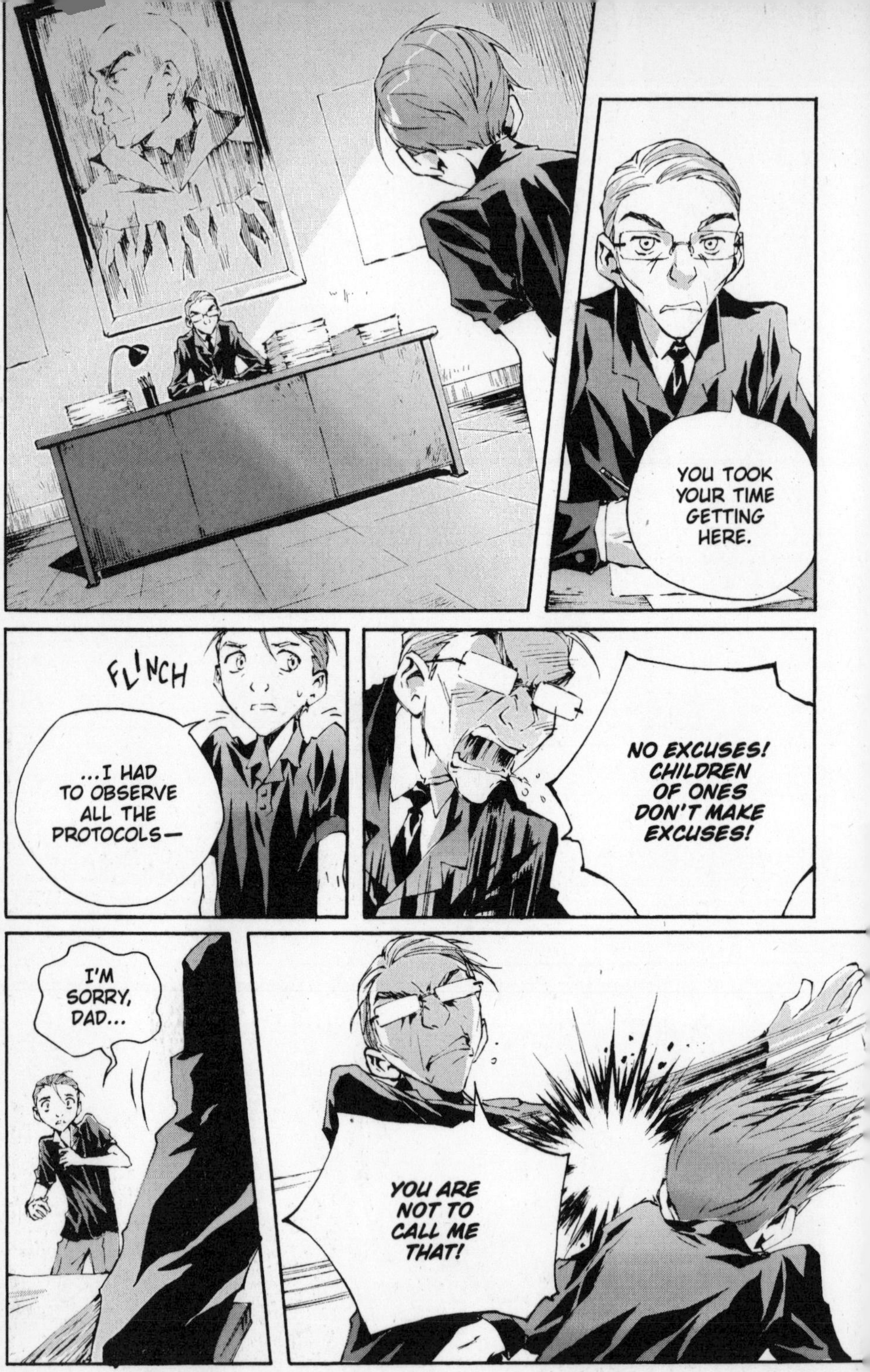
YOU TOOK YOUR TIME GETTING HERE.
FLINCH
...I HAD TO OBSERVE ALL THE PROTOCOLS—
NO EXCUSES! CHILDREN OF ONES DON'T MAKE EXCUSES!
I'M SORRY, DAD...
YOU ARE NOT TO CALL ME THAT!

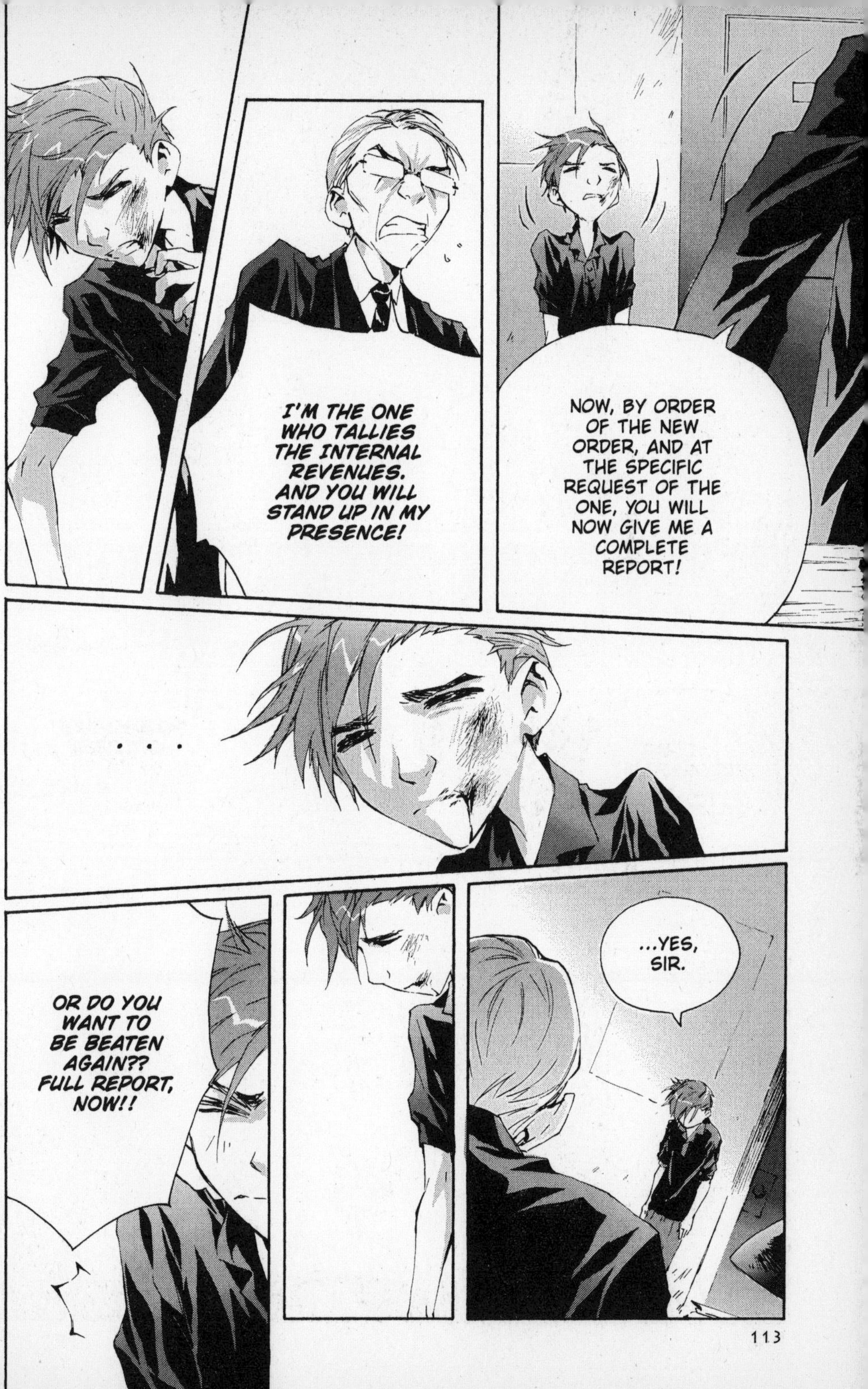

I'M THE ONE WHO TALLIES THE INTERNAL REVENUES. AND YOU WILL STAND UP IN MY PRESENCE!
NOW, BY ORDER OF THE NEW ORDER, AND AT THE SPECIFIC REQUEST OF THE ONE, YOU WILL NOW GIVE ME A COMPLETE REPORT!
...
OR DO YOU WANT TO BE BEATEN AGAIN?? FULL REPORT, NOW!!
...YES, SIR.

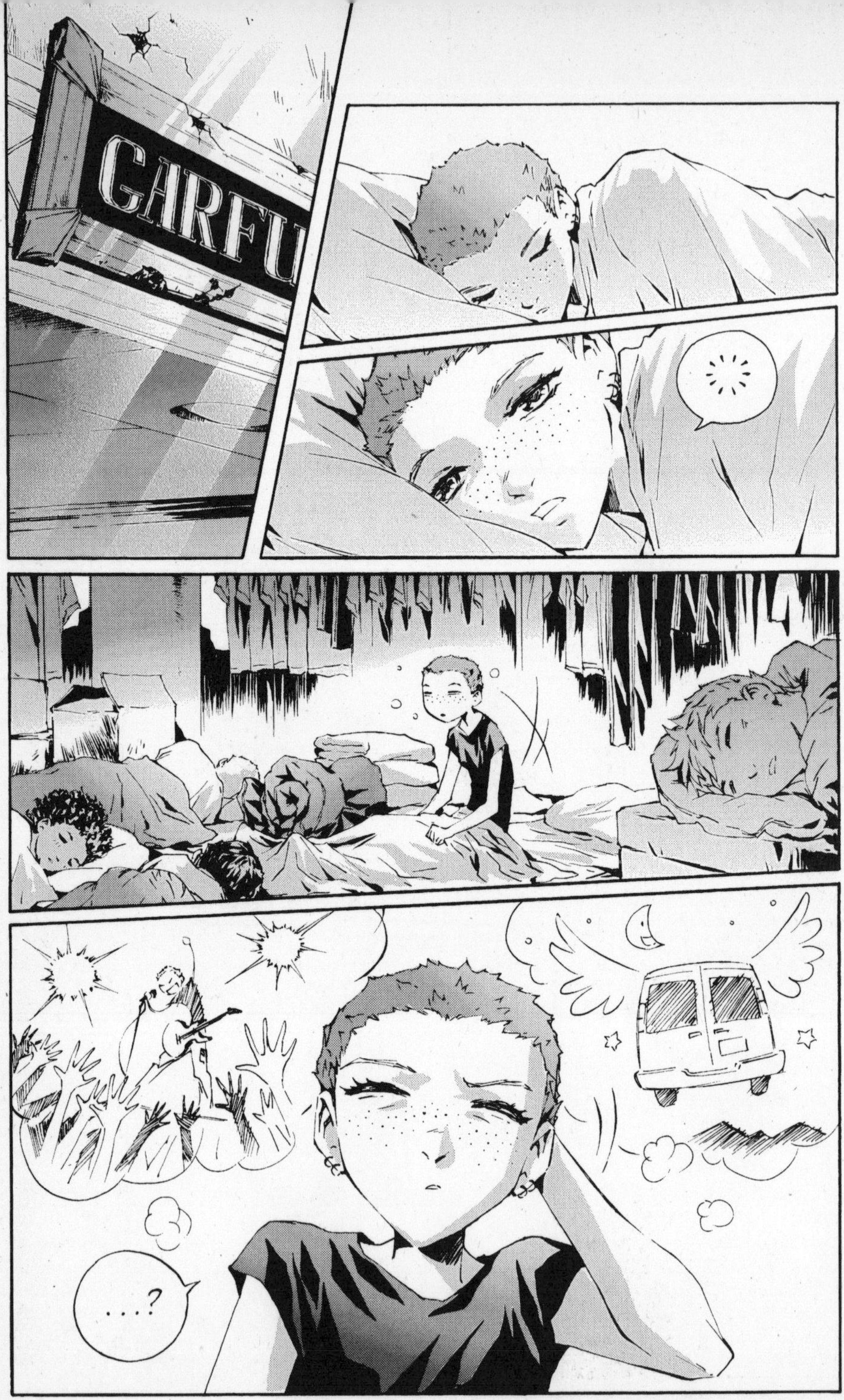
GARFU
...?

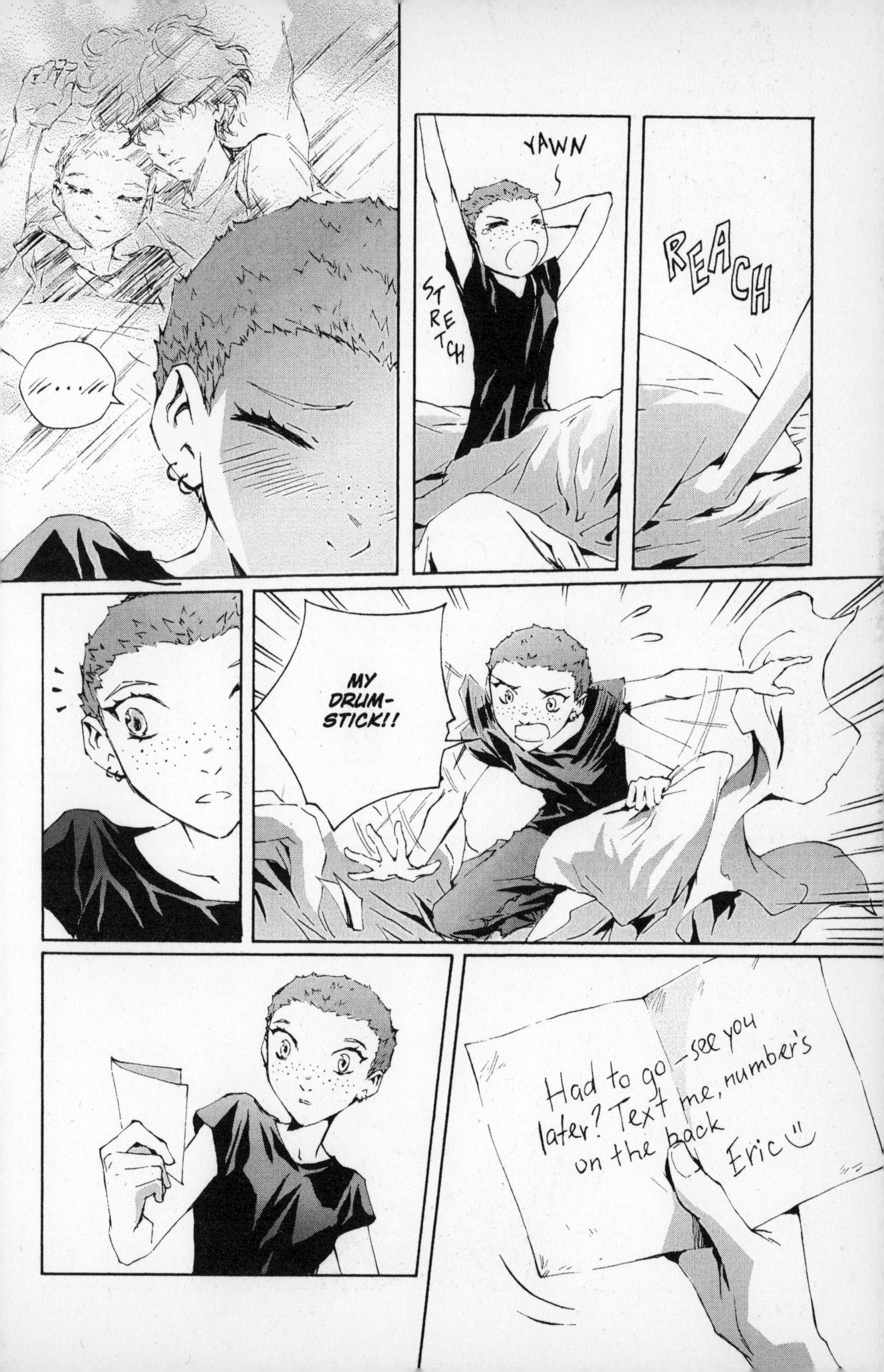

...
YAWN
STRETCH
REACH
MY DRUM-STICK!!
Had to go—see you later? Text me, number's on the back
Eric

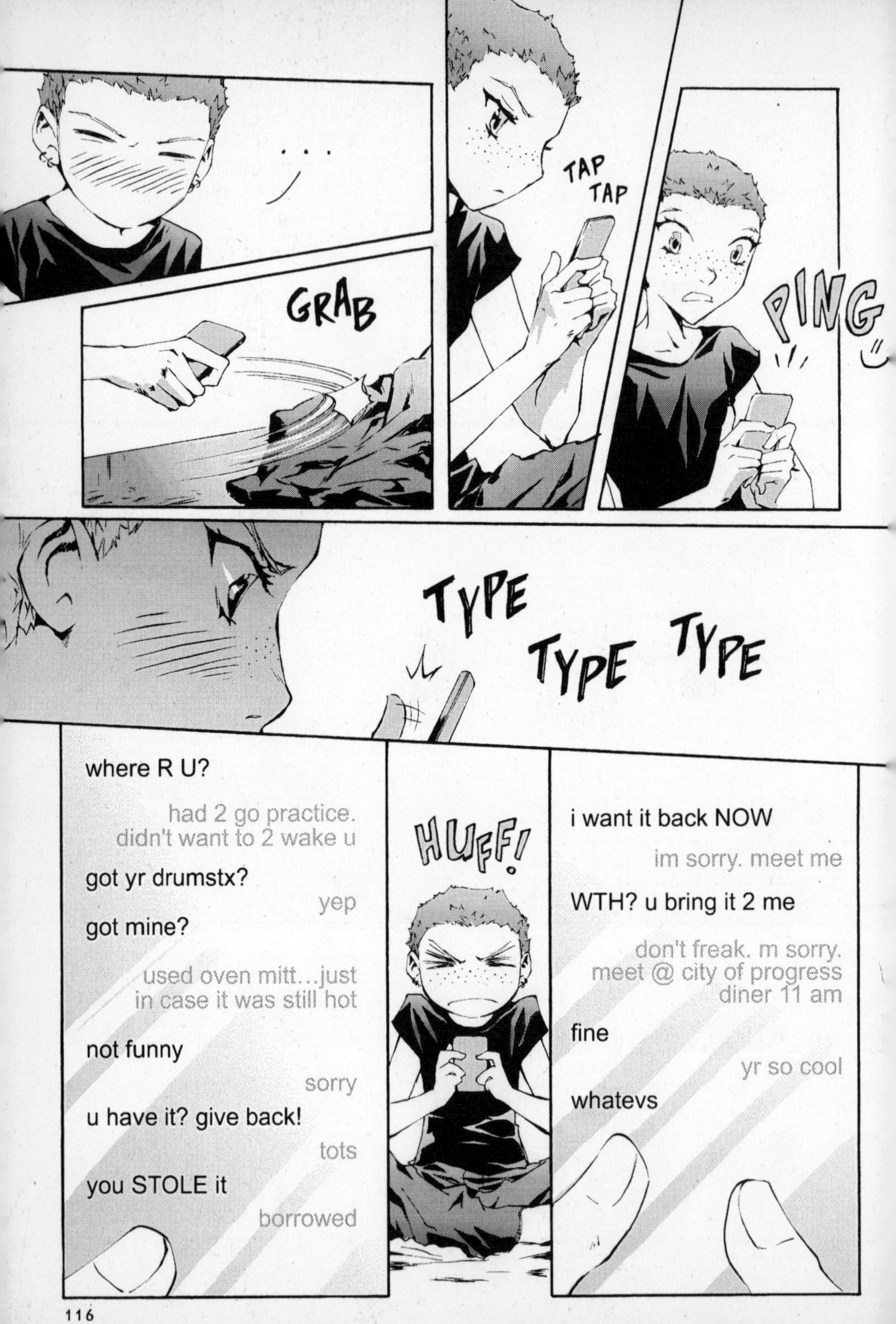
...
GRAB
TAP TAP
PING
TYPE TYPE TYPE
where R U?
had 2 go practice. didn't want to 2 wake u
got yr drumstx?
yep
got mine?
used oven mitt...just in case it was still hot
not funny
sorry
u have it? give back!
tots
you STOLE it
borrowed
HUFF!
i want it back NOW
im sorry. meet me
WTH? u bring it 2 me
don't freak. m sorry. meet @ city of progress diner 11 am
fine
yr so cool
whatevs

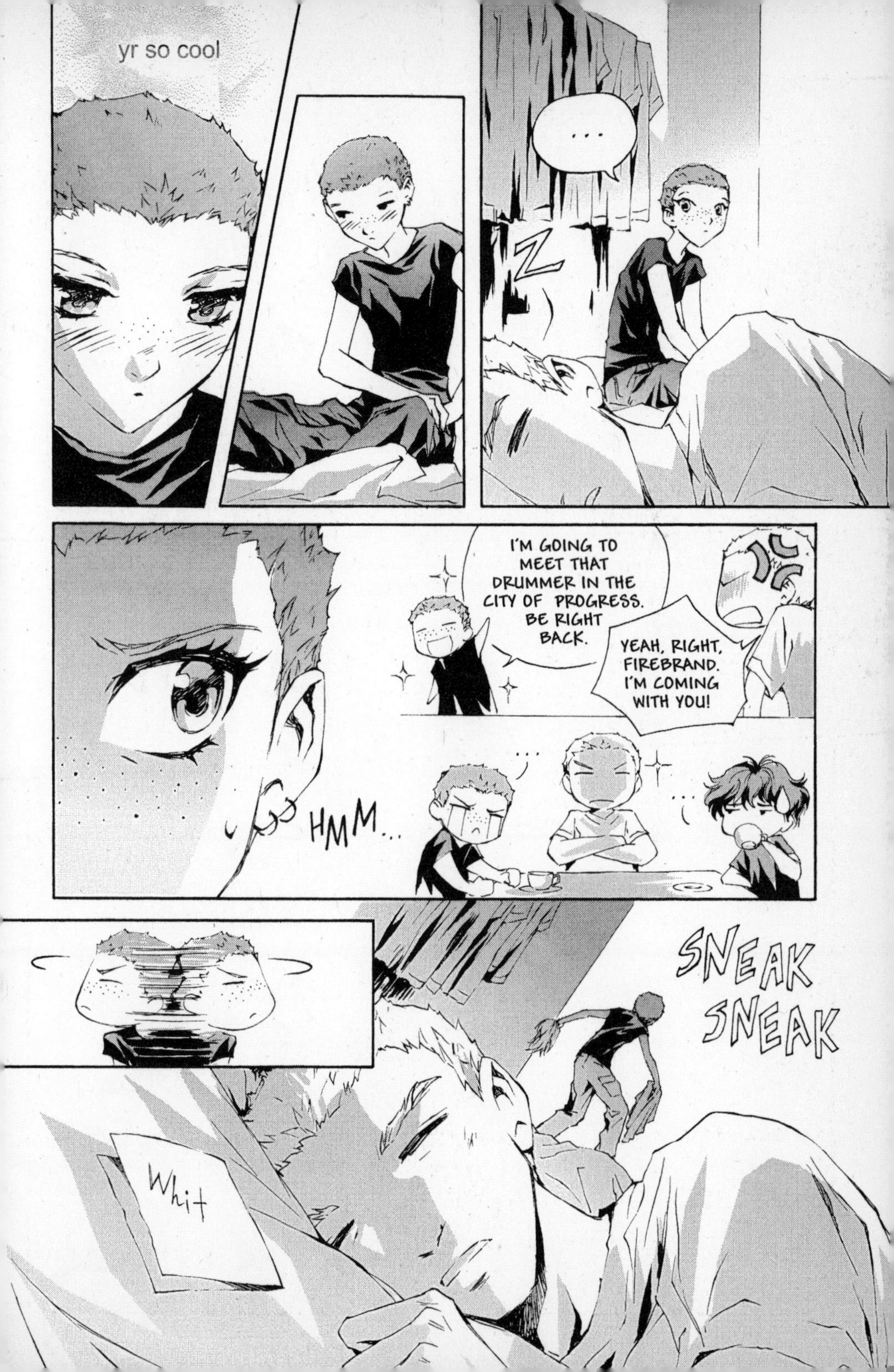
yr so cool
...
Z
I'M GOING TO MEET THAT DRUMMER IN THE CITY OF PROGRESS. BE RIGHT BACK.
YEAH, RIGHT, FIREBRAND. I'M COMING WITH YOU!
HMM...
...
...
SNEAK SNEAK
Whit

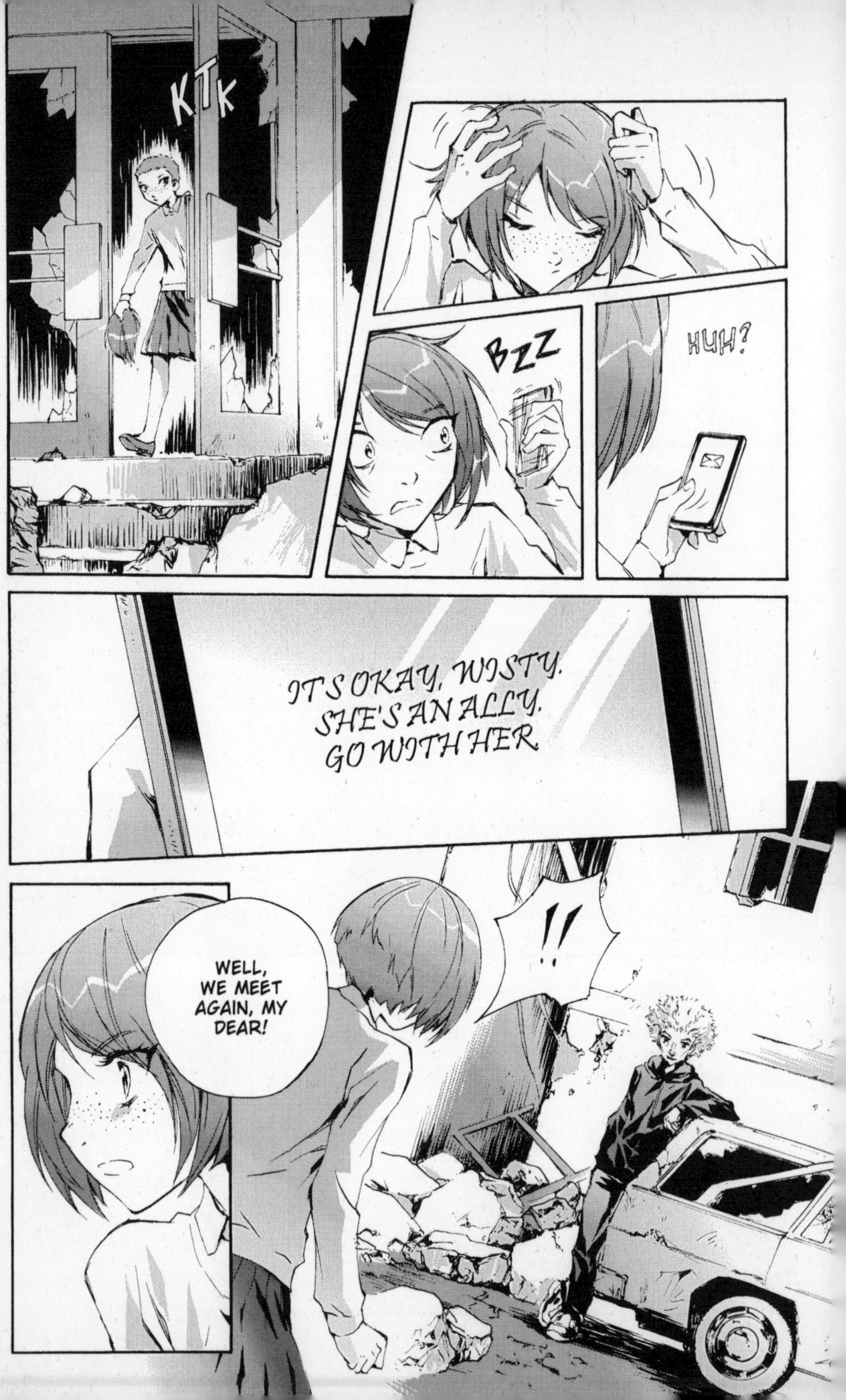
KTK
BZZ
HUH?
IT'S OKAY, WISTY. SHE'S AN ALLY. GO WITH HER.
WELL, WE MEET AGAIN, MY DEAR!
!!

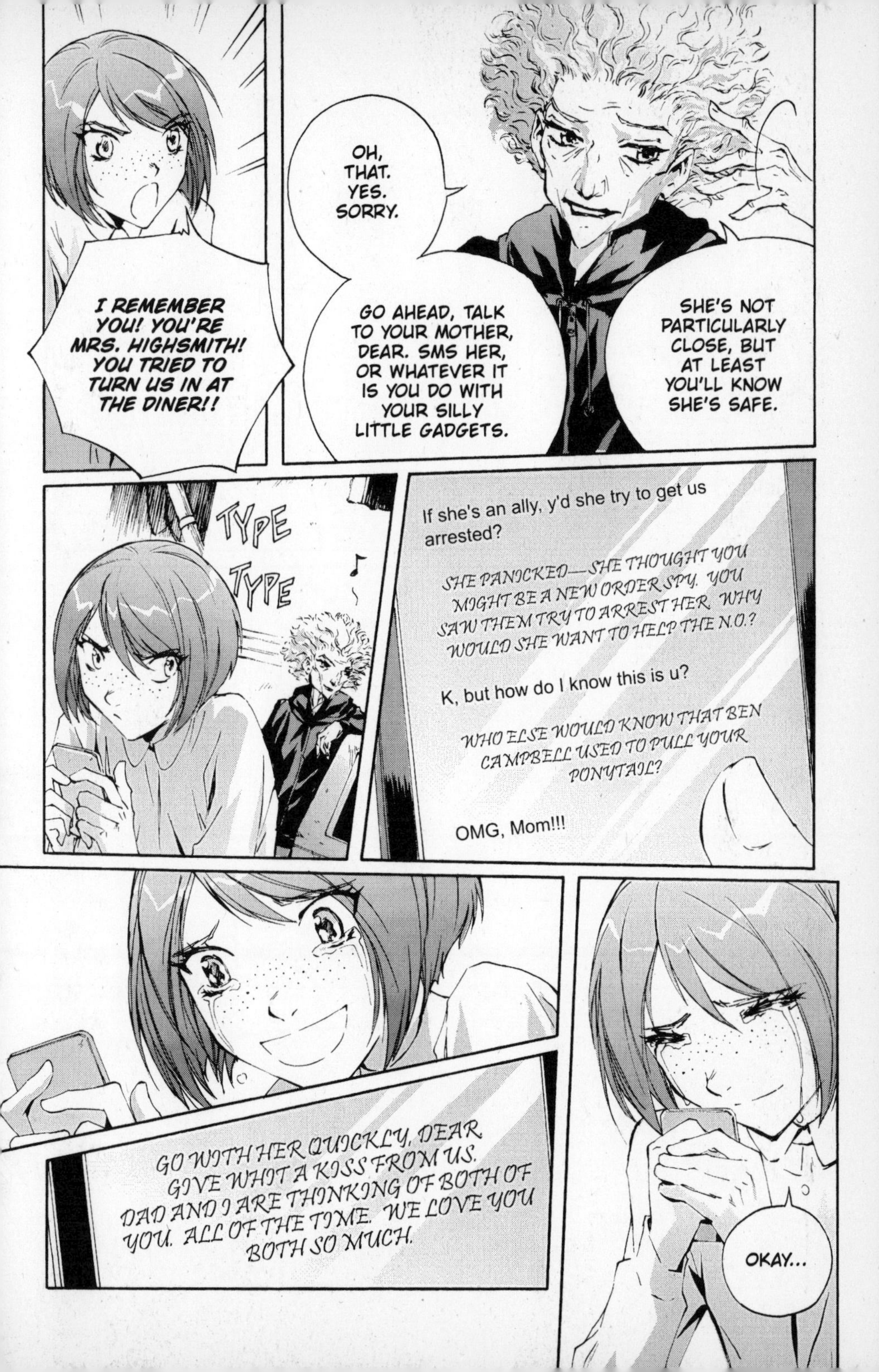
I REMEMBER YOU! YOU'RE MRS. HIGHSMITH! YOU TRIED TO TURN US IN AT THE DINER!!
OH, THAT. YES. SORRY.
GO AHEAD, TALK TO YOUR MOTHER, DEAR. SMS HER, OR WHATEVER IT IS YOU DO WITH YOUR SILLY LITTLE GADGETS.
SHE'S NOT PARTICULARLY CLOSE, BUT AT LEAST YOU'LL KNOW SHE'S SAFE.
TYPE TYPE
If she's an ally, y'd she try to get us arrested?
SHE PANICKED—SHE THOUGHT YOU MIGHT BE A NEW ORDER SPY. YOU SAW THEM TRY TO ARREST HER. WHY WOULD SHE WANT TO HELP THE N.O.?
K, but how do I know this is u?
WHO ELSE WOULD KNOW THAT BEN CAMPBELL USED TO PULL YOUR PONYTAIL?
OMG, Mom!!!
GO WITH HER QUICKLY, DEAR. GIVE WHIT A KISS FROM US. DAD AND I ARE THINKING OF BOTH OF YOU. ALL OF THE TIME. WE LOVE YOU BOTH SO MUCH.
OKAY...

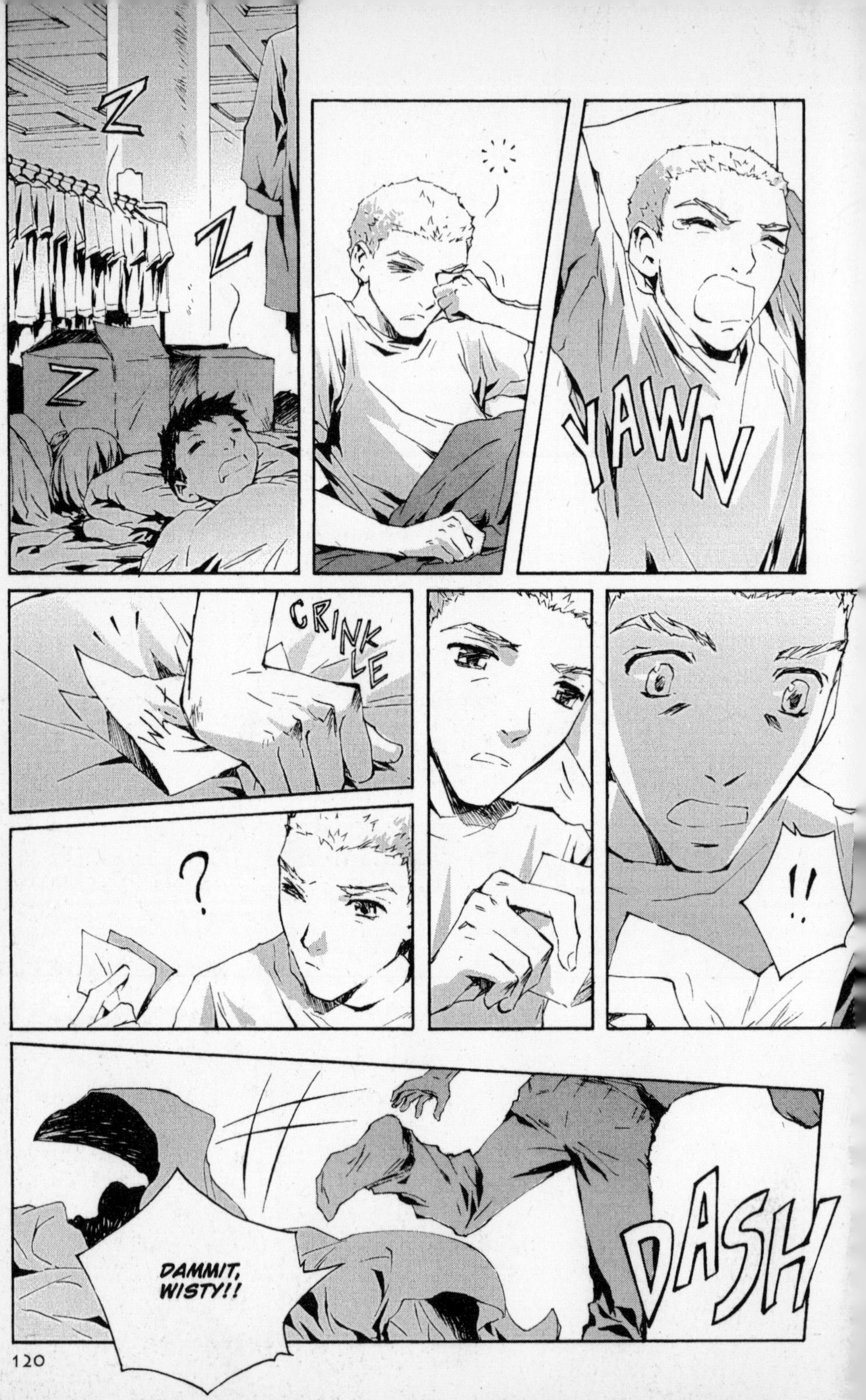
Z
Z
Z
YAWN
CRINKLE
?
!!
DASH
DAMMIT, WISTY!!

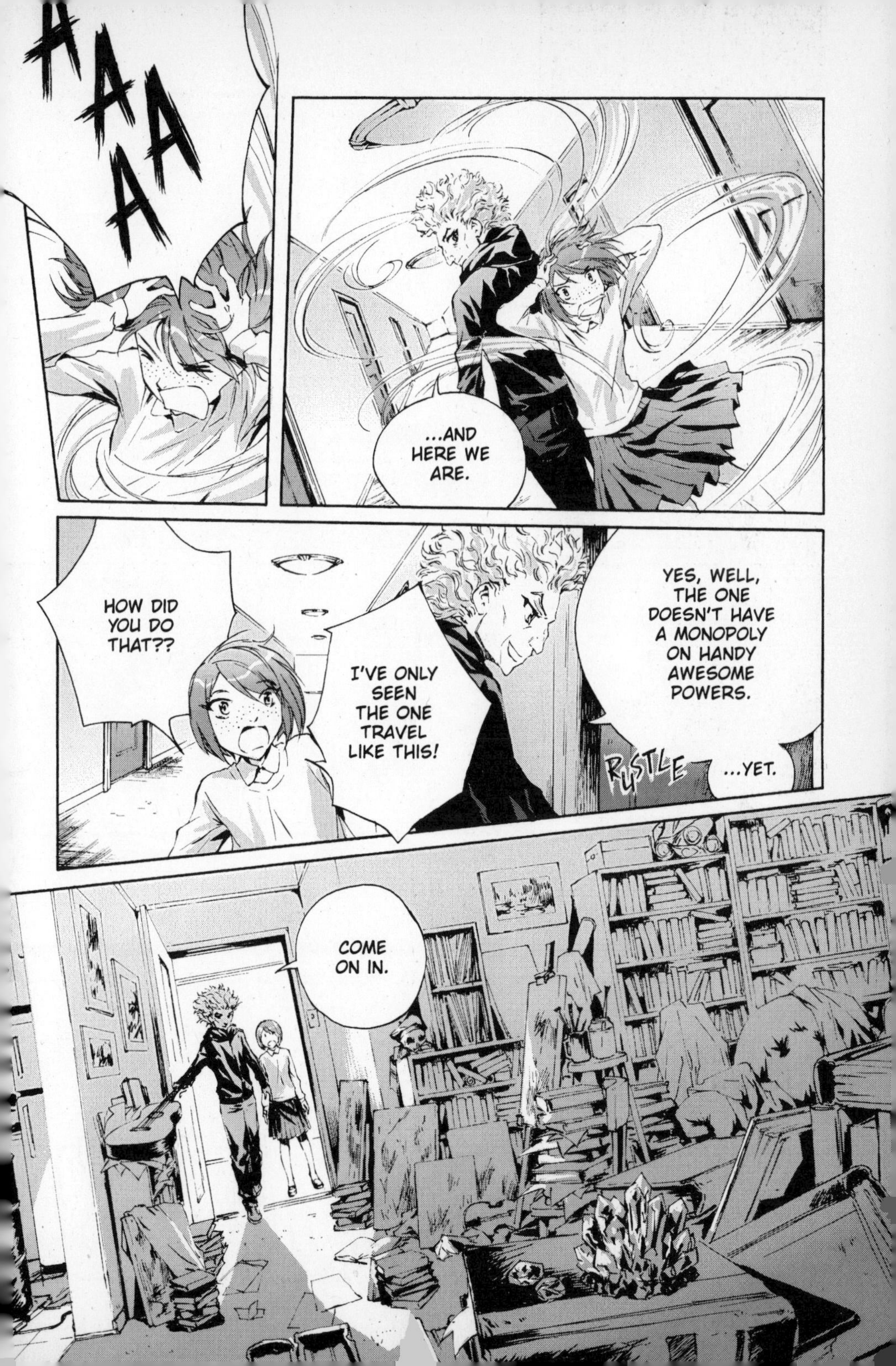
HAAAA
...AND HERE WE ARE.
HOW DID YOU DO THAT??
I'VE ONLY SEEN THE ONE TRAVEL LIKE THIS!
YES, WELL, THE ONE DOESN'T HAVE A MONOPOLY ON HANDY AWESOME POWERS.
RUSTLE
...YET.
COME ON IN.

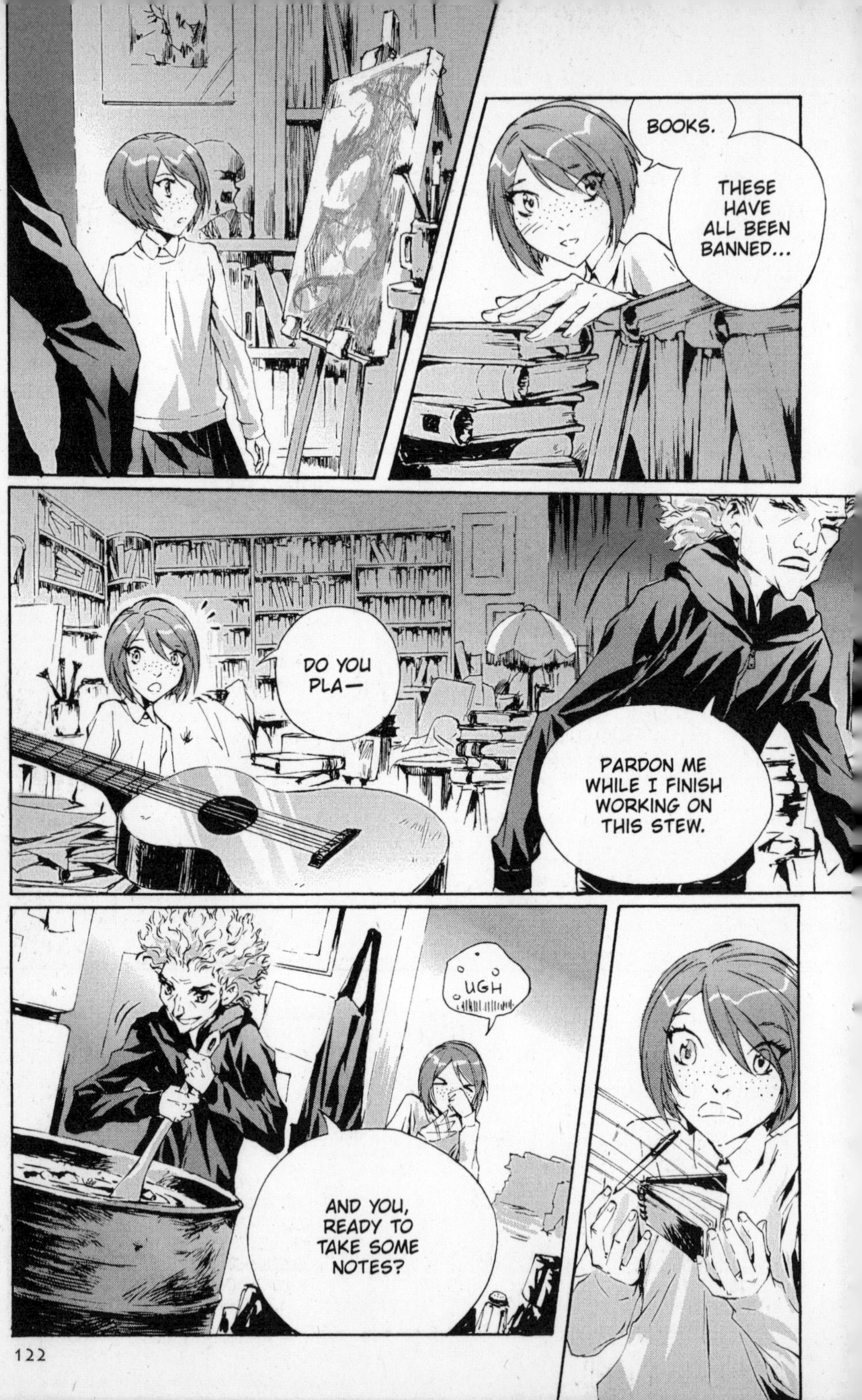

BOOKS.
THESE HAVE ALL BEEN BANNED...
DO YOU PLA—
PARDON ME WHILE I FINISH WORKING ON THIS STEW.
AND YOU, READY TO TAKE SOME NOTES?
UGH

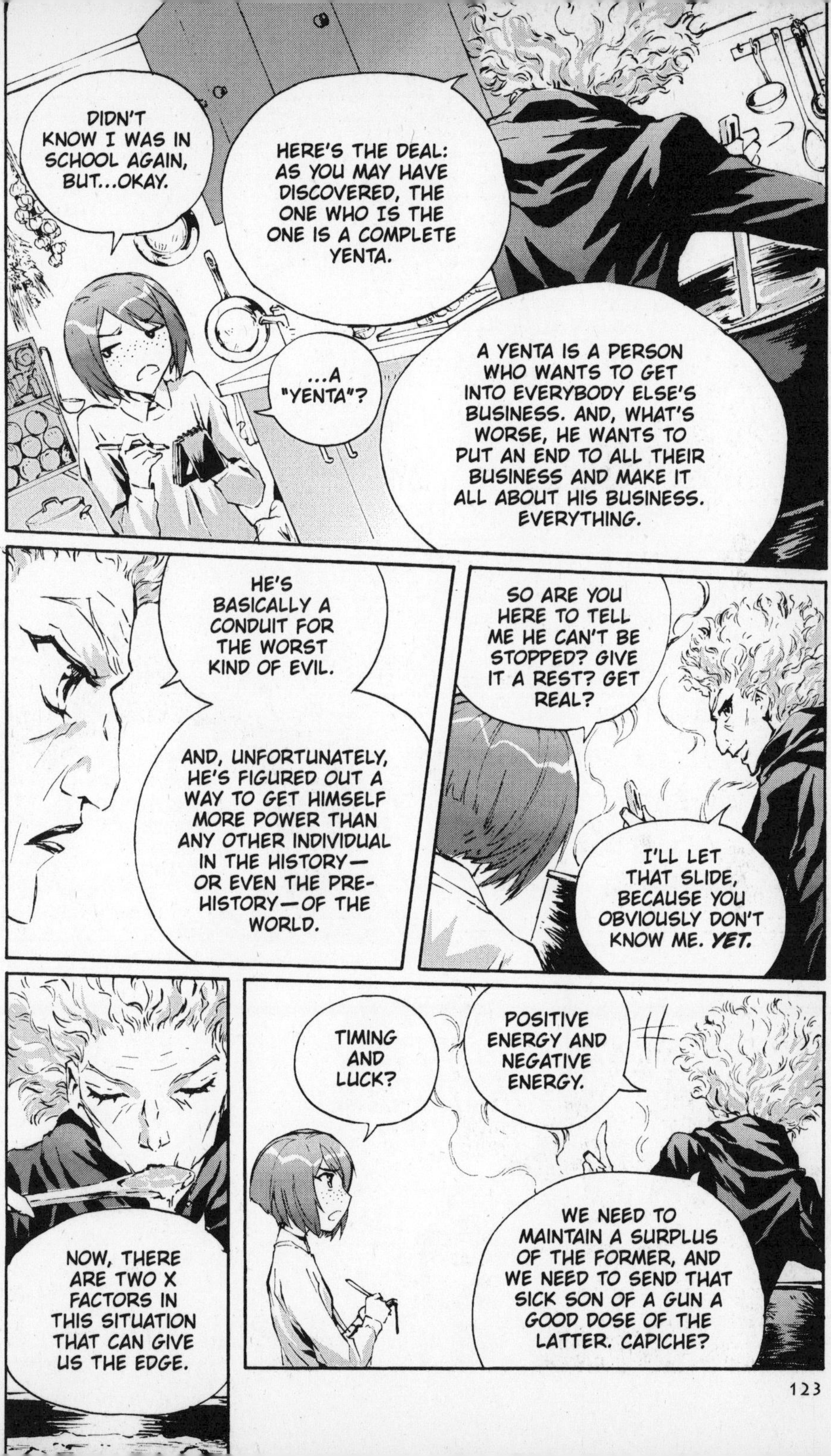
DIDN'T KNOW I WAS IN SCHOOL AGAIN, BUT...OKAY.
HERE'S THE DEAL: AS YOU MAY HAVE DISCOVERED, THE ONE WHO IS THE ONE IS A COMPLETE YENTA.
...A "YENTA"?
A YENTA IS A PERSON WHO WANTS TO GET INTO EVERYBODY ELSE'S BUSINESS. AND, WHAT'S WORSE, HE WANTS TO PUT AN END TO ALL THEIR BUSINESS AND MAKE IT ALL ABOUT HIS BUSINESS. EVERYTHING.
HE'S BASICALLY A CONDUIT FOR THE WORST KIND OF EVIL.
AND, UNFORTUNATELY, HE'S FIGURED OUT A WAY TO GET HIMSELF MORE POWER THAN ANY OTHER INDIVIDUAL IN THE HISTORY—OR EVEN THE PRE-HISTORY—OF THE WORLD.
SO ARE YOU HERE TO TELL ME HE CAN'T BE STOPPED? GIVE IT A REST? GET REAL?
I'LL LET THAT SLIDE, BECAUSE YOU OBVIOUSLY DON'T KNOW ME. *YET.*
NOW, THERE ARE TWO X FACTORS IN THIS SITUATION THAT CAN GIVE US THE EDGE.
TIMING AND LUCK?
POSITIVE ENERGY AND NEGATIVE ENERGY.
WE NEED TO MAINTAIN A SURPLUS OF THE FORMER, AND WE NEED TO SEND THAT SICK SON OF A GUN A GOOD DOSE OF THE LATTER. CAPICHE?

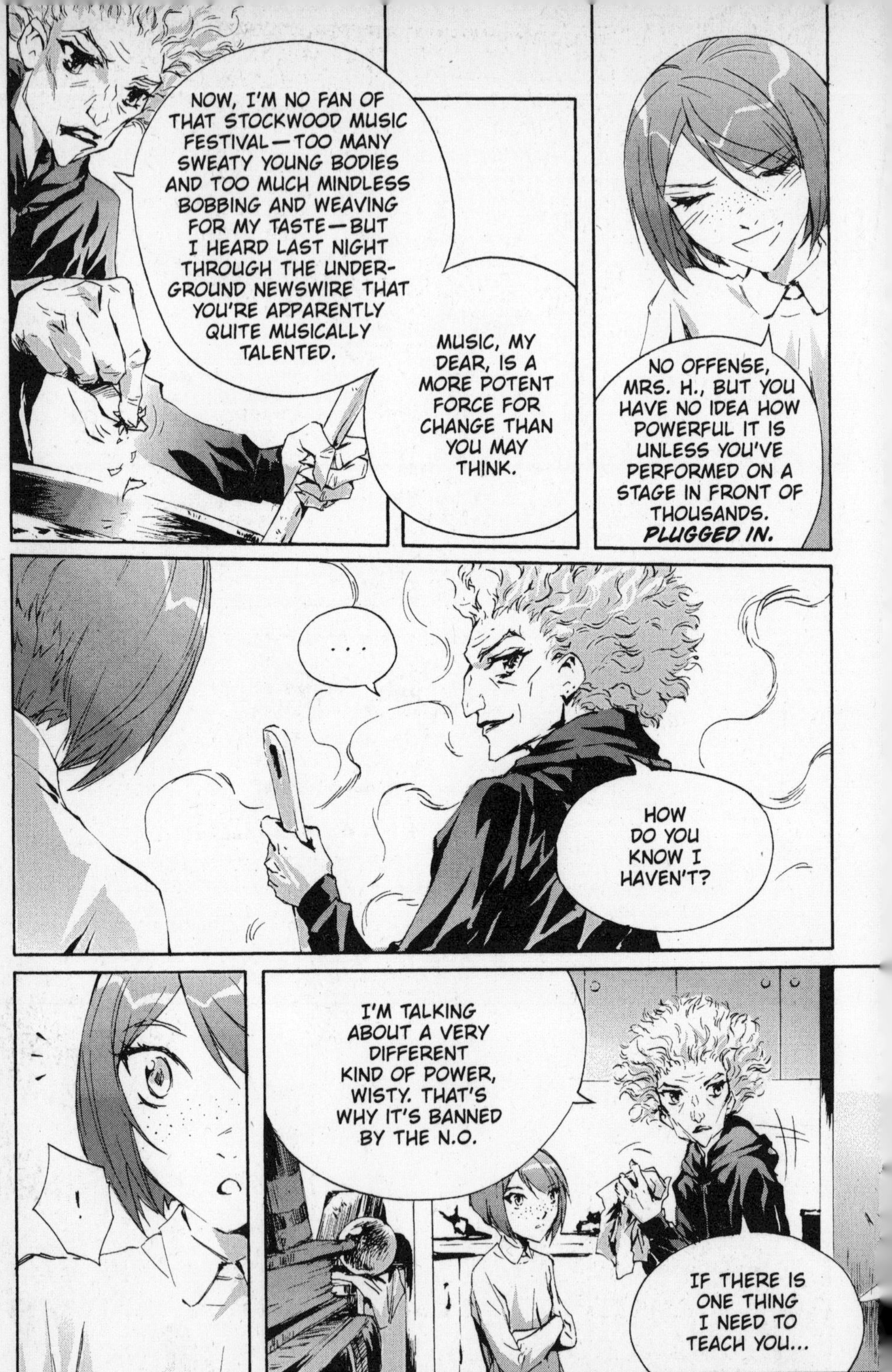
NOW, I'M NO FAN OF THAT STOCKWOOD MUSIC FESTIVAL—TOO MANY SWEATY YOUNG BODIES AND TOO MUCH MINDLESS BOBBING AND WEAVING FOR MY TASTE—BUT I HEARD LAST NIGHT THROUGH THE UNDERGROUND NEWSWIRE THAT YOU'RE APPARENTLY QUITE MUSICALLY TALENTED.
MUSIC, MY DEAR, IS A MORE POTENT FORCE FOR CHANGE THAN YOU MAY THINK.
NO OFFENSE, MRS. H., BUT YOU HAVE NO IDEA HOW POWERFUL IT IS UNLESS YOU'VE PERFORMED ON A STAGE IN FRONT OF THOUSANDS. *PLUGGED IN.*
. . .
HOW DO YOU KNOW I HAVEN'T?
!
I'M TALKING ABOUT A VERY DIFFERENT KIND OF POWER, WISTY. THAT'S WHY IT'S BANNED BY THE N.O.
IF THERE IS ONE THING I NEED TO TEACH YOU...

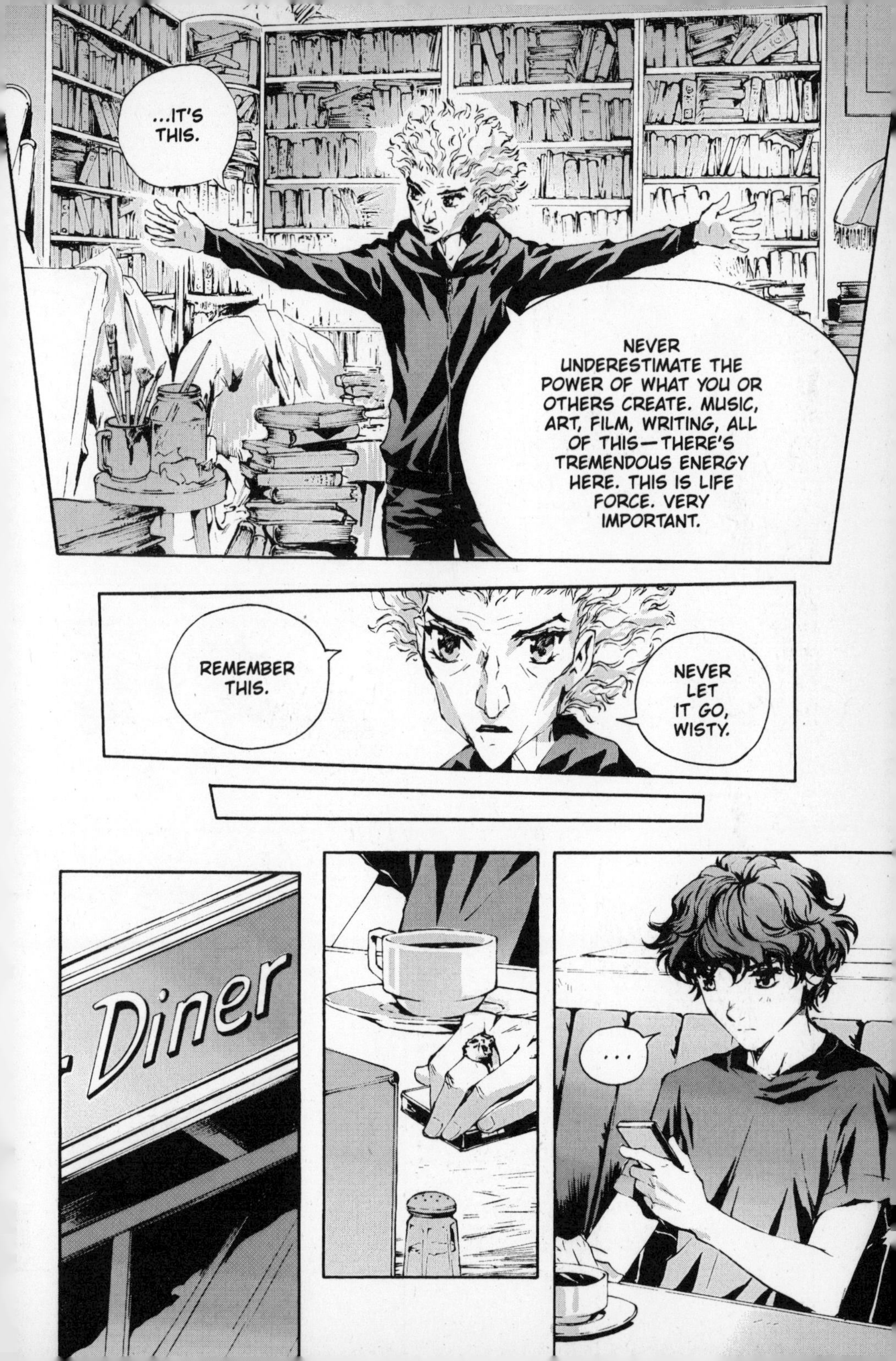
...IT'S THIS.
NEVER UNDERESTIMATE THE POWER OF WHAT YOU OR OTHERS CREATE. MUSIC, ART, FILM, WRITING, ALL OF THIS—THERE'S TREMENDOUS ENERGY HERE. THIS IS LIFE FORCE. VERY IMPORTANT.
REMEMBER THIS.
NEVER LET IT GO, WISTY.
Diner
...

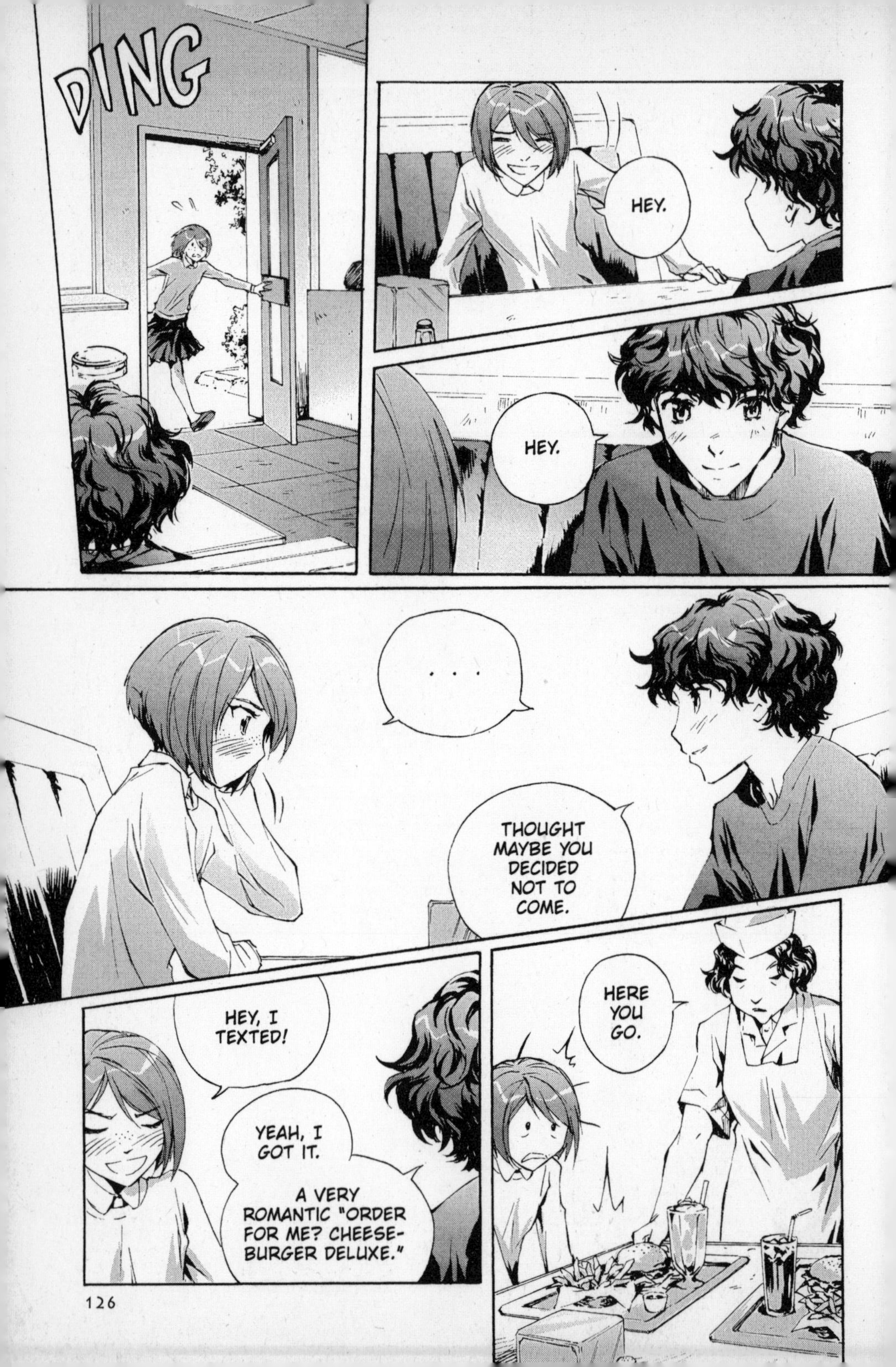
DING
HEY.
HEY.
. . .
THOUGHT MAYBE YOU DECIDED NOT TO COME.
HEY, I TEXTED!
YEAH, I GOT IT.
A VERY ROMANTIC "ORDER FOR ME? CHEESE-BURGER DELUXE."
HERE YOU GO.

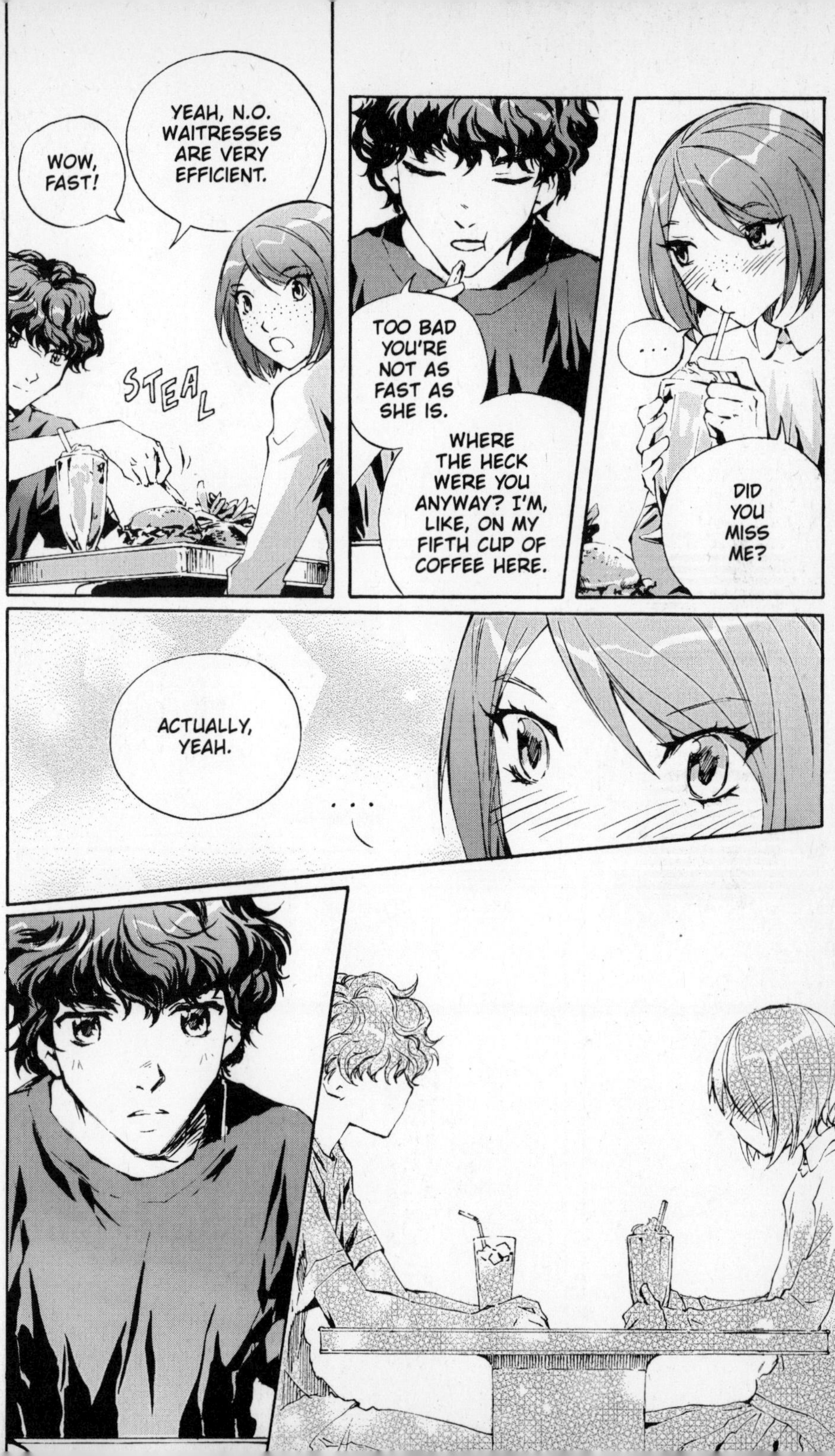
WOW, FAST!
YEAH, N.O. WAITRESSES ARE VERY EFFICIENT.
STEAL
TOO BAD YOU'RE NOT AS FAST AS SHE IS.
WHERE THE HECK WERE YOU ANYWAY? I'M, LIKE, ON MY FIFTH CUP OF COFFEE HERE.
...
DID YOU MISS ME?
ACTUALLY, YEAH.
...

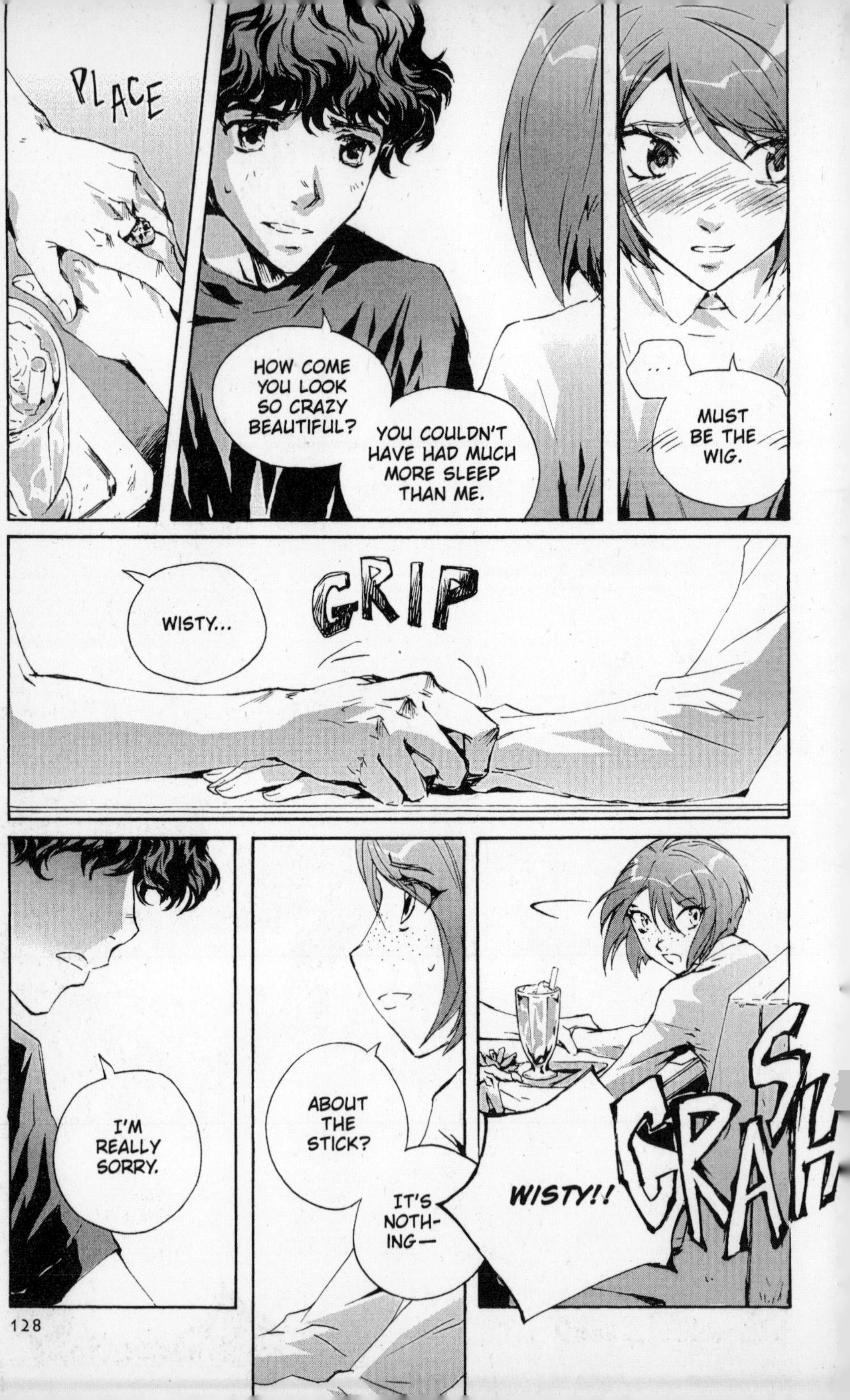
PLACE
HOW COME YOU LOOK SO CRAZY BEAUTIFUL?
YOU COULDN'T HAVE HAD MUCH MORE SLEEP THAN ME.
...
MUST BE THE WIG.
WISTY...
GRIP
I'M REALLY SORRY.
ABOUT THE STICK?
IT'S NOTH-ING—
WISTY!!

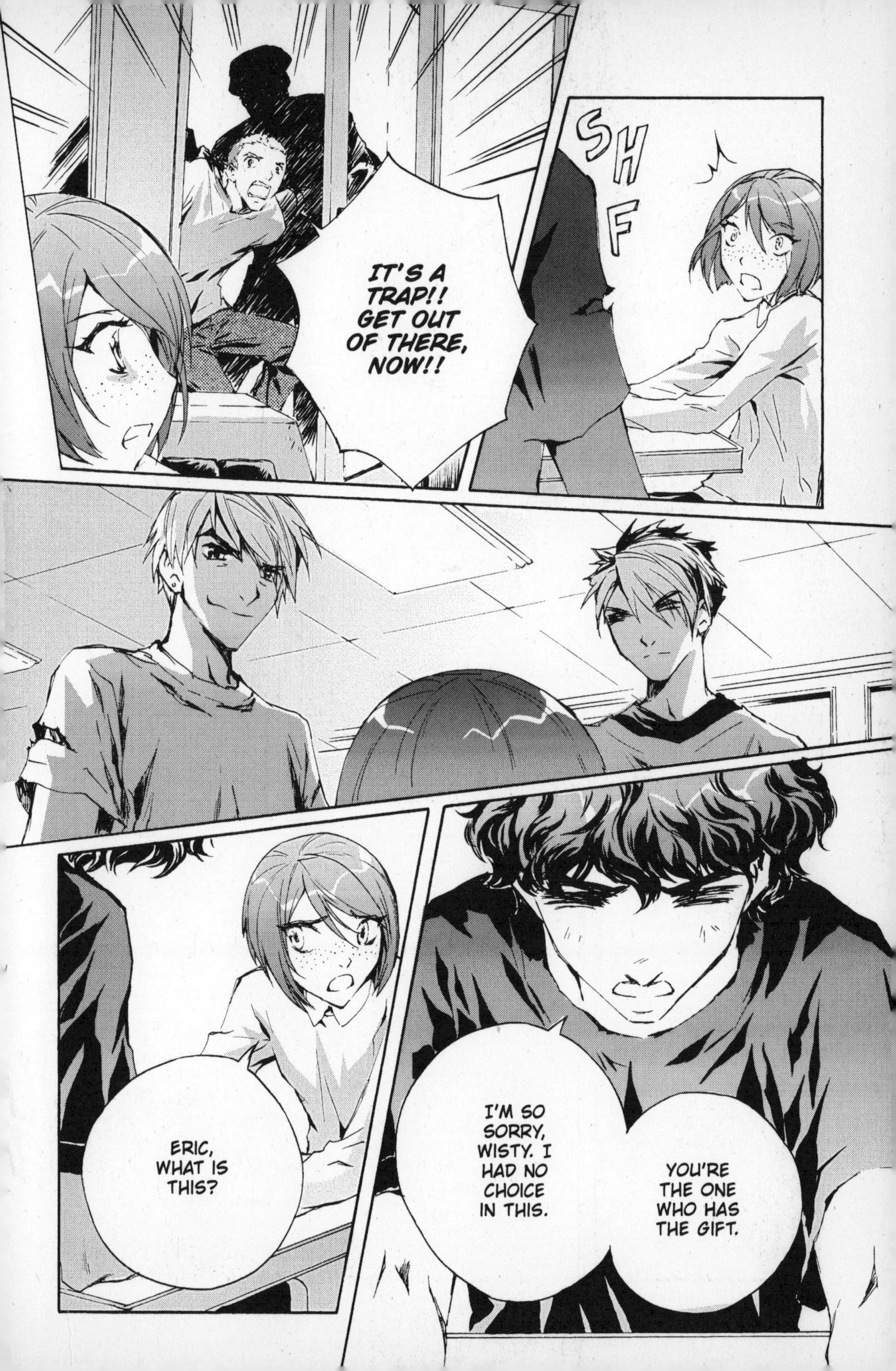
IT'S A TRAP!! GET OUT OF THERE, NOW!!
SHF
ERIC, WHAT IS THIS?
I'M SO SORRY, WISTY. I HAD NO CHOICE IN THIS.
YOU'RE THE ONE WHO HAS THE GIFT.

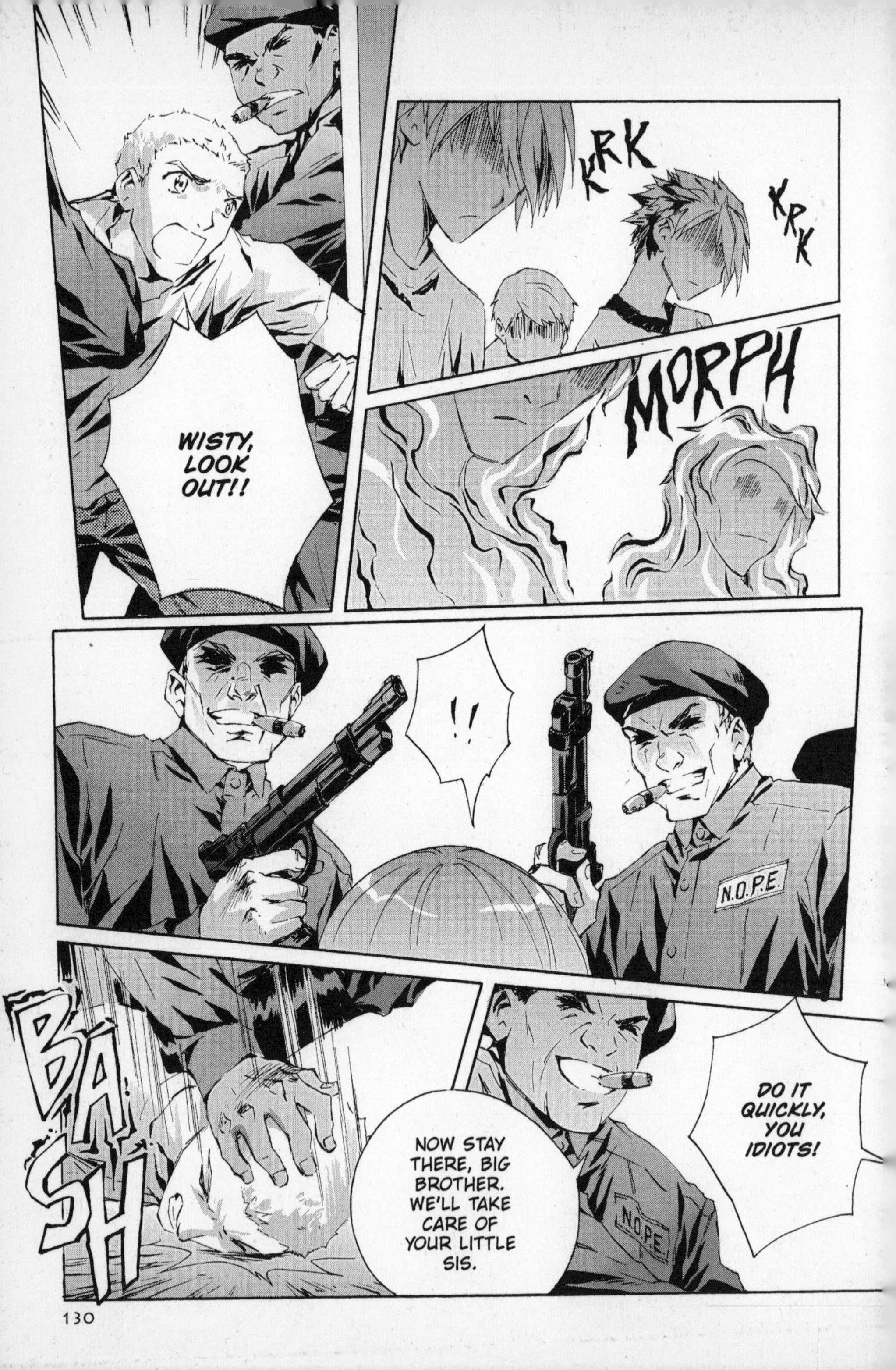
WISTY, LOOK OUT!!
KRK
KRK
MORPH
!!
BASH
NOW STAY THERE, BIG BROTHER. WE'LL TAKE CARE OF YOUR LITTLE SIS.
N.O.P.E.
DO IT QUICKLY, YOU IDIOTS!

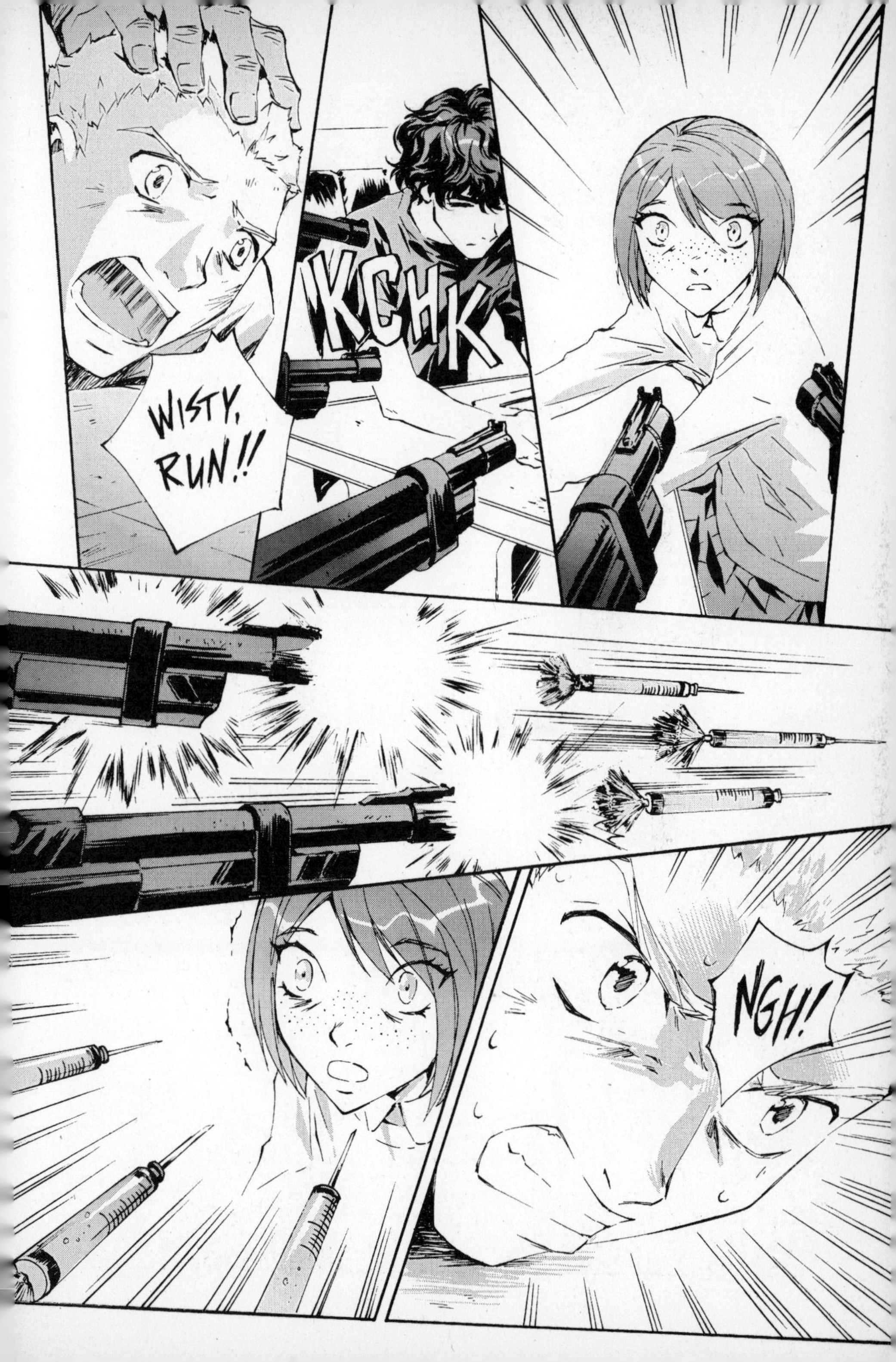
WISTY, RUN!!
KCHK
NGH!

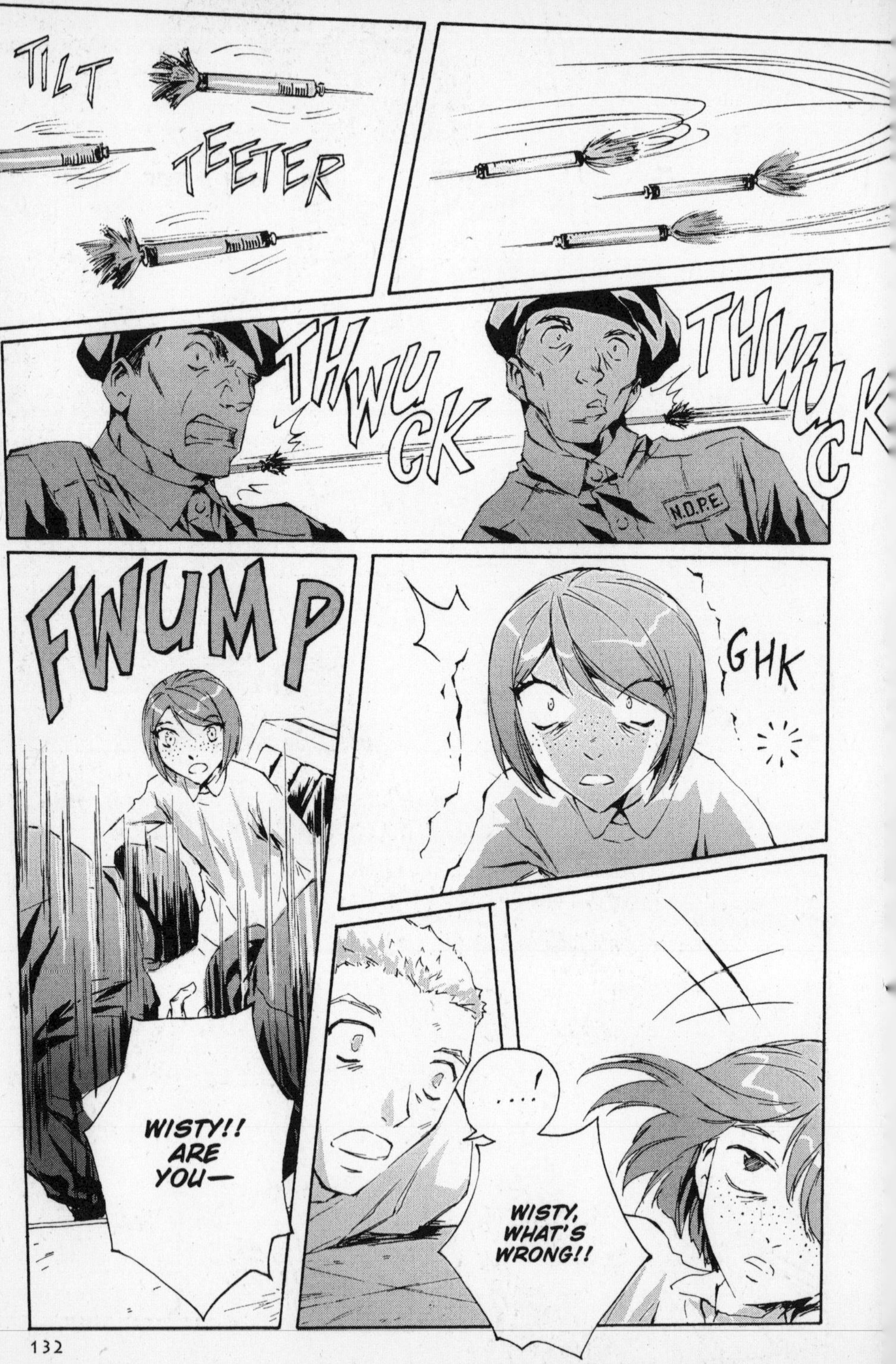
TILT
TEETER
THWUCK
THWUCK
FWUMP
WISTY!! ARE YOU—
GHK
....!
WISTY, WHAT'S WRONG!!

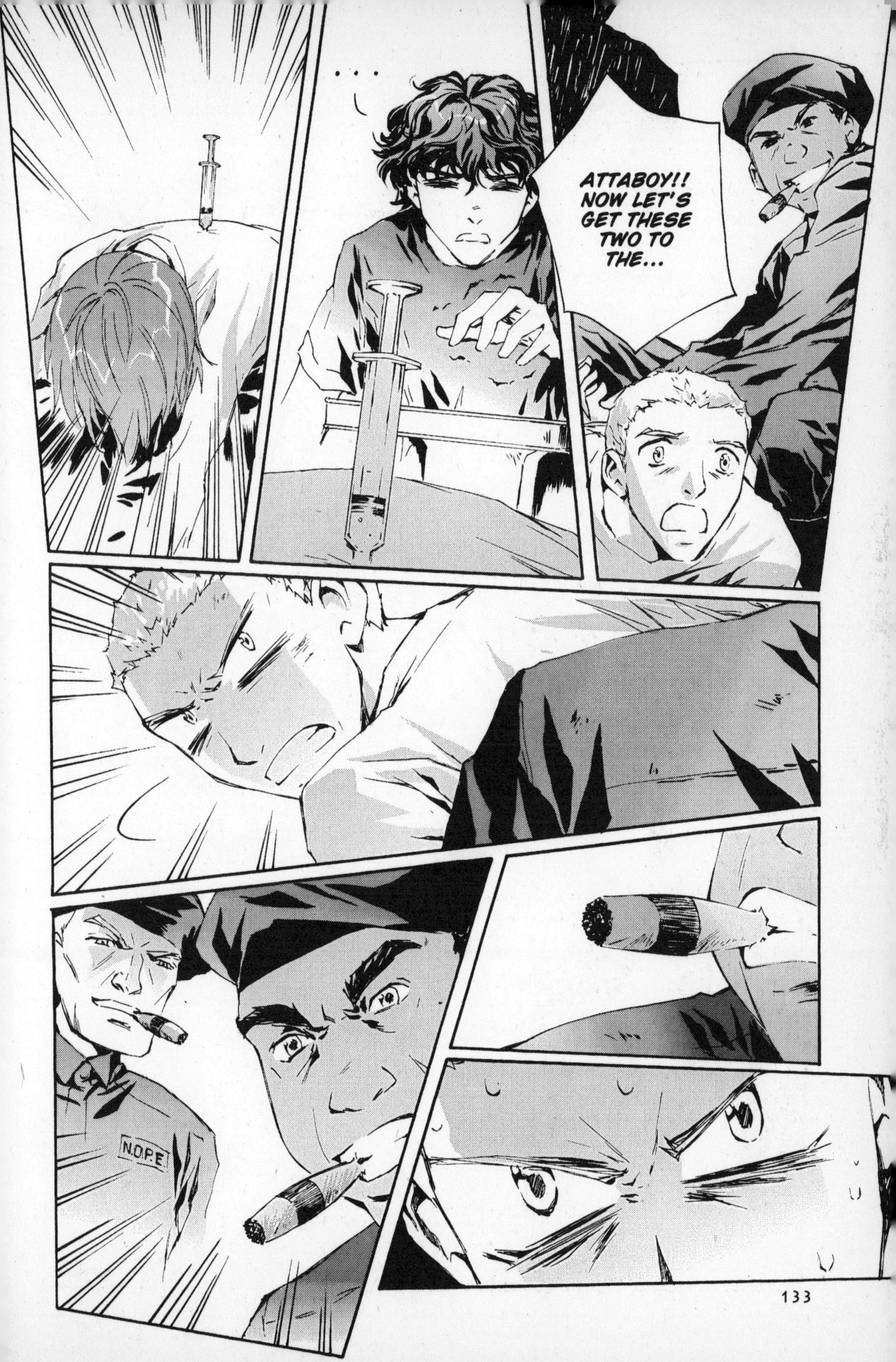
...
ATTABOY!! NOW LET'S GET THESE TWO TO THE...
N.O.P.E

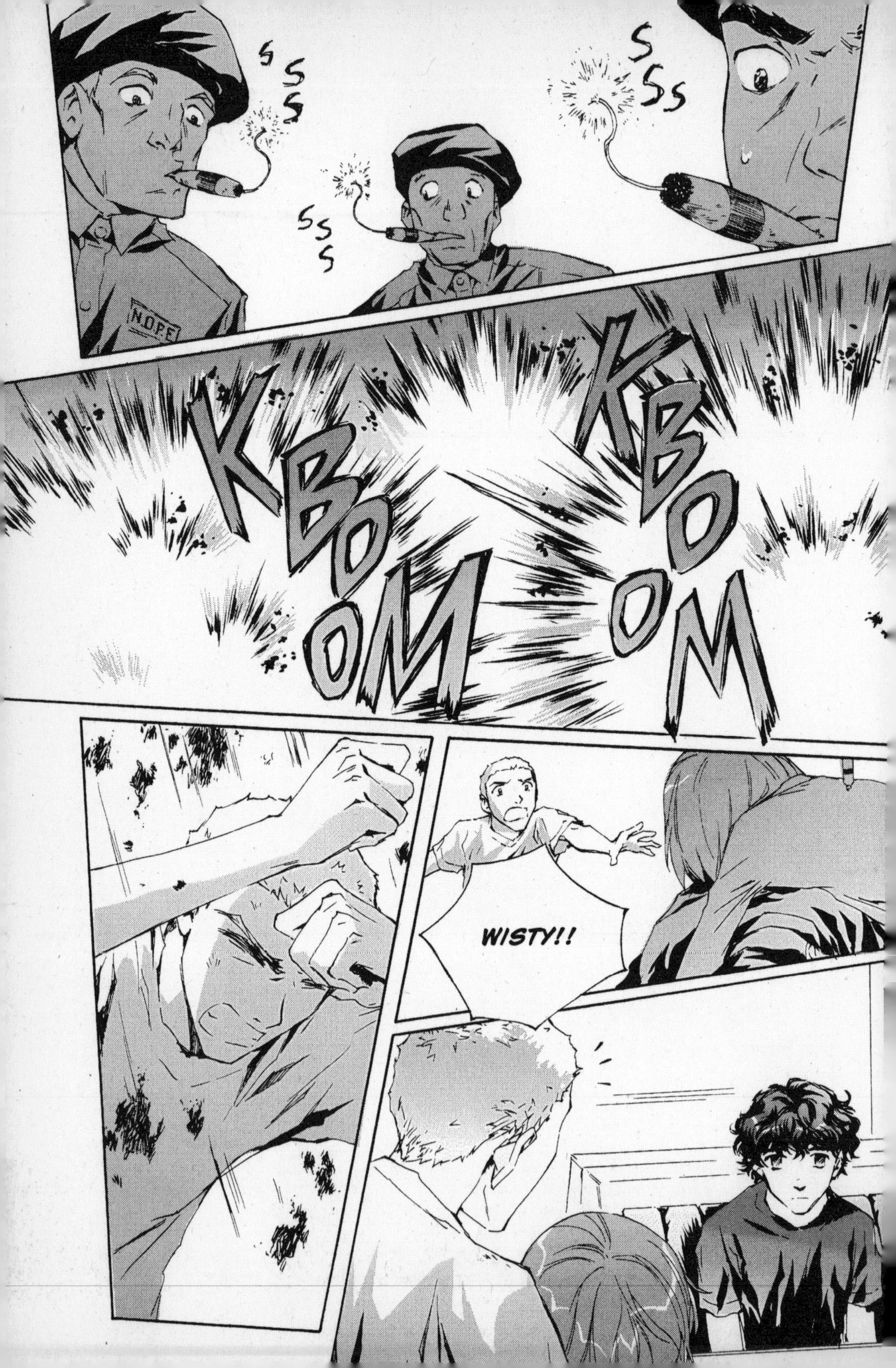
SSS
N.O.P.E.
SSS
SSS
KBOOM
KBOOM
WISTY!!

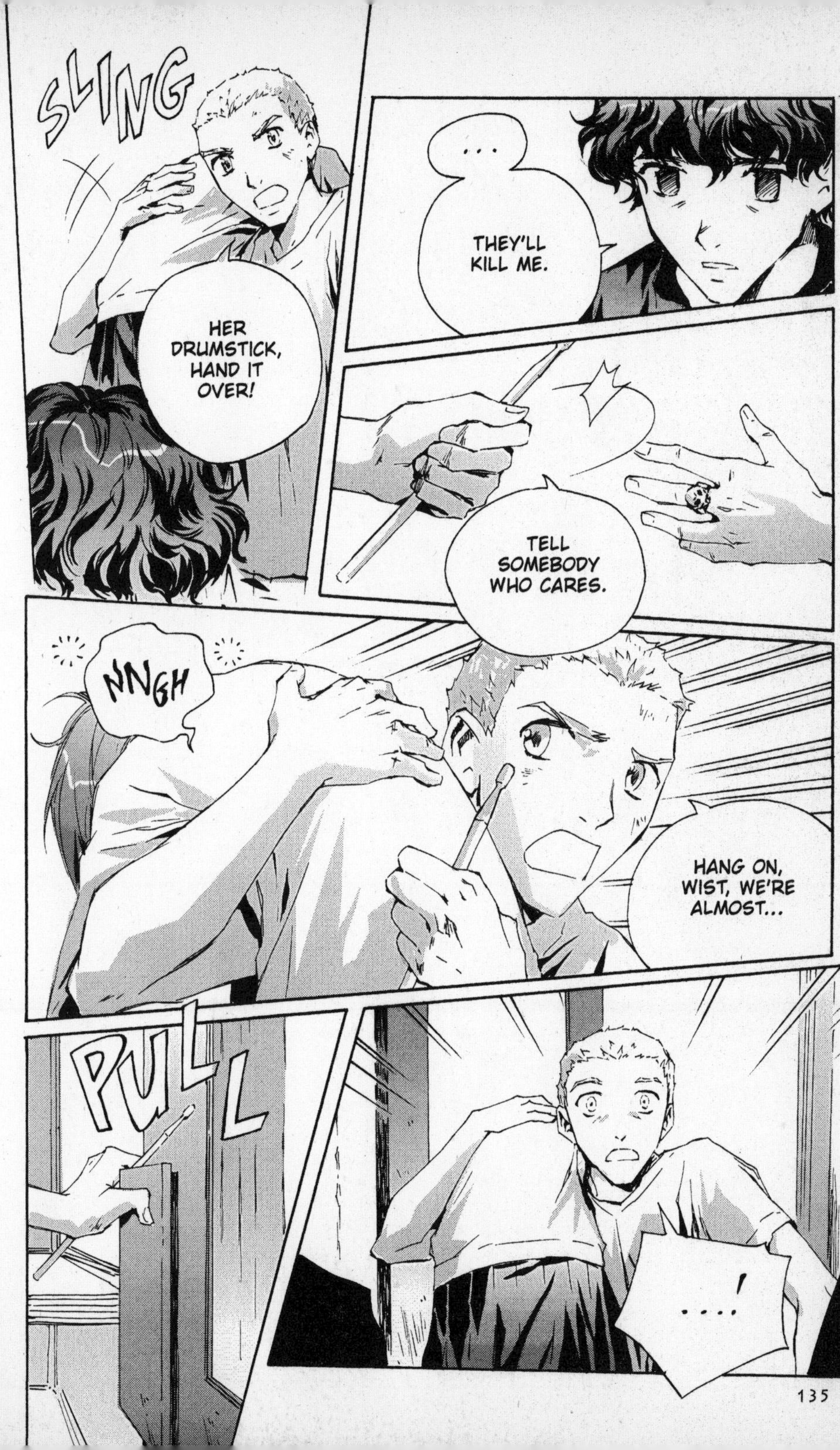
SLING
HER DRUMSTICK, HAND IT OVER!
...
THEY'LL KILL ME.
TELL SOMEBODY WHO CARES.
NNGH
HANG ON, WIST, WE'RE ALMOST...
PULL
....!

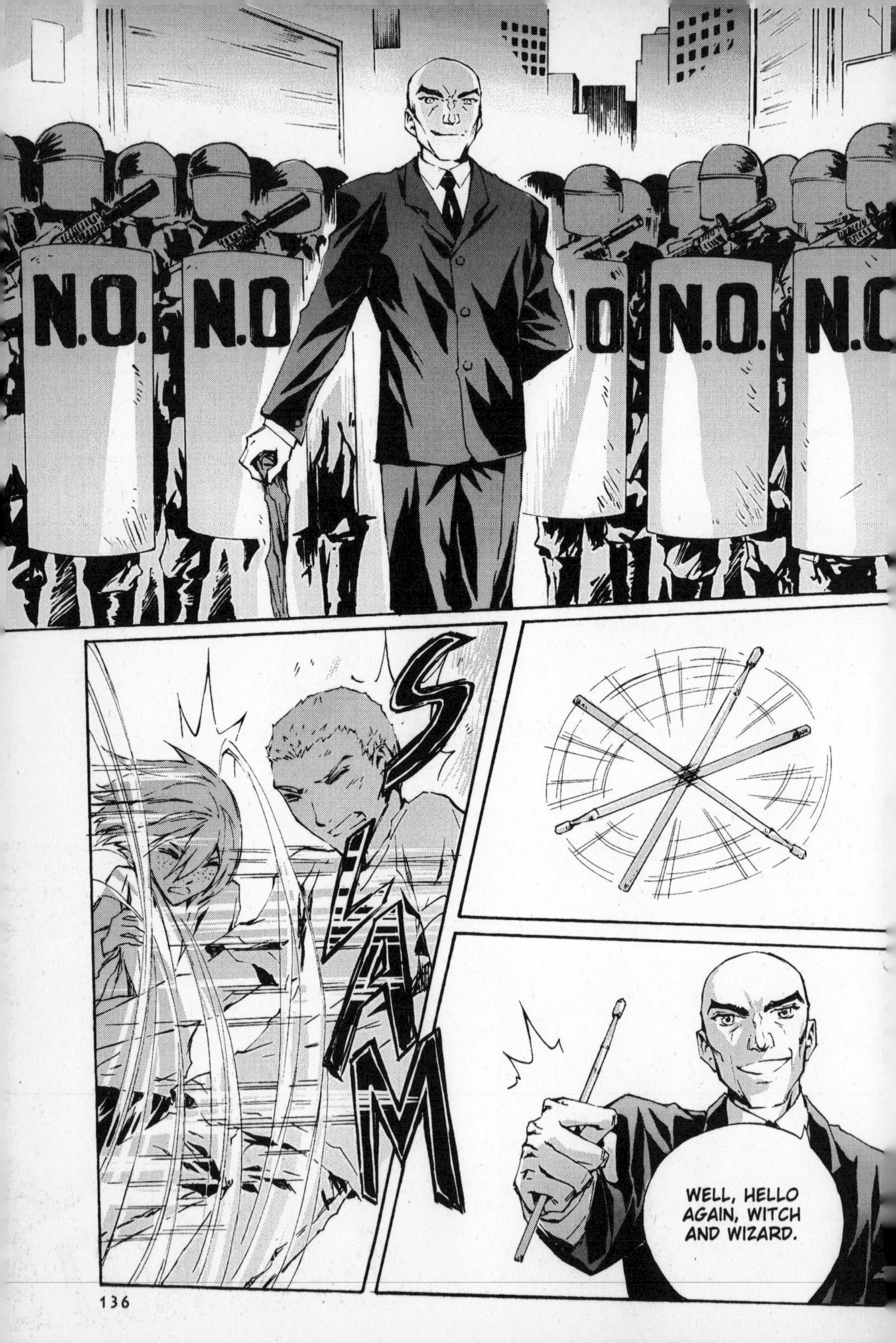
N.O.
SLAM
WELL, HELLO AGAIN, WITCH AND WIZARD.

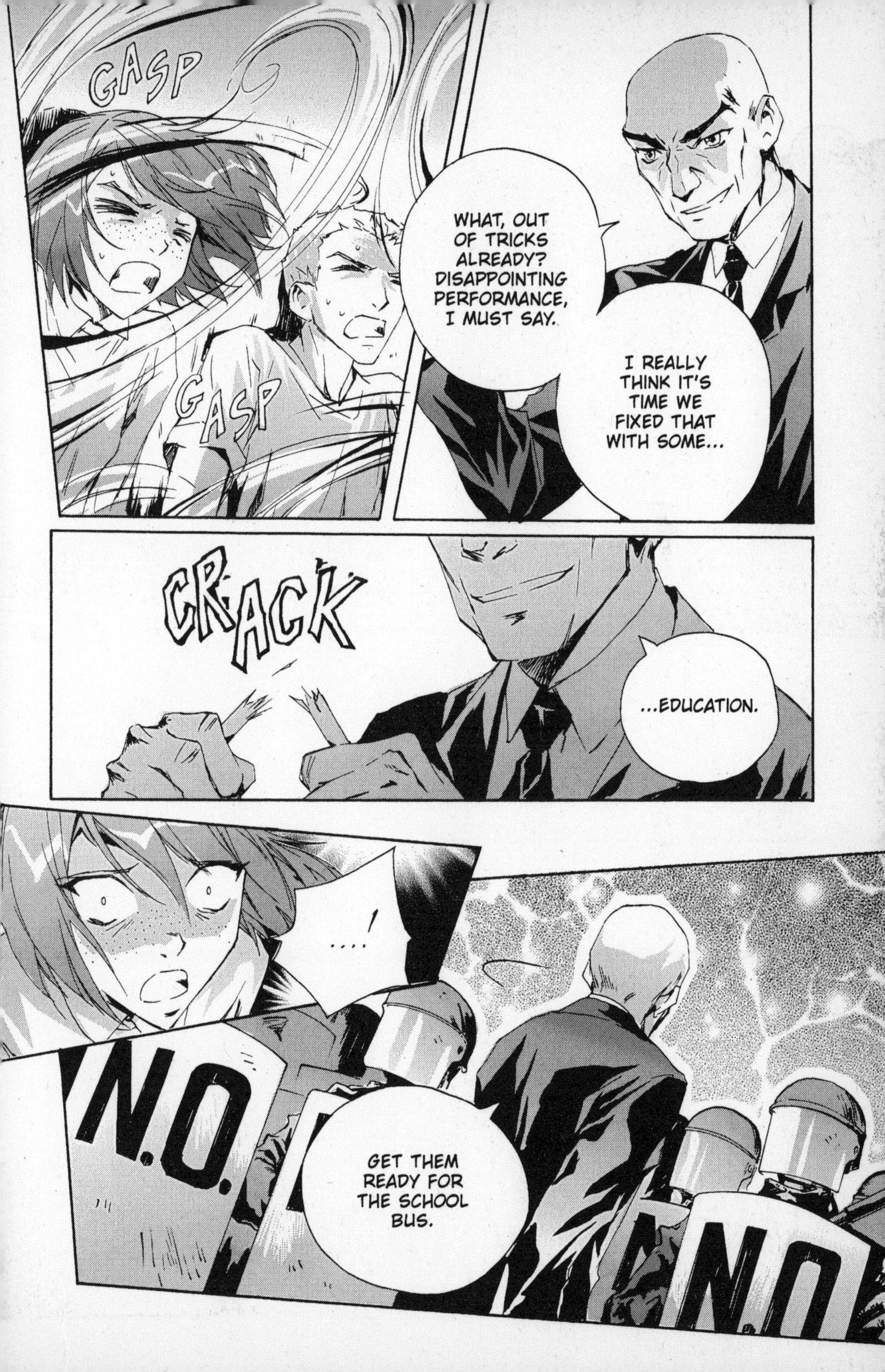
GASP
GASP
WHAT, OUT OF TRICKS ALREADY? DISAPPOINTING PERFORMANCE, I MUST SAY.
I REALLY THINK IT'S TIME WE FIXED THAT WITH SOME...
CRACK
...EDUCATION.
....!
N.O.
GET THEM READY FOR THE SCHOOL BUS.
N.O.

WITCH & WIZARD

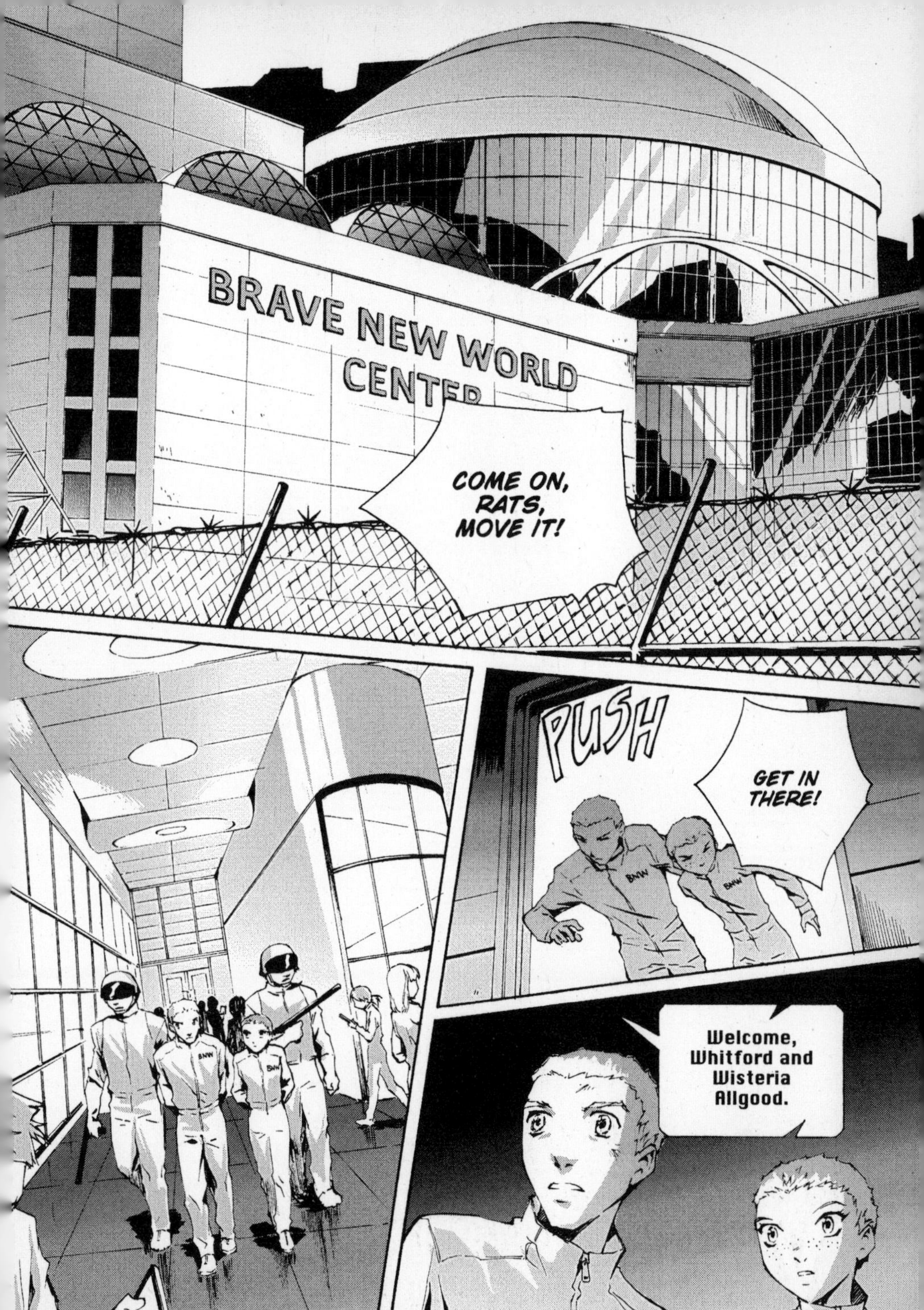
BRAVE NEW WORLD CENTER
COME ON, RATS, MOVE IT!
PUSH
GET IN THERE!
BNW
BNW
Welcome, Whitford and Wisteria Allgood.

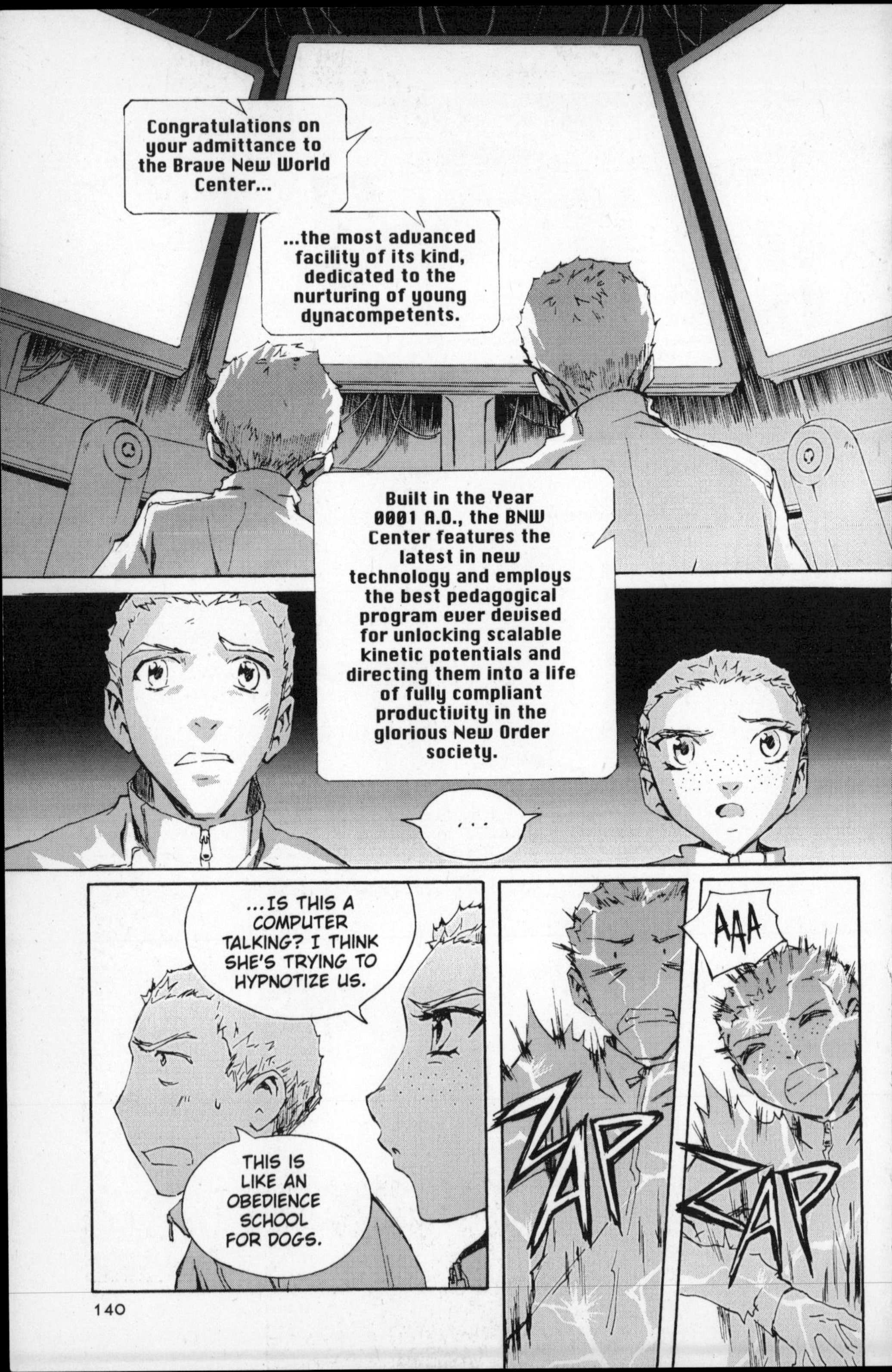
Congratulations on your admittance to the Brave New World Center...
...the most advanced facility of its kind, dedicated to the nurturing of young dynacompetents.
Built in the Year 0001 A.O., the BNW Center features the latest in new technology and employs the best pedagogical program ever devised for unlocking scalable kinetic potentials and directing them into a life of fully compliant productivity in the glorious New Order society.
...
...IS THIS A COMPUTER TALKING? I THINK SHE'S TRYING TO HYPNOTIZE US.
THIS IS LIKE AN OBEDIENCE SCHOOL FOR DOGS.
AAA
ZAP
ZAP

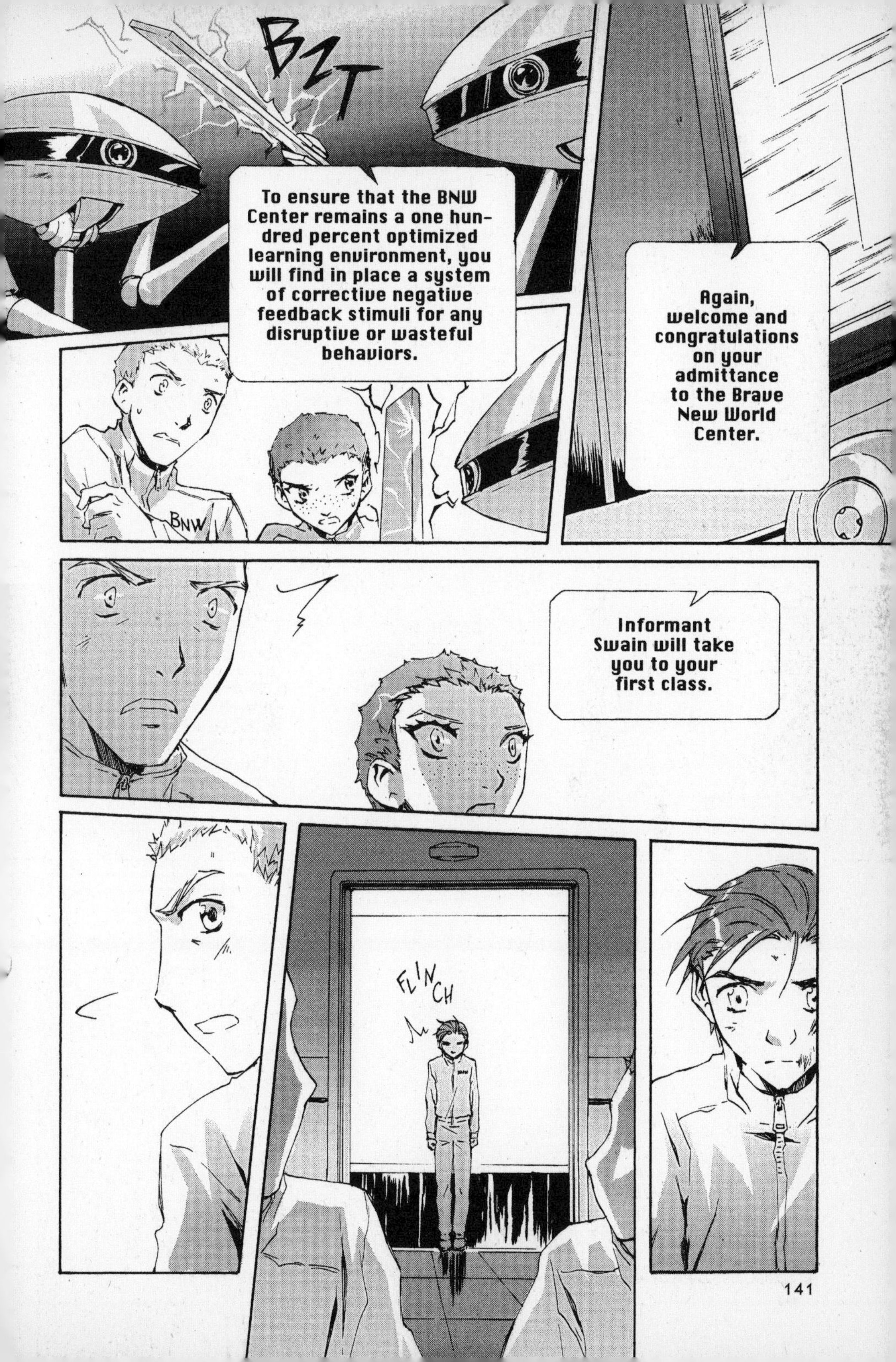
BZT
To ensure that the BNW Center remains a one hundred percent optimized learning environment, you will find in place a system of corrective negative feedback stimuli for any disruptive or wasteful behaviors.
BNW
Again, welcome and congratulations on your admittance to the Brave New World Center.
Informant Swain will take you to your first class.
FLINCH

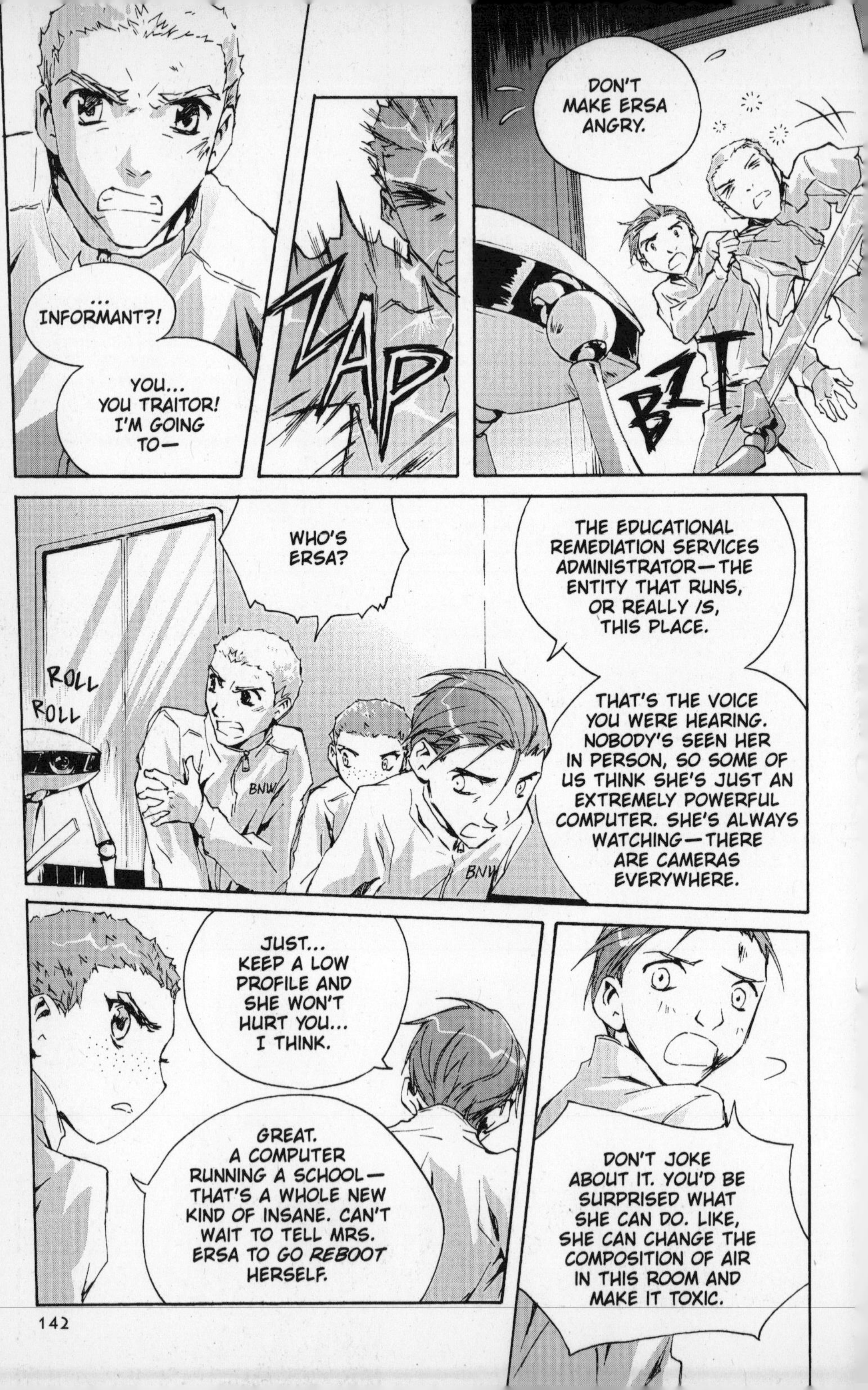

...INFORMANT?!
YOU... YOU TRAITOR! I'M GOING TO—
ZAP
DON'T MAKE ERSA ANGRY.
BZZT
ROLL ROLL
WHO'S ERSA?
THE EDUCATIONAL REMEDIATION SERVICES ADMINISTRATOR—THE ENTITY THAT RUNS, OR REALLY *IS*, THIS PLACE.
THAT'S THE VOICE YOU WERE HEARING. NOBODY'S SEEN HER IN PERSON, SO SOME OF US THINK SHE'S JUST AN EXTREMELY POWERFUL COMPUTER. SHE'S ALWAYS WATCHING—THERE ARE CAMERAS EVERYWHERE.
BNW
BNW
JUST... KEEP A LOW PROFILE AND SHE WON'T HURT YOU... I THINK.
GREAT. A COMPUTER RUNNING A SCHOOL—THAT'S A WHOLE NEW KIND OF INSANE. CAN'T WAIT TO TELL MRS. ERSA TO GO *REBOOT* HERSELF.
DON'T JOKE ABOUT IT. YOU'D BE SURPRISED WHAT SHE CAN DO. LIKE, SHE CAN CHANGE THE COMPOSITION OF AIR IN THIS ROOM AND MAKE IT TOXIC.

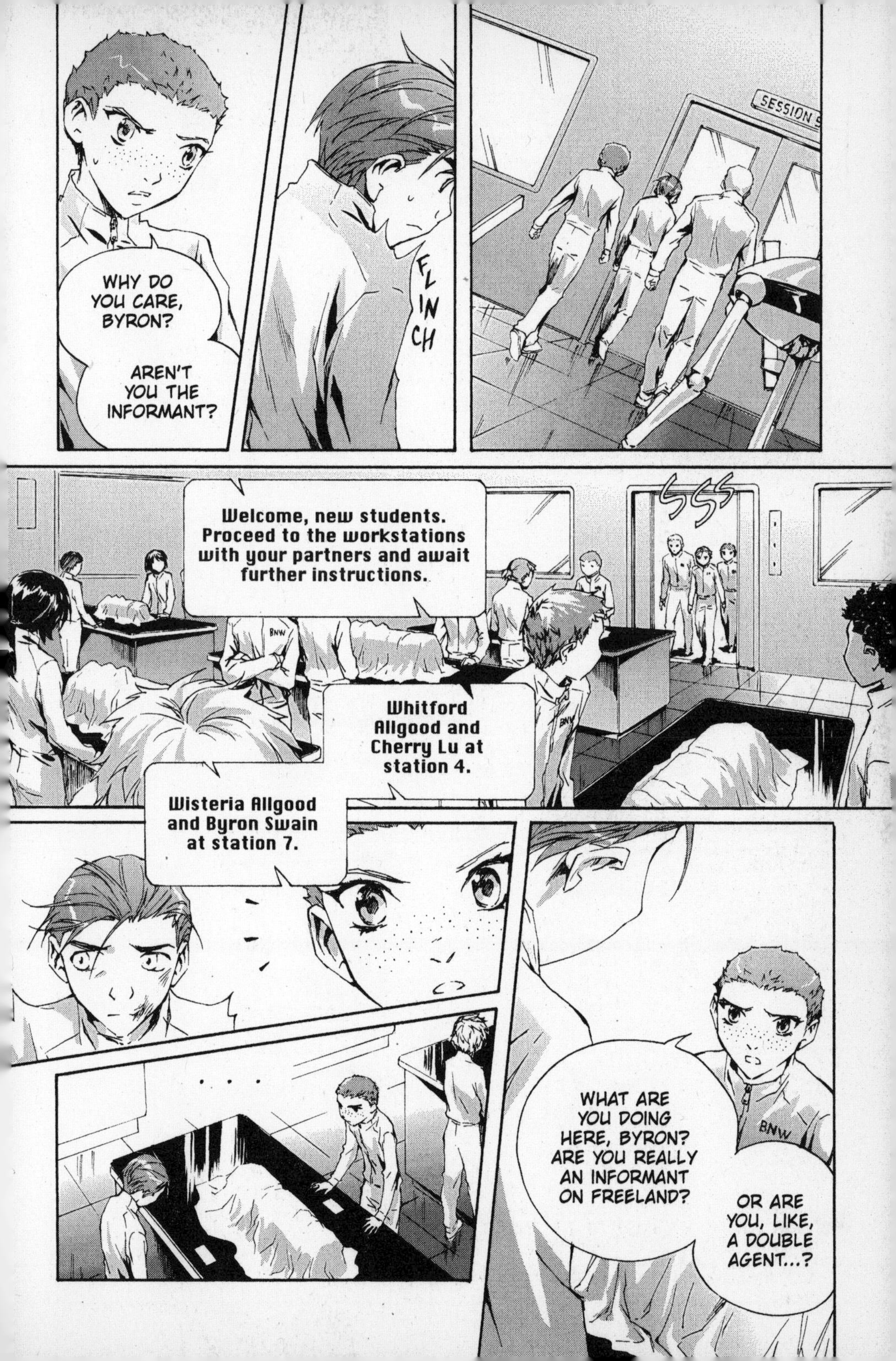
WHY DO YOU CARE, BYRON?
AREN'T YOU THE INFORMANT?
FLINCH
SESSION 5
Welcome, new students. Proceed to the workstations with your partners and await further instructions.
SSS
BNW
Whitford Allgood and Cherry Lu at station 4.
Wisteria Allgood and Byron Swain at station 7.
. . .
WHAT ARE YOU DOING HERE, BYRON? ARE YOU REALLY AN INFORMANT ON FREELAND?
OR ARE YOU, LIKE, A DOUBLE AGENT...?

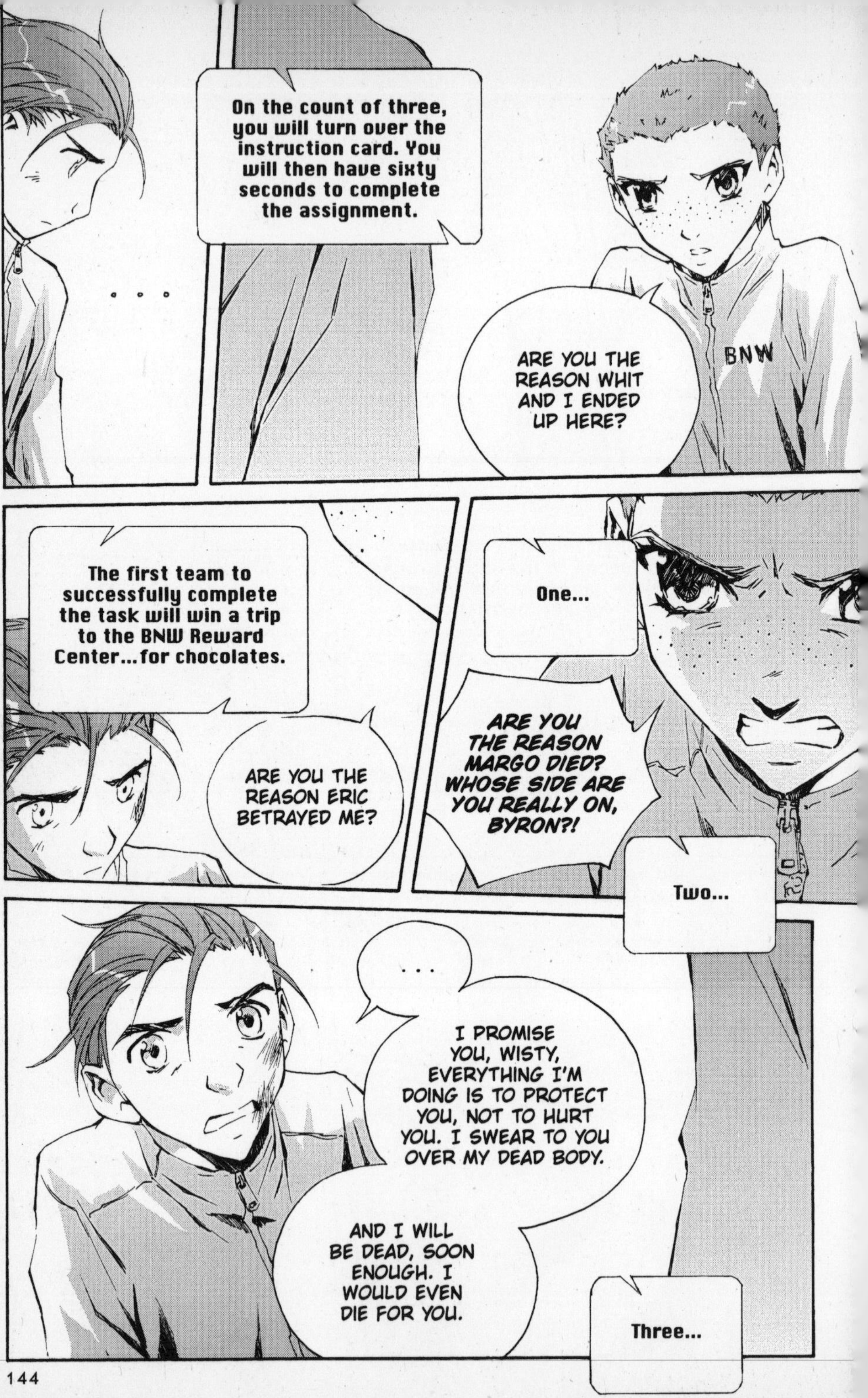

On the count of three, you will turn over the instruction card. You will then have sixty seconds to complete the assignment.
. . .
ARE YOU THE REASON WHIT AND I ENDED UP HERE?
The first team to successfully complete the task will win a trip to the BNW Reward Center...for chocolates.
ARE YOU THE REASON ERIC BETRAYED ME?
One...
ARE YOU THE REASON MARGO DIED? WHOSE SIDE ARE YOU REALLY ON, BYRON?!
Two...
. . .
I PROMISE YOU, WISTY, EVERYTHING I'M DOING IS TO PROTECT YOU, NOT TO HURT YOU. I SWEAR TO YOU OVER MY DEAD BODY.
AND I WILL BE DEAD, SOON ENOUGH. I WOULD EVEN DIE FOR YOU.
Three...

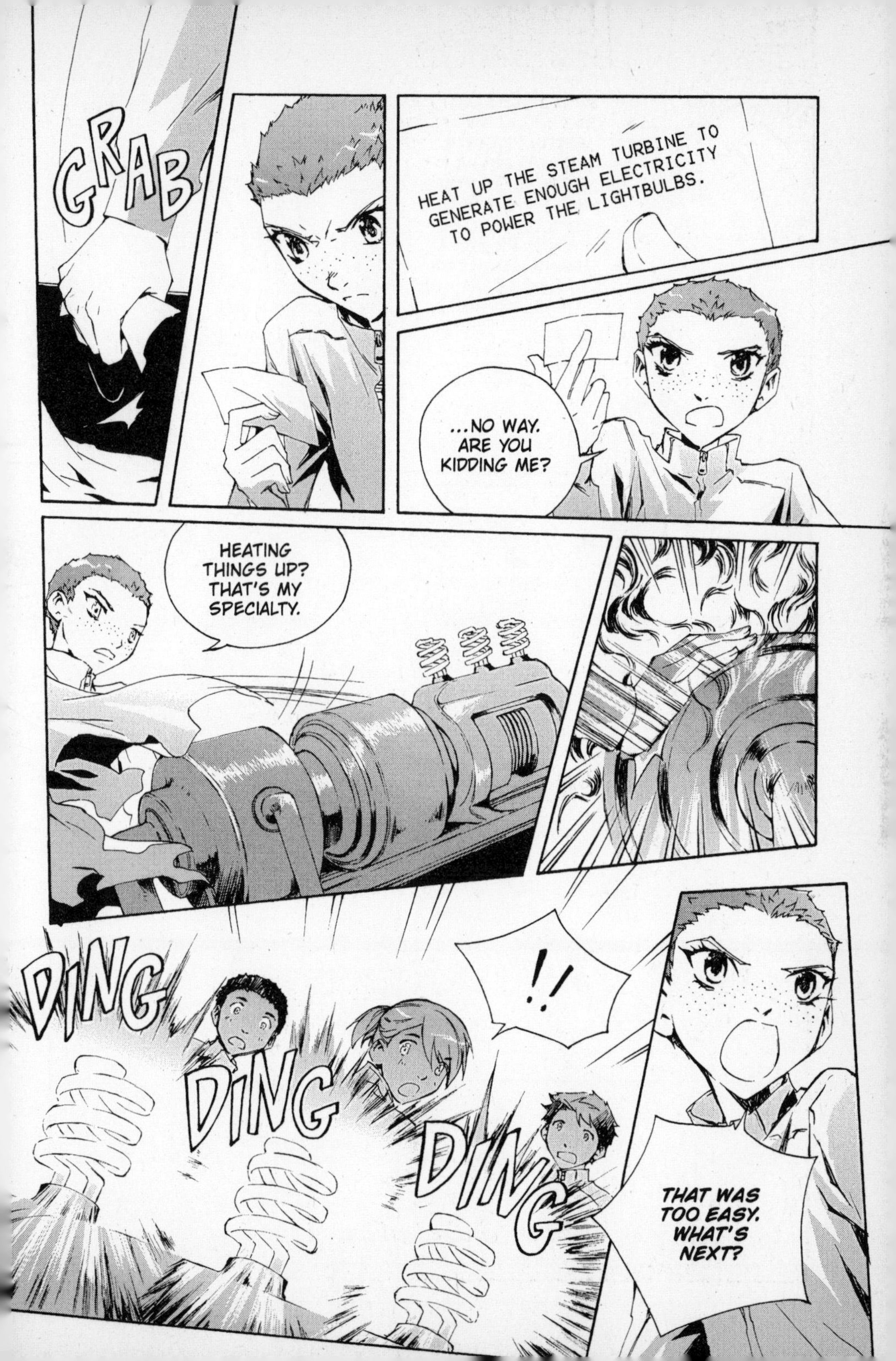
GRAB
HEAT UP THE STEAM TURBINE TO GENERATE ENOUGH ELECTRICITY TO POWER THE LIGHTBULBS.
...NO WAY. ARE YOU KIDDING ME?
HEATING THINGS UP? THAT'S MY SPECIALTY.
DING
DING
DING
!!
THAT WAS TOO EASY. WHAT'S NEXT?

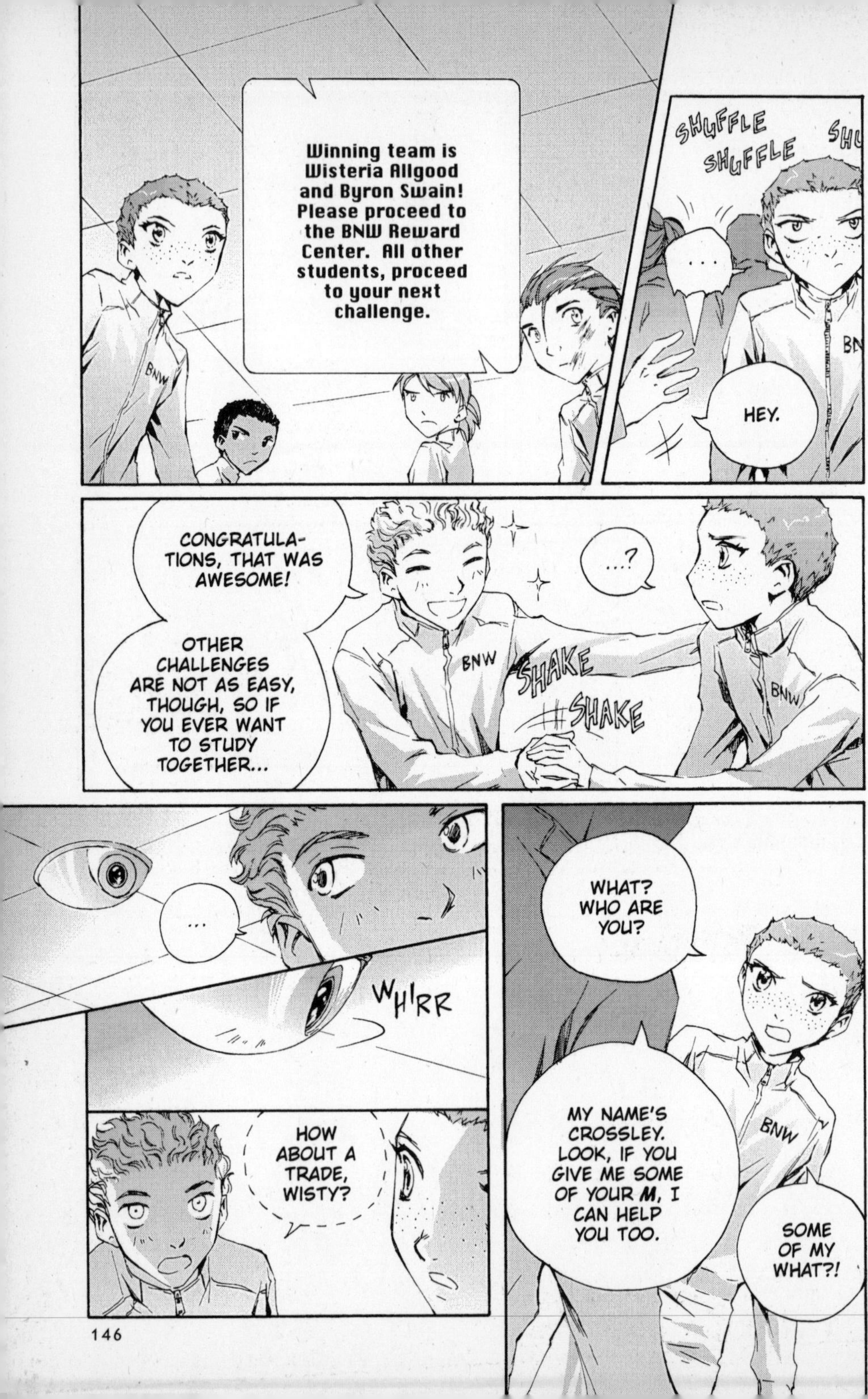

Winning team is Wisteria Allgood and Byron Swain! Please proceed to the BNW Reward Center. All other students, proceed to your next challenge.
BNW
SHUFFLE
SHUFFLE
...
HEY.
CONGRATULA-TIONS, THAT WAS AWESOME!
OTHER CHALLENGES ARE NOT AS EASY, THOUGH, SO IF YOU EVER WANT TO STUDY TOGETHER...
...?
BNW
SHAKE
SHAKE
BNW
...
WHIRR
HOW ABOUT A TRADE, WISTY?
WHAT? WHO ARE YOU?
MY NAME'S CROSSLEY. LOOK, IF YOU GIVE ME SOME OF YOUR *M*, I CAN HELP YOU TOO.
SOME OF MY WHAT?!
BNW

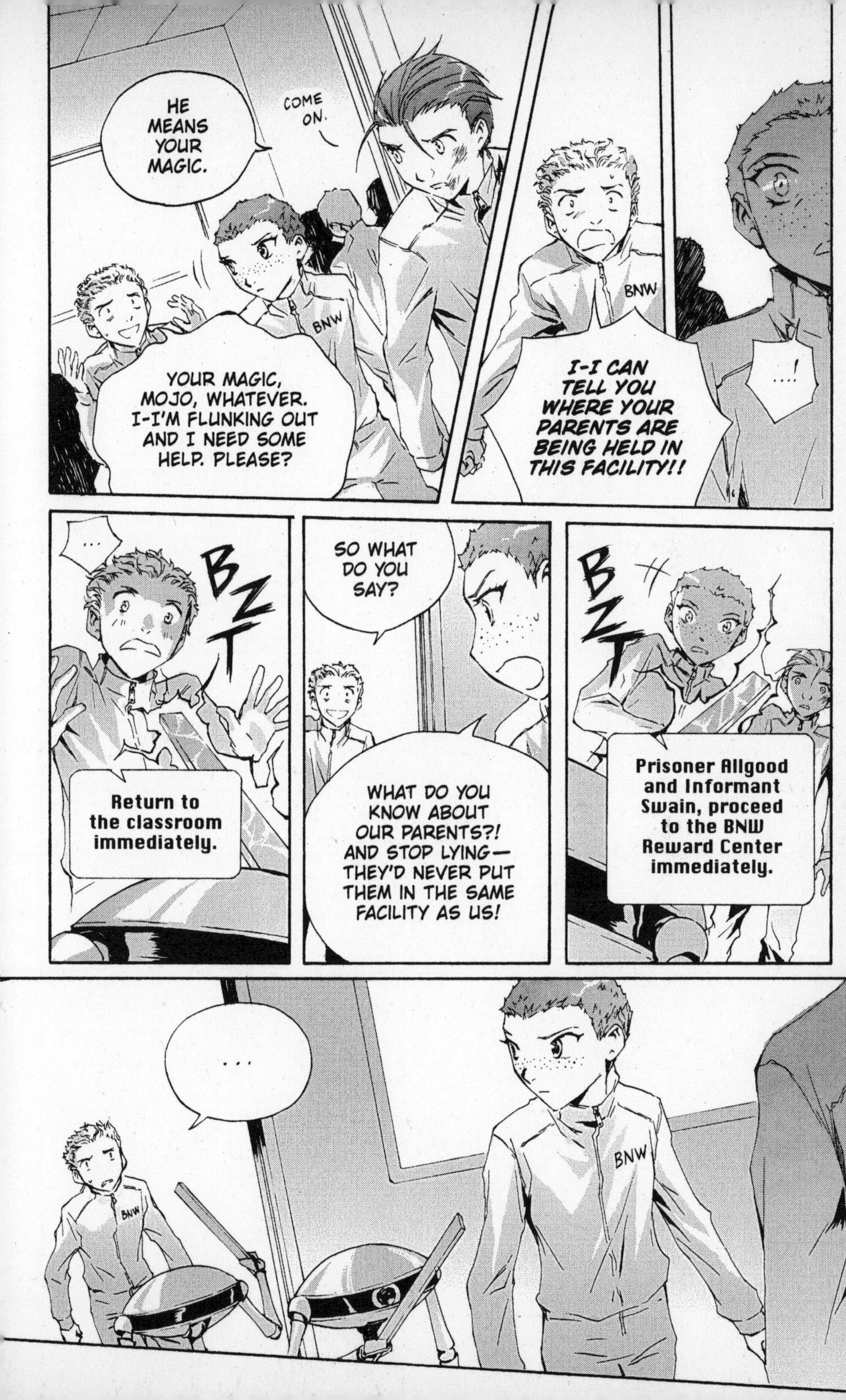
HE MEANS YOUR MAGIC.
COME ON.
YOUR MAGIC, MOJO, WHATEVER. I-I'M FLUNKING OUT AND I NEED SOME HELP. PLEASE?
I-I CAN TELL YOU WHERE YOUR PARENTS ARE BEING HELD IN THIS FACILITY!!
...!
...
BZT
Return to the classroom immediately.
SO WHAT DO YOU SAY?
WHAT DO YOU KNOW ABOUT OUR PARENTS?! AND STOP LYING—THEY'D NEVER PUT THEM IN THE SAME FACILITY AS US!
BZT
Prisoner Allgood and Informant Swain, proceed to the BNW Reward Center immediately.
...

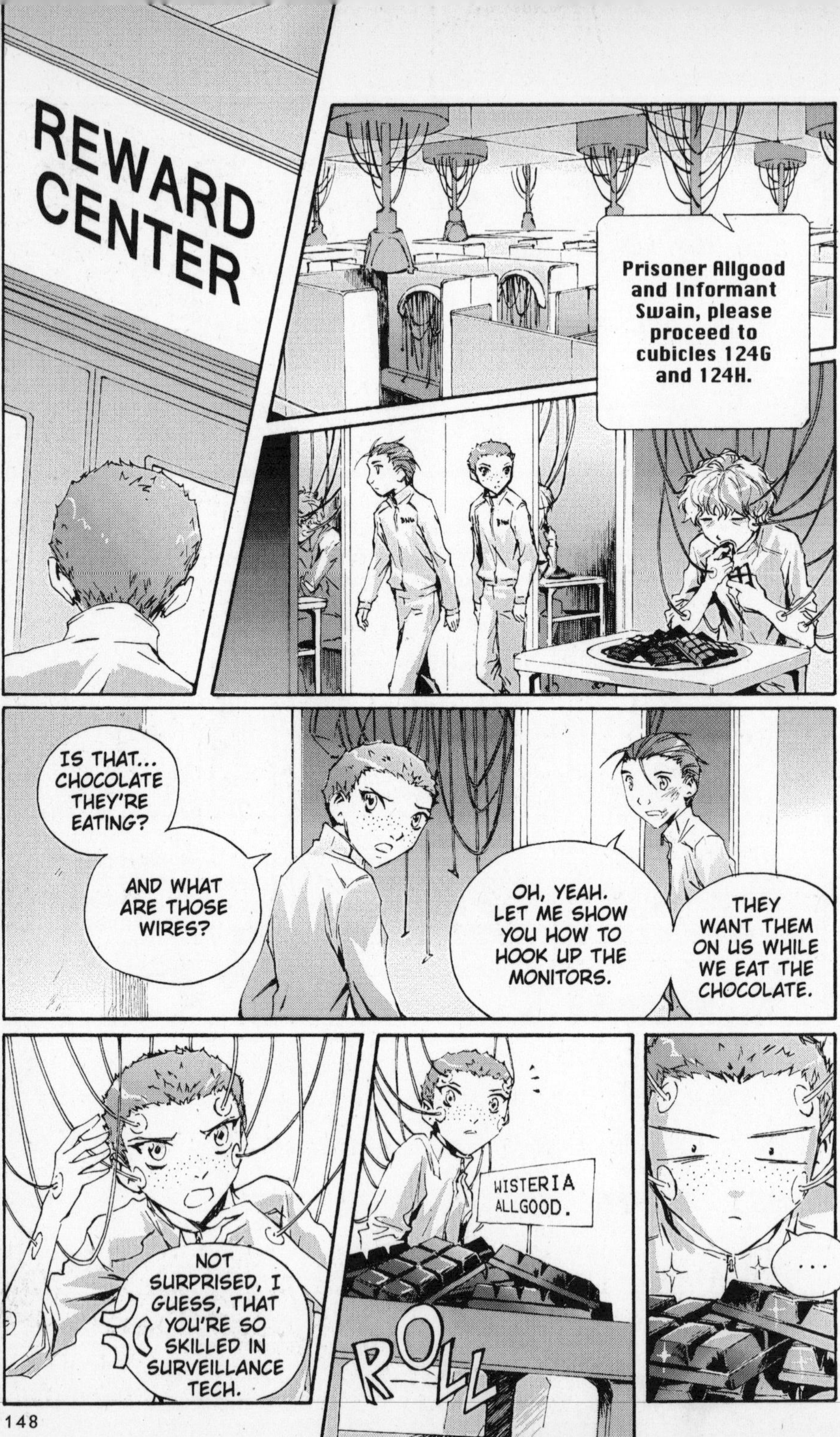
REWARD CENTER
Prisoner Allgood and Informant Swain, please proceed to cubicles 124G and 124H.
IS THAT... CHOCOLATE THEY'RE EATING?
AND WHAT ARE THOSE WIRES?
OH, YEAH. LET ME SHOW YOU HOW TO HOOK UP THE MONITORS.
THEY WANT THEM ON US WHILE WE EAT THE CHOCOLATE.
NOT SURPRISED, I GUESS, THAT YOU'RE SO SKILLED IN SURVEILLANCE TECH.
WISTERIA ALLGOOD.
ROLL
...

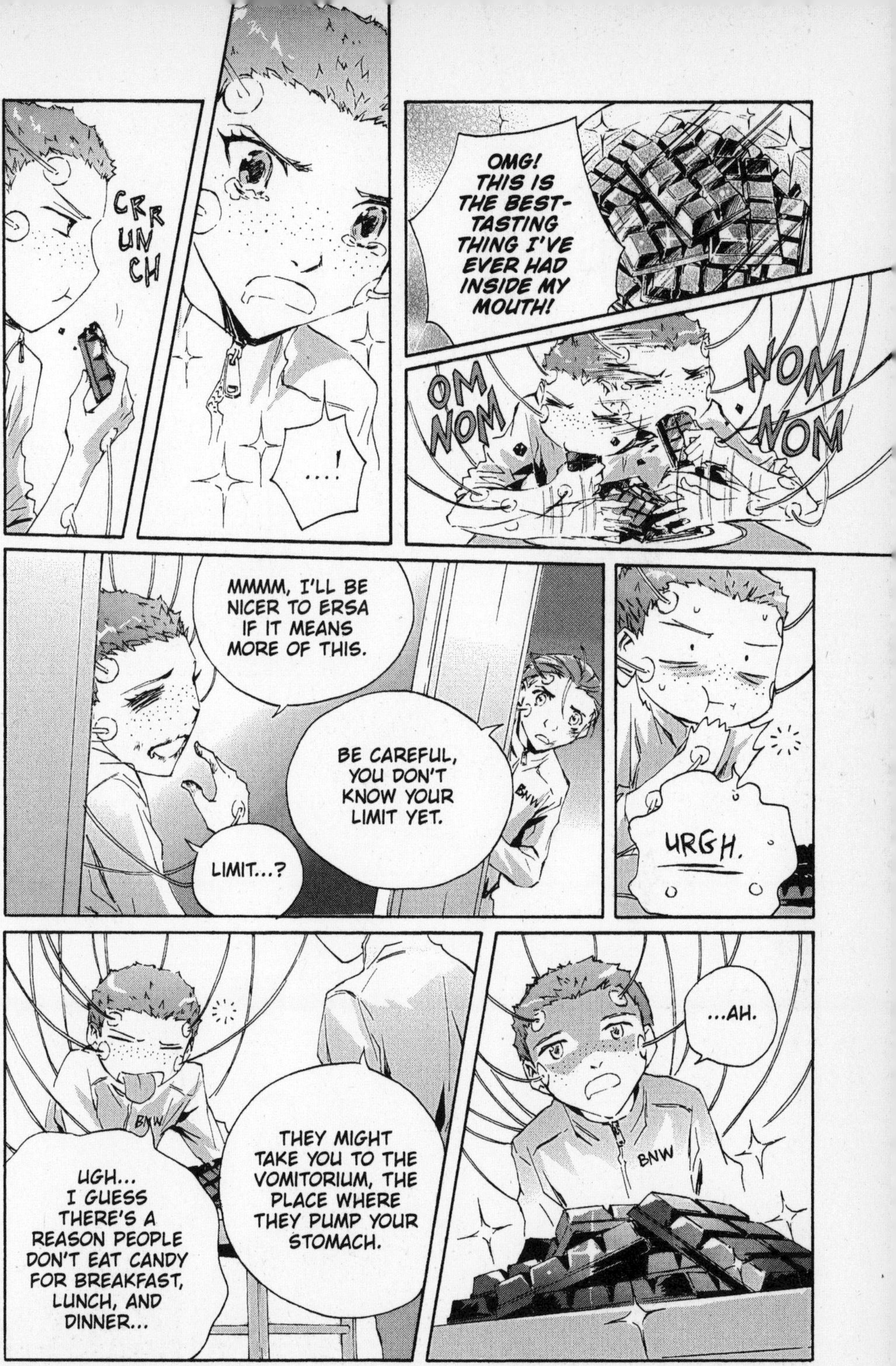
CRRUNCH
....!
OMG! THIS IS THE BEST-TASTING THING I'VE EVER HAD INSIDE MY MOUTH!
OM NOM
NOM NOM
MMMM, I'LL BE NICER TO ERSA IF IT MEANS MORE OF THIS.
BE CAREFUL, YOU DON'T KNOW YOUR LIMIT YET.
BNW
LIMIT...?
URGH.
BNW
UGH... I GUESS THERE'S A REASON PEOPLE DON'T EAT CANDY FOR BREAKFAST, LUNCH, AND DINNER...
THEY MIGHT TAKE YOU TO THE VOMITORIUM, THE PLACE WHERE THEY PUMP YOUR STOMACH.
...AH.
BNW

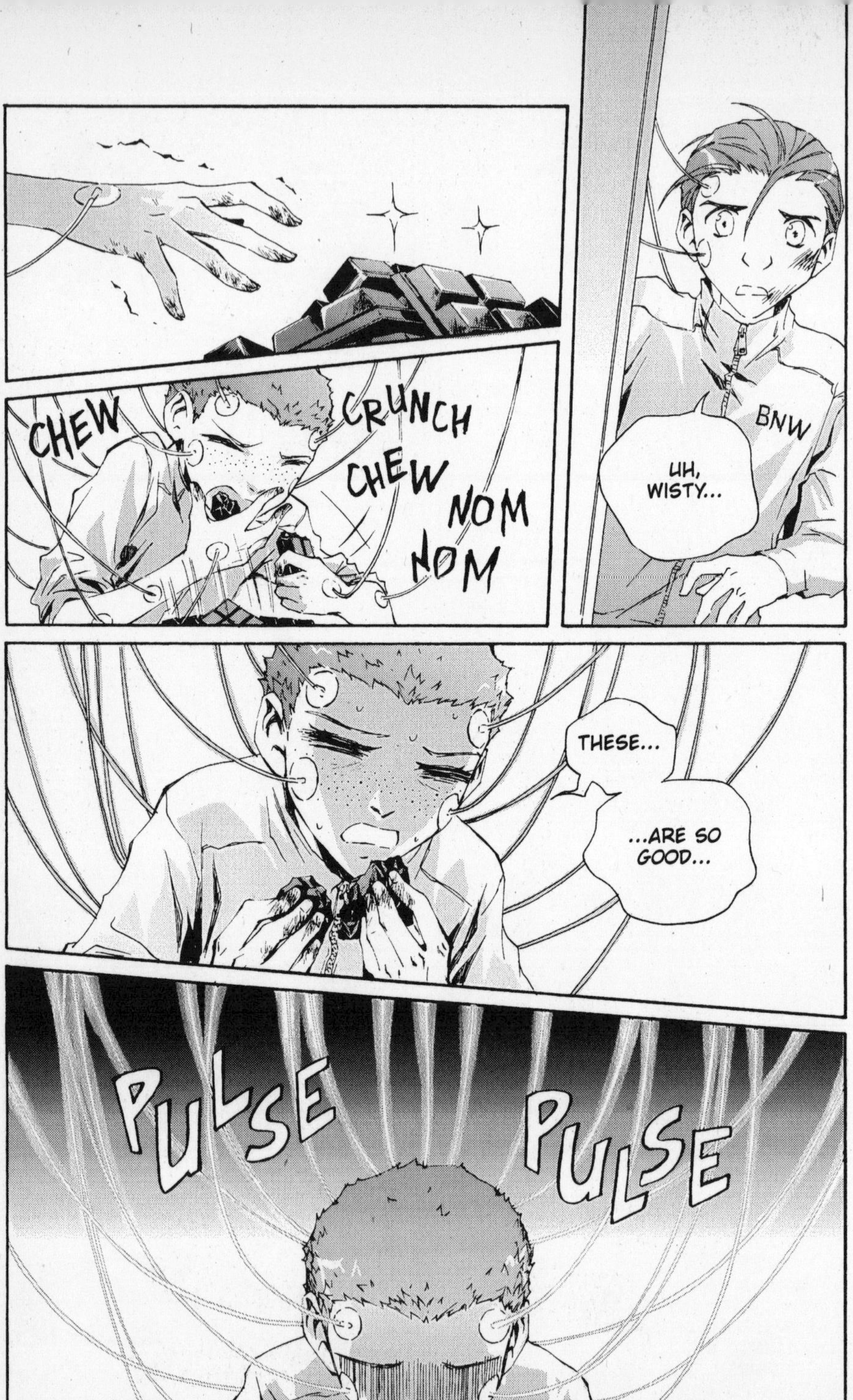

CHEW
CRUNCH
CHEW
NOM
NOM
BNW
UH, WISTY...
THESE...
...ARE SO GOOD...
PULSE
PULSE

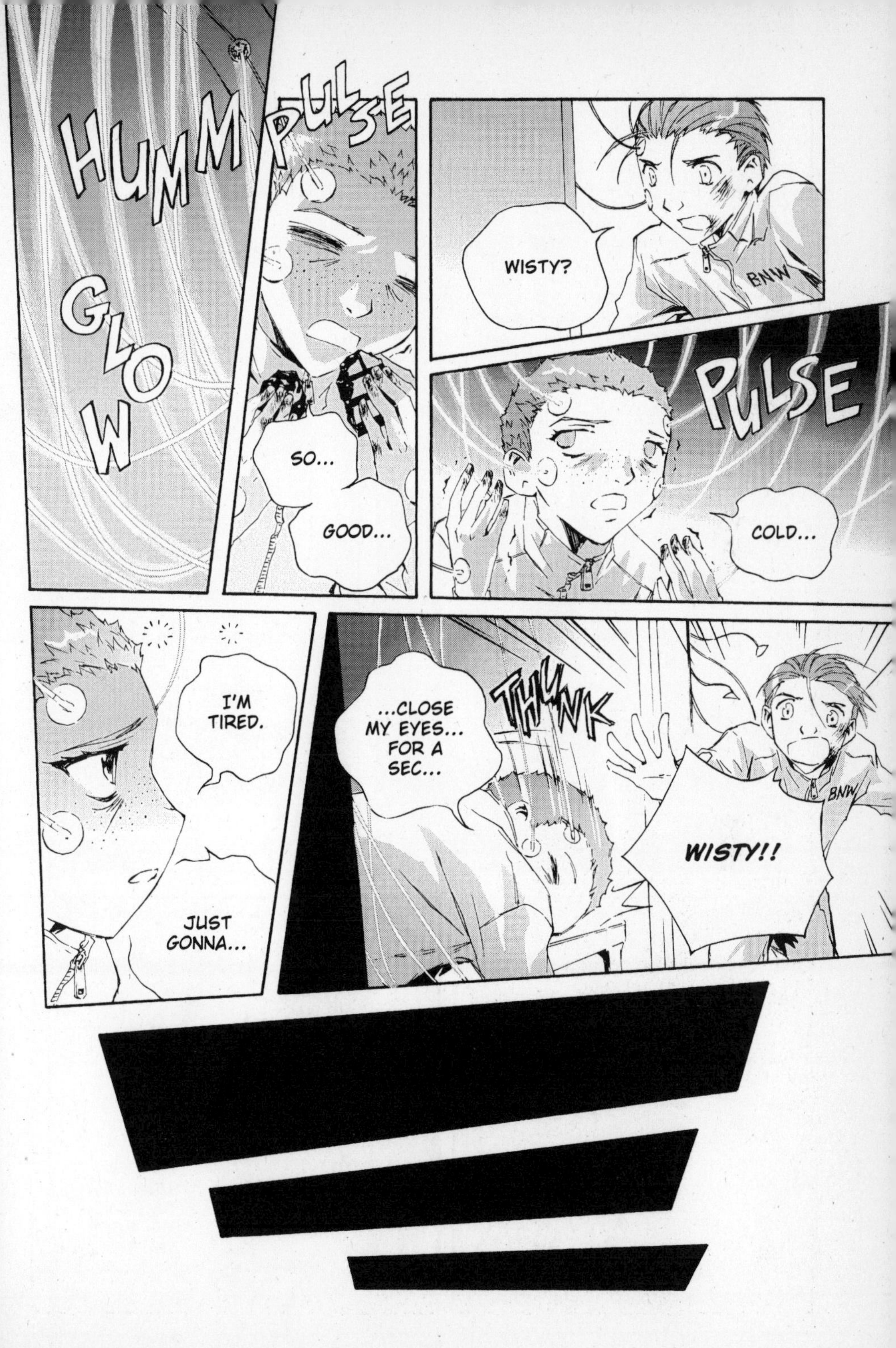
HUMM
GLOW
PULSE
SO...
GOOD...
WISTY?
BNW
PULSE
COLD...
I'M TIRED.
JUST GONNA...
...CLOSE MY EYES... FOR A SEC...
THUNK
BNW
WISTY!!

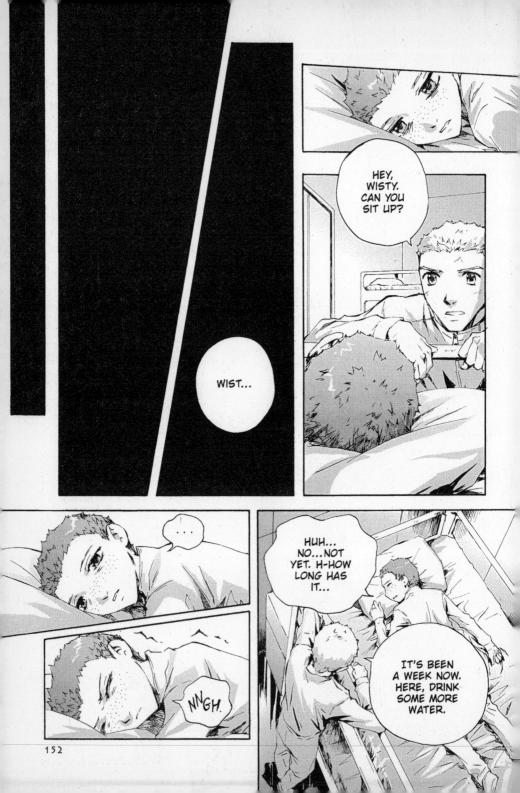

HEY, WISTY. CAN YOU SIT UP?

WIST...

...

NNGH.

HUH... NO...NOT YET. H-HOW LONG HAS IT...

IT'S BEEN A WEEK NOW. HERE, DRINK SOME MORE WATER.

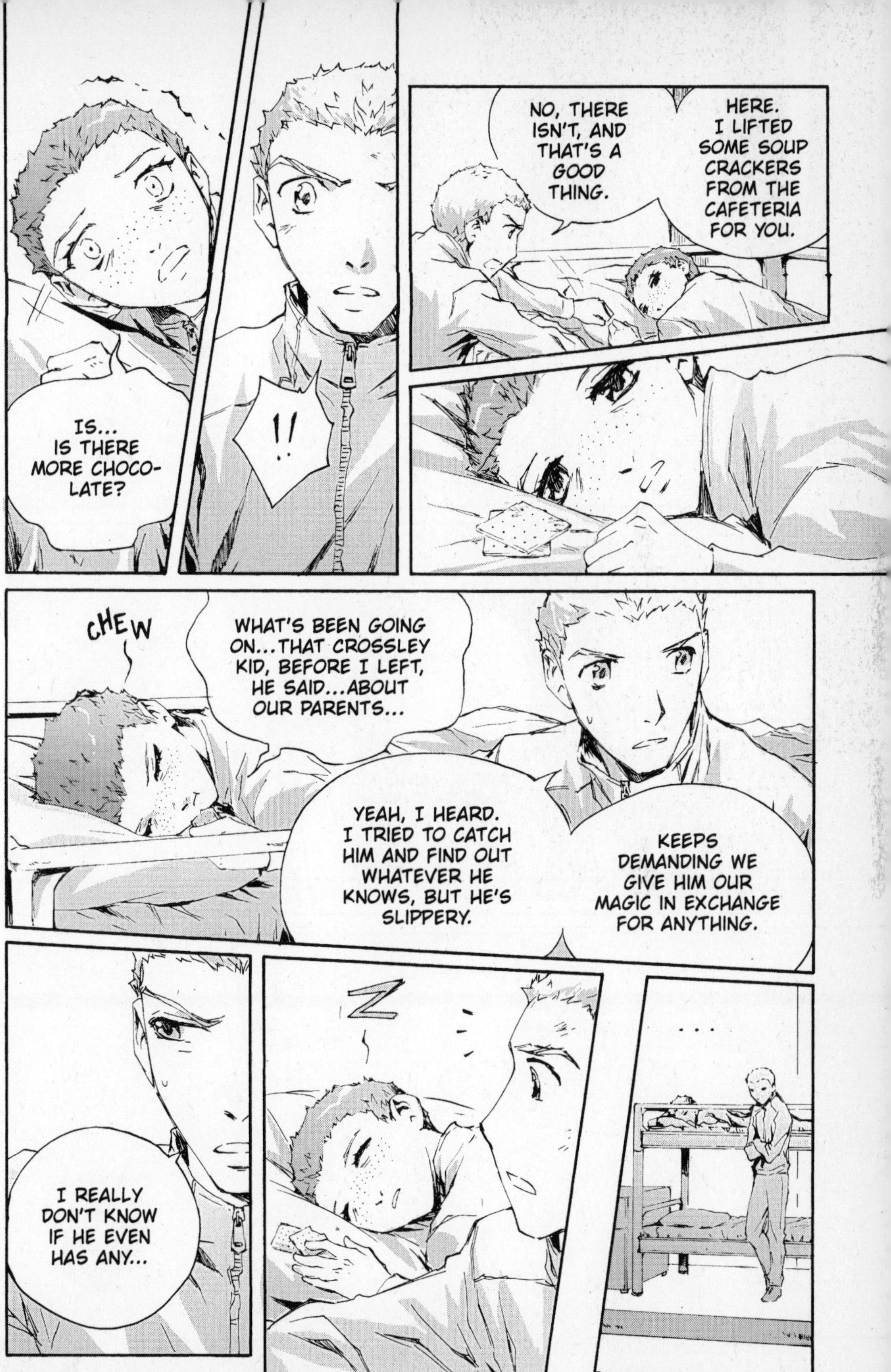
IS... IS THERE MORE CHOCO-LATE?
!!
NO, THERE ISN'T, AND THAT'S A GOOD THING.
HERE. I LIFTED SOME SOUP CRACKERS FROM THE CAFETERIA FOR YOU.
CHEW
WHAT'S BEEN GOING ON...THAT CROSSLEY KID, BEFORE I LEFT, HE SAID...ABOUT OUR PARENTS...
YEAH, I HEARD. I TRIED TO CATCH HIM AND FIND OUT WHATEVER HE KNOWS, BUT HE'S SLIPPERY.
KEEPS DEMANDING WE GIVE HIM OUR MAGIC IN EXCHANGE FOR ANYTHING.
I REALLY DON'T KNOW IF HE EVEN HAS ANY...
Z
...

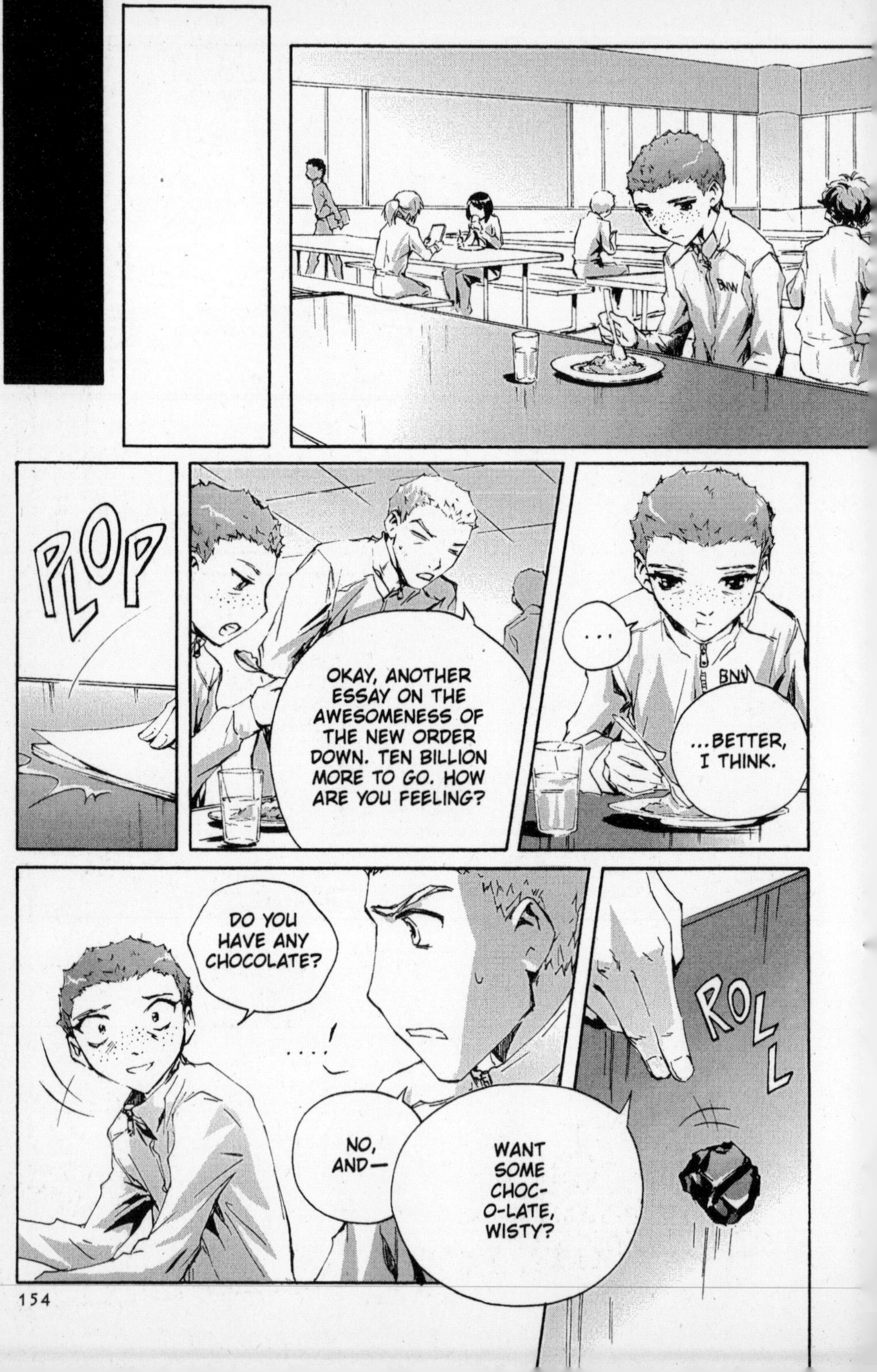
PLOP
OKAY, ANOTHER ESSAY ON THE AWESOMENESS OF THE NEW ORDER DOWN. TEN BILLION MORE TO GO. HOW ARE YOU FEELING?
...
...BETTER, I THINK.
DO YOU HAVE ANY CHOCOLATE?
...!
NO, AND—
WANT SOME CHOC-O-LATE, WISTY?
ROLL

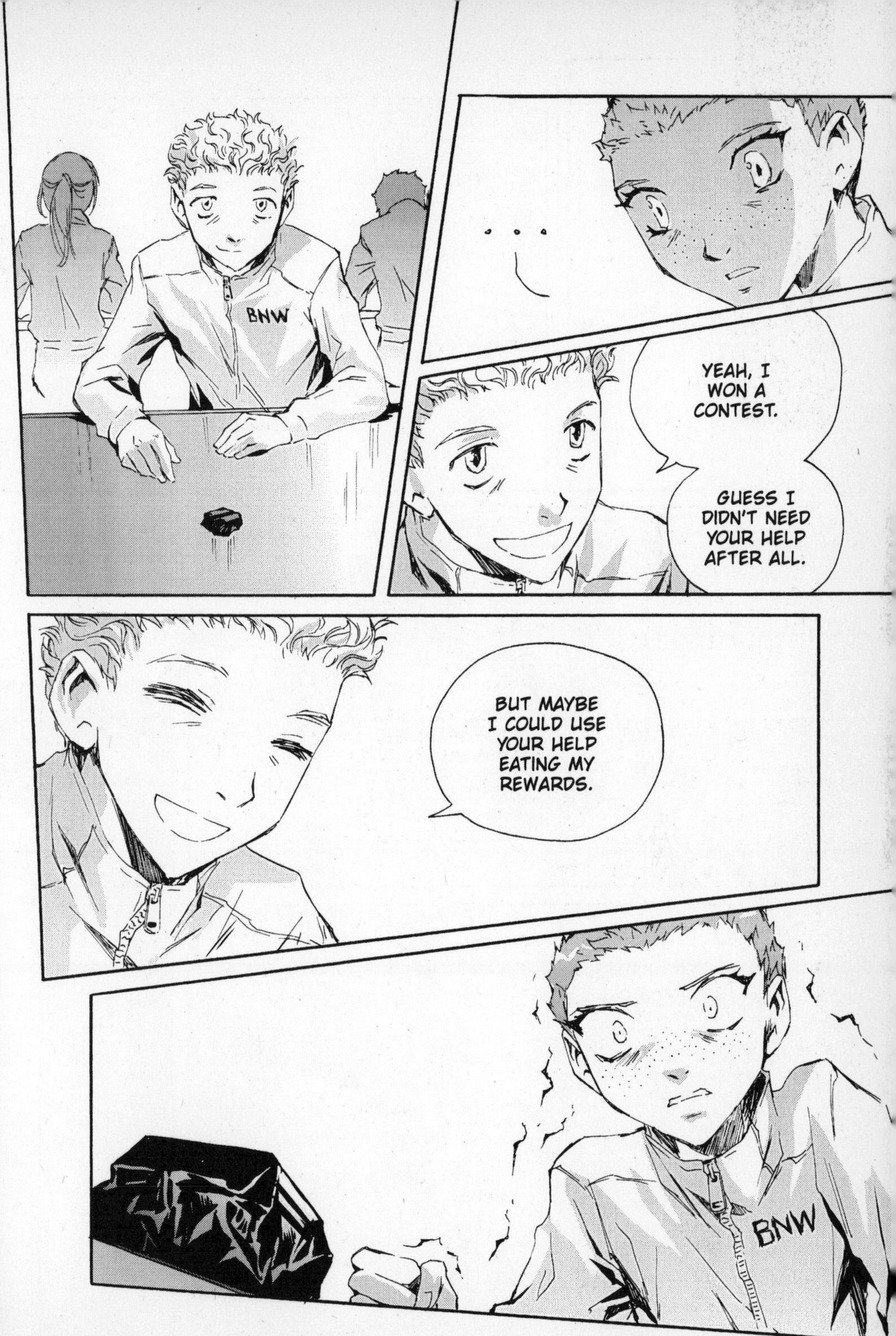
. . .
YEAH, I WON A CONTEST.
GUESS I DIDN'T NEED YOUR HELP AFTER ALL.
BUT MAYBE I COULD USE YOUR HELP EATING MY REWARDS.

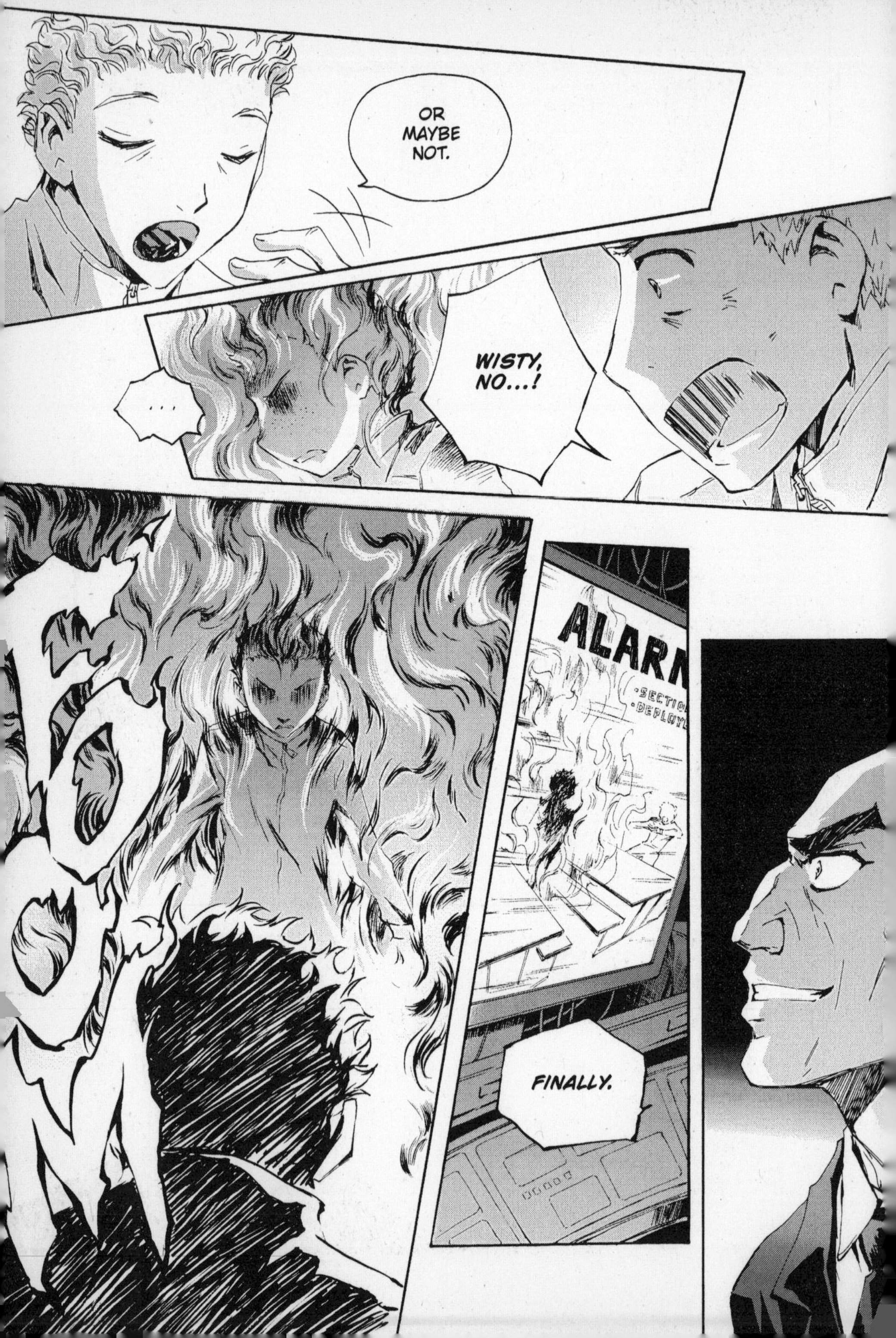
OR MAYBE NOT.
...
WISTY, NO...!
FINALLY.

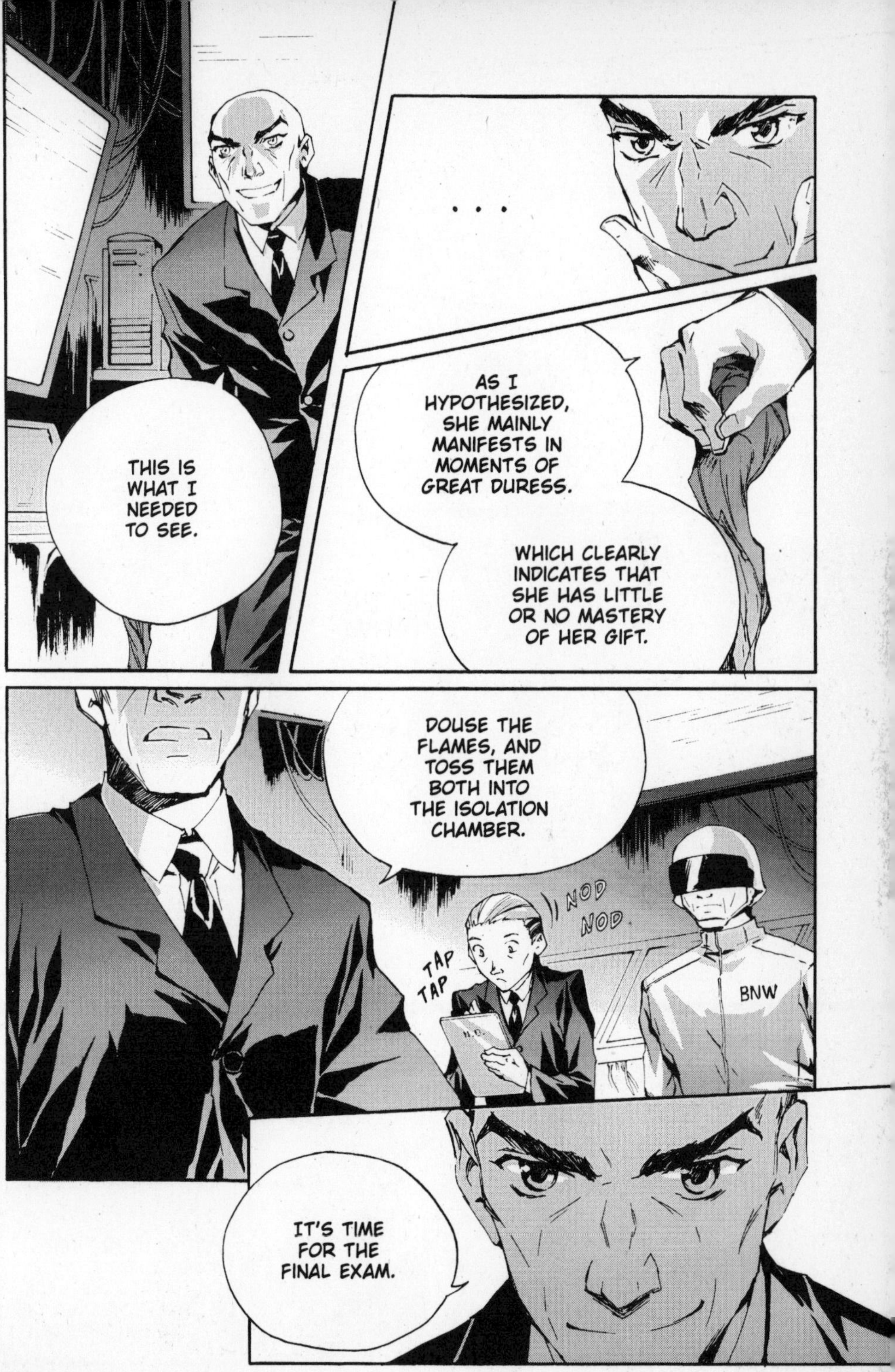

THIS IS WHAT I NEEDED TO SEE.
. . .
AS I HYPOTHESIZED, SHE MAINLY MANIFESTS IN MOMENTS OF GREAT DURESS.
WHICH CLEARLY INDICATES THAT SHE HAS LITTLE OR NO MASTERY OF HER GIFT.
DOUSE THE FLAMES, AND TOSS THEM BOTH INTO THE ISOLATION CHAMBER.
NOD NOD
TAP TAP
BNW
IT'S TIME FOR THE FINAL EXAM.

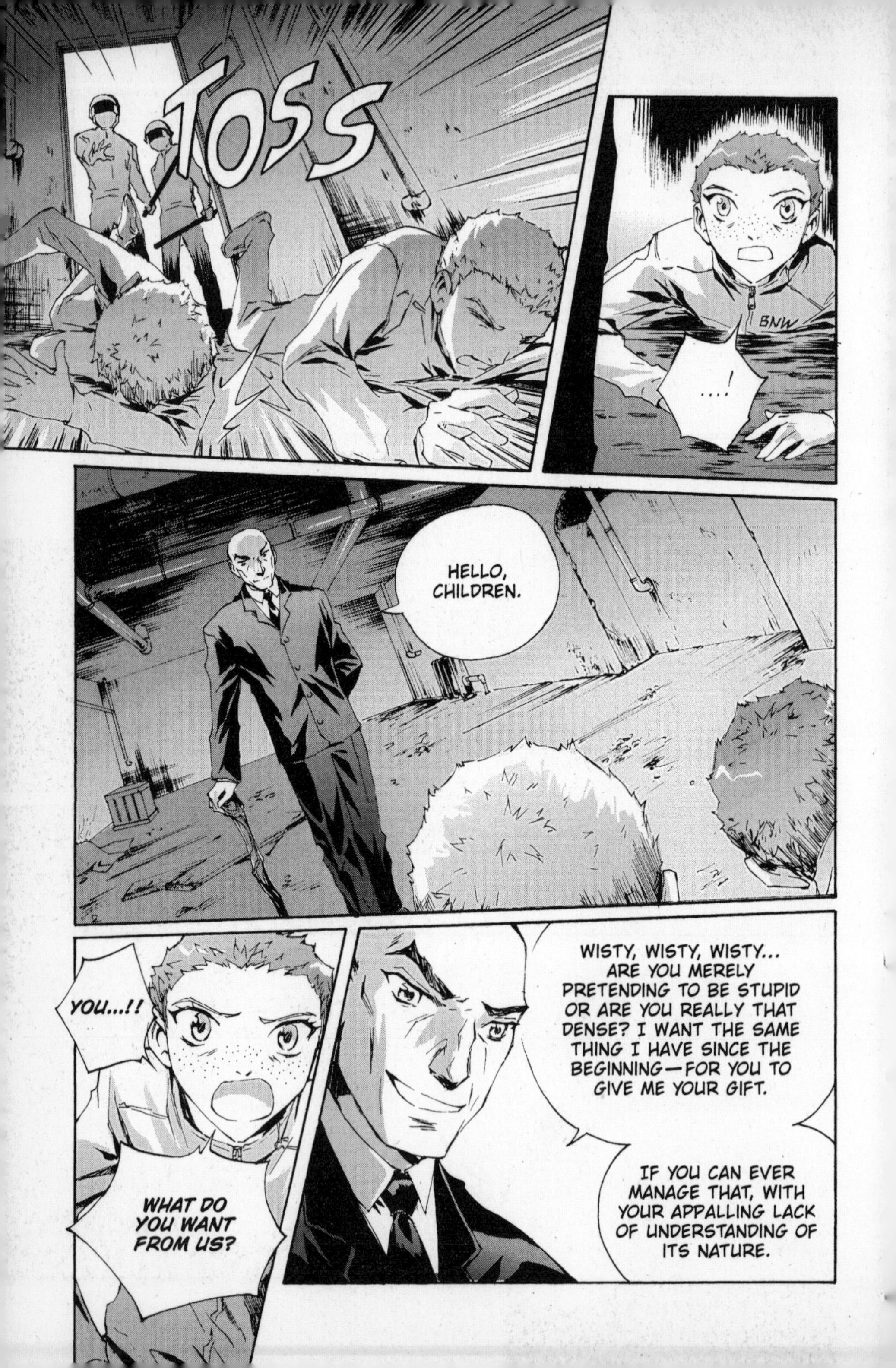
TOSS
BNW
...!
HELLO, CHILDREN.
YOU...!!
WHAT DO YOU WANT FROM US?
WISTY, WISTY, WISTY... ARE YOU MERELY PRETENDING TO BE STUPID OR ARE YOU REALLY THAT DENSE? I WANT THE SAME THING I HAVE SINCE THE BEGINNING—FOR YOU TO GIVE ME YOUR GIFT.
IF YOU CAN EVER MANAGE THAT, WITH YOUR APPALLING LACK OF UNDERSTANDING OF ITS NATURE.

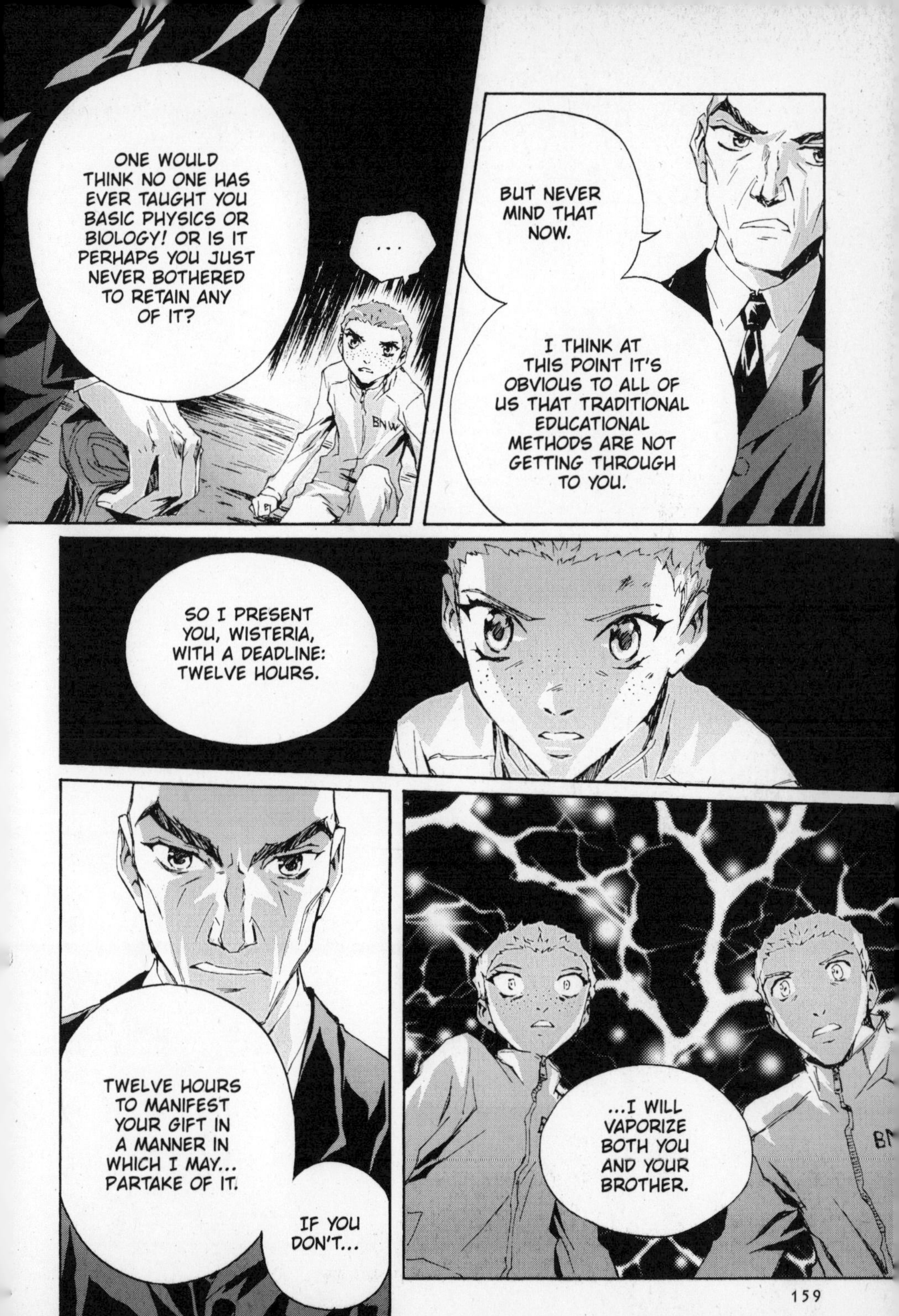
ONE WOULD THINK NO ONE HAS EVER TAUGHT YOU BASIC PHYSICS OR BIOLOGY! OR IS IT PERHAPS YOU JUST NEVER BOTHERED TO RETAIN ANY OF IT?
...
BUT NEVER MIND THAT NOW.
I THINK AT THIS POINT IT'S OBVIOUS TO ALL OF US THAT TRADITIONAL EDUCATIONAL METHODS ARE NOT GETTING THROUGH TO YOU.
SO I PRESENT YOU, WISTERIA, WITH A DEADLINE: TWELVE HOURS.
TWELVE HOURS TO MANIFEST YOUR GIFT IN A MANNER IN WHICH I MAY... PARTAKE OF IT.
IF YOU DON'T...
...I WILL VAPORIZE BOTH YOU AND YOUR BROTHER.

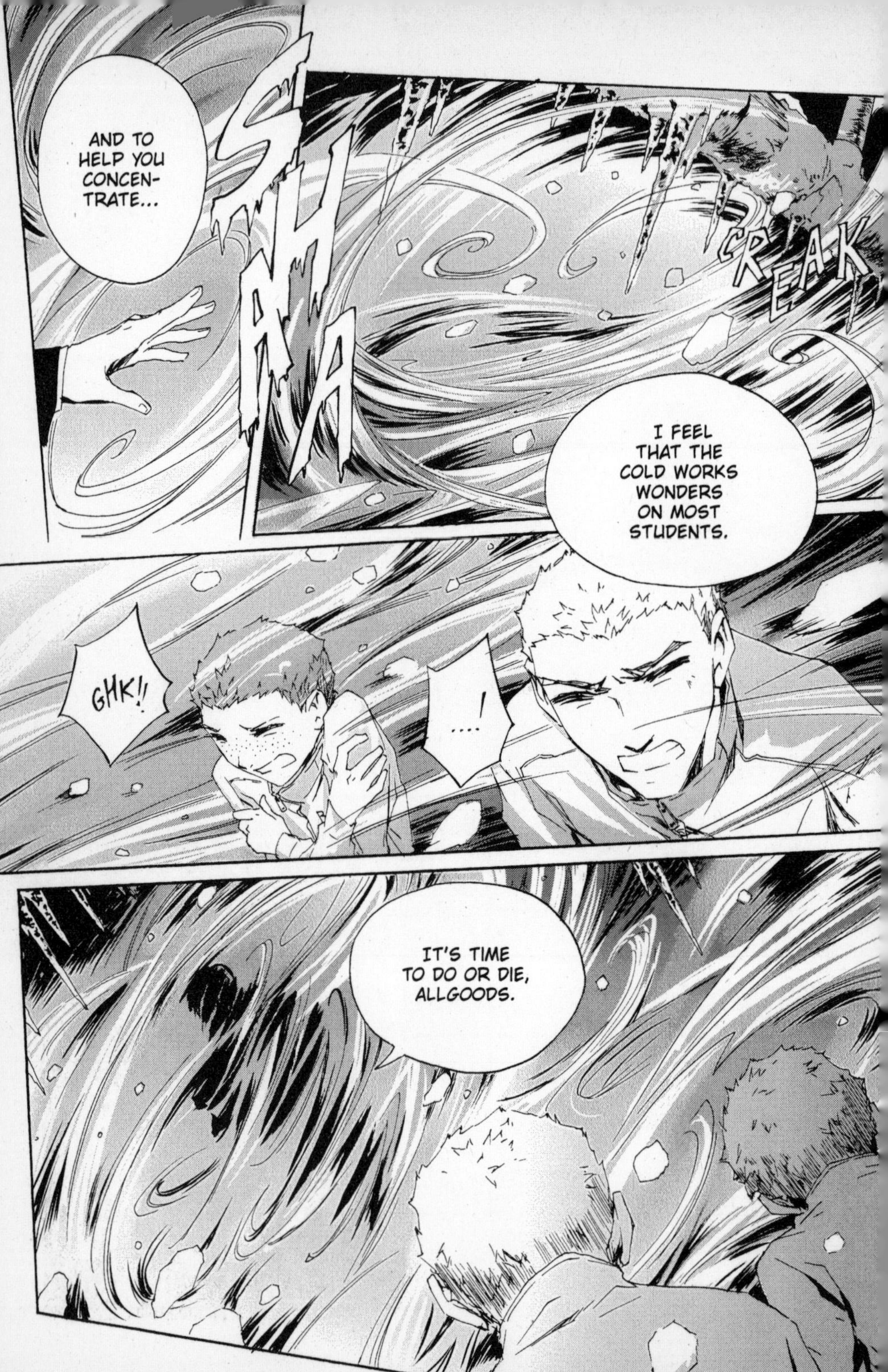
AND TO HELP YOU CONCEN-TRATE...
SHAA
CREAK
I FEEL THAT THE COLD WORKS WONDERS ON MOST STUDENTS.
GHK!!
....!
IT'S TIME TO DO OR DIE, ALLGOODS.

WITCH & WIZARD

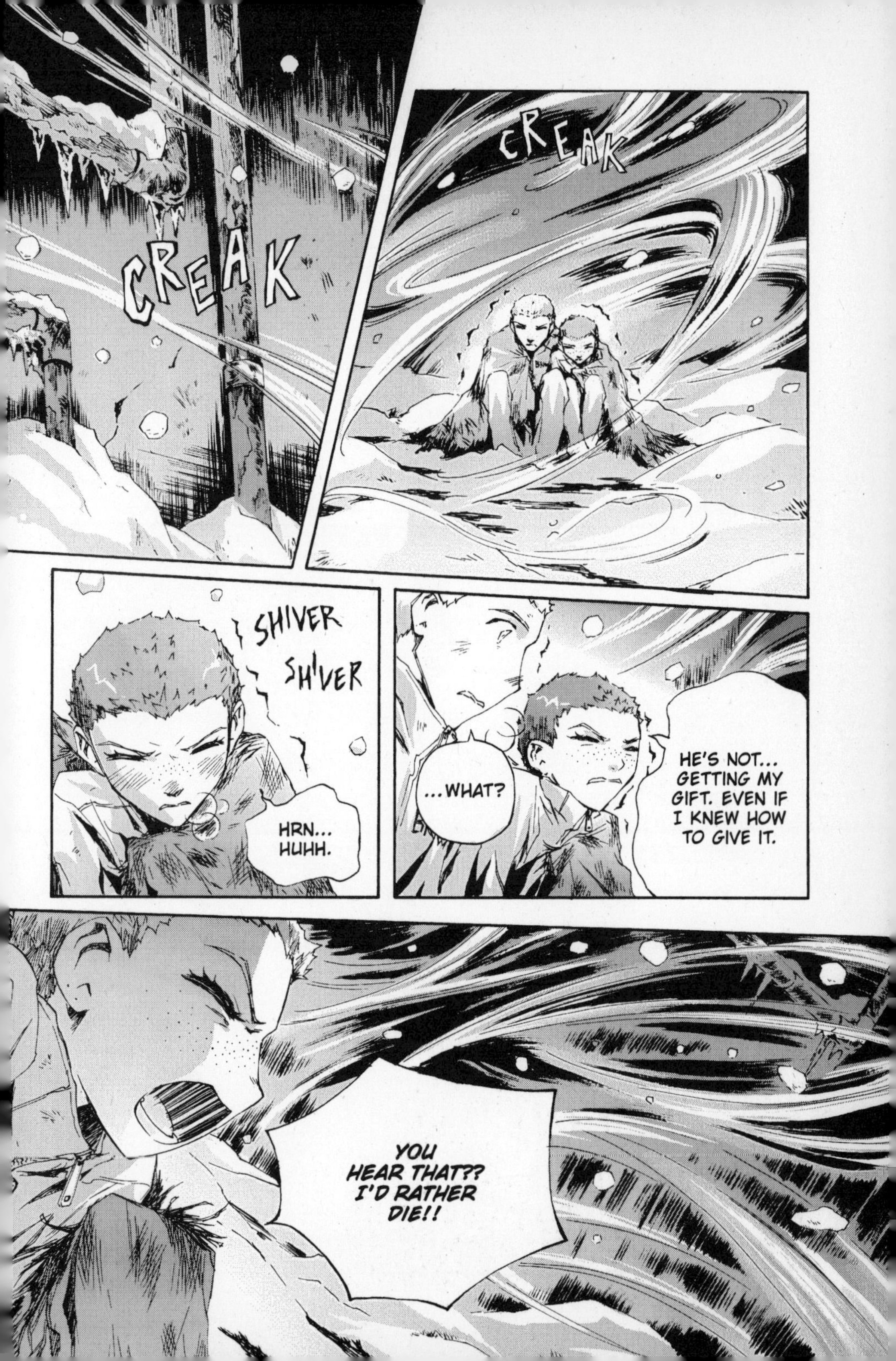
CREAK
CREAK
SHIVER
SHIVER
HRN... HUHH.
...WHAT?
HE'S NOT... GETTING MY GIFT. EVEN IF I KNEW HOW TO GIVE IT.
YOU HEAR THAT?? I'D RATHER DIE!!

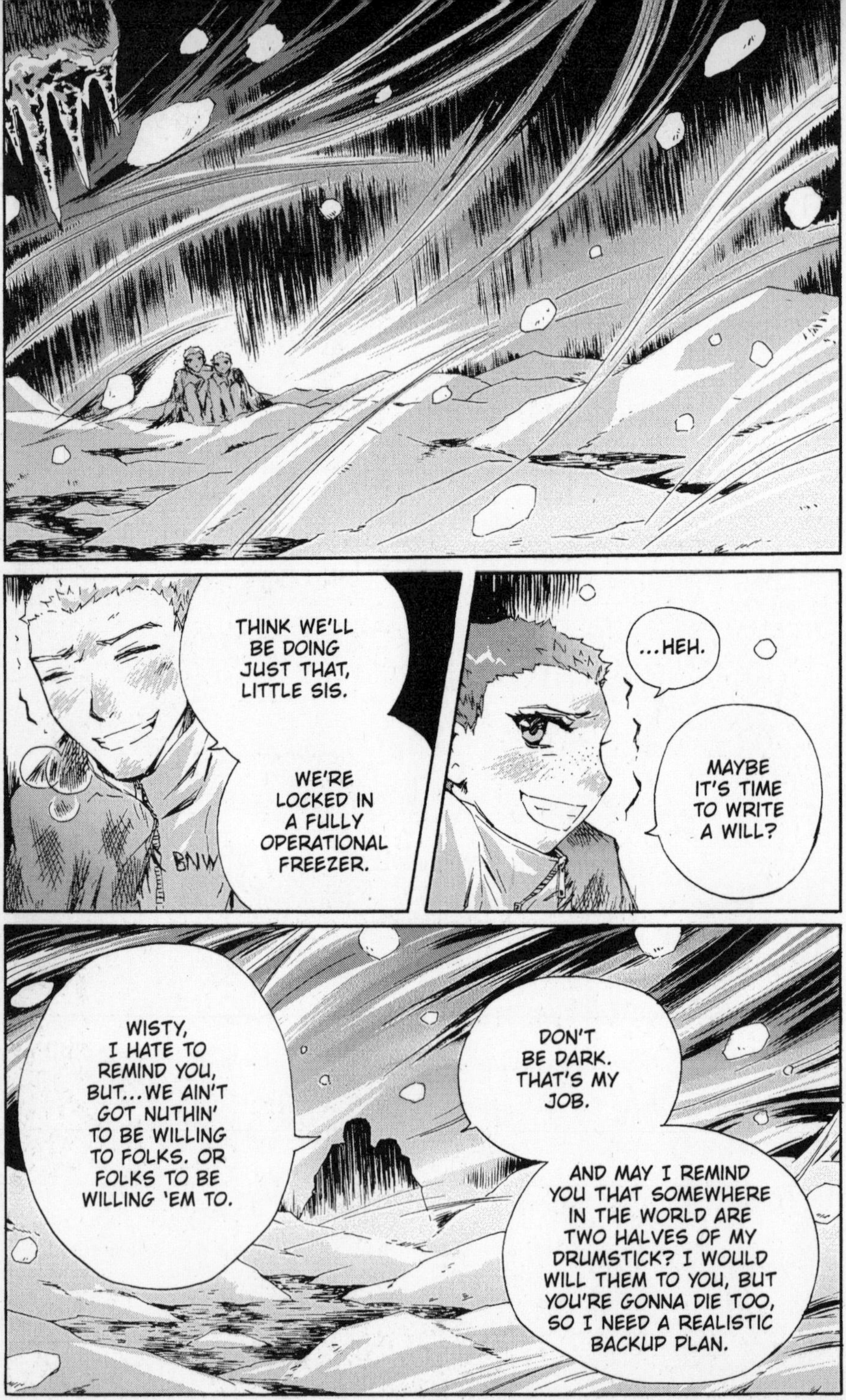
THINK WE'LL BE DOING JUST THAT, LITTLE SIS.
WE'RE LOCKED IN A FULLY OPERATIONAL FREEZER.
BNW
...HEH.
MAYBE IT'S TIME TO WRITE A WILL?
WISTY, I HATE TO REMIND YOU, BUT...WE AIN'T GOT NUTHIN' TO BE WILLING TO FOLKS. OR FOLKS TO BE WILLING 'EM TO.
DON'T BE DARK. THAT'S MY JOB.
AND MAY I REMIND YOU THAT SOMEWHERE IN THE WORLD ARE TWO HALVES OF MY DRUMSTICK? I WOULD WILL THEM TO YOU, BUT YOU'RE GONNA DIE TOO, SO I NEED A REALISTIC BACKUP PLAN.

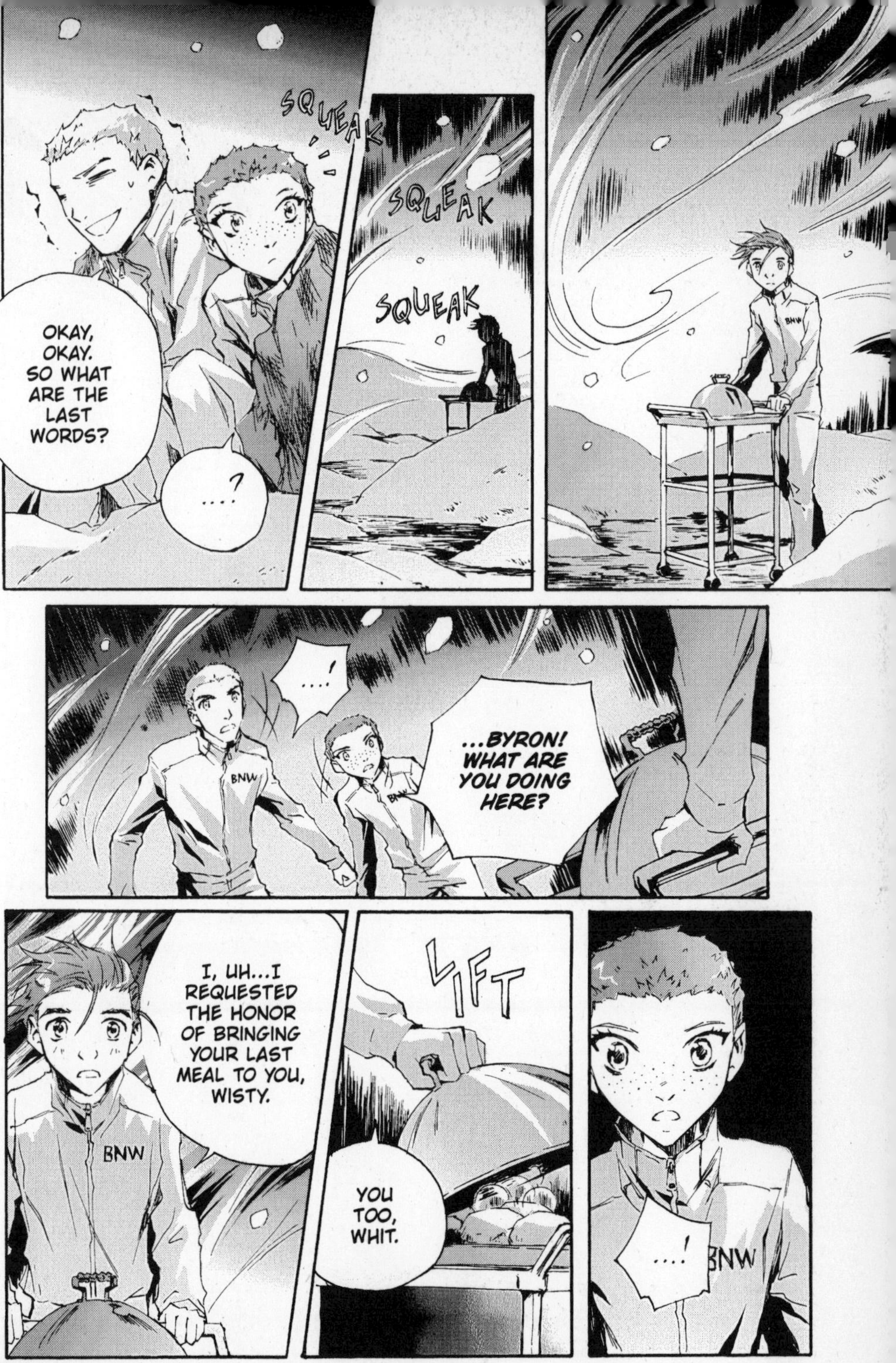
SQUEAK
OKAY, OKAY. SO WHAT ARE THE LAST WORDS?
...?
SQUEAK
SQUEAK
...!
...BYRON! WHAT ARE YOU DOING HERE?
I, UH...I REQUESTED THE HONOR OF BRINGING YOUR LAST MEAL TO YOU, WISTY.
LIFT
YOU TOO, WHIT.
...!

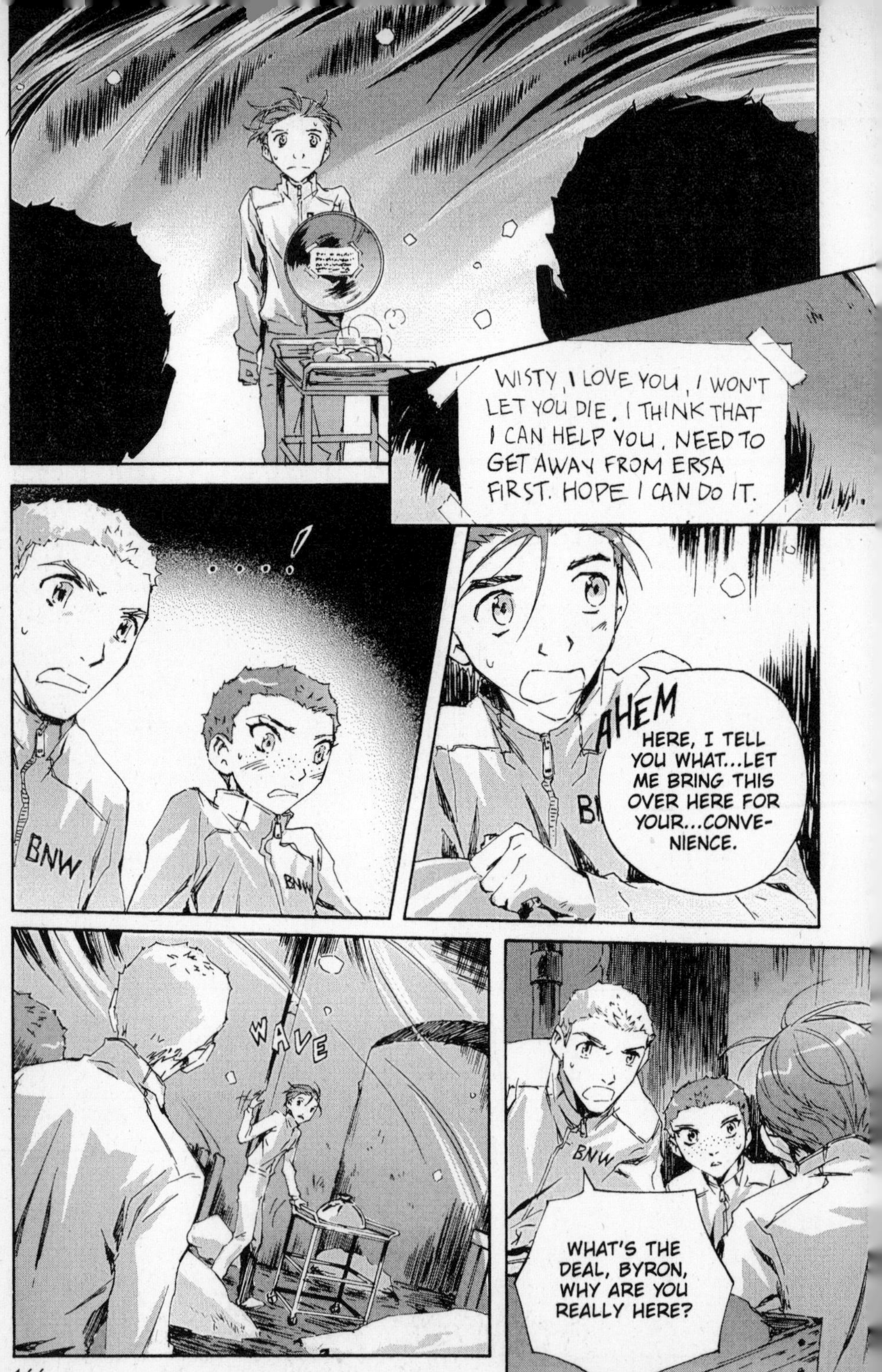
WISTY, I LOVE YOU, I WON'T LET YOU DIE. I THINK THAT I CAN HELP YOU. NEED TO GET AWAY FROM ERSA FIRST. HOPE I CAN DO IT.
BNW
....!
BNW
BNW
AHEM
HERE, I TELL YOU WHAT...LET ME BRING THIS OVER HERE FOR YOUR...CONVE-NIENCE.
WAVE
BNW
WHAT'S THE DEAL, BYRON, WHY ARE YOU REALLY HERE?

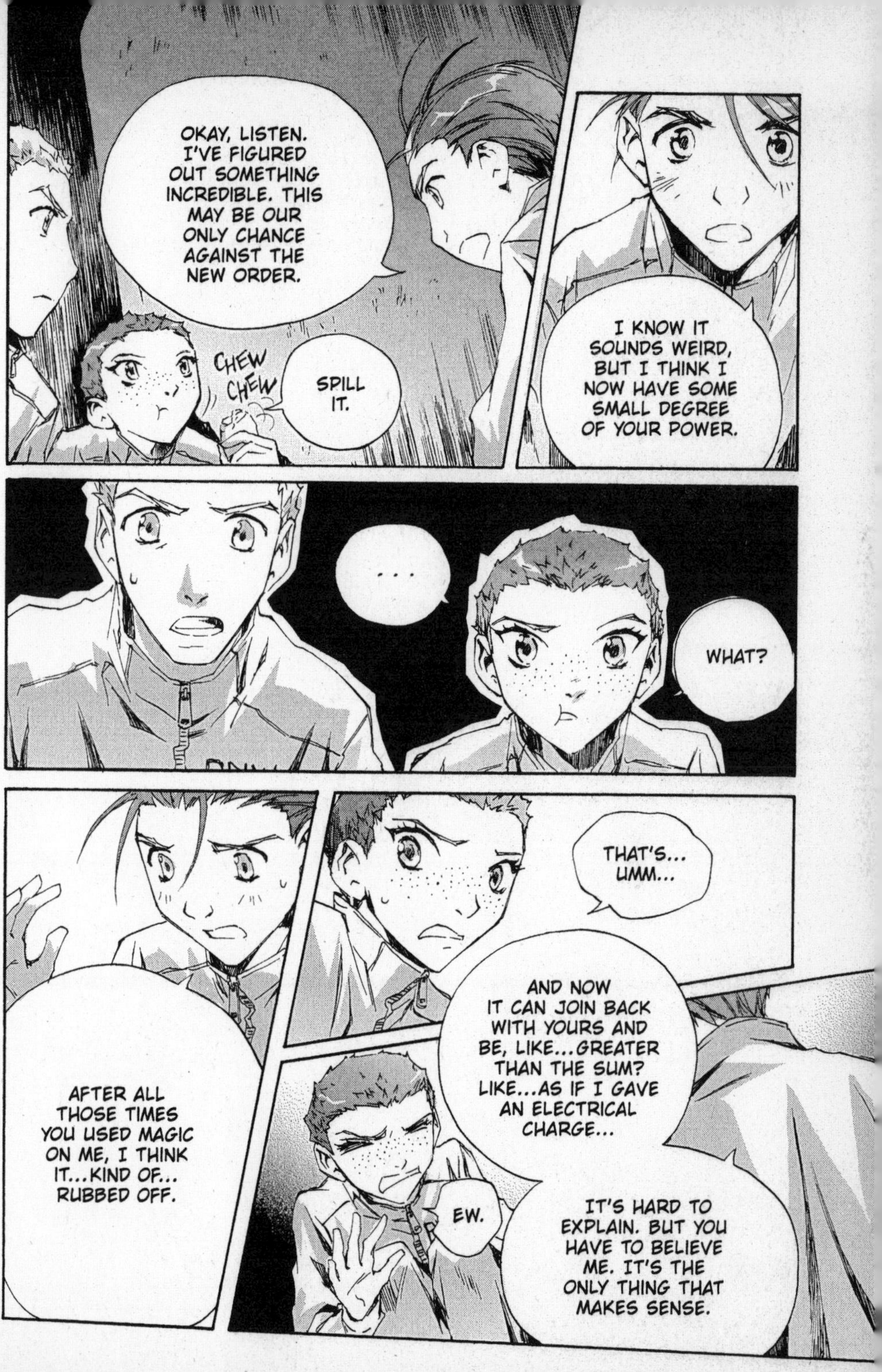
OKAY, LISTEN. I'VE FIGURED OUT SOMETHING INCREDIBLE. THIS MAY BE OUR ONLY CHANCE AGAINST THE NEW ORDER.
CHEW CHEW
SPILL IT.
I KNOW IT SOUNDS WEIRD, BUT I THINK I NOW HAVE SOME SMALL DEGREE OF YOUR POWER.
...
WHAT?
AFTER ALL THOSE TIMES YOU USED MAGIC ON ME, I THINK IT...KIND OF... RUBBED OFF.
THAT'S... UMM...
AND NOW IT CAN JOIN BACK WITH YOURS AND BE, LIKE...GREATER THAN THE SUM? LIKE...AS IF I GAVE AN ELECTRICAL CHARGE...
EW.
IT'S HARD TO EXPLAIN. BUT YOU HAVE TO BELIEVE ME. IT'S THE ONLY THING THAT MAKES SENSE.

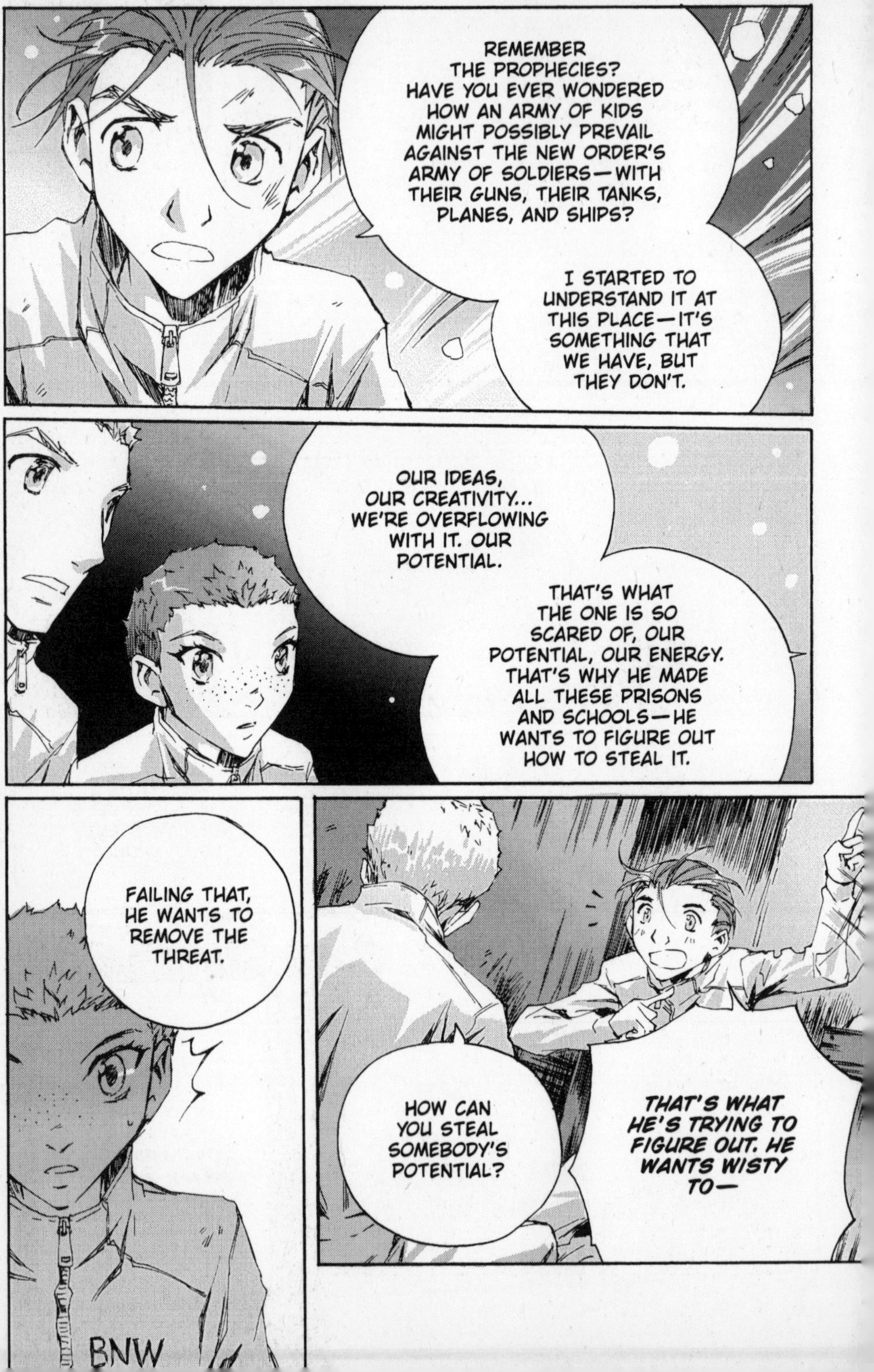
REMEMBER THE PROPHECIES? HAVE YOU EVER WONDERED HOW AN ARMY OF KIDS MIGHT POSSIBLY PREVAIL AGAINST THE NEW ORDER'S ARMY OF SOLDIERS—WITH THEIR GUNS, THEIR TANKS, PLANES, AND SHIPS?
I STARTED TO UNDERSTAND IT AT THIS PLACE—IT'S SOMETHING THAT WE HAVE, BUT THEY DON'T.
OUR IDEAS, OUR CREATIVITY... WE'RE OVERFLOWING WITH IT. OUR POTENTIAL.
THAT'S WHAT THE ONE IS SO SCARED OF, OUR POTENTIAL, OUR ENERGY. THAT'S WHY HE MADE ALL THESE PRISONS AND SCHOOLS—HE WANTS TO FIGURE OUT HOW TO STEAL IT.
FAILING THAT, HE WANTS TO REMOVE THE THREAT.
BNW
HOW CAN YOU STEAL SOMEBODY'S POTENTIAL?
THAT'S WHAT HE'S TRYING TO FIGURE OUT. HE WANTS WISTY TO—

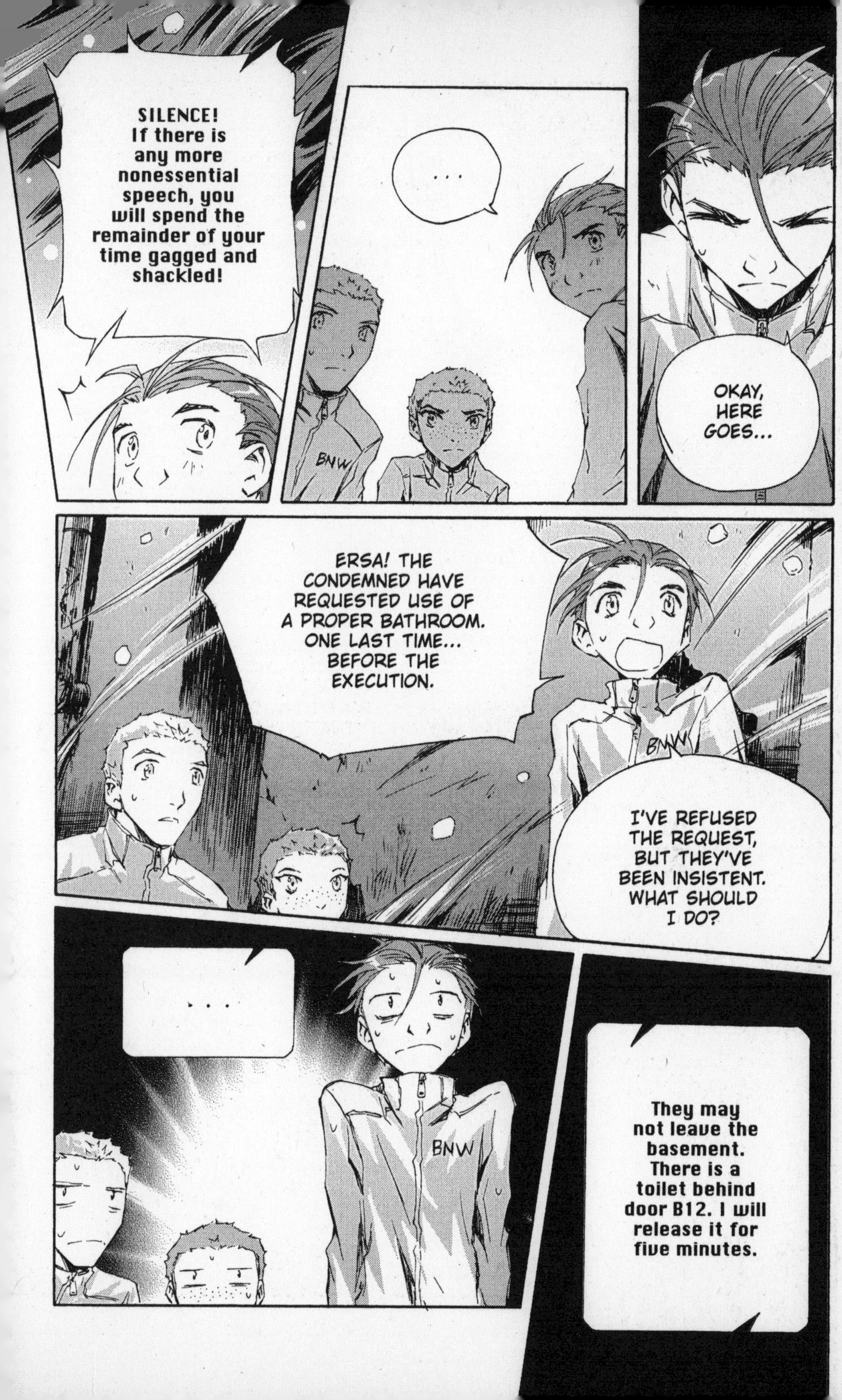
SILENCE! If there is any more nonessential speech, you will spend the remainder of your time gagged and shackled!
...
OKAY, HERE GOES...
BNW
ERSA! THE CONDEMNED HAVE REQUESTED USE OF A PROPER BATHROOM. ONE LAST TIME... BEFORE THE EXECUTION.
BNW
I'VE REFUSED THE REQUEST, BUT THEY'VE BEEN INSISTENT. WHAT SHOULD I DO?
...
BNW
They may not leave the basement. There is a toilet behind door B12. I will release it for five minutes.

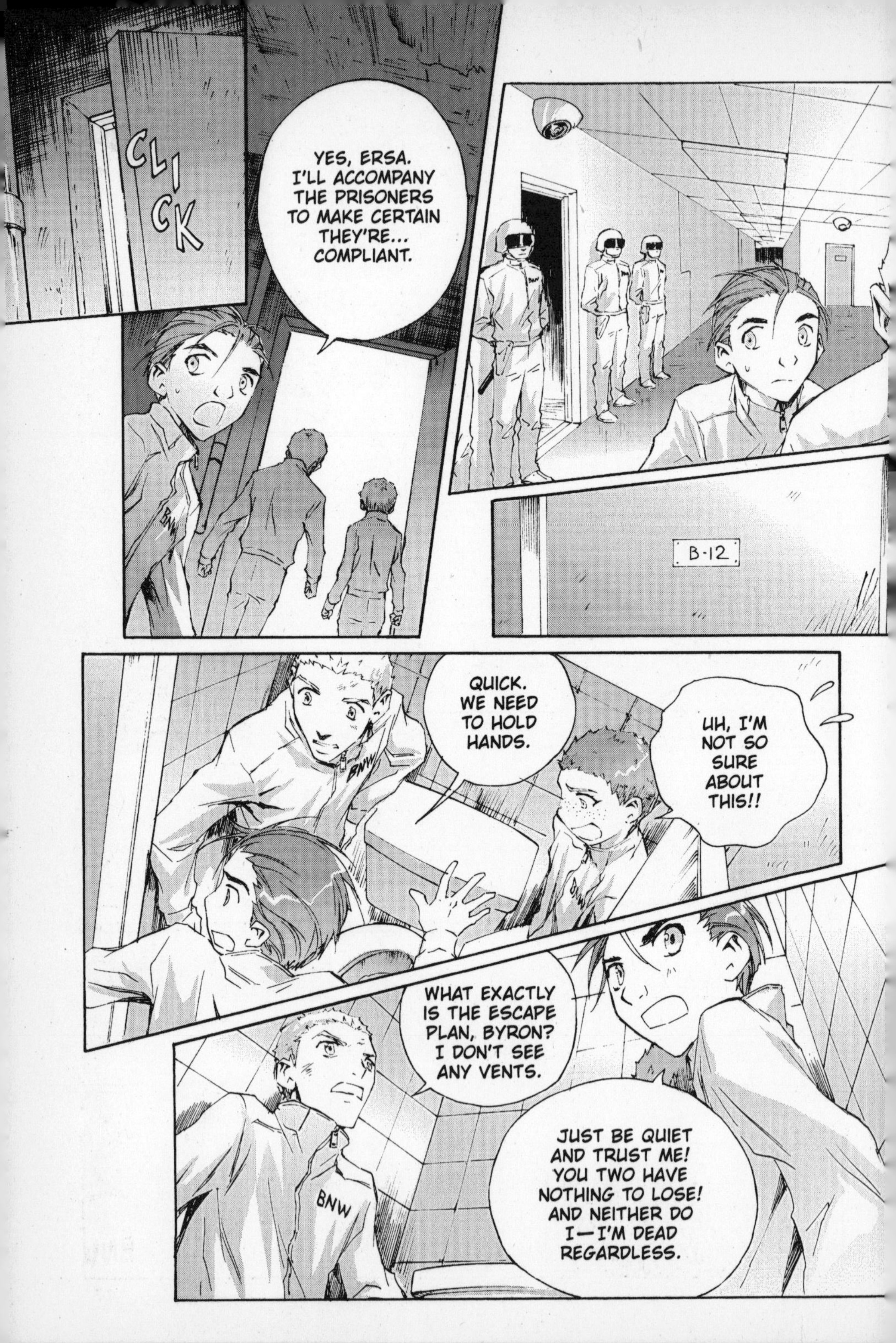
CLICK
YES, ERSA. I'LL ACCOMPANY THE PRISONERS TO MAKE CERTAIN THEY'RE... COMPLIANT.
B-12
QUICK. WE NEED TO HOLD HANDS.
UH, I'M NOT SO SURE ABOUT THIS!!
WHAT EXACTLY IS THE ESCAPE PLAN, BYRON? I DON'T SEE ANY VENTS.
JUST BE QUIET AND TRUST ME! YOU TWO HAVE NOTHING TO LOSE! AND NEITHER DO I—I'M DEAD REGARDLESS.

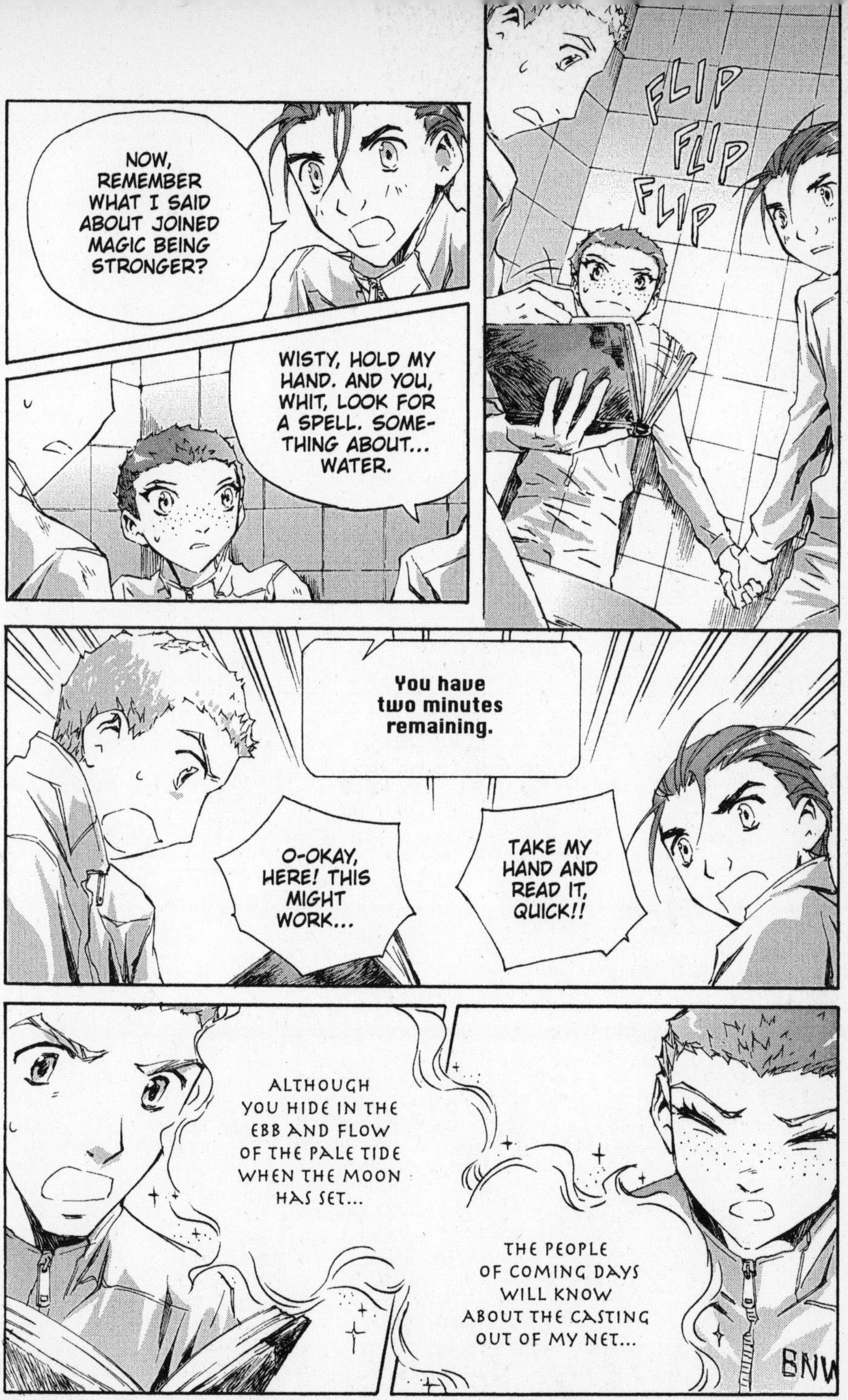
NOW, REMEMBER WHAT I SAID ABOUT JOINED MAGIC BEING STRONGER?
WISTY, HOLD MY HAND. AND YOU, WHIT, LOOK FOR A SPELL. SOMETHING ABOUT... WATER.
FLIP FLIP FLIP
You have two minutes remaining.
O-OKAY, HERE! THIS MIGHT WORK...
TAKE MY HAND AND READ IT, QUICK!!
ALTHOUGH YOU HIDE IN THE EBB AND FLOW OF THE PALE TIDE WHEN THE MOON HAS SET...
THE PEOPLE OF COMING DAYS WILL KNOW ABOUT THE CASTING OUT OF MY NET...
BNW

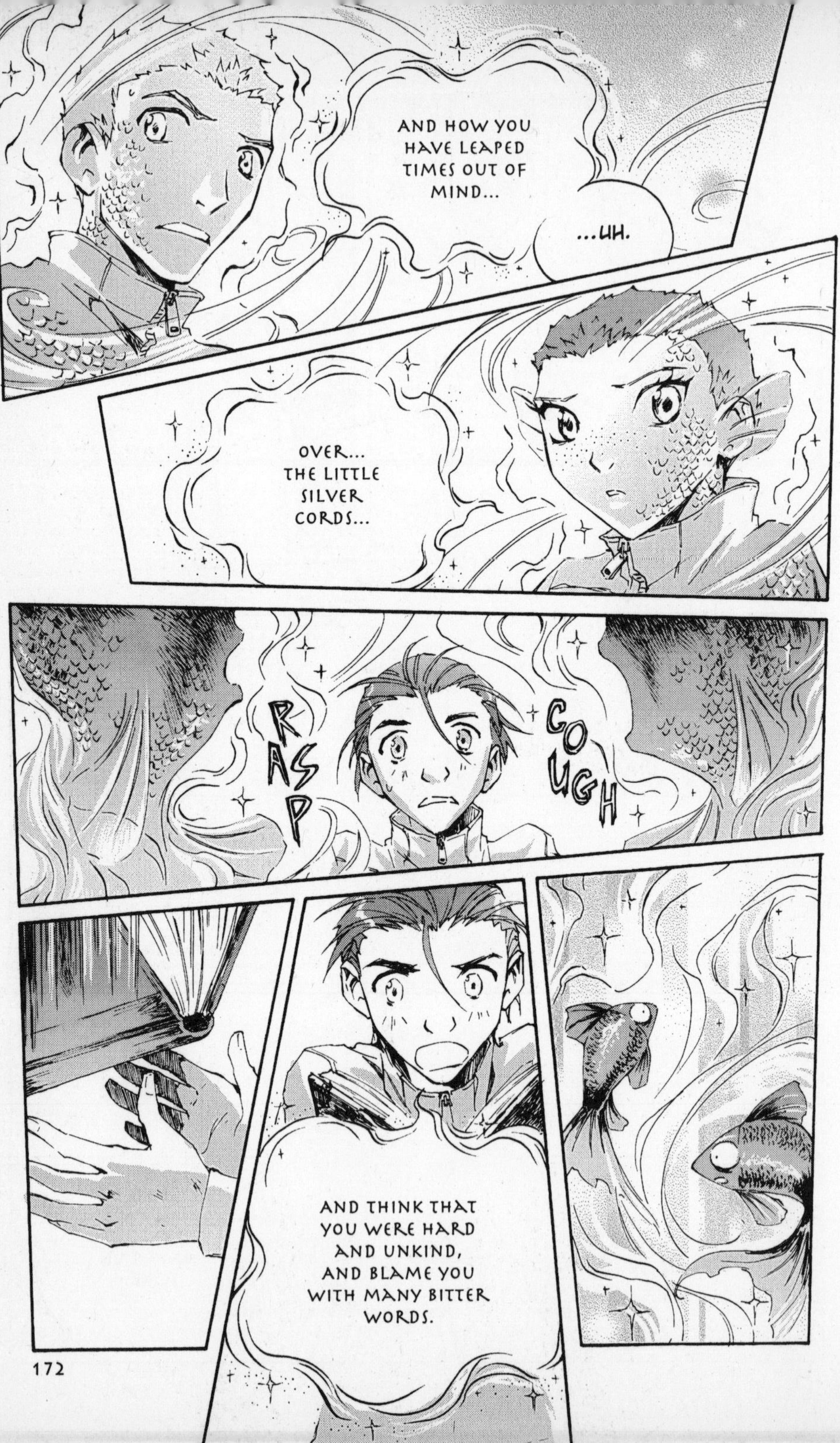
AND HOW YOU HAVE LEAPED TIMES OUT OF MIND...
...UH.
OVER... THE LITTLE SILVER CORDS...
RASP
COUGH
AND THINK THAT YOU WERE HARD AND UNKIND, AND BLAME YOU WITH MANY BITTER WORDS.

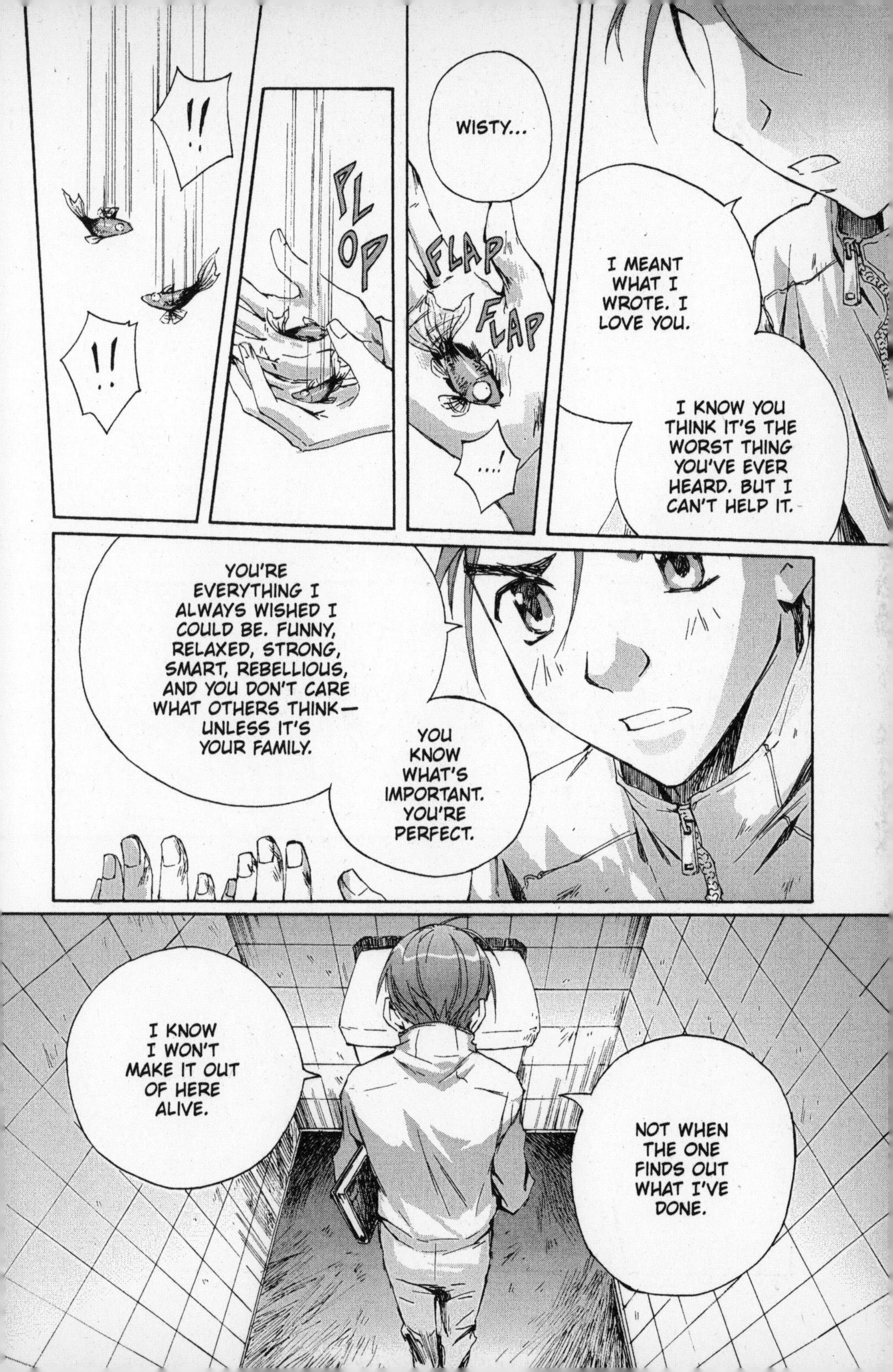
!!
!!
PLOP
WISTY...
FLAP FLAP
...!
I MEANT WHAT I WROTE. I LOVE YOU.
I KNOW YOU THINK IT'S THE WORST THING YOU'VE EVER HEARD. BUT I CAN'T HELP IT.
YOU'RE EVERYTHING I ALWAYS WISHED I COULD BE. FUNNY, RELAXED, STRONG, SMART, REBELLIOUS, AND YOU DON'T CARE WHAT OTHERS THINK—UNLESS IT'S YOUR FAMILY.
YOU KNOW WHAT'S IMPORTANT. YOU'RE PERFECT.
I KNOW I WON'T MAKE IT OUT OF HERE ALIVE.
NOT WHEN THE ONE FINDS OUT WHAT I'VE DONE.

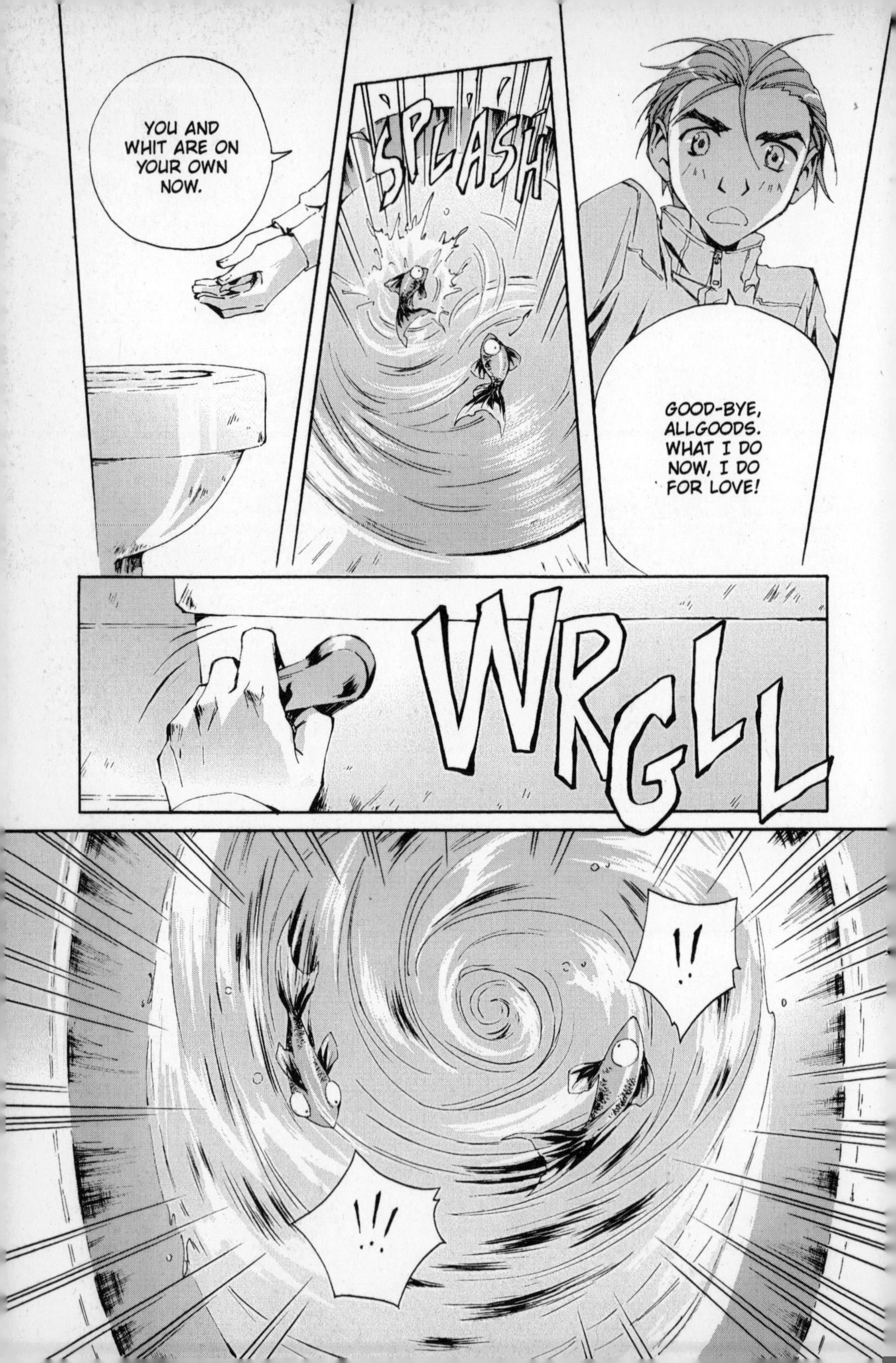
YOU AND WHIT ARE ON YOUR OWN NOW.
SPLASH
GOOD-BYE, ALLGOODS. WHAT I DO NOW, I DO FOR LOVE!
WRGLL
!!
!!!

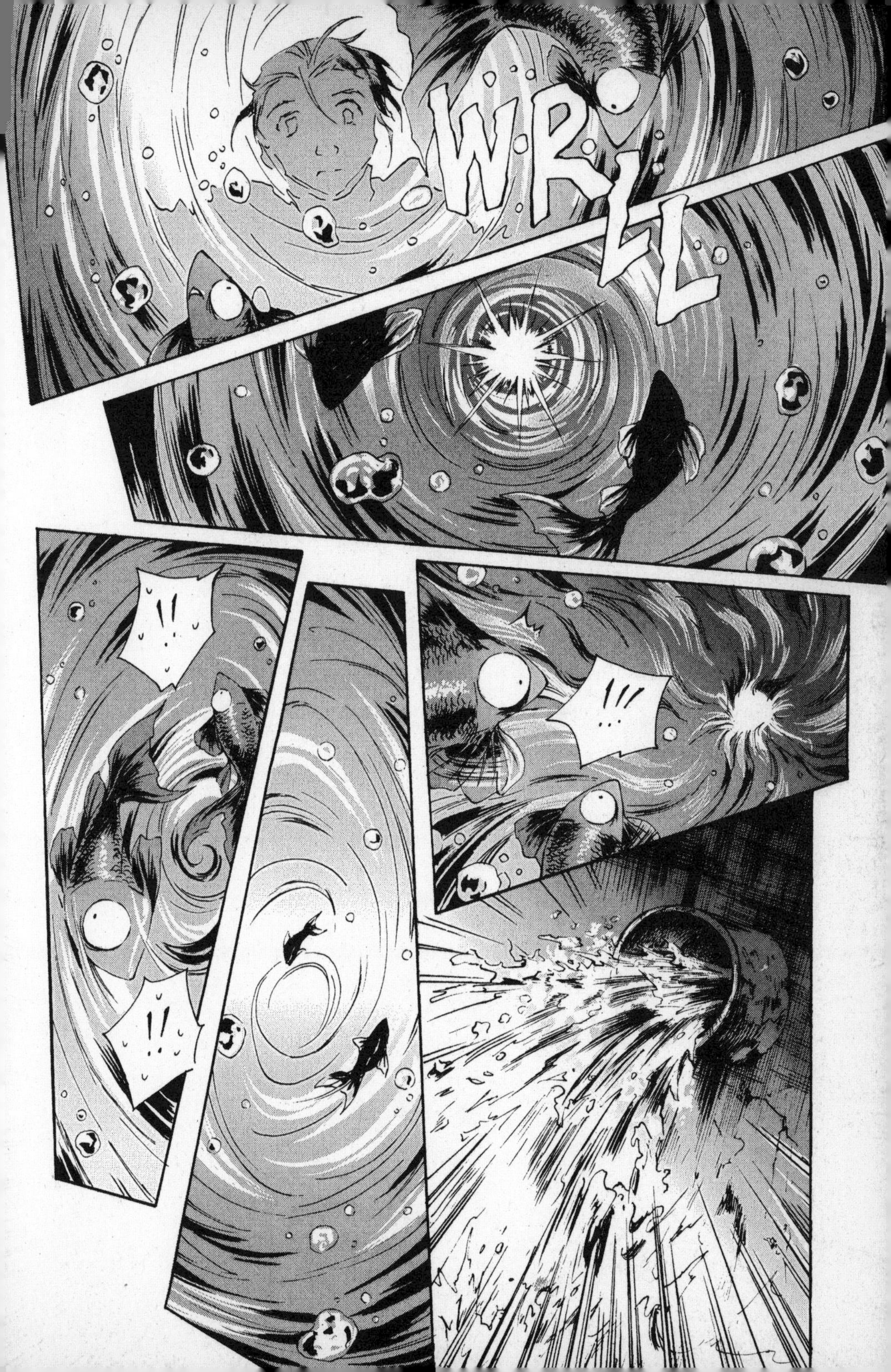
WRILL
!!
!!
!!!

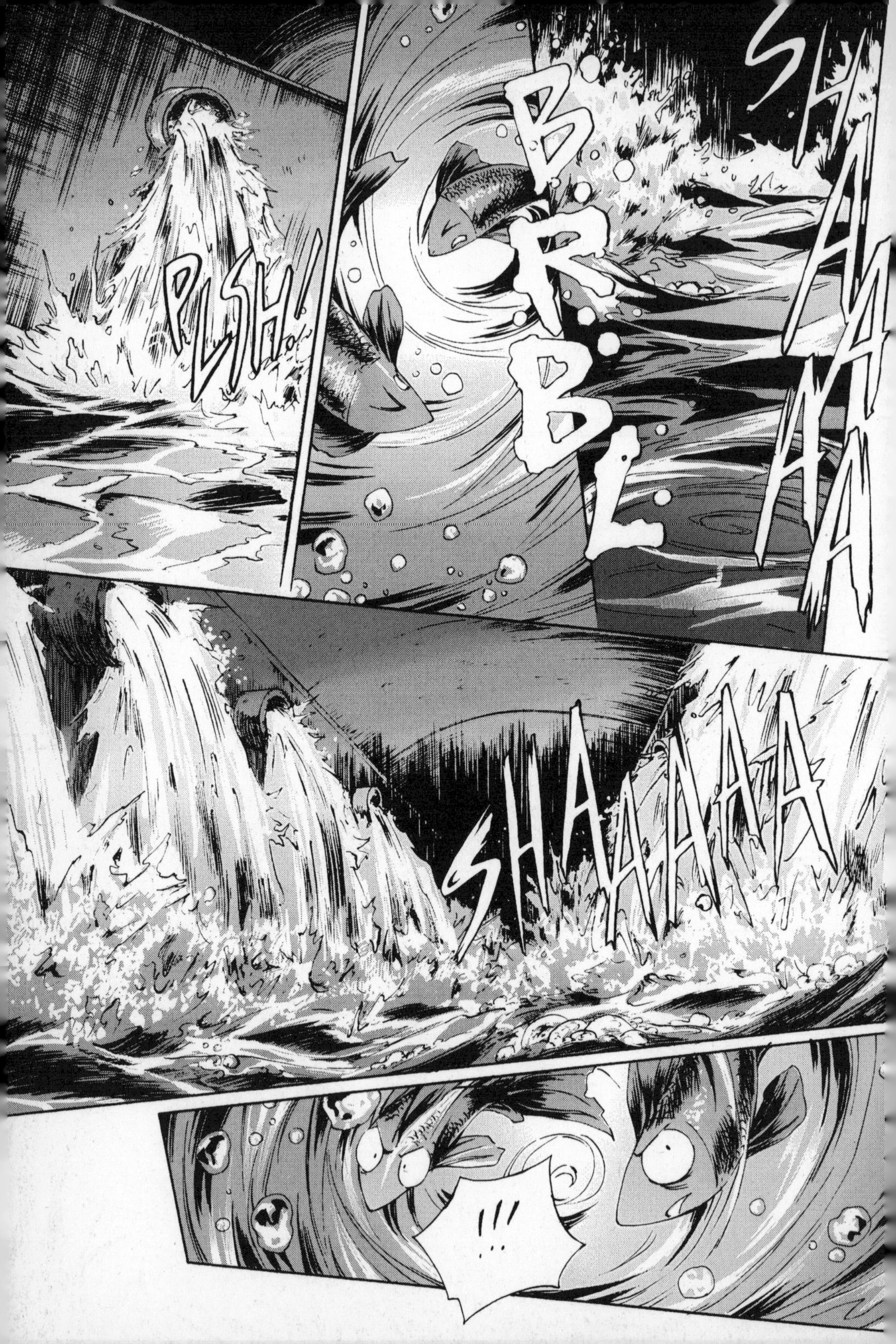
SHAAAAA
BRBBL
PLSH!
SHAAAAA
!!!

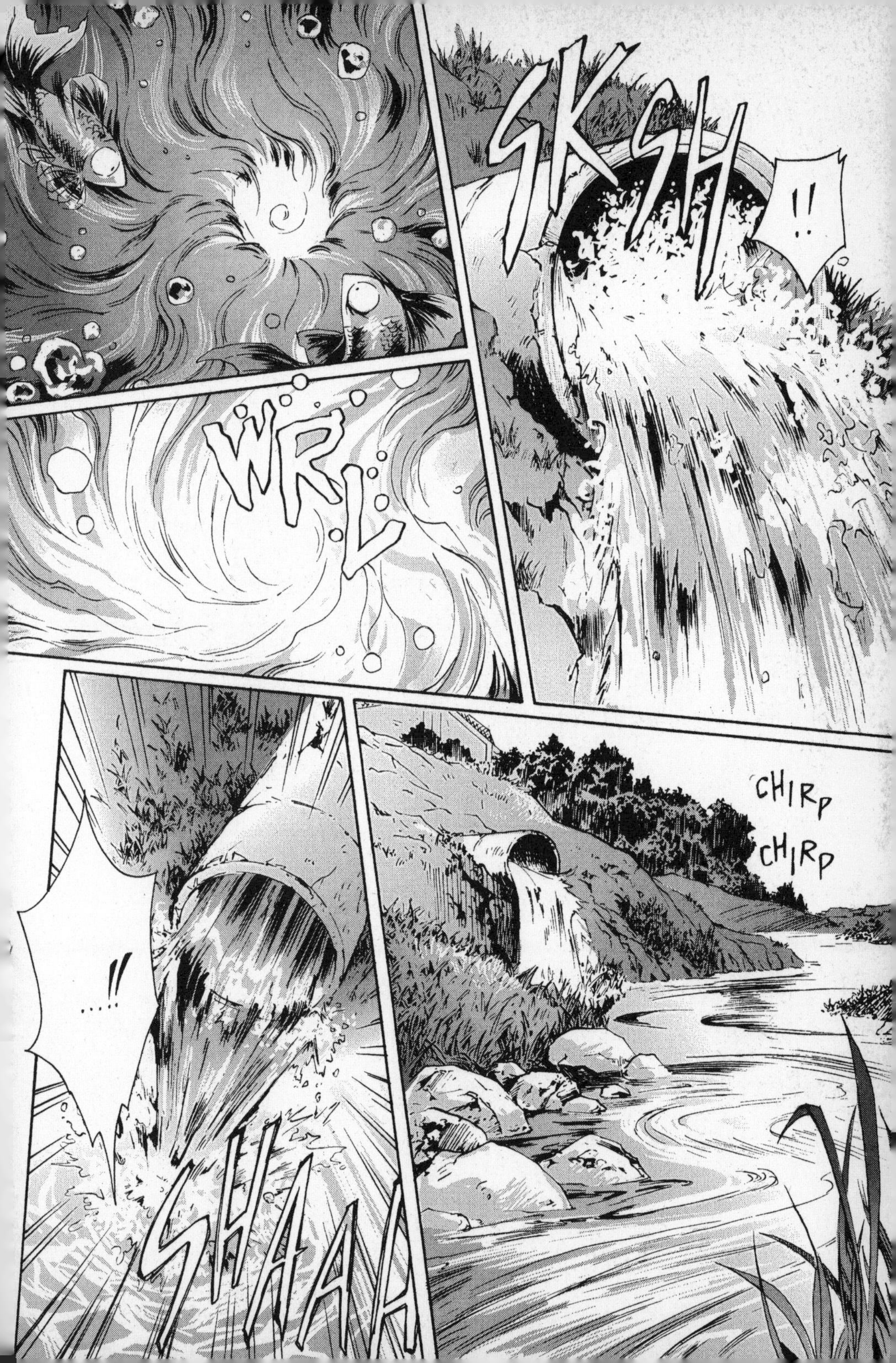

WRL
SKSH
!!
...!!
SHAAA
CHIRP
CHIRP

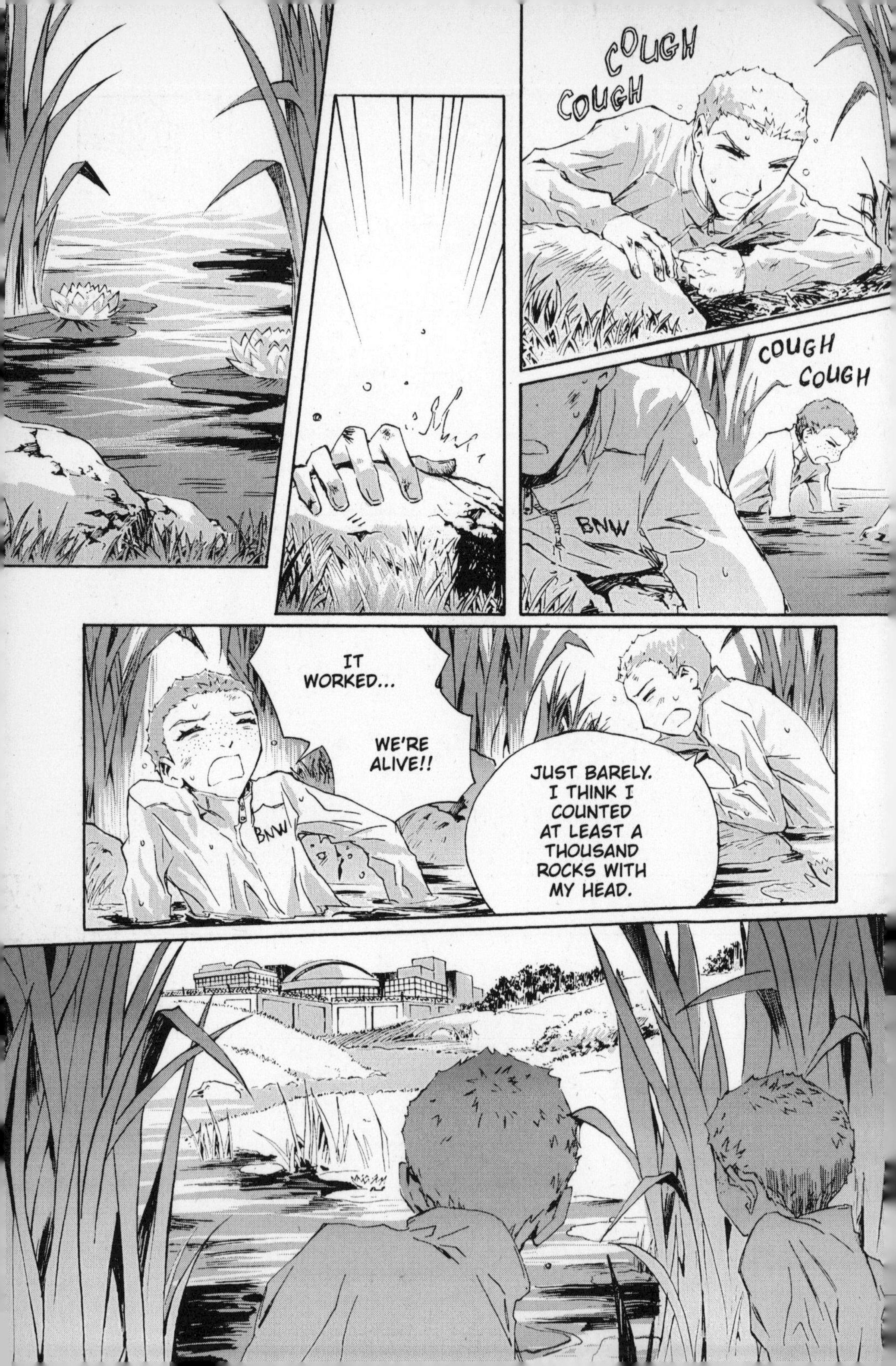
COUGH COUGH
COUGH COUGH
IT WORKED...
WE'RE ALIVE!!
JUST BARELY. I THINK I COUNTED AT LEAST A THOUSAND ROCKS WITH MY HEAD.

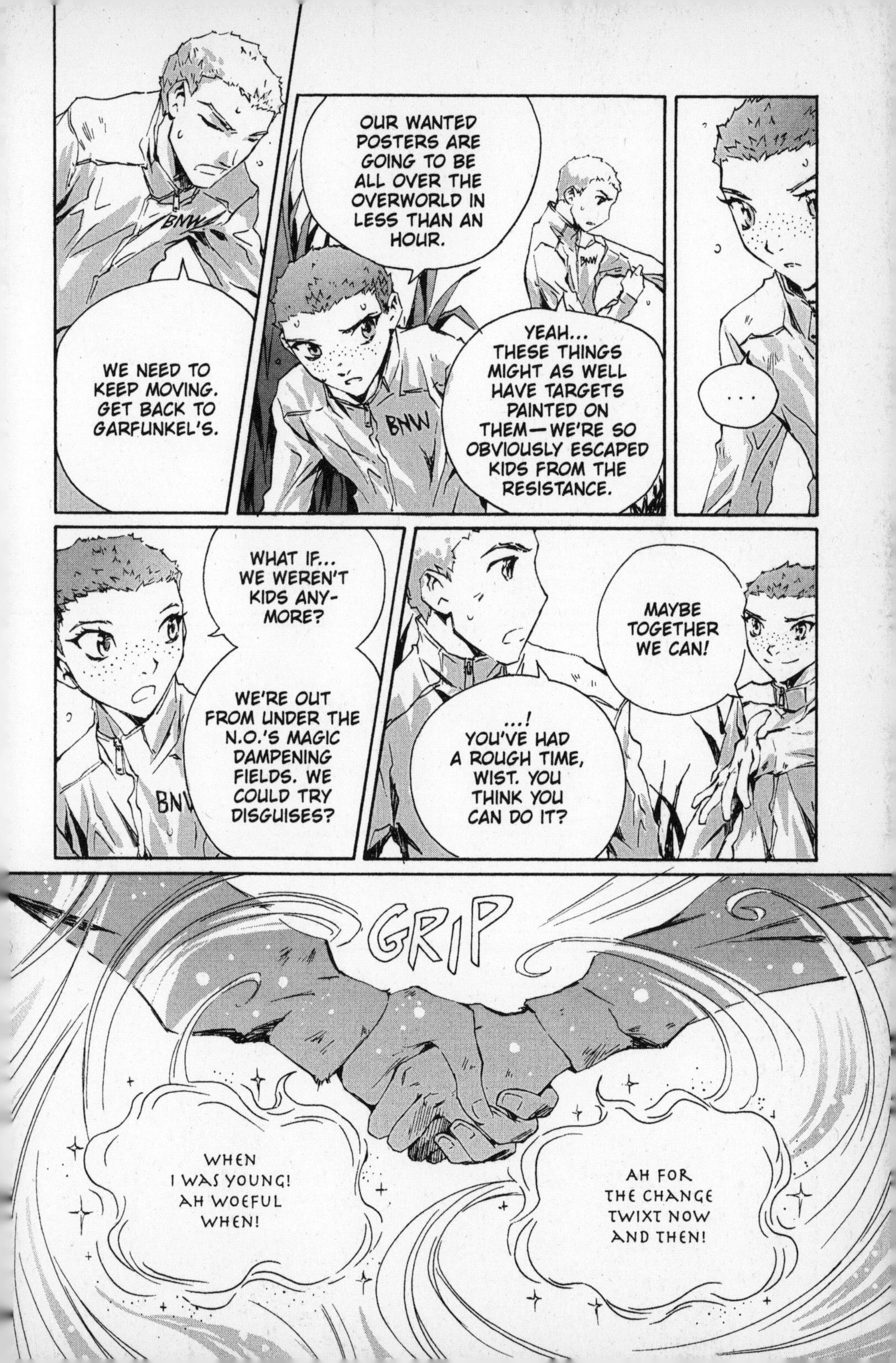
WE NEED TO KEEP MOVING. GET BACK TO GARFUNKEL'S.
OUR WANTED POSTERS ARE GOING TO BE ALL OVER THE OVERWORLD IN LESS THAN AN HOUR.
YEAH... THESE THINGS MIGHT AS WELL HAVE TARGETS PAINTED ON THEM—WE'RE SO OBVIOUSLY ESCAPED KIDS FROM THE RESISTANCE.
...
WHAT IF... WE WEREN'T KIDS ANY-MORE?
WE'RE OUT FROM UNDER THE N.O.'S MAGIC DAMPENING FIELDS. WE COULD TRY DISGUISES?
...! YOU'VE HAD A ROUGH TIME, WIST. YOU THINK YOU CAN DO IT?
MAYBE TOGETHER WE CAN!
GRIP
WHEN I WAS YOUNG! AH WOEFUL WHEN!
AH FOR THE CHANGE TWIXT NOW AND THEN!

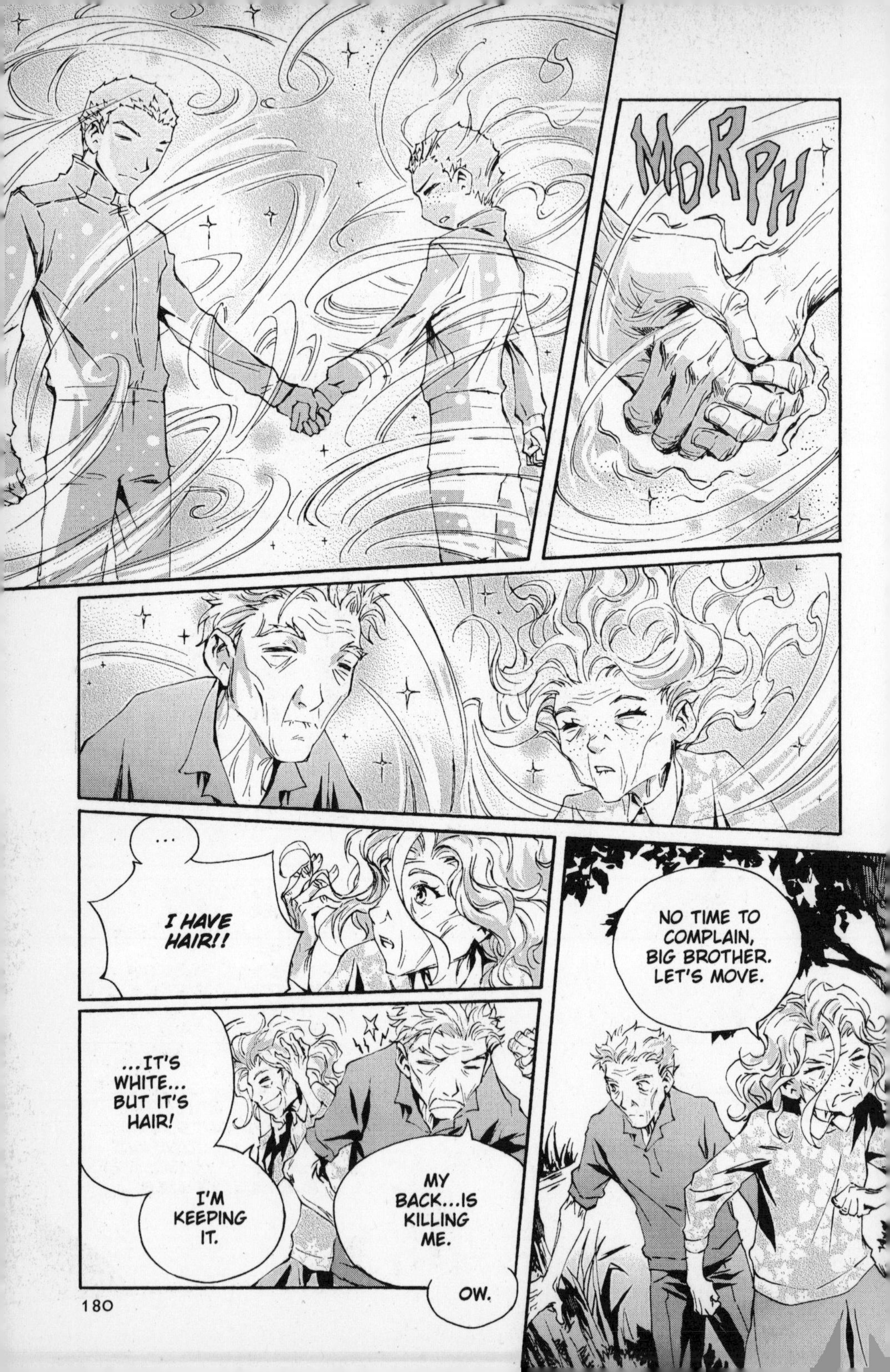
MORPH
...
I HAVE HAIR!!
...IT'S WHITE... BUT IT'S HAIR!
I'M KEEPING IT.
MY BACK...IS KILLING ME.
OW.
NO TIME TO COMPLAIN, BIG BROTHER. LET'S MOVE.

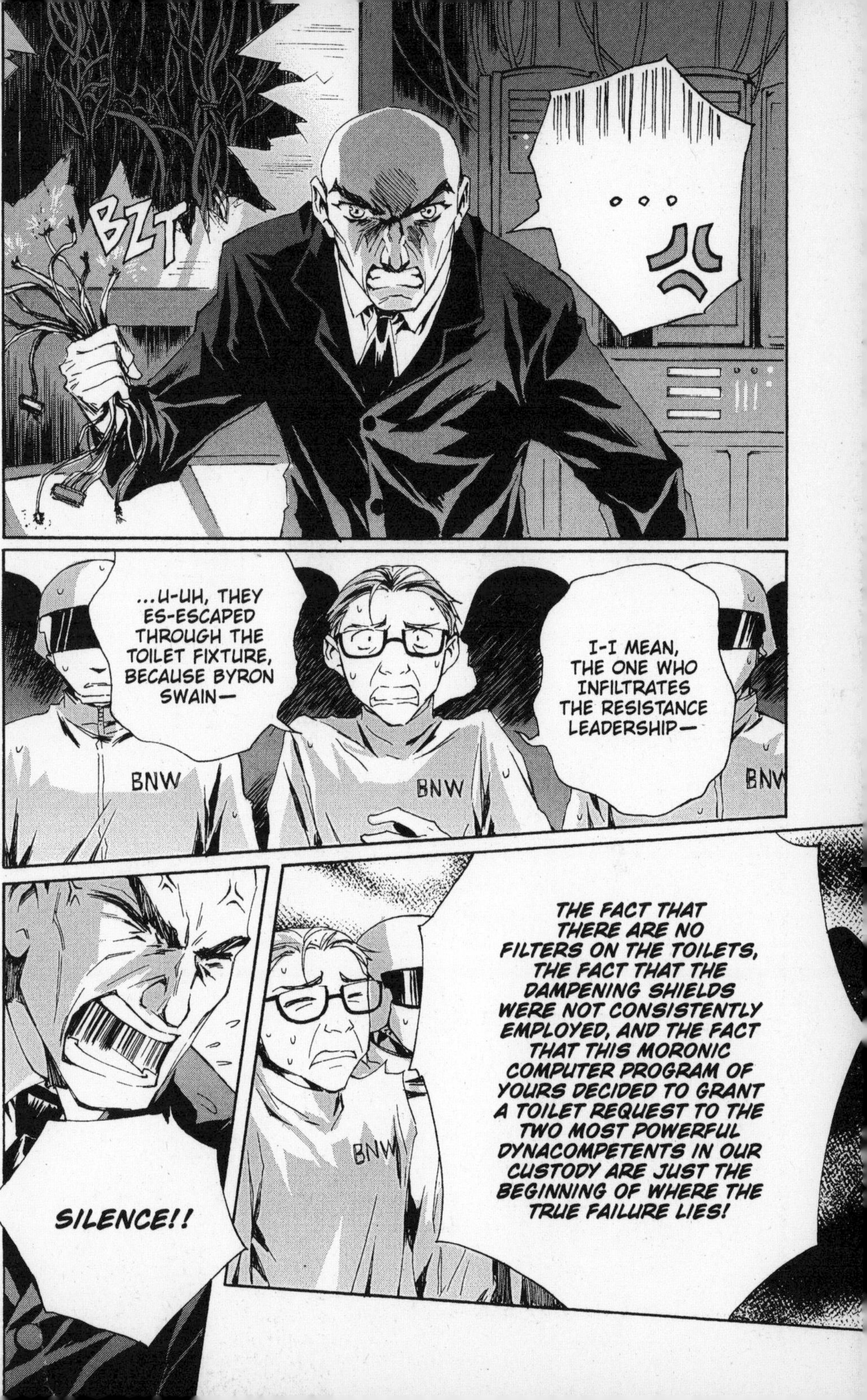
BZT
...
...U-UH, THEY ES-ESCAPED THROUGH THE TOILET FIXTURE, BECAUSE BYRON SWAIN—
BNW
BNW
I-I MEAN, THE ONE WHO INFILTRATES THE RESISTANCE LEADERSHIP—
BNW
SILENCE!!
BNW
THE FACT THAT THERE ARE NO FILTERS ON THE TOILETS, THE FACT THAT THE DAMPENING SHIELDS WERE NOT CONSISTENTLY EMPLOYED, AND THE FACT THAT THIS MORONIC COMPUTER PROGRAM OF YOURS DECIDED TO GRANT A TOILET REQUEST TO THE TWO MOST POWERFUL DYNACOMPETENTS IN OUR CUSTODY ARE JUST THE BEGINNING OF WHERE THE TRUE FAILURE LIES!

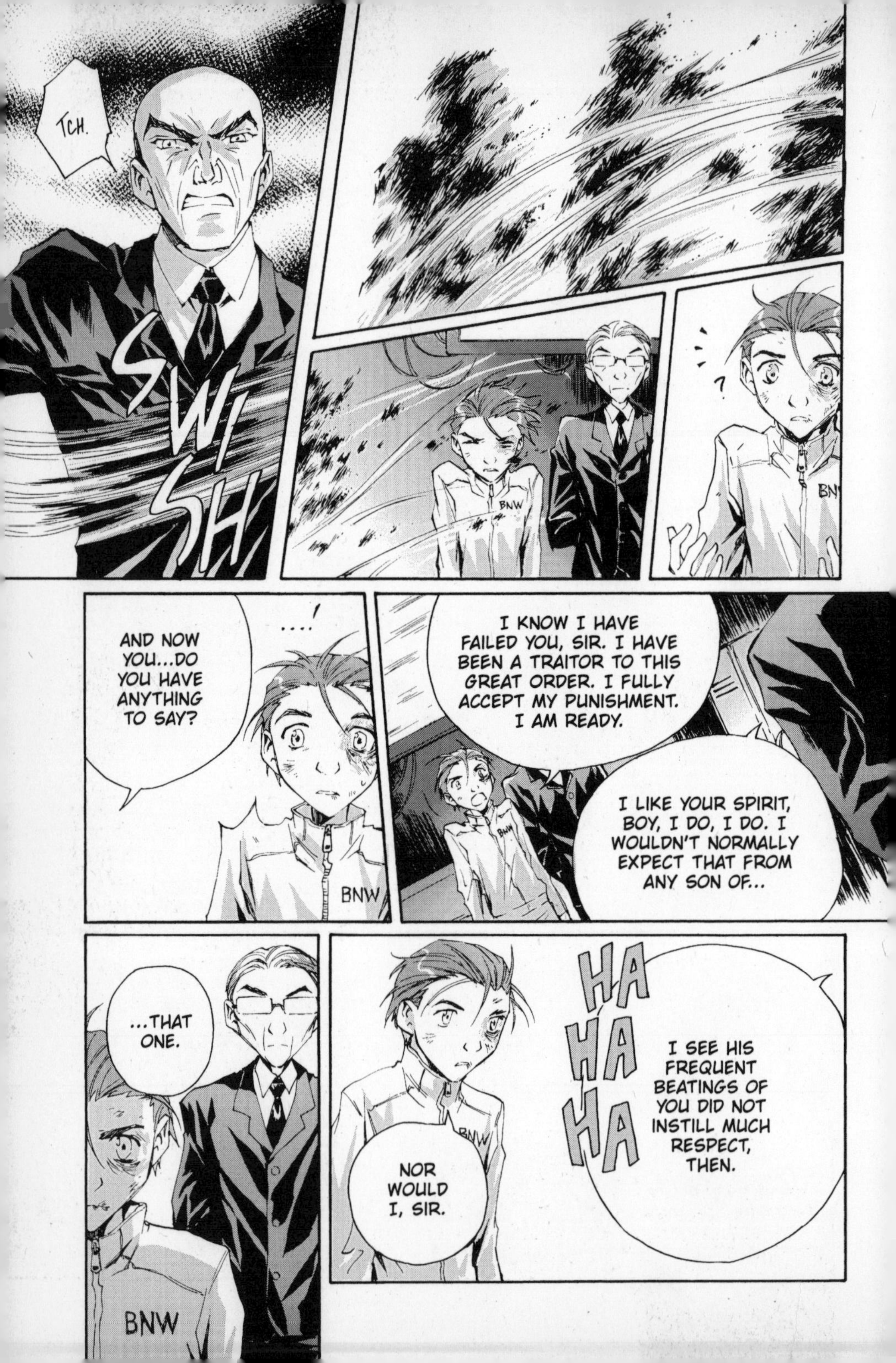
TCH.
SWISH
BNW
?
BN
AND NOW YOU...DO YOU HAVE ANYTHING TO SAY?
....!
BNW
I KNOW I HAVE FAILED YOU, SIR. I HAVE BEEN A TRAITOR TO THIS GREAT ORDER. I FULLY ACCEPT MY PUNISHMENT. I AM READY.
BNW
I LIKE YOUR SPIRIT, BOY, I DO, I DO. I WOULDN'T NORMALLY EXPECT THAT FROM ANY SON OF...
...THAT ONE.
BNW
HA HA HA
I SEE HIS FREQUENT BEATINGS OF YOU DID NOT INSTILL MUCH RESPECT, THEN.
BNW
NOR WOULD I, SIR.

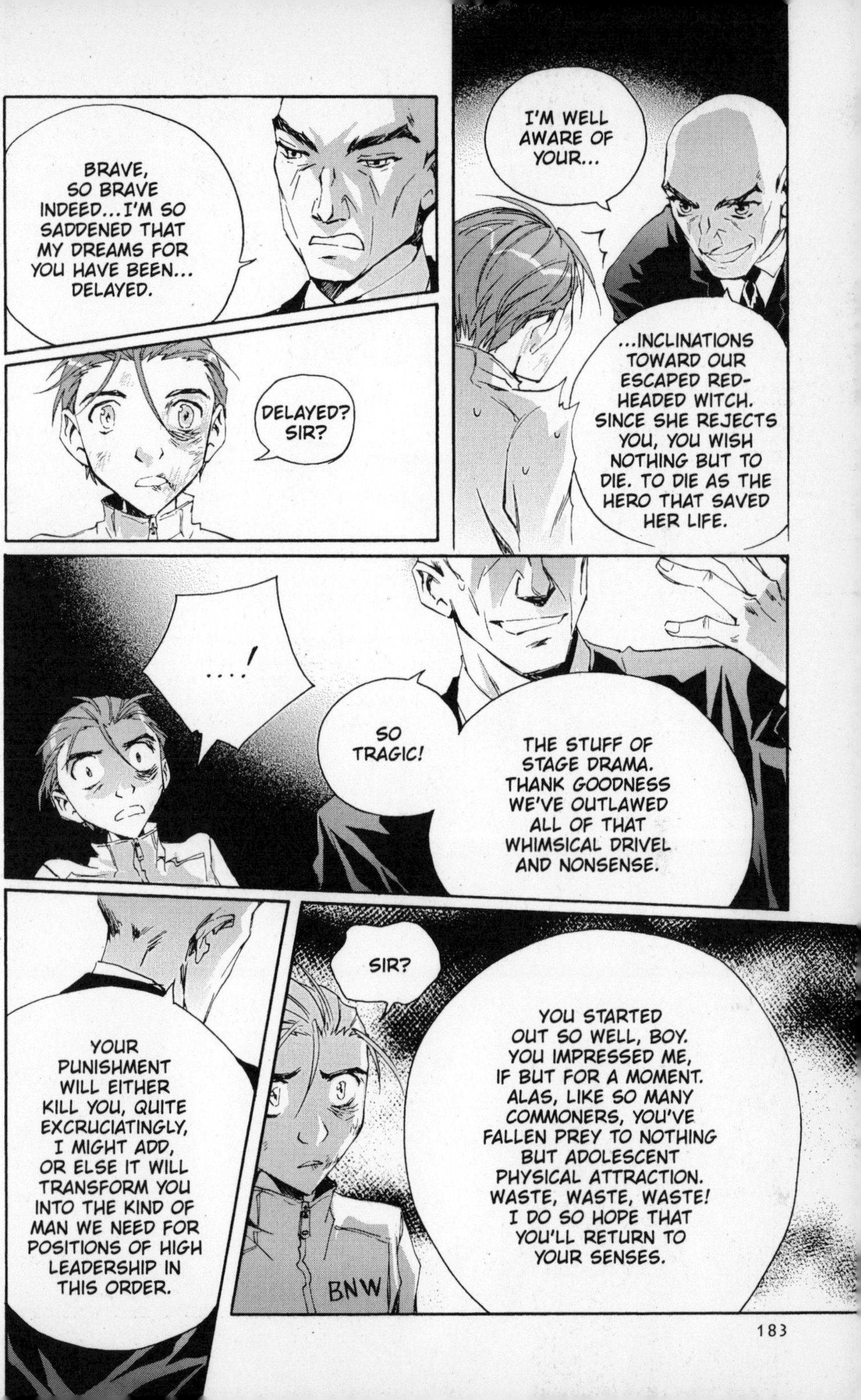
BRAVE, SO BRAVE INDEED...I'M SO SADDENED THAT MY DREAMS FOR YOU HAVE BEEN... DELAYED.
DELAYED? SIR?
I'M WELL AWARE OF YOUR...
...INCLINATIONS TOWARD OUR ESCAPED RED-HEADED WITCH. SINCE SHE REJECTS YOU, YOU WISH NOTHING BUT TO DIE. TO DIE AS THE HERO THAT SAVED HER LIFE.
...!
SO TRAGIC!
THE STUFF OF STAGE DRAMA. THANK GOODNESS WE'VE OUTLAWED ALL OF THAT WHIMSICAL DRIVEL AND NONSENSE.
YOUR PUNISHMENT WILL EITHER KILL YOU, QUITE EXCRUCIATINGLY, I MIGHT ADD, OR ELSE IT WILL TRANSFORM YOU INTO THE KIND OF MAN WE NEED FOR POSITIONS OF HIGH LEADERSHIP IN THIS ORDER.
SIR?
YOU STARTED OUT SO WELL, BOY. YOU IMPRESSED ME, IF BUT FOR A MOMENT. ALAS, LIKE SO MANY COMMONERS, YOU'VE FALLEN PREY TO NOTHING BUT ADOLESCENT PHYSICAL ATTRACTION. WASTE, WASTE, WASTE! I DO SO HOPE THAT YOU'LL RETURN TO YOUR SENSES.
BNW

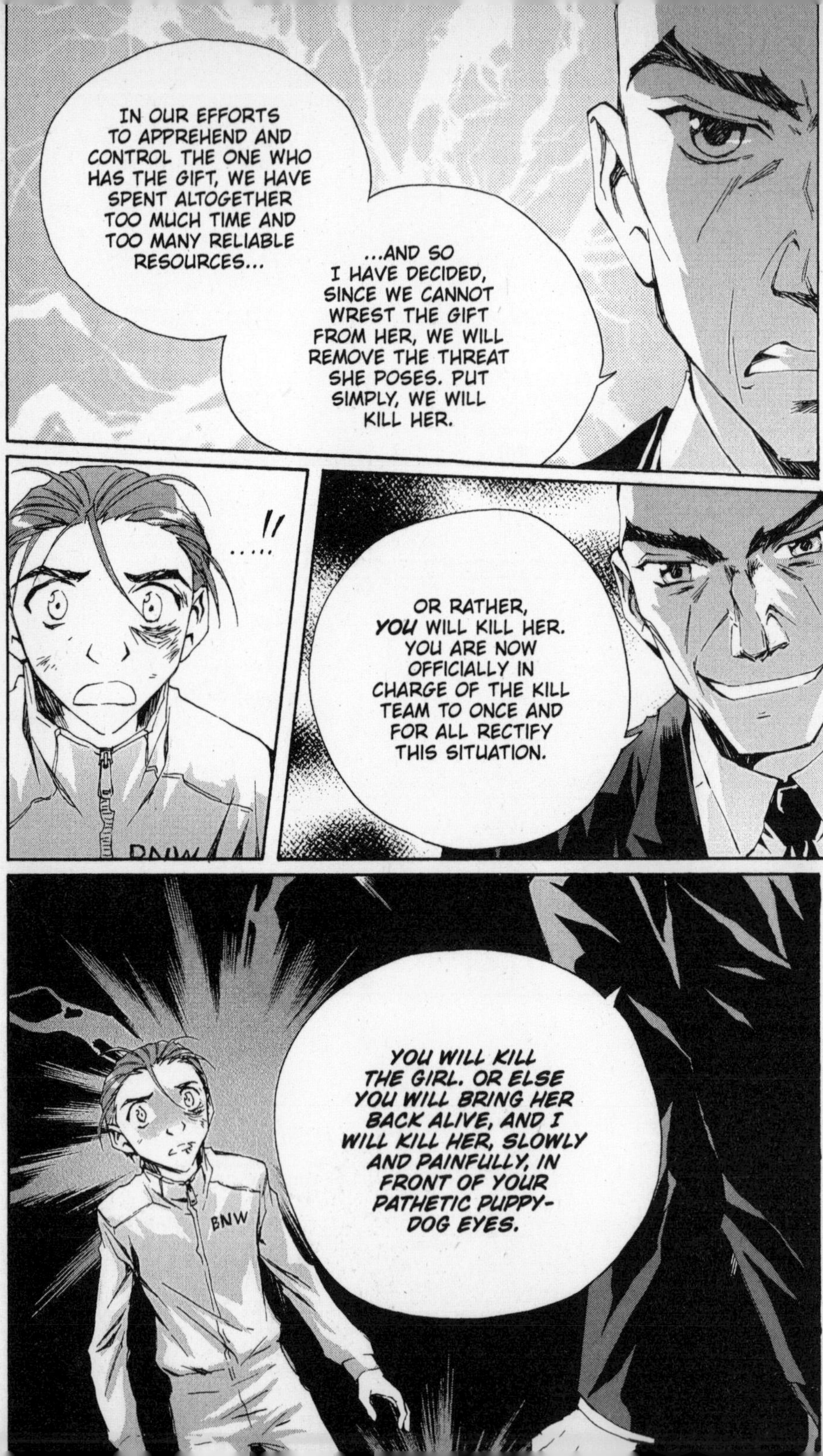
IN OUR EFFORTS TO APPREHEND AND CONTROL THE ONE WHO HAS THE GIFT, WE HAVE SPENT ALTOGETHER TOO MUCH TIME AND TOO MANY RELIABLE RESOURCES...
...AND SO I HAVE DECIDED, SINCE WE CANNOT WREST THE GIFT FROM HER, WE WILL REMOVE THE THREAT SHE POSES. PUT SIMPLY, WE WILL KILL HER.
....!!
OR RATHER, *YOU* WILL KILL HER. YOU ARE NOW OFFICIALLY IN CHARGE OF THE KILL TEAM TO ONCE AND FOR ALL RECTIFY THIS SITUATION.
BNW
YOU WILL KILL THE GIRL. OR ELSE YOU WILL BRING HER BACK ALIVE, AND I WILL KILL HER, SLOWLY AND PAINFULLY, IN FRONT OF YOUR PATHETIC PUPPY-DOG EYES.

WITCH & WIZARD

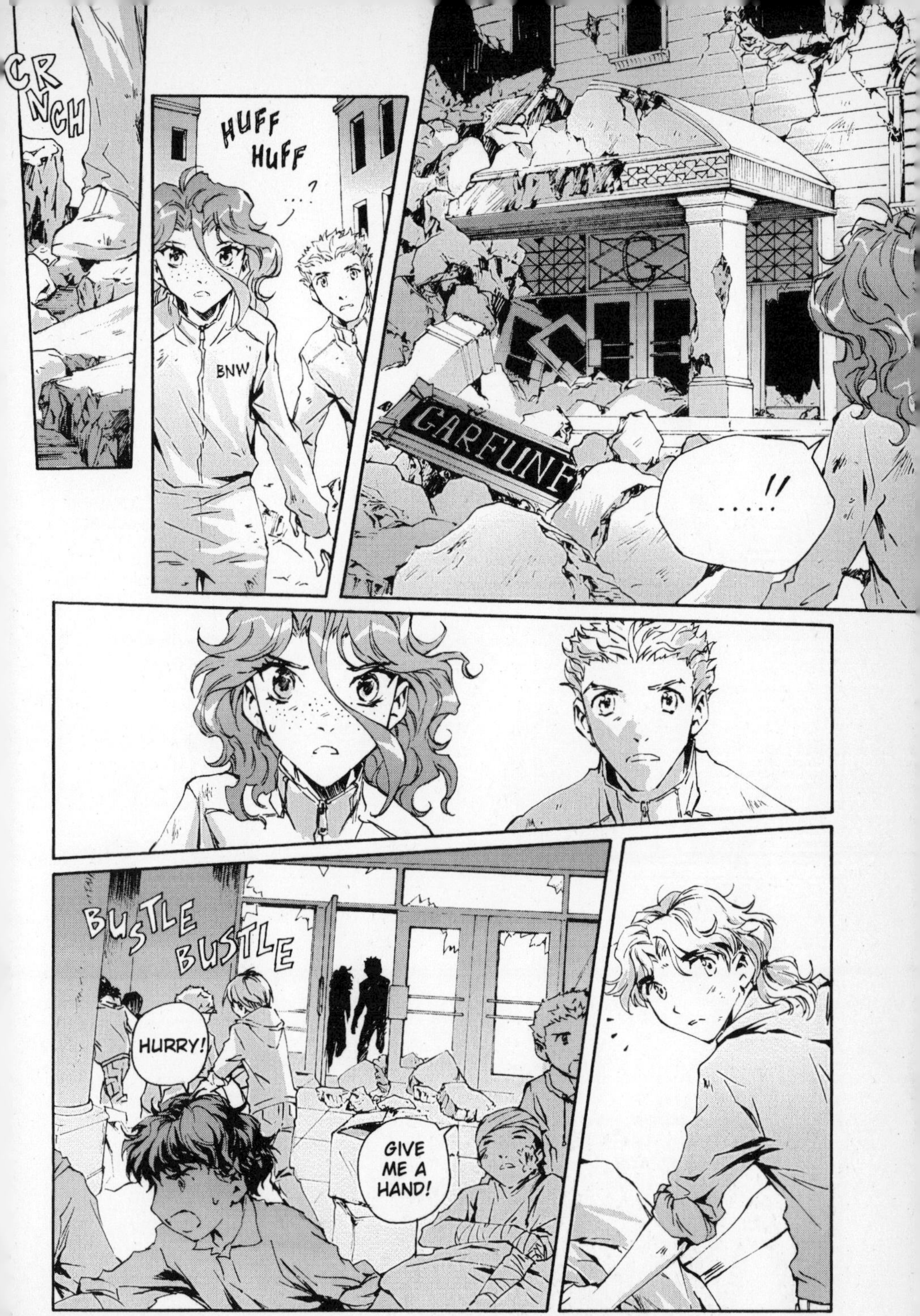
CRNCH
HUFF HUFF
...?
GARFUNF
...!!
BUSTLE BUSTLE
HURRY!
GIVE ME A HAND!

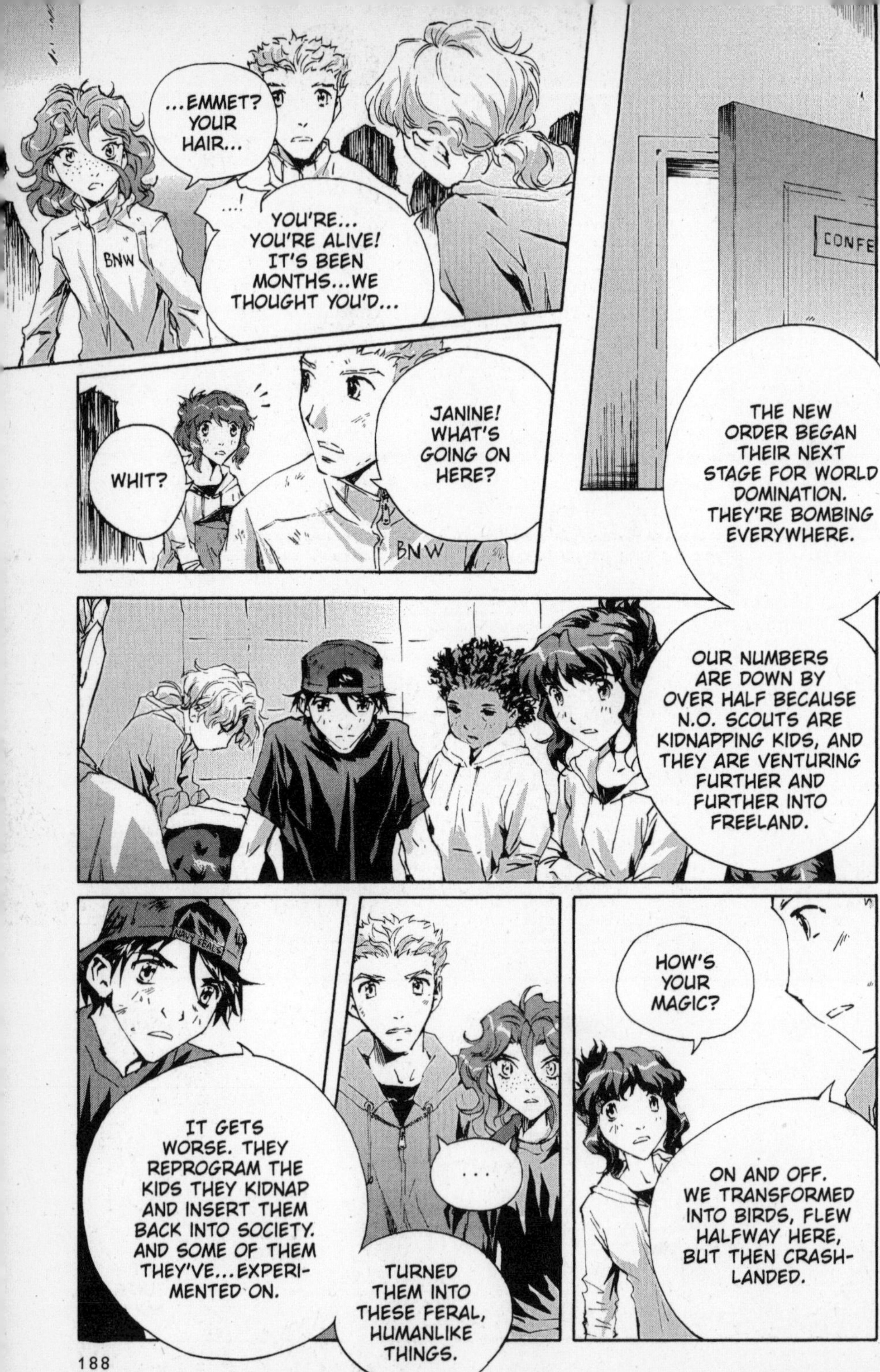
...EMMET? YOUR HAIR...
...!
YOU'RE... YOU'RE ALIVE! IT'S BEEN MONTHS...WE THOUGHT YOU'D...
CONFE
WHIT?
JANINE! WHAT'S GOING ON HERE?
THE NEW ORDER BEGAN THEIR NEXT STAGE FOR WORLD DOMINATION. THEY'RE BOMBING EVERYWHERE.
OUR NUMBERS ARE DOWN BY OVER HALF BECAUSE N.O. SCOUTS ARE KIDNAPPING KIDS, AND THEY ARE VENTURING FURTHER AND FURTHER INTO FREELAND.
IT GETS WORSE. THEY REPROGRAM THE KIDS THEY KIDNAP AND INSERT THEM BACK INTO SOCIETY. AND SOME OF THEM THEY'VE...EXPERI-MENTED ON.
...
TURNED THEM INTO THESE FERAL, HUMANLIKE THINGS.
HOW'S YOUR MAGIC?
ON AND OFF. WE TRANSFORMED INTO BIRDS, FLEW HALFWAY HERE, BUT THEN CRASH-LANDED.

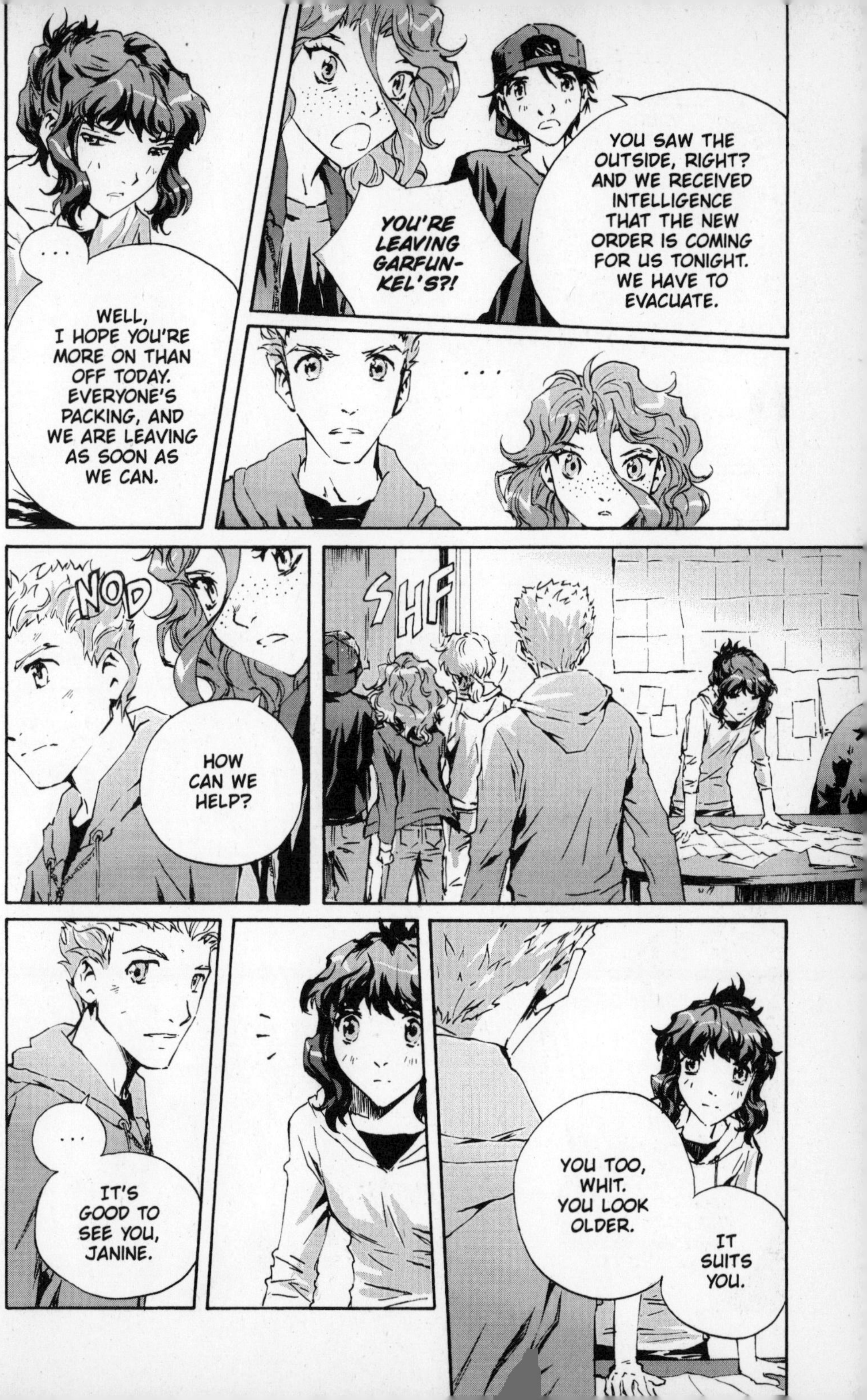
...
WELL, I HOPE YOU'RE MORE ON THAN OFF TODAY. EVERYONE'S PACKING, AND WE ARE LEAVING AS SOON AS WE CAN.
YOU'RE LEAVING GARFUN-KEL'S?!
YOU SAW THE OUTSIDE, RIGHT? AND WE RECEIVED INTELLIGENCE THAT THE NEW ORDER IS COMING FOR US TONIGHT. WE HAVE TO EVACUATE.
...
NOD
HOW CAN WE HELP?
SHF
...
IT'S GOOD TO SEE YOU, JANINE.
YOU TOO, WHIT. YOU LOOK OLDER.
IT SUITS YOU.

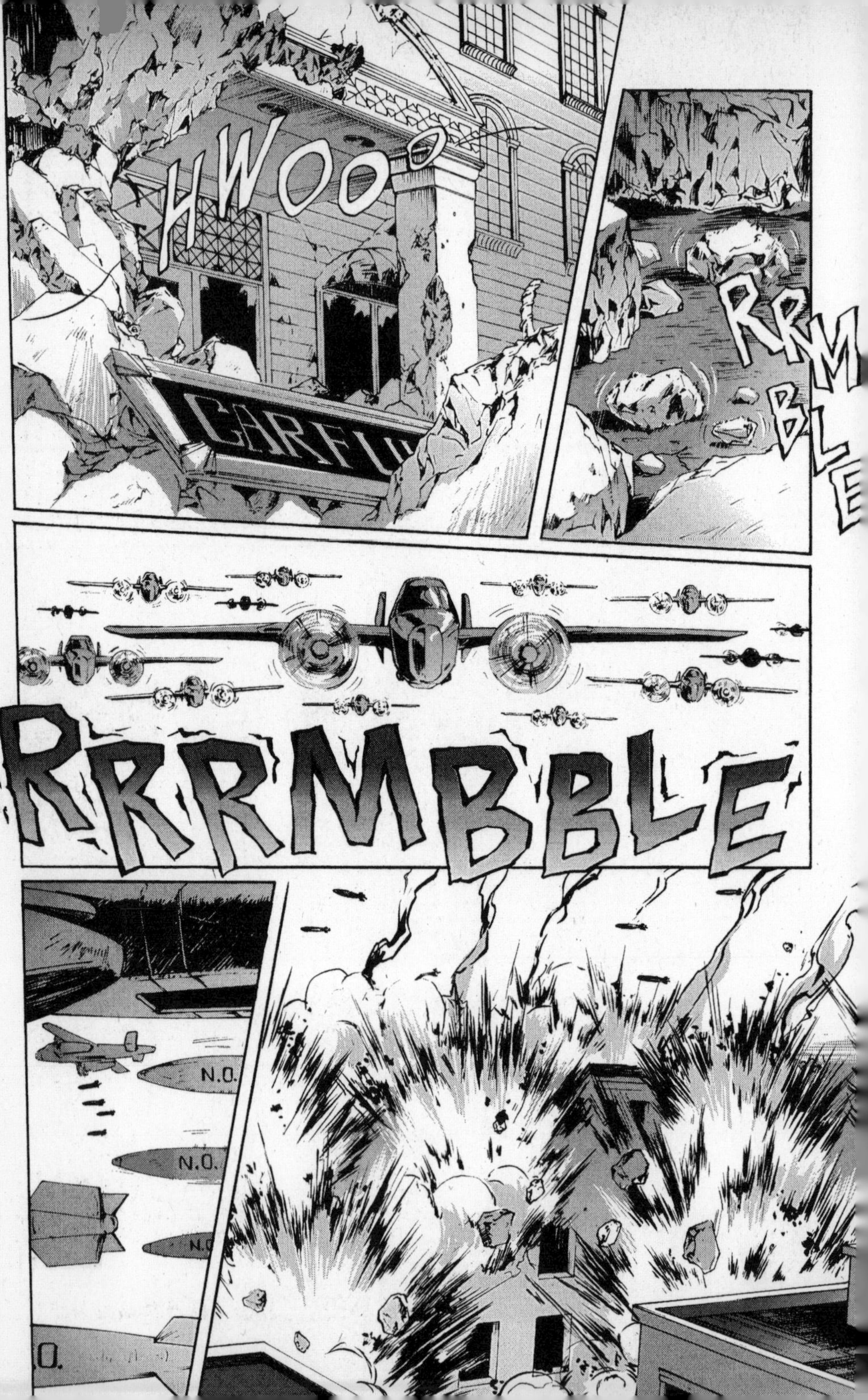
HWOOO
CARFU
RRMBLE
RRRMBBLE
N.O.
N.O.
N.O.

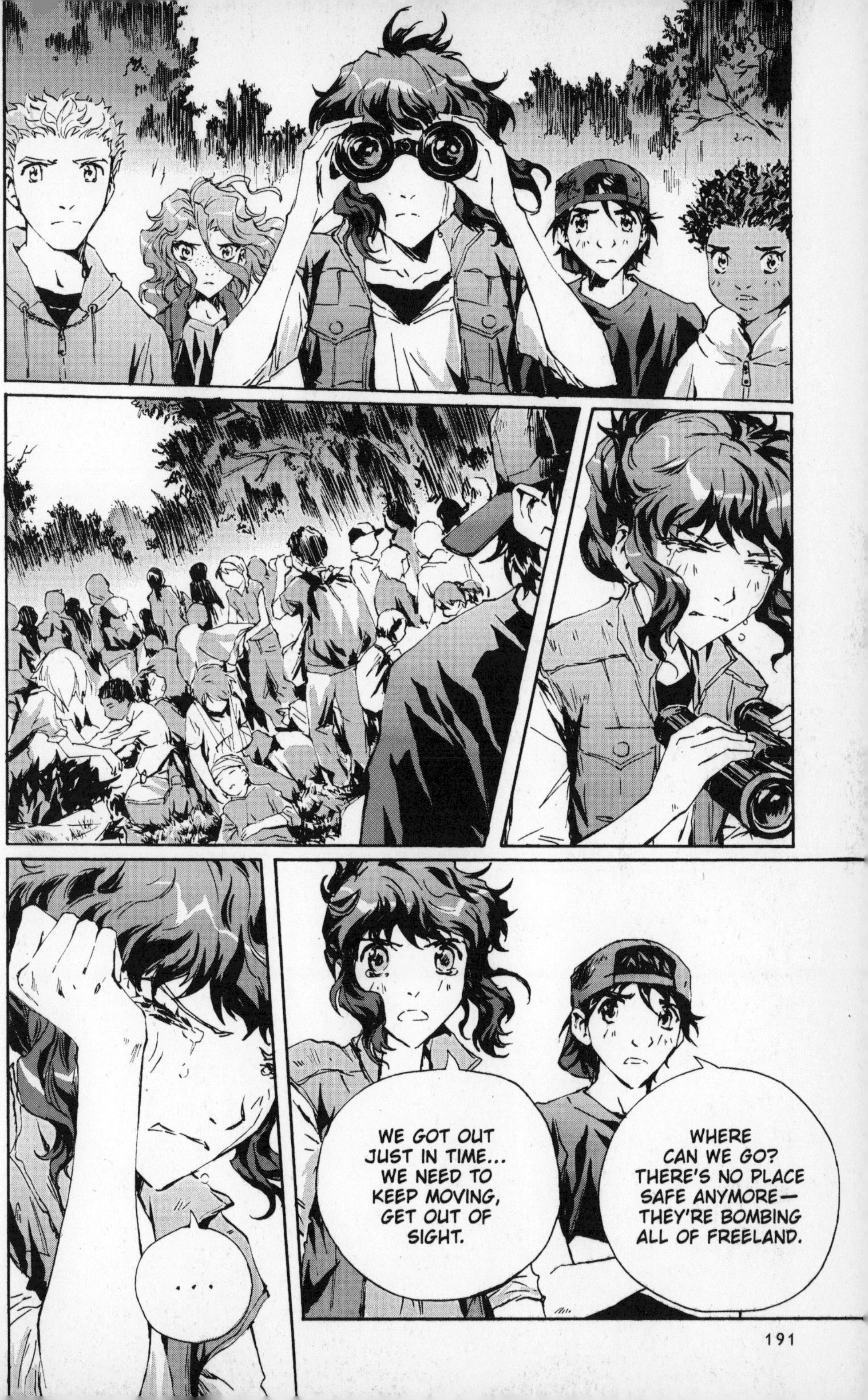
...
WE GOT OUT JUST IN TIME... WE NEED TO KEEP MOVING, GET OUT OF SIGHT.
WHERE CAN WE GO? THERE'S NO PLACE SAFE ANYMORE— THEY'RE BOMBING ALL OF FREELAND.

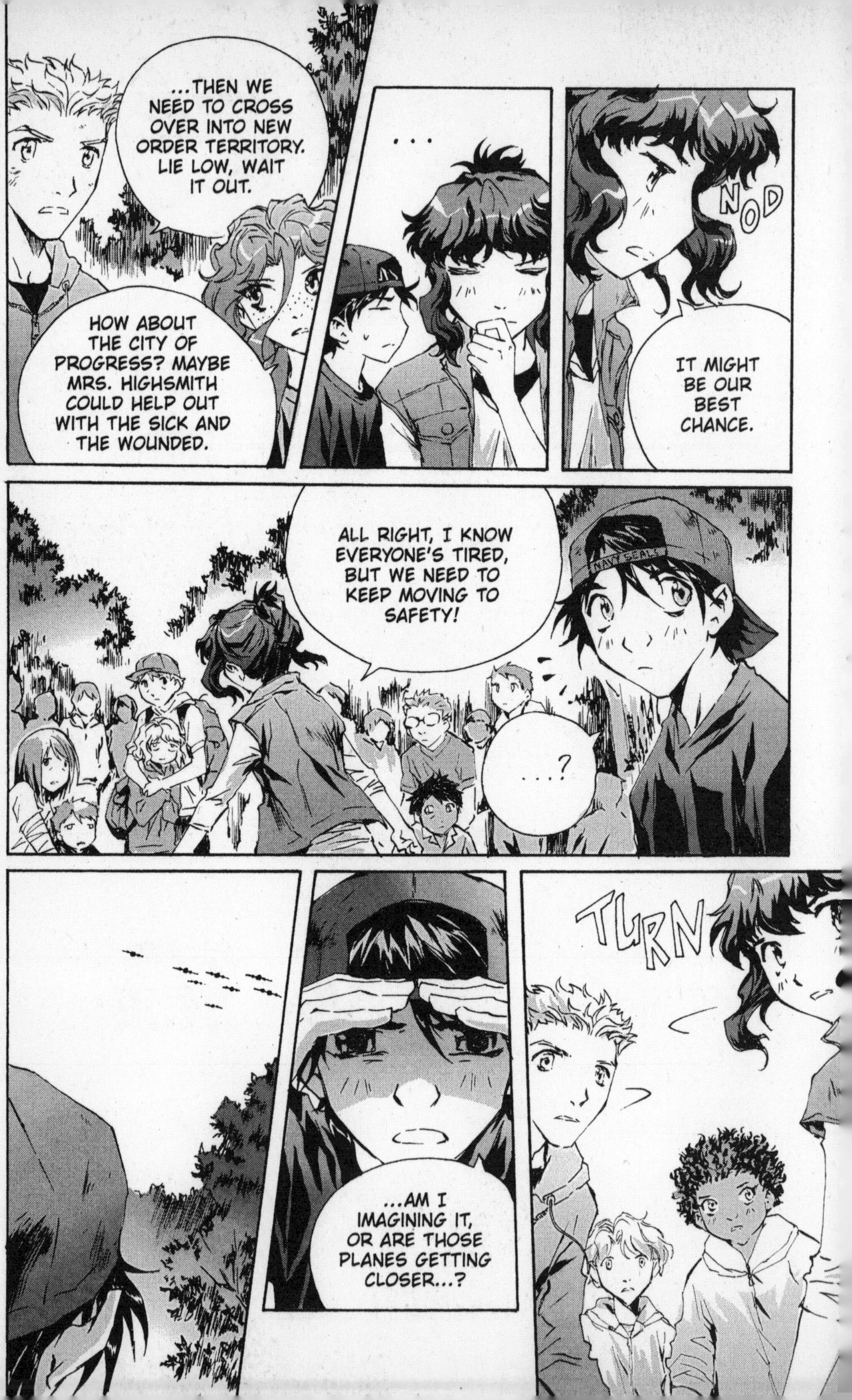
...THEN WE NEED TO CROSS OVER INTO NEW ORDER TERRITORY. LIE LOW, WAIT IT OUT.
HOW ABOUT THE CITY OF PROGRESS? MAYBE MRS. HIGHSMITH COULD HELP OUT WITH THE SICK AND THE WOUNDED.
...
NOD
IT MIGHT BE OUR BEST CHANCE.
ALL RIGHT, I KNOW EVERYONE'S TIRED, BUT WE NEED TO KEEP MOVING TO SAFETY!
NAVY SEALS
...?
...AM I IMAGINING IT, OR ARE THOSE PLANES GETTING CLOSER...?
TURN

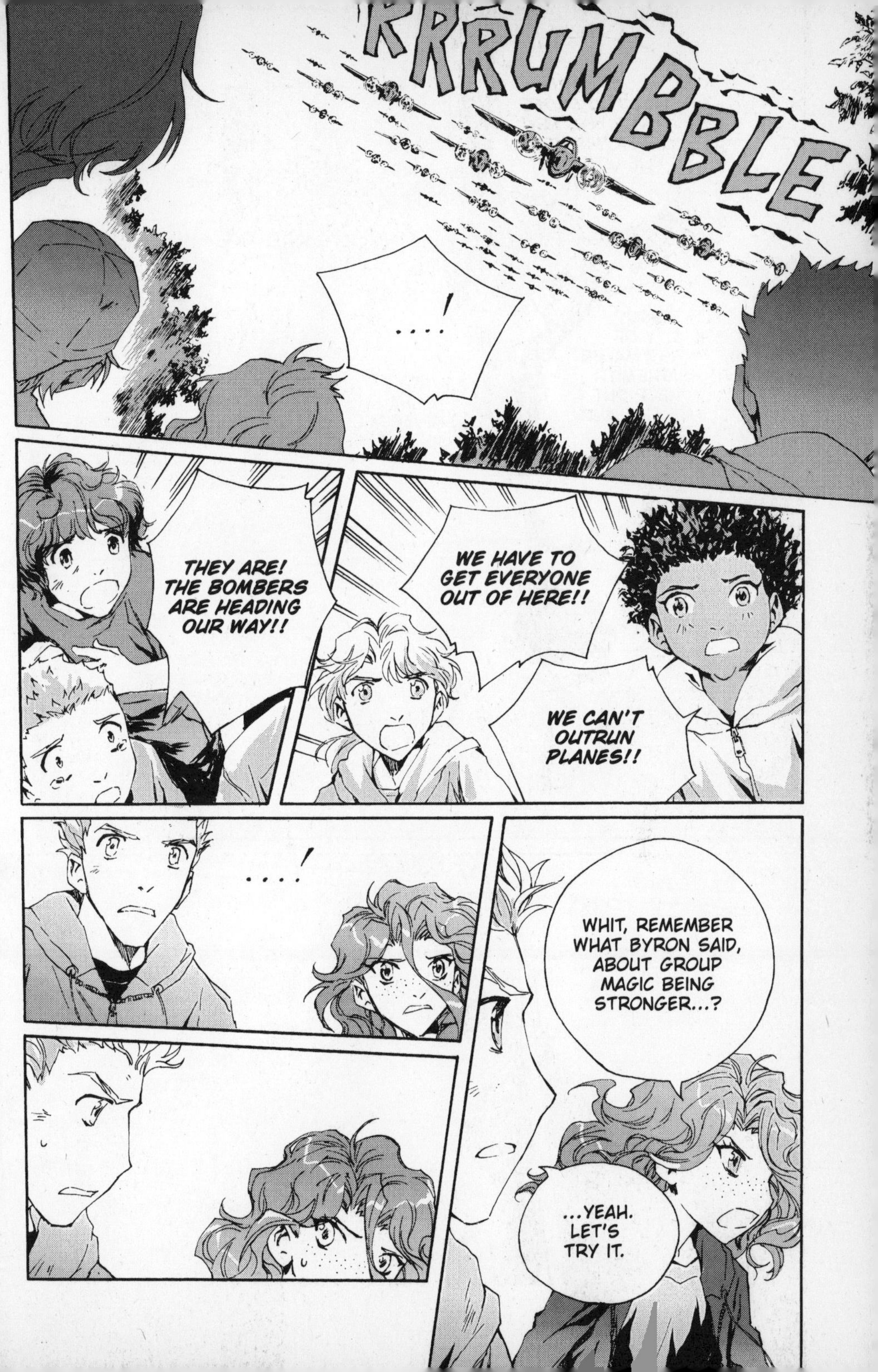

KRRUMBBLE
....!
THEY ARE! THE BOMBERS ARE HEADING OUR WAY!!
WE HAVE TO GET EVERYONE OUT OF HERE!!
WE CAN'T OUTRUN PLANES!!
....!
WHIT, REMEMBER WHAT BYRON SAID, ABOUT GROUP MAGIC BEING STRONGER...?
...YEAH. LET'S TRY IT.

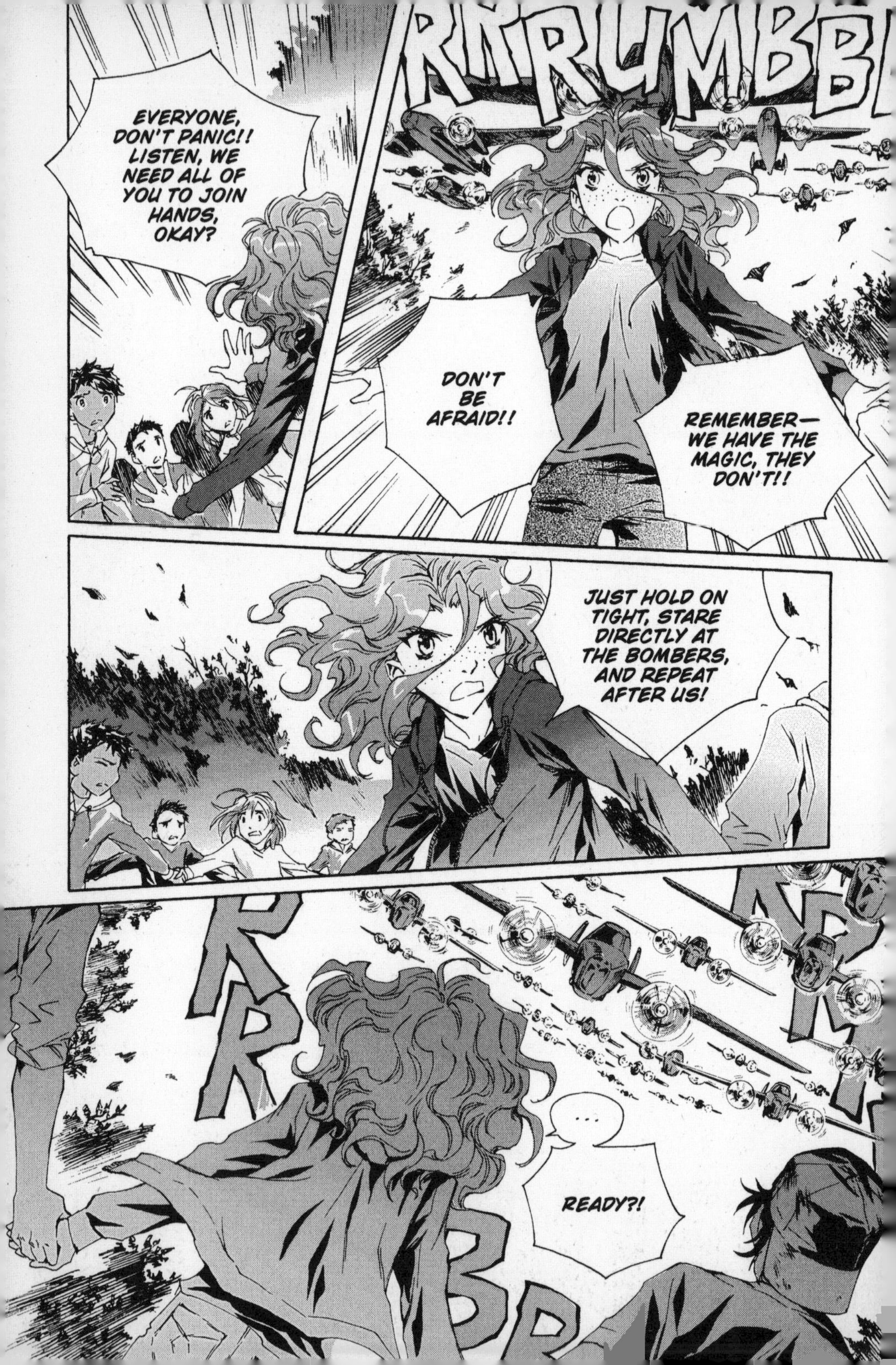
EVERYONE, DON'T PANIC!! LISTEN, WE NEED ALL OF YOU TO JOIN HANDS, OKAY?
RMRUMBB
DON'T BE AFRAID!!
REMEMBER— WE HAVE THE MAGIC, THEY DON'T!!
JUST HOLD ON TIGHT, STARE DIRECTLY AT THE BOMBERS, AND REPEAT AFTER US!
...
READY?!

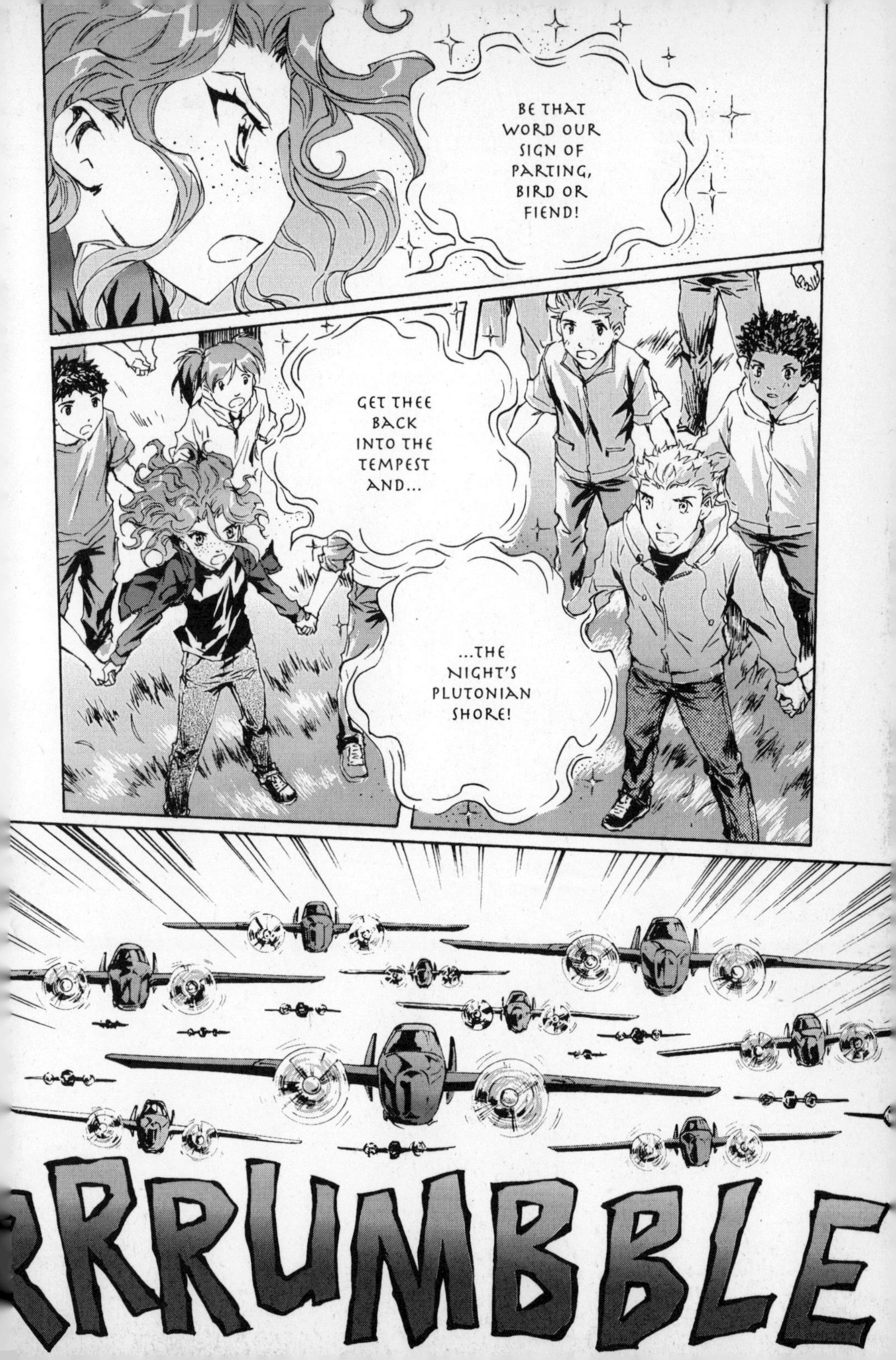
BE THAT WORD OUR SIGN OF PARTING, BIRD OR FIEND!
GET THEE BACK INTO THE TEMPEST AND...
...THE NIGHT'S PLUTONIAN SHORE!
RRRUMBBLE

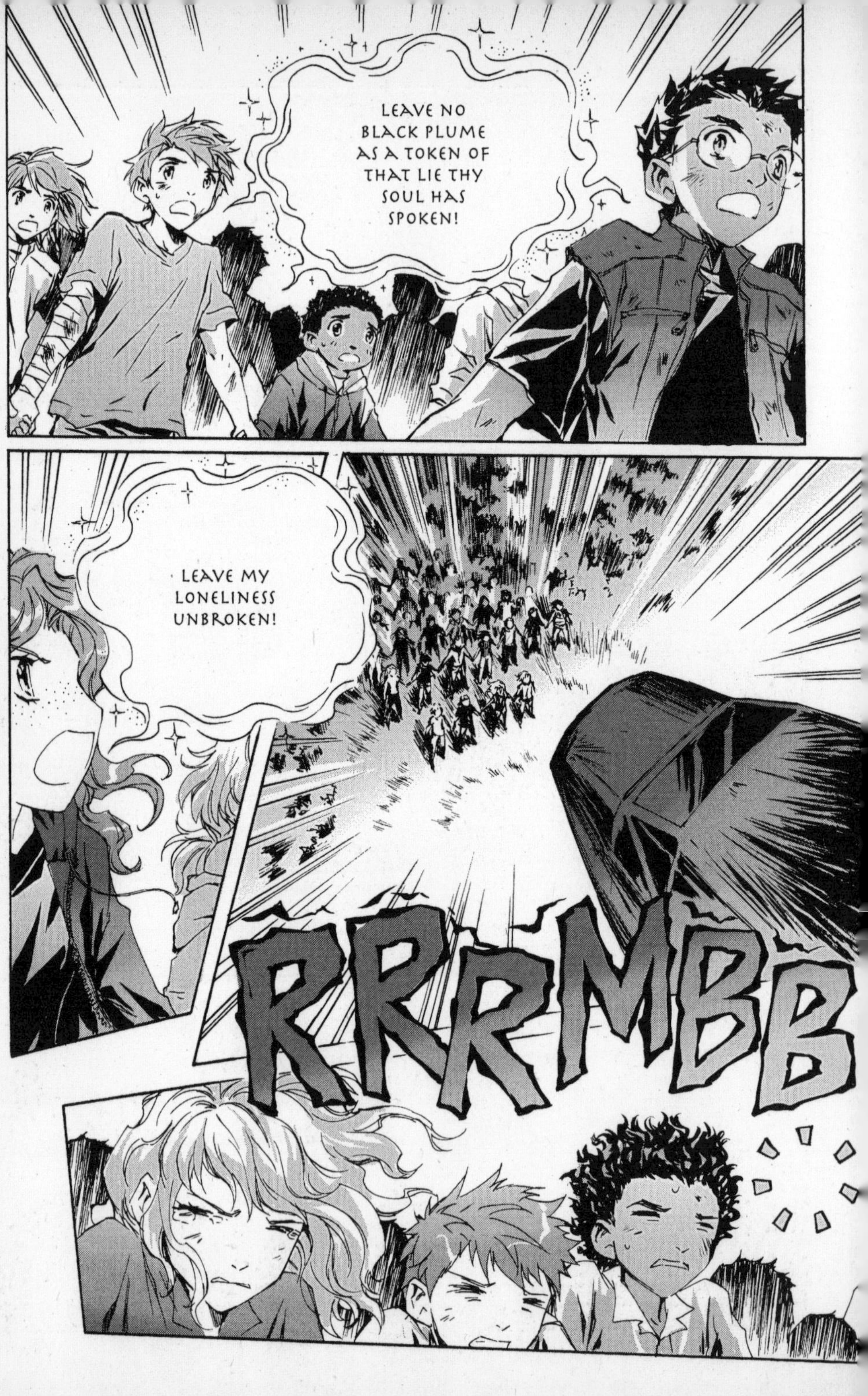
LEAVE NO BLACK PLUME AS A TOKEN OF THAT LIE THY SOUL HAS SPOKEN!
LEAVE MY LONELINESS UNBROKEN!
RRRMBB

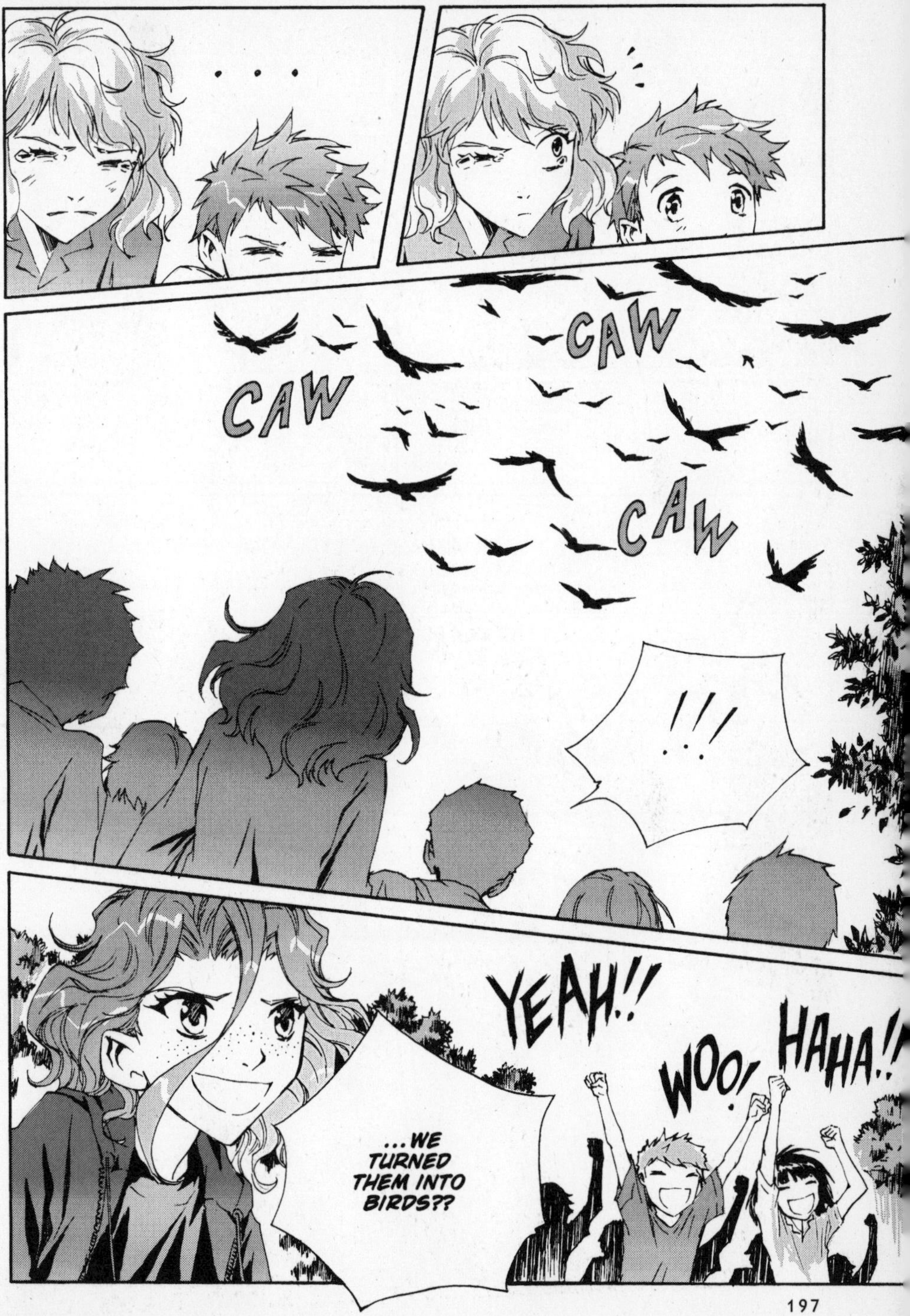
. . .
CAW
CAW
CAW
!!!
YEAH!!
WOO!
HAHA!!
...WE TURNED THEM INTO BIRDS??

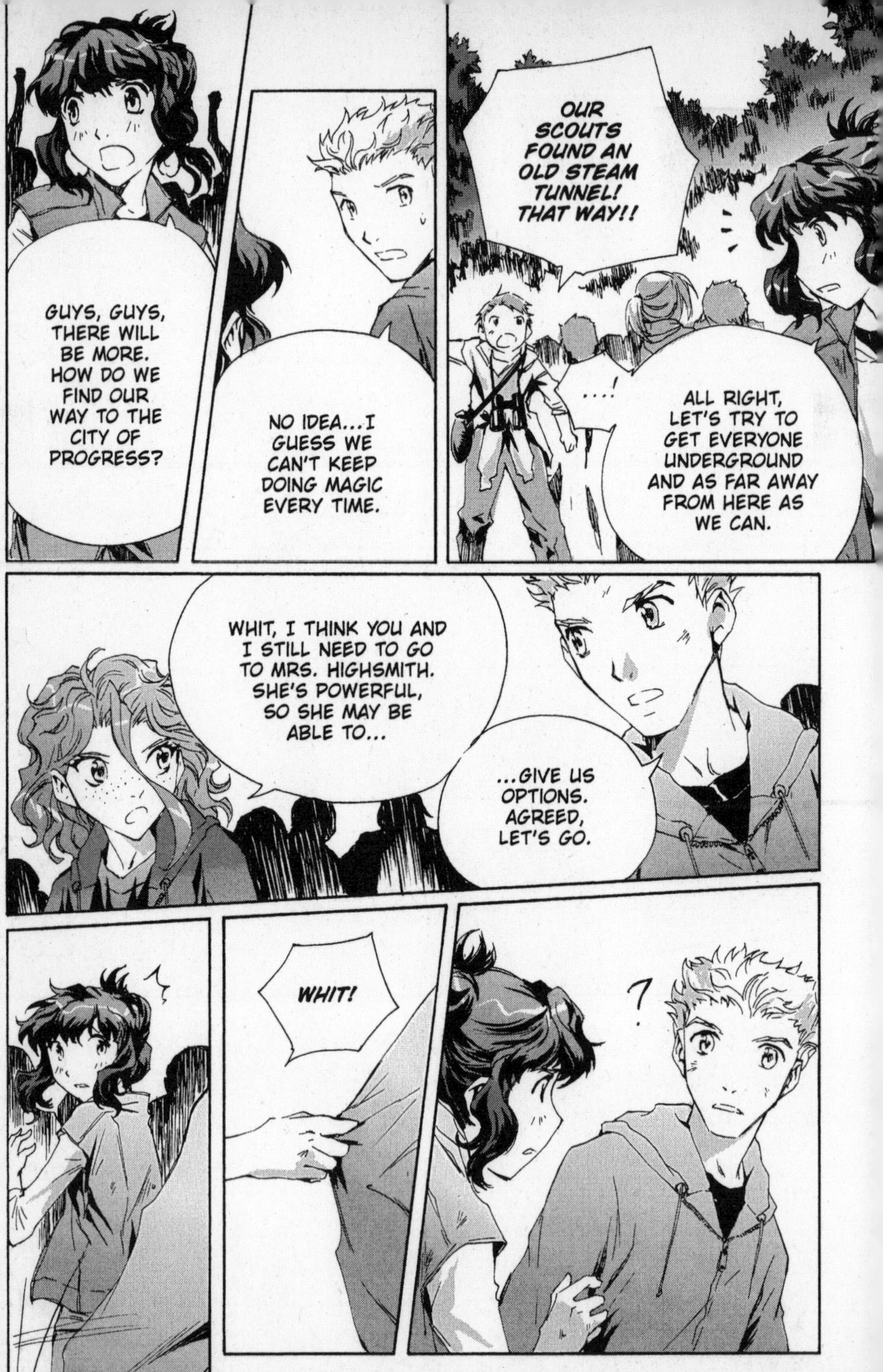
GUYS, GUYS, THERE WILL BE MORE. HOW DO WE FIND OUR WAY TO THE CITY OF PROGRESS?
NO IDEA...I GUESS WE CAN'T KEEP DOING MAGIC EVERY TIME.
OUR SCOUTS FOUND AN OLD STEAM TUNNEL! THAT WAY!!
...!
ALL RIGHT, LET'S TRY TO GET EVERYONE UNDERGROUND AND AS FAR AWAY FROM HERE AS WE CAN.
WHIT, I THINK YOU AND I STILL NEED TO GO TO MRS. HIGHSMITH. SHE'S POWERFUL, SO SHE MAY BE ABLE TO...
...GIVE US OPTIONS. AGREED, LET'S GO.
WHIT!
?

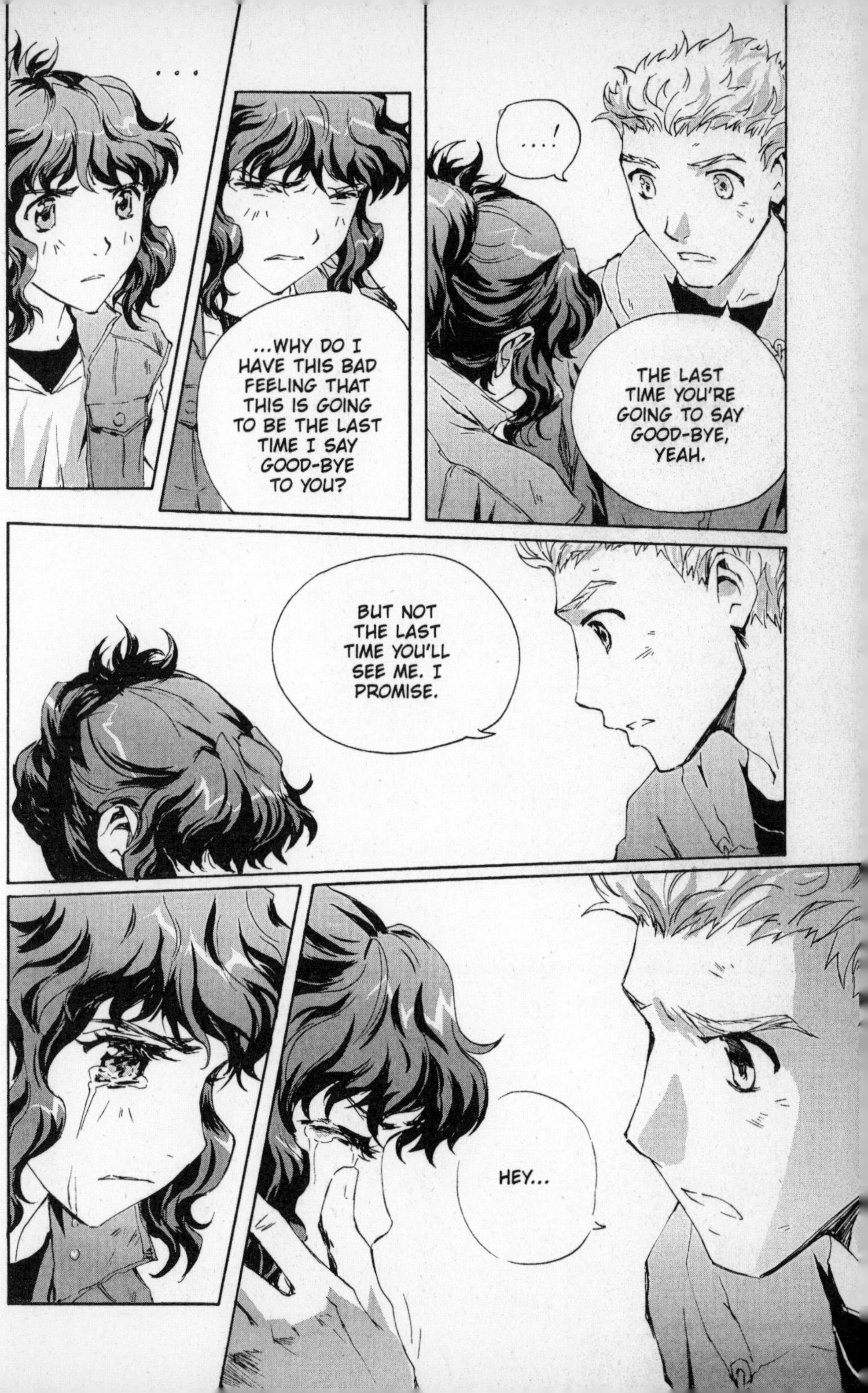

...
...WHY DO I HAVE THIS BAD FEELING THAT THIS IS GOING TO BE THE LAST TIME I SAY GOOD-BYE TO YOU?
...!
THE LAST TIME YOU'RE GOING TO SAY GOOD-BYE, YEAH.
BUT NOT THE LAST TIME YOU'LL SEE ME. I PROMISE.
HEY...

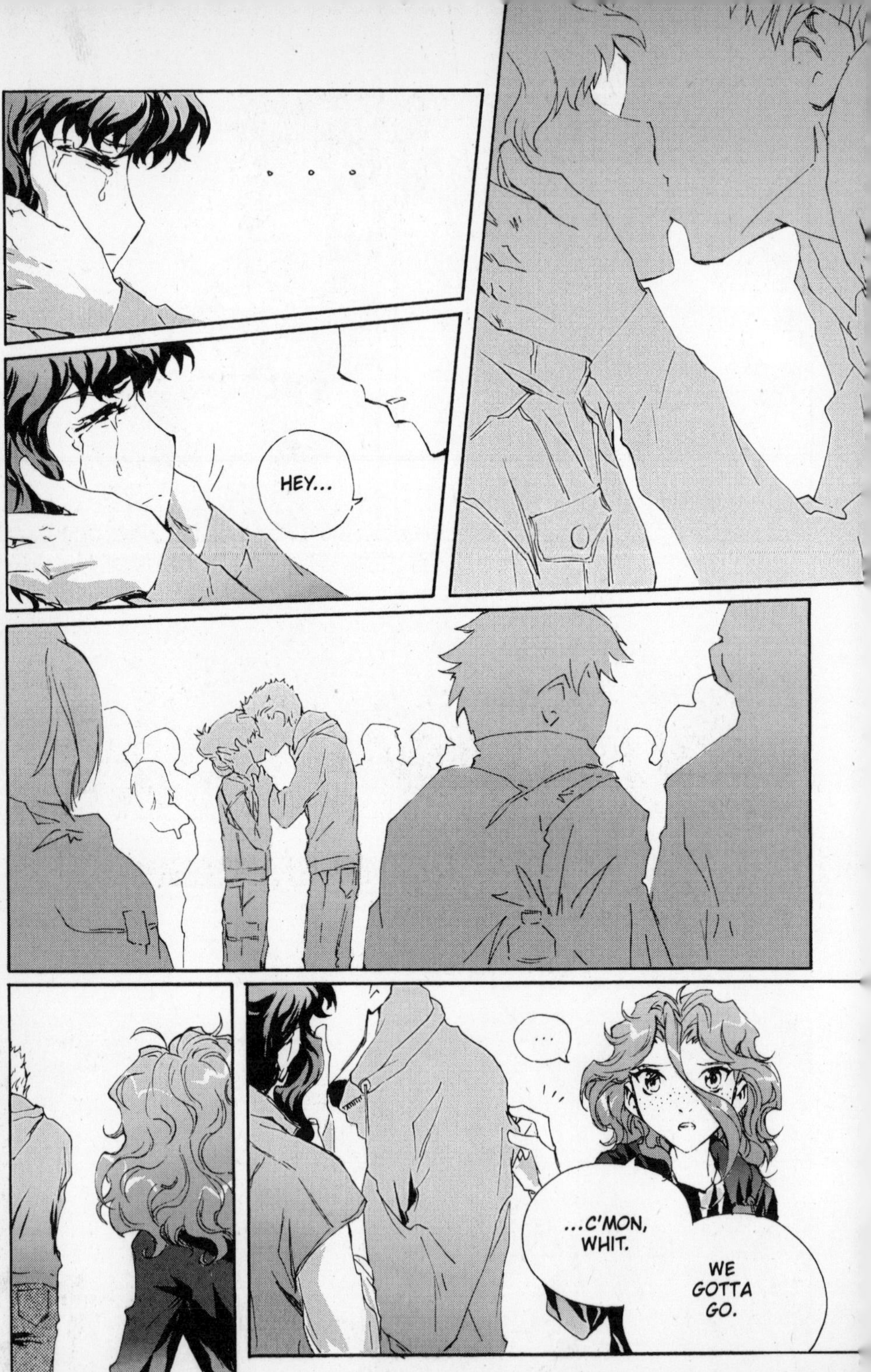
. . .
HEY...
...
...C'MON, WHIT.
WE GOTTA GO.

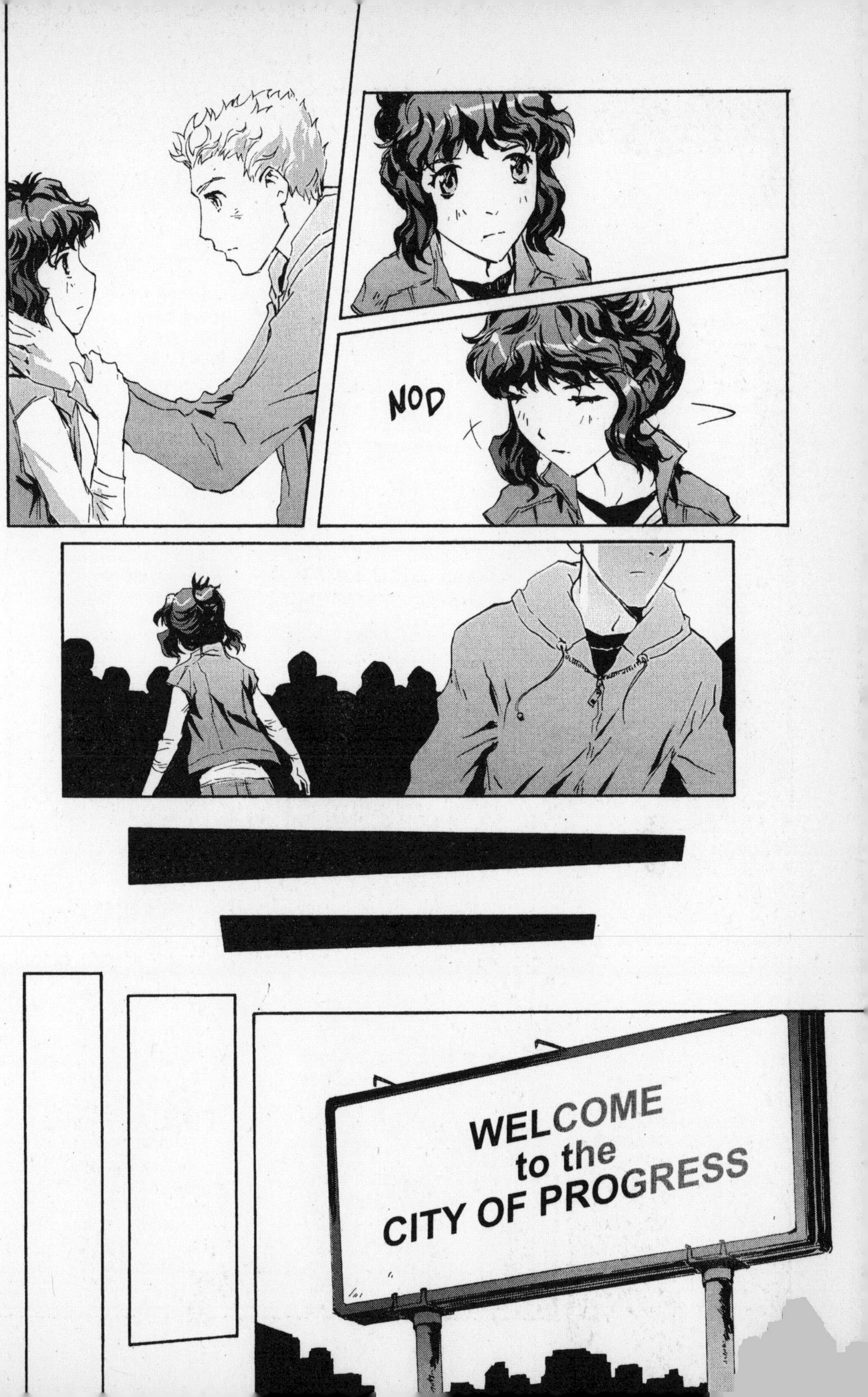
NOD
WELCOME
to the
CITY OF PROGRESS

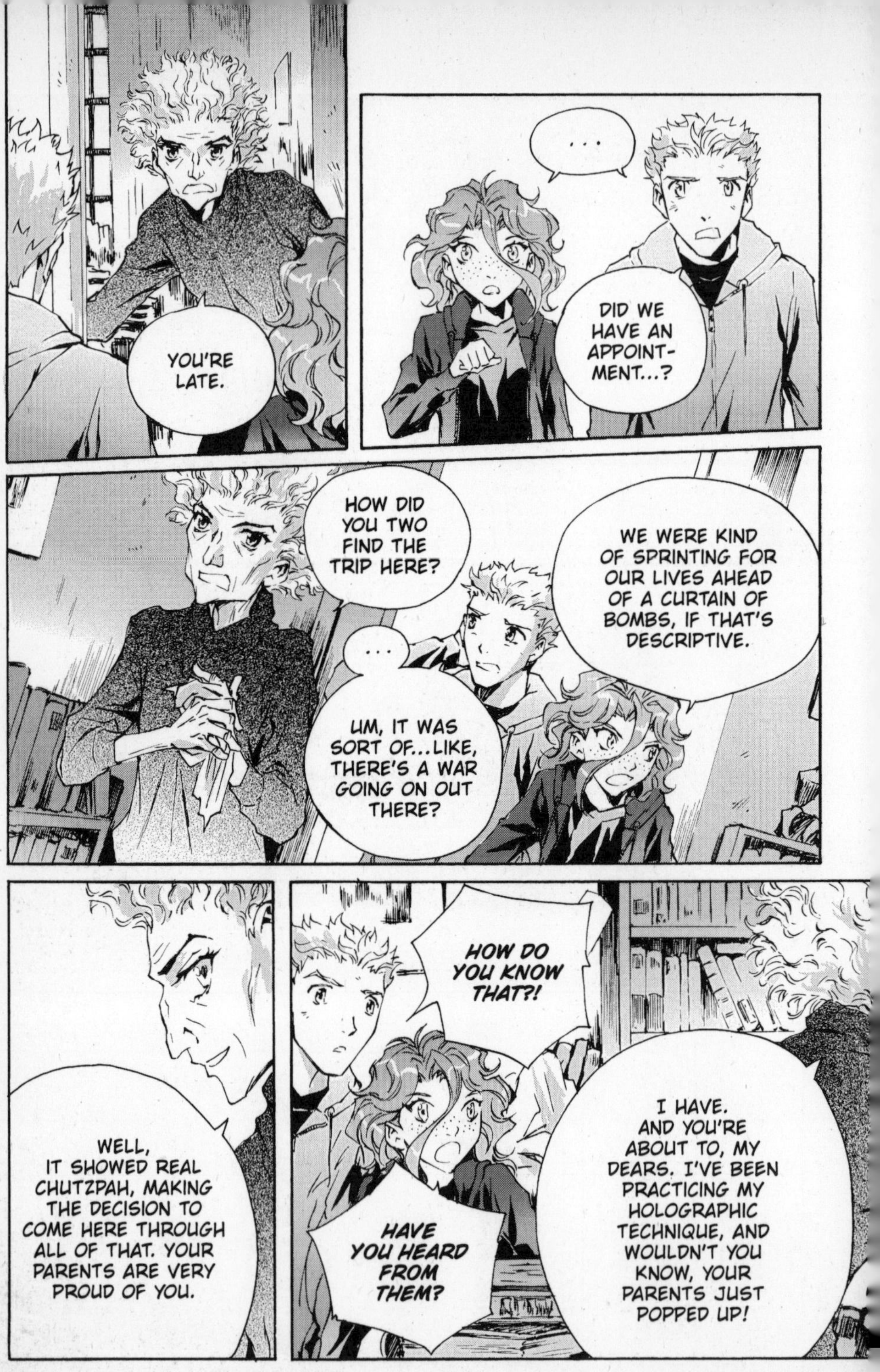
YOU'RE LATE.
...
DID WE HAVE AN APPOINT-MENT...?
HOW DID YOU TWO FIND THE TRIP HERE?
...
UM, IT WAS SORT OF...LIKE, THERE'S A WAR GOING ON OUT THERE?
WE WERE KIND OF SPRINTING FOR OUR LIVES AHEAD OF A CURTAIN OF BOMBS, IF THAT'S DESCRIPTIVE.
WELL, IT SHOWED REAL CHUTZPAH, MAKING THE DECISION TO COME HERE THROUGH ALL OF THAT. YOUR PARENTS ARE VERY PROUD OF YOU.
HOW DO YOU KNOW THAT?!
HAVE YOU HEARD FROM THEM?
I HAVE. AND YOU'RE ABOUT TO, MY DEARS. I'VE BEEN PRACTICING MY HOLOGRAPHIC TECHNIQUE, AND WOULDN'T YOU KNOW, YOUR PARENTS JUST POPPED UP!

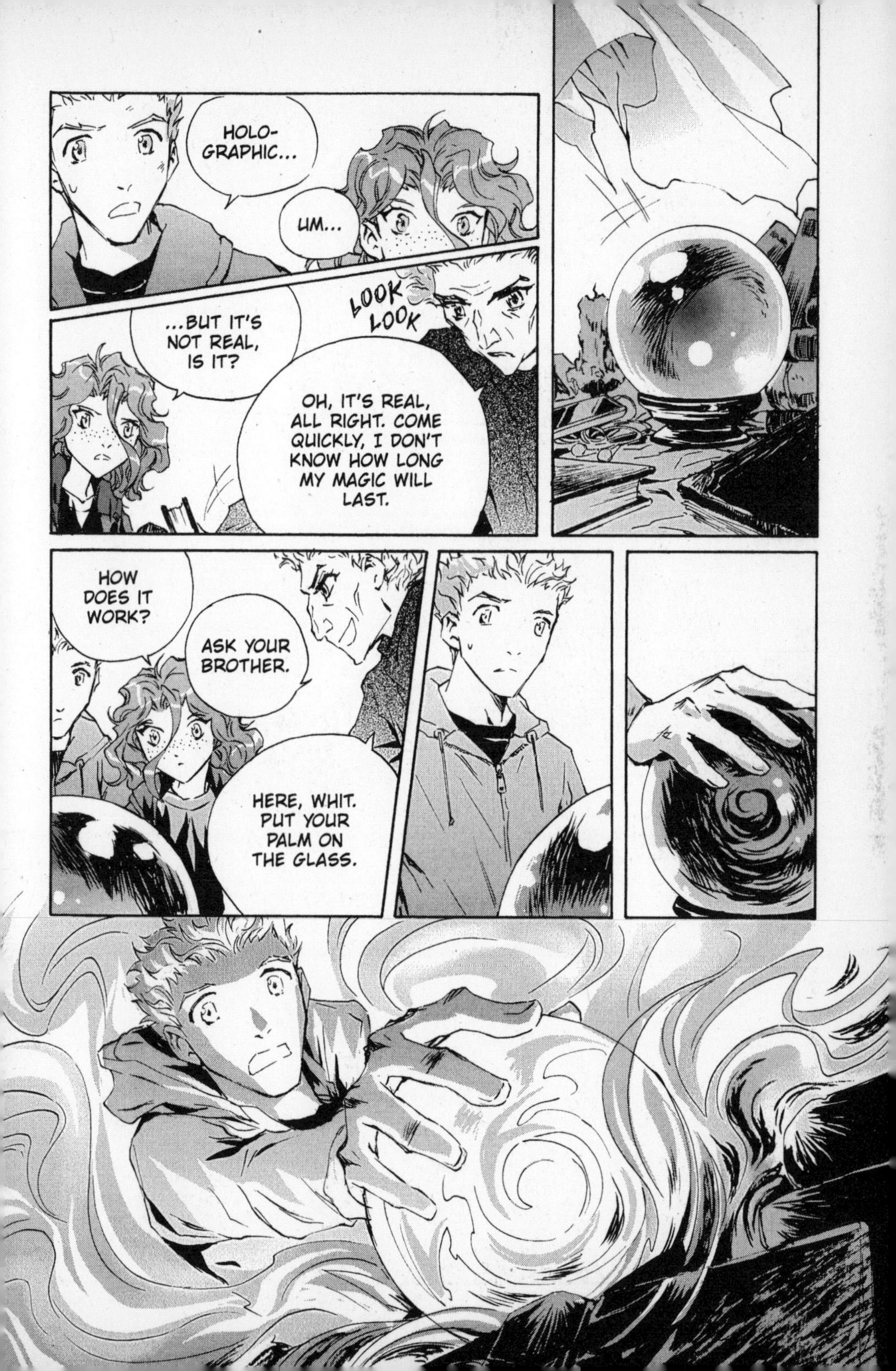
HOLO-
GRAPHIC...
UM...
...BUT IT'S NOT REAL, IS IT?
LOOK LOOK
OH, IT'S REAL, ALL RIGHT. COME QUICKLY, I DON'T KNOW HOW LONG MY MAGIC WILL LAST.
HOW DOES IT WORK?
ASK YOUR BROTHER.
HERE, WHIT. PUT YOUR PALM ON THE GLASS.

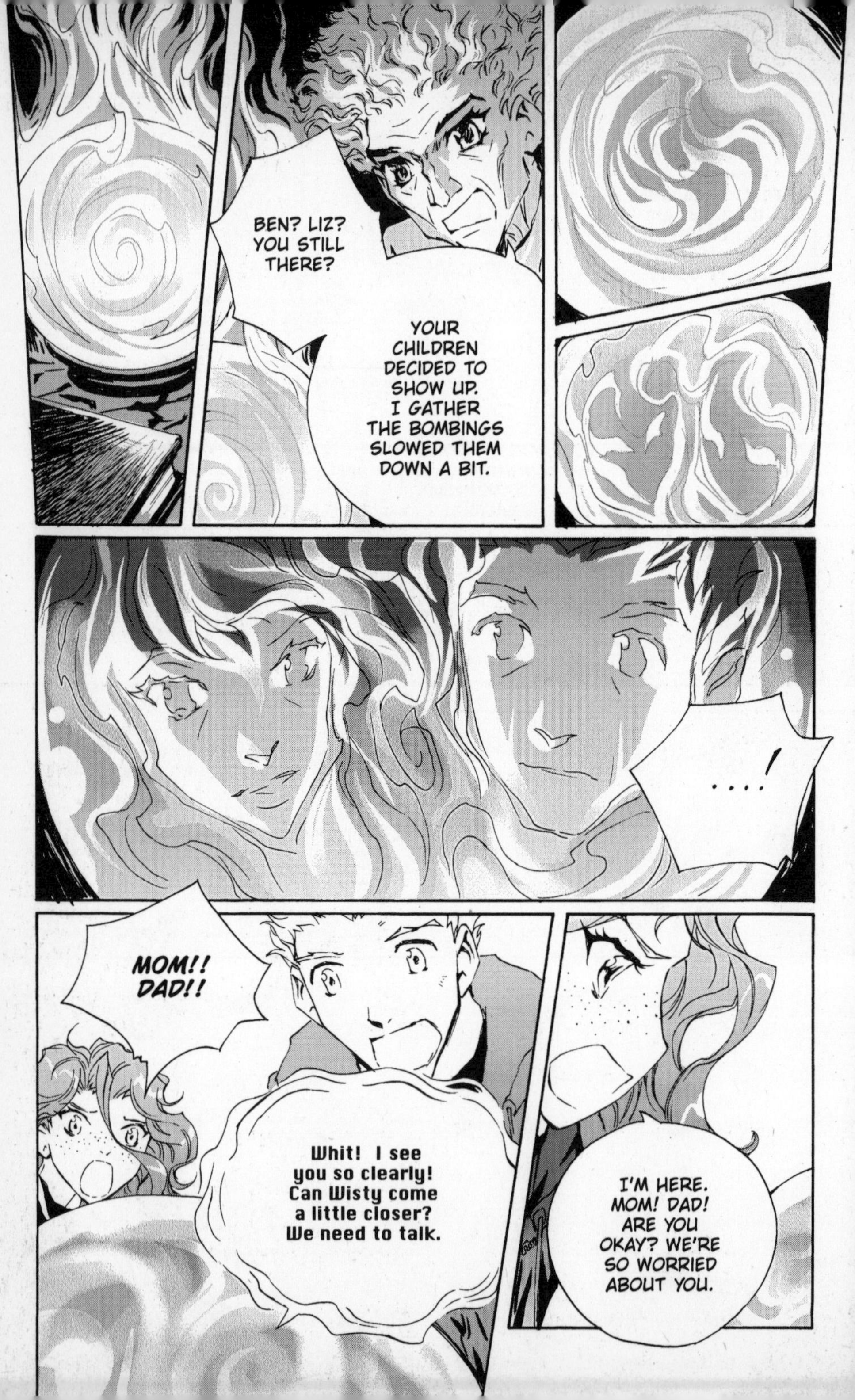
BEN? LIZ? YOU STILL THERE?
YOUR CHILDREN DECIDED TO SHOW UP. I GATHER THE BOMBINGS SLOWED THEM DOWN A BIT.
....!
MOM!! DAD!!
Whit! I see you so clearly! Can Wisty come a little closer? We need to talk.
I'M HERE. MOM! DAD! ARE YOU OKAY? WE'RE SO WORRIED ABOUT YOU.

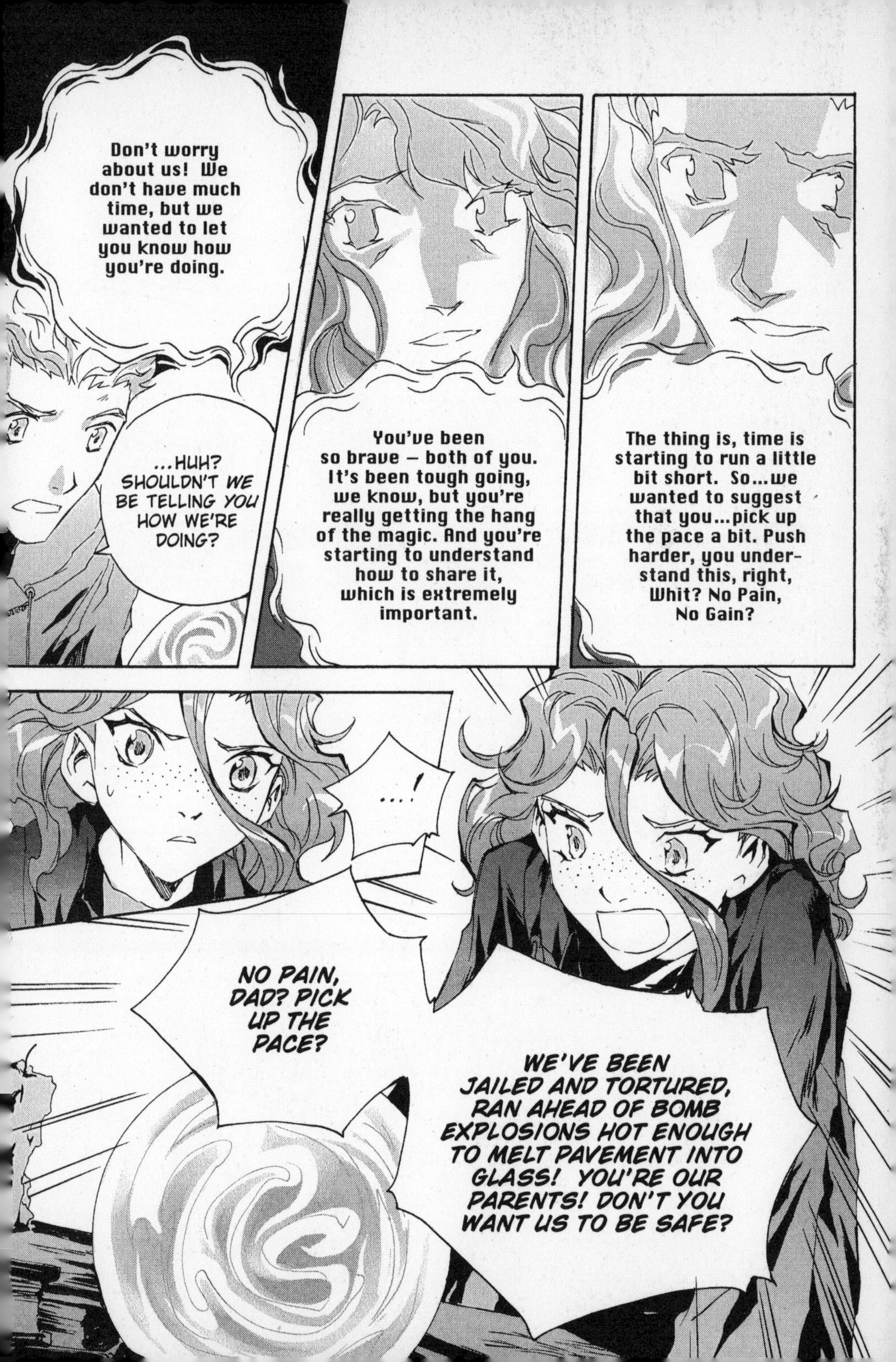
Don't worry about us! We don't have much time, but we wanted to let you know how you're doing.
...HUH? SHOULDN'T *WE* BE TELLING *YOU* HOW WE'RE DOING?
You've been so brave – both of you. It's been tough going, we know, but you're really getting the hang of the magic. And you're starting to understand how to share it, which is extremely important.
The thing is, time is starting to run a little bit short. So...we wanted to suggest that you...pick up the pace a bit. Push harder, you understand this, right, Whit? No Pain, No Gain?
...!
NO PAIN, DAD? PICK UP THE PACE?
WE'VE BEEN JAILED AND TORTURED, RAN AHEAD OF BOMB EXPLOSIONS HOT ENOUGH TO MELT PAVEMENT INTO GLASS! YOU'RE OUR PARENTS! DON'T YOU WANT US TO BE SAFE?

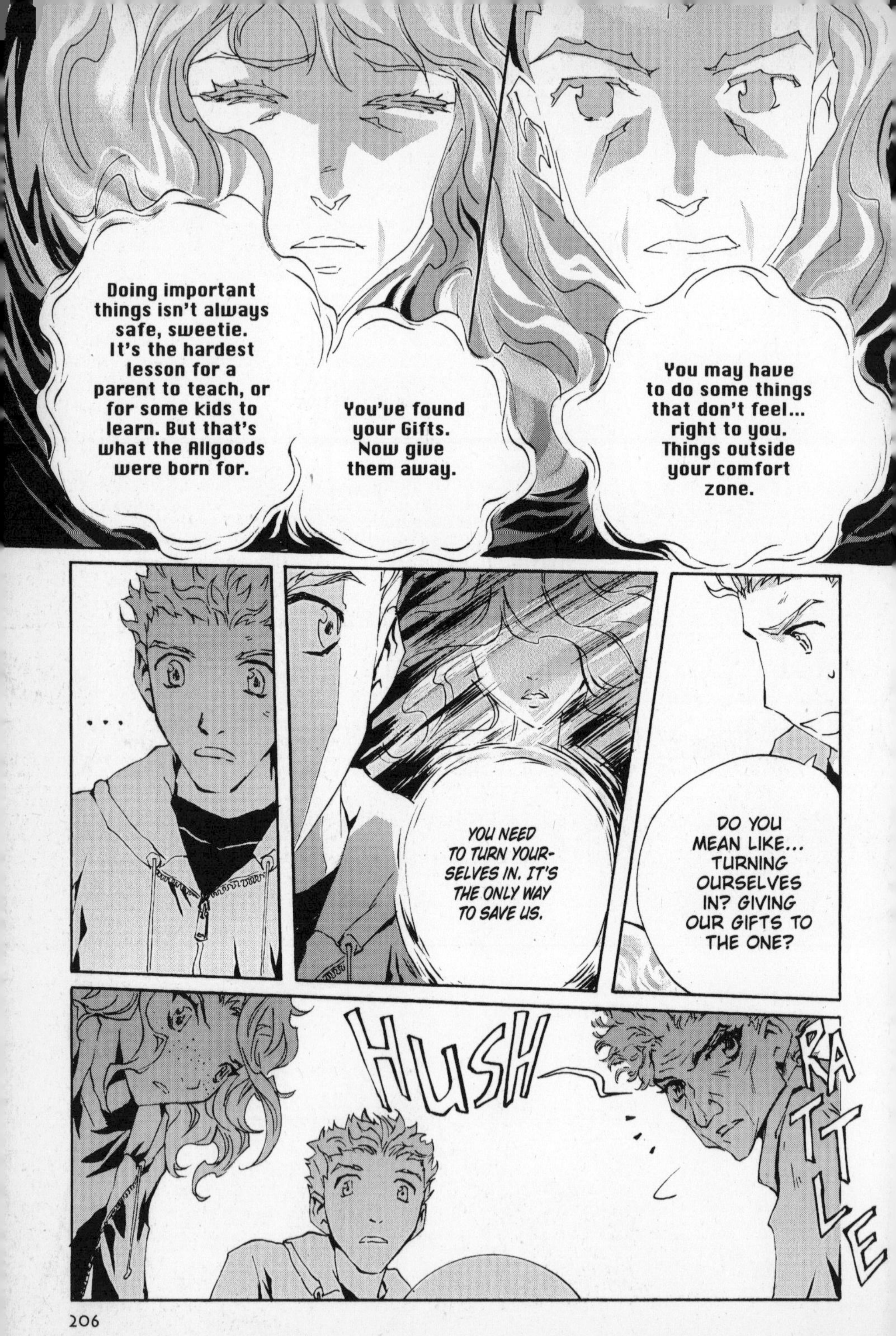
Doing important things isn't always safe, sweetie. It's the hardest lesson for a parent to teach, or for some kids to learn. But that's what the Allgoods were born for.
You've found your Gifts. Now give them away.
You may have to do some things that don't feel... right to you. Things outside your comfort zone.
...
YOU NEED TO TURN YOURSELVES IN. IT'S THE ONLY WAY TO SAVE US.
DO YOU MEAN LIKE... TURNING OURSELVES IN? GIVING OUR GIFTS TO THE ONE?
HUSH
...
RATTLE

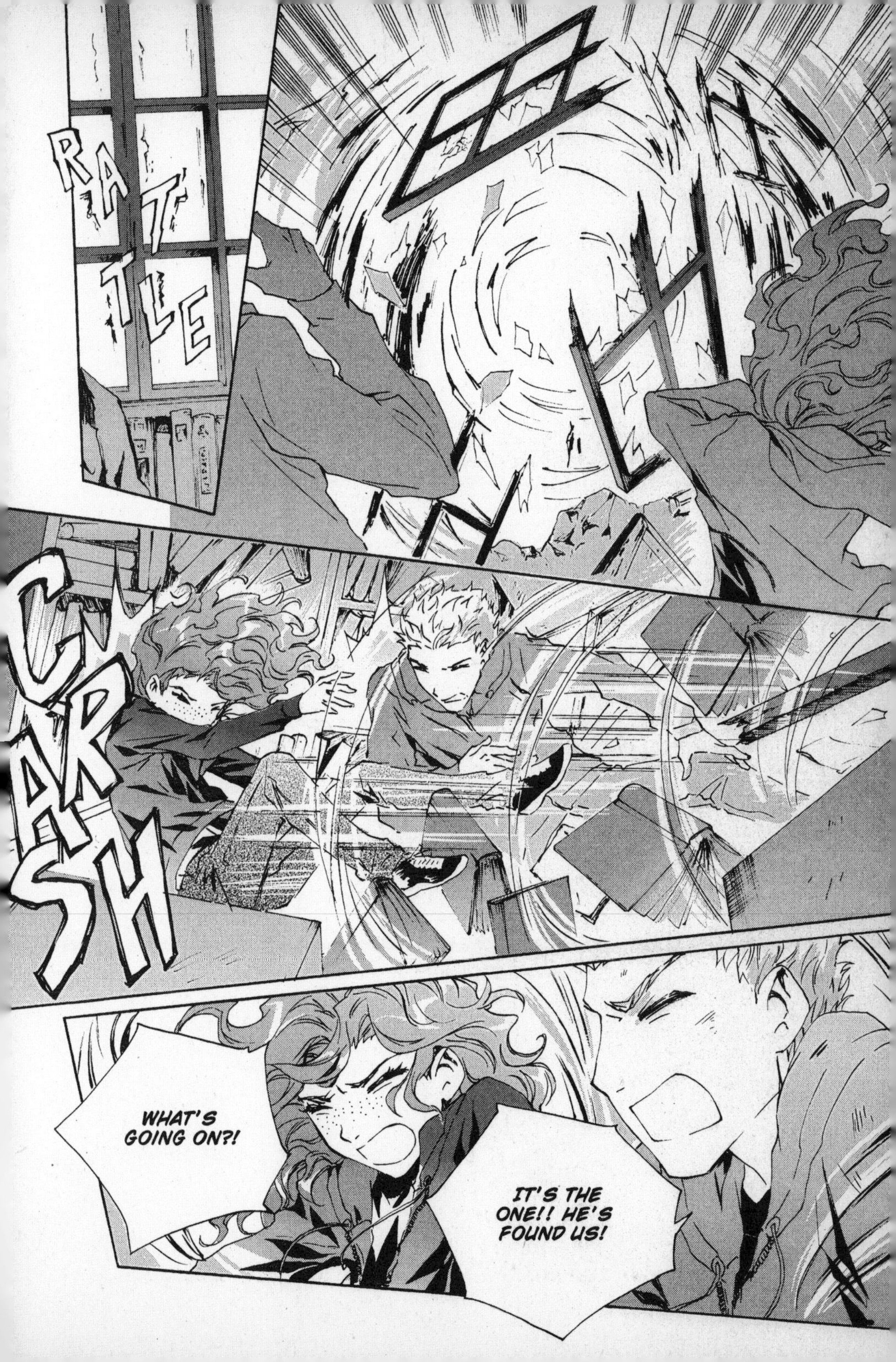
RATTLE
CRASH
WHAT'S GOING ON?!
IT'S THE ONE!! HE'S FOUND US!

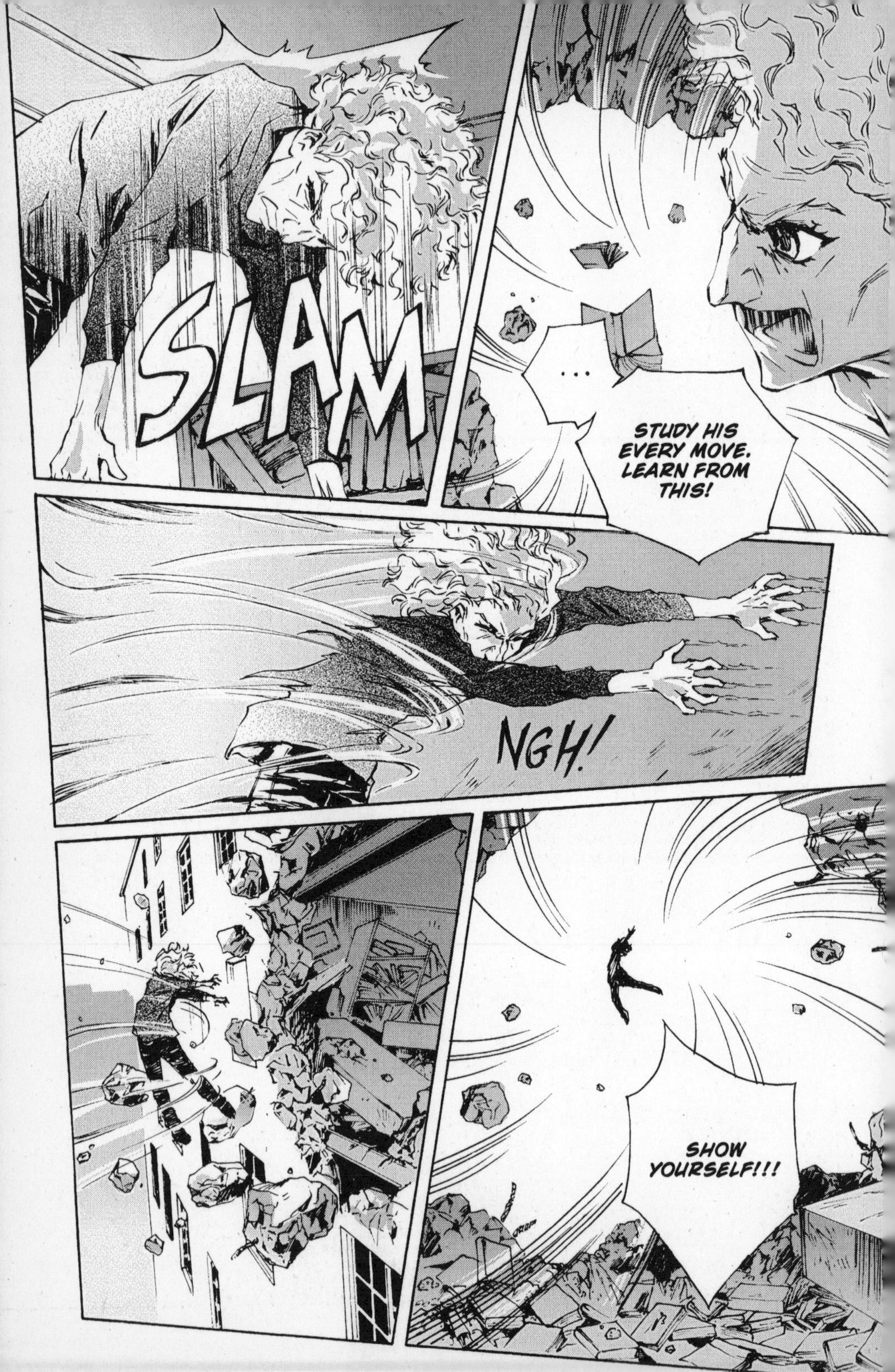
SLAM
...
STUDY HIS EVERY MOVE. LEARN FROM THIS!
NGH!
SHOW YOURSELF!!!

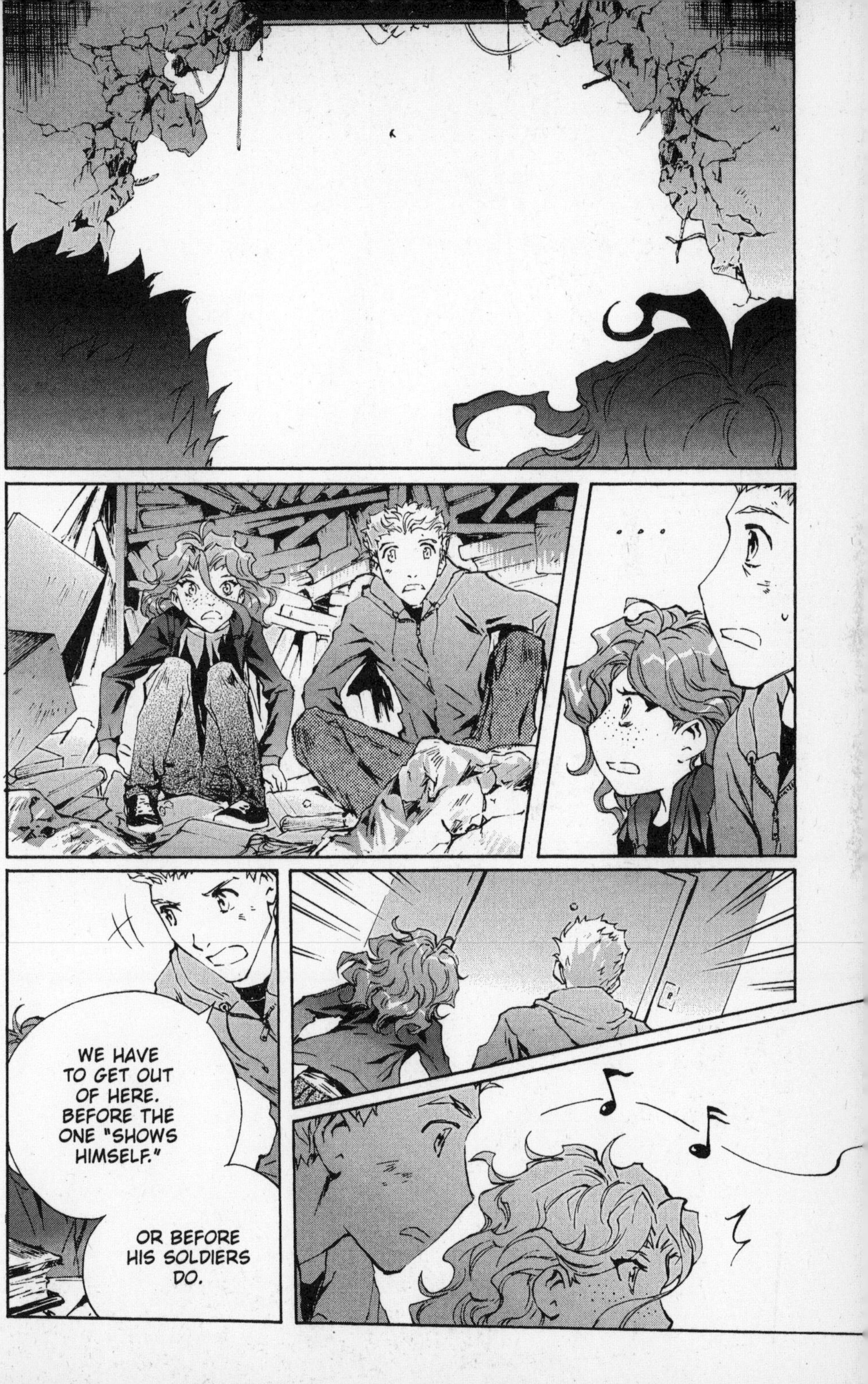
. . .
WE HAVE TO GET OUT OF HERE. BEFORE THE ONE "SHOWS HIMSELF."
OR BEFORE HIS SOLDIERS DO.

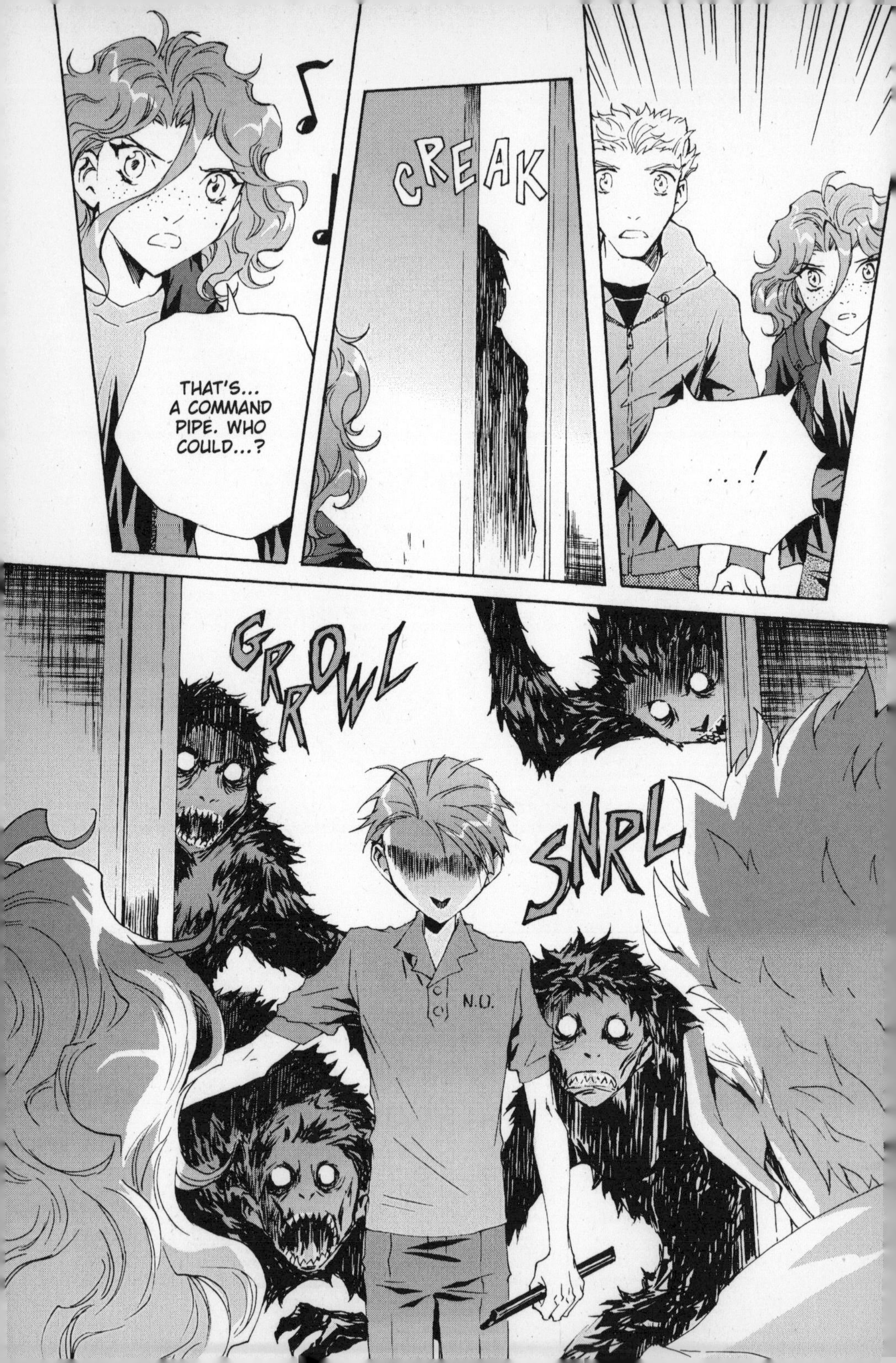
THAT'S... A COMMAND PIPE. WHO COULD...?
CREAK
...!
GRROWL
SNRL
N.O.

WITCH & WIZARD

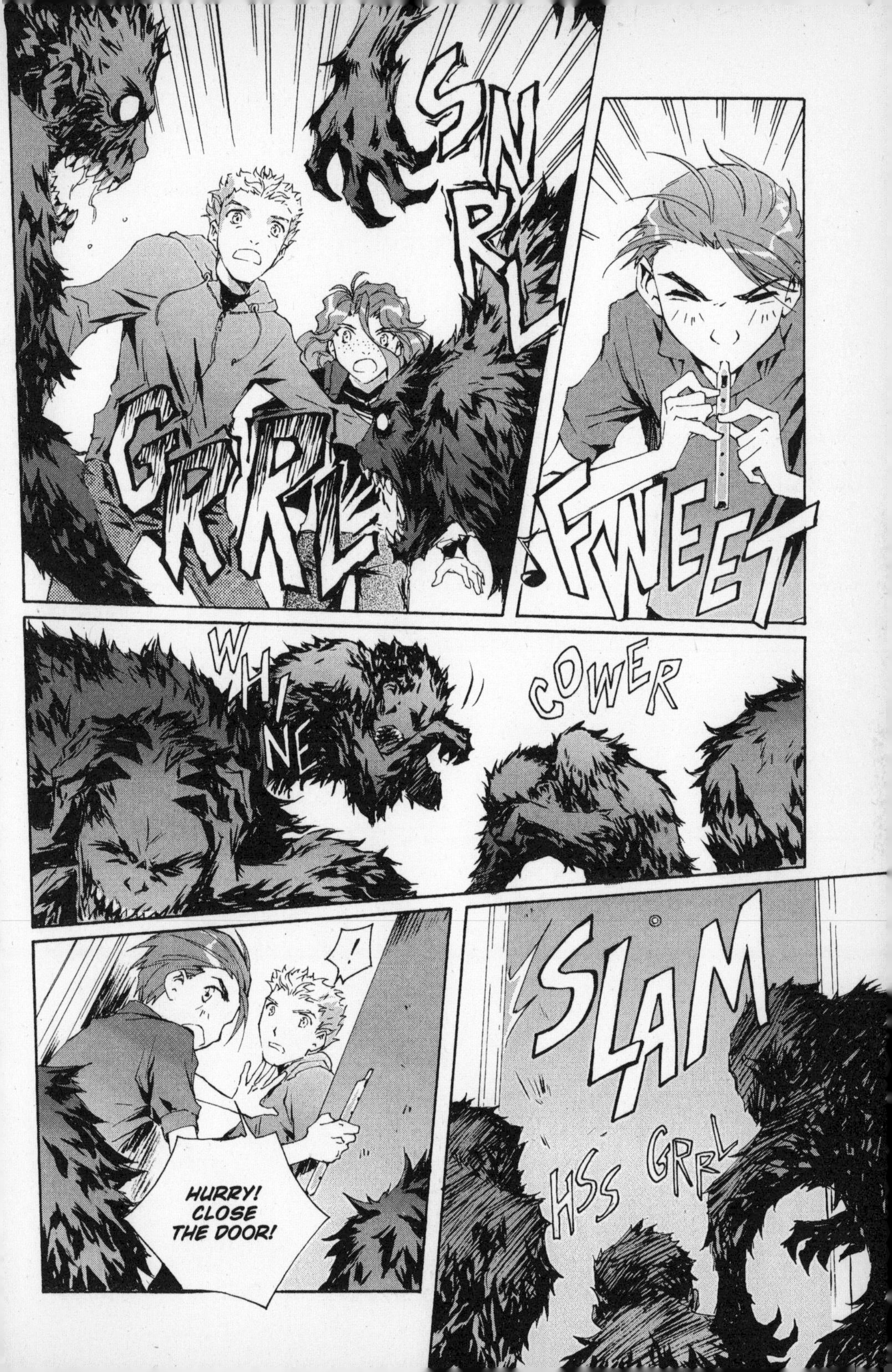
SNRRL
GRRRL
FWEET
WHINE
COWER
!
HURRY! CLOSE THE DOOR!
SLAM
HSS GRRL

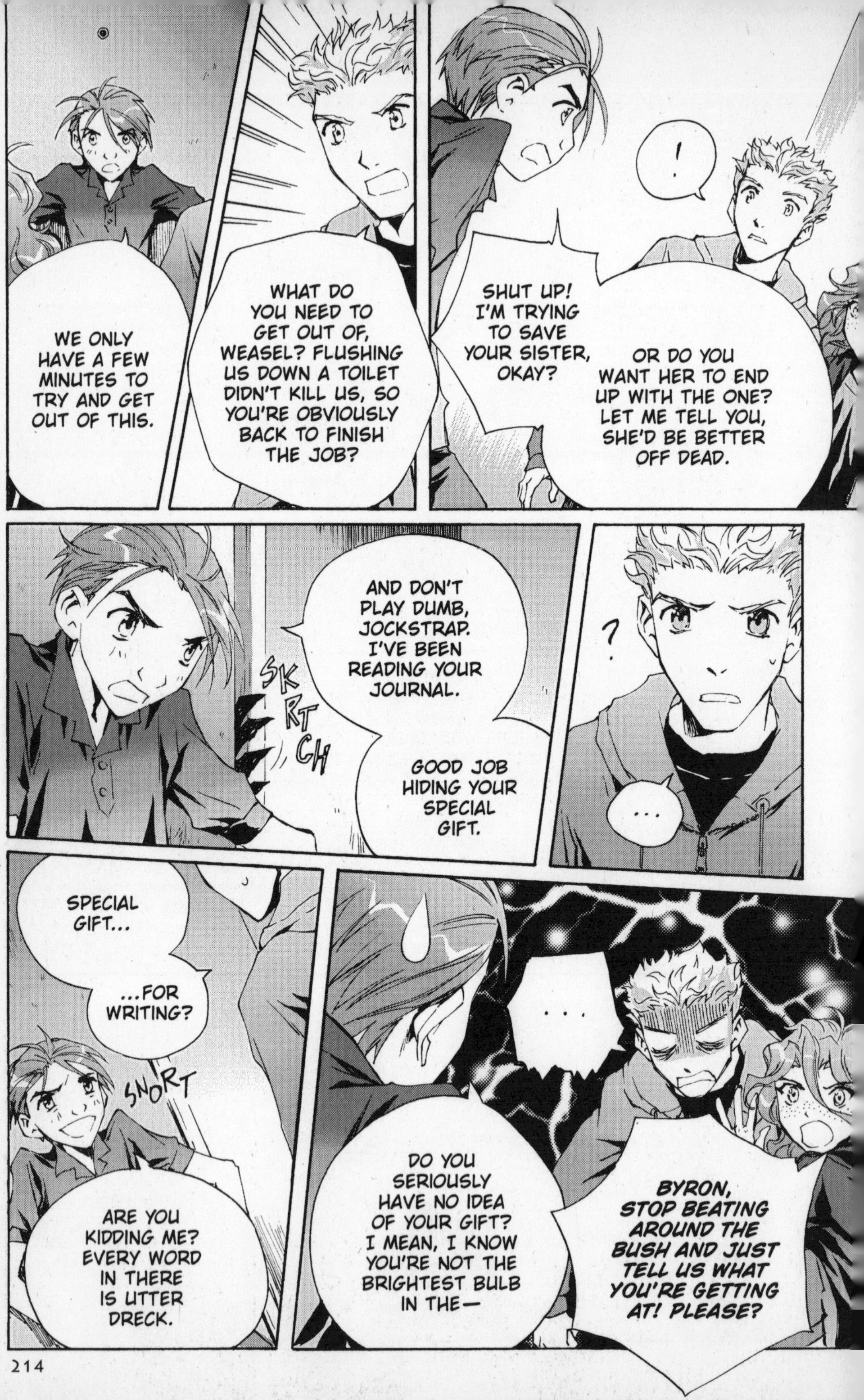

WE ONLY HAVE A FEW MINUTES TO TRY AND GET OUT OF THIS.
WHAT DO YOU NEED TO GET OUT OF, WEASEL? FLUSHING US DOWN A TOILET DIDN'T KILL US, SO YOU'RE OBVIOUSLY BACK TO FINISH THE JOB?
SHUT UP! I'M TRYING TO SAVE YOUR SISTER, OKAY?
!
OR DO YOU WANT HER TO END UP WITH THE ONE? LET ME TELL YOU, SHE'D BE BETTER OFF DEAD.
AND DON'T PLAY DUMB, JOCKSTRAP. I'VE BEEN READING YOUR JOURNAL.
SKRTCH
GOOD JOB HIDING YOUR SPECIAL GIFT.
?
...
SPECIAL GIFT...
...FOR WRITING?
SNORT
ARE YOU KIDDING ME? EVERY WORD IN THERE IS UTTER DRECK.
...
DO YOU SERIOUSLY HAVE NO IDEA OF YOUR GIFT? I MEAN, I KNOW YOU'RE NOT THE BRIGHTEST BULB IN THE—
BYRON, STOP BEATING AROUND THE BUSH AND JUST TELL US WHAT YOU'RE GETTING AT! PLEASE?

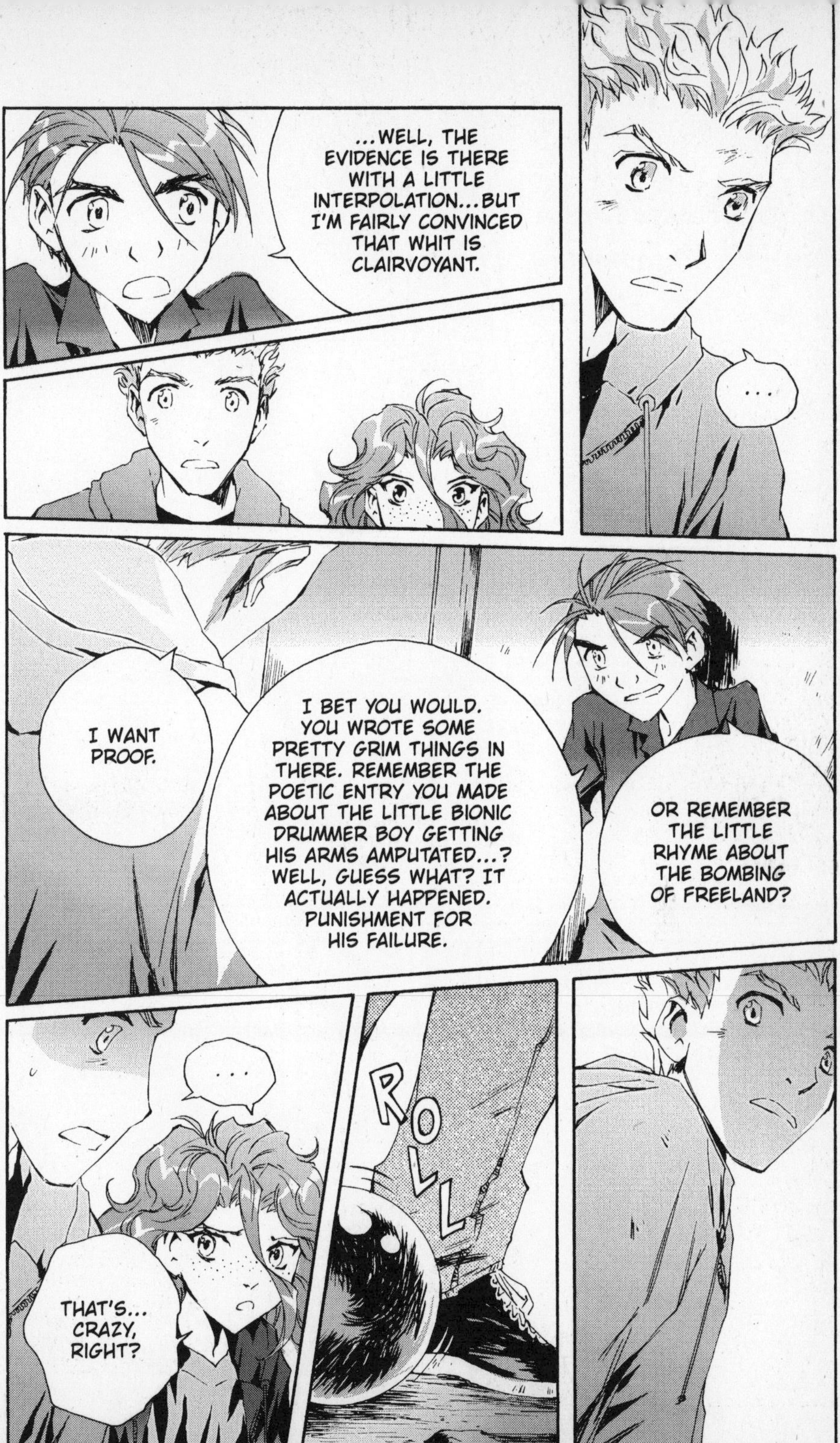
...WELL, THE EVIDENCE IS THERE WITH A LITTLE INTERPOLATION...BUT I'M FAIRLY CONVINCED THAT WHIT IS CLAIRVOYANT.
...
I WANT PROOF.
I BET YOU WOULD. YOU WROTE SOME PRETTY GRIM THINGS IN THERE. REMEMBER THE POETIC ENTRY YOU MADE ABOUT THE LITTLE BIONIC DRUMMER BOY GETTING HIS ARMS AMPUTATED...? WELL, GUESS WHAT? IT ACTUALLY HAPPENED. PUNISHMENT FOR HIS FAILURE.
OR REMEMBER THE LITTLE RHYME ABOUT THE BOMBING OF FREELAND?
...
THAT'S... CRAZY, RIGHT?
ROLL

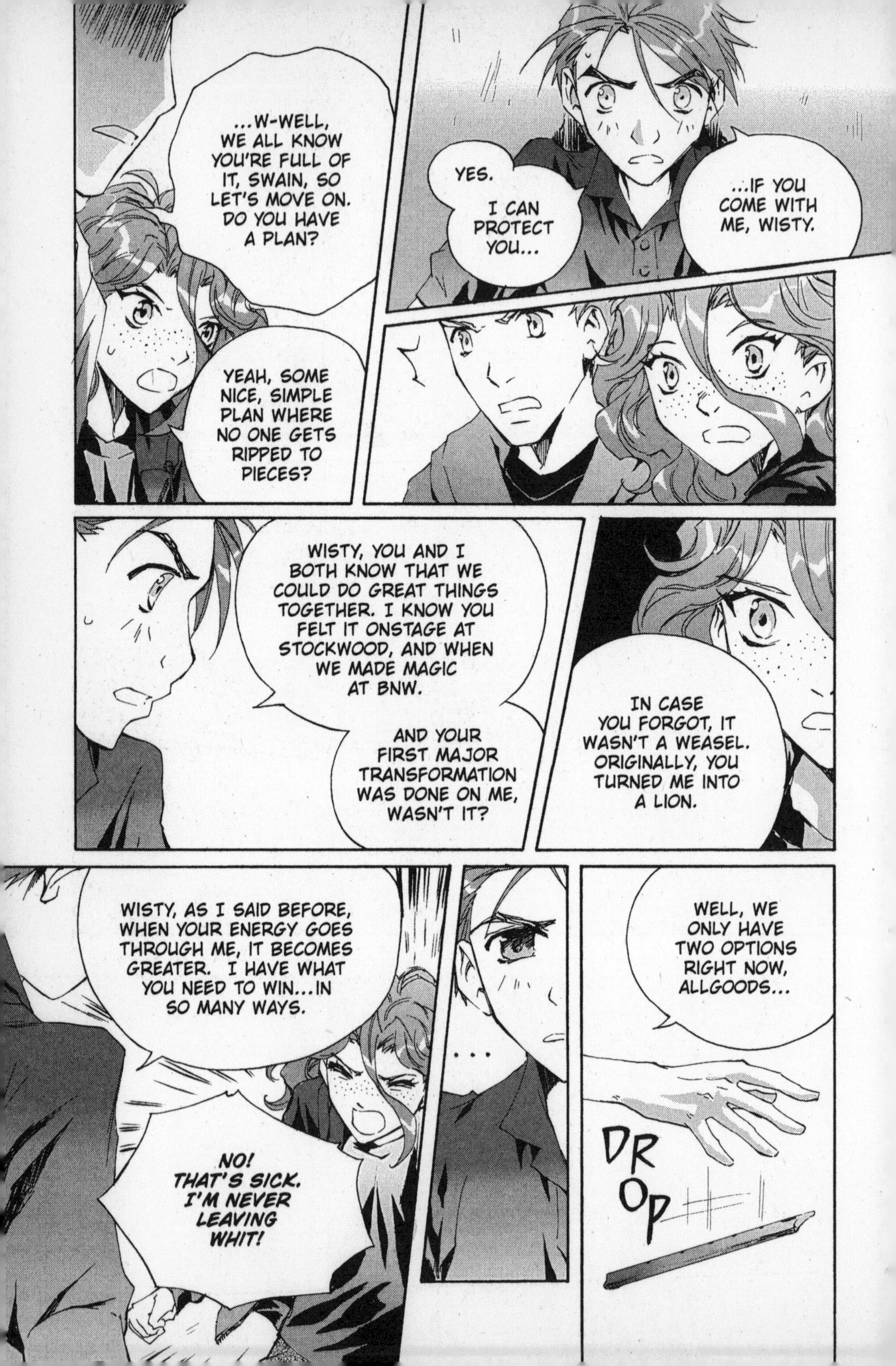
...W-WELL, WE ALL KNOW YOU'RE FULL OF IT, SWAIN, SO LET'S MOVE ON. DO YOU HAVE A PLAN?
YEAH, SOME NICE, SIMPLE PLAN WHERE NO ONE GETS RIPPED TO PIECES?
YES.
I CAN PROTECT YOU...
...IF YOU COME WITH ME, WISTY.
WISTY, YOU AND I BOTH KNOW THAT WE COULD DO GREAT THINGS TOGETHER. I KNOW YOU FELT IT ONSTAGE AT STOCKWOOD, AND WHEN WE MADE MAGIC AT BNW.
AND YOUR FIRST MAJOR TRANSFORMATION WAS DONE ON ME, WASN'T IT?
IN CASE YOU FORGOT, IT WASN'T A WEASEL. ORIGINALLY, YOU TURNED ME INTO A LION.
WISTY, AS I SAID BEFORE, WHEN YOUR ENERGY GOES THROUGH ME, IT BECOMES GREATER. I HAVE WHAT YOU NEED TO WIN...IN SO MANY WAYS.
NO! THAT'S SICK. I'M NEVER LEAVING WHIT!
...
WELL, WE ONLY HAVE TWO OPTIONS RIGHT NOW, ALLGOODS...
DROP

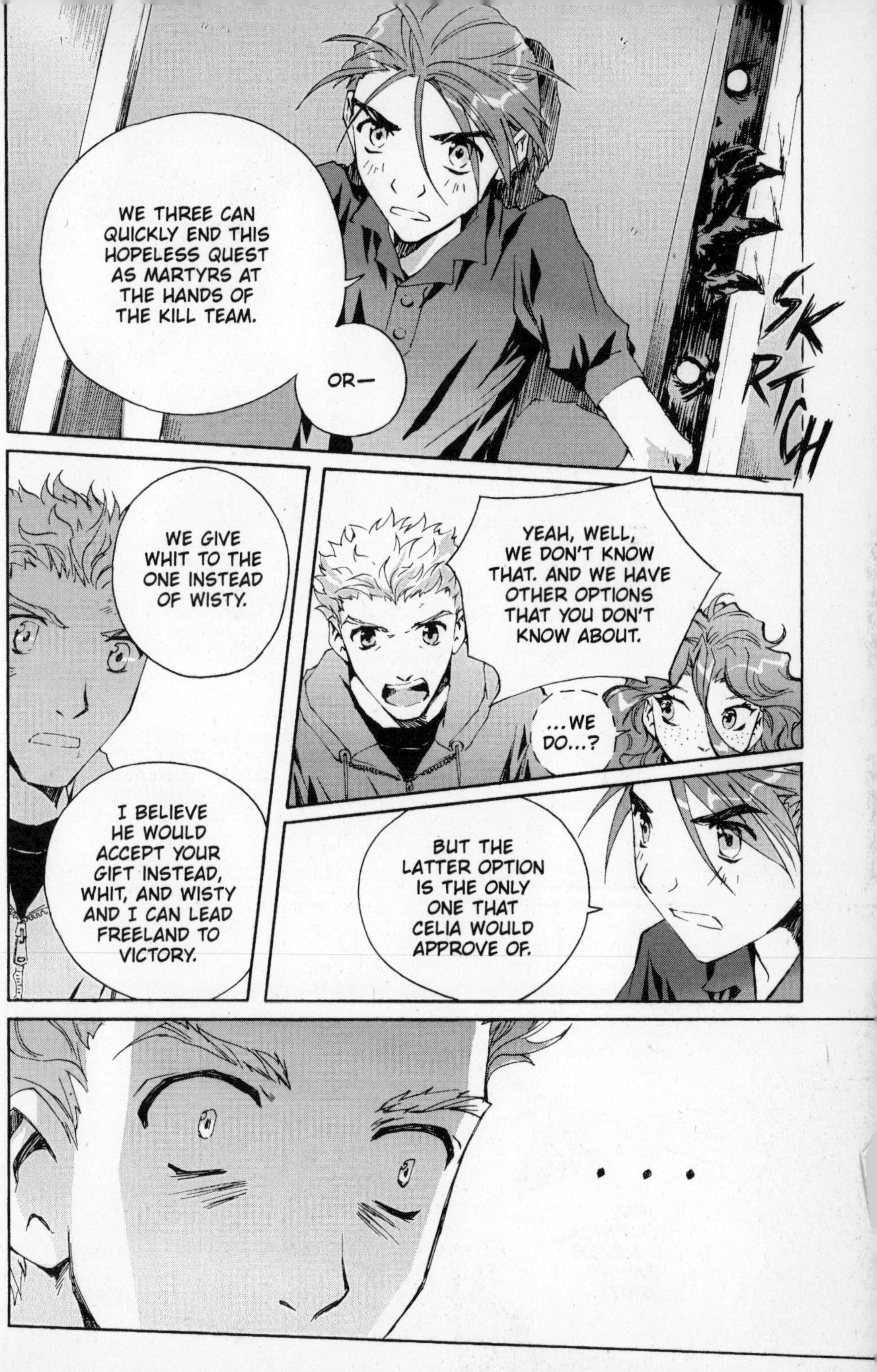
WE THREE CAN QUICKLY END THIS HOPELESS QUEST AS MARTYRS AT THE HANDS OF THE KILL TEAM.
OR—
SKRTCH
WE GIVE WHIT TO THE ONE INSTEAD OF WISTY.
I BELIEVE HE WOULD ACCEPT YOUR GIFT INSTEAD, WHIT, AND WISTY AND I CAN LEAD FREELAND TO VICTORY.
YEAH, WELL, WE DON'T KNOW THAT. AND WE HAVE OTHER OPTIONS THAT YOU DON'T KNOW ABOUT.
...WE DO...?
BUT THE LATTER OPTION IS THE ONLY ONE THAT CELIA WOULD APPROVE OF.
. . .

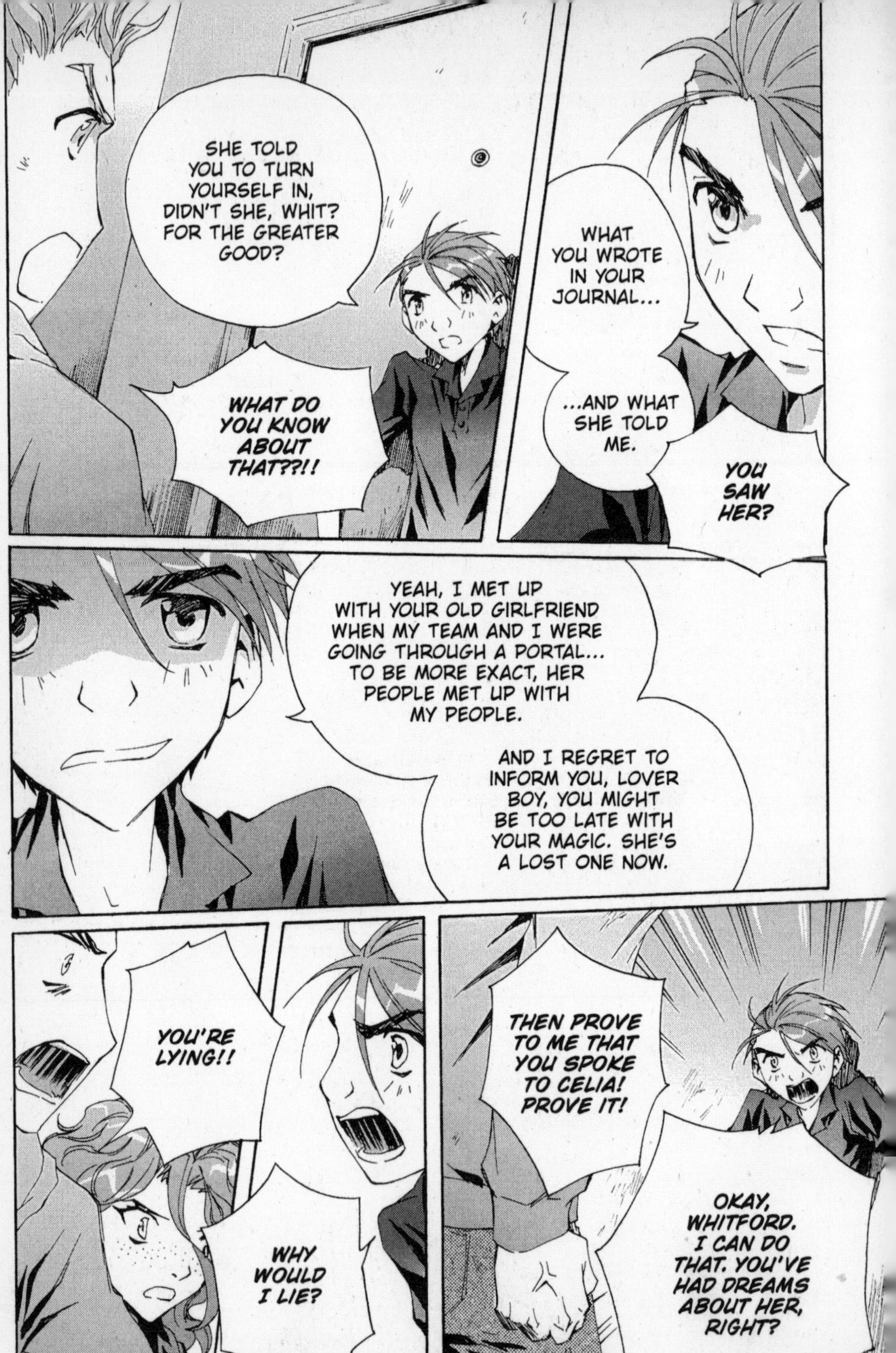
SHE TOLD YOU TO TURN YOURSELF IN, DIDN'T SHE, WHIT? FOR THE GREATER GOOD?
WHAT DO YOU KNOW ABOUT THAT??!!
WHAT YOU WROTE IN YOUR JOURNAL...
...AND WHAT SHE TOLD ME.
YOU SAW HER?
YEAH, I MET UP WITH YOUR OLD GIRLFRIEND WHEN MY TEAM AND I WERE GOING THROUGH A PORTAL... TO BE MORE EXACT, HER PEOPLE MET UP WITH MY PEOPLE.
AND I REGRET TO INFORM YOU, LOVER BOY, YOU MIGHT BE TOO LATE WITH YOUR MAGIC. SHE'S A LOST ONE NOW.
YOU'RE LYING!!
WHY WOULD I LIE?
THEN PROVE TO ME THAT YOU SPOKE TO CELIA! PROVE IT!
OKAY, WHITFORD. I CAN DO THAT. YOU'VE HAD DREAMS ABOUT HER, RIGHT?

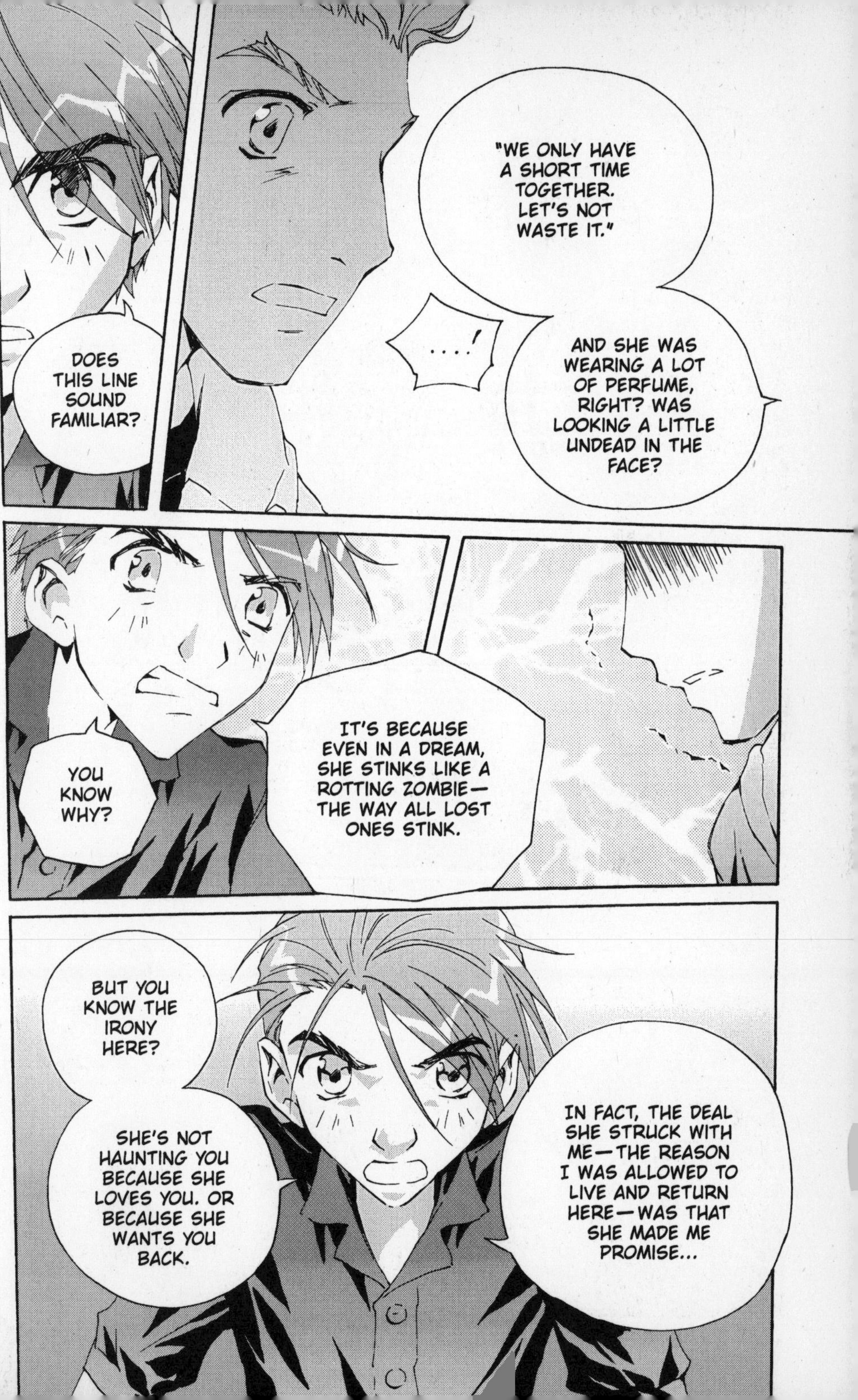
DOES THIS LINE SOUND FAMILIAR?
"WE ONLY HAVE A SHORT TIME TOGETHER. LET'S NOT WASTE IT."
....!
AND SHE WAS WEARING A LOT OF PERFUME, RIGHT? WAS LOOKING A LITTLE UNDEAD IN THE FACE?
YOU KNOW WHY?
IT'S BECAUSE EVEN IN A DREAM, SHE STINKS LIKE A ROTTING ZOMBIE—THE WAY ALL LOST ONES STINK.
BUT YOU KNOW THE IRONY HERE?
SHE'S NOT HAUNTING YOU BECAUSE SHE LOVES YOU. OR BECAUSE SHE WANTS YOU BACK.
IN FACT, THE DEAL SHE STRUCK WITH ME—THE REASON I WAS ALLOWED TO LIVE AND RETURN HERE—WAS THAT SHE MADE ME PROMISE...

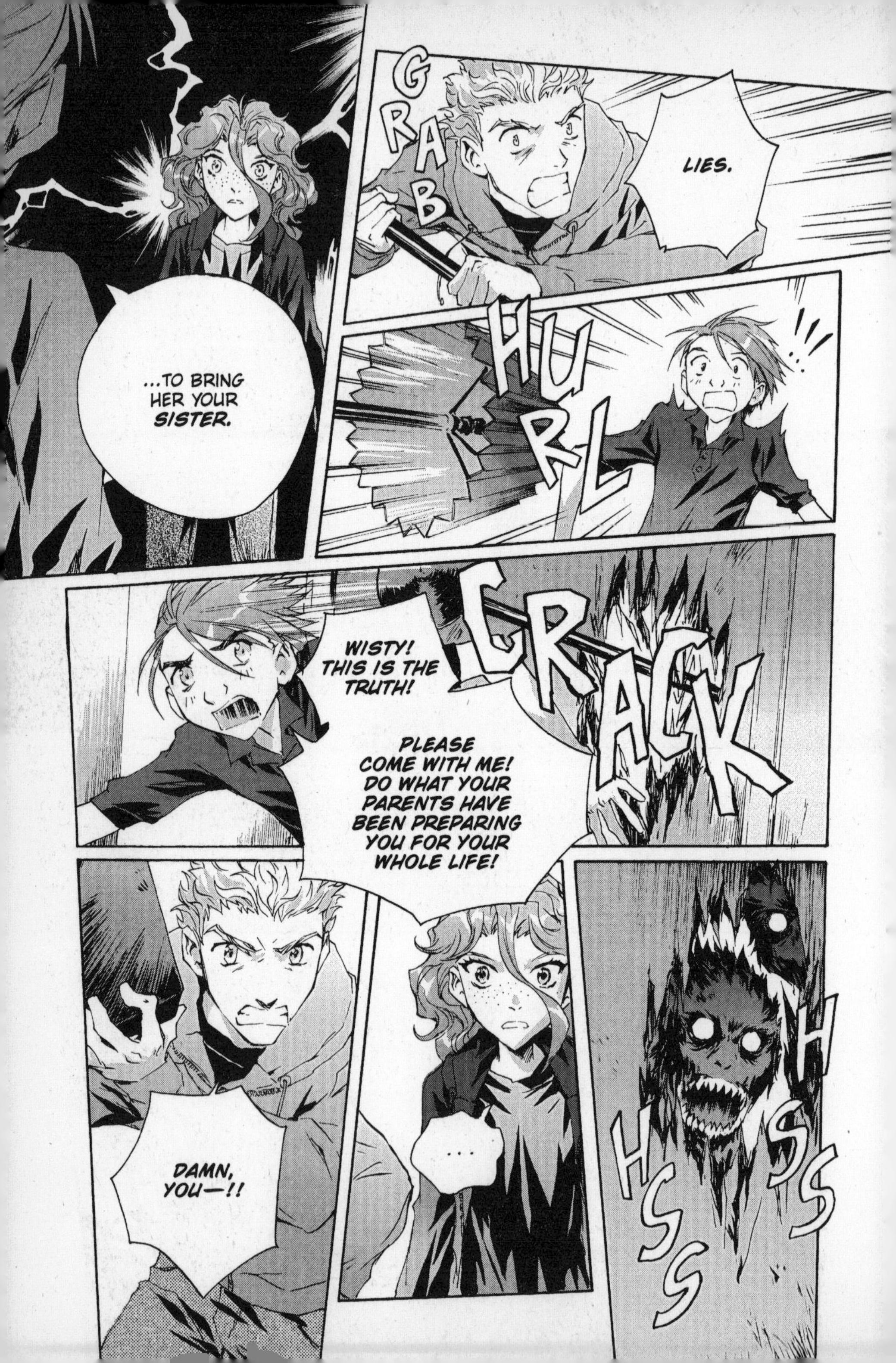
...TO BRING HER YOUR SISTER.
GRAB
LIES.
HURL
!!
WISTY! THIS IS THE TRUTH!
CRACK
PLEASE COME WITH ME! DO WHAT YOUR PARENTS HAVE BEEN PREPARING YOU FOR YOUR WHOLE LIFE!
DAMN, YOU—!!
...
HHSSSS
HSSS

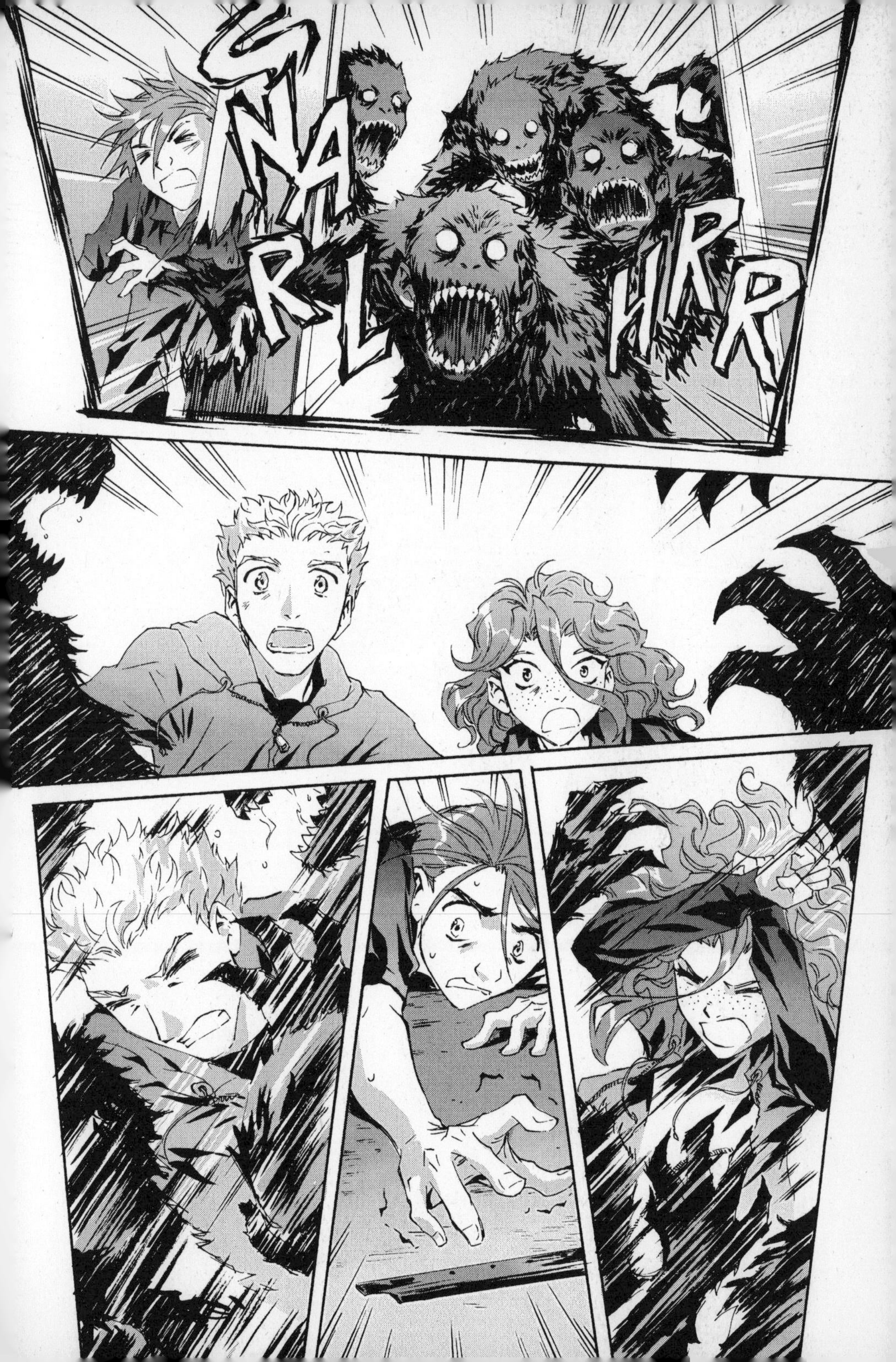
SNARL
HRR

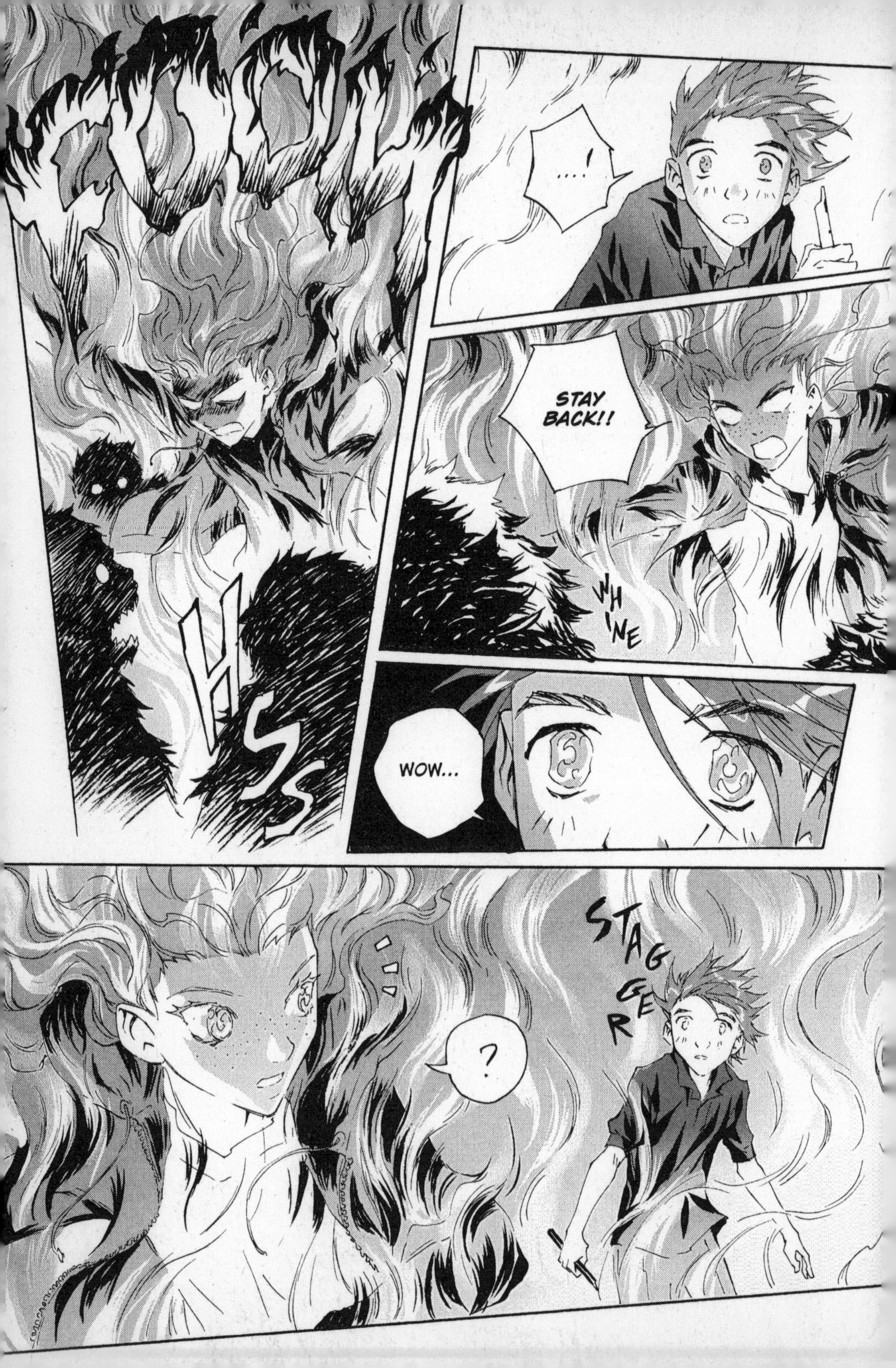

....!
STAY BACK!!
WHINE
WOW...
...
?
STAGGER

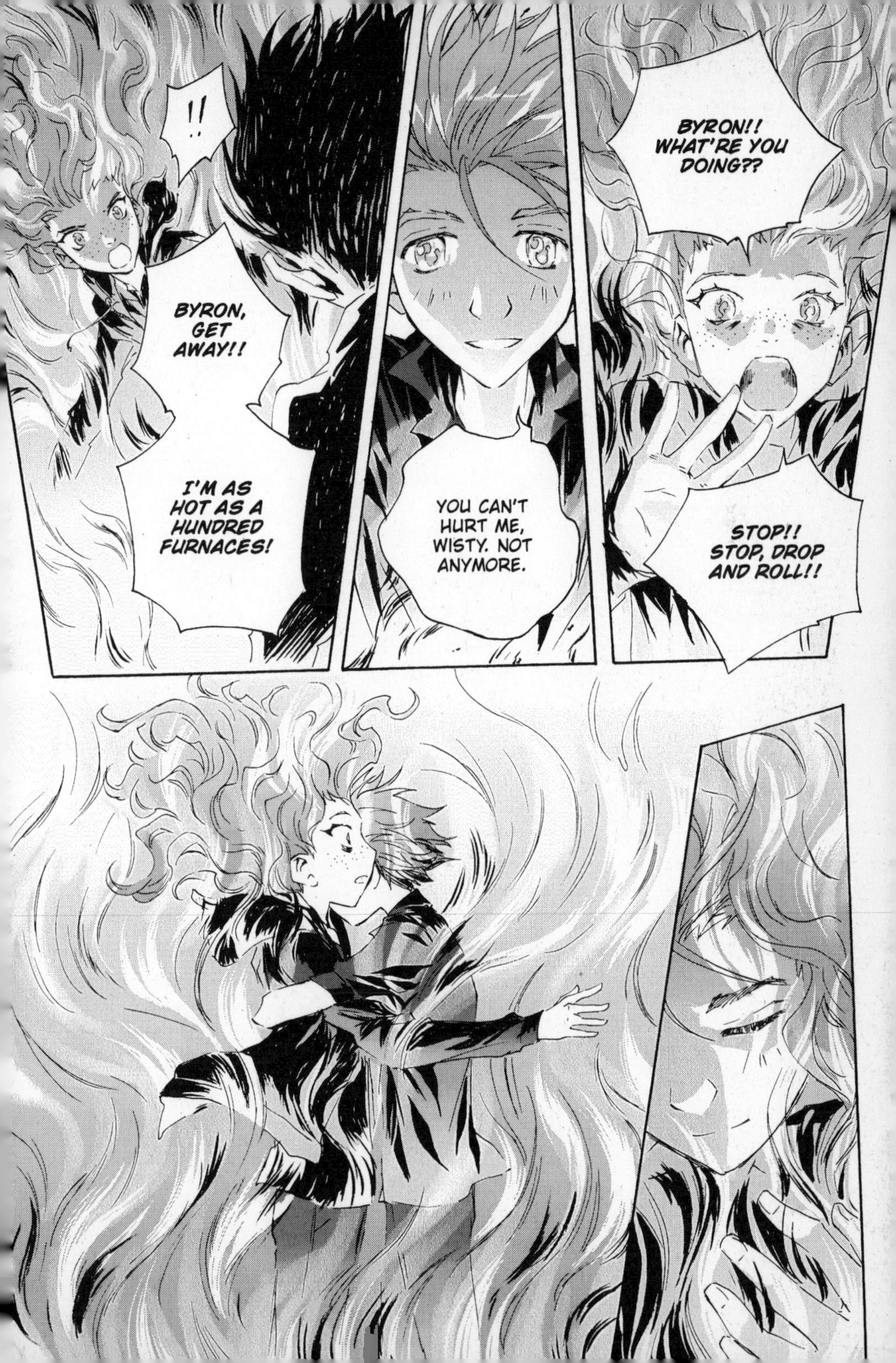
!!
BYRON, GET AWAY!!
I'M AS HOT AS A HUNDRED FURNACES!
YOU CAN'T HURT ME, WISTY. NOT ANYMORE.
BYRON!! WHAT'RE YOU DOING??
STOP!! STOP, DROP AND ROLL!!

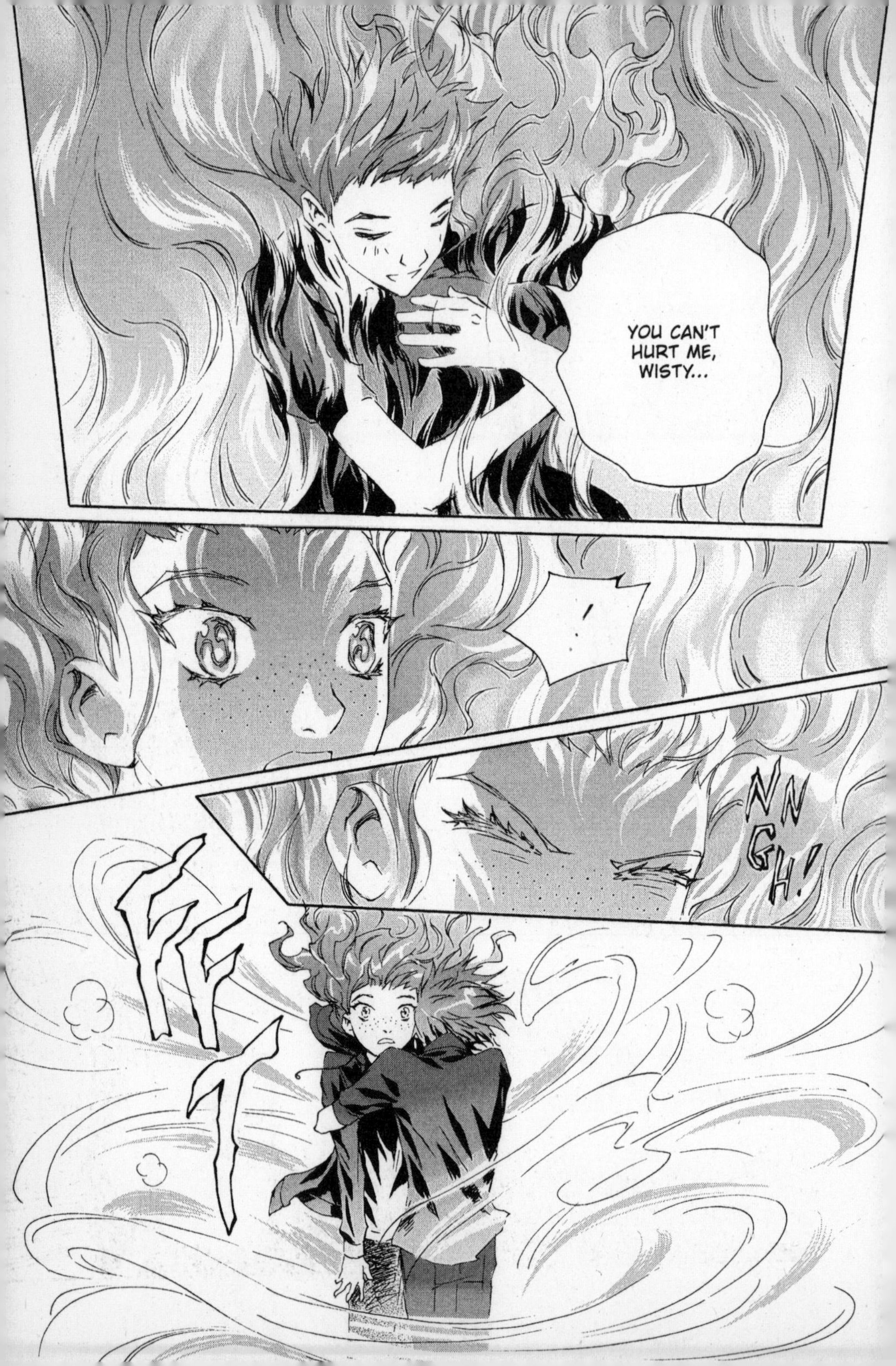
YOU CAN'T HURT ME, WISTY...
!
NNGH!

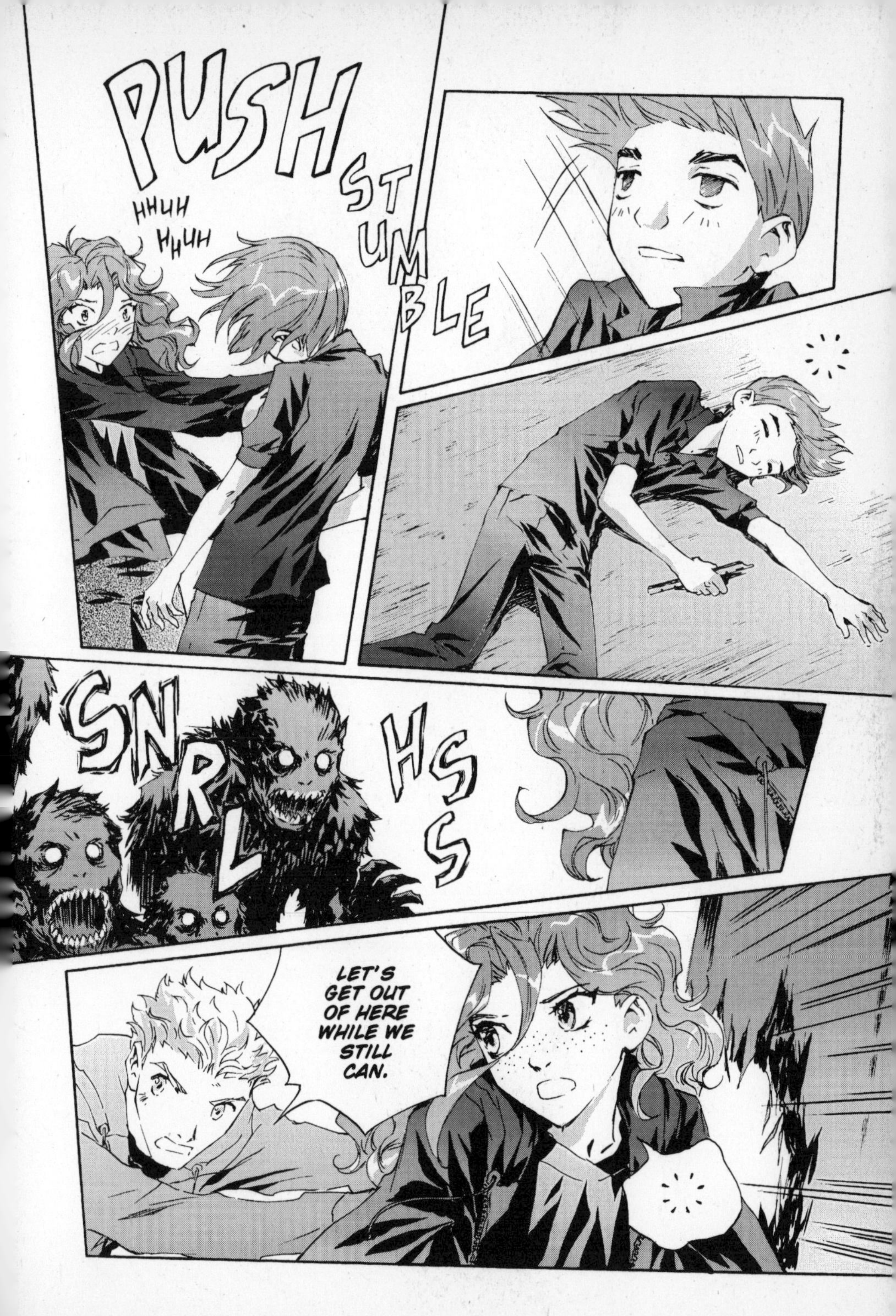
PUSH
HHUH HHUH
STUMBLE
SNRL
HSS
LET'S GET OUT OF HERE WHILE WE STILL CAN.

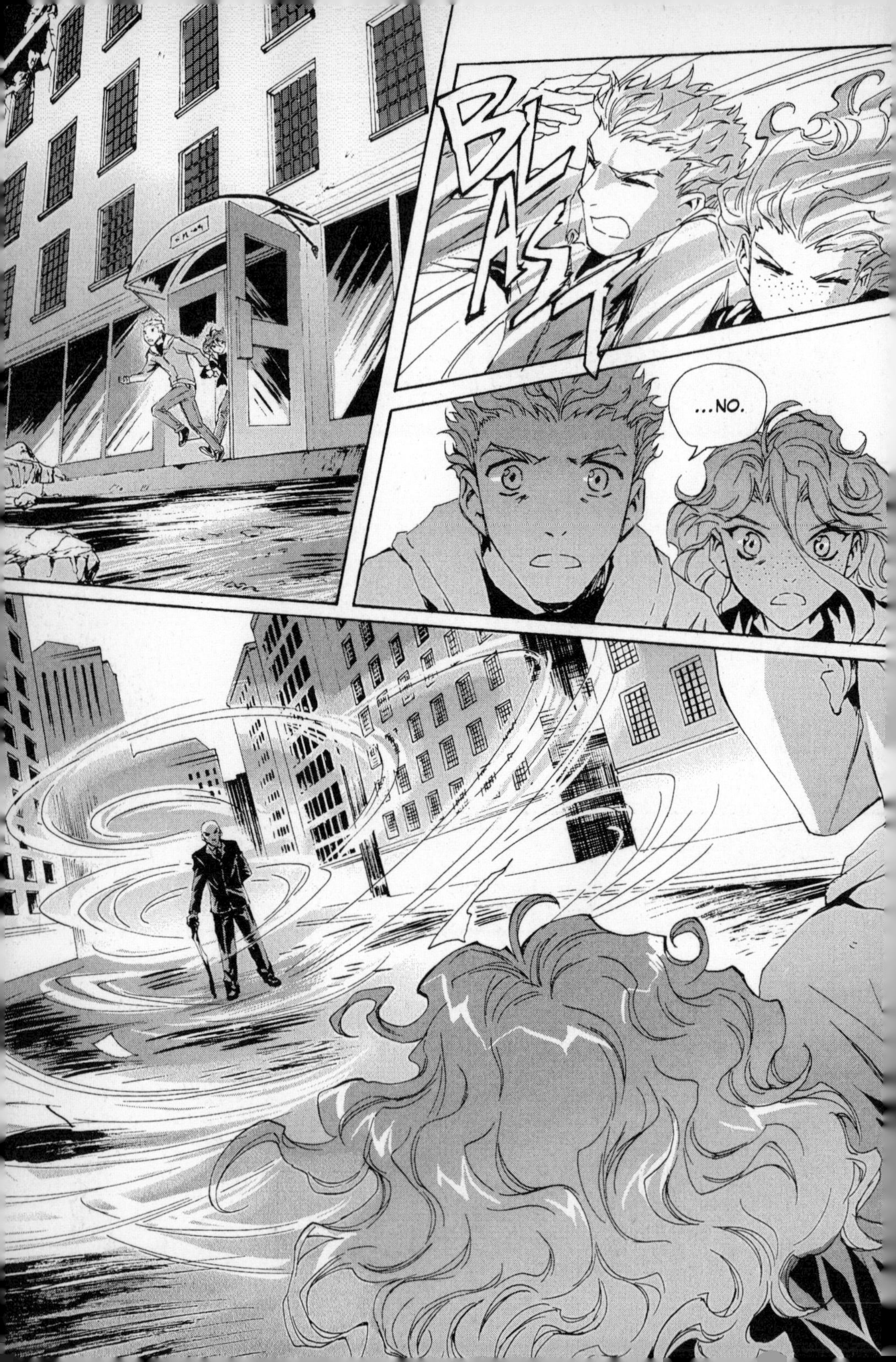
BLAST
...NO.

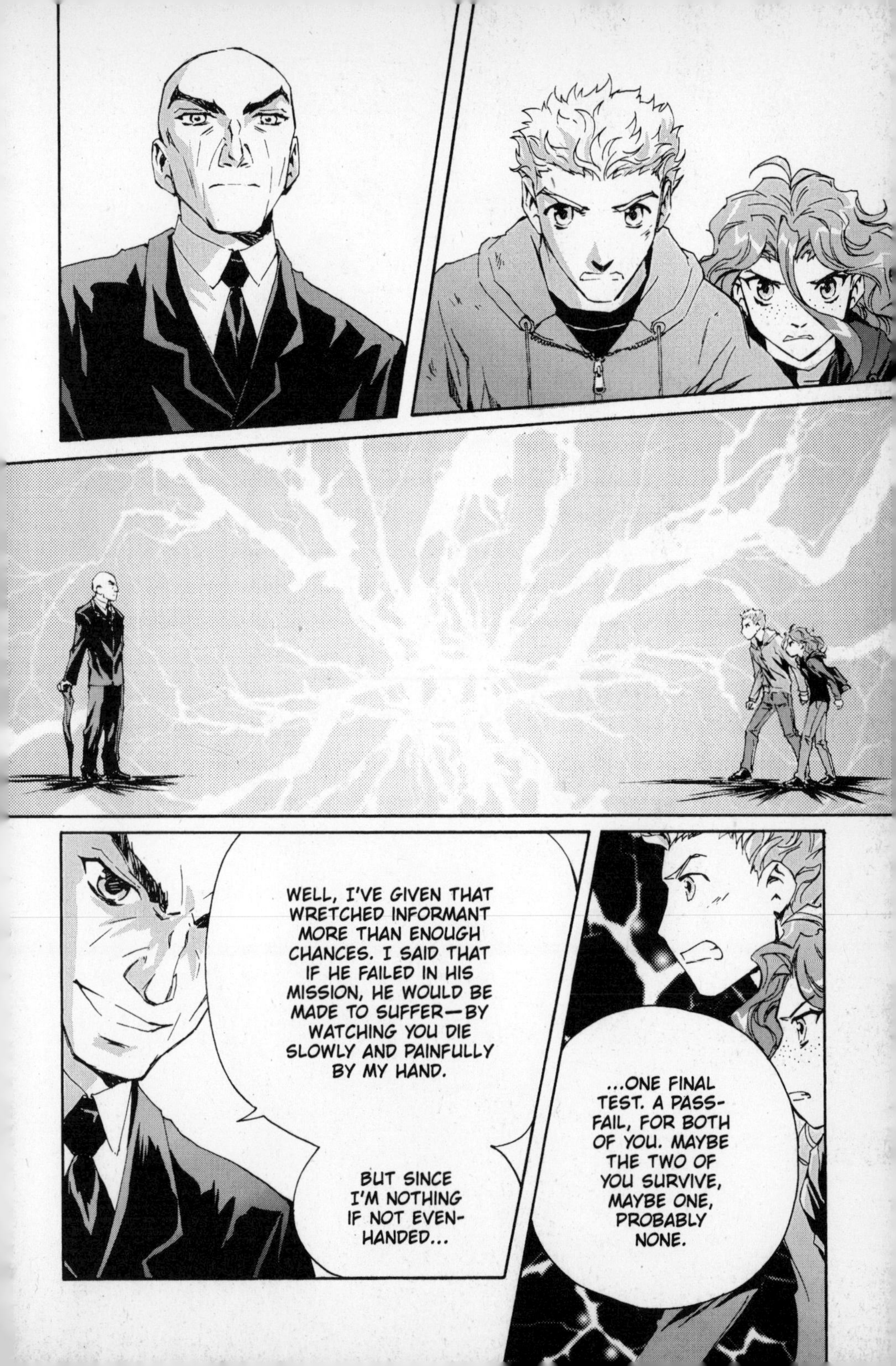
WELL, I'VE GIVEN THAT WRETCHED INFORMANT MORE THAN ENOUGH CHANCES. I SAID THAT IF HE FAILED IN HIS MISSION, HE WOULD BE MADE TO SUFFER—BY WATCHING YOU DIE SLOWLY AND PAINFULLY BY MY HAND.
BUT SINCE I'M NOTHING IF NOT EVEN-HANDED...
...ONE FINAL TEST. A PASS-FAIL, FOR BOTH OF YOU. MAYBE THE TWO OF YOU SURVIVE, MAYBE ONE, PROBABLY NONE.

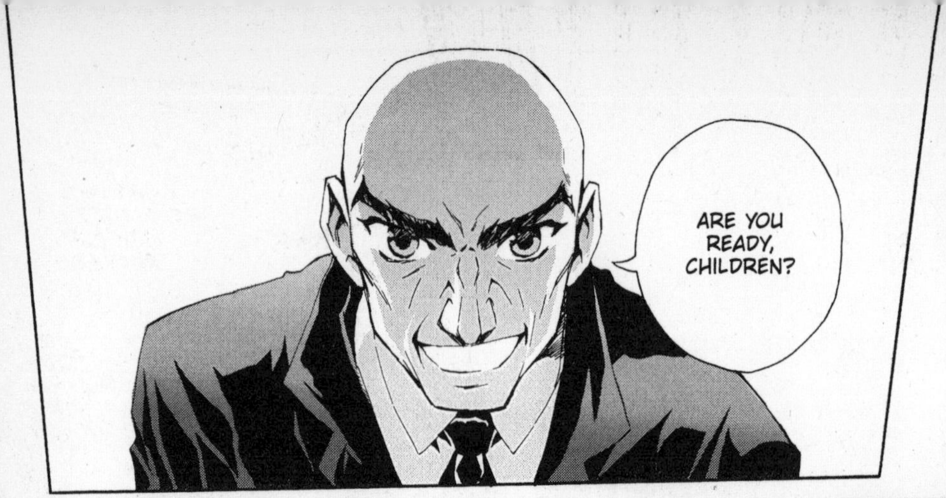
ARE YOU READY, CHILDREN?
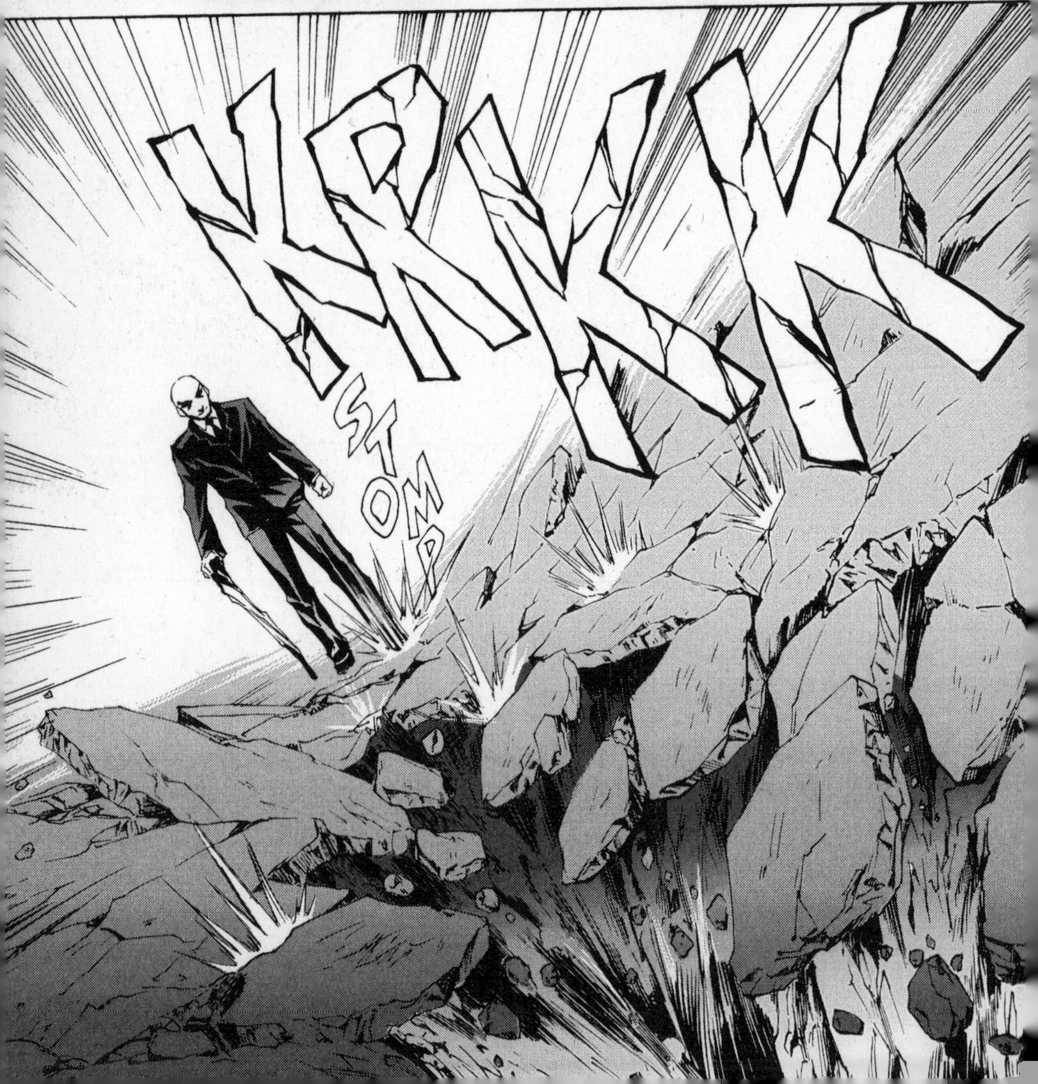
STOMP

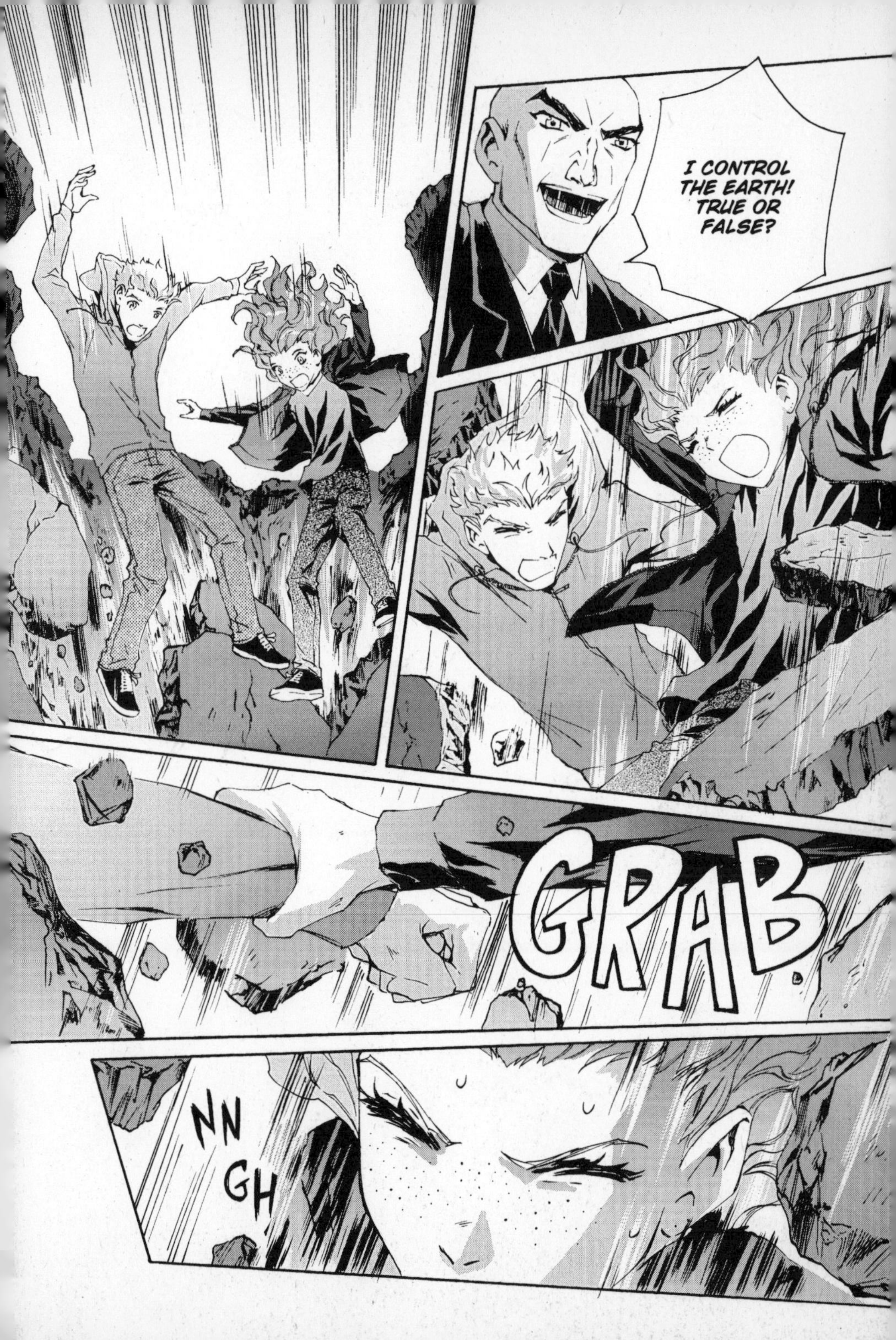
I CONTROL THE EARTH! TRUE OR FALSE?
GRAB
NNGH

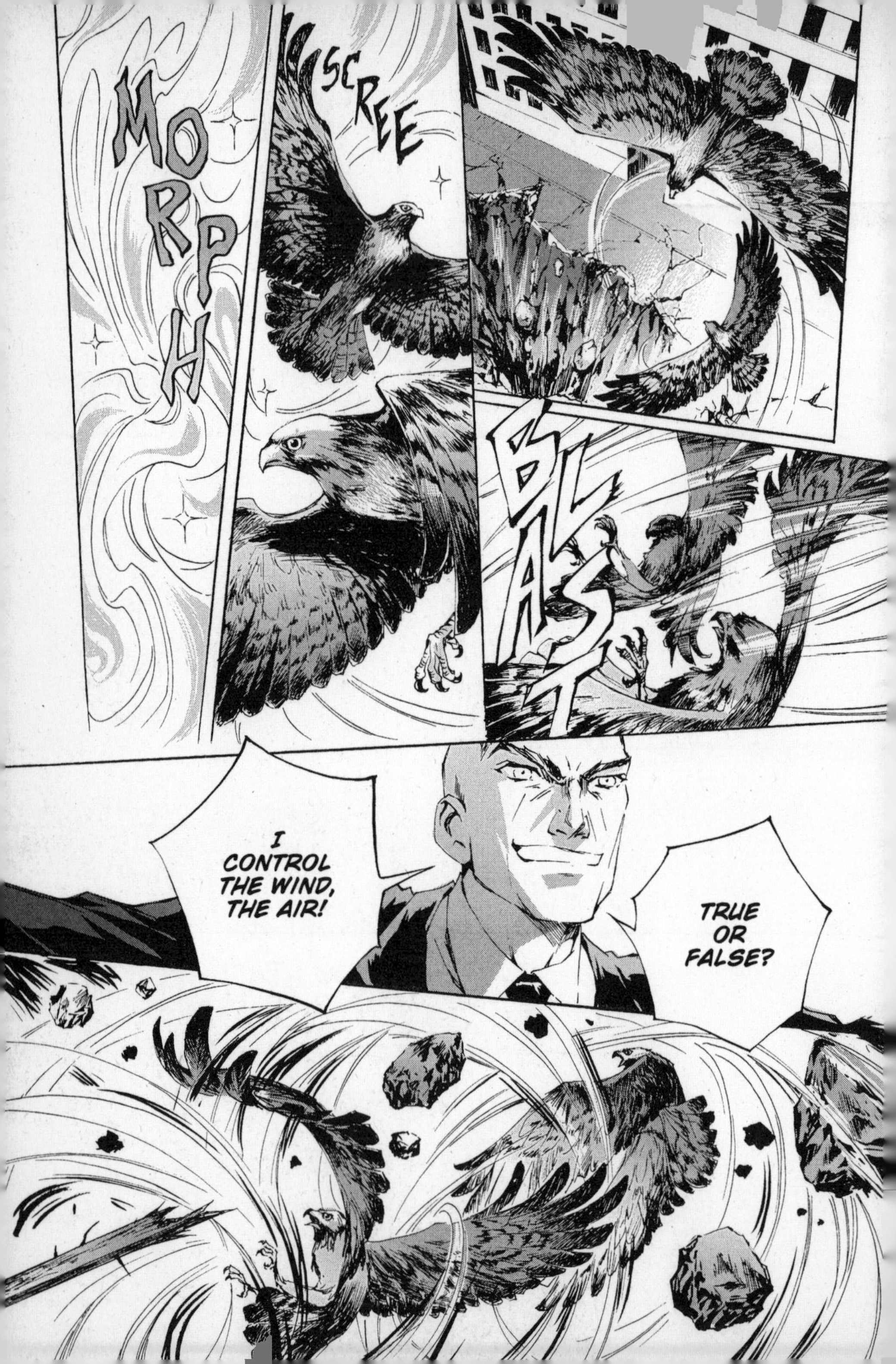
MORPH
SCREE
BLAST
I CONTROL THE WIND, THE AIR!
TRUE OR FALSE?

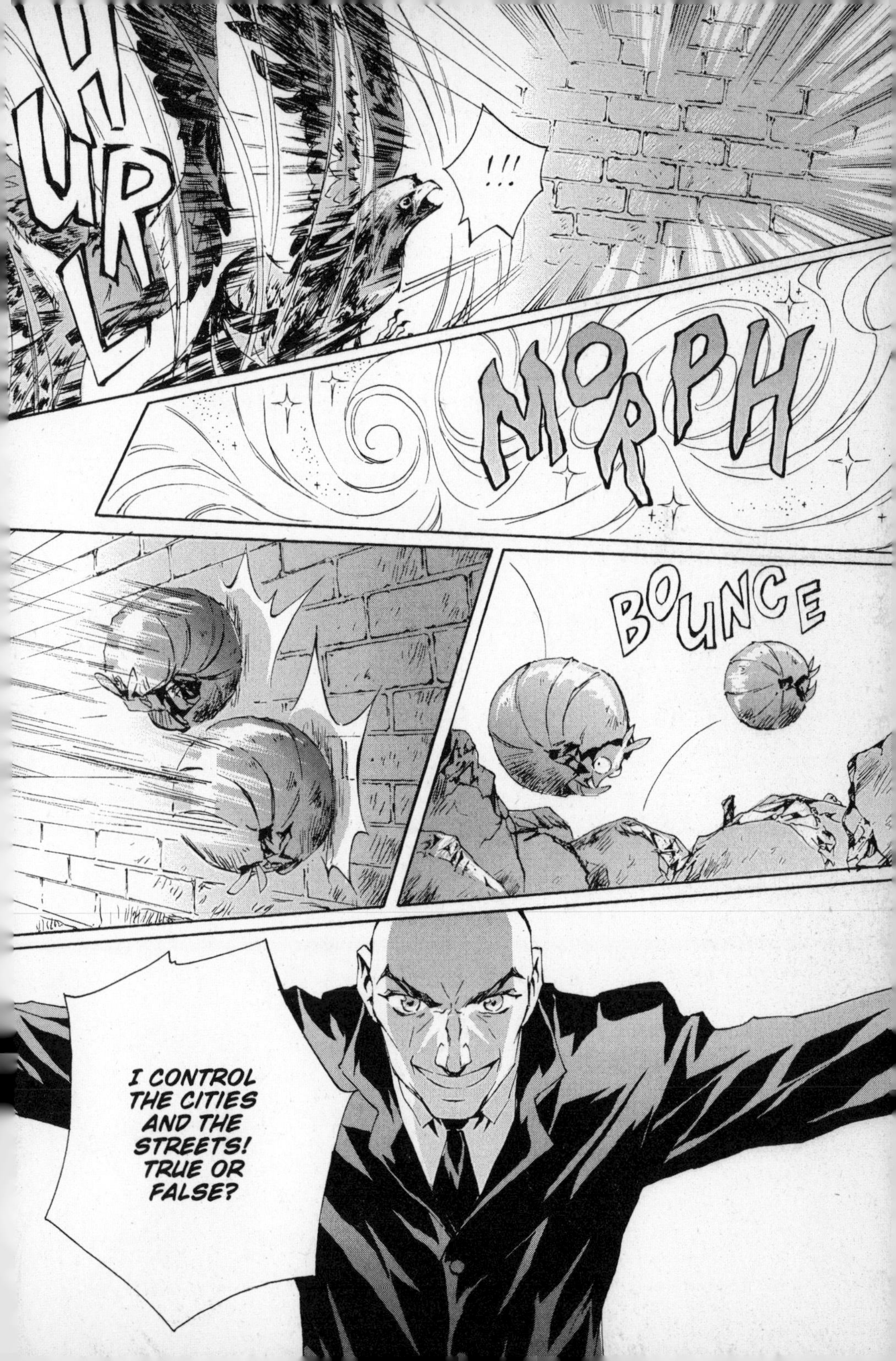
HURL
!!!
MORPH
BOUNCE
I CONTROL THE CITIES AND THE STREETS! TRUE OR FALSE?

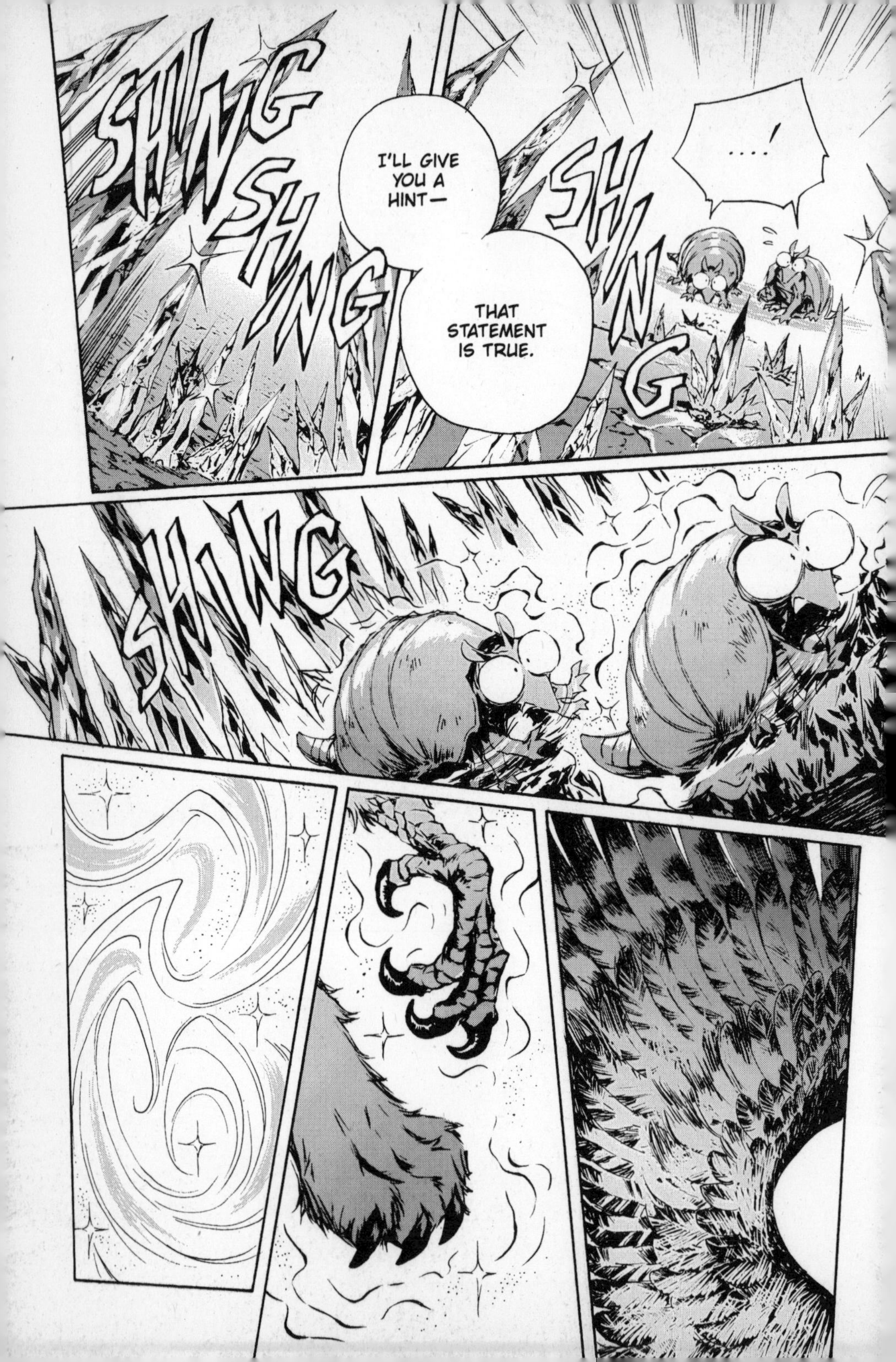
SHING
SHING
I'LL GIVE YOU A HINT—
THAT STATEMENT IS TRUE.
SHING
....!
SHING

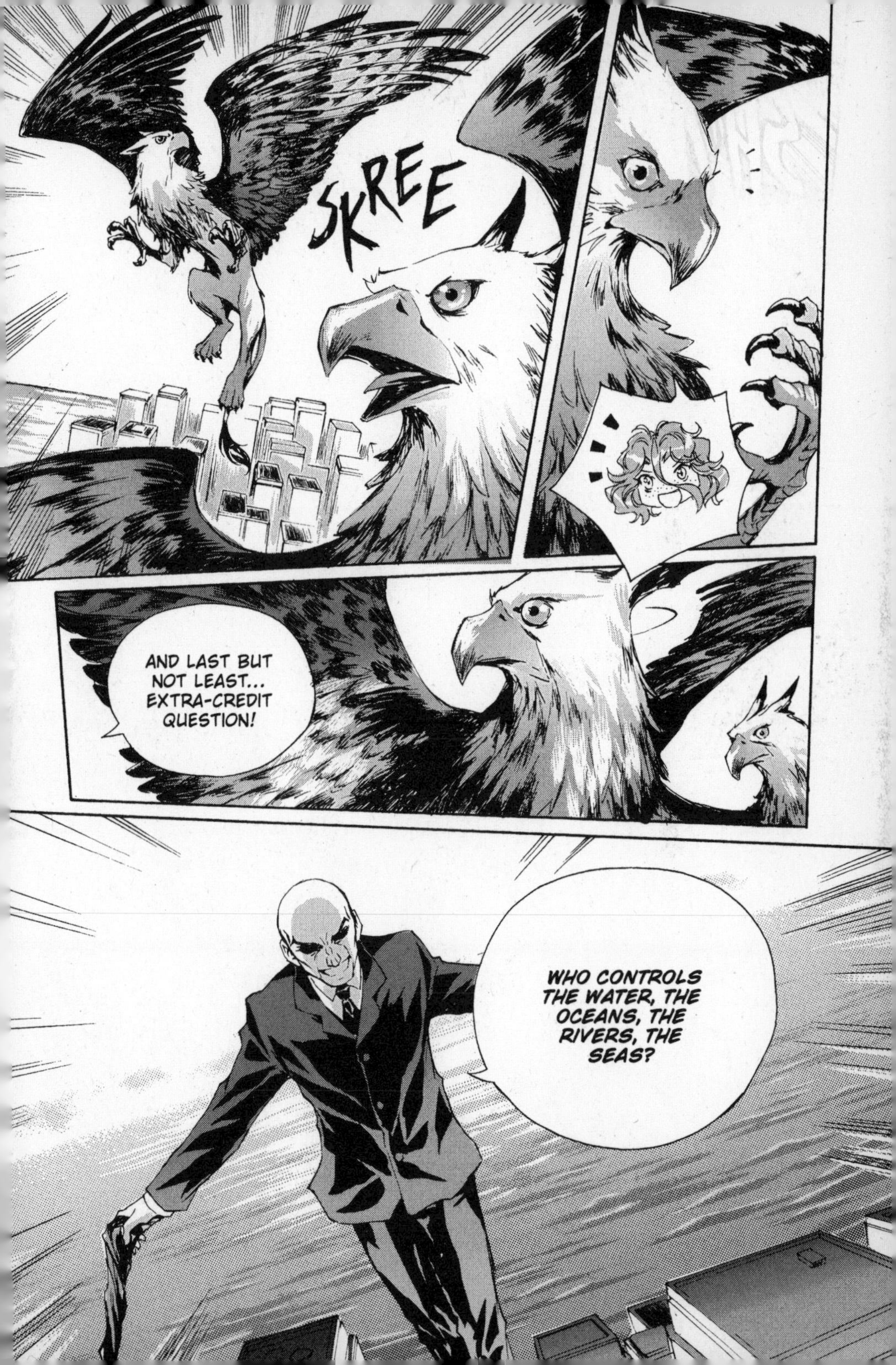
SKREE
AND LAST BUT NOT LEAST... EXTRA-CREDIT QUESTION!
WHO CONTROLS THE WATER, THE OCEANS, THE RIVERS, THE SEAS?

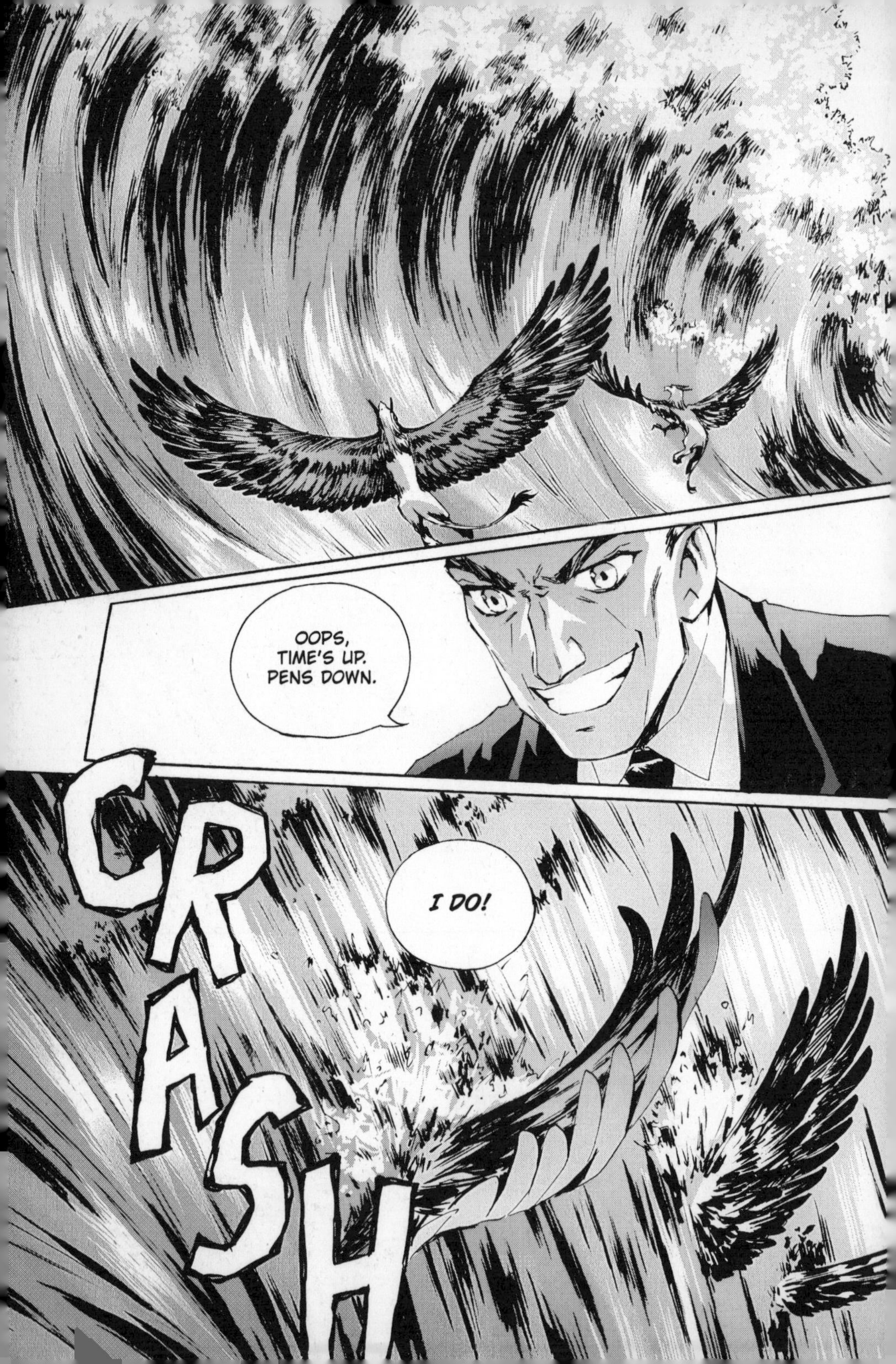
OOPS, TIME'S UP. PENS DOWN.
CRASH
I DO!

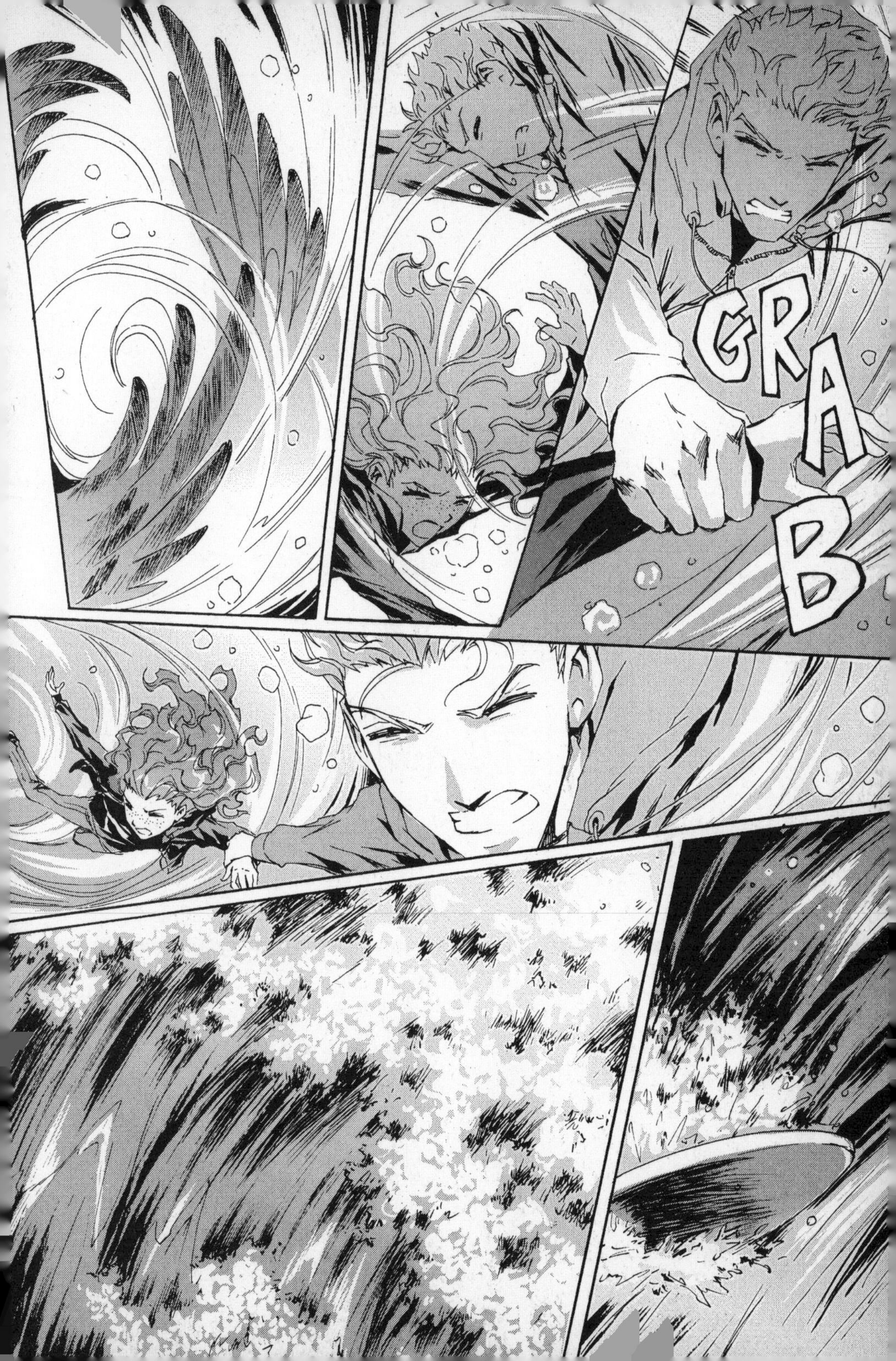
GRAB

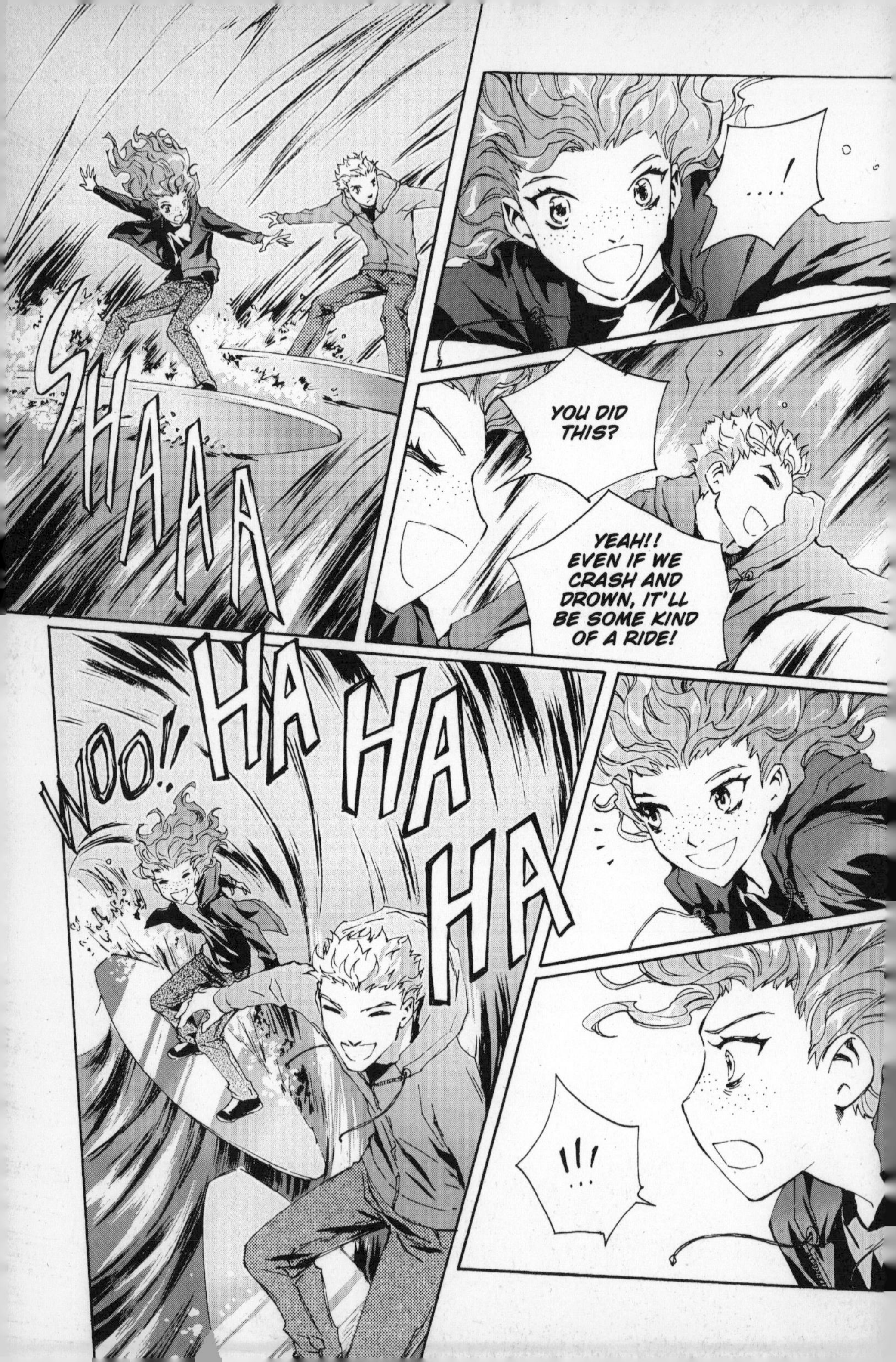
SHAAA
...!
YOU DID THIS?
YEAH!! EVEN IF WE CRASH AND DROWN, IT'LL BE SOME KIND OF A RIDE!
WOO!! HA HA HA HA
!!!
...

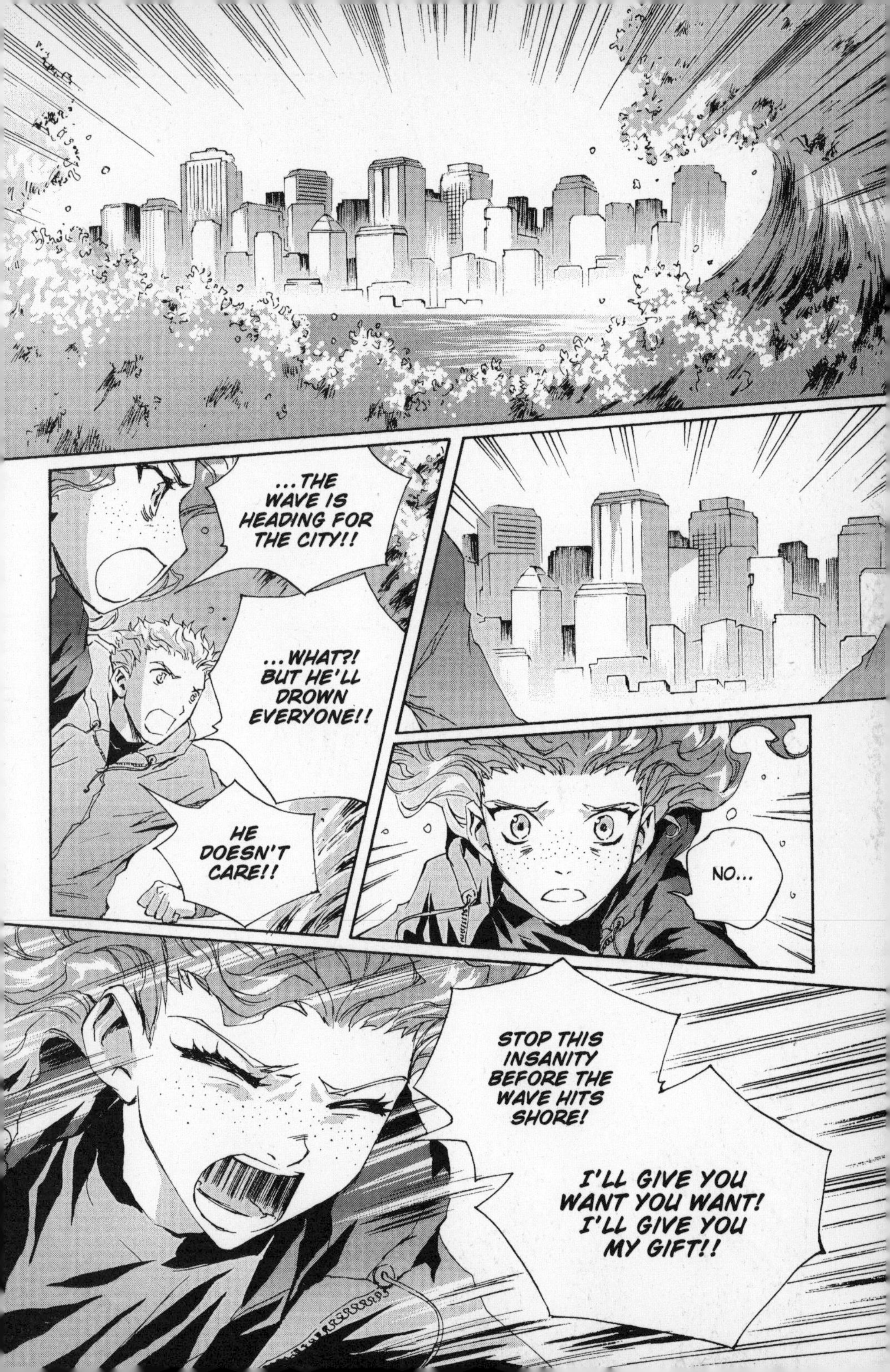
...THE WAVE IS HEADING FOR THE CITY!!
...WHAT?! BUT HE'LL DROWN EVERYONE!!
HE DOESN'T CARE!!
NO...
STOP THIS INSANITY BEFORE THE WAVE HITS SHORE!
I'LL GIVE YOU WANT YOU WANT! I'LL GIVE YOU MY GIFT!!

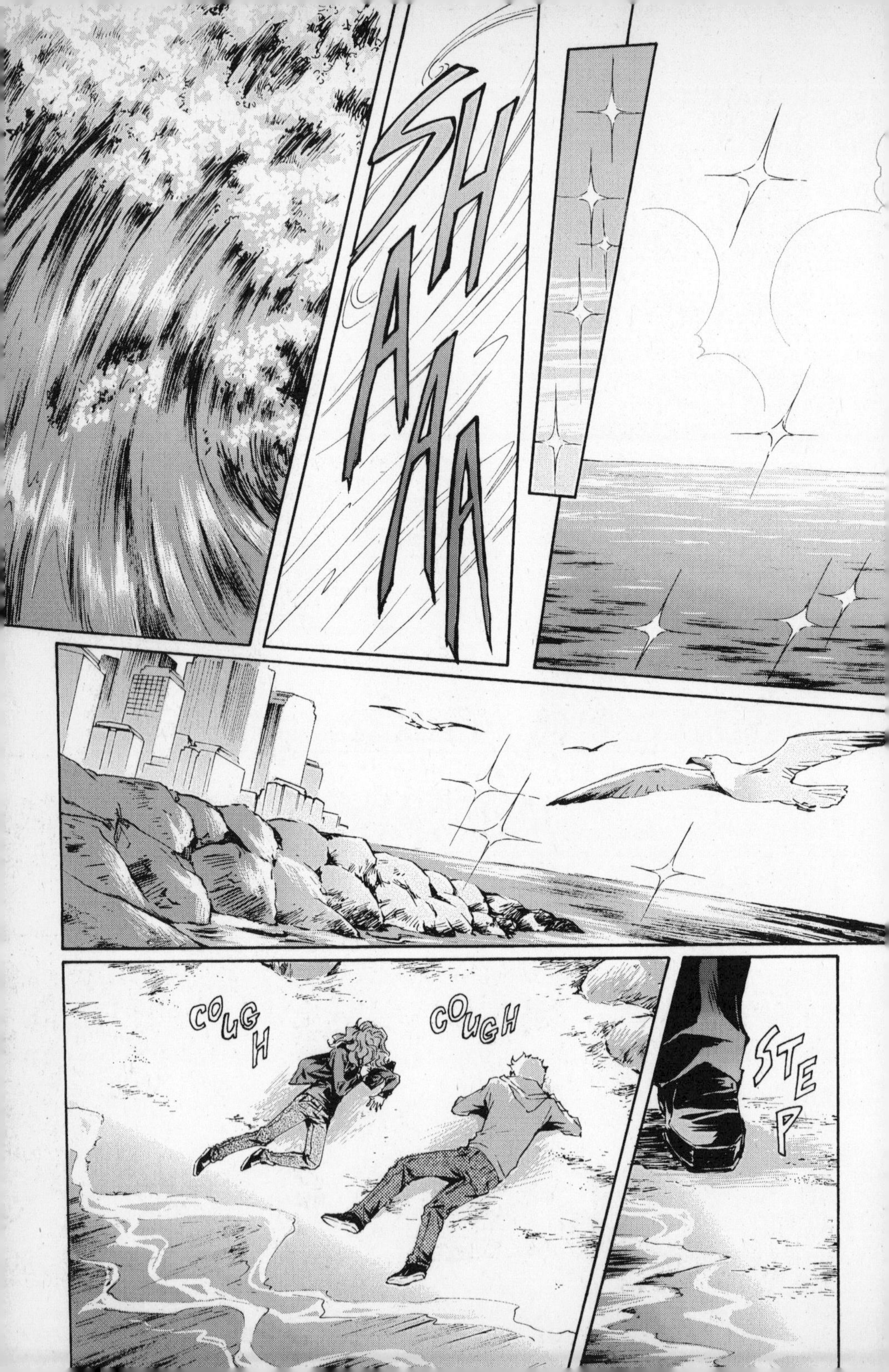
SHAAAA
COUGH
COUGH
STEP

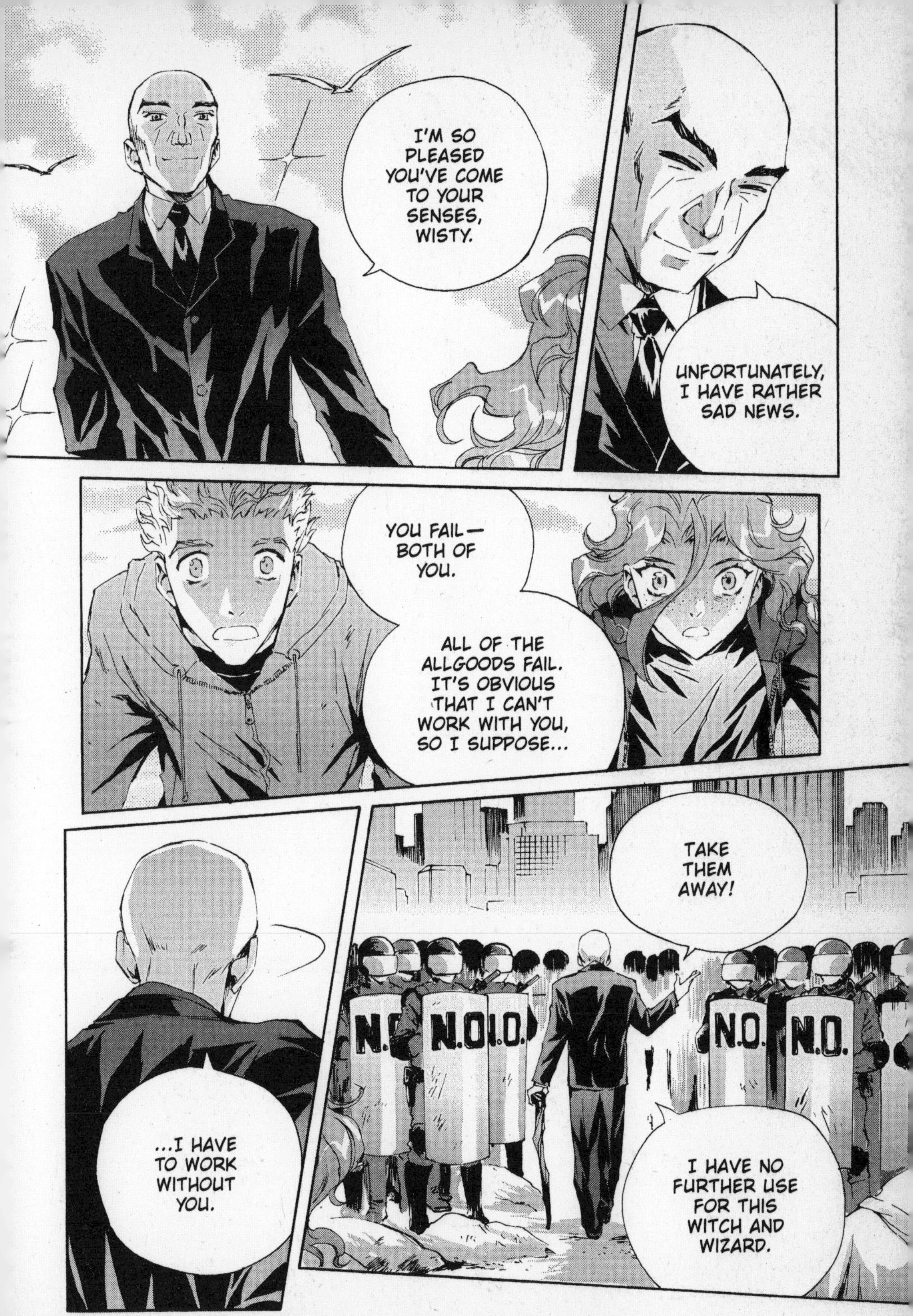
I'M SO PLEASED YOU'VE COME TO YOUR SENSES, WISTY.
UNFORTUNATELY, I HAVE RATHER SAD NEWS.
YOU FAIL— BOTH OF YOU.
ALL OF THE ALLGOODS FAIL. IT'S OBVIOUS THAT I CAN'T WORK WITH YOU, SO I SUPPOSE...
...I HAVE TO WORK WITHOUT YOU.
TAKE THEM AWAY!
N.O.
N.O.
N.O.
N.O.
N.O.
I HAVE NO FURTHER USE FOR THIS WITCH AND WIZARD.

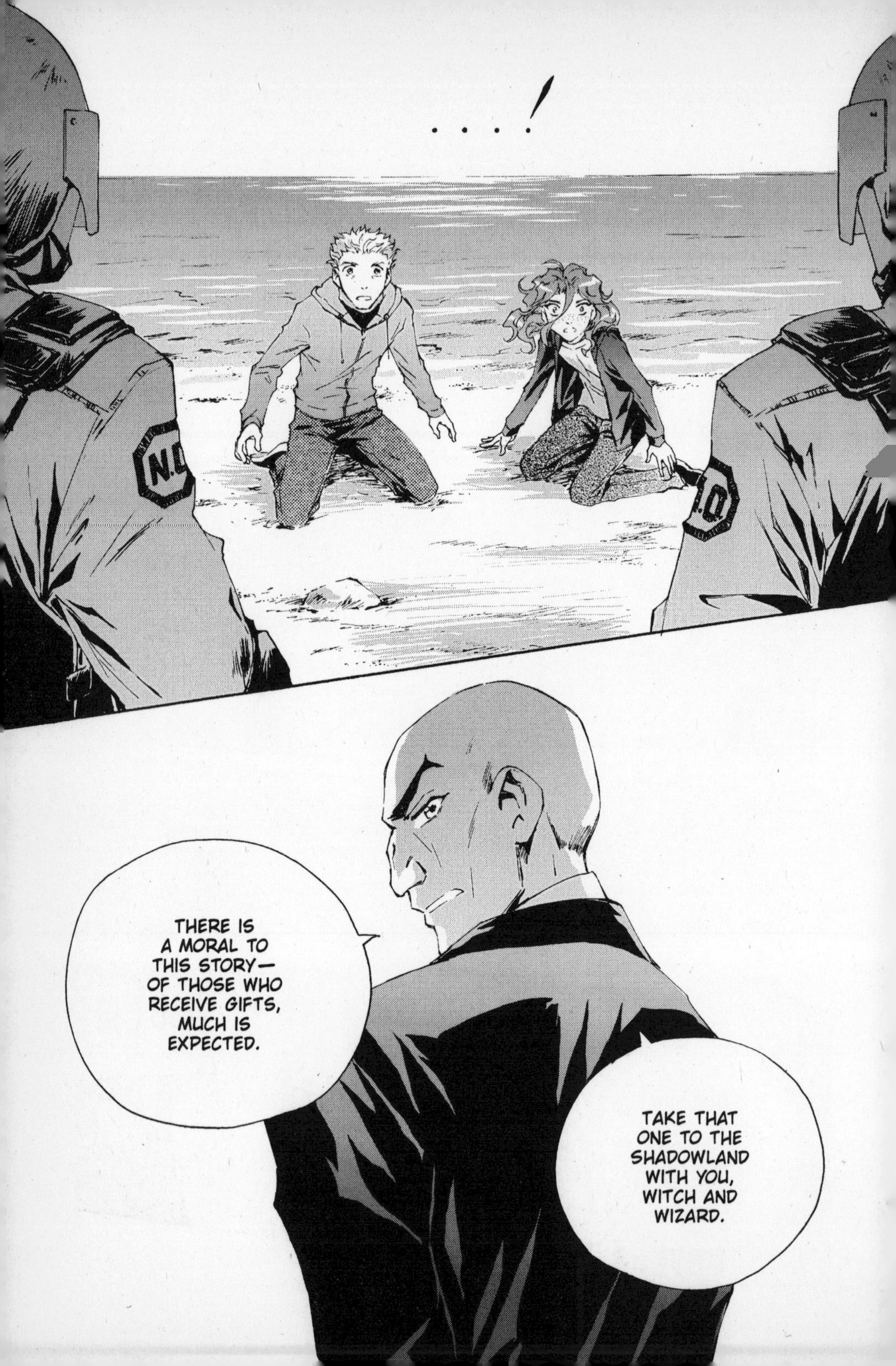
. . . . !
N.O.
N.O.
THERE IS A MORAL TO THIS STORY— OF THOSE WHO RECEIVE GIFTS, MUCH IS EXPECTED.
TAKE THAT ONE TO THE SHADOWLAND WITH YOU, WITCH AND WIZARD.

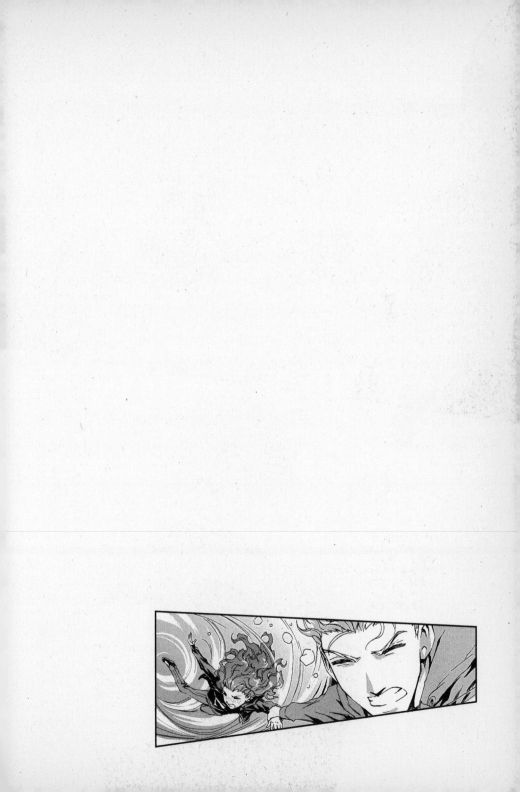

WITCH & WIZARD

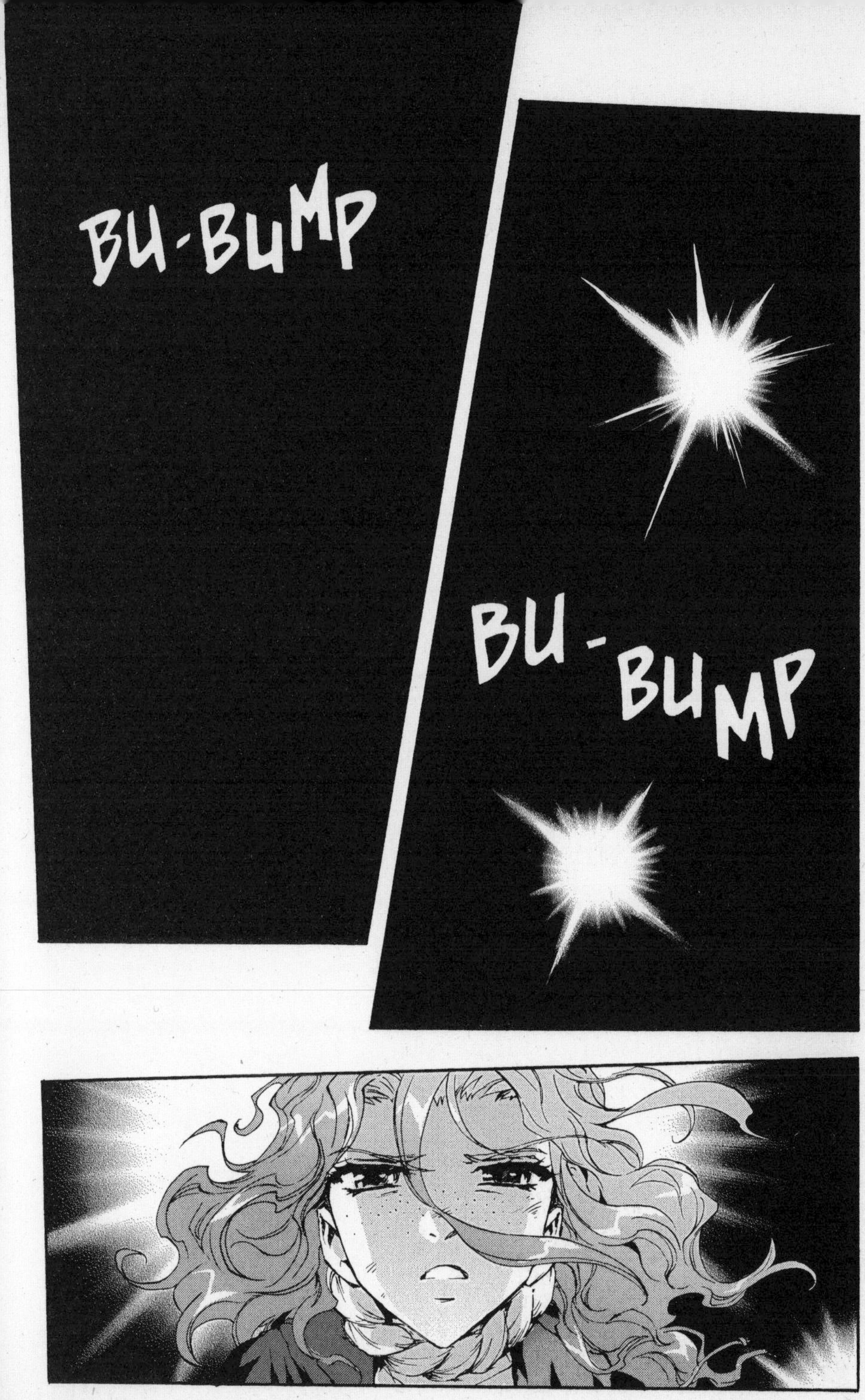
BU-BUMP
BU-BUMP

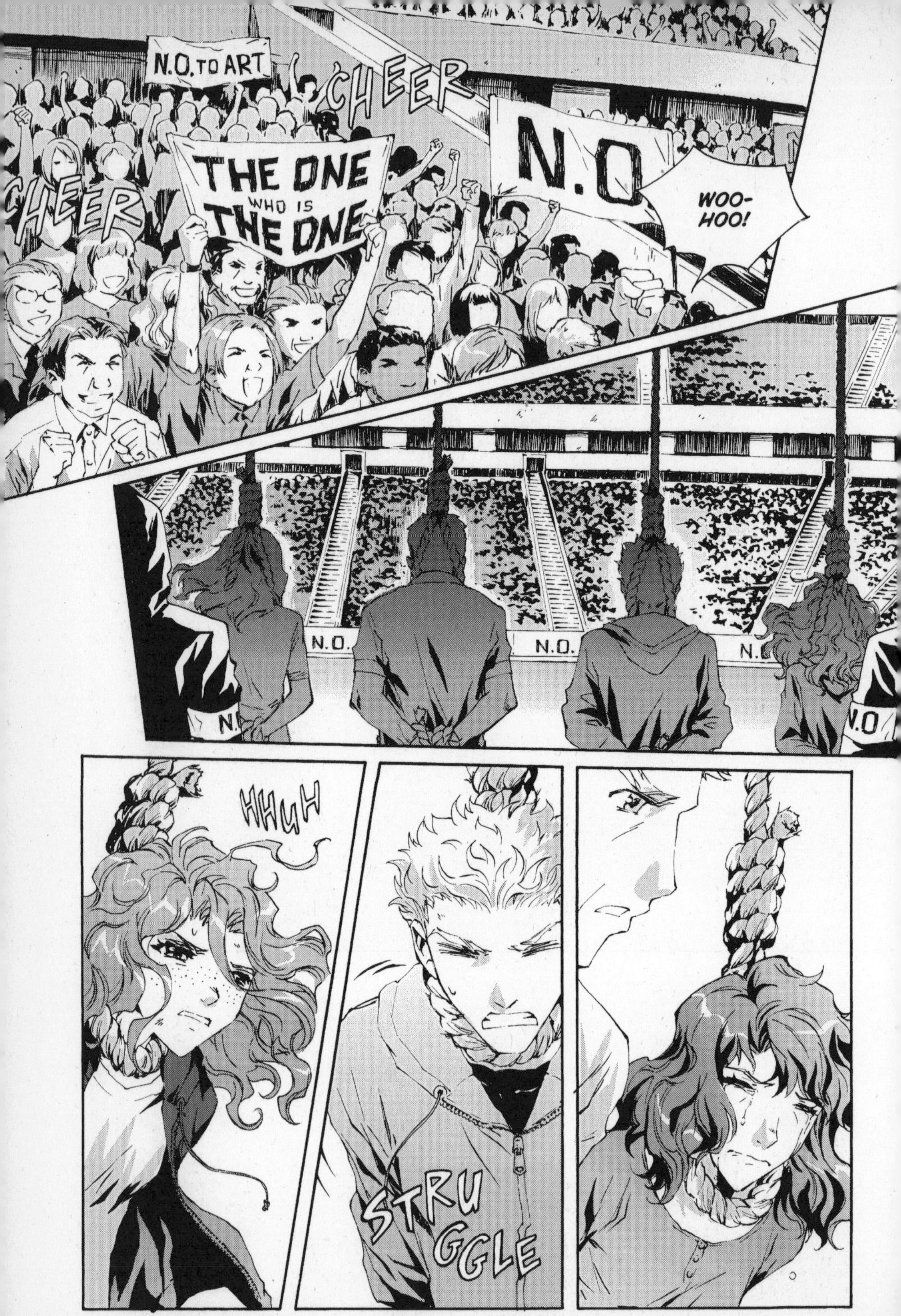
N.O. TO ART
CHEER
THE ONE WHO IS THE ONE
CHEER
N.O
WOO-HOO!
N.O.
N.O.
N.O
N.O
N.O
HHUH
STRUGGLE

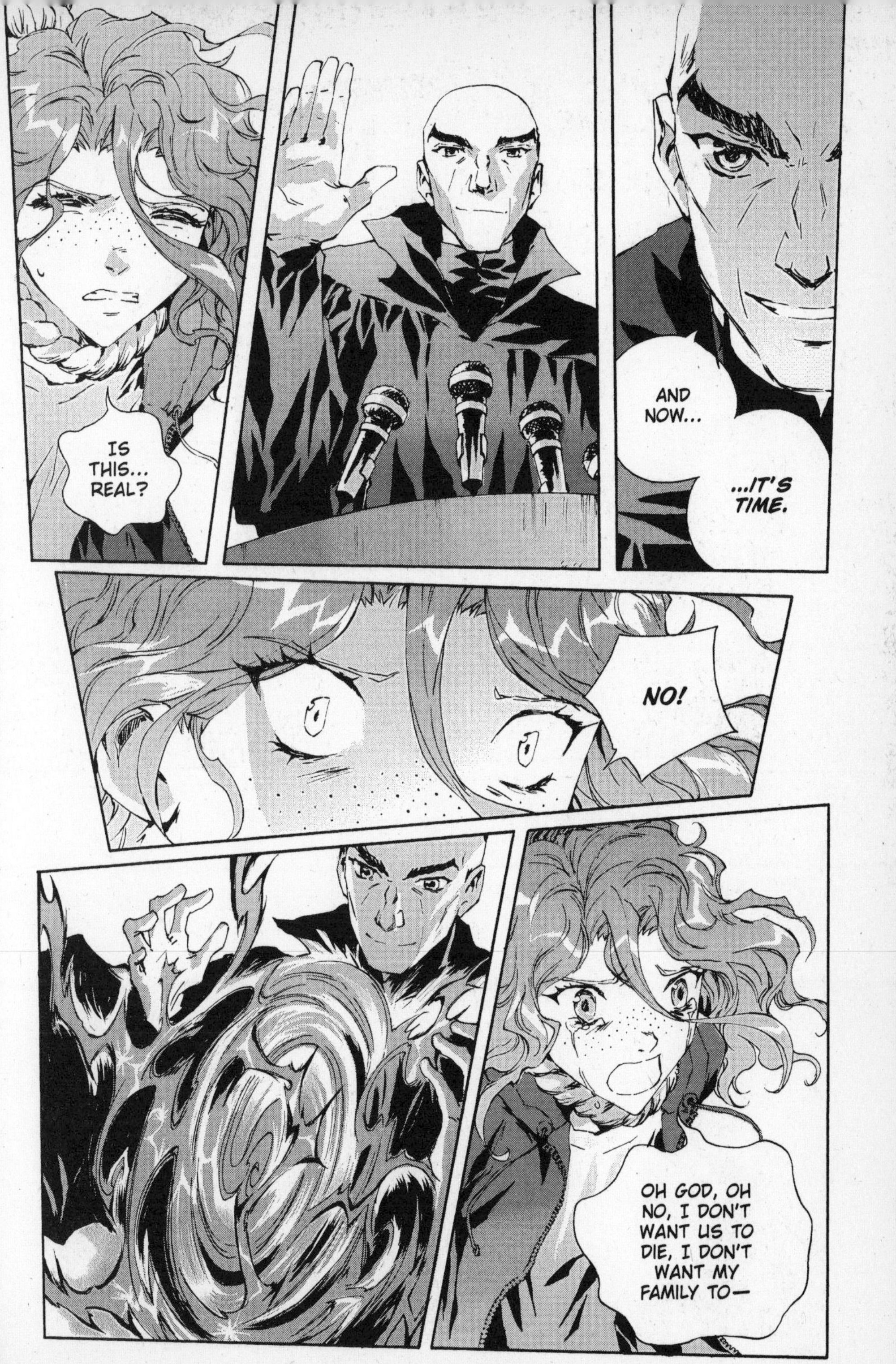
IS THIS... REAL?
AND NOW...
...IT'S TIME.
NO!
OH GOD, OH NO, I DON'T WANT US TO DIE, I DON'T WANT MY FAMILY TO—

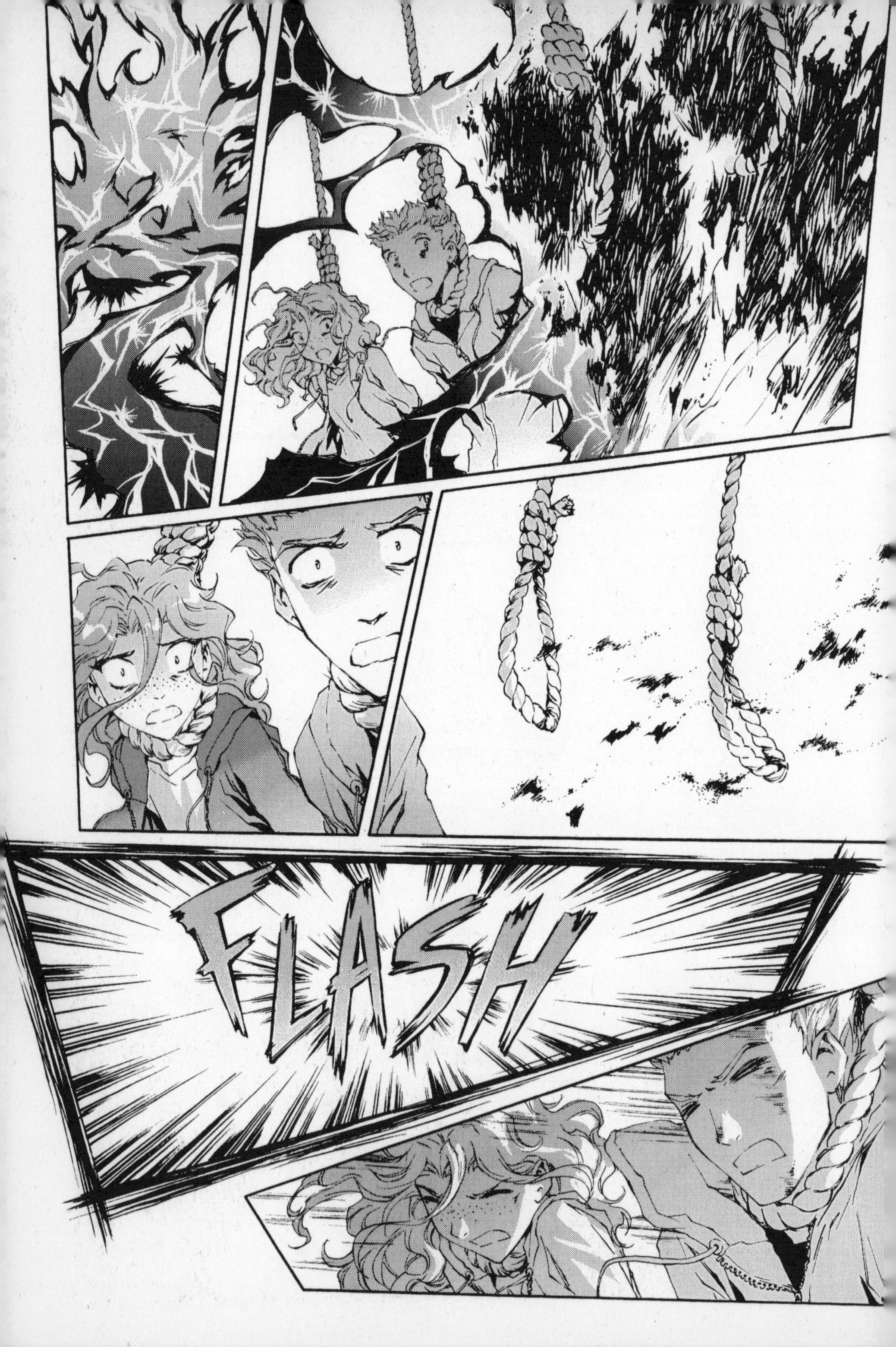
FLASH

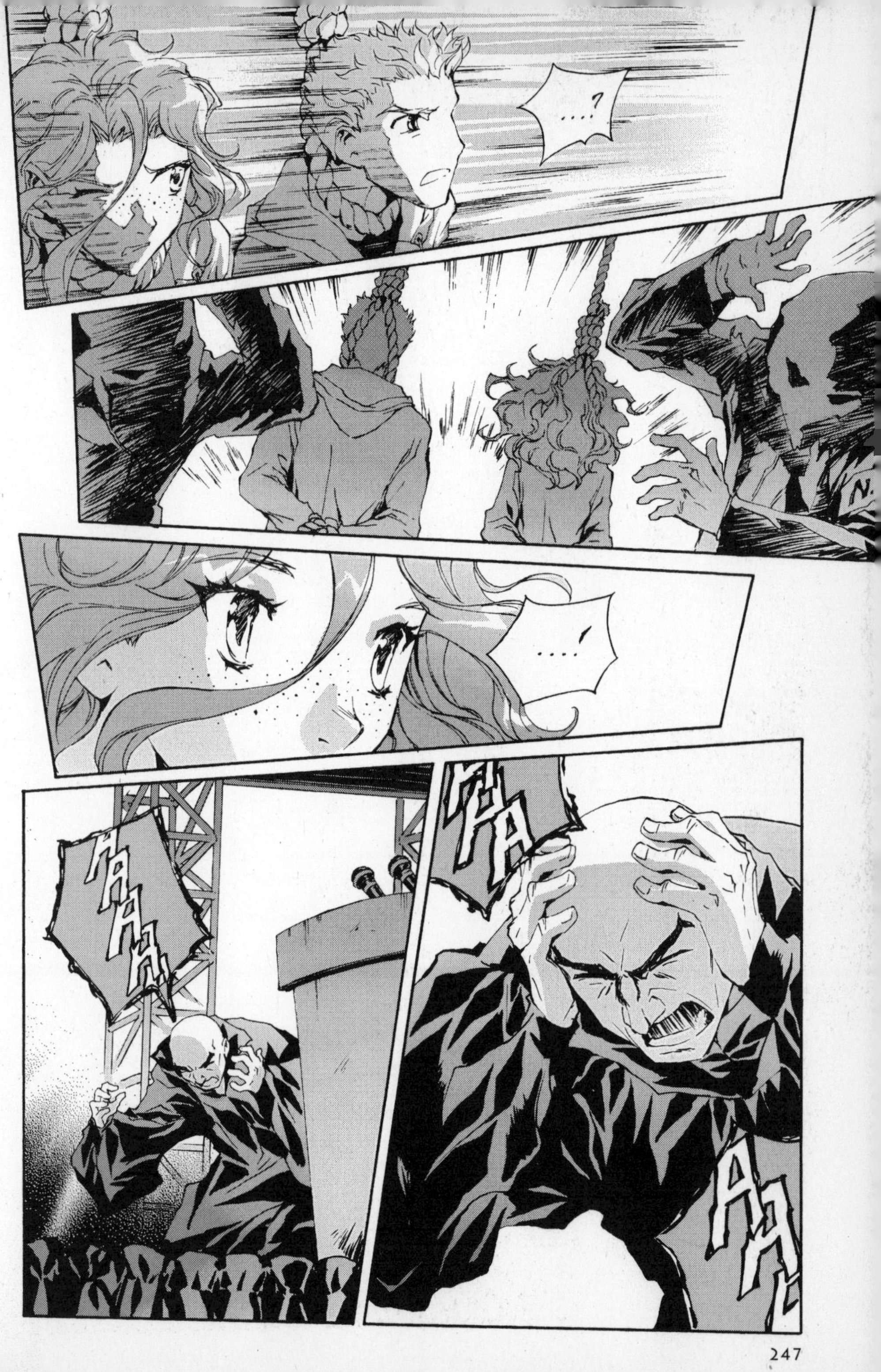
...?
...!
AAAAA
AA

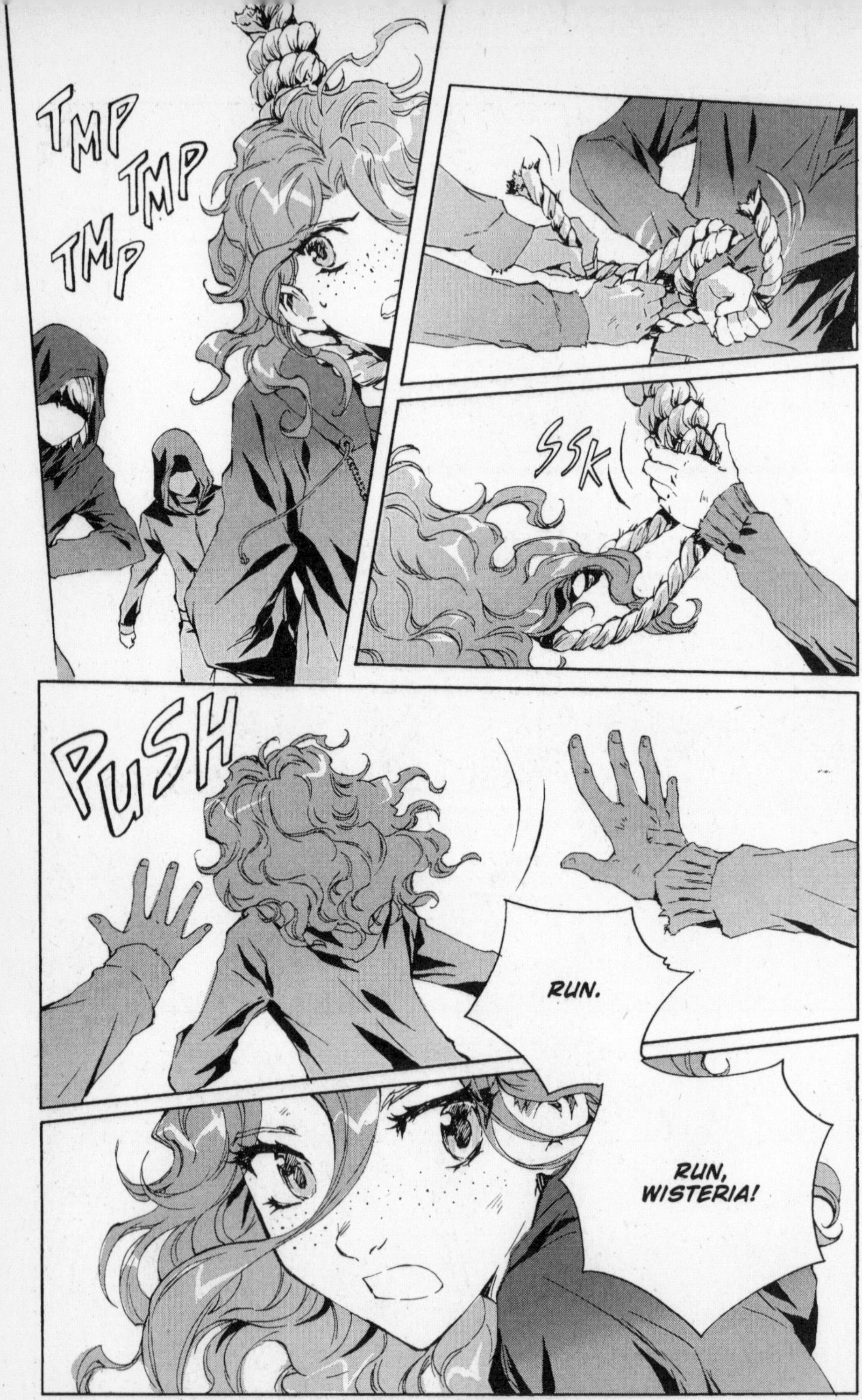
TMP TMP
TMP TMP
SSK
PUSH
RUN.
RUN, WISTERIA!

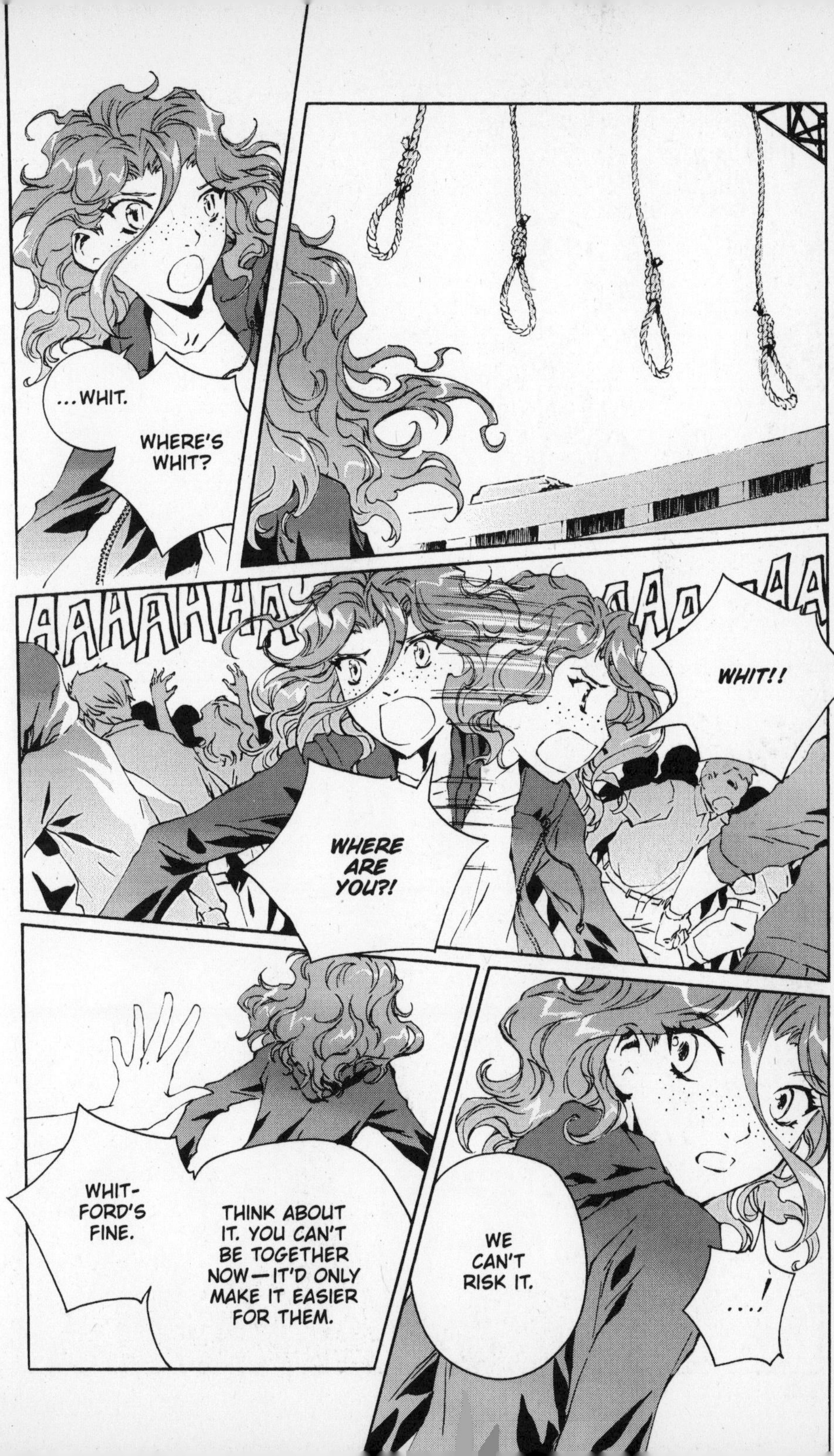

...WHIT.
WHERE'S WHIT?
AAAAAAAAAAAAAAAAA
WHIT!!
WHERE ARE YOU?!
WHIT-FORD'S FINE.
THINK ABOUT IT. YOU CAN'T BE TOGETHER NOW—IT'D ONLY MAKE IT EASIER FOR THEM.
WE CAN'T RISK IT.
...!

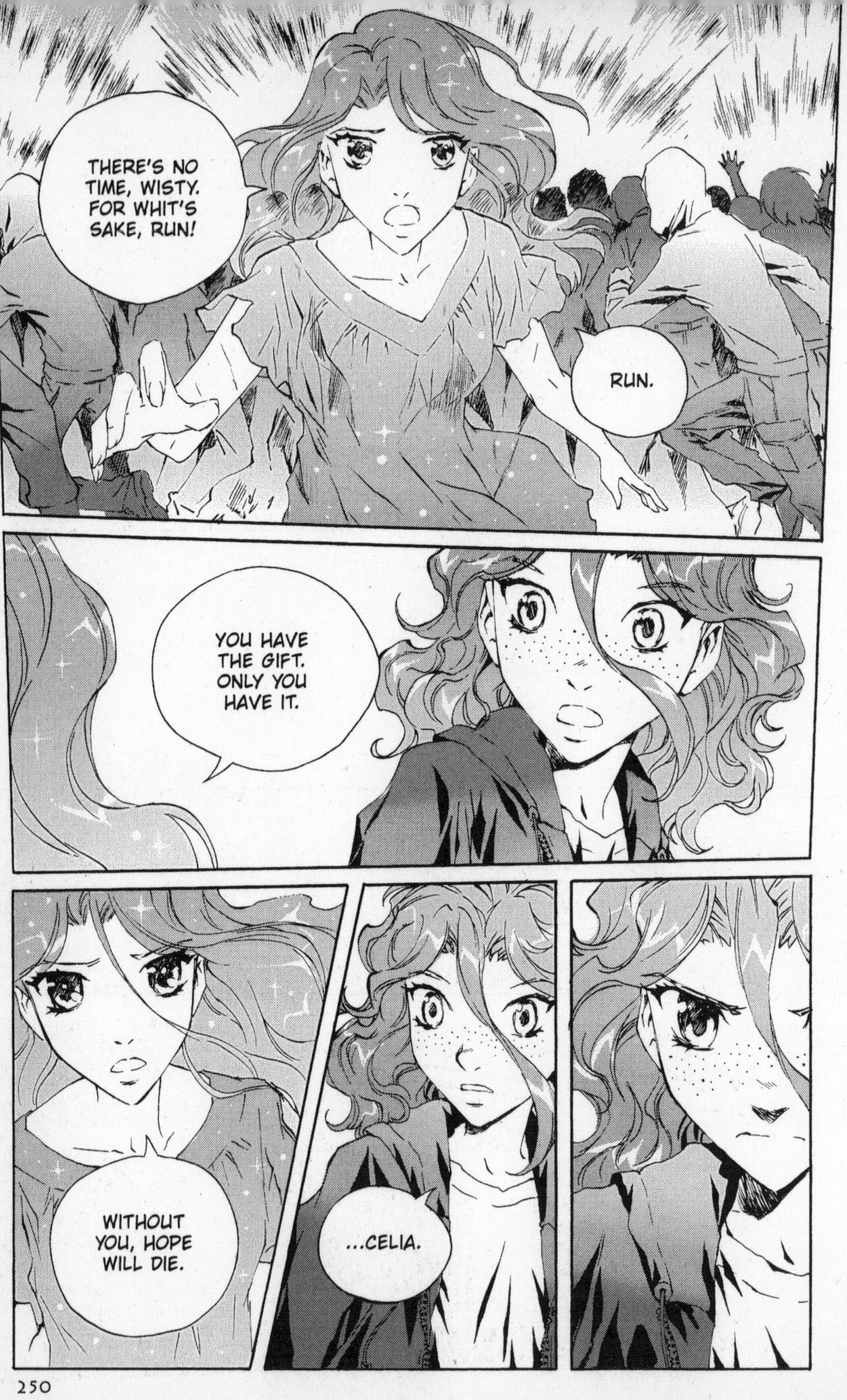
THERE'S NO TIME, WISTY. FOR WHIT'S SAKE, RUN!
RUN.
YOU HAVE THE GIFT. ONLY YOU HAVE IT.
WITHOUT YOU, HOPE WILL DIE.
...CELIA.

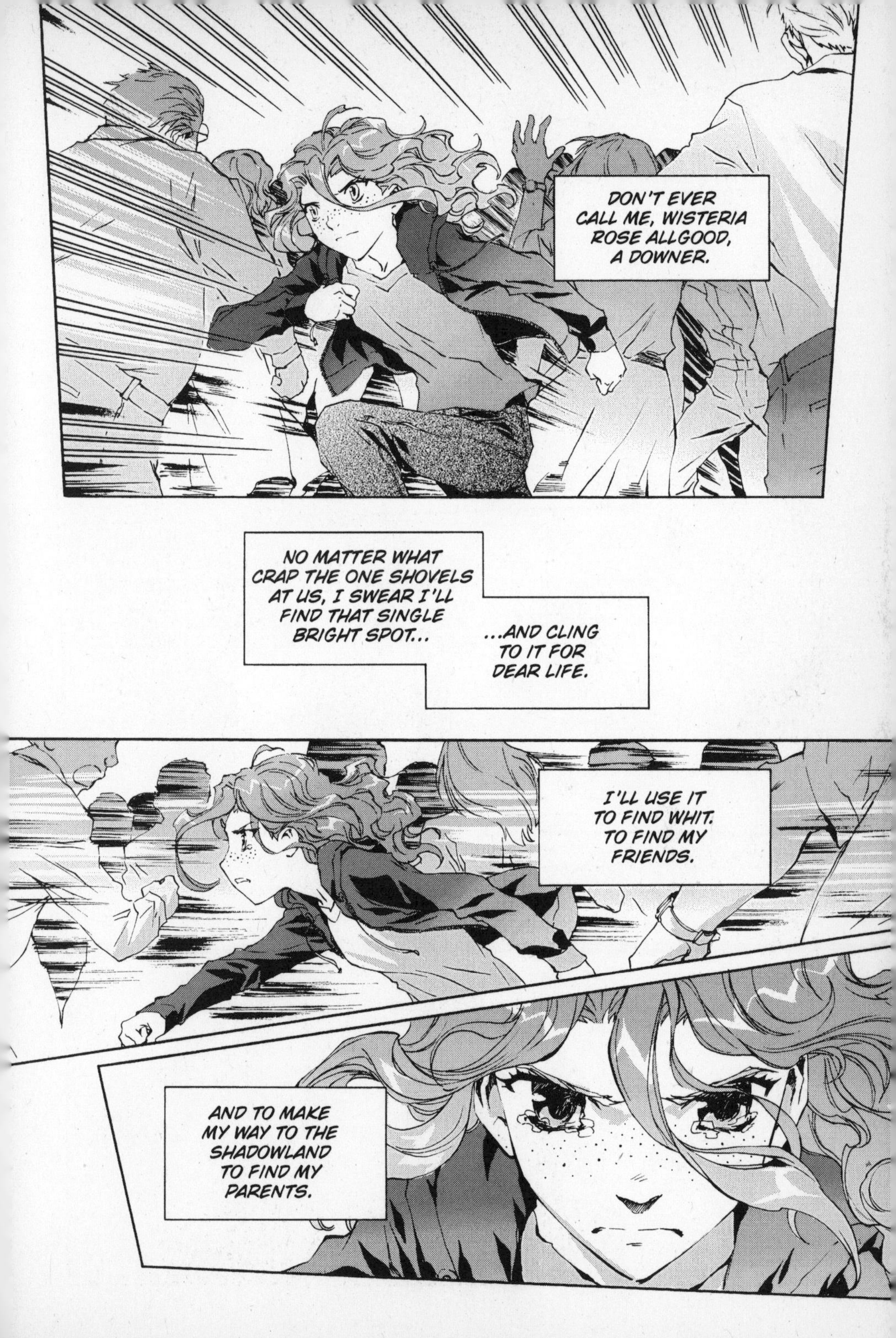
DON'T EVER CALL ME, WISTERIA ROSE ALLGOOD, A DOWNER.
NO MATTER WHAT CRAP THE ONE SHOVELS AT US, I SWEAR I'LL FIND THAT SINGLE BRIGHT SPOT...
...AND CLING TO IT FOR DEAR LIFE.
I'LL USE IT TO FIND WHIT. TO FIND MY FRIENDS.
AND TO MAKE MY WAY TO THE SHADOWLAND TO FIND MY PARENTS.

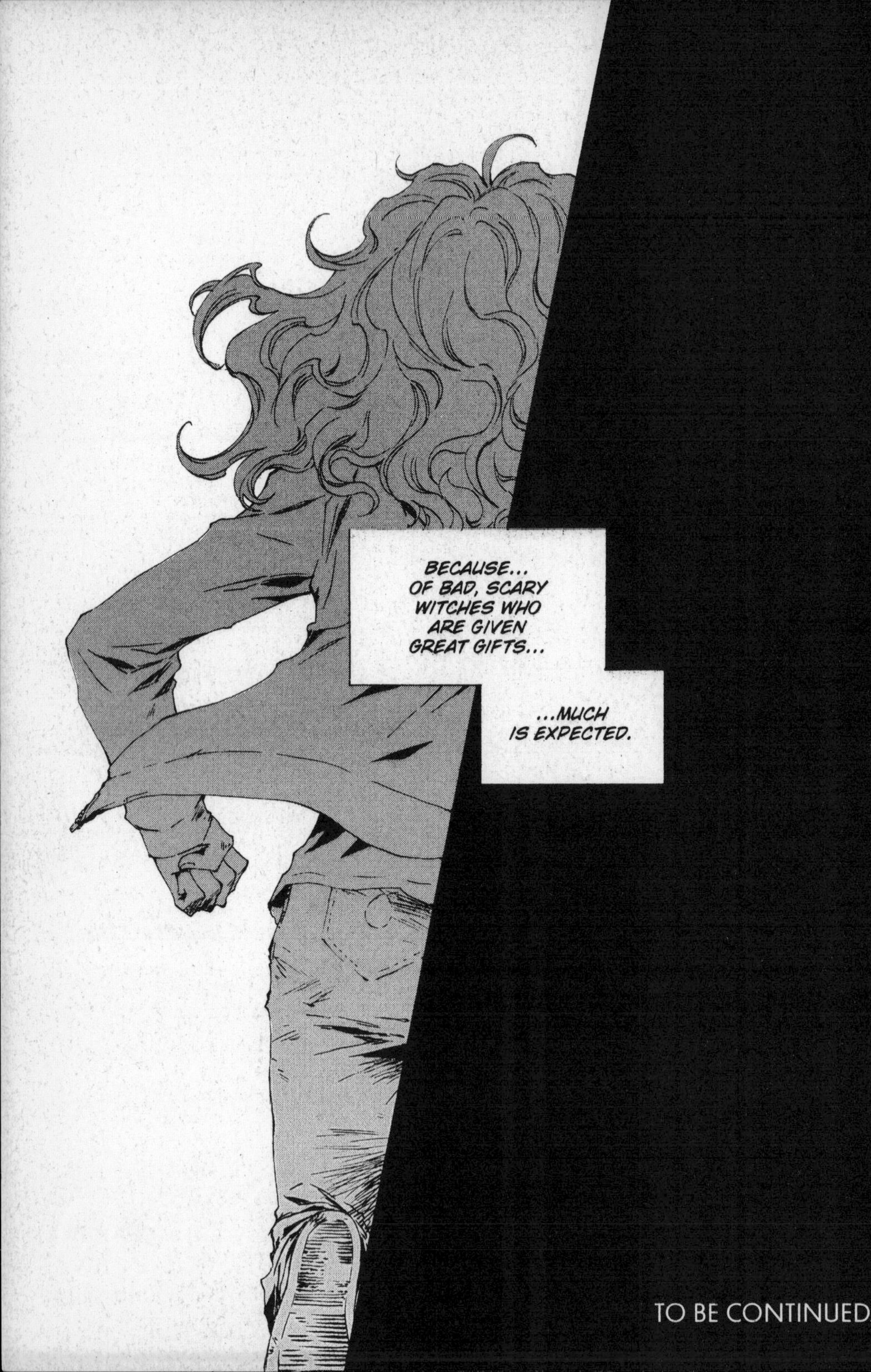
BECAUSE... OF BAD, SCARY WITCHES WHO ARE GIVEN GREAT GIFTS...
...MUCH IS EXPECTED.
TO BE CONTINUED

WITCH & WIZARD

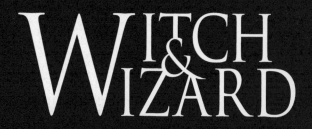

WITCH & WIZARD

EVERYTHING HAS CHANGED.
THE FATE OF THE WORLD NOW DEPENDS ON THEM....

READ THE NOVELS THAT STARTED IT ALL.

THE *NEW YORK TIMES*
Bestselling Series

NEW! Now Available in Hardcover

Available Now in Paperback

Available Now in Paperback

DON'T WAIT FOR THE MOVIE. READ THEM NOW.

WWW.WITCHANDWIZARD.COM

DANIEL X

THE GREATEST SUPERHERO OF THEM ALL

THE DANGEROUS DAYS OF DANIEL X

DANIEL X: WATCH THE SKIES

DANIEL X: DEMONS AND DRUIDS

DANIEL X: GAME OVER

DANIEL X: ARMAGEDDON
On Sale 10/15/12

ALSO AVAILABLE:

DANIEL X: ALIEN HUNTER GRAPHIC NOVEL

DANIEL X: THE MANGA, VOL. 1

DANIEL X: THE MANGA, VOL. 2

DANIEL X: THE MANGA, VOL. 3 NEW!

ACTION! ADVENTURE! ALIENS!

WWW.DANIEL-X.COM

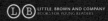

LITTLE, BROWN AND COMPANY
BOOKS FOR YOUNG READERS

B08490B

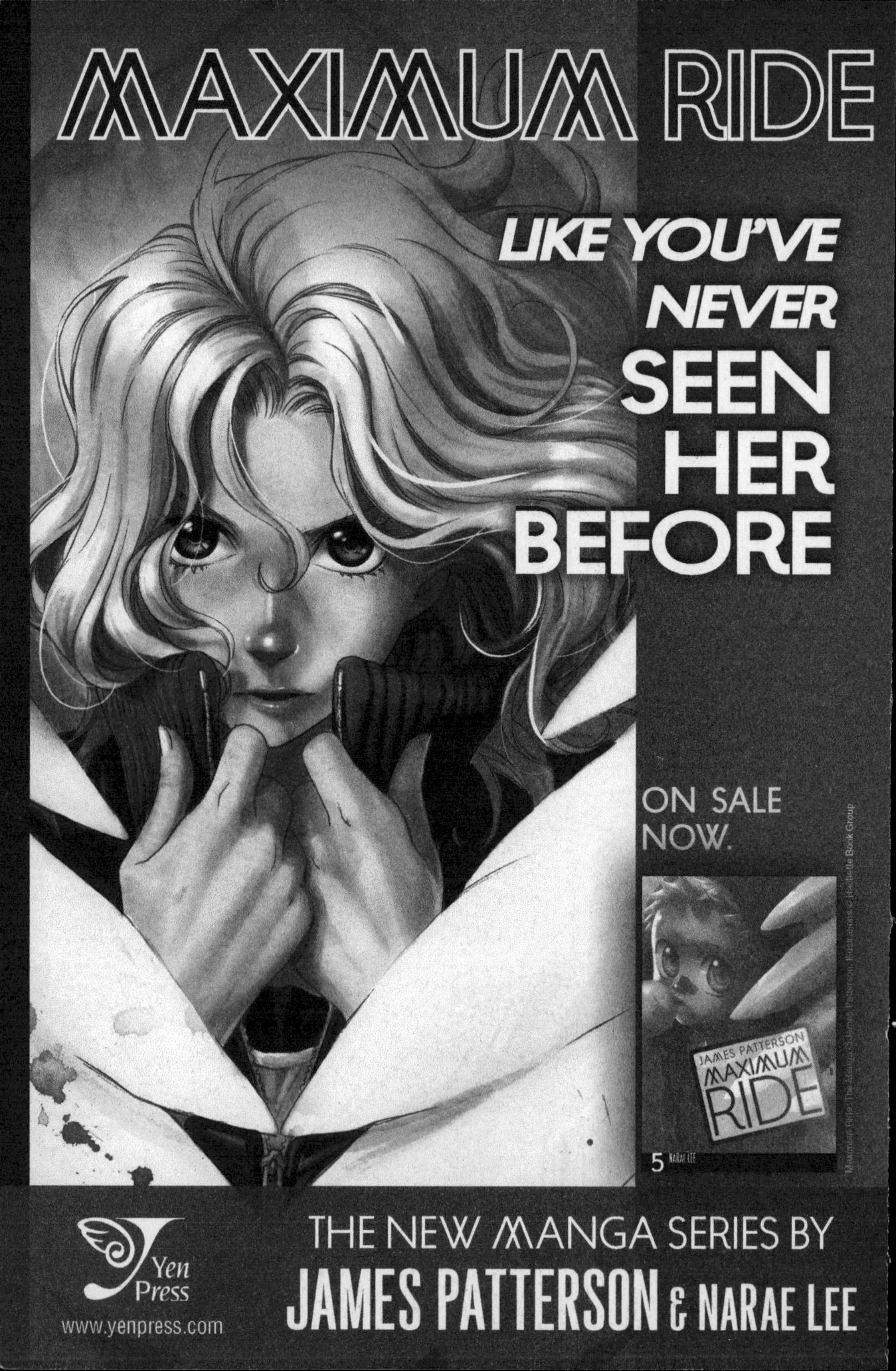

MAXIMUM RIDE
LIKE YOU'VE NEVER SEEN HER BEFORE
ON SALE NOW.
JAMES PATTERSON
MAXIMUM RIDE
5
NARAE LEE
Maximum Ride: The Manga © James Patterson. Illustrations © Hachette Book Group
Yen Press
www.yenpress.com
THE NEW MANGA SERIES BY
JAMES PATTERSON & NARAE LEE

WITCH & WIZARD: THE MANGA②

JAMES PATTERSON
WITH NED RUST
& SVETLANA CHMAKOVA

Adaptation and Illustration: Svetlana Chmakova

Inking/toning assistant: Dennis Lo
Toning assistant: Eric Kim

Lettering: JuYoun Lee

WITCH & WIZARD, THE MANGA, Vol. 2 © 2012 by James Patterson

Illustrations © 2012 Hachette Book Group, Inc.

Yen Press
Hachette Book Group
237 Park Avenue, New York, NY 10017

www.HachetteBookGroup.com
www.YenPress.com

Yen Press is an imprint of Hachette Book Group, Inc. The Yen Press name and logo are trademarks of Hachette Book Group, Inc.

First Yen Press Edition: June 2012

ISBN: 978-0-316-11991-7

10 9 8 7 6 5 4 3 2 1

BVG

Printed in the United States of America